MANAGEMENT DIMENSIONS

NEW CHALLENGES OF THE MIND

Owen B. Hardy, FACHE
National Health Care Planning Advisor
Ernst & Whinney
Chicago, Illinois

R. Clayton McWhorter, FACHE
Chairman and Chief Executive Officer
HealthTrust Inc.—The Hospital Company
Nashville, Tennessee

CLAYTON
ASSOCIATES, LLC

Library of Congress Cataloging in Publication Data

Hardy, Owen B.
Management dimensions: new challenges of the mind/Owen B. Hardy,
R. Clayton McWhorter.
p. cm.
Bibliography: p.
Includes index.
ISBN: 0-87189-760-1
1. Health services administration. I. McWhorter, R. Clayton.
II. Title.
RA971.H29 1988
658--dc19

88-3306
CIP

Editorial Services: Ruth Bloom

Library of Congress Catalog Card Number: 88-3306
ISBN: 0-87189-760-1

Printed in the United States of America

1 2 3 4 5

Dedication

To the professional associates with whom we have worked over the last three decades and, not least, to the members of our families.

Table of Contents

v

List of figures

. . . and tables . . .

. . . and exhibits

Preface

Management Dimensions: New Challenges of the Mind presents a previously ignored conceptual framework for understanding a highly important and complex discipline. As serious students of management for many years, we have been particularly impressed with the absence of a coherent system for classifying the various functions which management embraces. This absence, we maintain, has prevented many persons, including some in top executive positions, from clearly comprehending the numerous aspects of management as a discipline and the relationships among these aspects. That this deficiency has impaired the quality of management as practiced by many managers of business enterprises appears rather certain.

For the entire extent of our careers, we have believed that one's ability to conceive an appropriate organizational course, establish realistic goals and objectives, and then accomplish such goals and objectives in an efficient manner constitutes the basic measure of one's success as a manager. This being so, we have tried, as managers, to give equal emphasis to planning and to the activities of implementation. Both our experiences and thoughtful consideration of these two elements of management—planning and implementation—lead us to believe that one without the other is largely useless. Further thought suggests that planning and the activities of implementation compose two primary classes of management functions.

Because one cannot foresee the future with sufficient clarity to plan perfectly and because a host of problems occur in implementation, managers encounter situations that require them to respond adaptively in the best manner possible, often within a relatively short time. Indeed, when any manager analyzes the activities he or she undertakes over a period of days or months, it will be found that appreciable time is consumed in responding adaptively to uncontrolled and often uncontrollable environmental conflicts.

We present in this text the notion that all management activities of whatever kind or nature can be subsumed under three basic classes of functions, excepting certain legal functions or duties attached to the positions of executives, agents, or boards of directors in corporations. These classes are planning, activities of implementation, and adaptive responses. This book addresses each of these classes, or *management elements* as we subsequently call them, and their major subdivisions.

We conclude the book with a somewhat detailed chapter on integrity and social responsibility. Certainly, the whole of business management in the free world depends on both of these. When one considers the recent rash of revelations about insider trading and the general dishonesty of many persons in high management positions, the importance of these subjects seems to loom larger than at any previous time in modern history.

We primarily discuss management from an academic standpoint based on our previous study and our extensive research of the literature. However, we incorporate many accounts of our personal experiences as managers, with emphasis on the experiences of one of us, who recently served as president and chief operating officer of the Hospital Corporation of America and now holds the position of chairman and chief executive officer of HealthTrust Inc. We believe that the combination of academic study, research, and practical experiences as executives has allowed us to prepare a book that will be useful both for students and active practitioners of management.

Our joint authorship of this book emanated from an association and friendship lasting over 30 years. We participated equally in its preparation and wish to share equal credit, if credit accrues, or blame, if readers have serious disagreement with our views.

Finally, we wish to thank the thousands of persons who have either worked for us or with us in various organizations during our careers. With their help, we have been able to shape some definitive, positive views, both practical and philosophical, regarding management as a discipline and as a mentally challenging profession. These views have served us well, and we hope sharing them with others advances their understanding of management and proves helpful in its practice.

Owen B. Hardy
R. Clayton McWhorter
May 1988

Acknowledgments

Over the course of writing and preparing this book, a number of people helped us. We especially wish to thank the following:

Anne Hardy	Bettye Daugherty
Shalom DuBow	Richard Gaston
James Morell	Paul Rutledge
John Abendshien	George M. Garrett
Barbara Garvin	Lucien Roberts
Laura West	Lawrence P. Lammers
Kenneth C. Donahey	Brenda Nowlan
Chuck Kown	Kathy McInerney
Thomas H. Bain	Brenda Bonert
Debbie Dorsky	Scott Mercy
Ernest Bacon	Dennis Meulemans
Kerry Jackson	Rodney True
Paul Fenaroli	

In addition to those who provided direct assistance, a number of friends gave us considerable encouragement and moral support. We especially wish to thank the following:

James Lifton	Barbara Natal
Richard Kasten	David West
Norman D. Burkett	John Fidler
Norman D. Burkett, Jr.	Sam Feazell
Lee Mootz	Peter Rogan
Sam Glenney	David Shade
Douglas M. Parker	Lynda Barber
David Shanahan	Linda Simon
Robert Harrison	Gail Warden
David P. Buchmueller	Glenn Hogan
Frederick H. Gibbs	

Part I

A Functional Perspective

The ready comprehension of any functional discipline requires subsuming similar activities under a relatively few broad classes. Management is no exception, and many authorities have made such attempts but have achieved only limited success. In fact, confusion still abounds regarding the true nature of management (including its central theme and its elements) and how it should best be practiced by individual managers.

The first chapter presents a conceptual framework embracing three major classes, or elements, under which all management activities can be easily subsumed. Additionally, we identify and briefly discuss a number of major activities under each class. We hope this will lead to a much clearer and easier understanding of management than has heretofore been possible.

Many have claimed that the skills of management are transferable from one type of business enterprise to another. We agree with this view, and our discussions, not only in Chapter 1 but throughout the book, give support to it. If management does indeed constitute a distinct, understandable discipline, separate from the operational knowledge required for a particular type of business, and if a manager proposing to transfer from one type of business to another does indeed understand that discipline, there is no reason why the transfer should not be successful. It is even possible that at some point in the future, a truly professional body of skilled managers may evolve, the individuals of which will be able to manage any type of organized endeavor. We are far from that point at present, but the realization of this vision may be brought closer by the concepts explained in this book.

The preceding remarks should not be taken to mean we think management will ever be a separate science, as some have believed. To the contrary, strong evidence indicates it will never achieve this status. However, it may increasingly become a separate discipline, one that, for purposes of comprehension, assumes the existence of a structure composed of distinct but interrelated elements which are, in turn, composed of interrelated but easily identifiable subelements. In the first chapter, we outline the subsumptions inherent in such a structure.

1

Chapter 1

Management: structure and definitions

Elements of Management
in Corporations

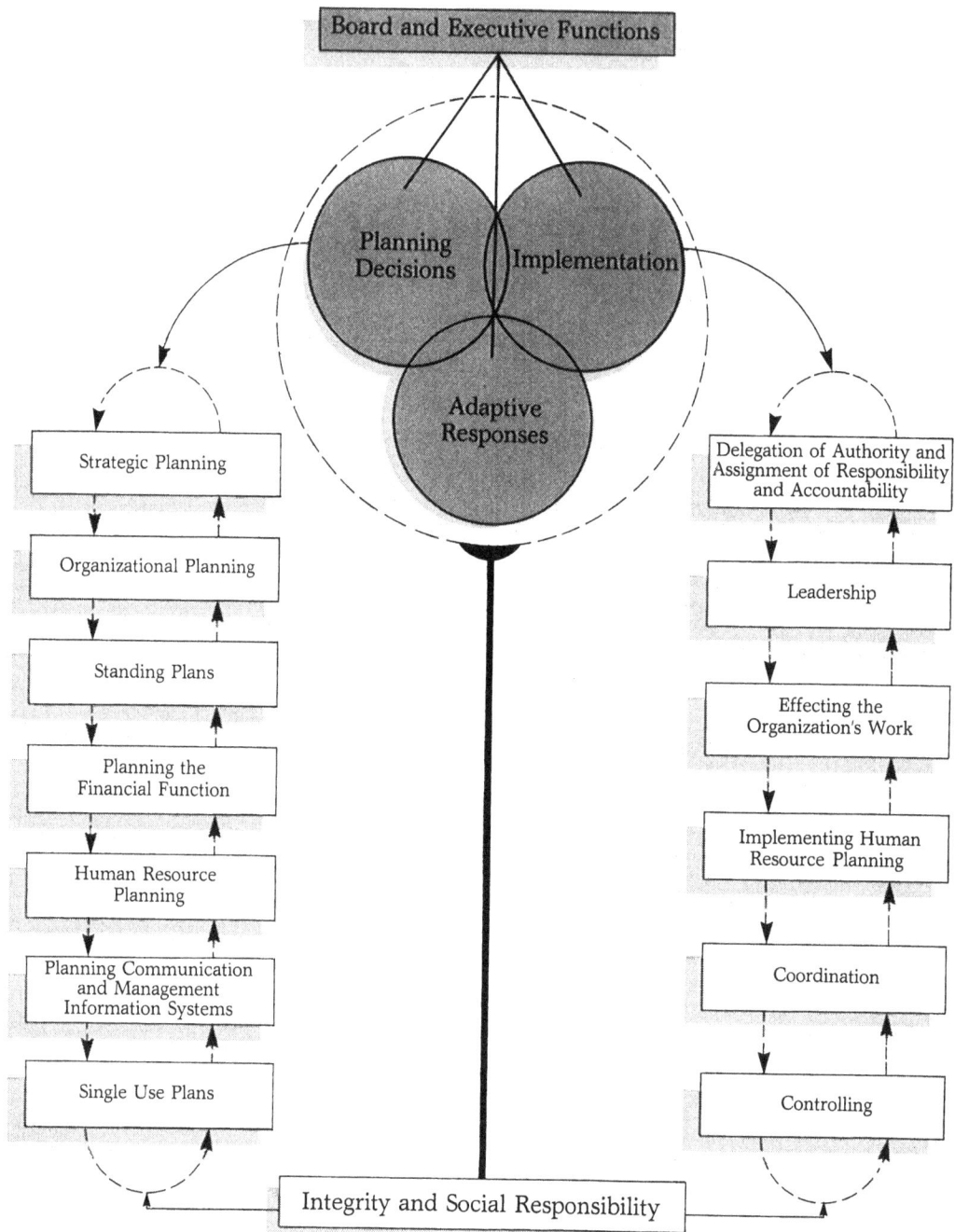

Board and Executive Functions

Planning Decisions

Implementation

Adaptive Responses

Strategic Planning

Organizational Planning

Standing Plans

Planning the Financial Function

Human Resource Planning

Planning Communication and Management Information Systems

Single Use Plans

Delegation of Authority and Assignment of Responsibility and Accountability

Leadership

Effecting the Organization's Work

Implementing Human Resource Planning

Coordination

Controlling

Integrity and Social Responsibility

1

Background

Academicians have written the vast majority of books on management. Philosophers have published some very thoughtful material peripherally related to the subject, and a broad range of behavioral scientists and technologically oriented individuals have made worthwhile contributions. Practitioners have written a variety of articles, but relatively few have authored books compared with the number engaged in management, and these books make up only a small part of the whole body of management literature now in existence.

The current scarcity of books by practitioners is understandable. A manager's basic role is to conceive objectives and get them accomplished within an organizational context. Writing is an essential part of a manager's work, but it is a means to an end, not an end in itself. Most nonpractitioner authors have had to develop practical skills in assembling large amounts of structured information about given subjects and reporting it in an orderly, understandable format. In this regard, managers are at a disadvantage, and they usually lack the competencies of professional writers. Also, the time demands of managers leave few opportunities for authorship. Thus, circumstances inevitably tend to exclude from the literature many of the ideas and opinions of the most successful managers.

As a result of the skewed distribution of authorship, with most of the authors coming from academia, management has been presented from such a broad variety of viewpoints that one can easily become lost in the complex maze of expressed opinions. Beginning students and practitioners are especially aware of the absence of a valid, widely accepted management concept, the corresponding absence of structure, the absence of clearly defined relationships among management's diverse aspects, and the resulting confusion. This confusion has led many to believe management possesses enigmatical complexities nearly defying rational understanding.

We admit the complexities of management and believe its study presents new intellectual challenges. However, its broad structure is relatively simple. Because few have recognized its simple structure and many have presented peripherally related aspects as being the central theme of management, the perception has seemingly prevailed that management is abstruse.

Perhaps the tortuous evolution of management both as a subject and a discipline over the last century has contributed to the nearly overwhelming mass of often contradictory and uncertain opinions voiced today. Our investigations reveal that this may be at least partially true.

Peter Drucker, one of the most brilliant academicians of our time, defined management in one of his early books thus: "The first definition of management is therefore that it is an economic organ, indeed the specifically economic organ of an industrial society. Every act, every decision, every deliberation of management has as its first dimension an economic dimension."[1] In the same text, he opined, "Management . . . is a practice, rather than a science or a profession, though containing elements of both."[2]

By 1974, Drucker had broadened his concept of management to include institutions other than those whose mission is primarily economic. In 1974, he stated, "Management is the specific organ of the new institution, whether business enterprise or university, hospital or armed service, research lab or government agency."[3]

Over the course of his long career writing on the subject, Drucker has variously referred to management as work (a definition with which most managers would surely agree), a discipline, a social function embedded in a culture, tasks, people, and "the organ of leadership, direction and decision in our social institutions."[4]

If one considers that Drucker, who perhaps is the most eminent writer on management of the previous four decades, seems somewhat perplexed about precisely defining management, and then one surveys a portion of the vast literature on the subject now available, one can only conclude that ideas about it are nearly as numerous as the proverbial sands of the seashore. Arguments began years ago about each of the following issues, among others:

- Is management an art or a science or a combination of the two?

- Is management a social science or a science basically concerned with more precise work measurements?

- Does management include part or all of the activities of a manager?

- Does management require adherence to identifiable management principles or does it require adaptation to the demands of a situation?

- Does management involve the direction and control of human resources alone or a combination of both human and material resources (within an organizational context)?

- Is management a systematic process or a responsive coordination?

- Is management a twentieth century invention or an ancient concept designed to extend the authority and control of rulers and other various officials over vast numbers of people, especially in work situations?

Although many authorities try to define management (but with considerable differences, as we will demonstrate later), others seem to deliberately avoid such attempts. For purposes of systematic study, explanation, and teaching, some authorities divide the total tasks of a manager into certain elements. Although unanimity of opinion is lacking, four or five elements most frequently receive recognition. Those authors who cite five elements often include planning, organizing, directing, staffing, and controlling. Those who cite only four sometimes omit staffing, viewing that function as part of organizing. In a recent volume, Newman and Warren named four elements—organizing, planning, measuring and controlling, and activating—and proceeded to analyze them as subprocesses of the whole of management.[5] Some authors have identified as many as ten elements.

Not only has there been a diversity of opinion regarding the elements of management (among those who try to define the subject as well as those who do not), but many authors have had difficulty explaining the relationships that occur among the elements that they identify. Such difficulty has occurred since Fayol first attempted to group "all activities to which industrial activities give rise" into six classes shortly after the turn of the century.[6] Fayol called one of the six classes "managerial activities" and stated that the functions in this class could be divided into elements which he labeled "planning, organization, command, coordination and control."[7] Perhaps Fayol, the first prominent writer who viewed management as a process, had as much success as any later writer in correctly classifying management functions and in subsequently describing each class and the relationships that occur among them.

Questions and answers

Why have disagreements and confusion existed among writers who have attempted to explain management as a process composed of "elements" or "functional groups"?

Could it be because so much overlapping occurs among the elements usually identified? Could it be because many management functions fail to fit into the classes or elements that for generations now writers have been prone to identify? Could it be that the classification systems are not clearly or intelligibly based on the actions that organizational managers take and have been taking for centuries? Finally, does there exist a system of classifying management functions that allows more accurate classification of the activities that managers undertake?

To each of these questions, the answer is yes. Yes, overlapping occurs among the elements that authorities currently identify as composing management; yes, many management functions fail to fit into these elements; yes, the elements traditionally cited do not constitute an understandable circular or linear system and cannot be used to graphically present an intelligible process flow. The answer to the final question is also yes. Indeed, we will present in this book an alternate classification system that we believe is more accurate and useful than any previous one.

Before we outline the structure of management as we view it, we will take a serious look at its true nature. We will consider the ideas of various prominent authorities and we will frame a definition of management which is relevant to modern theories about the subject.

Management defined

The vast majority of leaders throughout recorded history have practiced management, for every successful organized endeavor requires it (see Table 1-1). However, conscious attention to better methods for accomplishing organized work did not occur until the eighteenth century and the advent of the factory system, which resulted from the introduction of power-driven (steam) machinery. Adam Smith, in *The Wealth of Nations*, clearly wrote about methods of management, as did Sir James Stewart in *An Inquiry into the Principles of Political Economy*, which also contained opinions about power and authority, work methods, and incentive wages.

An increase during the nineteenth century of theorizing about management resulted in many publications. Noteworthy among these were the writings of Henry R. Towne, president of the Yale and Towne Manufacturing Company for over 40 years, the writings of Captain Henry Metcalfe, manager of a U.S. Army arsenal, and the writings of Frederick Halsey. Towne instituted many modern management methods in his company as early as 1870. His dissertation, "The Engineer as an Economist," may have been the impetus for Frederick W. Taylor to undertake the development of scientific management as the major task of his life. Captain Henry Metcalfe published *The Cost of Manufacturers and the Administration of Workshops, Public and Private* in 1885. This book was immediately acclaimed as an important step forward in thinking about management (then called administration), and in fact it still is sometimes used in teaching management students early in their course of study. Frederick Halsey gained recognition in 1891 for a paper presented before the American Society of Engineers about a wage payment plan. The plan won wide approval and served as a model for wage administration in industry both in this country and Great Britain for a number of years.

Unquestionably, the automation of printing was responsible for the proliferation of knowledge about management during the late nineteenth century and for the explosive dissemination which began early in the twentieth century and continues today. In this current age of the computer (the forerunner of which was invented by another authority on management, Charles Babbage, in the nineteenth century), electronic data processing will continue to revolutionize the practice of management. However, a revolutionary role as large or even larger has been played by the printing press. But for it, many "reinventions of the wheel" would still be occurring.

Frederick W. Taylor
Frederick W. Taylor, an American engineer and executive and management consultant, was either the first or among the first to attempt a definition of management—early in the twentieth century. (Henri Fayol, a Frenchman and a contemporary of Taylor's, also attempted a definition, one that certainly was clearer and more precise.)

Taylor, the father of "scientific management," stated that managers should give planning much greater emphasis as a centralized function of management and devised four basic principles of scientific management

Table 1-1

Management in Recorded History

Period	Practitioners	Location	Recognition As a Discipline	Noted Expositors
10,000 B.C. to 500 B.C.	Rulers, Explorers, Builders, Merchants, Military Leaders, and Religious Leaders	China, Egypt, Babylonia, Hebrew Kingdoms, Persia, other nations of the Middle East	Unlikely before 600 B.C. Possible from 600 to 500 B.C.	Ptah-hotep (an Egyptian King's Visier); Jethro (Moses' father-in-law); Hammurabi (a Babylonian ruler); Chow (a Chinese Prime Minister); Sun Tzu (a Chinese general)
499 B.C. to 500 A.D.	Rulers, Explorers, Builders, Merchants, Military Leaders, Religious Leaders, and Governmental Officials	China, Egypt, Babylonia, Macedonia, Greece, Persia, other nations of the Middle East and the Roman Empire	Yes, especially after 400 B.C.	Socrates, Plato, Xenophon, Cato, Varro, and various Roman writers
501 to 1500	Kings; Lords; Vassals; Church and Monastery Officials; Merchants; Builders; Bankers; Managers of arsenals, warehouses, ship outfitters, and other commercial and industrial ventures; and Military Leaders	China, the Middle East, and throughout Europe	Yes	Alfarabi and Ghazali (both Islamic philosophers) and Barbarigo (a Venetian merchant)
1501 to 1900	Kings, Governmental Officials, Military Leaders, Merchants, Industrialists, Church Officials, Builders, Explorers, and Managers of a growing number of organized efforts	Spread from Europe, the Middle East and the Far East throughout the world; native to some populations of the New World, e.g., the Aztec Nation	Yes	Sir Thomas More, Machiavelli, Adam Smith, Sir James Stewart, Thomas Jefferson, Eli Whitney, James Watt, Robert Owen, Charles Babbage, Henry Pool, Henry E. Metcalfe, Henry R. Towne, Frederick Halsey, Frederick W. Taylor, F. B. Gilbreth
1901 to Present	The managers of all organized efforts	Worldwide	Yes	The Gilbreths, Gant, Church, Parsons, Tead, Sheldon, Fisher, Mayo, Follett, Mooney, Barnard, Urwick, Weber, McGregor, Maslow, Likert, Argyris, Simon, Drucker, and many others

Note: This table was compiled by the authors primarily from *The History of Management Thought* by C.S. George, Jr., Prentice-Hall, Inc., © 1968.

which, in combination, defined the nature of such management. Taylor's four principles were these:

1. Develop a science for each element of a man's work, which replaces the old rule-of-thumb method.

2. Scientifically select and then train, teach, and develop the workman, whereas in the past he chose his own work and trained himself as best he could.

3. Heartily cooperate with the men so as to insure all of the work being done in accordance with the principles of the science which has been developed.

4. There is an almost equal division of the work and the responsibility between the management and the workmen. The management takes over all work for which they are better fitted than the workmen, while in the past almost all of the work and the greater part of the responsibility were thrown upon the men.[8]

In his *Principles of Scientific Management*, published in 1911, Taylor also described certain management techniques, which he contrasted with his defining principles. These, even yet, possess considerable relevance, and they also provide help in understanding his definition of scientific management:

• Time study, with the implements and methods for properly making it.

• Functional or divided foremanship and its superiority to the old-fashioned single foreman.

• The standardization of all tools and implements used in the trades, and also of the acts or movements of workmen for each class of work.

• The desirability of a planning room or department.

• The "exception principle" in management.

• The use of slide rules and similarly timesaving implements.

• Instruction cards for the workman.

• The task idea in management, accompanied by a large bonus for the successful performance of the task.

• The "differential rate."

• Mnemonic systems for classifying manufactured products as well as implements used in manufacturing.

• A routing system.

• Modern cost system.[9]

Henri Fayol

Fayol, in his famous book *Administration Industrielle et Generale*, which was first published in 1916, stated that all industrial undertakings could be divided into the following six basic groups:

1. Technical activities (production, manufacture, adaptation).

2. Commercial activities (buying, selling, exchange).

3. Financial activities (search for and optimum use of capital).

4. Security activities (protection of property and persons).

5. Accounting activities (search for and optimum use of capital).

6. Managerial activities (planning, organization, command, co-ordination, control).

According to Fayol, "Be the undertaking simple or complex, big or small, these six groups of activities or essential functions are always present. The first five are well known—a few words will be enough to demarcate their respective spheres—but the managerial group calls for further explanation."[10]

After explaining the elements of each of these groups, Fayol goes on to define managerial activities:

> To manage is to forecast and plan, to organize, to command, to co-ordinate and to control. To foresee and provide means examining the future and drawing up the plan of action. To organize means building up the dual structure, material and human, of the undertaking. To command means maintaining activity among the personnel. To co-ordinate means binding together, unifying and harmonizing all activity and effort. To control means seeing that everything occurs in conformity with established rule and expressed command.[11]

Since 1916, many writers have segmented management into functional elements, basically following Fayol. Even today most works that cover management theory still cite Fayol's divisions or derivations of them. Why? For the simple reason that no better system of taxonomy has gained favor or even been devised. Also, the cited functions do occur in organizations, and despite the shortcomings of the various existing schemes of classification, they are better than nothing at all. At least some useful order is provided for purposes of investigation and instruction. Considerable difficulties occur, however, in explaining management as an ongoing process, for there is no straightforward way in which each element relates one to the others, either within a system that takes input and produces output over time or one that is closed and characterized by functional circularity.

Recent developments

In 1935, Harry A. Hopf, a noted management consultant, presented a paper at the Sixth International Congress for Scientific Management held in London. In this paper, he defined management as "the direction of a business enterprise through the planning, organizing, coordinating, and controlling of its human and material resources, toward the achievement of a predetermined objective."[12] Obviously, Fayol's influence remained strong.

In 1961, two noted academicians, William H. Newman and Charles E. Summer, Jr., declared in *The Process of Management* that "managing is a social process. It is a *process* because it comprises a series of actions that lead to the accomplishing of objectives. It is a *social* process because these actions are principally concerned with relations among people."[13] Newman and Summer stated further that "a highly useful way of dividing up the total task of management is in terms of organizing, planning, leading, and controlling. Although all are closely interrelated, each of these elements of managing can be analyzed as a sub-process."[14] Again, one notes Fayol's influence.

In 1969, another academician, Ernest Dale, stated that management was frequently defined as "getting things done through other people."[15] Dale also stated that management was often regarded as "decision making." However, in describing management as a total set of activities, he reverted to Fayol's methodology of functional divisions. In *Management: Theory and Practice*, Dale divided management activities into the categories of planning, organizing, staffing, direction, control, innovation, and representation.[16]

In 1971, in the second edition of *Essentials of Management*, Joseph L. Massie, Acting Dean of the College of Business and Economics, University of Kentucky, stated,

> The chief characteristic of management is the integration and application of the knowledge and analytical approaches developed by numerous disciplines. . . . Simply stated, management "gets things done through other people." For the purpose of this book, management is defined as the *process* by which a cooperative group directs action towards common goals.[17]

In step with Fayol and his academically trained followers, Massie then noted certain functions of management and named and discussed seven of them:

1. *Decision making*—the process by which a course of action is consciously chosen from available alternatives for the purpose of achieving a desired result.

2. *Organizing*—the process by which the structure and allocation of jobs is determined.

3. *Staffing*—the process by which managers select, train, promote and retire subordinates.

4. *Planning*—the process by which a manager anticipates the future and discovers alternative courses of action open to him.

5. *Controlling*—the process that measures current performance and guides it toward some predetermined goal.

6. *Communicating*—the process by which ideas are transmitted to others for the purpose of effecting a desired result.

7. *Directing*—the process by which actual performance of subordinates is guided toward common goals.[18]

More recently, in 1978, William J. Ronan, former chairman of the Port Authority of New York and New Jersey as well as a noted authority on management, stated the following:

> Management in the second half of the twentieth century is accordingly a developing discipline and a focus of attention in the free enterprise world, the socialist world, the semi-state-planned economies, the developed world, and the developing world. It is a significant factor in the international world—in the international and regional organizations established among the nations for a wide spectrum of purposes. (Management may be defined as the purposeful utilization of manpower, money, energy, technology, and materials to accomplish collective objectives.) The objectives may be to produce goods and services, construct works, raise money, make profits, achieve economic plans, maintain law and order, balance competing interests, assure national or international security, conduct research and development, or audit performance. This litany does not specify or detail all the myriad possible objectives. It serves to show, however, the universality of the management problem.[19]

Current thought

In the tradition started by Fayol and adhered to by many academicians, Brown and Moberg, of the University of Oregon and University of Santa Clara respectively, wrote the following in their book *Organization and Management: A Macro Approach*, published in 1980:

> Basically, management is marshalling both human and material resources towards common organizational goals. Traditionally, this process has been divided into several broad activities. The more technical or analytic side of management involves goal-setting for the organization, planning the internal activities to accomplish the goals, and controlling those activities so that the end results are the desired ones. Each of these in turn involves technical knowledge and many specific skills. Some managers specialize in one or another of these functions.
>
> The other basic aspect of management involves dealing with people. This is a very large topic, and we shall address it here insofar as it involves the broader aspects of organizations. Specifically, we shall examine the functions of staffing, directing, and supervising employees.
>
> For most managers it is essential to be knowledgeable in both the technical and human aspects of the overall manage-

ment process. This is so because management involves a highly varied set of activities in which both types of skills are needed. Such job variety is a common element of management whether one looks at a supervisor in a manufacturing plant, a department head of a state welfare agency, or an executive in a large corporation. Wherever found, management is a critical, driving force in organizations, a vital dimension to organizational success.[20]

In his excellent text *Management* (second edition published in 1982), James A.F. Stoner, of Fordham University, continued the trend of defining management as a process composed of certain elements. Stoner identified the same elements as Newman and Summer did in 1961:

> Management is the process of planning, organizing, leading, and controlling the efforts of organization members and of using all other organizational resources to achieve stated organizational goals.
> A process is a systematic way of doing things. We define management as a process because all managers, regardless of their particular aptitudes or skills, engage in certain interrelated activities in order to achieve their desired goals.[21]

One of the most popular books about management in recent years is *In Search of Excellence*, written by two management consultants, Thomas J. Peters and Robert H. Waterman, Jr. Although the authors do not define management explicitly, they do state it is an art essentially concerned with the motivation of organizational members and that the skills of managing people are transferable. Based on research (unfortunately not clearly described) involving some 62 American companies of diverse origins and missions, the book emphasizes the need for business corporations to observe eight "basic principles" to stay on "top of the heap," which presumably means to attain and maintain a state of excellence (loosely defined as readiness and ability to innovate in the face of change).[22]

More than most current volumes about management, *In Search of Excellence*, published in 1982, rightly emphasizes the role which the behavioral sciences can play in management and traces both early and recent work that applies the behavioral sciences. Four of the pioneers were Elton Mayo, Douglas McGregor, Herbert Simon, and James March, and their work has been paralleled or supplemented by the work of a host of others, such as Rensis Likert, Chris Argyris, Abraham Maslow, Gordon Lippitt, and Karl Weick.

In an extremely informative, up-to-date text prepared primarily for teaching management in universities, Steers, Ungson, and Mowday offer a definition of management that is strictly within the tradition that regards management as a process. They state management is "the process of planning, organizing, directing and controlling the activities of employees in combination with other organizational resources to accomplish stated organizational goals."[23] It is interesting to note, however, that these authors designed their book, *Managing Effective Organizations*, around a "triadic model of management/organizational effectiveness," with the focus on technical competencies, behavioral competencies, and strategic competencies.[24] The book contains few descriptions of the relationships among planning, organizing, directing, and controlling—possibly owing to reasons to which we have already referred.

Truths and fallacies

Prior to setting forth what we believe to be a useful definition as well as certain explanations referenced to management, we shall respond to a number of oft-quoted statements about the subject that have been made by various authorities during the last century.

1. *Management is an art.* The common usages of the word *art* are various and all are imprecise. At the very least, assessing the statement would require knowing which definition is being referred to. *Black's Law Dictionary* states that art is a "systematic application of knowledge or skill in effecting a desired result; also, an employment, occupation or business requiring such knowledge or skill."[25] In these senses, management is very definitely an art.

2. *Management is a science or is becoming a science.* Management has not been, is not now, and will not become a separate science. However, application of the scientific method can be made to many management problems. Operations research is a classic example of the application of other sciences to problems of management. A manager should be knowledgeable about a number of behavioral sciences and apply their precepts when the situation so indicates. Knowledge of mathematics and statistics has considerable usefulness. But this is not to say that management is a science in itself, and we remain convinced it never will be.

3. *Management is a profession and its skills are transferable.* Given our perception of the current nature of management and both *Webster's* and *Black's* definition of the word *profession*, we believe management is indeed a profession. Black defines a profession as "a vocation, calling, occupation, or employment involving labor, skill, education, special knowledge, and compensation or profit, but the labor and skill involved is predominately mental or intellectual, rather than physical or manual."[26] In that sense, management is a profession. We also believe that management skills and knowledge are transferable, especially at the top echelons of organizations. Don Mac-Naughton's successful transfer from the head of Prudential to chairman and CEO of Hospital Corporation of America is a case in point. Even at lower management levels, one can still distinguish between technical knowledge required for a particular position and management knowledge and skills, which are transferable.

4. *Management is a discipline which can be learned.* Our most prestigious universities have codified management into a teachable body of knowledge and have long offered management courses to students. Some students learn faster than others. Some become top managers with limited formal training and others boast numerous degrees but turn out to be also-rans. However, much the same is true of other disciplines, e.g., engineering, medicine, education, etc.

5. *Management is people.* Many voice this cliché, which is largely true. A manager gets most of his or her tasks accomplished through other people, and if a manager performs operating work, it is separate from management. However, responsibility and accountability for managing money, real estate, and other physical assets rest with management personnel, and thus management is not just "people." Recently, most unbiased authorities have recognized this and include the direction and control of all material resources of an organization within the boundaries of management.

6. *Management is a social function and the organ of social institutions.* This is true only if management is taken to apply solely to social institutions. Of course, if one considers the term *social institution* to refer to every organized effort of humans, the statement is indisputable. However, the term *social* is confusing or ambiguous according to many people, and we believe that words and phrases that are more precise and less controversial should be used. For example, deploying nuclear missiles, planning for their use, or actually using them requires management of organized efforts; we are not sure that such management should be called a social function within a social institution.

7. *Management is practice.* We believe when Drucker wrote his pioneering book *The Practice of Management*, he was referring to management as a profession. Furthermore, we believe this statement is basically correct.[27]

8. *Management is "getting things done through other people."* In large part this is true, but as noted in (5) above, management also concerns the direction and control of all material assets possessed by an organization.

9. *Management is a process.* The word *process* has been defined as "a systematic series of actions directed to some end . . . a continuous action, operation, or series of changes taking place in a definite manner." Given that definition, if management is practiced as we think it should be, it can be characterized as a process. That process can be easily understood if one thinks of it as composed of two basic phases: the planning of actions and their implementation. One can display the process graphically, as we have done later in this chapter.

10. *Management is a system.* In their insightful book *The Theory and Management of Systems*, Johnson, Kast, and Rosensweig define a system as "an organized or complex whole; an assemblage or combination of things or parts forming a complex or unitary whole."[28] This definition serves as a suitable description of a formal organization, and these authors state that the typical business organization is directly comparable to an open system which "maintains a constant state while the matter and energy which enter it keep changing"[29] Additionally, they state that "the business organization is a man-made system which has a dynamic interplay with its environment—customers, competitors, labor organizations, suppliers, government, and many other agencies. Furthermore, the business organization is

a system of interrelated parts working in conjunction with each other to accomplish a number of goals, both those of the organization and those of individual participants."[30] These authors do not state that management itself is a system. They merely argue that viewing a business organization as a system facilitates the understanding of its management, the effectiveness of which is thereby increased. We believe that management is not a system. Management is better viewed as a process occurring within organizations. Formal organizations themselves can be viewed as systems, mostly as open systems, but possibly in a few instances as closed systems. The commonly used term *systems approach to management*, which is often heard, merely alludes to the fact that management builds its functions around the concept that an organization (in contrast to management) is an open system. Many behavioral scientists have viewed organizations as social systems and "management as a system of cultural interrelationships."[31] While we recognize the great importance of the behavioral sciences as tools for managers, along with others, and while we know that building a value-laden corporate culture attracts, retains, and motivates quality personnel, we still maintain that management itself is more a process than a true system—even a system of cultural interrelationships.

11. *Management is decision making.* Many theorists have viewed decision making (including decision making that concerns future courses of management action, which we call planning) as nearly equivalent to management. Certainly no more important element of management exists than decision making. But even though it is a *sine qua non* of management, it does not compose the whole of management, or vice versa. All decisions, to be useful in management, need to be carried out. Thus, without implementation decision making in business organizations is largely useless.

Our definition

Over the last three decades, the term *management* has been used to designate the body of managers in various business organizations (i.e., those who manage as opposed to those who perform operating work, either technically skilled or manual work). What is the characteristic that distinguishes a manager and a nonmanager? Few authorities have made the distinction clear. We believe that when an organizational member has one or more persons under his or her control or supervision, then he or she is part of management, regardless of whether the position is "line" or "staff." In some small organizations, a person may be an officer or possess responsibility for the handling of vital material assets and still be classified as part of "management," even with no reporting subordinates. However, we believe responsibility for the tools of one's trade, though they may be expensive, does not make an operator a manager.

Suppose that a pathologist in a clinical laboratory spends 95 percent of worktime at the microscope doing clinical tasks, yet is responsible for the work of a dozen technicians. That pathologist is a member of management. Is the pilot of a five million dollar aircraft who has five flight attendants reporting to him or her in flight a member of management? We think not, for the in-flight reporting is temporary; the flight attendants actually report to someone else within the organizational structure. The pilot is essentially an operator, and the aircraft, though very expensive, is merely a tool of the trade.

Thus, the term *management* has come to have two meanings. Sometimes it is used to refer to the body of organizational managers and other times to the functions of managers. Thus, no simple one sentence definition of management could possibly be adequate. This fact has stymied many who have tried to give a pithy characterization. The following, though a bit lengthy, catches the essence of our own view of management.

> *In either formal or informal organizations, management consists of the various activities performed by those who have accepted the responsibility for setting organizational objectives and accomplishing them through the use of authority and various other means. The activities performed are largely mental or intellectual and include communicating with subordinates about the assignment and accomplishment of tasks. Those engaged in management activities have the responsibility for and use of all organizational resources—both human and material—in setting and pursuing objectives.*

As a whole, management is both the driving force and the regulator of all organizational actions; without it there would be no way an organization could exist. It has come to be, if not the most important function in modern society, then one of the most important.

The structure of management

Conceptualizing the elements

The basic structure of management can be best understood by viewing it as a whole composed of related components. To the extent they have viewed it this way, management analysts have approached the subject correctly. To draw an analogy, had the blindfolded men, in the story, who touched parts of the elephant been permitted to view the whole animal first, their perceptions of it would have been far different and much more accurate. Again, it is better to first "see" the forest before beginning to investigate its various kinds of vegetation. Even more to the point, it is not by accident that study of the various parts and systems of the human body starts in the first year of medical school with instruction on the anatomy and physiology of a whole human being. In short, understanding the whole facilitates understanding the individual components and their relationships, whether the whole being studied is a science, system, process, or any other kind of subject. Management is no exception. However, as already noted, those attempting to analyze management as a process (which it is) have not identified its most basic elements.

From a conceptual viewpoint, managing the various resources under one's control in a formal organization differs very little from conducting one's personal life. An individual human, within his or her environment, consciously or unconsciously contemplates and decides what actions should be taken to satisfy perceived needs and then attempts to perform these actions. Two broad categories of function are essential: (1) planning (reflective thought), including both short- and long-range planning, with a focus on decision making; and (2) implementing actions to carry out plans and decisions, including many typical human activities. Purposeful decisions (in contrast to vagaries) are basically of two types: (1) those deliberately made and implemented with a distinct objective in mind, and (2) those made as a reaction to uncontrolled and usually dissatisfactory elements within the environment.

With regard to management in organizations, every functional activity performed by managers can be subsumed under three basic categories. Activities of two of the categories should and usually do predominate in most organizations, but activities of the third category must receive attention, because planning is often imperfect and obstacles inevitably arise that are not or even cannot be foreseen. As a result, choices have to be made among available alternatives, usually urgently and immediately.

The two main categories of management functions are *planning* and *activities of implementation*. We designate the third category, which involves some decision making that cannot truly be called planning, as *adaptive responses*. Thus, the three broad categories of management functions are

1. *planning*, of every kind

2. *implementing activities*, some of which are in direct pursuance of objectives established in planning and some of which are only indirectly related to such objectives

3. *adaptive responses*, usually occasioned by unforeseen exigencies or by imperfect planning

We graphically present these three functional categories in Figure 1-1. This figure allows anyone having the barest qualifications for becoming a manager to easily comprehend the structure of management. This way of presenting the structure not only helps in understanding management as an integrated whole but also leads to a better understanding of the component functions of management.

The perspective gained by considering the structure in the way we suggest is justified by the increase in ability to forecast and plan with greater accuracy and certainty than ever before. Planning, rather than being merely one of many elements of management (which is the view of most authorities), can now be seen as the great driving force of all formal organizations that it is. Data resources of all types for all enterprises offer infinitely more and better data than at any previous period, and the ability to process data and secure needed information is beyond the wildest imaginings of a half century ago.

The following warning should be noted: *Those managers who fail to recognize how computers can enhance all types of planning will eventually lose out to those who do recognize this.*

Despite the fact that we may now be living in a period of more uncertainty than ever before, the ability to forecast has greatly improved organizational abilities to exercise control over the future. The assumed fact of more uncertainty requires, however, that organizations plan

Figure 1-1

The Three Basic Elements of Management

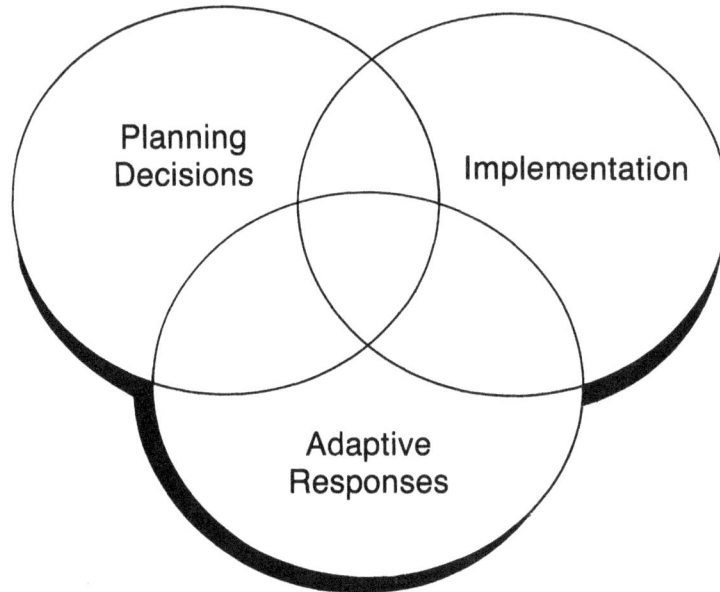

appropriately. For successful maintenance of organizational viability and vitality, planning is no longer optional—it is imperative.

Although all organizational management functions can be subsumed under one of the three categories cited, we consider board and executive functions separately. This is because board members and executives of corporations, in addition to their management functions, have special legal functions and duties as well as certain unique legal relationships with shareholders, employees, and the corporation itself. Because this book primarily concerns management in corporations, we devote a whole chapter (Chapter 2) to the management and legal functions of top corporate positions. Figure 1-2 depicts our concept of the elements of management in corporations as they relate to board and executive functions.

Planning

Nature and perspective

From earliest antiquity to the present, those who have held responsibility for the organized efforts of small groups, vast armies, multinational industrial empires, health care enterprises, educational systems, and a variety of modern day corporations have planned in varying degrees what was to be done; who was to do it; how the implementing actions would be carried out; when the actions would be undertaken, performed, and possibly completed; where the implementation would occur; and, in most instances, what volumes and types of human and material

Figure 1-2

Basic Elements of Management in Corporations

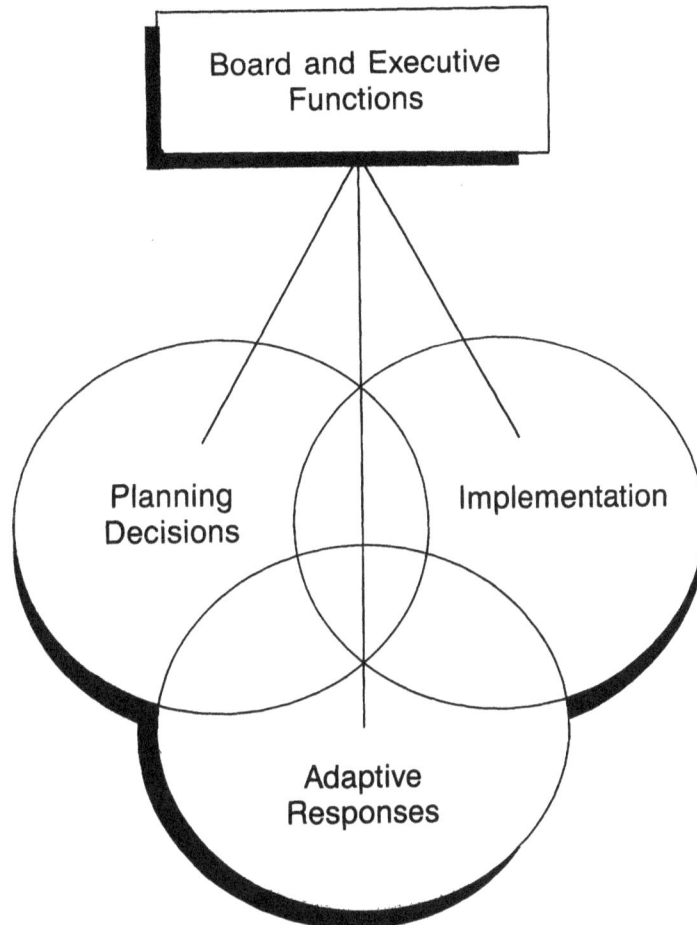

resources would be required. Planning may vary from that being made on a day-to-day basis to that covering extremely long periods, even many years. Planning may occur solely in the mind of a single individual and never be reduced to writing; it may reflect the consensus of a group and result in extensive documentation; it may occur as an informal or a formal activity; it may be effective or ineffective, efficient or inefficient; and it may result in social benefit or social harm. In all of these instances, however, the initial act of all management transpires—planning.

Planning which occurs in organizations, however, must be communicated in some form and by some means; if not communicated, it might just as well not have occurred. Those who will carry out organizational actions must somehow receive information about what is expected of them. Even in covert operations, an unexplained order for a secret agent to travel to a particular destination implies that a plan (probably part of a larger plan) has been made for the agent to do so; he or she could not have been directed where to go otherwise.

One reason that planning occupies such an important place in management is that no purposeful organizational effort can occur without it. As we have already noted, voluntary actions of humans result from deciding what to do and then doing it. In the case of individual actions, however, communication with others is often unnecessary. It *is* necessary for organizational efforts, at least in some form and to some extent.

Definition

Our research indicates writers have defined planning in nearly as many ways as management, but one of the briefest definitions seems to be more nearly correct than any other: *Planning is the making of decisions about future courses of actions.* Thus, all planning is decision making. Planning and decision making are not synonymous, however, for decision making sometimes involves choosing among several possible alternatives without any orientation to future courses of action.

Types of planning

Many types of planning occur in various organizations. In the health care field, we have even seen plans formulated for planning, and to good advantage. Planning is invariably a process—sometimes merely a thought process, but sometimes a process so detailed that highly involved techniques are required, such as the Critical Path Method or Program Evaluation and Review Technique (PERT). Long-term strategic planning of large corporations almost always benefits from the applications of such scheduling tools.

The key types of planning usually done by successful major corporations and other large-scale organized efforts, both at the outset and over the continuing life cycle, are as follows:

1. *Strategy Planning:* includes mission and role planning; short- and long-range program planning; the formulation of goals and objectives, both short- and long-term; forecasting and environmental assessments; planning for feedback on progress occurring toward mission fulfillment, goals, and objectives

2. *Organizational Planning:* includes initial and ongoing planning of all factors involved in departmentation, decentralization, job design, delegation, and structural design

3. *Standing Plans:* includes policies, standard operating procedures, standard methods, and rules; these serve to guide repetitive activities, including all phases of managerial and operational work as well as the conduct of employees on the job and various facets of company-employee or organization-member interfaces

4. *Planning the Financial Function:* includes formulation of financial objectives; planning to perform desirable financial analyses (ratio and other) on an ongoing basis; planning financial records and controls; projection of needs for short-term operating funds, such as cash flow and cash budgets; preparation of balance sheets and pro forma statements of income, expense, working capital, and the source and use of funds; preparation of anticipatory break-even charts; planning for the

acquisition of assets for both short- and long-term use; inventory planning; preparation of valuation methods; formulation of all operating and capital budgets; the several aspects of tax planning; planning for auditing and risk management

5. *Human Resource Planning*: includes planning for organization of personnel functions; ongoing forecasting of personnel needs; formulation of personnel policies (broadly construed); construction of procedures and methods for employee recruitment, selection, and performance appraisal; planning of educational and training programs; planning for financial compensation; planning motivational and productivity programs; planning for occupational safety; preparation of policies for dealing with labor unions, where indicated

6. *Planning Communication Networks and Management Information Systems*: includes planning of all factors related to means, modes, and channels of communication, both internal and external; timing; the means and methods of providing relevant and timely data and information to operational personnel and all managers for purposes related to operational work and all facets of management, particularly planning and executive decision making

7. *Single Use Plans*: includes one-time-through plans, such as those developed in planning, design, and construction programs; planning to develop and initiate marketing of a new product; planning to merge with another organization; all other planning for a definable single action, either on an emergency or nonemergency basis

The above seven major categories of planning do not include all planning that takes place in organizations, but they do include most. Planning literally dominates the worklife of many key executives and plays a major role in the work of all managers. Some planning, especially planning that occurs only in the minds of managers, is not easily classifiable; on the other hand, some planning is subsumable under two or more of the above categories.

The pervasive nature of planning prevents the classification of all of it for precise study. But since planning is the beginning point of all management and it provides direction and guidance throughout the life of every organization, it should be examined from the most advantageous perspective possible. Our categorization of types, while not perfect, establishes a basis for study and understanding and we hope it will lead to further thought and investigation by our readers.

Implementation

Background and definition

After appropriate decisions (plans) have been made regarding specific work to be done or actions to be accomplished, managers then face the tasks needed to carry out the decisions. This applies to every aspect of planned activities, of whatever kind, that are performed in organizations.

It applies to both staff work and operating work, from the most technical jobs to cleaning the floors.

We have elected to use *implementation* to refer to the efforts involved in the carrying out of plans. This is due primarily to a lifelong habit. We considered using *execution*, which might have served our purposes just as well. However, J.P. Barger previously defined that term as "a collection of activities by which a manager puts into being his own plans for his own job."[32] We intend *implementation* to have a broader meaning. The definition we prefer, which conforms closely to Webster's definition, is as follows:

> *Implementation consists of all those management activities that contribute to realizing previously made plans or decisions.*

We discuss most of the major activities involved in implementation in the six chapters that constitute Part IV, which is appropriately titled "Implementation."

Approaches to implementation

Managers use many approaches in getting work or tasks accomplished. The approach chosen depends on the nature of the work, its volume, the limitations on time and resources, and the characteristics and qualifications of those available to do the work.

The first act of implementation is the same for all approaches. This is the assignment of tasks to particular individuals. For each task, the assignment may start at the top of a bureaucratic hierarchy or at lower levels, but it must ultimately be communicated to the person who will actually perform the task, either alone or with others.

Assigning work is inescapable, but it can be done in a number of ways, some more suitable for a given situation than others. If management by objectives (MOB) has been adopted, the assignment may involve an agreement by the manager and the subordinate on the objective to be attained. Using job descriptions is a common method, as is using verbal communications. Specific instructions (orders), either verbal or written, can also be used. Contracts are common in setting the terms of employment of key executives.

After assignment, managers have many ways of seeing that the work is accomplished. The best way (or ways) usually depends on how the assignment was made. One of the oldest ways, dating back to the beginning of recorded history, is supervision. Another time-honored way that is still prevalent makes use of various leadership techniques. The exercise of authority and the application of power and force typify other older forms; disciplinary actions or the threat of them represent their manifestations.

In more modern times, a combined "carrot and stick" approach has been widely used. Most recently, as people within organizations have developed a greater need for esteem and self-actualization, attention has turned toward those things that increase job satisfaction, including a variety of intangible motivators and adequate pay. The idea is that the initiative of the performer should serve as the basic impelling force ensuring work accomplishment.

Effecting group synergy through use of research findings related to group dynamics represents one of the most recent hopes for increasing the productivity of persons working in groups.

Presently, except at the most menial task levels, relatively few managers employ close supervision as a technique for getting work done. Supportive supervision may still be employed at levels where clearcut delegation of work is not possible.

Regardless of how work assignments are made and methods for task execution are selected, managers must make sure three things are clearly settled at the time of assignment: (1) authority, (2) responsibility, and (3) accountability. Although this may seem elementary, cases of erroneous, incomplete, or ineffective settlement of these things occur surprisingly often.

At most, if not all, levels of management, it doesn't matter whether management by objectives has been perfected and extended to the most routine work, even to work that nearly defies measurement, or whether specific objectives have remained unformulated. In any case, *who* is to do the work must be confirmed and, almost always, issues of authority, responsibility, and accountability must be worked out. If this is not done, the probability of later problems is considerably increased.

In all cases, the assigning manager has a responsibility to keep track of progress in terms of appropriate and hopefully measurable factors. Time, quality, quantity, and cost are among the most common factors, but there are many others. Monitoring progress may be done as a part of the control process described in most academic texts on management. Visual inspection and verbal and written reports are the most prevalent methods of tracking.

Although a given control method for specific situations must be determined through careful planning, its application is a part of implementation.

Every manager has a coordinating responsibility in getting work done through others, and coordination is a characteristic element of implementation. Coordination can be expertly planned—the better the plan, the better the coordination. However, the best planning seldom covers every aspect of implementation. Voluntary cooperation and coordination can be achieved through motivational factors, but managers almost always must personally engage in on-the-spot coordinating efforts where two or more persons are involved in related work tasks.

Vertical communication and horizontal communication are important for coordination in particular and serve as another distinct tool in implementation. During planning, managers devise networks and methods, but during implementation they themselves must become effective communicators and see that the networks and methods are used and that they function properly.

Implementation embraces many activities, some of which are rare and do not fall neatly into any of the categories we mention in Chapters 10–15. Other activities might be placed in two or more categories. However, texts on management note the vast majority of actions for which managers have responsibility during implementation, and these can easily be obtained and studied for further information.

Adaptive responses

Relevance and importance

Adaptive responses is a new term applied to a category of management functions about which little has been written. Insofar as we are aware, no author has used it as the heading for a major category of management or operating functions. A number of authorities have employed such terms as *contingency responses, adaptivising, adaptive changes,* and *adaptations,* all of which we discuss briefly in Chapter 16. None of these terms, we believe, suggests clearly that managers spend appreciable amounts of valuable time in responding adaptively to a variety of situations arising in day-to-day management. The need to frame and implement adaptive responses arises especially in the thousands of small organizations where planning receives little formal attention. But even in many medium and large organizations, "putting out fires" takes up appreciable management time. In all organizations, no matter how much planning is accomplished, situations occur that require managers to "wing it" for a time. Where managers have formulated and pursued wrong decisions, they must then make requisite changes or reversals (adaptive responses), which may necessitate, especially in large firms, actions extending over long periods of time.

Perfect planning is difficult, if not impossible, to achieve, and managers often reach a point beyond which intense planning efforts should be reduced. Because of the constraints of personnel time and costs, it behooves managers to postpone some decision making until implementation is in process, during which time necessary responses to environmental occurrences can be determined. This technique has aptly been called *adaptivising.*[33] In adaptivising, managers routinely make adaptive responses to unforeseen environmental obstacles or opportunities.

The uncertain, sporadic nature of some businesses, such as small architectural and consulting firms, often prevents effective planning. Businesses with a routine-service orientation, such as hospitals, are often thrown into confusion when crises arise. The sudden death or resignation of a key executive or specialist nearly always necessitates a broad range of adaptive responses. Many otherwise well-planned military operations may encounter the unforeseen and require adaptive responses to thwart a threat or exploit an opportunity. In all of these instances, managers or leaders must respond adaptively to the environmental circumstances encountered.

We stress that adaptive responses usually occur as a result of some new or unforeseen environmental condition; the responses are usually required immediately or urgently. They may take the form of changes in previous plans or of new plans or decisions quickly made. Their objective is to avoid undesirable results or to reap attractive rewards. Adaptive responses comprise (1) planning, primarily short-term (planning decisions); (2) nonfunctional decisions (those involving mere choices); and (3) implementing actions (implementation).

Definition

In Chapter 16, we define adaptive responses as *managerial reactions to unforeseen environmental occurrences.* Although adaptive responses are composed of elements similar to those of other phases of management, their causes are completely different, their urgency is usually far greater, and they are usually unique in some aspect.

Other considerations

One of the responsibilities of all managers, whether explicitly stated or merely implied, is to remain constantly on the alert for opportunities which have not been anticipated in plans. Likewise, managers must also be vigilant concerning unforeseen threats to objectives currently being pursued. Thus, effective managers do not single-mindedly plan and implement, even though these two functions are clearly keys to success in the running of organizations. Managers must understand the importance of this third element of management and be able to make successful adaptive responses to a variety of unforeseen environmental exigencies.

Owing to pressures that sometimes quickly build, managers often execute adaptive responses poorly and ineffectively. In a majority of instances, they probably execute them inefficiently. One of the purposes of this book is to identify adaptive responses as an element of management, isolate them as a class for study, focus the attention of managers and students of management on them, and outline procedures for their timely and effective formulation.

Events which necessitate adaptive responses do not necessarily occur singly. The worklives of most managers include periods when unexpected occurrences are nearly overwhelming. Such periods test not only a manager's intelligence and capabilities but a manager's basic stamina and courage. Thus, a procedure for formulating adaptive responses must take into consideration the amount of time and resources available.

Managers can handle many, if not most, unforeseen events quickly and within the constraints of available time. Usually in such cases, the appropriate responses are easily determined and the required resources are available or can be procured promptly. Appropriate responses can be quickly framed and executed with no organizational coordination required (except perhaps the coordination of immediate subordinates). The process includes a fast mental review (reflective thought), followed by a decision and directions to act.

However, some matters in large organizations affect other managers standing in both vertical and horizontal relationships and they cannot be resolved through existing policies or protocol. These should be subjected to a rather formal process (one that can easily be learned and followed), with adaptations to accommodate the peculiarities of each situation as required.

Our current knowledge of statistics and of human nature, plus our ability to process information in milliseconds, allows us to forecast the future and plan better than ever. In addition, the same factors which have brought improved planning have also vastly increased the efficiency of implementation. Yet it is still necessary to frame adaptive responses to those events impossible to foresee. When adaptive responses are needed, a manager will be more likely to react properly if he or she can recognize that the problematic event is not dealt with by existing plans and can then follow an orderly procedure for resolution. Later in this book, we discuss some of the issues concerning the recognition and resolution of unforeseen problems in an attempt to aid managers in dealing with them.

Summary

Writers have defined management in a variety of ways depending on their viewpoints. In addition, writers have variously conceived the structure of management and the elements that compose it. As a result, there exists no universally agreed upon model of management as a process. Although both academicians and practitioners are more sophisticated regarding certain aspects of management (owing to technology, research, and experience), the management-theory jungle that Harold Koontz wrote about in 1961 remains almost as dense as ever.[34]

We believe this state exists largely because the basic elements of the management process have been misidentified. We suggest that management is composed of two basic categories of function: planning and implementation. No purposeful action can be done in any organization without there first having been a plan made for doing it. The plan may not have been made correctly and may even be detrimental to the organization. Nonetheless, all purposeful action results from a plan of some sort, no matter how simple in content or how quickly made.

The other *sine qua non* of management, implementation, is composed of all activities that contribute to realizing the plans that have been made. All plans (i.e., decisions about future courses of action) are useless unless they are carried out. It is no surprise that these twin categories, planning and implementing, include most management functions. Furthermore, planning and implementing activities are often closely associated and even intertwined in a work situation. Nonetheless, each can be clearly identified only through superficial analysis.

We have identified a third category of management, which we entitle *adaptive responses*. This category includes all reactions to events and occurrences that arise because of a lack of appropriate planning, mistakes in planning, or unforeseen environmental factors (either internal or external to the organization). Although such reactions are themselves composed primarily of planning and implementation, we believe their dissimilarity to deliberately made plans and controlled implementation merits studying them separately. In most cases, they are characterized by urgency, a short timeframe for planning, decision making, and implementation; and nonrecurrence (or uniqueness).

These three categories, then, include all the functions that make up the process of management: planning, implementation, and adaptive responses. Because of certain legal functions and duties that boards of directors and executives in corporations possess by law (regarding shareholders, employees, the public, and the corporation itself), we have elected to discuss board and executive functions in a separate chapter. However, all the management functions exercised by boards of directors and by executives fall in the same three categories.

Notes

1. Peter F. Drucker, *The Practice of Management* (New York: Harper & Row, 1954), 8.
2. Maurice Wormser, "Private Corporations," in *Modern American Law*, vol 4, ed. Eugene A. Gilmore (Chicago: Blackstone School of Law, 1965), 100.
3. Peter F. Drucker, *Management: Tasks, Responsibilities, Practices* (New York: Harper & Row, 1973, 1974), 5.

4. Ibid., 17.

5. William H. Newman, Kirby E. Warren, and McGill, *The Process of Management*, 4th ed. (Englewood Cliffs, N.J.: Prentice-Hall, 1977), 12–14.

6. Henri Fayol, *General and Industrial Management* (London: Sir Isaac Pitman and Sons, 1967), 3.

7. Ibid.

8. Frederick W. Taylor, *Principles of Scientific Management* (New York: Harper & Bros., 1911), 36–37.

9. Ibid., 129–130.

10. Fayol, *General and Industrial Management*, 3.

11. Ibid., 5–6.

12. Henry Arthur Hopf, "Management and the Optimum," in *Classics in Management*, ed. Harward F. Merrill (New York: American Management Association, 1960), 358.

13. William H. Newman and Charles E. Summer, Jr., *The Process of Management* (1961), 9. Reprinted by permission of Prentice-Hall, Inc., Englewood Cliffs, N.J.

14. Ibid., 10. Reprinted by permission of Prentice-Hall, Inc., Englewood Cliffs, N.J.

15. Ernest Dale, *Management: Theory and Practice*, 2d ed. (New York: McGraw-Hill, 1969), 4.

16. Ibid., 5–7.

17. Joseph L. Massie, *Essentials of Management*, 2d ed. (1971), 4. Reprinted by permission of Prentice-Hall, Inc., Englewood Cliffs, N.J.

18. Ibid., 6–7. Reprinted by permission of Prentice-Hall, Inc., Englewood Cliffs, N.J.

19. William J. Ronan, "The New Dimensions of Management," in *Management for the Future*, ed. Lewis Benton (New York: McGraw-Hill, 1978), 247–56.

20. Warren B. Brown and Dennis J. Moberg, *Organization Theory and Management: A Macro Approach* (New York: Wiley, 1980), 6.

21. James A.F. Stoner, *Management*, 3rd ed. (1982), 8. Reprinted by permission of Prentice-Hall, Inc., Englewood Cliffs, N.J.

22. Thomas Peters and Robert H. Waterman, Jr., *In Search of Excellence* (New York: Harper & Row, 1982).

23. Richard M. Steers, Gerardo R. Ungson, and Richard T. Mowday, *Managing Effective Organizations* (Boston: Kent Publishing Company, 1985), 29.

24. Ibid., p. VI.

25. *Black's Law Dictionary*, 4th ed., s.v. "art."

26. Ibid., s.v., "profession."

27. Drucker, *The Practice of Management*, 370–92.

28. Richard A. Johnson, Fremont E. Kast, and James E. Rosenzweig, *The Theory and Management of Systems*, 2d ed. (New York: McGraw-Hill, 1967), 4.

29. Ibid., 11.

30. Ibid.

31. Ibid., 12.

32. J.P. Barger, "The Managing Process," in *Handbook of Business Administration*, ed. H.B. Maynard (New York: McGraw-Hill, 1967), 1–5.

33. Brown and Moberg, *Organization Theory and Management*, 280.

34. Harold Koontz, "The Management Theory Jungle," *Journal of the Academy of Management*, December 1961, pp. 174–188.

Part II

Exercising the Corporate Franchise

Corporations control the major portion of business and industry in this nation and throughout the Western world. They are all somewhat similar with respect to formation, legal status, and structure. The second chapter discusses the functions of those who have legal responsibility for the conduct of the corporate business: board members and executives.

Boards and their appointed executives both initiate and maintain the exercise of all corporate franchises. Their actions are central to the success or failure of any corporate venture. Because of the importance of these actions and their unique relationship to the management of corporations and consequently to the bulk of business activities, we have set them apart for discussion.

Although boards and executives perform the same management functions that prevail throughout all management (i.e., functions classifiable as planning, implementation, or adaptive responses), they have an added responsibility not clearly and routinely vested in managers at lower management levels. These we designate *legal functions and duties,* and we discuss them in addition to planning, implementation, and adaptive responses.

Boards and executives represent the power and driving force of the corporations they serve. They have been called the fulcrum of activities, the nerve center, the soul, or the heart of the corporate body. The individuals may not be indispensable, but the positions they hold and the functions they perform clearly are. The positions are repositories of functional power conferred directly by the state and thus, in this nation, by society as a whole.

Over the last several years, some have expressed rather severe criticism of the actions or lack of actions of boards of directors in corporations. Although there will always be poorly constituted boards, as well as ineffective executives, the freedom now allowed in board formation and action is probably beneficial to corporate management overall. Possibly we are biased owing to our having worked with unusually objective, honest, and forward-thinking board members. However, we think not. Rather, we believe the current climate that is created by allowing relationships to form among board members and executives as they see fit outweighs in the long run any benefits that might occur from imposing restrictions, as some have suggested.

Chapter 2

Board and executive functions

33

Elements of Management
in Corporations

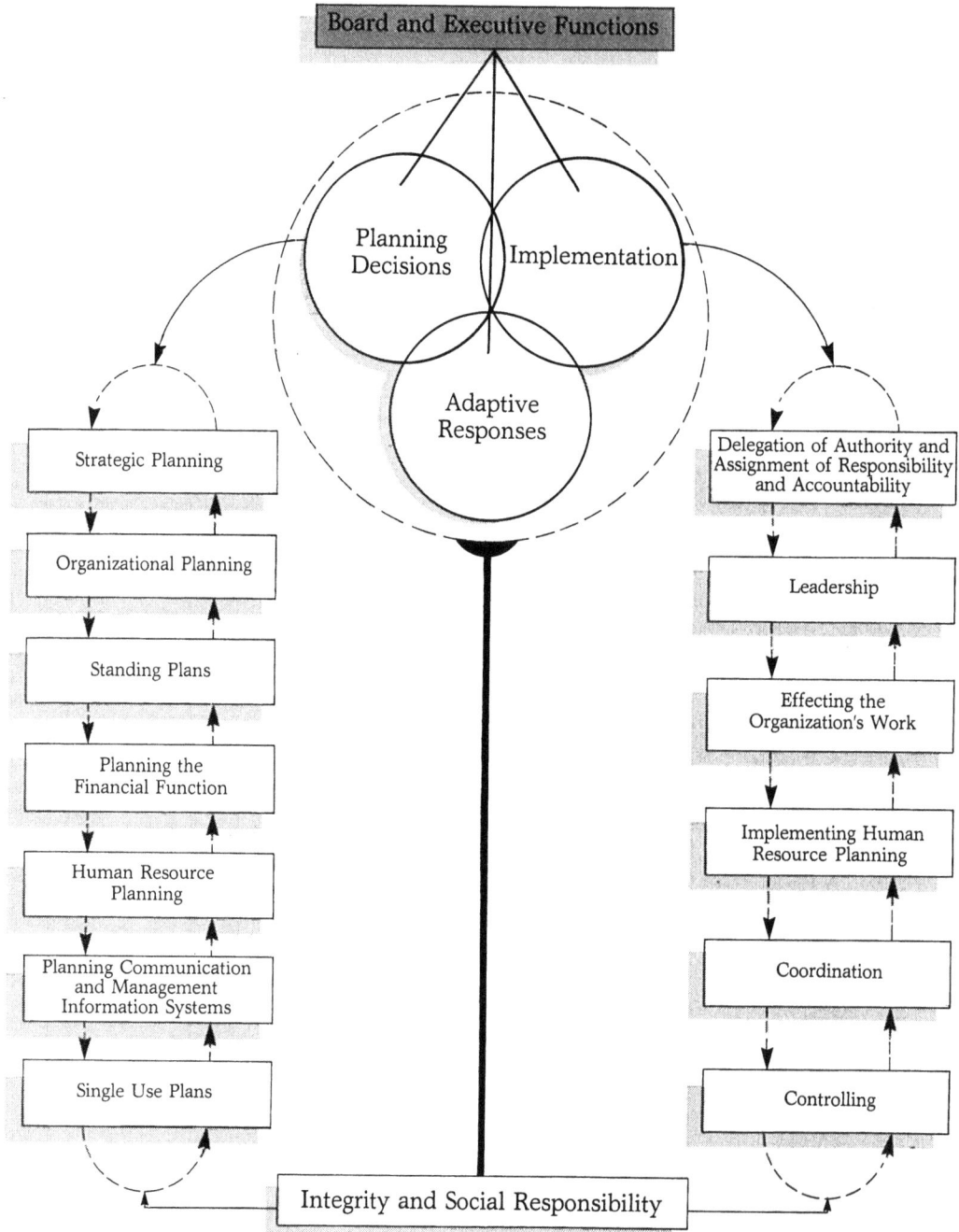

Board and Executive Functions

Planning Decisions

Implementation

Adaptive Responses

Strategic Planning

Organizational Planning

Standing Plans

Planning the Financial Function

Human Resource Planning

Planning Communication and Management Information Systems

Single Use Plans

Delegation of Authority and Assignment of Responsibility and Accountability

Leadership

Effecting the Organization's Work

Implementing Human Resource Planning

Coordination

Controlling

Integrity and Social Responsibility

2

Focus of terms

Organizations of many types exist throughout the world and for a variety of purposes. In this book, we discuss formal and informal organizations, especially formal organizations such as businesses. Although we hope our opinions may be useful to persons associated with any type of organized endeavor, our primary intent is to provide insights regarding the management of business firms. In this chapter, we confine our comments exclusively to business firms, with an emphasis on private corporations. Such corporations control the major portion of industry, trade, and commercial services in the Western world, although their number is much less than the number of partnerships and individual entrepreneurs. We focus on corporations not only because of their business volumes but also owing to the fact that they possess some legal aspects unlike those of partnerships and other business firms. To discuss all types of organizations with regard to their top managers and boards (for those that have boards) would be a monumental task. Therefore, we decided to limit discussion to board and executive functions as we understand them to exist in private corporations. Even so, there may be some conclusions we draw that are pertinent to other types of corporations or businesses. In particular, persons involved with public or quasi-public corporations may find some of our comments useful.

Corporations can derive their right of existence from any one of the fifty states. In the early part of the nineteenth century, the Supreme Court of the United States, in *Trustees of Dartmouth College v. Woodward*,[1] held that a corporate charter was a contract within the meaning of the constitutional provision that no state may pass any law impairing the obligations of a contract. Many authorities have believed, and believe even today, that the Court erred and that the granting of a corporate charter only constitutes a franchise or a privilege granted by a sovereign state to incorporators authorizing them to do business as a legal entity.[2] Nonetheless, *Trustees of Dartmouth College v. Woodward* put all states into a predicament with regard to controlling the actions of corporations. Shortly after this decision, the states began to include in corporate charters, as they were granted, provisions to amend, alter, or rescind them at the discretion of the state. This practice continues today. Without it, states might have serious problems in controlling the actions of corporations.

Whether one regards the charter of a corporation as a franchise granted by a state or as ''a contract between the state and the corporation, between the corporation and the stockholders, and between the stock-holders and the state"[3] really makes little difference for our purpose here. In either instance, the charter of a corporation represents the authority under which a corporation exists and is enabled to do business. It forms a locus of power—power derived from the state and delegated by it to the corporation. The filing of the charter creates a new and separate legal person, recognized by the state as such. In effect, a new, legally distinct citizen is born, with a life and identity separate from its parent share-holders.

What does a corporation have the power to do? The prevailing view holds that a corporation possesses powers specified in the corporate charter, and most states require that the overall type of business the incorporators expect to conduct be described fairly accurately in the charter. Many would-be incorporators choose Delaware as the state of choice in which to incorporate, for Delaware grants charters that do not have restrictions on types of business or combinations of business (there is a broad range of other advantages as well). An incorporator or incorpo-rators will obtain a corporate charter in Delaware, employ a "registered agent" resident in that state, and then establish headquarters, branch offices, or subdivisions in any other state that is desired.

A board of directors, whose members are usually elected by the stockholders, exercises the powers stipulated in the corporate charter and defined in the laws of the state which created the corporation (see Figure 2-1). (In most nonstock corporations organized for the conduct of some type of business, which are usually not-for-profit, directors are elected by the "members," and "membership" is acquired according to stipulations in the corporate charter and bylaws.)

Subject to the charter provisions, the bylaws adopted by the stock-holders or members, and the state laws, the board of directors has vested in it the authority or power to conduct such business as the corporation may be allowed to undertake. True, the board can only act as a group, but, sitting as a group, it has the power to manage the business, even in disregard of the wishes of the stockholders or members, as the case may be. (Some states do not allow directors to act by unanimous vote without officially convening.)

The board of directors in turn elects a president and other officers of the corporation—such officers as may seem appropriate—to manage the day-to-day business of the corporation. The president is usually dele-gated the authority and assigned the responsibility commensurate with the requirements of operating the business. However, other officers who may be named receive such authority and responsibility as are specifically given by the board or required by state law.

Who are the executives of a corporation? Here, again, we have an instance of a very loosely used management term. Some older manage-ment texts refer to all managers, even down to the level of supervisors, as *executives*. Others ignore the term altogether. Chester Barnard, in his remarkable text *The Functions of the Executive*, stated

> The functions of the executive . . . are those of control, manage-ment, supervision, administration, in formal organizations. These functions are exercised not merely by high officials in such organizations but by all those who are in positions of control of

Figure 2-1

Basic Corporate Management Structure

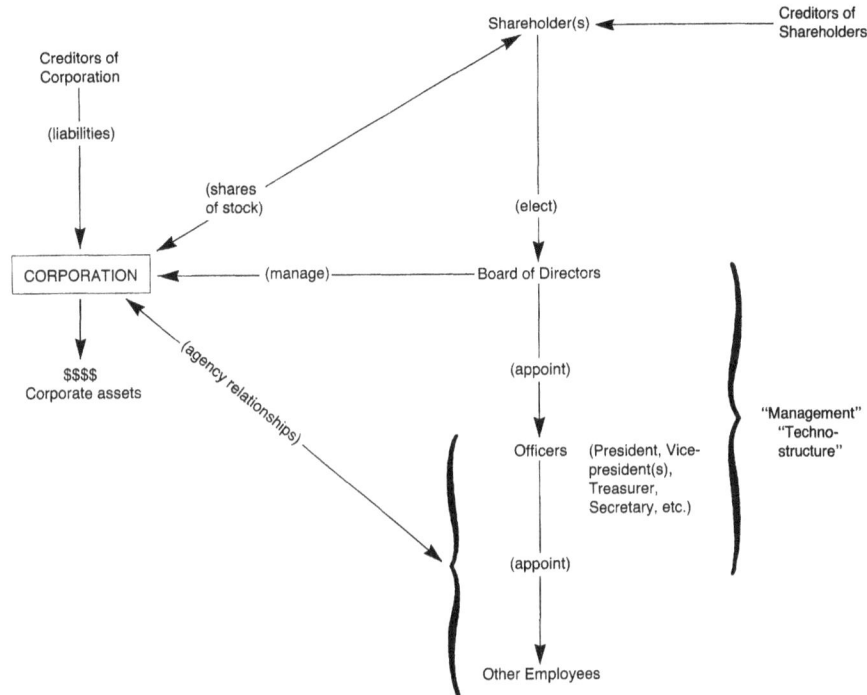

Source: Reprinted from *Laws of Corporations* by H.G. Henn and J.R. Alexander, p. 467, with permission of West Publishing Company, © 1983.

whatever degree. In the large-scale and complex organizations, the assistants of executives, though not themselves executives, are occupied in the work of executives. . . . On the other hand it not infrequently occurs that high officials in organizations, though known as executives and occupying important positions, exercise few or unimportant and incidental executive functions, and at least some work of all executives is not executive in the sense which concerns us.[4]

Certainly, Barnard states forthrightly what he considers executive functions to be: control, management, supervision, and administration. But these functions themselves are unclear. One might conclude that all who exercise executive functions are therefore executives, but Barnard eliminates this possibility by stating "assistants to executives, though not themselves executives, are occupied in the work of executives." Thus, we are left in a quandary as to who, in formal organizations, should be rightfully considered executives.

Steers, Ungson and Mowday provide a useful definition of *executive management*. In categorizing managers by level, they identify executive management, middle management, and first-line management, which they define as follows:

- *Executive Management:* Executive managers are those relatively few senior administrators who are responsible for establishing long-term objectives as well as general operating policies to ensure that the objectives are met. Executive managers can usually be identified by their titles, such as chief executive officer (CEO), president, and vice-president.

- *Middle Management:* Middle managers are largely responsible for interpreting the general, long-range objectives set down by executive management and translating them into concrete specific goals for various decisions and departments. Middle managers often supervise the activities of other lower-level managers.

- *First-line Management:* First-line managers, or supervisors, are largely responsible for carrying out the day-to-day activities within the various departments to ensure that short-term goals are met. Such positions are often the place where new college graduates receive their first assignment.[5]

Brown and Moberg, although they do not define the term *executive* as such, define the term *executive structure* as "the design of the organizations at the top of the hierarchy."[6]

Based upon the preceding opinions and our personal experience, we consider the executives in private corporations to be the chief executive (usually called the CEO or president), who reports directly to the board of directors, and those managers who report directly to the chief executive. If individuals other than the chief executive have direct appointments from the board as officers of the corporation and retain a direct reporting relationship to the board, they, too, should be considered executives. So should chief executive officers of largely independent plants, divisions, or subsidiaries of corporations, together with managers who report directly to them (see Figure 2-2).

De jure and usually de facto authority to do business in a private corporation vests in a corporate charter; a board of directors, elected by stockholders, has the right and obligation to exercise the authority specified in the charter and in state law; the board of directors then usually appoints a president and vests in him or her the authority and assigns the responsibility to operate the business. Other officers, who may report directly to the board or to the president, may also receive appointments for specific purposes. The president, in turn, appoints a top echelon of managers, all of whom we shall define as executives.

Having defined boards of directors and executives and having identified their relationship within private corporations, we can now examine their functions, both from the standpoint of the law and of operating practices.

Board functions

Overview

Many authorities on management ignore the role of boards of directors in the management of corporations. Yet, the law clearly holds that these

Figure 2-2

Management Levels
in Corporations

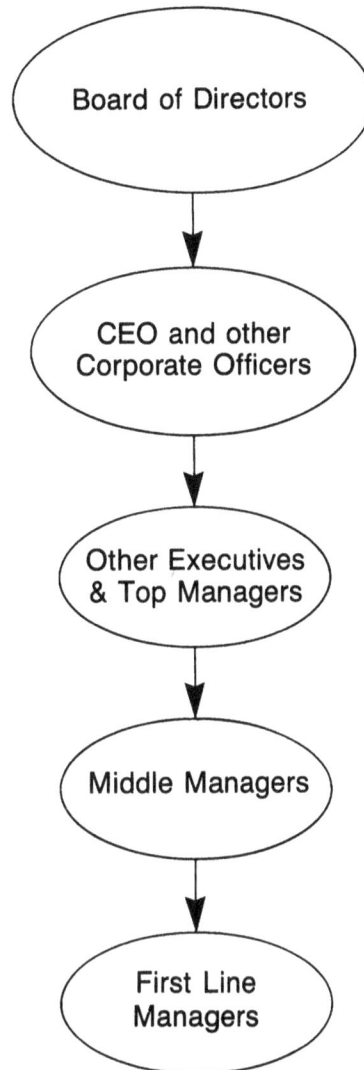

```
        ┌─────────────────────┐
        │   Board of Directors │
        └──────────┬──────────┘
                   │
                   ▼
        ┌─────────────────────┐
        │    CEO and other     │
        │  Corporate Officers  │
        └──────────┬──────────┘
                   │
                   ▼
        ┌─────────────────────┐
        │   Other Executives   │
        │    & Top Managers    │
        └──────────┬──────────┘
                   │
                   ▼
        ┌─────────────────────┐
        │   Middle Managers    │
        └──────────┬──────────┘
                   │
                   ▼
        ┌─────────────────────┐
        │     First Line       │
        │      Managers        │
        └─────────────────────┘
```

boards, elected by the shareholders, possess all of the authority and all of the responsibility to manage that is contained in the corporate charter and required by state law. That the majority of the Fortune 500 companies, for example, have boards which depend upon hired executives to perform the actual tasks of management and which, according to at least one authority, are somewhat passive does not detract from the legal fact of their pre-eminence regarding both authority and responsibility.[7] However, directors usually exercise their legal management functions only when duly convened as a board,[8] and for this reason alone the implementation of management decisions is left largely to managing officers and agents. See Figure 2-3 for a simple portrayal of the functions of a corporate board.

Figure 2-3

**Functions of the
Board of Directors**

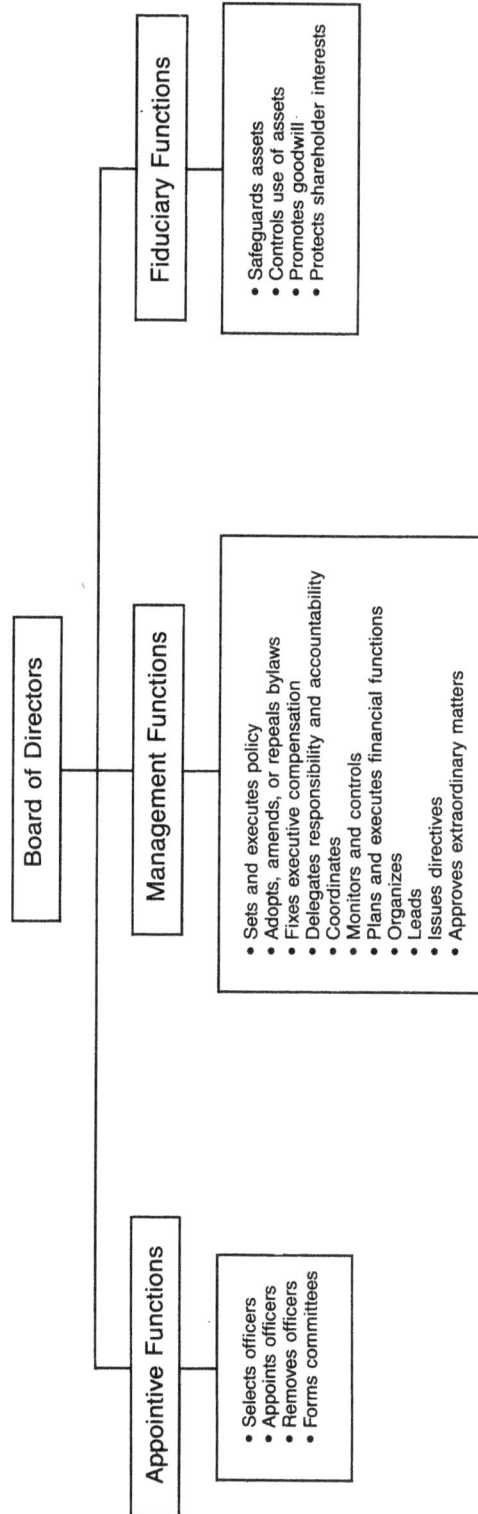

Board of Directors

Appointive Functions

- Selects officers
- Appoints officers
- Removes officers
- Forms committees

Management Functions

- Sets and executes policy
- Adopts, amends, or repeals bylaws
- Fixes executive compensation
- Delegates responsibility and accountability
- Coordinates
- Monitors and controls
- Plans and executes financial functions
- Organizes
- Leads
- Issues directives
- Approves extraordinary matters

Fiduciary Functions

- Safeguards assets
- Controls use of assets
- Promotes goodwill
- Protects shareholder interests

Relationship of board to shareholders

Although shareholders elect the directors and can remove them with or without cause, directors are not the agents of the shareholders.[9] And although the position of directors is similar to that of a trustee, in the strict sense they are not trustees.[10] Indeed, their relationship to shareholders is *sui generis* [one of a kind].[11] Directors occupy a fiduciary relationship, both to the corporation and its shareholders.[12]

"Within the scope of their authority—that is, in regulating the ordinary business affairs of the corporation—the power of the directors is supreme, and the stockholders have no right to dictate to them or to order them to do or not to do certain acts."[13] Although this is generally thought to be true at the present time, many tests of the matter have occurred in the courts of this nation and in Britain.

In general, during the terms of office of directors, the shareholders cannot remove them, either singly or as a body. At annual meetings of shareholders, which are held primarily for the election of directors, the removal of directors and the election of others can and do occur.[14] "Shareholders elect the board of directors, who manage the corporation by determining corporate policy and appointing officers to execute [implement] such policy. Separation of ownership (in the shareholders) and management (in the board of directors and officers) is inherent in such approach."[15]

Shareholders generally engage in management functions (interpreted as legal rights of shareholders under state law) to a very limited extent, with such duties ordinarily encompassing only (1) electing and removing directors, usually at annual meetings; (2) approving, disapproving, or amending corporate bylaws; (3) framing and passing resolutions; (4) appointing independent auditors; and (5) deciding special or extraordinary corporate matters, e.g., merger, consolidation, dissolution, etc.[16] With regard to bylaws, provisions may be included "for the management and regulation of the corporation,"[17] so long as the provisions are not inconsistent with existing local laws and the corporate charter. In different states, either the incorporators, shareholders, or board of directors may initially adopt the bylaws.[18] "Notwithstanding any power in the board of directors to amend or repeal the by-laws, the shareholders usually retain inherent powers to do so."[19] Certainly the greatest effect shareholders have on the management of any corporation is to elect new directors when they become dissatisfied with existing ones.

Relationship of board to executives

Directors of the board "are responsible for the determination and execution of corporate policy, usually including . . . (b) selection, supervision, and removal of officers and possibly other executive personnel; (c) fixing of executive compensation, pension, retirement, etc. plans; . . . (e) delegation of authority for administrative and possibly other action."[20] These responsibilities, in most instances dictated by statute, largely determine the relationship between the board and executives.

The CEO almost invariably reports directly to the board of directors, although in many instances the board creates an executive committee for the CEO to consult during the time the board is not in session. Other officers appointed by the board (and most statutes provide at least for the election of vice-presidents, a secretary, and a treasurer) are delegated authority of various kinds and degrees. In the case of the secretary and the treasurer, the authority delegated has become rather standard. Regarding vice presidents, the authority often is focused on a particular function or area of corporate activity, such as the development and marketing of a particular product or service. Either pertaining statutes or corporate bylaws stipulate exactly whom the board of directors must appoint. "Actual authority [of officers] consists of any express authority delegated to them by the by-laws or by the board of directors and the implied authority inherent to their respective offices. Directors are under a duty of due care in supervising officers."[21]

The relationship of the board to executives depends somewhat on whether a particular executive is also a member of the board. Nearly always in large corporations, the CEO is a member of the board and in many instances is either elected as its president or serves in that capacity under bylaws or by statute. In most instances, it is up to the CEO to see to it that the board receives timely, accurate information pertinent to all matters to be considered on a prepared agenda.

> The chief executive will be careful to keep his board happy by not shifting the regular meeting date, having too many long meetings (two or three hours should be the rule) or calling too many special meetings (which may indicate a lack of planning ability on his part). He will also see to it that the meetings are productive.[22]

Unquestionably, boards of directors can contribute much to corporate management because of their individual experiences and other unique qualifications (which were hopefully ascertained and used as reasons for election). The wise chief executive will find a way to profit from these qualifications.

Harold Geneen, a former head of ITT, has been extremely critical of boards of directors and their relationships to company officers.[23] While we have the utmost respect for him, we do not share his view that board-executive relationships need nearly universal revamping. Certainly, one can deplore certain conflicts of interest that often arise, and his cautions can be appreciated. However, persons who worship at the altar of selfishness will probably gravitate toward compromise in most situations in which they find themselves. Furthermore, no matter how the relationship is restructured, self-interest will have its say. And note that avariciousness is not confined to any social or economic class.

Irving S. Shapiro, who is a former chairman of the board and chief executive officer of the Du Pont Company and who has served on HCA's board since 1981, holds a more moderate view about the functions of directors than Geneen's. In his recent book *America's Third Revolution*, Shapiro considers the functions of boards:

> The thrust of this chapter [titled "The Climate Inside"] is that the foundations of the present system are sound, the methods of governance are defensible in terms of both ethics and democratic principle, and the proposed curatives are more dangerous than any disease from which the private sector suffers.

Some changes are needed to remedy past mistakes and reflect new conditions, but such changes should come in an orderly way and are being made. Pat formulas for "restructuring" [boards] should be viewed with great skepticism, on the grounds that what fits one corporation may not be suited to another. The drastic reforms suggestions ought to be opposed *in toto* for they would yield the worst of all possible outcomes.[24]

We believe the traditional relationships which statutes or bylaws specify between executives (officers) and boards are generally satisfactory. If they aren't, one thing seems certain: They will not change much faster than the constitution of this nation. That being the case, both boards and executives must make the best of the existing situation, which they can easily do through complete honesty, exemplary ethics, mutual trust, and a determination to produce positive results through efficient management. The initiative for all of this should come primarily from the CEO and other company officers, who must realize that boards are not executive bodies and hence are forced more toward reaction than action. This being so, a good CEO and his or her retinue of executives must always try to *draw out* the very best from their board. This requires refraining from deception, painting rosy pictures when there are none, and putting personal objectives above those of the corporation.

As to relations between the board and executives who are appointed exclusively by and report directly to the CEO, they vary widely and depend on certain interests of the board and the CEO. However, boards should diligently keep abreast of the capabilities and accomplishments of these executives, and those who produce outstanding results should occasionally receive audiences with and appropriate recognition by the board itself. The CEO should also see to it that this occurs. Any perceptive CEO knows that his or her performance depends largely on the performance of the other executives directly below his or her own position. Finally, a board should remove any CEO (or other executive) who stays on top through repression of subordinates or deliberate employment of less competent persons in executive positions.

Functions of the board

Richard M. Paget, a senior partner of Cresap, McCormick and Paget, divides the functions a board performs into two basic categories: (1) formal legal functions and (2) special functions.[25] Paget further divides formal legal functions into two subcategories: "(1) responsibilities for safeguarding and controlling the use of corporate assets; and (2) duties involved in discharging legal obligations to manage the affairs of the business."[26]

As regards safeguarding and controlling the use of corporate assets, the law clearly holds that the board of directors stands in a fiduciary relationship to the corporation. Shareholders "own" the property and other assets, whereas the board of directors possesses them and is responsible for safeguarding them.

As far as legal obligations concerning the management of the business, boards are required to select, supervise, and remove executives (when necessary), determine their compensation, and devise pension and retirement plans. In addition, boards are responsible for

(a) policy decisions with respect to products, services, prices, wages, labor relations; . . . (d) determination of dividends, financing, and capital charges; . . . (f) possible adoption, amendment and repeal of by-laws; (g) possible participation along with shareholders in approving various extraordinary corporate matters [mergers, dissolution, disposal of property, etc.]; and (h) supervision and vigilance, for the welfare of the whole enterprise.[27]

As to special functions, we agree with Mr. Paget that among the most valuable functions performed by directors, both as individuals and as members of a formal body, is providing advice to the CEO.[28] Both authors of this book over many years have dealt with boards which were fortunate to have outstanding individuals as members. Not only did these board members help shape and guide the businesses we were managing, but they helped us to mature, both personally and professionally. One of us, as a consultant, has not had a direct relationship with a board for several years, but the other, while serving as president and chief operating officer of HCA, had a close relationshp with HCA's board of directors and, in fact, held membership on that board until formation of HealthTrust Inc. HCA's board, in our opinion, has on it some of the top management talent in the nation.

The selection of the outside members of HCA's board has been based first and foremost on the specific contributions each individual could make as a part of a mature, action-oriented, policy-making body. No two members have possessed identical backgrounds (i.e., education, skills, and experience), but most have served as top executives or board members of large corporations. All are noted for being highly independent thinkers. The careful selection process is largely due to the efforts of Don MacNaughton, a recognized authority on the functions of boards, and Dr. Thomas F. Frist, Jr., who currently serves as chairman of HCA's board and as its chief executive officer.

The many demonstrations of farsighted and independent resolve by HCA's board clearly show that the current methods of membership selection, the generally recognized limits on board responsibilities, and the allowable board-executive relationships can easily accommodate the best action-oriented decision making possible in today's business world.

In a sense, board appointments have paralleled HCA's need for management knowledge at particular points in its history. Strategic planning moves have resulted in certain requirements for specialized knowledge and opinions, and one of the functions of board members has been to supply that knowledge. For example, Robert Anderson, chairman of the board and CEO of Rockwell International, has extensive experience in dealing with a variety of government agencies, and HCA's policies in this regard have benefited since he accepted an appointment in 1971. Carl Reichardt, chairman and CEO of Wells Fargo Company and Wells Fargo Bank, N.A., joined HCA's board in 1972 at a time when capital formation was an overriding issue for the firm. Frank Cary, former chairman of IBM, was added when the need for in-depth knowledge about data processing became apparent. He was joined in 1984 by Joe B. Wyatt, chancellor of Vanderbilt University, whose expertise in data processing is well known.

Irving Shapiro, former chairman and CEO of Du Pont and an authority on antitrust law, received his appointment in 1981 when HCA's problems in the antitrust arena surfaced. Owen B. Butler, chairman of Proctor and Gamble Company's board, and Donald V. Seibert, retired chairman and CEO of J.C. Penney Company, were appointed when marketing responses to the current wave of consumerism in health care became necessary. More recently, Martin Feldstein, professor of economics at Harvard and former chairman of President Reagan's Council of Economic Advisors, agreed to serve and give guidance concerning current world economics. Clifton C. Garvin, Jr., retired chairman and CEO of Exxon Corporation, recently joined HCA's board as a replacement for the late John deButts; he will undoubtedly lend advice in an area already well known in the oil industry—that of maturing lines of business. Outpatient care is rapidly expanding, but inpatient care seems to have matured with respect to its demand.

Other current outside HCA board members, such as Frank Borman, Eastern Airlines' former top executive; Frank Royal, M.D.; John Thornton, M.D.; Barbara Clark, of the Massey Companies; and Charles J. Kane, chairman of the board of the Third National Corporation (in Nashville) were all elected to provide expertise in areas where needs have been particularly apparent.

In reviewing its membership composition, no reasonable mind could conclude that HCA's board would ever be a "rubber stamp" for HCA's management. Indeed, in the past this combination of incisive minds has provided a tremendous challenge to all appointed officers. As a group, the board has possessed full awareness of its authority and responsibilities, and one of its prime concerns has been to perform in accordance with its legal duties.

Paget has noted another special function of boards: making sure "programs are being followed to develop successful management [talent]."[29] Although this is certainly a board duty, we have always been so concerned about this ourselves that we have not had to rely heavily on boards. Make no mistake: Any manager's immediate subordinates hold the key to his or her success—or undoing.

The last special function listed by Paget is the board's duty to check on management's results. This is definitely one of the board's legal obligations and is a part of the control process.[30] As noted elsewhere, a failure by managers to control is virtually equivalent to a failure to manage. We abhor dictatorial controls, we reject them, and if they had emanated from our boards, we would have protested. However, we have appreciated the control measures to which we have had to adhere. The necessity to measure up oneself is invariably appreciated by one's subordinates when they prepare reports about their own efforts to meet objectives or other predetermined standards of performance.

Boards perform their functions both through convening regularly and through a committee structure. Boulton states that a "monitoring function is being carried out through . . . committees that parallel the management structure of the executive organization."[31] He suggests that an organization committee can review the legal liabilities and responsibilities of the corporation; an audit committee can review the accuracy of financial and operating information (and, we would add, the timeliness of that information) and ensure that controls and auditing procedures are appropriate; an executive committee can review corporate objectives and policies as well as critical decisions that relate to them; a strategy review committee can study the nature and adequacy of business strategies to meet corporate objectives and satisfy corporate policies; a compensation and human resources committee can review the sufficiency of organizational development, productivity, and motivational systems; and a corporate relations and ethics committee can monitor the effects of corporate actions on the corporation's committees and environment (and on the corporate culture itself).[32]

Although Boulton did not mention a finance committee, we regard that as one of the most important committees which any board appoints. However, as Paget notes, "it is generally a mistake to include both an executive committee and a finance committee in the board structure of the average corporation, because it is extremely difficult to define the respective limits of responsibility of these two groups."[33]

The committee structure of HCA's board is typical of most large corporations and reflects the experience of its members. Committees have met bimonthly (or at the call of the chairperson) in conjunction with the board meeting—except the executive committee, which has met in the intervening month. Five committees have composed the entire structure: (1) audit, (2) compensation and benefits, (3) executive, (4) nominating, and (5) social responsiveness. The names of the committees indicate the functions carried out, so no elaboration seems necessary. We note that the executive committee has had rather broad authority to act on matters that otherwise might have been considered by a meeting of the full board had such a meeting been possible to hold. It has also possessed the power to monitor financial functions (in line with Paget's suggestion quoted above).

Certainly, the committee approach to monitoring corporate functions is a sound one. Such monitoring not only fulfills the board's legal responsibility but assists the CEO in keeping all executives (as defined in this book) constantly alert. Figure 2-3 provides a brief summary of the functions of a corporate board.

Executive functions

We have defined the class of executives of a corporation as consisting of (1) the chief executive officer (CEO), (2) other officers of the corporation who are appointed by its board and who then report either to the board or the CEO, (3) other managers who report directly to the CEO, and (4) heads of largely independent plants, divisions, or other subsidiaries, together with their immediate subordinates. Thus, executives constitute the top-level management of the corporation. Of course, corporations are organized in numerous ways and our definition may not "fit" some corporations as well as others (e.g., in some cases managers would be considered executives under our definition, but could not plausibly be placed in the top level).

Executive functions fall into two basic categories: (1) management functions and (2) legal functions and duties (see Figure 2-4). Some may

Figure 2-4

Executive Functions in Corporations

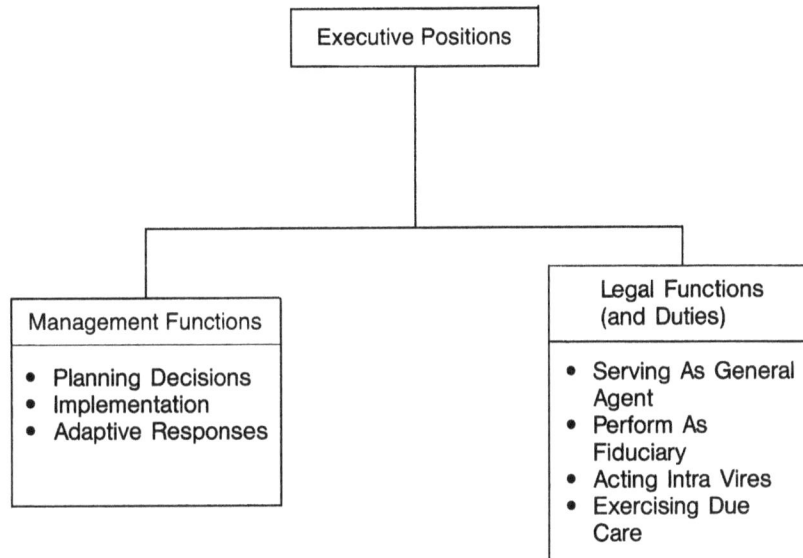

```
                        ┌─────────────────────┐
                        │ Executive Positions │
                        └──────────┬──────────┘
                                   │
              ┌────────────────────┴────────────────────┐
              │                                          │
   ┌──────────┴──────────┐                   ┌───────────┴───────────┐
   │ Management Functions │                   │    Legal Functions    │
   │                      │                   │     (and Duties)      │
   │ • Planning Decisions │                   │ • Serving As General  │
   │ • Implementation     │                   │   Agent               │
   │ • Adaptive Responses │                   │ • Perform As          │
   │                      │                   │   Fiduciary           │
   │                      │                   │ • Acting Intra Vires  │
   │                      │                   │ • Exercising Due      │
   │                      │                   │   Care                │
   └──────────────────────┘                   └───────────────────────┘
```

question whether a text about management should consider legal functions. One could also question whether a text on management should consider such subjects as operations research, industrial engineering, and the social sciences. We strongly believe that all of the above are involved in management and that one cannot be an outstanding executive without understanding legal functions and duties, especially at the CEO level. In our opinion, far too few texts on management try to elucidate the legal milieu within which executives must function.

Management functions

The general management functions of executives fall into the same categories as those for other managers. Executives (1) plan, (2) implement their plans, and (3) respond adaptively to situations where control is lacking.

Uniqueness of executive positions
Although the classifications of functions may be the same, executives' perspective, opportunities, and obligations regarding overall corporate performance differ greatly from those at lower organizational levels. Executives must have a panoramic view of all of their corporation's functions; other personnel may concern themselves with only some of these functions. In a sense, executives must consider all parts as they relate to the whole; others need only consider how one part relates to the whole.

Harold Geneen states that "top management, headed by the chief executive, is in effect the fulcrum of the company. Pressures for performance are exerted upon him from the top and from the bottom of the organization."[34] Geneen's words, from our viewpoint, are perfectly true.

The position of top management and the role it plays in every organization have some unique aspects not possessed by the positions and roles of other managers at lower echelons. This is precisely the reason we have chosen to discuss executive functions separately. Executives truly form the nerve center of a corporation. With the CEO at the head, they are the basic source of authority for all corporate management (once they have received this authority from the board of directors). They occupy positions at the top, and since the beginning of history humans have looked to the top for leadership in all types of organized endeavors (whether it was forthcoming or not).

This looking to the top occurs naturally. In the way our society is organized (with corporations as integral parts), it confers legitimacy. Furthermore, it has proven to be of great benefit, because a leaderless flock lacks the kind of identifiable mindset that allows it to act as an organized whole. Executives may not be the soul of an organization, but they have a better opportunity to express the organization's soul, especially in the case of corporations, than any other person or group of persons. Executives also possess greater responsibilities than other managers, for responsibility cannot be delegated. CEOs, for example, possess responsibility for the acts of their subordinates in addition to responsibility for their own acts.

Since confronting the responsibilities of being president and chief operating officer of a large corporation, one of us stated, "It is like being a director of a very large orchestra. Each instrument grouping must make its appropriate contribution in perfect harmony with the others."[35] This comment basically agrees with the comment of Harold Geneen quoted above.

Other differences between executives and lower echelon managers may be related to the greater need for perceptiveness on the part of executives regarding all of the internal and external relationships a corporation possesses or should possess. Although planning, implementation, and the framing of adaptive responses may reflect this perceptiveness, it is separate from these functions. It is, in part, a matter of having a certain kind of attitude toward the world in which one lives and functions. Without a necessary sensitivity, which is due to one's basic nature, keenness of perception and skill at conceptualizing, one can be a good executive but it is doubtful one can be a great executive. One way of putting this is that being a great executive depends on more than just corporate results; it depends on being a certain kind of person and on acting in certain responsible ways regarding one's fellow human beings.

If executives possess greater responsibilities than other managers, they also possess greater opportunities, not only opportunities for realizing corporate mission, goals and objectives but also opportunities for framing and modifying them in response to environmental change. We discuss such opportunities in the following account of the three categories of executive management functions: planning, implementation, and adaptive responses.

Planning
Essentially, executives have ultimate responsibility for planning of every type throughout a corporation's hierarchy of managers. The focus of

executives, however, must be on the mission of the corporation and its goals and top objectives rather than on in-the-trenches operational planning. While in theory they may not be responsible for the formulation of top policies (which is the board's duty), in fact executives usually formulate policies or collaborate in formulating policies for approval by the board, with subsequent promulgation being done by the board, the CEO, or another appropriate executive.

Executives must plan for longer terms than other managers, and thus their planning sets the tone, the climate, and the general direction for strategic, operational, and all other types of planning in the corporation. They also deal with unknowns and unknowables more than do others. Because of this, every executive has a responsibility for getting the very best available information, both in order to plan and to make on-the-spot decisions. We decry those who accept false theories of leadership, including the view that a true business leader can smell out opportunities, wade ashore amid a hail of bullets, and go on to lead the troops to a glorious victory. (More likely, such a "leader" drowns in a flood of criticism, swamped by failures.) No, we believe any leader worthy of the name plans and makes decisions based on facts to the extent that this is feasible. Having said this, we admit that because executives must plan for longer time periods and because short-term information has more validity than long-term, they will often have to proceed with planning in the absence of vital information.

Some executives fall into the trap of spending such a long period seeking information on which to build a plan that the optimal time for planning and implementation passes by. This may occur because they have failed to give previous consideration to procedures for obtaining information. They may have also failed to give anyone the responsibility for settling on a procedure or for getting information. However, we know from our own experience that good information, especially information that pertains to periods beyond five years, can be in extremely short supply.

Lee Iacocca has said, "I may act on my instincts—but only if my hunches are supported by the facts. . . . Obviously, you're responsible for gathering as many relevant facts and projections as you possibly can. But, at some point you've got to take that leap of faith."[36] These comments suggest the view about the executive's role in planning that we are trying to convey.

Alvin Toffler's book *The Adaptive Corporation* recounts AT&T's attempt, beginning in 1968, to look beyond the present and discern the general nature of the future. Top management hired Toffler to do this, and in a remarkable and famous report, he predicted AT&T's break-up fairly accurately.[37] While we doubt many corporations will need to hire someone like Alvin Toffler to prepare such a report, Toffler's employment indicates the kind of planning responsibility that top executives have, including the responsibility to try to peer into the future, starting with what might be called zero-base strategic planning. This latter type of planning involves annually re-examining basic assumptions about the mission and goals of a corporation (see Chapter 3).

Do executives spend more of their professional time in planning than do other managers, and if so, should they? The answer to both parts of the question is yes. Indeed, on the whole, executives still do not spend as much time in planning as they should. In major corporations, at least one-third of an executive's time can well be spent in planning, and possibly as much as 50 or 60 percent, depending on the situation.

Throughout this text, we emphasize the need for executives of major corporations to plan well into the future (say, 5 years ahead) and to formulate an outlook for strategic planning for possibly as long as 10 to 15 years ahead. However, we want to stress that this should not detract from operational planning of all types that is needed to gain such short-range objectives as those related to increasing earnings. Executives must ensure there are adequate planning sessions that include subordinates who are on the firing line. Earnings and profits lost today are seldom replaced by those anticipated in the long term. Managers must meet all budgeted earnings for the short term (quarterly and annually) *and* stakeout claims for the long term—certainly for three to five years ahead.

Implementation

Implementation is covered in detail in Part IV of this book, which contains chapters on delegation of authority and assignment of responsibility and accountability, leadership, effecting the organization's work, implementating, human resource planning, coordination, and controlling. Executives, like other managers, have functions in all these areas. However, the scope of an executive's tasks and the style used in implementation are different than for lower echelon managers.

In organizational planning (see Chapter 4), executives determine the basic organizational structure of a corporation and the degree of decentralization of authority by considering various aspects of management (e.g., decision making, planning, control, etc.). Following this, implementation of the plans occurs. Implementation is done by obtaining agreements or coming to an understanding with those to whom delegations of authority and assignments of responsibility and accountability are made. A written format should be used and usually a clearly and specifically worded job description should be set down.

In getting work accomplished, executives both direct and lead, and they may employ influence, authority, and power as required. However, executives occupy positions where leadership can be effective (and their actions hopefully will demonstrate this).

Geneen has commented extensively on business leadership. He states,

> A leader leads his people; a commander commands them. . . .
> In the long run, I am certain that it [commanding] is coun-
> terproductive . . . under those conditions. . . . The person who
> heads a company should realize that his people are not really
> working for him; they are working *with* him for themselves.
> They have their own dreams, their own need for self-fulfill-
> ment. . . . He [the CEO] has to prove to them that he is working
> as hard as they are, that he is competent in his own role as chief
> executive, that he will not lead them over the cliff and jeopardize
> their livelihoods, that he can be relied upon to reward them
> properly and fairly, that he is willing to share the risks as well as
> the rewards of their enterprise.[38]

Iacocca has indirectly referred to leadership as follows: "In addition to being decision makers, managers also have to be motivators. . . . The only way you can motivate people is to communicate with them. . . . My policy has been to be democratic all the way to the point of decision."[39]

Successful executives conscientiously devote time to coordination. They must be extremely perceptive regarding the formal arrangement of the organization's divisions or departments. Also, they must understand the essential elements of voluntary coordination and be good communicators, both in speaking and writing.

We have emphasized repeatedly that planning and controlling are essential to getting work accomplished on time, within budget, and of intended quantity and quality. Executive control necessarily involves reporting by exception to some extent, or else one becomes lost in a sea of reports. Yet, a competent executive must devote time to implementing an effective procedure for reporting key information (especially about results) and must take the time to study the information received.

Executives must exert control through using a reporting system and should spend less time in direct observation than a supervisor, for example. However, seeing and being seen from time to time proves beneficial, not only for the executive but for his or her subordinates.

Adaptive responses

The more skill executives exercise in planning, the less time they will devote to adaptive responses. "Putting out fires" constitutes a way of life for some executives, seemingly because they choose such a management style. Some achieve a certain flamboyance in thrashing around, exercising their authority and power, and exhibiting their importance. Perhaps this makes them feel a certain exhilaration. However, this style of management eventually takes its toll in failing to provide direction for a company. Appropriate planning allows executives to act so as to increase the chance of success and decrease the need to be forever reacting to the vicissitudes of the environment.

On the other hand, no executive can plan so thoroughly that all eventualities will be foreseen (nor should one attempt to do so). As already stated, many executive decisions about the future necessarily involve a longer lead time than do those of other managers. This being so, some of the decisions will be risky and require changes, even though prudent efforts may have been devoted to planning (gathering appropriate data, considering alternatives, etc.). On-the-spot responses will sometimes have to be made to changed or unforeseen circumstances. In such instances, executives must undertake short-range planning or make immediate selections from among existing alternatives. (We have already noted that all planning is decision making—about future actions over varying time periods—but that not all decision making is planning. Some decision making merely involves choosing from among largely similar alternatives.) Of course, if there is time, one should try to obtain the relevant facts. Where time is short, one may have to draw on experience. Perhaps that's why most top corporate executives have reached or passed middle age.

In framing adaptive responses, not only does an executive need the skills of a good decision maker, but he or she must have what might be crudely called "guts." This characteristic, whatever the term used, is not so important for making immediate decisions as for seeing that the decisions are carried out (i.e., for the implementation element of adaptive responses).

When one makes decisions in framing adaptive responses that require immediate action, there may be little or no time available to gain a consensus among subordinates. This is another reason to plan well and avoid adaptive responses. However, one will inevitably be faced with this situation, and one must simply act without a consensus. Iacocca may overstate the case, but after describing how he tries to maintain a democratic spirit by listening to subordinate opinions, etc., he states, "I then became the ruthless commander."[40] Certainly, in responding to exigent situations, one may have to exercise authority. If so, it should be done unhesitant. Wavering under pressure can undermine one's leadership and decrease the probability of a successful implementation.

Legal functions and duties

Legal functions

Executives have express authority to perform management functions and, in the case of the CEO, authority implied by virtue of the position occupied. The authority vested in executives is through delegation by the board of directors "pursuant to statute, the articles of incorporation, by-laws and resolutions of the board."[41]

At the present time, in some larger corporations, boards have virtually abdicated their rights to manage, and according to a number of authorities, they do "little more than ratify, or 'rubber stamp' the actions and even policy decisions of the officers."[42] In these cases, not only do officers and other executives possess the authority delegated to them expressly, but they possess considerable implied authority. This implied authority, "which may not be inconsistent with express authority, may be said to be 'presumptive,' 'inherent' or exist 'by virtue of office,' or it might result from general custom or the practice of the particular corporation (with the acquiescence of directors or shareholders)."[43]

Customarily, the CEO possesses authority to conduct the business transactions of a corporation by virtue of the office, while vice-presidents have only the authority that has been expressly delegated, usually through bylaws and board resolutions.[44] Other officers and executives have only express authority, and this varies widely according to what is needed, or believed to be needed, for achieving objectives.

Executives, mostly by express authority, function as agents of a corporation. Managers at lower corporate levels can also be given authority as agents, and likewise even purchasing agents and salesmen. The CEO, however, functions very much as a general manager, and as such has the broad authority (and the responsibility) of a general agent. A general agent can be defined as "an agent authorized to conduct a series of transactions involving continuity of service."[45] In contrast, a special agent only receives directions "to conduct a single transaction or a series of transactions not involving continuity of services."[46]

It may be helpful to define the term *agent:* "An agent is one who acts for and on behalf of another person called the principal, in the same manner as the principal might himself act in the particular matter in which the authority is conferred."[47] In years past, the agent-principal relationship was used primarily in forming contracts with third parties; in modern corporate law an agent can be presumed to act on behalf of a principal in a number of ways.

As agents of a corporation, executives perform a broad variety of functions. In many instances, executives stand in a fiduciary relationship to the corporation and owe fiduciary duties not only to the corporation but sometimes also to shareholders.

Legal duties
The legal duties of executives (together with directors and sometimes controlling shareholders) can be subsumed under three general categories: "(a) to act *intra vires* and within their respective authority, (b) to exercise due care and (c) to observe applicable fiduciary duties."[48]

Intra vires *actions:* To act *intra vires* broadly means to engage only in that business which the corporate charter allows the corporation to do. *Ultra vires* actions are those beyond the terms of the charter. "For any loss [by officers and other executives] to the corporation resulting from their engaging the corporation in *ultra vires* activities, they are, in some jurisdictions, absolutely liable and in other jurisdictions, liable only if they were negligent as to the scope of their corporate powers."[49] This sounds somewhat frightening, but as a matter of fact litigation rarely occurs, except when executives engage in fraud or other illegal activities.

Duties of due care: Generally, the law defines due care as acting in the manner of a reasonably prudent person in a similar situation. Executives can be found remiss in circumstances where due care is owed, either through acts of commission or omission. "However, they are not insurers and are not liable for errors of judgment or mistakes while acting with reasonable diligence, care and skill."[50]

Fiduciary duties: Executives owe certain fiduciary duties to the corporations they serve. These duties have been defined more through decisional law than statutes, but some states now specifically record by statute the fiduciary duties owed to corporations within their borders. The kinds of violation of fiduciary duty by executives are generally as follows:[51]

1. competing with the corporation

2. usurping corporate opportunity (where one diverts to oneself an opportunity rightfully belonging to the corporation)

3. allowing a conflict of interest (where one has an interest in the outcome of a transaction that could conflict with one's primary duties to the corporation)

4. engaging in insider trading of stock (primarily regulated by the federal Securities and Exchange Commission)

Although our discussion of the legal functions and duties of executives has necessarily been brief, hopefully we have called to our readers' attention the fact that, from the standpoint of the law, executives do not merely perform in the role of an employee. In the traditional employee-employer relationship, no agency powers accrue or form and no fiduciary duties exist. Indeed, the roles of executives and directors involve many legal implications, of which they should be aware. This is the reason a corporate attorney (or attorneys) regularly attends the board meetings of any major corporation.

At the same time, executives should not allow unnecessary fear of the law to prevent them from acting aggressively on behalf of the corporation. Some attorneys, we believe, are overly cautious for fear that their own positions may be at stake if executives incur legal problems. In such cases, the attorney's position may be safe, but the executive, by trying to avoid every potential legal snare, may put at risk his or her own job, which is, after all, to achieve certain results.

Summary

We have limited our discussion here to board and executive functions in private corporations. However, our remarks may have relevance for some members of other types of organizations.

Each corporation derives its existence, legal power, and authority to do business from one of the fifty states, and each corporate charter documents the scope of such powers and authority. The shareholders (owners of a corporation) elect and authorize a board of directors to manage it, and the board in turn has the power to appoint officers (including a CEO) who act for it in carrying forward the business. Delegations of authority by the board of directors to executives may be contained in statutes, the corporate charter, corporate bylaws, and board resolutions.

We intend that the term *executive* refer to the following: the CEO; board appointed officers who report either directly to the board or to the CEO; other officers or managers who report directly to the CEO; the heads of largely independent plants, divisions, etc.; and their immediately subordinate managers. In other words, executives are the top managers and officers, including the CEO.

The corporate board of directors, elected by the shareholders, possesses all of the power and authority, as well as all of the responsibility for operating the corporation. Directors serve neither as trustees nor agents of the shareholders, although they possess a fiduciary relationship to them.

Shareholders do not directly control the directors, even though at annual shareholder meetings they elect them and can remove them (which rarely occurs). In fact, one of the main items of business at annual shareholder meetings is reflected in the election of directors. Shareholders affect the decisions of directors to some extent by virtue of their power to approve and amend bylaws, frame and pass resolutions, and approve or disapprove special or extraordinary corporate matters. In the course of ordinary business, however, directors act without being much constrained by shareholders.

Legally, a board of directors sets policy, controls the CEO, and appoints officers and such other executives as may be necessary. In actual practice, the executive staff, especially the CEO, usually assists the board in making policy, and where a board elects to pursue a passive role (as some do), executives may make policy as a matter of course.

Boards also routinely determine dividends, policy on financing and capital changes, and sometimes changes in bylaws. They may also act with shareholders in approving extraordinary matters, and they determine the compensation and retirement provisions for executives. In effect, boards have the responsibility to supervise the corporation and vigilantly protect its general welfare.

Executives perform the same basic functions of management that all managers do, namely planning, implementation and the framing of adaptive responses. In addition, they serve as agents of the corporation, either general or special, and as such possess a strong fiduciary relationship to the corporation.

Executive positions, especially that of the CEO, are at the top of the management hierarchy. These positions form the corporation's nerve center and their occupants hopefully provide its leadership. Executives must consider all parts of the corporation and how each should mesh with all the others. Other managers are more concerned with how a single part relates to the whole.

In planning, executives must devote time and energy not only to quarterly and annual plans but to those which are longer term, even those looking 5, 10, or 15 years into the future. Each type of planning discussed in this text will be of concern to the effective executive, and he or she should see to it that an ongoing orderly planning process exists.

Executives delegate authority for hands-on management to others. They also decide on the basic degree of decentralization and then implement decentralization plans through new policies, through changes in formal organizational structure, and through agreements with subordinate managers regarding delegations of authority and assignments of responsibility and accountability.

Executives direct, exercise authority, and provide leadership in getting the actual work of the organization accomplished. They devote conscious effort to coordination and establishing systems of communication. All highly successful executives institute effective systems of control and ensure that a reporting system delivers to them such timely information as will be needed to keep the firm on target regarding its mission, goals, and objectives.

Inevitably, executives must concern themselves with adaptive responses, but the time devoted to "putting out fires" can be drastically reduced by appropriate planning. Success in making adaptive responses results from recognizing when they should be made, making good decisions, and following up the decisions with effective implementation (a part of which is exercising appropriate control).

Executives have both express and implied authority for performing their functions. Express authority is explicitly stated in formal documentation. Implied authority is consistent with express authority, but unlike the latter it is presumed to inhere in the office or to result from custom or from the practice of the particular corporation (i.e., it is not explicitly set out).

Three general duties include all the specific legal duties of executives to corporations: (1) to act *intra vires* and within delegated authority, (2) to exercise due care, and (3) to observe applicable fiduciary duties. Four kinds of violation of fiduciary duty comprise the great majority of actual violations. These are (1) competing with the corporation; (2) usurping corporate opportunity; (3) allowing a conflict of interest in planning and making other decisions, and (4) engaging in insider trading of stock. Certainly, all executives have a duty to become sufficiently aware of the law to avoid serious legal entanglements, both with regard to themselves and the corporations they represent.

Notes

1. 4 Wheat. 518 (U.S.), Leading Illustrative Cases.
2. Maurice Wormser, "Private Corporations," in *Modern American Law*, vol. 4, ed. Eugene A. Gilmore (Chicago: Blackstone School of Law, 1965), 110.
3. *Black's Law Dictionary*, 4th ed., s.v. "charter."
4. Chester I. Barnard, *The Functions of the Executive* (Cambridge, Mass.: Harvard University Press, 1966), 6.
5. Richard M. Steers, Gerardo R. Ungson, and Richard T. Mowday, *Managing Effective Organizations* (Belmont, Calif.: Kent Publishing Company, 1985), 30–31.
6. Warren B. Brown and Dennis J. Moberg, *Organization Theory and Management* (New York: Wiley, 1950), 664.
7. Harold Geneen with Alvin M. Moscow, *Managing* (Garden City, N.Y.: Doubleday, 1984), 252.
8. Harry C. Henn and John R. Alexander, *Laws of Corporations* (St. Paul, Minn.: West Publishing Company, 1983), 564.
9. Ibid., 563.
10. Ibid.
11. Ibid.
12. James L. Vincent, "Role of the Corporate Secretary," in *Handbook of Business Administration*, ed. H.B. Maynard (New York: McGraw-Hill, 1967), 13–15.
13. Wormser, "Private Corporations," 180.
14. Henn and Alexander, *Laws of Corporations*, 511.
15. Ibid., 490.
16. Ibid., 491–517.
17. Ibid., 513.
18. Ibid., 573.
19. Ibid.
20. Ibid., 563.
21. Ibid., 571.
22. Richard M. Paget, "The Board of Directors," in *Handbook of Business Administration*, ed. H.B. Maynard (New York: McGraw-Hill, 1967), 3–19.
23. Geneen, *Managing*, 249–66.
24. Irving S. Shapiro with Carl B. Kaufmann, *America's Third Revolution* (New York: Harper & Row, 1984), 235.
25. Paget, "The Board of Directors," 3–18.
26. Ibid.
27. Henn and Alexander, *Laws of Corporations*, 563.
28. Paget, "The Board of Directors," 3–18.
29. Ibid.
30. Ibid., 3–19.
31. William R. Boulton, *Business Policy* (New York: Macmillan, 1984), 137.
32. Ibid., 138–39.
33. Paget, "The Board of Directors."
34. Geneen, *Managing*, 87.

35. Comment of R.C. McWhorter after becoming executive vice-president for operations at HCA, May 1984.

36. Lee Iacocca with William Novak, *Iacocca* (New York: Bantam Books, 1984), 50.

37. Alvin Toffler, *The Adaptive Corporation* (New York: McGraw-Hill, 1985), 1–174.

38. Geneen, *Managing*, 145–46.

39. Iacocca, *Iacocca*, 52.

40. Ibid.

41. Henn and Alexander, *Laws of Corporations*, 593.

42. Ibid.

43. Ibid., 595–96.

44. Ibid.

45. Harold Gill Reuschlein and William A. Gregory, *Agency and Partnership* (St. Paul, Minn.: West Publishing Company, 1980), 14.

46. Ibid.

47. William A. Ferguson, "Agency," in *Modern American Law*, vol. 2, ed. Eugene A. Gilmore (Chicago: Blackstone School of Law, 1963), 2.

48. Henn and Alexander, *Laws of Corporations*, 611.

49. Ibid., 620.

50. Ibid., 621.

51. Ibid., 625–63.

Part *III*

Planning Decisions

In its purest form, planning is a mental activity: thinking. Many aspects of planning may be recorded, either on paper or in electronic data banks, and countless calculations and evaluations may be done by computer, but invariably the end product of planning—a decision or decisions—involves human thought. Even in cases where arguably computers do make decisions and render orders based on them, humans planned that this should be done and made decisions in the process.

Planning results from *purposeful thinking*, as opposed to vagaries, daydreams, reveries, or other purposeless thought. Purposeful thinking occurs as a response to desire or the need for self-preservation, and even in the latter desire is present—the desire for continued life and well-being. Desire generates purposeful thought: The mind perceives a need in the form of an objective or goal and immediately confronts the problem of attainment. The problem of attainment, then, is the fundamental cause of purposeful thought.

The reflective thought process described by the philosopher John Dewey is equivalent to purposeful thought. According to Dewey, the reflective thought process has the following six phases (the sixth phase is described in the quotation after the list below):

1. *suggestions*, in which the mind leaps forward to a possible solution;

2. an intellectualization of the difficulty or perplexity that has been *felt* (directly experienced) into a *problem* to be solved, a question for which the answer must be sought;

3. the use of one suggestion after another as a leading idea, or *hypothesis*, to initiate and guide observation and other operations in collection of factual material;

4. the mental elaboration of the idea or supposition as an idea or supposition (*reasoning* in the sense in which reasoning is a part, not the whole, of inference); and

5. testing the hypothesis by overt or imaginative action.[1]

59

Dewey clearly perceived the reflective thought process as planning (making decisions about future courses of action); this is evident in his suggested sixth phase.

> It has been suggested that reflective thinking involves a look into the future, a forecast, an anticipation, or a prediction, and this should be listed as a sixth aspect or phase. As a matter of fact, every intellectual suggestion or idea is anticipatory of some possible future experience, while the final solution [or decision] gives a definite set toward the future.[2]

In commenting on the benefits of the reflective thought process, Dewey made a statement in 1933 that will always be worthy of note: The reflective thought process "converts action that is merely appetitive, blind, and impulsive into intelligent action."[3] Clearly, Dewey regarded the reflective thought process as a rational planning model for individual human beings. And humans are the basic units of all organizations, some of whom—managers—are charged with a key role of planning.

The rational decision-making process, possibly derived from Dewey's reflective thought process or from the scientific method, has also been advanced as a model for making both planning and nonfunctional decisions. This process is usually regarded as having four steps, or phases when used for planning exclusively:

1. The problem is diagnosed and the mission, objectives, or goals are defined.

2. Alternative solutions or courses of action are determined and set forth.

3. The relative feasibility of each of the alternative solutions or courses of action is analyzed and tested.

4. The most feasible solution or plan is selected.

The scientific method, possibly the progenitor of all reflective, rational planning methodologies, can be traced directly to Galileo (1564-1642) and Bacon (1561-1626). Scientific investigators have used the method worldwide since the days of Galileo and Bacon, and it is recognized as being largely responsible for thrusting humankind into the atomic age and to the far reaches of space.[4] In essence, the scientific method makes use of the following steps:

1. The problem to be investigated is defined.

2. Pertinent facts are obtained (observation).

3. Hypotheses are formulated.

4. The hypotheses are tested (experiment).

5. A theory is constructed on the basis of the hypothesis which seems best.

6. The theory is submitted to wider testing, either in an experimental situation or in the real world.

The Re-entry Systems Department of General Electric Company used the "systems approach" to planning in the late 1950s and throughout most of the 1960s in their space contracts. General Electric and Gordon A. Freisen International, Inc. first introduced this methodology to health care planning in the late 1960s, and since that time derivations of it have been used throughout the health care field. In fact, the methodology for strategic planning described in Chapter 3 is such a derivation.

Figure III-1 outlines the systems approach to planning, and readers can easily grasp its applicability in numerous instances where complex plans must be devised. Regarding use in corporations, its adaptability to various levels of cognizance will become obvious.

Figure III-1

The Systems Approach to Planning

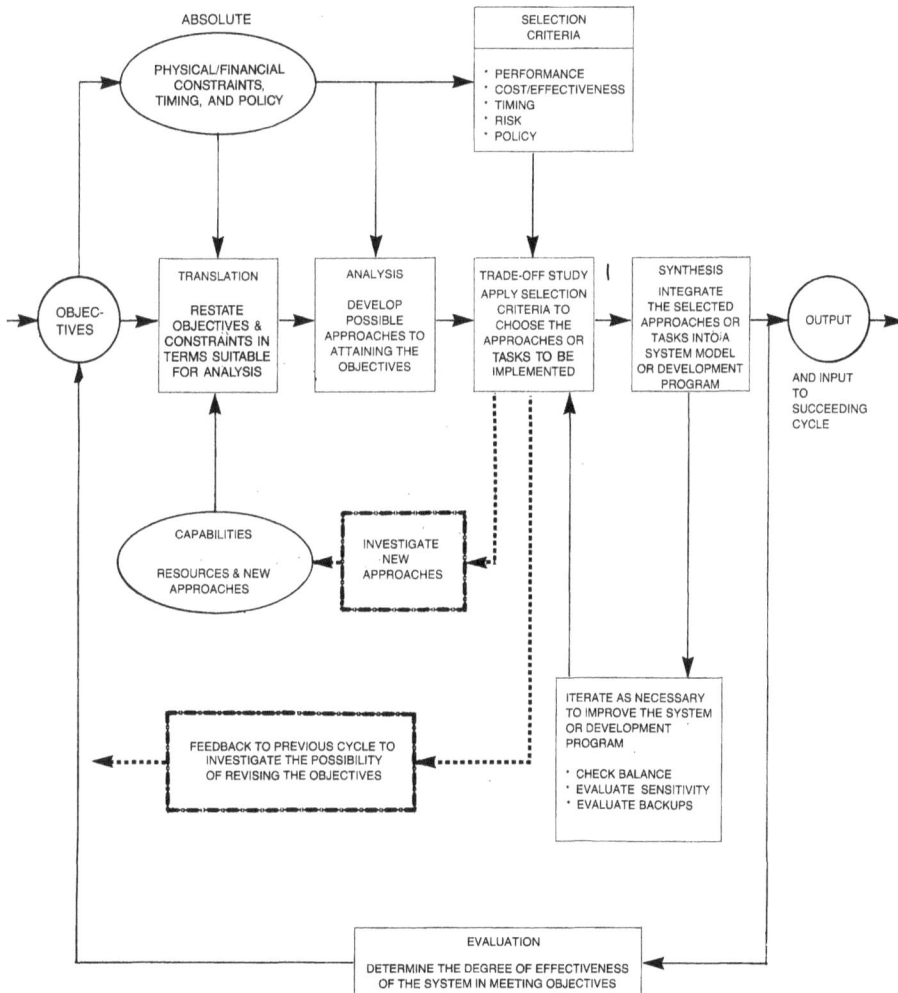

Courtesy of: Re-entry Systems Department, General Electric Company.

The systems approach has been shown to be adaptable for designing operational systems (lending validity to its name) and also for planning—if the objective of that planning is to identify, describe, and eventually adopt an ongoing activity or process.

The analysis or design of a system centers upon definitions of who (if humans are involved), when, what, where, and how. We have noted several times in this text definitions of the same kinds are integral to a complete plan.

As readers review the various types of planning outlined in the next seven chapters, they should remember that all plans possess several characteristic components, and the determination of each requires a planning decision or decisions. These components are as follows:

1. designation of a person or persons who will perform one or more envisioned tasks (who)

2. determination of a timeframe in which performance will take place (when)

3. specification of tasks to be done (what)

4. designation of the place or places where tasks will be done (where)

5. definition of the procedure, process, or method by which tasks will be done (how)

6. quantification of expected expenditures and associated asset gains, if applicable (how much)

Some of the decisions relating to one or more of these components may be merely implicit in the communications to those who will perform the intended tasks. Some may be made at different times or by different decision makers than others, but on the completion of the tasks, analysis will invariably reveal that all were made—either rationally or irrationally, timely or untimely, efficiently or inefficiently, and correctly or incorrectly. Successful implementation usually results from decisions that were made rationally, timely, efficiently, and correctly.

Notes

1. John Dewey, *How We Think* (Boston: Heath, 1933), 117.
2. Ibid., 117.
3. Ibid., 17.
4. Owen B. Hardy, "Systematic Process Applied to Health Care Planning," *Hospital Administration* 16 (Winter 1971): 13.

Chapter 3

Strategic planning

Elements of Management
in Corporations

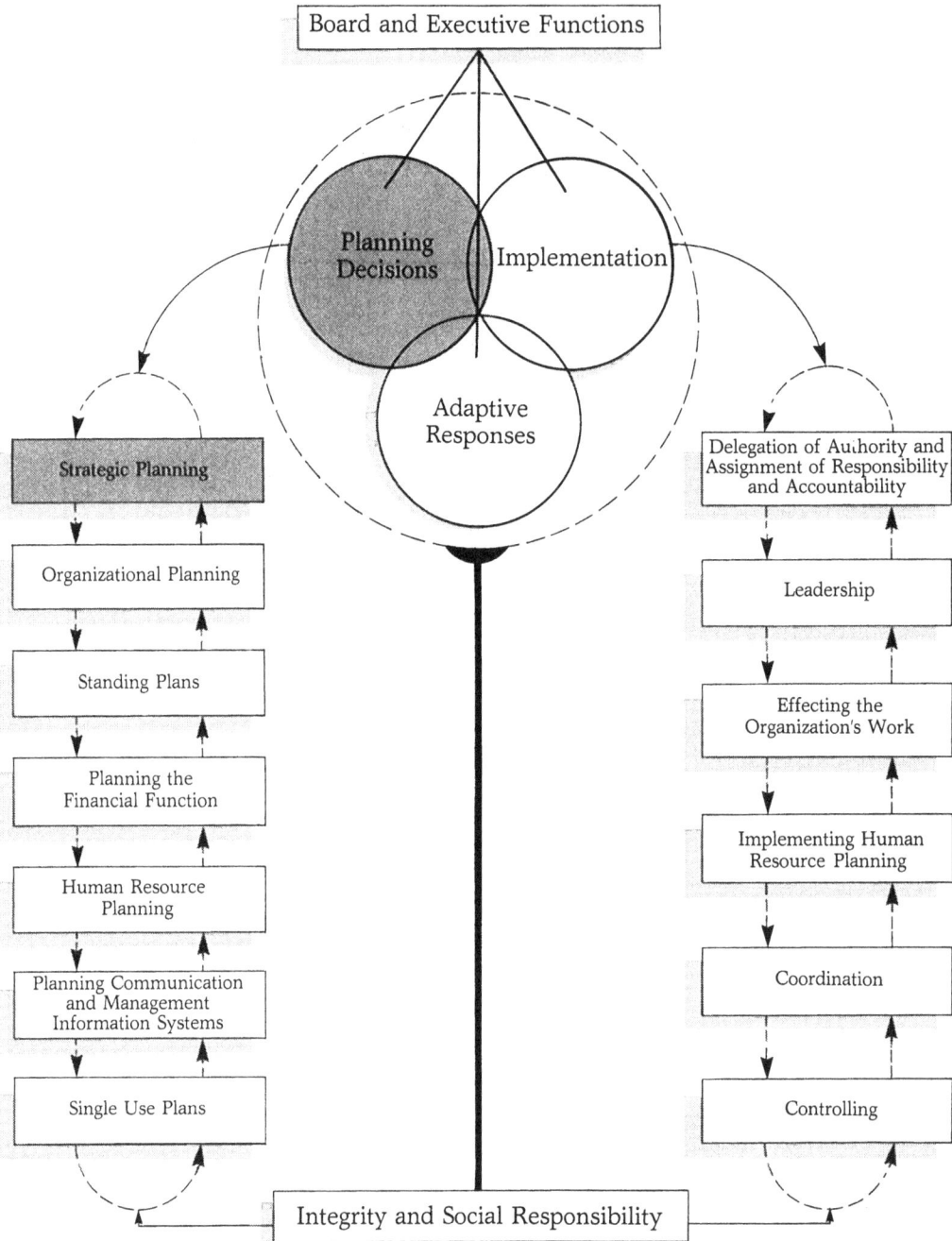

Board and Executive Functions

Planning Decisions

Implementation

Adaptive Responses

Strategic Planning

Organizational Planning

Standing Plans

Planning the Financial Function

Human Resource Planning

Planning Communication and Management Information Systems

Single Use Plans

Delegation of Authority and Assignment of Responsibility and Accountability

Leadership

Effecting the Organization's Work

Implementing Human Resource Planning

Coordination

Controlling

Integrity and Social Responsibility

3

Need, situation, and benefits

Given the amount of competition among business enterprises today, no management function possesses greater importance than strategic planning, except of course the actions which implement such planning. As we move forward into the twenty-first century, the organizations that will dominate our society and culture and achieve a high degree of success—as measured in economic terms and by other standards, both qualitative and quantitative—will do so through a process of sound strategic planning. Having stated this somewhat pedantically, we fear our readers will merely pass over the subject, dismissing it as among those "things we wish we could do but probably won't have time to do—and besides we don't quite understand it." Therefore, we express some honest and straightforward opinions below in the hope of getting the attention of our readers, especially top officials of corporations and business units.

Many corporations and other business firms in this nation still fly by the seat of their pants. If strategic planning ever occurs outside the individual brains of top officers, it occurs in brief, usually informal conferences, and it is typically based on information little better than "hunches" or on the witnessed success of a few other firms in the same line of business (so-called copycatting). Even when a formal process is followed for developing strategies based on appropriate data and information, the derelictions are so numerous that the results are questionable.

The volume and quality of opinions recorded in management literature about strategic planning appear to be inversely proportional to the importance of the subject. Although some authors on management now recognize the critical necessity to plan strategically, most remain silent. This may be due to a lack of understanding about the strategic planning process or a failure to appreciate that the intensity of business competition has reached levels seldom, if ever, experienced. It may be partly due to a lack of realization that the current abundance of immediately available demographic data and pertinent business information, together with the existence of appropriate computer programs, has made it possible to investigate almost instantaneously virtually any course of business action relating to market consumption, demand and growth, and competitive threat. Thus, any business organization with revenues in the thousands or millions of dollars can indeed formulate highly rational decisions about future strategic courses of action within a relatively short time. Such was not the case even two decades ago.

HCA has viewed strategic planning as so critical that a recent mandate required every hospital in the owned system to formulate an individual strategic plan by the close of 1987 and to continue with ongoing planning for the foreseeable future. Those hospitals which have pioneered programs of strategic planning have conclusively proven its merits, thus justifying the mandate. We believe an appropriate program of strategic planning can yield the following benefits to the vast majority of business firms:

1. conclusive identification of business opportunities

2. valid assessment of competition

3. correct evaluation of organizational capabilities and disabilities

4. clear recognition of constraints, both internal and external to the organization

5. adoption of *optimal* corporate goals and business objectives in light of opportunities, competitive threats, organizational strengths, and internal and external constraints

6. orderly, controlled movement into a planned future, with avoidance of hasty, ill-conceived courses of action

7. structured marshalling of all resources—capital, plant, equipment, goods and personnel—within a common program of implementation to attain adopted goals and objectives

In essence, strategic planning allows pursuit of deliberately selected, feasible goals and objectives through planned organizational actions having a high probability of success. A firm can *act* based on valid and reliable information rather than *react* to the vicissitudes of fortune resulting from ignorance, the designs of hostile competitors, or adventitious environmental occurrences.

Definitions

Possibly one reason strategic planning has not received the emphasis it deserves is that considerable confusion still exists regarding its definition. It is small wonder that many business executives don't know how to carry forward a strategic planning process when they don't clearly understand what strategic planning is or why they should do it.

There are three related terms being applied to planning today. Each of these has been variously defined, which has caused considerable confusion among executives. The terms are (1) *long-range planning*, (2) *marketing*, and (3) *strategic planning*. Although mere definitions can't completely clarify the nature and purpose of each, at least they provide a point of departure for detailed discussion.

However, we should also emphasize that definitions in themselves are not of great importance, especially for matters of practice. *Rather, achieving results is what stands as the basic criterion of any goal-oriented plan which requires implementing actions.* What one calls the planning that is done to determine a firm's mission, goals, and objectives and subsequently to achieve them is a minor issue. The important thing is to adopt a formal planning process, involve key line managers (adequately supported by staff in appropriate planning units), and use reliable information to arrive at rational conclusions about what the organization should be doing to attain its goals and objectives.

Long-range planning

Most frequently, the term *long-range planning* refers to the mission and goals of an organization that are to be attained within five to ten years. Firms that engage in long-range planning usually gear short-range plans (say, for the period one month to one year) to the longer range goals and objectives, and if managers formally document plans, as they should, they may include short-range plans with long-range plans within the same manual or document.

In the hospital field, long-range planning has for years meant, to many executives, facility planning. More recently, it has tended to mean program planning, owing primarily to experience with the ill-fated National Health Planning and Resources Development Act (P.L. 93-641).

Stoner calls strategic planning a long-range planning process and thereby, probably unwittingly, adds to the confusion. In Stoner's defense, he clearly recognizes the importance of strategic planning and sets forth a lucid and authoritative presentation of it in his recent book, simply entitled *Management*.[1] Linneman also gives an excellent presentation of strategic planning in a book with the unfortunate title *Shirt-Sleeved Approach to Long Range Planning*.[2]

Marketing

MacStravic defines marketing as "the design and management [by a given organization] of exchange relationships with important publics."[3] Kotler has stated, "Marketing is the analysis, planning, implementation and control of carefully formulated programs designed to bring about voluntary exchange of values with target markets for the purpose of achieving organizational objectives."[4] He has also stated, "Marketing is human activity directed at satisfying needs and wants through exchange processes."[5] Thus, both authors imply in their definitions that marketing includes both strategic planning and the implementation of it. To some extent, each provides an example of an authority on a single element of management attempting to bring the whole under the purview of that element. In our view, strategic planning clearly comprises the formulation of programs for establishing desirable exchange relationships with all categories of people necessary to the success of an organization; thus, strategic planning includes the planning required for marketing. In its strictest sense, marketing is concerned with the actions that are needed to implement plans for selling something (establishing exchange relationships). All dictionaries support this interpretation and none indicate that marketing is essentially a planning function.

Strategic planning

Brandt states, "Strategic planning is a line management activity centered in getting the right people, agenda, and information together on a timely schedule in order to make decisions that commit cash and people to market place positioning assignments extending beyond the current operating cycle."[6] This is essentially a correct definition.

Linneman states, "Strategic planning . . . involves looking into the future and deciding what the basic future of your business ought to be. It may result in a strategy that, over time, brings about fundamental change in your business. The point of strategic planning is to decide a course today that will get the company where it wants to be tomorrow."[7] Again, this is essentially correct.

Stoner rightly states, "Strategic planning is the process of selecting an organization's goals; determining the policies and strategic programs necessary to achieve specific objectives en route to the goals; and establishing the methods necessary to assure that the policies and strategic programs are implemented."[8] After acknowledging that this definition borrows from that of George A. Steiner and John B. Miner,[9] Stoner claims that "this comprehensive definition might be distilled into a shorter one: Strategic planning is the formalized, long-range process used to define and achieve organizational goals."[10] Here Stoner misses the mark. Among other things, when he uses the word *achieve*, he suggests that such planning includes implementation. As we have stated repeatedly, planning is planning and implementing is implementing. Although the two may directly interface and intertwine, they remain distinct.

A fellow hospital executive, Lee Domanico, has formulated one of the best definitions of strategic planning we have found. Its essential correctness makes it usable for any business (with deletions of specific references to hospitals). The author acknowledges assistance from the consulting firm of Booz, Allen & Hamilton. The modified definition is this: "Strategic planning encompasses . . . program planning, and also includes . . . mission identification, goal setting, market strategy, image building . . . a comprehensive planning data base, assessment of prime competitors . . . cooperative and political planning. Strategic planning must be highly integrated into existing planning and operating functions."[11] The statement that strategic planning must be highly integrated into operating functions does not exactly express our belief or the belief of several other authors, but the issue is minor. We believe strategic planning interfaces with and merges into operational planning; it is instead operational planning that must be highly integrated with operating functions. Operational planning directly results in implementing actions, and we devote two full chapters to it (see Chapters 5 and 9 on standing plans and single use plans, respectively, and see the sections of Chapter 6 on management planning, operating budgets, and financial budgets).

Why organizations fail to plan

Before we set forth our definition of strategic planning, to which we have devoted some careful thought, we will briefly review why strategic planning remains deficient throughout the business world.

Numerous reasons exist as to why managers do not perform appropriate strategic planning. We have listed some of them below in what we believe is their order of occurrence:

1. *Top executives do not understand the process.* Their idea of a strategic planning session is a brainstorming weekend retreat. While such retreats are probably better than nothing, mature consideration of pertinent information goes lacking.

2. *Top executives bog down in operations and believe they do not have time to devote to strategic planning.* One reason managers become bogged down in operations is the lack of appropriate planning, especially strategic planning.

3. *The chief executive officer believes his or her instincts are invariably correct, or nearly so, and consequently disdains strategic planning.* Alas, these executives nearly invariably have some rude awakenings in store.

4. *One or more of the organization's top executives are "job holding" and are fearful changes may occur which will cause them to lose their positions.* For the most part, such organizations merely react to the environment, and by failing to take charge of their future, they often lose control of it—and also lost are the jobs of the very executives who were afraid to plan. This lends support to the simple but sound principle: In most situations, act rather than react.

5. *Top executives understand the process and intend to pursue it, but allow either real or imagined political situations to disrupt or nullify it.* To avoid political interference, proper organizing at the outset of the process is essential.

6. *The proper mindset is absent at the start of the process, although executives understand the process and can obtain appropriate information.* Some executives, rather than entering into the process with the proper attitude for problem solving, allow a variety of preconceived notions, personal likes and dislikes, apprehensions and other assorted emotions to prevent them from objectively evaluating alternative goals and courses of action. Although humans have considerable difficulty being totally objective, most of us, at least on specific occasions, can commit ourselves to processes requiring nearly complete objectivity, such as the process of strategic planning.

7. *Executives and other managers fail to obtain required pertinent information for testing and selecting alternatives.* Some executives do not know what information is required, where it is located, or how to obtain it. In most businesses, pertinent data are more available than ever before and can more easily be used to generate information necessary for strategic planning.

8. *Executives do not value the importance of "timing" enough with respect to strategic planning.* In most organizations, strategic planning should be done on an ongoing basis, but start-up nearly always necessitates

intensified efforts. Also, based on budget cycles, executives must update existing goals and objectives within a limited time, and this updating process requires specific time commitments. In any event, executives sometimes begin the formal process at the wrong time, pursue it over too long or too short a time, or fail to conclude it in time to reflect the impact of adopted goals and objectives on budget and other pro forma financial statements.

9. *Top executives sincerely believe strategic planning is not worth the required effort.* This belief may be true where the business is a purely adaptive one and where the owners do not want it to grow any faster than their adaptations to the environment allow. Such firms typically are very small operations. In most instances, throughout the entire business continuum, strategic planning is well worth the effort.

10. *The level of intelligence and knowledge required to do strategic planning is not present in the organization.* We add this because strategic planning does require some detailed thought, reflection, and conceptualization. There may be firms, probably small, which actually do not have the expertise to get the job done.

The above are certainly a majority of reasons why many organizations do not carry out strategic planning at all or fail to carry it out appropriately. In some cases, of course, more than one reason may apply.

Our definition

A definition should be precise but also express the full meaning of the term being defined. In the case of *strategic planning,* a number of definitions exist, but most fail to set forth the full meaning. For example, we could have simply said, "Strategic planning is making decisions about future courses of action." While this is true, making such decisions is common to all planning. We have tried to focus on strategic planning as a more or less singular type of planning that is done for rather specific purposes. Our definition follows:

> *Strategic planning constitutes a process undertaken by an organization to formulate mission, goals, and objectives for future time periods extending from one to five or more years. It requires rational and creative decision making and involves finance, productivity, sales, procurements, personnel needs and responsibilities, performance dates, locations, and programs for implementation. It further involves creation of an appropriate data base; demographic, statistical, and financial analyses; projections, predictions, and forecasts; assessments of competition and other environmental elements; and selections among alternative goals and courses of action.*

Several authorities have rightly said that strategic planning provides answers to the following questions as the process unfolds:

1. Where have we been?

2. Where are we now?

3. Where do we want to go?

4. How do we get there?

Contemplating these four questions may be slightly misleading, however, for one might not appreciate that strategic planning must possess considerable specificity, especially in terms of who, when, what, where, how, and how much (if funds are required). Implementation necessitates a great amount of detail, particularly with reference to the control process. Readers will note that our definition of strategic planning gives due consideration to who, when, what, where, how, and how much, the essential issues for any complete plan.

Organizing for strategic planning

Principles for organizing

The appropriate way to organize for strategic planning will differ from one organization to another, depending on the current and anticipated structure, the size, the products or services, the technologies employed, the current and anticipated responsibilities of key executives, and the geographic locations of organizational elements.

However, managers should respect some few general guidelines in all situations:

1. Those top managers who will have responsibility for implementing the plan should be intimately involved in its formulation. If not, the probability of cooperation and coordination during implementation will be greatly reduced.

2. The responsibility for creation of an appropriate data and information base should be assigned to a single person. In large organizations, this person will require adequate support staff. He or she should not be part of the planning group but should serve as staff to the group. Many firms employ consultants to assist in creating the data and information base.

3. The chief financial officer of the organization or business unit doing the planning should be present at all meetings of the planning group and usually should be a member of the group. This officer ought to have responsibility for presenting all financial information, as opposed to other information flowing from the data base mentioned in (2). In some instances, the chief financial officer also makes use of consultants.

4. The plan developed had best evolve through a group process, with the top executive officer guiding the process and retaining the right of

veto. This officer should not, however, dictate to the group, for reasons related to (1) above.

5. The planners should constitute a formalized group in the eyes of organizational members, with managers at the hierarchical level just below having access to their superiors serving the group.

6. The planning group should organize itself, with the chief executive officer serving as chairperson unless he or she desires otherwise and appoints someone else. An appointed secretary should record all minutes of the group, except when instructed to refrain from doing so for purposes of confidentiality.

7. The group should establish policy at the outset regarding the confidentiality of discussions, of decisions, and of information developed by and for the group.

8. Scheduling regular meetings of the group is preferable to keeping members "on-call." However, the chief executive officer should hold called meetings as deemed necessary.

The importance of group planning

Most firms intending to grow engage in strategic planning, regardless of what it is called, how it is done, or how it is later implemented. Sometimes the chief executive officer, who may also be the owner in closely held corporations, engages in such planning almost exclusively. Even in corporations with publicly held stock, some chief executives still devise future strategies by themselves. Often such individuals do achieve success, as well as considerable recognition for foresight and leadership. However, not much attention has been paid to the probably much greater number of cases where *poor* results were achieved almost exclusively because of the *poor* foresight of a single individual. Two or more heads are usually better than one, no matter how brilliant the one may be.

Herbert Simon has observed, "It is impossible for the behavior of a single isolated individual to reach any high degree of rationality."[12] Evidence obtained under controlled laboratory conditions clearly supports Simon's opinion. Many years ago, Marjorie Shaw investigated the ability of individuals as compared with the ability of small groups in solving complex problems involving a series of steps, all of which had to be correct to obtain the right answer. The groups generally reached a much larger proportion of correct solutions than individuals.[13] Since Shaw's day, many investigations have supported the finding of her study. There is truly a greater success rate in problem solving by correctly sized groups as compared to individuals.

Some individuals falsely reason that a methodical pursuit of rational decision making (which is essentially equivalent to strategic planning) by a group impedes the creative decisions of brilliant individuals. This reasoning borders on being absurd. It is chiefly advanced by those who want to take all the credit for success, but if left to their own abilities, usually face accepting the blame for failure. Finding a scapegoat provides an alternative. Readers can reach their own conclusions about which alternative, in the case of failure, is most often selected.

The effects of structure

The current and anticipated structure of a firm affects strategic planning, since this planning must be accomplished not only at the highest levels of the organization but at the levels where operations are directly controlled and largely independent budgets set. Most small business firms have a single profit center and therefore should undertake only one strategic planning effort for the entire organization. Many organizations, however, have geographic profit centers, and in these organizations each center should prepare a strategic plan. The profit centers for some manufacturing or industrial firms may be particular plants producing one or more products. In HCA and HealthTrust Inc., every hospital is a profit center, and each formulates an individual strategic plan annually. HCA also has several distinct profit centers at the corporate level and each of these has planned strategically (e.g., the management, psychiatric, and owned-hospital companies). In any event, where more than one hierarchical level carries on strategic planning, the top-level plans should set a broad direction or course for the firm by specifying a mission (or missions). They should also include some specific goals that the whole organization can strive to meet. These goals may apply to particular business units or profit centers as well as to the firm as a whole.

Communications

In large organizations where each hierarchical level plans strategically, managers must hold continuous discussions both up and down the line or coordination will suffer severely. This is absolutely necessary in one specific area: the allocation of capital funds on rational bases. For example, an individual hospital in HealthTrust Inc. need not base a major portion of its strategic plan on a sizeable plant addition to house several vertically integrated services when requirements for obtaining the funds cannot be met through the corporate capital fund allocation process.

Other than constant communication to assure that no plans conflict at different hierarchical levels, the actual process used to strategically plan is the same at all levels. At each level, managers should form a planning group, and although it would be impossible to state here the composition of all possible groups, the general principles we have already noted should serve to set appropriate organizational guidelines in each separate case.

Funds for planning

Strategic planning in very small one-profit-center firms may not require any budgeted funds for its initiation. In larger firms, where millions and even billions of dollars may be under consideration, planning efforts will obviously require budgeted funds, and stinginess regarding such funds, especially for planning at corporate levels, is inadvisable. Some small profit centers should exercise great caution about budgeting dollars for planning, but they also should not be penny wise and pound foolish. Very simply, when any business unit prepares a multimillion-dollar expense budget, it should have the greatest degree of certainty that the products or services it proposes to sell are those that will return all of the expenses incurred, plus a competitive profit. Also, if a business organization wants to expand its product or service lines, the expansion should be based on something other than wishful thinking and the competitive urge. Therefore, the very process which will allow a firm to determine probabilities of success should not be treated like a penniless orphan.

The strategic planning process

Processes described by others

Although most authorities who have published their thoughts about strategic planning espouse generally similar views, to our knowledge no two have agreed specifically on a single process. Many writers have simply described what they have seen in various organizations, which may or may not constitute the most effective process. We intend to outline very briefly some basic characteristics appropriate to all strategic planning and to discuss in some detail the process we recommend, which we have distilled from planning that occurred in hundreds of hospitals, long-term care institutions, ambulatory care facilities, and retail drug businesses.

Planning process characteristics

When anyone, for any business, starts to develop a strategic plan, the process adopted should conform to the following guidelines:

1. *Investigations rationally or scientifically conducted, which will yield objective conclusions, should form the basis of the process adopted.* We have observed adaptations of four related processes which can serve usefully in major strategic planning processes: (a) John Dewey's reflective thought process, (b) the scientific method, (c) the rational decision-making process, and (d) the systems approach to planning and systems development as originally documented by a department of the General Electric Company. We briefly discussed each of these in the introduction to Part III. Each advances hypotheses or alternative courses of action for comparison and selection based on factual evidence concerning feasibility and constraints.

2. *The process should be preconceived and formalized, with responsibilities of participants clearly outlined and agreed upon.* This forces conduct of the process to be organized and thorough rather than eclectic and hit-or-miss. The formalization should be presented through diagrams and verbal explanations.

3. *Sequenced steps in the order they occur in making a rational decision and then pursuing a course of action should serve to guide the process from investigative phases to implementation.* Such sequencing is implicit in the four processes mentioned in (1) above and in the adaptation of the planning process we shall shortly discuss.

4. *The process should be geared directly to operational planning, and operational planning should result in the implementation of the strategic plan.* No plan is worth the paper it is written on unless it can be implemented. Therefore, the steps from the planning stage through implementation are

just as important as the strategic plan itself. Whatever an organization plans to do should have a good probability of being implemented through operational planning, which includes both operational and financial budgeting.

5. *Iterations of the planning work must be possible, both in the budget cycle during which the process is initiated and in subsequent years.* This provides for strategic planning to be conducted on an ongoing basis.

6. *The same process should be usable at each level of an organization's hierarchy where strategic planning will be conducted.* The process we will describe is so usable.

7. *The process should be susceptible of being scheduled, and such scheduling should be formally done from year to year.* The time allocated for going through the process will vary from firm to firm. However, seldom should even small firms set less than a month, and large corporations may well consume an appreciable part of the budget cycle, leaving time to devise operational plans only for those strategic actions that need to be undertaken during the current cycle.

Mission, goals, and objectives

Many business firms, management consultants with various backgrounds, and possibly a majority of authors on management processes use the terms *aim, purpose, goal, mission,* and *objective* synonymously, or nearly so. Others differentiate among the terms variously, so that considerable confusion now exists. We prefer to use the following terms as defined below, for reasons that will become apparent:

- *Mission:* The raison d'être of an organization. Its basic purposes, which the aggregate goals and objectives are intended to attain. HCA's mission is shown in Exhibit 3-1. This statement of mission is framed and displayed in appropriate locations at both corporate and division headquarters. An organization's top-level management—in the case of corporations, the board of directors—should prepare and adopt the formal mission statement.

- *Goals:* The broad ends toward which the efforts of the organization as a whole or specific divisions of it are directed. Planners should provide for quantification of achievement so as to allow measurement of degrees of success or failure for specific time periods. The determination of goals ought to originate within an organization's higher levels. HCA has established a set of ten permanent goals and, on an ongoing basis, has formulated time-related goals concerning such things as the establishment of new business lines, the achievement of a given debt-to-equity ratio, the acquisition of vertically related businesses for integration into the hospital system, etc. HCA's permanent goals are shown in Exhibit 3-2.

- *Objectives:* These are specific ends to be accomplished within a given timeframe and for which there is some way of quantifying the degree of

Exhibit 3-1

HCA's Mission

HCA The Healthcare Company

MISSION

To attain international leadership
in the health care field.

•

To provide excellence in health care.

•

To improve the standards of
health care in communities in which
we operate.

•

To provide superior facilities and
needed services to enable physicians to best
serve the needs of their patients.

•

To generate measurable benefits for:

The Company
Medical Staff
The Employee
The Investor
and, most importantly,

THE PATIENT

Source: Reprinted with permission of Hospital Corporation of America.

---

achievement. Planners should always formulate the statement of an objective so it can serve as a yardstick by which success can be measured during implementation. Planners can formulate objectives at any level of an organization, but most frequently they are formulated at work unit or profit center levels.

Zero basing

Owing to the volatility of today's markets and the rapid evolution occurring in technology, all managers should regard the goals and objectives of a given organization within the context of a "zero base." Even a company's basic mission should receive critical scrutiny from time to time as to its continued viability and vitality. Managers will not be required to

Exhibit 3-2

HCA's Goals

HCA The Healthcare
Company

GOALS

1. To demonstrate that the free enterprise system can provide a high quality of health care at a reasonable cost.

2. To achieve international leadership and to maintain a reputation for excellence in the health care field.

3. To develop an organizational climate of productivity that provides each individual the opportunity to make an increasingly significant contribution to the organization with appropriate personal rewards.

4. To maintain a position of trust, confidence, respect and compassion to our patients, employees, and the communities we serve.

5. To further develop a flexible, responsive, professional organization capable of meeting the needs of and realizing the opportunities within the health care field.

6. To develop sufficient profit to support the growth of the company and compensate investors for their risk and use of their money.

7. To maintain a strong, viable financial position which will continue to deserve the respect of and give confidence to the financial and investment communities.

8. To continually examine the health care industry for appropriate opportunities for growth, growing according to definitive plans based upon pragmatic research.

9. To attract to HCA intelligent, enthusiastic, loyal, trustworthy employees who can identify closely with HCA's philosophy and goals, and be capable of making a significant contribution to the achievement of HCA objectives.

10. To provide a climate, facilities and services in which physicians can practice medicine in a manner which contributes to superior health care.

Source: Reprinted with permission of Hospital Corporation of America.

make adaptations in planning processes in order to implement the zero base concept. All that is required is a vigilant commitment that no line of business, no program of marketing, and no internal methodologies for performing will be free of scrutiny or be allowed to assume a sacred cow status (with regard to profitability, state-of-the-art criteria, or market share percentages).

At least annually, as preparations advance for beginning the strategic planning cycle, managers should both individually and collectively question all activities of the company. Then, as strategic planning goes forward, suspicions evoked by zero base scrutiny can be investigated within the first three steps of the strategic planning process described below.

Steps in the strategic planning process

The following steps are diagrammed in Figure 3-1.

Step 1: tentative formulation of mission, goals, and objectives

Most authorities simply state that the first step should be to set objectives. Of course, thinking about what a business organization ought to be doing occurs within some frame of reference. Often that frame of reference is constituted by what executives personally desire to achieve. These desires can be motivated variously, including a concern for competitive bottom line profits. Other motivations include personal prestige and the desire to travel (believe it or not). For example, some failed international ventures have been based on little more than a desire by top executives to boast about "international operations." Partly because of such cases, we state that planners should *tentatively* formulate mission, goals, and objectives in Step 1.

Another frame of reference used in formulating the mission, goals, and objectives is what the business currently engages in doing. "Do we want to continue what we're doing and base our strategy on that?" "Do we want to add one or more lines of business?" "Do we want to expand on a horizontal basis?" "Do we want to effect an expansion with vertically integrated businesses?" "Do we want to change our product mix?" All of these questions are usually asked in the tentative formulation of mission, goals, and objectives in existing organizations.

Figure 3-1

The Strategic Planning Process in Seven Steps

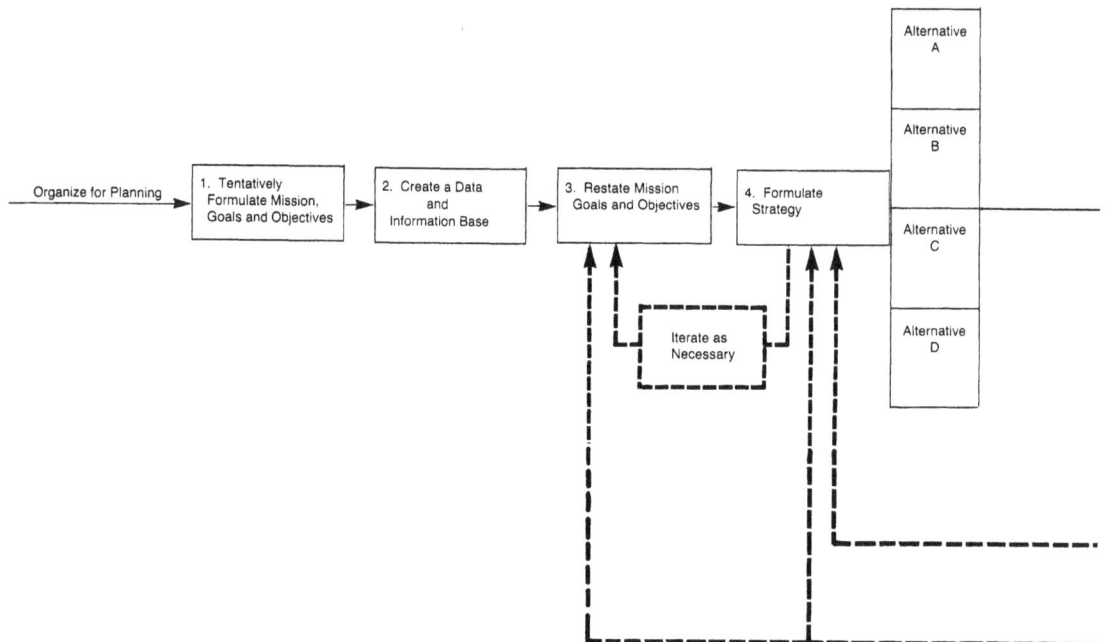

Other frames of reference within which tentative formulations may be made include these: the experiences of executives elsewhere; observed societal trends; known markets the organization can tap with known available resources; observed successes or failures of others; the results of research and development, either internal or external to the planning organization; competitive threats; and observable returns on investments. There are many others besides these.

One reason formulations should be tentative in organizations having more than one level of strategic planning is that layered goals and objectives must not conflict. There must be communication up and down the hierarchical levels to prevent such conflict, and companywide planning should keep goals and objectives at lower levels from becoming completely fixed until those at top levels have received approval. This does not mean that tentative formulations of goals and objectives at lower levels should await finalization of formulations at the top. Indeed, in the case of existing organizations, planning at all levels ought to proceed simultaneously—unless for some unusual reason lower levels had best hold their efforts in abeyance. By proceeding simultaneously, pertinent information and data can be sent both up and down the line to assure that planning at all levels is of better quality and that operational coordination will be improved.

Those who engage in the planning processes should word their tentative mission statements and statements of goals and objectives carefully and precisely so that they can usefully be considered in light of a pertinent data and information base, which is described next.

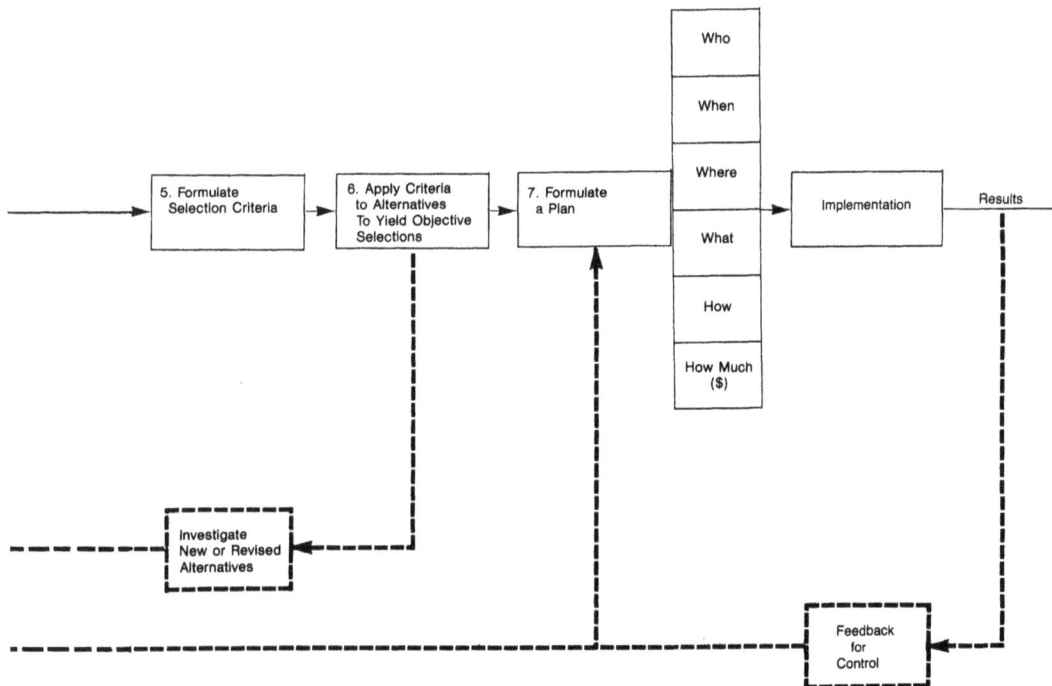

Step 2: creation of a data and information base

Some call this step *situation analysis* and others call it *identification of constraints*. The latter designation seems to have negative connotations, but we have no argument with *situation analysis*. However, because creating a data and information base is precisely what occurs in this step, we elected to entitle the step in the way we have.

The data and information to be assembled must reflect the past, the present, and educated predictions about the future. Data or information about the past should, in most cases, cover a period of three to five years so that valid trends can be traced. The questions "Where have we been?" and "Where are we now?" should be answered using as many pertinent facts as is feasible. However, it is possible for a planning group to become completely lost in a maze of data or oversupplied. Some kinds of data may be interesting but not much use.

Every business has areas unique to itself where data should be gathered, trend analyses performed, and projections or predictions of future outcomes made. The following areas are ones that most businesses generally find pertinent. Note that we do not claim these are the only areas pertinent to strategic planning.

Past and present financial data and information

- *Sales volumes by category of product or service.* Most business enterprises study trends related to distinct product and service sales and base future actions upon them, at least in part. Both dollars and numerical volumes should be tracked, if possible. This information, when related to market saturation points and estimated in dollars and numerical volumes for a specific product or service, proves especially valuable.

- *Relative profitability by planning unit.* Trends of relative profitability (by hospital) have served, together with considerations related to capital allocations, as a prime basis for programs of divestiture by HCA. Planners can easily express relative profitability by planning unit both in terms of total dollar contribution and profit margin. The determination of profit margin, of course, results from dividing net profit after taxes by sales, thus yielding the profit per dollar of sales.

- *Return on investment (ROI).* Annual trends of this ratio by plant or profit center often serve as one of the prime bases for capital investment strategies. Investors also closely watch this ratio.

- *Other financial ratios.* Depending upon the organization, planners may pay attention to the trends of other financial ratios, such as specific liquidity, leverage, and activity ratios.

Market area analyses

- *Population growth and demographic environments.* Population growth (or decline) in the sales or service area of a particular business is generally useful to know. Such trends can be extrapolated into the future by several statistical methods to ascertain sales possibilities in future years. However, planners now usually rely on commercial data companies to provide population projections and demographic analyses. Analysis of past trends still proves useful, if only to ascertain whether a market appears to be saturated on a year-by-year basis.

- *Actions and capabilities of competitors.* Analyses of competitor sales or services by product type, together with their product capabilities, may be useful, especially when referenced to a specific area. HCA has closely watched the occupancy rates of competing hospitals, for example. Typically, not-for-profit facilities cannot quickly reach decisions to expand nor quickly obtain the necessary money. Investor-owned systems (if not bureaucratically paralyzed) can usually make decisions promptly and rather easily obtain capital funding. In this regard, HCA has over the years had the capability to intervene and rapidly expand, ready to absorb growing demand before competitors could make use of the opportunity.

  The actions and capabilities of competitors within a given geographic area are useful to know. Many retail businesses, for example, locate the position of competitors on a sales area map, determine the total area demand for a given product or products, determine the amount of that demand met by local retailers, and make judgments about what percentage might be possible to capture both from local competitors and from current outflows to other areas.

  Many businesses fail simply because the competition was not initially adequately assessed. This occurs despite the fact that business directories are available in most libraries and can be used to ascertain exact sources of information about any industry or trade existing in the nation, by specific geographic area. For example, the *Dun and Bradstreet Reference Book* lists approximately three million businesses of various types, together with ratings of them. Dun and Bradstreet publishes this book several times a year. McLaughlin, in his recent book *Building Your Business Plan*, has devoted an entire chapter to competitive data sources, which gives detailed instructions for pursuing sources of information.[14]

Current market demand analyses

- *Estimates of total market demand, by product and by geographic area, for a period of time equal to the organization's budget cycle.* This information proves useful in making projections of future market volumes related to specific products under certain assumed marketing strategies.

- *Market shares by sales or service area.* Every planning unit should know the trends of its market share for a specific sales or service area so as to judge the results of past efforts. For example, each hospital in both HCA and HealthTrust Inc. must keep track of its total patient admissions, patient days, and outpatient visits relative to total admissions, patient days, and outpatient visits for the population of a specific geographic area it serves. Regardless of numerical volumes and profitability, any hospital can then keep track of whether it is holding its own, losing ground, or gaining on the competitors. Marketing and other strategies can be developed accordingly.

Facilities and manpower

- *Existing capabilities of facilities and equipment.* Many planning units ignore the capabilities of existing facilities and equipment to accommodate growth of existing operations and to initiate new ones. Unless capital funds can be obtained to expand facilities and obtain new equipment, opportunities for growth can be lost where full loadings have already been reached. Even where necessary capital funds can be acquired to accommodate profitable new or expanded productions, planners must determine the capabilities of existing facilities and equipment so as to calculate the amount and cost of any additional facilities and equipment that would be required.

- *Current manpower capabilities.* Obviously, planners must review existing manpower capabilities in order to consider the feasibility of attaining goals and objectives.

Other past and present considerations

- *Research and development reports.* Investigations and findings of R and D departments play a major role in planning for both new products or services and improvements to existing products or services. R and D may report new methods or procedures whereby productivity can be increased. Such reports, as well as others from R and D, should be considered carefully.

- *Productivity ratios by planning unit.* Where productivity ratios by planning unit are kept, these may form the basis for deciding on certain objectives related to expansion.

Projections and predictions

The following projections or predictions, based on stated assumptions, are generally useful to include in a data and information base.

- *Population numbers by age category, for specific sales or service areas, either existing or contemplated.* The volume of all retail sales and services, for example, depends on population numbers and ratios of consumption per unit of population.

- *Total market demand by product or service, by geographic area, for specific time periods (usually from one to ten years in the future).* Projections or predictions may be for shorter time periods than noted. The time period usually depends on how long it will take to begin production and sale of a product or service. One should also consider here the product life cycle for specific products. Most products or services go through phases of market introduction and market growth, maturity, and decline. Predictions of market demand will be more accurate if planners correctly assess the stage a product occupies in its product cycle and the length of time in each stage. The product cycle also has implications for devising strategy.

- *Market shares by sales or service area for discrete products and services or families of products and services.* These projections or predictions, used in conjunction with those mentioned above and immediately following, allow a business to estimate more accurately total sales volumes for target years.

- *Numerical volumes of specific product or service sales for target years.* Statisticians can extrapolate these based on past trends previously analyzed.

- *Dollar sales by category of product or service, plus pertinent financial ratios.* Estimates of dollar volumes, based on predicted prices and numerical volume, can be calculated by several methods. Financial ratios can be predicted based on past experience and the experience of others in the same or similar lines of business.

- *Future levels of productivity by product or service lines.* These predictions may be advantageous in estimating future production expenses and manpower and equipment needs.

- *Availability of capital dollars for investment in plant, equipment, and other items that can be capitalized.* Availability of capital will depend on those funds held as accumulated depreciation, derived from stock sales, and available from other sources, such as borrowing.

Step 3: restatement of mission, goals, and objectives

If, as is probable, there are opportunities and constraints revealed by the data and information base, the mission, goals, or objectives should be restated as required. We have on occasion needed to restate the mission, goals, and objectives all together, and others have had to do the same. Goals and objectives tend to be especially in need of revision at various levels of planning.

When the restatement is completed, there should be no basic conflict of goals and objectives throughout the layers of planning, if such layers exist. However, some divisions or planning units of organizations may compete with others in the same organization, in some instances as a calculated strategy to best outside competitors. HCA, for example, has had owned hospitals competing against other owned units, but duplications of offered services were allowed because HCA units would lose less business to each other than would be gained from several other competitors. Manufacturers of several different brands of cars pursue the same strategy.

Step 4: formulation of strategy

All strategies for attaining goals and objectives require determinations of who, when, what, where, and how. Planners must also consider the anticipated cost of a strategy. The purposes of devising strategies are three: (1) to allow direct comparisons among alternative strategies, (2) to achieve optimal control during implementation, and (3) to set the stage for the operational planning that will directly result in implementation.

In this step, some additional restatement of goals and objectives may be beneficial, for an evaluation of strategies for attaining them, as already reformulated, may reveal there is no feasible strategy. This does occur, but fortunately not often.

The basic purpose of this step is to devise alternative courses of action for attaining specific goals and objectives. The purpose of devising *alternative* courses of action is to allow objective comparisons among alternatives (taking account of all or most factors) so that the best one can be selected. Such comparison brings into the process the systematic scientific or rational approach to decision making.

> For best results in this phase . . . creativeness, keen insight, intuition and high intellectual capability are required. Because even near exhaustive examination or testing of all possible courses of action . . . would not be feasible from the standpoint of cost and time, usually only a limited number of alternatives are constructed for consideration. Thus, it is highly important that experienced persons capable of somewhat complex psychological activity be here employed to reduce to a minimum errors which will require needless effort for discovery in later steps and force the reformulation of additional alternatives. Of course, barring the disproving of a fallacious plan, activities could be directed on a wrong course and cause irreparable setbacks in the procurement of optimum goals.[15]

An outline of a format we have used in stating alternative courses of action, or strategies, for attaining objectives follows:

1. State the goals or objectives precisely.

2. State the division, department, or other operational unit responsible for attaining the goals and objectives (use specific names and titles).

3. State the timeframe for carrying out the actions necessary for accomplishment.

4. Name the site or sites where the actions will be carried out (if necessary).

5. Describe briefly the actions, in sequence if necessary (we have constructed basic Gantt charts here), that will be required to attain the goals and objectives.

6. Relate any necessary changes in policy.

7. Provide estimates of capital costs, if any, of implementing the strategy, plus estimates of operating revenues and expenses in terms of some measure.

All of this may appear formidable, but in practice it is actually very simple. Often an experienced planner can outline an alternative strategy on a single sheet of paper. In addition, it will sometimes be apparent that only one strategy is feasible.

Step 5: formalization of selection criteria

This step is usually easy to complete, for pertinent criteria tend to be obvious. It is an important step, however, and should be done through formal group decision making. Almost invariably a single person will omit at least one pertinent criterion that another will know to include. Some particular criteria often used to choose among alternatives in business enterprises are as follows:

- capital costs
- profitability
- cash flow
- required debt
- labor requirements
- timing
- flexibility
- quality
- adherence to acceptable policy

- operational costs
- return on investment
- life cycle costs
- acceptable debt/equity ratio
- growth potential
- risk
- product life cycle
- technical superiority
- avoidance of harmful consequences

Step 6: application of criteria to yield objective selections

For each goal or objective a planning unit establishes, planners should determine one best course of action for attaining it from among those formulated for consideration. Application of the criteria adopted in Step 5 to the alternative strategies developed in Step 4 is the method for doing this.

In considering the application of the criteria, one will discover that some are quantifiable and some are not. Dollars are always precisely quantifiable. Thus, financial criteria allow objective comparisons so long as only "apples" are involved. Product volumes constitute another quantifiable item, as does time. The application of several other criteria result in a simple yes or no answer. However, some criteria—such as quality, risk, avoidance of untoward consequences, and flexibility, to name four of those listed above—defy ready and completely accurate quantification. How, then, can these be rationally applied?

The answer lies in performance of a "factor" analysis, which brings some objectivity to what would otherwise be a completely subjective evaluation of the alternatives. Exhibit 3-3 displays a sample factor analysis work sheet. By getting a group consensus on the relative weights of each factor (i.e., the relative importance of each vis-à-vis the others), each member of the group can then score all factors and a definitive total number can be obtained for each strategy. By arriving at numbers for all strategies, direct comparisons result.

We have used this method of comparison on many occasions and found it useful in reaching a consensus among members of a planning group, which otherwise would have been very difficult to achieve.

Step 7: formulation of plan

This step involves drawing together all selected strategies for achieving goals and objectives into a coordinated plan for each individual planning unit and for the organization as a whole. The overall planning effort

Exhibit 3-3

Factor Analysis Worksheet
Hospital Corporation of America

Alternatives Relating to: _____

Alternative Being Scored: _____

Factor	Factor Weight	Score	Points
1.			
2.			
3.			
4.			
5.			
6.			
7.			
8.			
9.			
10.			
11.			
12.			
13.			
14.			
		Total Points:	

Factor Scores
Excellent = 4
Good = 3
Fair = 2
Poor = 1
Unsatisfactory = 0

Note: "Points" is the product of Weight and Score

Description of Alternative:

_____
_____
_____
_____
_____
_____
_____

Source: Reprinted with permission of Hospital Corporation of America.

---

should include preparation of a schedule for accomplishing all goals formulated at the top hierarchical level, together with schedules for accomplishing goals and objectives within specific planning units. Exhibit 3-4 displays a typical scheduling form. Note that one column is provided for designating the manager responsible for carrying out the strategy selected to obtain the stated goal or objective (Step 6). This manager's responsibility very definitely includes development of an operational plan for implementation.

In most instances, except where confidentiality is required, the strategic plan ought to be set out in a document, which should then be presented in a loose leaf binder as a manual for all involved members of management. The document should cover all the major parts of the plan.

Exhibit 3-4

Implementation Schedule

Statement of Goal or Objective: _____

Implementing Manager _____
Reporting To: _____

Task Number	Statement of Tasks	Date	Implementation Responsibility Assigned To:	Direct Expense Budget	Implementation Date (Final)	Written Progress Report(s) Due (Date)	Work to be Coordinated With:	Others to be Kept Informed	Manager Follow-up on (Date)	NOTES

All reports required for control purposes, except those presented in routine accounting, statistical, or other reports, should be clearly outlined in the planning manual, as should the route of transmittal.

There exists a great diversity of opinion about what the total contents should be of the planning manual mentioned above. At a maximum, it should only contain some or all of the data and information base, plus all subsequent formulations. At a minimum, it should include the selected strategies for attaining the goals and objectives of a specific planning unit, plus implementation schedules, all drawn together into a coordinated short- and long-range planning outline. If the planning manual contains all of the accumulated papers of the process, it should be organized by steps, similar to the way we have laid out the process above.

Follow-up to strategic planning

Most organizations, as follow-up to strategic planning, formulate various types of business or operational plans. In this book, we provide a chapter on single use plans and discuss several aspects of management planning done annually by HCA (see Chapters 9 and 6 respectively). Some businesses, of course, merely integrate the mission, goals, and objectives into their continuing operations if no basic realignments are required.

Summary

At this particular point in the history of organized business, no aspect of management has more relevance or importance than strategic planning. The giants of tomorrow in industry and commerce will be those firms today that objectively survey their competition and environment and determine strategies for successful expansion.

The hallmarks of appropriate strategic planning are (1) objectivity (as opposed to subjectivity); (2) application of a rational, structured, systematic process in determining courses of action to attain reasonable goals and objectives; (3) rational selections among alternative feasible courses of action; and (4) precise statements of mission, goals, objectives, and selected courses of action, with the forms of the statements such as to facilitate later application of the control process during implementation. In essence, goals and objectives are specific targets, and courses of action should be stated in terms of who, when, what, where, and how. Implementing costs must also be considered.

Before beginning strategic planning, a business must organize for the endeavor. *Those who do the planning must be those who will later have the responsibility for implementing it.* The best possible plan from an academic standpoint might be the worst possible plan from a practical standpoint if this principle is not followed.

In large organizations, strategic planning should be done simultaneously at different levels or within separate profit centers. In such instances, constant communication among the separate planning units, both up and down the line, becomes necessary so as to assure consonance among developed plans and coordination in implementation and in application of the control process.

After organizing and establishing lines of communication, seven basic steps make up an appropriate strategic planning process:

1. *Tentative formulation of mission, goals and objectives.* Initial formulation should be tentative, for objective data and information must be assembled and considered before concrete decisions can be made about formal adoption. Further, tentative formulations necessarily guide assembly of relevant data and information, but considerations of that data and information may indicate beneficial changes, deletions, and additions to initial formulations.

2. *Creation of a data and information base.* This base reflects past and present statistical and financial information, both internal and external to the planning organization, as well as projections or predictions of future trends. An objective survey of the competition must be made. Current and future capabilities in terms of finance, facilities, equipment, and manpower should be assessed. R and D reports and recommendations should receive careful consideration, together with current and projected productivity ratios.

3. *Restatement of mission, goals, and objectives.* Consideration should be given again to the tentatively formulated mission, goals and objectives, but this time in light of the data and information base. In some instances, a restated version, formulated for further evaluation as to possibility of attainment, may be desirable.

4. *Formulation of strategy.* Alternative strategies or courses of action to pursue in attaining the mission and specific goals and objectives should be formulated in terms of who, what, when, where, and how. Estimates of required capital and operational costs are most often necessary.

5. *Formalization of selection criteria.* Many criteria for evaluating alternative strategies developed in Step 4 are unique to particular organizations. However, some are widely used in a variety of situations, including capital costs, operational costs, profitability, return on investment, cash flow, life cycle costs, required debt, debt/equity ratio, labor requirements, growth potential, timing, risk, adherence to acceptable or established policy, avoidance of harmful consequences, flexibility, product cycle, quality, and technical superiority.

6. *Application of criteria to yield objective selections.* The criteria of Step 5, when applied to strategies developed in Step 4, allow selection of the optimal implementation strategy for the mission and for each specific goal and objective. Direct comparisons can be made regarding quantifiable criteria (dollars and numerical values). Where quantifications are not possible (e.g., quality, risk, flexibility, etc.), factor analysis offers a rational means of comparison.

7. *Formulation of plan.* The strategies selected in Step 6 should be drawn together, coordinated as to timing and responsibility for implementation, and, ideally, documented in a loose leaf planning manual. The

manual can facilitate ongoing planning and be used as a reference work by everyone concerned. The schedules drawn up as a part of this step should anticipate subsequent business or operational planning.

Actual implementation is the aim of all strategic planning. Thus, as follow-up, operational planning must be assigned to particular persons and be done according to the timetable specified in the strategic plan.

Notes

1. James A.F. Stoner, *Management*, 2d ed. (Englewood Cliffs, N.J.: Prentice-Hall, 1982), 101.
2. Robert E. Linneman, *Shirt-Sleeved Approach to Long Range Planning* (Englewood Cliffs, N.J.: Prentice-Hall, 1980).
3. Robin E. Scott MacStravic, "The Relationship between Planning and Marketing," in *Marketing for Hospitals in Hard Times*, ed. Lee F. Block (Chicago: Teach 'em, Inc., 1981), 2.
4. Philip Kotler, *Marketing for Non-Profit Organizations* (Englewood Cliffs, N.J.: Prentice-Hall, 1975), 5.
5. Philip Kotler, *Marketing Management, Analysis, Planning and Control*, 4th ed. (London: Prentice-Hall International, 1980), 19.
6. Steven C. Brandt, *Strategic Planning in Emerging Companies* (Reading, Mass.: Addison-Wesley, 1981), 4.
7. Linneman, *Long Range Planning*, 4.
8. Stoner, *Management*, 101.
9. George A. Steiner and John B. Miner, *Management Policy and Strategy* (New York: Macmillan, 1977), 7.
10. Stoner, *Management*, 101. Reprinted by permission of Prentice-Hall, Inc., Englewood Cliffs, N.J.
11. Lee Domanico, "Strategy Planning: Vital for Long Range Development," *Hospital and Health Services Administration*, Summer 1981, 26.
12. Herbert A. Simon, *Administrative Behavior* (New York: Macmillan, 1957), 79.
13. Marjorie E. Shaw, "A Comparison of Individuals and Small Groups in the Rational Solution of Complex Problems," *American Journal of Psychology* 44 (July 1932): 491–504.
14. Harold J. McLaughlin, *Building Your Business Plan* (New York: Wiley, 1985), 84–96.
15. Owen B. Hardy, "Systematic Processes Applied to Health Care Planning," *Hospital Administration* 16 (Winter 1971): 19.

Chapter 4

Organizational planning

Elements of Management
in Corporations

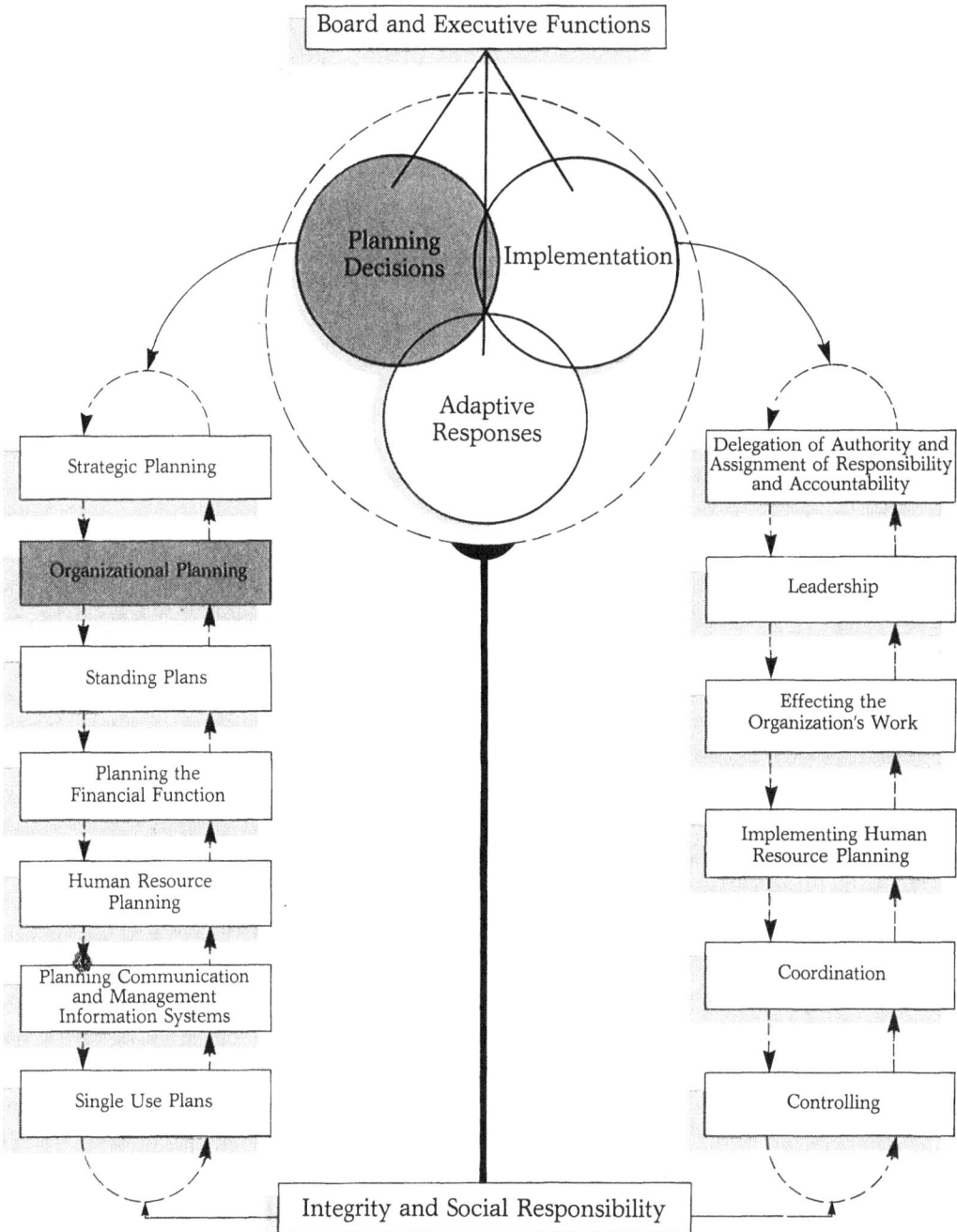

Board and Executive Functions

Planning Decisions

Implementation

Adaptive Responses

Strategic Planning

Organizational Planning

Standing Plans

Planning the Financial Function

Human Resource Planning

Planning Communication and Management Information Systems

Single Use Plans

Delegation of Authority and Assignment of Responsibility and Accountability

Leadership

Effecting the Organization's Work

Implementing Human Resource Planning

Coordination

Controlling

Integrity and Social Responsibility

4

Importance and responsibility

Those who engage in organizational planning must make decisions about what degree of structure should be imposed, not only initially but as such planning continues throughout the life of the organization. The appropriate degree of structure varies and is based on many factors. However, recorded research presents good evidence that definitive structure and pressure for performance, coupled with consideration for the welfare and needs of subordinates, result in higher performance and elevated morale.[1] Yet one must not overlook the fact that too much structure can be harmful, particularly too much personal supervision and too many picayune rules and regulations. Avoiding unnecessary aggravations and keeping initiatives from being stifled are valid goals of organizing.

Management literature presents research findings and authoritative opinions about appropriate degrees of structure, usually within the topic of leadership or the more general topic of organizing. Fortunately, many investigators have extensively studied organizing, and most texts contain worthwhile information about it. Few authors, however, differentiate between organizational planning and the implementation of that planning, as we do here. This may be largely owing to the fact that many only write about what they have studied or observed. Our own experience indicates that if one intentionally plans and then intentionally implements, with adaptive adjustments being made as implementation proceeds, one has a much greater chance of success than if one pursues a haphazard "organizing" approach.

Regarding the various recognized rights of owners, employees, customers, and the general public, all those who guide the "destiny" of a business organization have a continuing obligation to organize in such a manner that operational efficiency and control will be optimal and the needs of employees at every hierarchical level will be met, including needs related to self-actualization. Certainly, such goals present a challenge to all managers engaged in the actual tasks of organizational planning—a challenge that will require their best thinking.

Many, if not most, organizations do organizational planning only sporadically and often haphazardly. In some instances, the original plans and structure continue in use far beyond the point at which they lose their applicability, and the literature records many disasters that have occurred as a result. Admittedly, managers require considerable mental discipline and persistency to continually alter organizational structure as a business grows or as goals and objectives change, but no other option assures organizational health and the resultant efficiencies and control. To see to it that organizational planning remains a foremost consideration, top executives should identify it as one of their personal responsibilities and give it high priority. In corporations, boards of directors must continually monitor executive efforts at maintaining high-quality organizational planning.

Elements of organizational planning

Careful analysis reveals that organizational planning comprises five fairly distinct elements, each of which we will discuss in some detail later in this chapter. These elements are as follows:

1. *Departmentation.* This involves planning how operating work will be segmented into workable and manageable units.

2. *Decentralization.* This involves determining how management duties related to planning, implementation, and adaptive responses should be divided among persons and locations and deciding who should be delegated authority and assigned responsibility and accountability. Of course, planning for decentralization necessarily depends heavily on departmentation plans and vice versa.

3. *Considerations concerning state-of-the-art technology, operating systems, and operational procedures.* Almost inevitably some overlap occurs between this area and the devising of standing plans and of long-term program and single use plans, discussed in Chapters 5 and 9 respectively. We refer our readers to those chapters for additional information pertinent to organizational planning.

4. *Job design.* Individual jobs need to be designed so that the work flow within each segmented department can be well accommodated while at the same time the needs of the various managers and operational workers involved can be satisfied.

5. *Workplace functionality.* Too often, particularly in small businesses, managers ignore the functionality of facilities. Most buildings that house services or production should be planned so they are adaptable but also so they can actually function to accommodate the work flows that will be required by envisioned departments. No type of business should underestimate the importance of functionality in the workplace.

These, then, are the prime elements with which organizational planning must be concerned. Associated with each element are a number of considerations that may be pertinent to executives as they plan the structure and processes by which work tasks of every type will be assigned and coordinated within the totality of purposeful, controlled operations.

In this chapter, we do not discuss the several "principles" of classical organizational theory, nor do we dwell upon the theories of any of the behavioral theorists. Although all of these theories assist in understanding organizational planning, they are covered in many other texts, and we refer our readers there.

Also, we do not discuss the "systems approach," but we recognize its applicability to the third element of organizational planning: state-of-the-art technology, systems, and operating procedures. Nor do we discuss the more recently recognized "contingency approach to organizing," which addresses the question "What is the best type of organizational structure given specific situations and conditions?" Even so, the process outlined in this chapter is very similar to this approach. (For a clear explanation of the contingency approach to organizing, we refer our readers to Dessler's *Organization and Management*[2] or Webber's *Management*.[3])

Certainly, one cannot either plan or implement or make adaptive responses in a vacuum. Differences occur in the real world and every setting where organizational planning occurs has its unique features, to which planners must give account. Thus, one cannot plan according to a pat set of principles. The best one can do is to follow a process that takes into consideration at least a majority of the primary factors influencing a situation and leading to the resolution of as many problems as possible.

Undertaking organizational planning

One reason managers may perform organizational planning only sporadically is that the five previously named elements compose the total, and one must conceptualize each element based on a broad range of considerations (some of which we will discuss in this chapter). The subject can hardly be conceived as an integrated whole, and therefore it becomes necessary to study the elements individually and note a number of relationships among them. The problem is compounded by the fact that (1) managers may not know where to begin with study efforts, and (2) they may not or cannot devote the required time to planning efforts. As with strategic planning, managers must undertake organizational planning in a detailed, organized, methodical way and thereby, to the greatest extent possible, eliminate destructive mistakes, avoid tangential courses of action, and assure intended consequences.

Our purpose here is to outline a brief process by which organizational planning can be carried out. We cannot conclusively advise managers and students of management how to make time available for organizational planning. However, planning of the various types we have discussed in this text should occupy a major part of the worktime of top managers. From our own experience, we know that "putting out fires," or formulating necessary adaptive responses, greatly is reduced through appropriate planning, of which organizational planning is an important part.

The primary question which organizational planning should answer is very simple. Even so, managers sometimes fail to give it due consideration because of various pressures which may appear as threatening. The question is this: *How should this firm be organized so that its formally adopted mission, goals, and objectives can be most efficiently realized given the environment within which it must operate and the need to respond appropriately to the several groups whose "rights" must be respected?* It is easy to see that organizational planning must be a response to strategic planning and to the purposes of the individual organization. Of course, in established organizations, the manner in which structure has already been imposed constitutes a matter for consideration in strategic planning, but after such consideration has been given and the strategic plan adopted, organizational planning will then likely be affected by the strategic plan. In the initial stages of getting a new business organized, the strategic plan and organizational purposes should directly dictate organizational planning (including each of its several elements).

After realizing that organizational planning should be geared to strategic planning and its results, executives and managers at every level are ready to embark upon the process of organizational planning. This process is simple in concept, but it is critical that all of its steps be pursued and in essentially the manner and sequencing we outline here (see Figure 4-1). The flow of planning activities is completely logical. Furthermore, even though some academic authorities and knowledgeable practitioners have advanced arguments against it, our own experience confirms its efficacy.

Among those who hold a different opinion, Newman and Warren would have planners focus first on combining operating tasks into individual jobs, then on grouping jobs into work groups, and finally on consolidating work groups into departments.[4] Our objection to this rests on our view that one should first conceptualize an overall scheme of departmentation (based on the human job scale, of course) so as to take account of such factors as specialization and product differentiation (subsequently explained). To pursue the flow from a "bottom-up" starting point but without consideration of an overall scheme of departmentation into which all jobs will fit would surely result in an unbalanced, disjointed total organization, one where coordination would prove nearly impossible. This is especially true in large production-oriented businesses. The bottom-up approach can work very well in small organizations and some service organizations, such as consulting firms. In all of the "Big Eight" accounting firms and most legal firms, for example, organizational structure develops essentially around the jobs of largely independent partners or principals, and in these instances a bottoms-up approach works fine.

Our view about using a top-down approach in organizational planning does not ignore the fact that the design of individual jobs must be considered at the outset when planning departmentation is undertaken, and our process chart clearly reflects that necessity. We merely claim that if owners and organizers propose to start what they hope will be a large organization, they had best pursue the process outlined in Figure 4-1 and explained below. In existing medium and large organizations, the process has unquestionable validity.

Process of organizational planning

This section discusses the five basic elements of organizational planning presented as steps in a process, together with pertinent factors that must be considered as each step is undertaken.

Figure 4-1

The Process of Organizational Planning

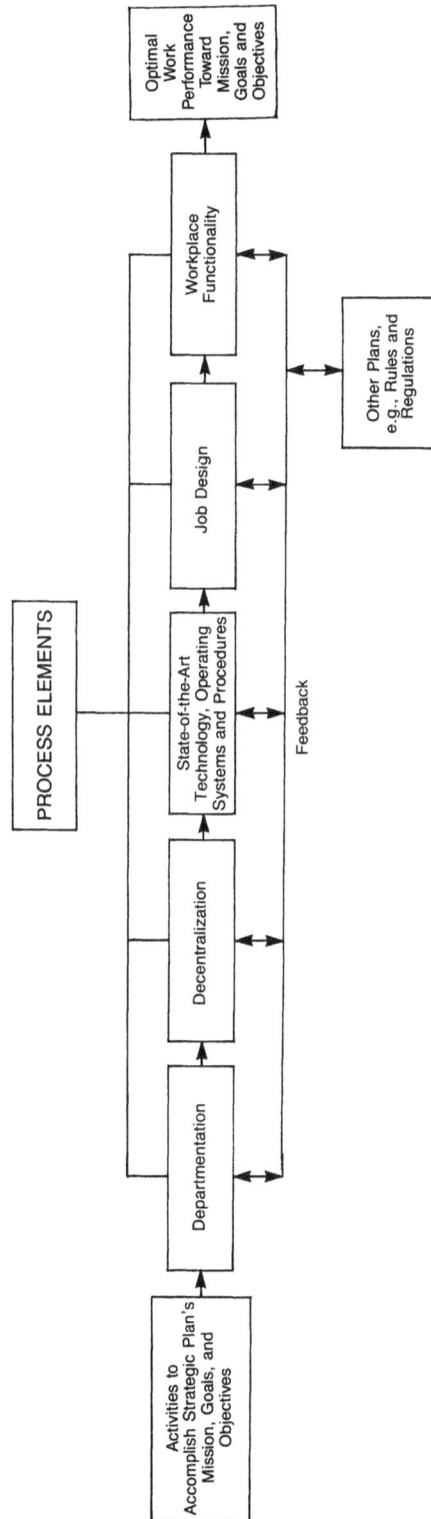

PROCESS ELEMENTS

Activities to Accomplish Strategic Plan's Mission, Goals, and Objectives → Departmentation → Decentralization → State-of-the-Art Technology, Operating Systems and Procedures → Job Design → Workplace Functionality → Optimal Work Performance Toward Mission, Goals and Objectives

Other Plans, e.g., Rules and Regulations

Feedback

Planning for departmentation

Departmentation, a term used by nearly all management authorities and practitioners, pertains to operating work (as opposed to the work of managers) and refers directly to grouping jobs into departments, divisions, plants, or other administrative units. More than any other organizational planning element, planning for departmentation determines the broad scheme of how an organization will actually operate.

What are the purposes of departmentation? Included among the many purposes are the following:

- to create manageable work units

- to realize the benefits of specialization regarding procurement of personnel and all facets of functional operations

- to focus on desirable outcomes regarding production and customers

- to respond to steps or phases of a production or other work process

- to respond to market demand by area or to the location of raw materials by area

- to realize the synergistic benefits of group work efforts

- to respond to the security and social needs of employees, as well as to the need to create coherent work groups

- to allow professional development among specialists

- to allow focused delegations of authority and assignments of responsibility and accountability to specific managers

Traditionally, managers have based departmentation on (1) functions, (2) types of products or services, (3) types of customers, or (4) geographic areas. Some authorities have cited types of equipment and designated processes (e.g., an assembly process) as two additional bases. In most instances, one can consider these under *functions*, and although we have no objections to recognizing these two additional bases, we have elected here to consider them under that heading.

Most sizeable organizations, for example those with 500 or more employees, deliberately plan their departmentation on more than one of these bases. As an example, HCA, with a broad variety of services and over 120,000 employees, has utilized all of them in its departmentation scheme. Most small organizations (say, those with less than 500 employees) departmentalize based on function, though some use an additional basis and some use none, e.g., closely held firms with a single owner-manager and only operating personnel. Even here, however, one usually finds that financial accounting is departmentalized, often on a contracted basis.

Recently, a significant number of firms originally organized on a functional basis have also added departments based on products, projects, or geographic regions. For example, one of us served as a project vice-president of a consulting firm largely organized on a functional basis. One department, a systems and research division, made significant contributions to each project, and there was a continuous vying among the project vice-presidents for the services of this division, sometimes to the point of absurdity.

For some time, HCA's organization reflected a matrix approach, with a number of functional departments based in Nashville that provided services to geographic divisions, which themselves contained "task force" groups of functional specialists. The problem of satisfactorily scheduling services for the geographic regions was encountered, and no acceptable solution appeared short of creating nearly independent geographic business units. This solution itself had problems: It would probably not be cost effective and would almost certainly create upheavals among personnel. HCA's organizational planners foresaw these problems, however, and efforts to resolve them continued.

Many large industrial organizations have evolved into matrix organizations as additional discrete product manufacturing has been undertaken (see Figure 4-2). They have almost invariably retained certain functions exclusively on a centralized basis for reasons related either to control or to cost.

Before commenting on each of the four prime bases for departmentation and on the combinations that may be applicable in individual situa-

Figure 4-2

Matrix Organization Structure for Chicago-based A/E Firm

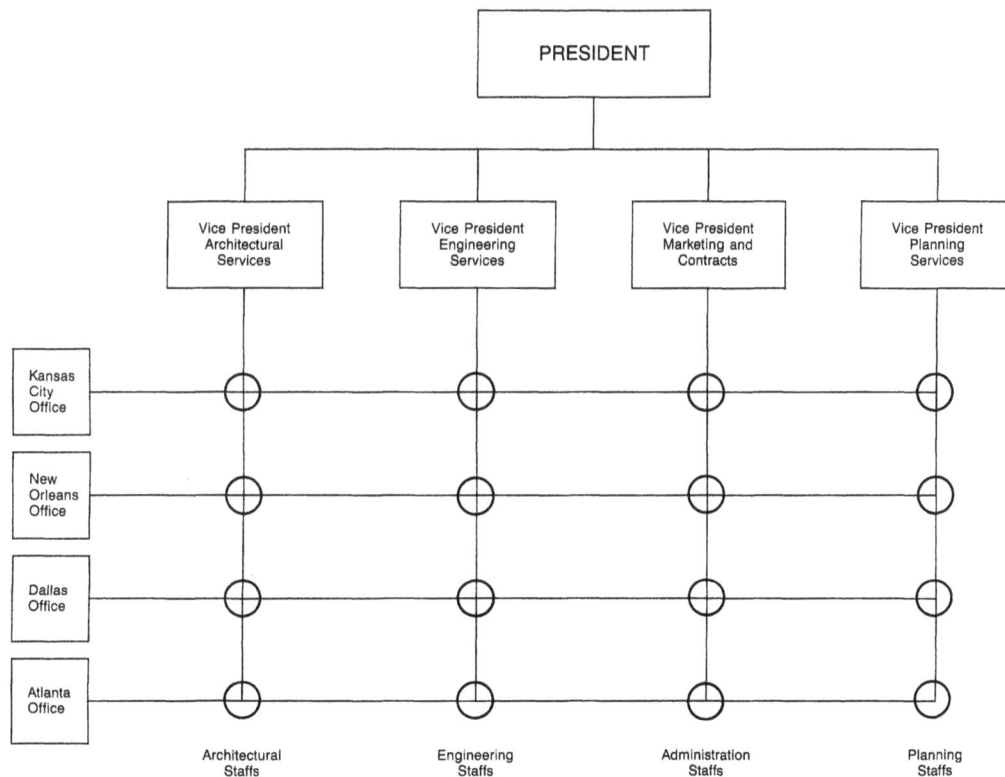

tions, we will mention several considerations that pertain to choosing among the alternatives. A choice usually must be made when any extensive organizational planning is undertaken. The pertinent considerations are as follows:

1. Will the contemplated departmentation scheme enhance employee motivation and need satisfaction or will it adversely affect them?

2. Will the basis for departmentation provide the optimal and most sustainable level of productivity among operations personnel? Will effective use be made of specialization?

3. Does the envisioned scheme of departmentation and the basis or bases for it provide for effective and easy coordination from input of resources to output of services or products within the context of the total operational system?

4. Can all types of management planning be effectively accomplished, and can the resulting plans be efficiently implemented? Can managers easily and effectively implement the control process?

5. Will the envisioned scheme of departmentation and the basis for it allow for easy expansion or contraction of operations? Will they be inappropriate for either one?

6. Will the departmentation scheme unnecessarily duplicate specialized operational skills or management talent?

7. Will the basis for departmentation promote customer satisfaction or will it lead to confusion among customers?

8. Will the departmentation envisioned adversely affect the environment where the work efforts are implemented?

9. Can best use be made of state-of-the-art technology, especially equipment, under the departmentation as envisioned?

10. In existing organizations, will proposed changes in the basis or bases for departmentation occasion intolerable upheaval among employees or established customers?

11. How will bottom-line profits be affected?

12. How will the public image be affected?

13. Will procurement of desirable operations or management personnel be adversely affected?

14. Can management confidently state that the proposed scheme of departmentation and its basis or bases will be the most effective in fulfilling the mission and attaining the adopted goals and objectives of the organization?

Certainly other considerations may apply in particular situations, perhaps uniquely in some cases. However, as various options are considered regarding departmentation, methodically posing the above questions with respect to each option will assure that, at the very least, major mistakes will not be made.

Departmentation by function

This type of departmentation remains probably the most prevalent. In fact, seldom does one encounter an organization where function has not been used as a basis for at least one department. Over a broad variety of business firms, functional specialization forms the basis for departmentation in one or more of the following: procurement, production, sales, finance, and human resource management. Figure 4-3 shows a typical organizational chart for a small firm departmentalized by the functions named.

Certain advantages accrue from departmentation by function, such as the following:

- The role of specialized, professional personnel is accentuated rather than de-emphasized. The advantages of task and process specialization can be easily obtained.

- Segmentation of whole functional process into logical steps or phases accommodates high-volume production.

- The enhanced ability to pinpoint errors or flaws in quality allows better control.

- Functional groupings afford better differentiation between operating personnel and service or staff personnel.

- Creation of multiple groups performing similar functions stimulates increased group productivity through intergroup competition, which can be easily fostered.

Figure 4-3

Departmentation by Function

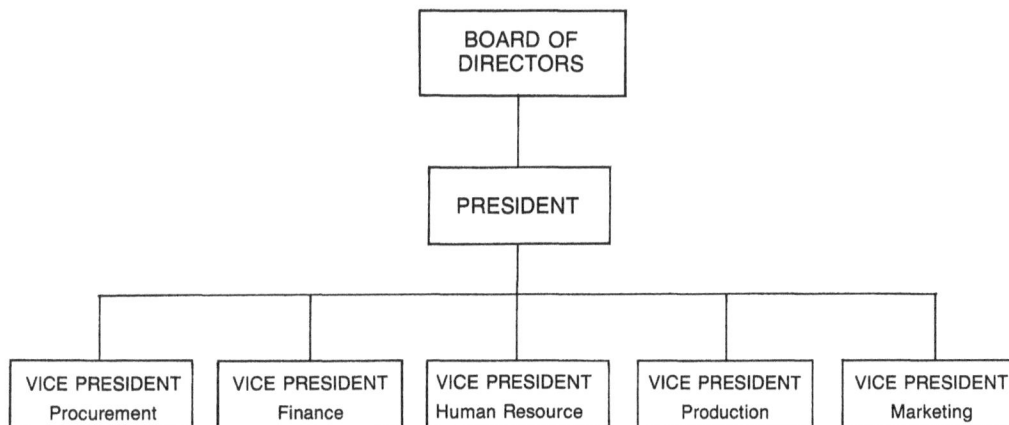

- Grouping functions homogeneously simplifies cost accounting.

- Operations follow traditional patterns and are readily understood by a broad range of persons "in the business."

- Managing one function rather than a variety obviously simplifies the work of assigned managers.

One disadvantage of departmentation based on function that has frequently been cited relates to coordination. If the efforts of one functional department are dependent upon those of another and both departments are headed by respective managers of equal status, then coordination may become a problem.

Hospitals are good examples of departmentation by function. Even in community hospitals, there will almost always be 40 to 50 functional units operating as departments, and the advantages we have cited are clearly perceptible. Offsetting the advantages, however, are disadvantages due to coordination problems arising daily despite best efforts in planning operational procedures.

See Figure 4-4 for the charted service departments of a typical 400-bed hospital. When one studies this chart, the statement by the philosopher Jacques Barzun that hospitals are among humankind's most complex organized efforts to date rings particularly true.[5]

Other disadvantages related to departmentation by function become apparent when smaller firms experience rapid and appreciable growth. Performance becomes difficult to evaluate, adaptive responses are not formulated as quickly owing to the need for approvals from central headquarters, planning of all types proceeds tediously, and coordination becomes more difficult to achieve.

Departmentation by product or service
Products manufactured or sold (or both) form the basis for departmentation in many instances. Large retail vendors often departmentalize based on products sold, such as men's clothing, women's clothing, sporting goods, jewelry, etc. General Motors represents probably the most frequently cited large corporation where departmentation has been accomplished based on products (both manufactured and sold). Their Pontiac, Chevrolet, Cadillac, and other product divisions are examples of "departments" resulting from this kind of departmentation.

Figure 4-5 displays the typical departmentation of a retail firm based on products sold. The advantages related to departmentation by product are several, including these:

- There is great flexibility concerning expansion of existing product lines or adding new ones. New and separate administrative units can be established. When retractions become necessary, the selective closing or sale of units affects remaining operations to a minimal degree.

- Accuracy and validity in evaluating performance are increased.

- Control is simplified.

Figure 4-4

Departmentation by Function in a 400-Bed Hospital

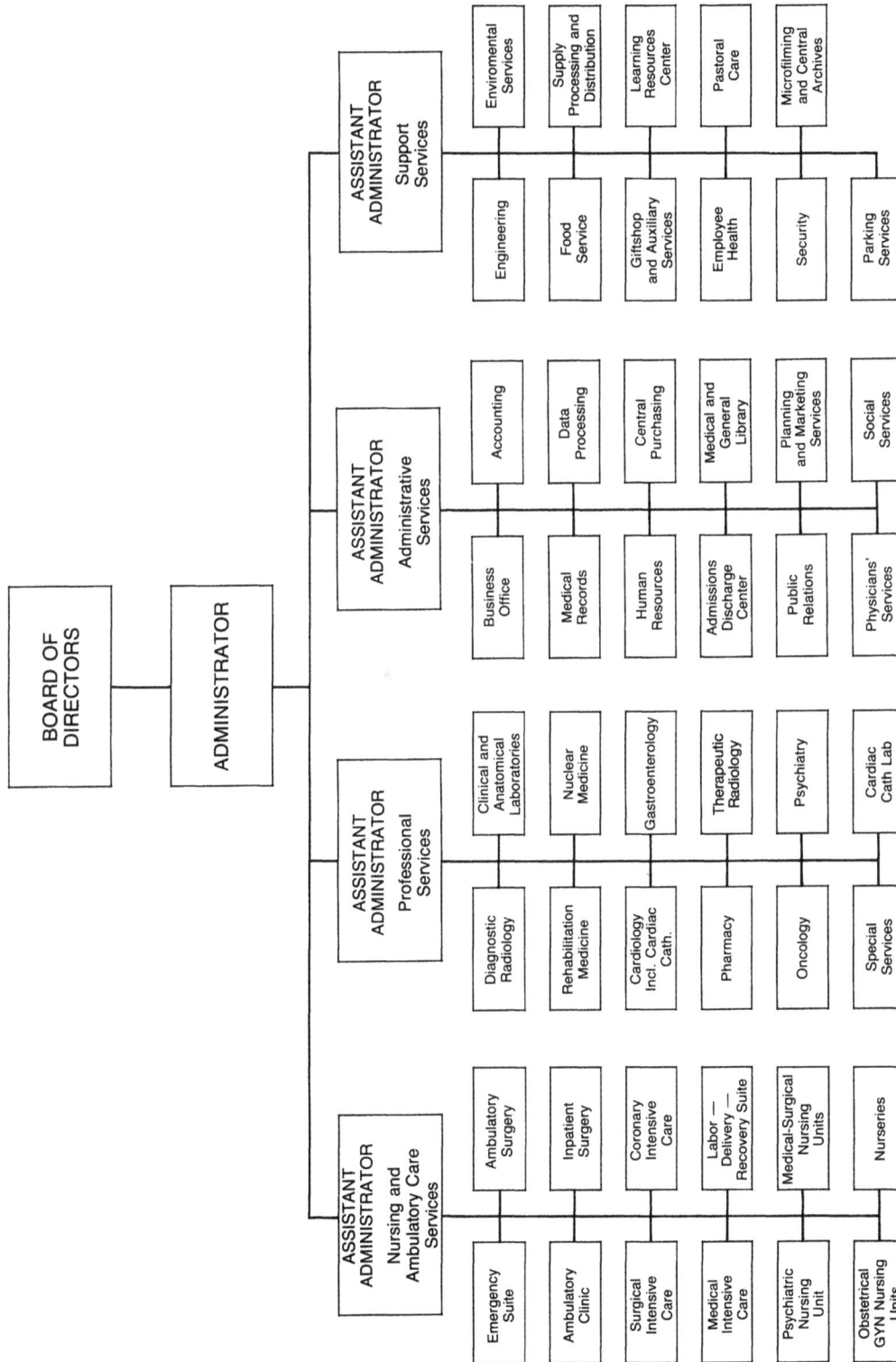

Figure 4-5

**Departmentation Based on
Product Specialization**

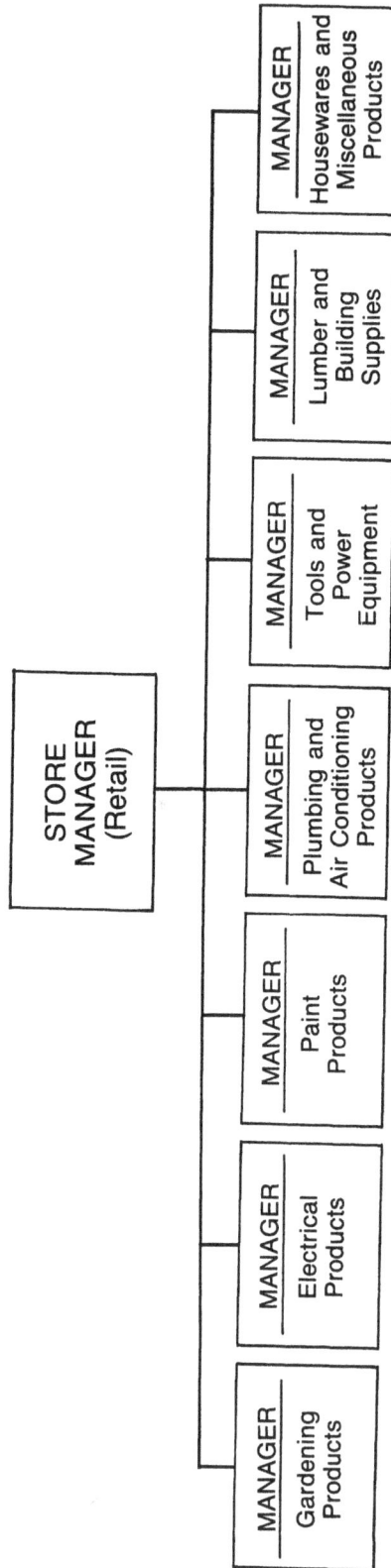

STORE
MANAGER
(Retail)

MANAGER
Gardening
Products

MANAGER
Electrical
Products

MANAGER
Paint
Products

MANAGER
Plumbing and
Air Conditioning
Products

MANAGER
Tools and
Power
Equipment

MANAGER
Lumber and
Building
Supplies

MANAGER
Housewares and
Miscellaneous
Products

- Departmentation by function can be done where it is advantageous. Witness the functional departmentation of many manufacturers (e.g., into departments of engineering, production and sales, etc.) that have departmentalized primarily on a product basis.

- Executive development is enhanced.

- Competition among divisions usually occurs, with the result that productivity increases.

- The need for close coordination to be exercised at the uppermost levels of the organization reduces, and self-coordination at division levels emerges.

- Marketing focuses more specifically.

- Motivation and needs satisfaction of a higher percentage of individuals employed becomes possible.

- The easier formulation of clear and specific strategic and business planning objectives nearly always occurs.

Disadvantages due to departmentation based on products or services include the lowered probability of a uniform corporate culture, the necessity for high volumes before such departmentation can occur, and the possibility that top executives, being so far removed from actual operations, may become lethargic or insensitive regarding the realities of operations. These disadvantages are, of course, unlikely to occur in small retail firms, but they can easily occur in large manufacturing operations.

Departmentation by types of customers
This basis for departmentation stands as the least utilized among the four bases cited, and yet, depending on the business being considered, it may be the most valid for some individual organizations. For example, some wholesalers also operate retail units, and departmentation based on customer types makes patent good sense. Sears operates a catalog business as well as a host of direct-sell retail stores. Most major seaports are the homes of vendors who sell to national and international customers. To assure satisfaction to various customers, they create separate administrative units to handle the problems of separate customer groups (e.g., domestic versus foreign customers).

The primary advantages of this basis for departmentation are in regard to marketing and to handling problems unique to separate customer groups. As for disadvantages, some loss of flexibility in operations may result, although probably not enough to offset the advantages. See Figure 4-6 for an illustration of departmentation based on customer specialization.

Departmentation by geographic location
This is a very common basis for departmentation. All of HCA's major national operations have used this as a basis in the creation of administrative units (together with two other bases—types of customer and

Figure 4-6

**Departmentation Based on
Customer Specialization**

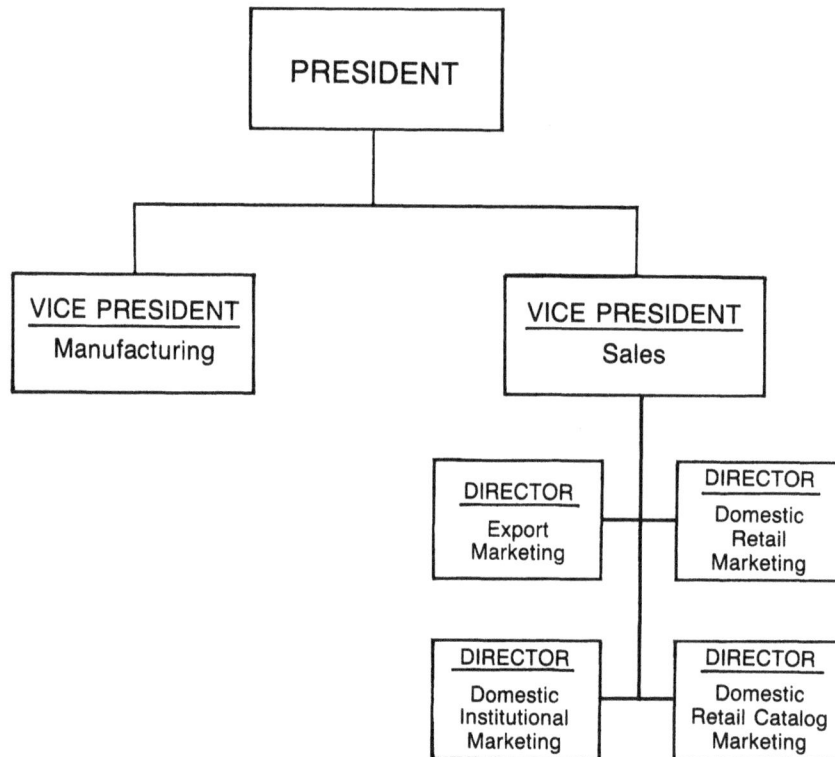

```
                    ┌─────────────────┐
                    │    PRESIDENT    │
                    └─────────────────┘
                             │
          ┌──────────────────┴──────────────────┐
┌───────────────────┐               ┌───────────────────┐
│  VICE PRESIDENT   │               │  VICE PRESIDENT   │
│   Manufacturing   │               │      Sales        │
└───────────────────┘               └───────────────────┘
                                             │
                           ┌─────────────────┼────────────┐
                    ┌───────────────┐  ┌───────────────┐
                    │   DIRECTOR    │  │   DIRECTOR    │
                    │    Export     │  │   Domestic    │
                    │   Marketing   │  │    Retail     │
                    │               │  │   Marketing   │
                    └───────────────┘  └───────────────┘
                    ┌───────────────┐  ┌───────────────┐
                    │   DIRECTOR    │  │   DIRECTOR    │
                    │   Domestic    │  │   Domestic    │
                    │ Institutional │  │ Retail Catalog│
                    │   Marketing   │  │   Marketing   │
                    └───────────────┘  └───────────────┘
```

types of service). International operations also have based their departmentation on geography and types of customers.

In early 1987, HCA's owned-hospital operations had 12 geographic
divisions, the psychiatric company had 4 districts, and the management
company had 4 regions which were further divided into 24 districts.
These various divisions, regions, and districts had considerable territorial
overlap owing to the decentralized nature of decision making throughout
HCA, which occasioned a certain amount of confusion as to who was
doing what and where. But top management tolerated the situation
because of considerations related to the marketing of differentiated services and to the entrepreneurial motivations of the several executives
involved. Thus, HCA's departmentation was not based solely on geography but to some extent on services. The main reason was that the
management of owned acute care hospitals, the contractual management
of general acute care hospitals owned by others, and the management of
owned psychiatric hospitals all differ considerably.

For several years, HCA considered creating four to six business units
on the basis of geography. All service operations would be combined
within these units, thus eliminating the existing national departmentation by service. However, if deemed desirable following creation of these
geographic units, further departmentation could have been based on

services. This geographic reorganization was not done owing to a number of negatives that became apparent through methodically applying the 14 criteria set forth previously in the section, Planning for Departmentation. Not the least of these negatives was the upheaval that would have been created by abandoning the existing organizational configuration. Figure 4-7 displays HCA's organization chart (for early 1987) regarding operations and Figure 4-8 shows the alternative that was actively considered.

Advantages sometimes attributable to departmentation based on geography are as follows:

- Those who are responsible for operations have their offices where the action is, and sensitivity to local situations can thus increase.

- "Marketing by territory" promotes flexibility in expansions and contractions and facilitates understanding by employees through simplification.

- Executives are kept highly motivated.

- Employees usually come from the local territory and can better relate to the local populace and local conditions.

- The public image probably will be enhanced and marketing will be more effective by having operations closer to the markets served.

Where a departmentation plan is inappropriately based on geography, one can envision a number of disadvantages. However, where markets clearly relate to dispersed territories, few disadvantages emerge. Some problems in planning invariably arise concerning which support services should be centralized and which should be geographically dispersed. These problems can become serious and sometimes may preclude creating additional divisions based on geography.

Planning for decentralization

This term refers to the division of management work and duties—as contrasted to operations work—that must occur in all organizations among established hierarchical levels. Specifically, decentralization refers to the delegation of authority and the assignment of responsibility and accountability to positions created and staffed to manage subordinates, who in some instances may be managers and in others operations personnel of one type or another. Usually, the only completely centralized firm is a one-person "organization." Someone who was the sole owner and manager of a business could conceivably employ a number of operations workers without delegating any authority or assigning any responsibility and accountability for any aspect of management, but this would be difficult to accomplish even if it was the goal.

The degree of decentralization in an organization is determined by the amount of authority delegated and the amount of responsibility and degree of accountability assigned to lower hierarchical levels as compared with the total amount of authority that has been vested by the state in the owners and organizers and usually transferred to a corporate board of

Figure 4-7

HCA's Department of Operations (1986) (Based on Geography and Types of Service)

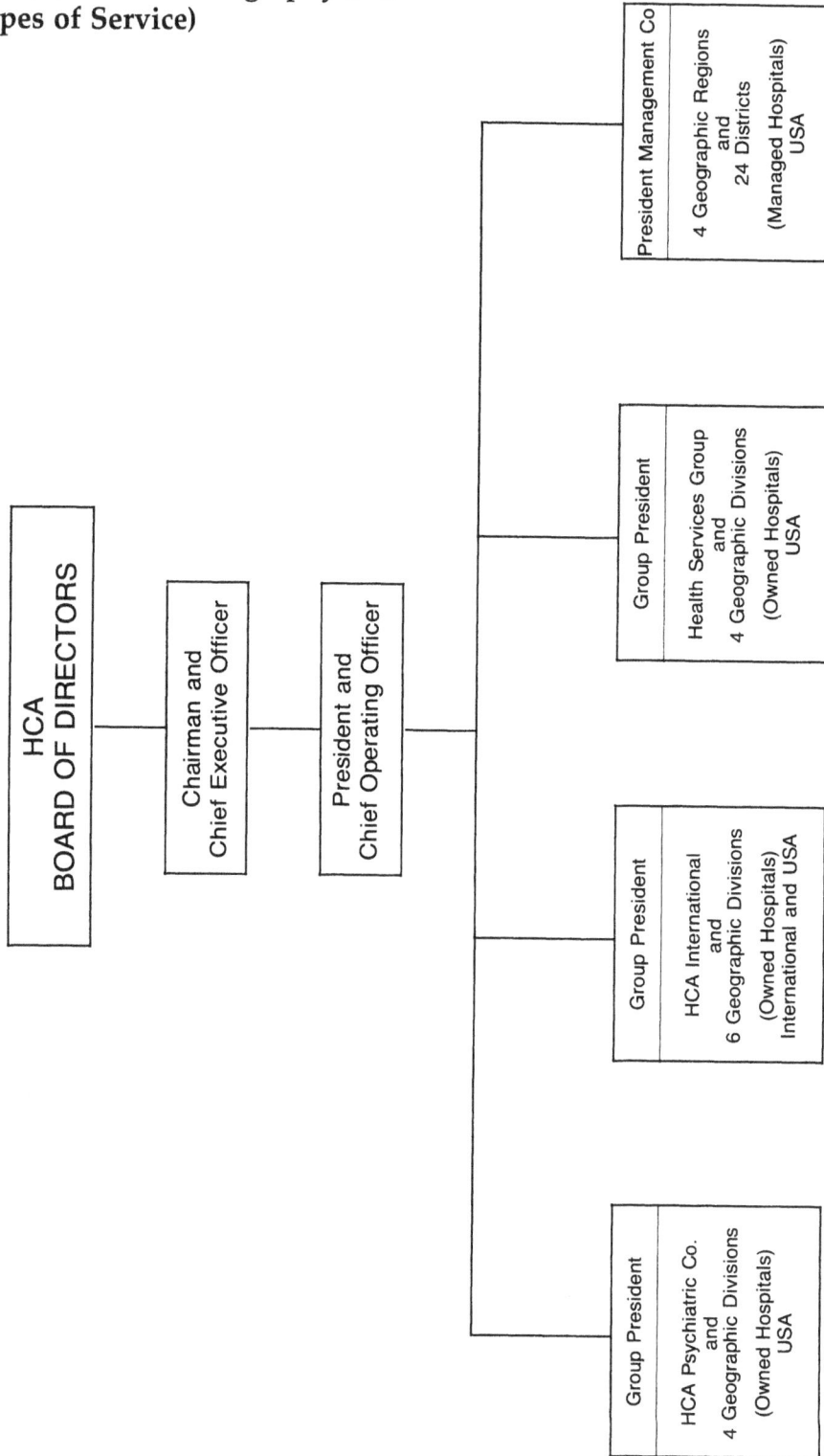

Source: Reprinted with permission of Hospital Corporation of America.

Figure 4-8

Alternative Departmentation of HCA's Operations (Based on Geographic Units)

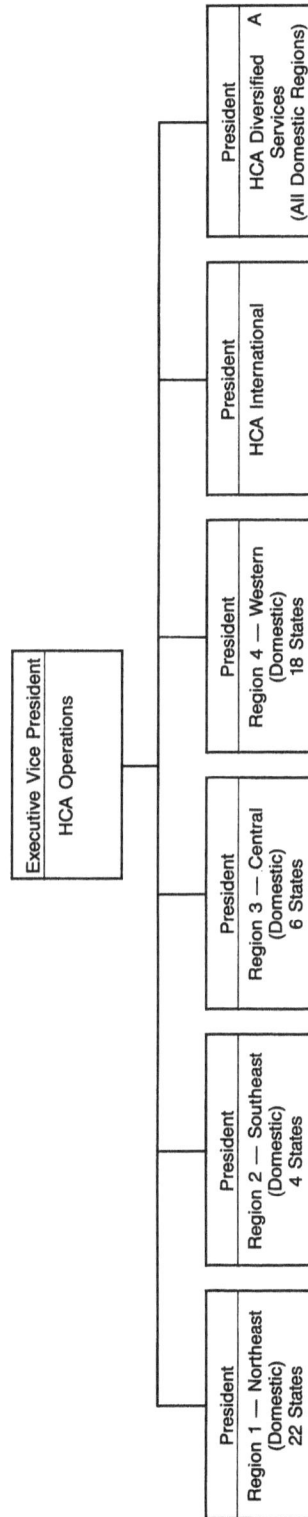

Executive Vice President HCA Operations						
President Region 1 — Northeast (Domestic) 22 States	President Region 2 — Southeast (Domestic) 4 States	President Region 3 — Central (Domestic) 6 States	President Region 4 — Western (Domestic) 18 States	President HCA International	President HCA Diversified Services (All Domestic Regions) A

Notes:
A. This department is based on product specialization rather than geography.

Source: Reprinted with permission of Hospital Corporation of America.

directors. Typically, the board of directors elects a president, who in turn appoints vice presidents and delegates authority and assigns responsibility and accountability to them for accomplishing specific operations. Further decentralization of authority, responsibility, and accountability may subsequently occur through the actions of vice presidents.

In this second step of organizational planning, a framework of management positions forms that will be related to departments already envisioned in the first step. For each of these positions, the authority necessary to accomplish the work of the relevant department will be determined and specified. Appropriate matching assignments of responsibility and accountability must correlate with delegated authority.

In this step, managers devise a hierarchy and framework of management positions reaching to the department level only. Further decentralization should await the conclusion of the third step, for a departmental framework must come into shape that is based on state-of-the-art technology, planned systems, and operating procedures. Thus, although planning for decentralization starts here, it extends through the third and fourth steps.

Planning for decentralization should include the following:

1. A determination must be made of the management positions required to manage all work and of a framework in which they are related to each other (most often a hierarchy). This determination should extend to the department level in this step and be completed by the conclusion of steps three and four, when operational procedures and the content of jobs will have been at least tentatively settled.

2. A determination must be made of the authority to be delegated and the responsibility and accountability to be assigned to each management position as determined in (1) above. Such authority, responsibility, and accountability should relate to the planned departments and to work actually to be performed either by individuals or groups. Essentially, this involves initial planning related to the job descriptions of managers. We outline in detail implementation of planning as it relates to this and the following two steps in the organizational planning process in Chapter 10, entitled "Delegation of Authority and Assignment of Responsibility and Accountability." We refer readers to that chapter, which sets forth specific actions required to implement the planning of decentralization as described in this chapter.

3. Although specific planning regarding managerial duties of both line and staff positions occurs in step four of the organizational planning process, planning for decentralization includes relating line and staff positions and determining what type of staff positions will be created, which duties will be assigned to each position, and which line position designated staff will report to. If functional authority will be assigned to certain staff positions, managers must also make this determination.

4. Consideration should be given to the system of lateral relationships and to the vertical relationships that must be created. One of the great problems of coordination within organizations that are hierarchical

(and most are) develops as a consequence of deficient lateral relationships among managers. Many authorities have pointed this out, and we ourselves discuss it further in Chapter 8 ("Planning Communication and Management Information Systems") and Chapter 14 ("Coordination").

5. A determination must be made of those positions which will be assigned responsibility for specific types of planning. We identify and discuss seven specific areas of planning in the course of this text, and responsibility for each should be settled. Of course, final decisions about responsibility should be reflected in the actual job designs of individual managers. This should receive consideration in step four *after* the tentative determinations of operational systems and procedures.

6. A determination must be made of the number of levels in the management hierarchy and the span of control which each management position at each level will possess. If a matrix organization seems applicable, a tentative determination should result from the output of the first two steps, with final determination occurring at the conclusion of the third step. Although we have deliberately excluded academic discussions of chain of command, numbers of hierarchical levels, and span of control, our own experience indicates the desirability of keeping the number of levels to a minimum and at the same time increasing span of control to a maximum (for each given situation). In our specialized field, we know that this principle reduces bureaucratic choking through providing better communication. By planning automatic controls on an impersonal basis and putting this principle into practice, operations will be considerably streamlined and the number of required managers will be reduced. This principle is also consistent with the inevitable trend toward self-control as national educational levels advance in all areas of specialization.

7. A determination must be made regarding the degree of centralization versus decentralization, including a determination of which management functions will remain centralized. Although the specific authority delegated and the responsibility and accountability assigned to each management position as they relate to divisions, departments, sections, etc., will determine the actual "degree of decentralization," managers should try to assess the extent of decentralization from a general or "philosophical" standpoint (i.e., one that reflects the philosophy of the organization).

State-of-the-art technology, operating systems, and operating procedures

All organizational planning must take into account the environment in which a business intends to operate, with particular focus on the technological environment. More specifically, the current and future state-of-the-art technology used by the planning organization both in operations and management functions must receive evaluation. Such evaluation involves procedures as well as equipment. In recent years, vast strides have been made in all facets of industrial operations, and service operations feature a dazzling array of electronic equipment of various types.

Automation has increased manyfold and numerous procedures accepted as modern two decades ago are now considered obsolete. Advances in technology have constantly changed production, transport, communications, and the way businesses operate in general. These changes have affected most work processes throughout the business world and, in turn, have affected the number and types of operators needed and the design of millions of operational jobs. Because of changing technology, which has so drastically affected procedures and jobs in operations, the types of skill and knowledge needed by managers have changed. More than any other technological development, the computer has dramatically changed operational processes and thereby affected the jobs of managers.

Job design, the next step of organizational planning, cannot intelligently proceed without first assessing the types of equipment that will be used in operations and without having some concrete knowledge of procedures to be followed in operations.

In framing work systems and devising procedures within departments and between departments, many firms now use specialists in management engineering (they can be considered a new generation of industrial engineers). Such specialists, if experienced in and qualified for working in a given service or industry, offer a tremendous advantage. In organizations already established, however, these specialists should provide room for participation in their systems and planning procedures for persons already employed and involved. If this is not done, a rebellion can occur—as often happens.

As already noted, some authorities, possibly from considerations related to the behavioral sciences, cite job design as being the first step in organization, preceding even the conceptualization of structure. This question immediately arises, especially in the case of operations: How can a job be designed without considering state-of-the-art technology, an operating system, and operational procedures? The answer is that it can't. Where work follows a process—as is the case in most industrial operations, hospitals, and a multitude of service organizations—the work system and procedures must first be planned before specific job content can be determined.

Many businesses operate overall as an open system. Figure 4-9 broadly portrays the concept of an open system (as described by Optner)[6] and introduces additionally the descriptive parameters inherent in the process.[7]

Many authorities have described in detail the techniques and processes used to design systems, and we will not discuss them here.

Job design

Brown and Moberg state, "Basically, job design is the part of organization structure that focuses on how tasks and responsibilities are combined in any one individual's assignments. More formally, we can define job design as *the assignments of task* activities, duties, and responsibilities to organizational members to accomplish organizational goals."[8] This definition is both valid and practical, although we have some disagreement with the word *assignment*. We believe that for any position there should be a mutually understood *agreement* between the superior and the subordinate about what the subordinate will be doing and what authority,

Figure 4-9

The Basic Concept of an Open System

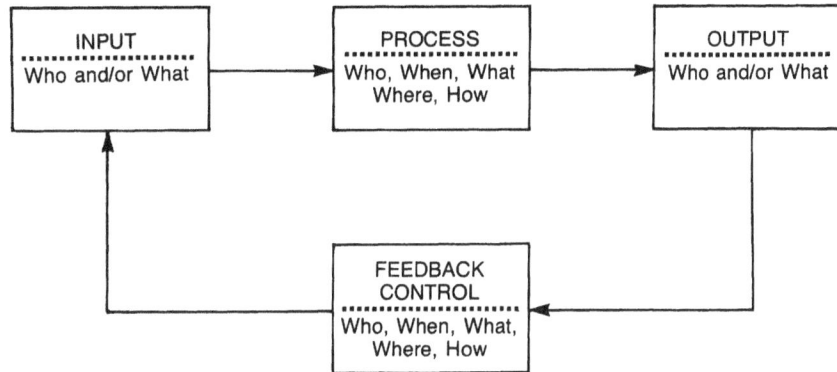

Source: Reprinted from *Hospital & Health Services Administration,* vol. 16, no. 1, p. 17, with permission of American College of Healthcare Executives, © Winter 1971.

responsibility, and accountability he or she will possess. Even though the job design previously worked out unilaterally by the superior may remain largely the same, some adjustments are often made, which help to avoid later aggravation for both parties. From a psychological standpoint, one advantage is that the subordinate willingly agrees to undertake a particular set of duties instead of being merely told, "Here's what you've got to do; good luck."

A job as designed and agreed upon with a subordinate should be set out in a job description. Exhibit 4-1 displays a typical job description prepared for and agreed to by a worker performing key operational duties within a supply processing and distribution system operating in a hospital. The work of this position is very closely geared to that of other positions to allow the smooth functioning of the entire system. Again, we point to the fact that had not the work inherent in the system and its procedures been determined previously, it would have been impossible for this job description to have been prepared.

Much jargon concerning job design has accumulated over the years. "*Job scope* refers to the number and variety of tasks included in any job."[9] *Job depth* "refers to the degree of influence employees have over their work environment to carry out their work without supervision."[10] *Job enlargement* and *job enrichment* are synonymous and refer to the adding of variety to job tasks and the making of provisions for greater autonomy. *Job rotation* means allowing individuals to shift from one job to another from time to time to relieve monotony. *Task identity* means that the job requires performing and completing an identifiable piece of work rather than doing, for example, rote spot welding on an assembly line. The fact that an employee can identify with and be responsible for a completed product has been shown to be psychologically rewarding (at least to a majority of employees). Often task identity is nearly impossible where specialization is carried to its ultimate degree, and managers may face decisions as to whether the benefits of specialization or of worker satisfaction are more important. In many instances, however, specialists take

Exhibit 4-1

Description of Job Duties

Effective Date _____
Revised Date(s) _____

For: (Name) _____

Title: Preparation and Sterilization Technician (1, 2, and 3)

Department: Supply Processing and Distribution

Division: Preparation and Sterilization

Reports to: _____

Code Number: _____

Approved by: _____

I. *Job Summary:* Works in the preparation and sterilization room exclusively in the preparation of packs and trays, following the receipt of sterile or sanitized items coming from decontamination and clean linen coming from the laundry. Delivers all terminally sterilized goods to the processed stores division. Rotates on two shifts according to schedule and according to position. Coordinates work with other technicians.

II. *Major Daily Tasks:*

1. Receives and sorts items coming from decontamination through the AMSCO Washer-Sterilizers, the Hi-Vac Sterilizer and manual clean-up room and checks visually for all defects.
   a. If defects are found, follows procedure for repair or discard as necessary.
   b. If item is free of defects, it will be assembled, packaged and terminally sterilized.

2. Receives and sorts all items passed by decontamination personnel through the Gas-Gravity Steam Sterilizer.
   a. If it is an ethylene oxide load, it will be placed in the aerator and then passed to processed stores if no further processing is required.
   b. If it is a gravity steam load, it will be cooled and processed according to procedure.

3. Monitors all sterilized loads for proper preparation temperature, pressure and exposure time.

4. Under direction of the RN Supervisor, checks, assembles and wraps all surgical packs and trays according to work sheets.

5. Terminally sterilizes all packs and trays according to procedures and then passes sterile items to the proper section of the processed stores division.

6. Performs biological monitoring of terminal sterilizers (weekly only) and of environment on a regular schedule, according to procedure.

III. *Minor Daily Tasks:*

1. Cleans work area daily, according to procedure.

2. Cleans terminal sterilizers, including door gasket, drain screen and trap.

3. Attends department meetings as directed.

4. Performs special assignments as directed.

IV. *Typical Assignments*

Position No. 1: 8:00 A.M. to 4:30 P.M.

1. Report to RN Supervisor.
2. Clean sterilizer, including gasket on door, drain screen and drain trap.
3. Change and date charts on all sterilizers daily.
4. Start gas sterilizer each morning when necessary.

Position No. 2: 8:00 A.M. to 4:30 P.M.

1. Report to Supervisor.
2. Assist in loading and unloading sterilizers when necessary.
3. Check linen for holes.
4. Fold special sheets by procedure.
5. Fan fold towels and package.
6. Make up basic packs.

5. Load and unload sterilizer when necessary.
6. Check, assemble and wrap all surgical trays according to inventory worksheets.
7. Package dressing sets as needed.
8. Flush distilled water through all special needles and instruments with a lumen before packaging.
9. Assemble and wrap Empyema bottles when necessary.
10. Assemble and package syringes.
11. Make up blow bottle sets as needed.
12. Operate water distiller when necessary.
13. Report to supervisor in charge on completed work assignments and on unfinished assignments, before going off duty.
14. Leave work area clean and neat.
15. Assist others as necessary. TEAMWORK.

7. Select and package instruments for special cases.
8. Check operative schedule for special packs and instruments for surgical cases.
9. Package individually wrapped instruments and supplies.
10. Place on shelf all instruments not used for sets.
11. Make up suture needle sets.
12. Package supplies for gas sterilization.
13. Check all catheters and tubing before packaging.
14. Do special assignments as given.
15. Place all sterile supplies on mobile shelving according to procedure.
16. Keep sterile supplies in proper rotation and remove any out-dated material, according to procedure.
17. Report to supervisor in charge on completed work assignments, and on unfinished assignments, before going off duty.
18. Leave work area clean and neat.
19. Assist others as necessary. TEAMWORK.

Position No. 3: 3:30 P.M. to Midnight

1. Report to day RN Supervisor and receive report of work on morning shift and status of work progress.
2. Assume charge of Preparation and Sterilization room when RN Supervisor departs.
3. Load and unload sterilizers when necessary.
4. Keep checking sterilizers to insure proper functioning. (Leave note if a certain sterilizer is not working properly and why it is not.)
5. Select and package instruments for all basic sets.
6. Select and package instruments for special cases.
7. Make up suture needle sets.

8. Check all catheters and tubing before packaging.
9. Flush distilled water through all special needles and instruments with a lumen before packaging.
10. Terminally sterilize as necessary.
11. Do special assignments as given.
12. Operate water distiller when necessary.
13. Give assistance to processing and distribution unit when needed (only in emergencies when only one person is in processing and distribution unit).
14. When an emergency operation is in progress after tour of duty (12:00 Midnight) remain in preparation and sterilization room.
15. Leave work area clean and neat.
16. Assist others. TEAMWORK.

V. *Authority*

The person filling either of the three basic positions as noted is delegated that authority necessary to perform the tasks as described, together with that delegated by the RN Supervisor necessary to perform specific other tasks.

VI. *Responsibility*

Responsibility is assigned for performing the tasks as noted, some under supervision and others independently.

VII. *Acknowledgment of Tasks To Be Performed, Delegated Authority and Assigned Responsibility*

I, __(Name)_____ , understand the tasks as outlined and hereby accept the authority delegated and responsibility assigned to me. I have studied the procedure manual for preparation and sterilization and have received appropriate on-site orientation. I am ready to assume the position of Preparation and Sterilization Technician on either of the three shifts as described, under appropriate instructions and supervision.

Signed _____

pride in their specialty if it is vitally important to a given system or procedure and particularly if it possesses some professional significance.

Brown and Moberg cite five characteristics of well-designed jobs based on recent research reported by J.R. Hackman.[11] These are:

1. skill variety

2. task identity

3. autonomy

4. opportunities for social interaction

5. knowledge of results

These characteristics are somewhat self-explanatory, and experienced managers will largely agree on their importance. Certainly they should receive attention during the course of job designing.

Providing many positions with feedback about performance (in regard to both quality and quantity) poses considerable difficulties. However, our experience indicates the great value of feedback and the importance of supplying it promptly, routinely, and impersonally.

Job design and redesign have recently received greatly increased attention because of the increased expectation of personnel that they should get some satisfaction from the work environment and the work itself. This is not surprising when one contemplates the continuously rising levels of education, the greater affluence of the nation as a whole, and the consciousness of individual worth currently so prevalent. With regard to the last point, we believe the decreasing size of American families is an important factor that is often overlooked. A change in any of these trends seems unlikely, and therefore the importance of intelligent attention to job design will undoubtedly increase.

Job boredom, the stultification of initiative, "blue collar blues," disenchantment with specialization, etc., are frequently cited as the undesirable side effects of narrow job scope resulting primarily from the job specialization inherent in many industrial work systems or procedures. To avoid these undesirable effects, job designers have attempted in recent years to enlarge or enrich jobs which seem to produce low worker morale. Not all such programs aimed at job enrichment have yielded positive results. In our opinion, failure to achieve unqualified success in all programs should have been expected. Resistance to change can emerge as a real psychological deterrent in many such programs, and program perfection is always very difficult to achieve (no matter what the program). Net results, not surprisingly, show some failures.

An example of the nearly universal resistance to change occurred during our early years in hospital administration. After having devised a new system for room scheduling at a hospital, one of us was asked by an admissions officer to designate the placement of a visual scheduling board. As the board was being uncrated, one admissions clerk, not having been informed of the impending installation, stated, "I don't know what it is, but it won't work." Although the remark was amusing and epitomized resistance to change, the admissions clerk should in fact have been previously told not only about the installation of the new scheduling board, but about the proposed changes as they affected existing procedures and the design of individual jobs.

Resistance to Change

"I don't know what it is, but it won't work here."

Our general thoughts about job enrichment programs and all other programs of job redesign are as follows:

1. Careful analysis must first be made of existing jobs within the context of an existing work system or procedure. Is it the job or the system and its procedures that have undesirable effects on employee productivity and morale? If only the job design itself is at fault, redesign may not be too difficult. If the system itself needs redesigning, the task will be much greater, and in many instances professional management engineers should be called upon to help. It must always be remembered that employee morale and job satisfaction are not the only factors to be considered. Productivity and the attainment of goals and objectives have, of course, a top priority.

2. Employees who will be affected should have an opportunity to make meaningful contributions to the redesign of systems, procedures, and jobs.

3. However a job may be redesigned, employees and managers who will be affected should agree upon its characteristics and the employees should willingly accept the changes. We believe that instances where such agreement cannot be achieved rarely occur. When they do, there are usually means by which reasonable adjustments can be made. Many firms have created programs of orientation, retraining, etc., to alleviate employee dissatisfaction with systems, procedures, and job redesigns.

4. Managers should restate the new job in a new formal job description that can stand as an agreement between superiors and subordinates. The job description should set out the tasks, the authority delegated, and the responsibility and accountability assigned.

Workplace functionality

Like job design, the architectural design of the workplace should facilitate the work systems and procedures to be performed. Many operations try to fit the flow of work into buildings that were designed for other purposes or that were poorly designed for the work they are supposed to accommodate. Bad workplace design can cause a business enterprise untold increased costs. Company officials may not even recognize the problem. Surprisingly, humans often think of buildings as given, fixed, unalterable. We have seen workplaces where people were "going around their elbows to get to their noses." As an example, one of us came across a hospital in Australia where circulating nurses were retrieving supplies and instruments to service an operating room at one level via stairways from a level below. Architects had intentionally designed the building in this manner!

> Interdepartmental relationships should determine basic architectural layout and the form of the building, taking into consideration pertinent constraints [usually related to the site]. Individual departmental design should add to the efficiency of functions to be performed. The sizes and shapes of respective rooms should specifically be planned to accommodate their functions, equipment requirements, and numbers and types of occupants.[12]

These words, though written about the design of hospitals, apply to the design of any workplace. The workplaces of industry and service operations should have a utilitarian character, and this ought to be clearly manifest in the architectural design. Of course, image is of great concern to many firms, and we will not disparage this factor. However, architectural monumentality should generally be reserved for structures housing corporate headquarters.

Although not related directly to functionality, optimal security and comfort of employees are important design considerations, as is aesthetics. Many have argued about the merits of aesthetics versus the merits of functionality, regarding them as being at variance. But they are not at variance, especially in the case of interior work spaces. "In truth, aesthetics and function can be synergistic, with at least part of beauty stemming from the fitness of design for purposes intended."[13]

Winston Churchill once stated, "We shape our buildings and then our buildings shape us." This is certainly true and the statement is a fitting complement to the adage that "form should follow function."

Form Follows Function*

*Credit is given to Gordon A. Friesen for the idea reflected in this cartoon.

Summary

Engaging in organizational planning is an obligation that the owners and managers of a business have to employees, customers, the general public, and themselves. Broadly speaking, an organizational structure should reflect the environment within which the organization exists and the work processes that are implemented in pursuit of the established goals and objectives. Determining the nature of the structure and the degree of decentralization is the basic purpose of organizational planning.

Organizational planning, which is essentially a process, includes five interrelated elements:

1. departmentation

2. decentralization

3. state-of-the-art technology, operating systems, and operating procedures

4. job design

5. workplace functionality

Managers traditionally have based departmentation on one or more of the following in individual organizations: (1) functions, (2) types of products or services, (3) types of customers, and (4) geographic areas. Some organizations have superimposed a departmentation based on products upon a functional departmental structure to achieve what is commonly known as a matrix organization. Many organizations use two or more of the bases cited.

In planning for departmentation, a number of criteria are relevant for selecting the most desirable basis or bases. Such criteria should be methodically considered.

Departmentation by function constitutes by far the most prevalent basis for organizing, and it is rare to find any sizeable organization that has not used it. The vast majority of small- and medium-size organizations (roughly, those with 500 employees or less) make use of departmentation by function almost exclusively. As an organization grows, however, departmentation by function becomes unwieldy and may inhibit growth. Breaking this yoke has often been traumatic.

Departmentation by product is advantageous for many organizations, from those engaged in modest retail sales to giant multinational enterprises. General Motors is the most commonly cited large organization so structured. Departmentation by type of customer is probably the least common, but even so many organizations, including Sears, build around customer specialization. Departmentation by geographic location has been the primary basis for HCA's structure, and many other organizations that obtain customers by locating in new territories eventually departmentalize in this manner.

Matrix organizations usually form to make full use of costly, functionally specialized, centralized departments and to retain overall control at corporate headquarters. There are many troublesome operational aspects inherent in a matrix organization, but in some cases the advantages outweigh the disadvantages.

Planning for decentralization involves determining a framework of management positions as these relate to the operational units established in departmentation. Further, it involves dividing the total authority granted to the organization to do business among the management positions so established, as well as assigning appropriate responsibility and accountability to each position. This planning should take into account the number of needed hierarchical levels, the required span of control of each position, and the numerous principles of classic management theory (all of which have been shown to be particularly elastic over the years). It should also take into account various theories advanced by the behavioral scientists, especially those pertaining to motivation and need satisfaction.

Before individual jobs can be designed, managers must give consideration to state-of-the-art technology, operating systems, and operating procedures. If team play is to occur, one must first devise the "play" and then devise accordingly the roles of the "players" (keeping in mind, of course, the capabilities of the players). As a result, some trade-offs certainly must be made, based on the individual talents, idiosyncrasies, and desires of the players. However, organizations should be a systematically operating whole, not an eclectic collection of individuals.

The design of each job should be consistent with the departmentation scheme, the planned operating systems and procedures, and the needs of employees. A particular design specifies what one individual in a given position will do and how the work of that individual should interrelate with the work of others. After an initial formulation, managers should have individual discussions with jobholders to finalize the design. On the basis of such discussions, completed job descriptions will constitute employees' agreements with management regarding the work they will do.

"Form should follow function" is often quoted but then ignored in the design of facilities to accommodate the basic work processes of an organization. This adage should truly guide physical plant planning and design.

See Chapter 5 for information regarding the role of standing plans in the planning and definition of organizational structure.

Notes

1. Ross A. Webber, *Management* (Homewood, Ill.: Richard D. Irwin, Inc., 1975), 192–94.

2. Gary Dessler, *Organization and Management* (Reston, Va.: Reston Publishing Company, 1982), 12–90.

3. Webber, *Management*, 431–39.

4. William H. Newman and Kirby E. Warren, *The Process of Management*, 4th ed. (Englewood Cliffs, N.J.: Prentice-Hall, 1977), 20–36.

5. Jacques Barzun, quoted from telephone interview, November 1966.

6. Stanford L. Optner, *Systems Analysis for Business and Industrial Problem Solving* (Englewood Cliffs, N.J.: Prentice-Hall, 1965), 41.

7. Owen B. Hardy, "Systematic Processes Applied to Long Range Planning," *Hospital Administration* 16 (Winter 1971), 17.

8. Warren B. Brown and Dennis J. Moberg, *Organization Theory and Management* (New York: Wiley, 1980), 137.

9. Ibid., 137.

10. Ibid.

11. Brown and Moberg, *Organization and Management*, p. 148, citing J.R. Hackman, "Work Design," in *Improving Life at Work*, ed. J.R. Hackman and J.L. Suttle (Santa Monica, Calif.: Goodyear, 1977).

12. Owen B. Hardy and Lawrence P. Lammers, *Hospitals: The Planning and Design Process* (Rockville, Md.: Aspen, 1977), 79.

13. Ibid., 7.

Chapter 5

Standing plans

Elements of Management
in Corporations

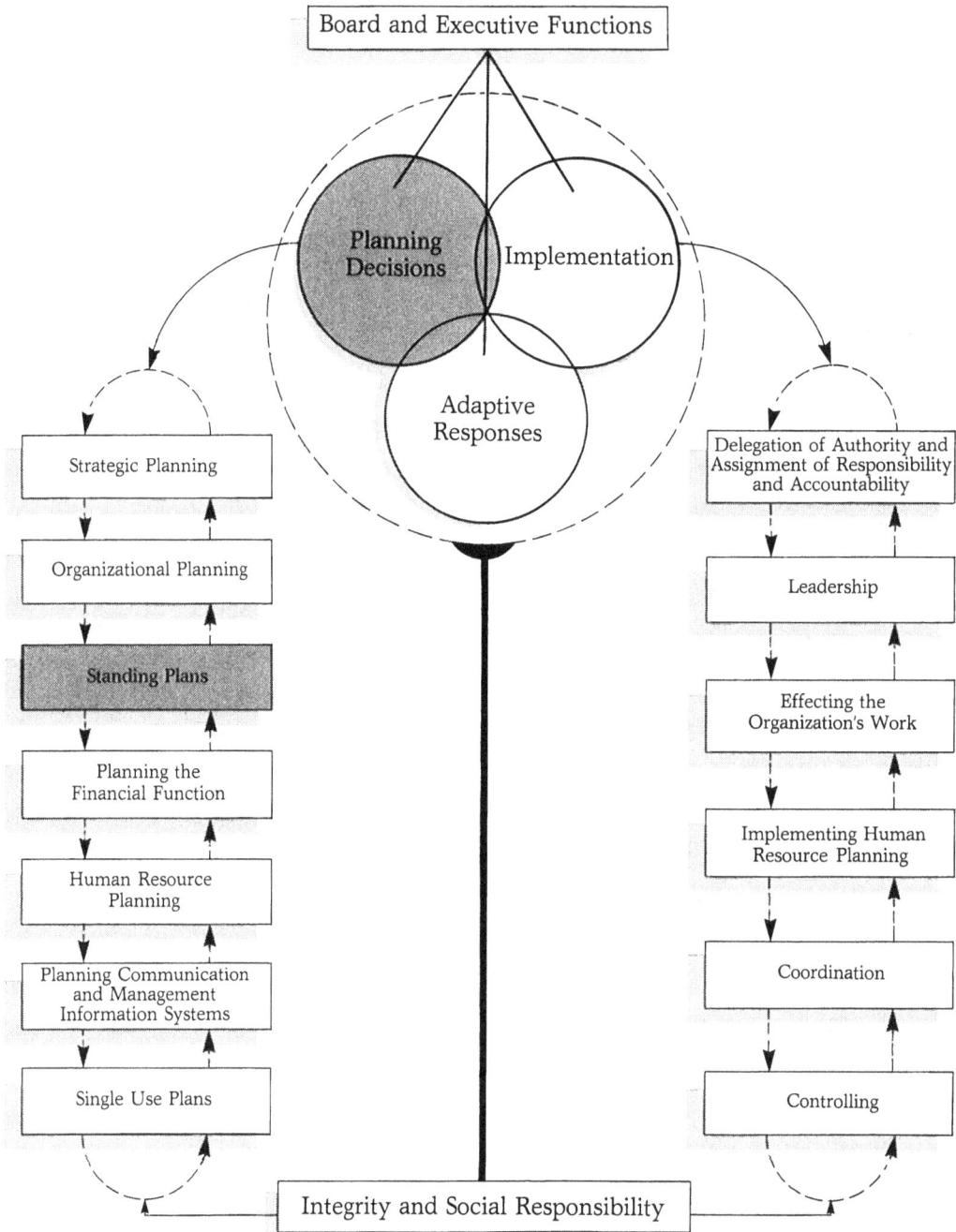

Board and Executive Functions

Planning
Decisions

Implementation

Adaptive
Responses

Strategic Planning

Organizational Planning

Standing Plans

Planning the
Financial Function

Human Resource
Planning

Planning Communication
and Management
Information Systems

Single Use Plans

Delegation of Authority and
Assignment of Responsibility
and Accountability

Leadership

Effecting the
Organization's Work

Implementing Human
Resource Planning

Coordination

Controlling

Integrity and Social Responsibility

5

Perspective

Standing plans in formal organizations have some six basic functions:
(1) to establish directional guideposts for the formulation of other plans,
including goals and objectives; (2) to organize and coordinate repetitive
actions that can be predicted to occur during implementation of plans and
adaptive responses; (3) to provide limits within which employee efforts
will be directed, whether repetitive or not; (4) to set parameters for
decision making and for delegated authority at each organizational level;
(5) to provide standards (or yardsticks) by which results achieved
through the implementation of plans can be measured; and (6) to assure
that all actions taken are orderly, legal, and ethical.

Standing plans, if followed, provide for consistency in the execution
of all phases of management and act as a centripetal force in organizing.
Through standing plans, other planning becomes partially predictable
and the character of an organization is explicitly or implicitly defined.
These plans serve as organizational stabilizers and preclude many tangential courses of action that might have been taken in the pursuit of
continuing goals and objectives. Probably more than any other conscious
act of management, devising standing plans lays the foundation of the
organizational culture.

Many standing plans are in effect decisions that limit the range of
other decisions made at lower hierarchical levels. For example, HCA has
had a policy that a division vice president annually can spend up to a fixed
dollar sum in capital funds as he or she chooses. This constitutes a limit to
both authority and decision making and specifies a point below which
authority to spend capital dollars is decentralized and above which is
centralized. As already noted in Chapter 4, on many occasions policies
establish degrees of decentralization in a variety of areas and set precon-
ditions for the design of jobs.

Standing plans are called by a variety of names in business firms and
other organizations. Some of the more common are *policies, procedures,
rules, regulations, methods, practices, creeds, laws, principles, guides* (or *guidelines*), *adopted beliefs, standards, standing orders,* and *approved approaches* or
protocols. In this chapter we will discuss only four categories of standing
plans, but these categories include the kinds of standing plans found in
the vast majority of organizations (although nomenclature and definitions vary quite widely). The four categories we shall define and discuss
are (1) policies, (2) procedures, (3) methods, and (4) rules. (See Figure 5-1.) For each of these categories, we have relied primarily on our

Figure 5-1

A Hierarchy of Standing Plans

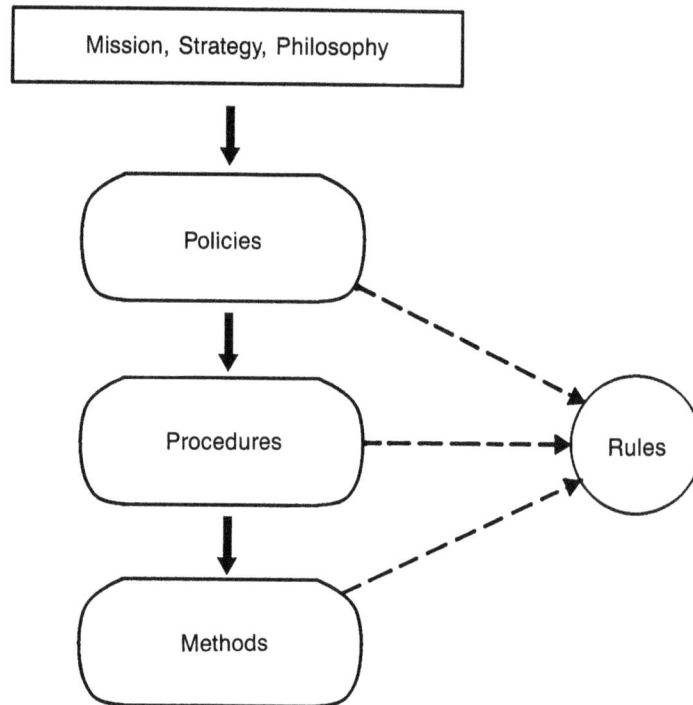

years of experience and observation for definitions, explanations of relationships, and suggested formulations. However, we have also researched the subject quite thoroughly and have set forth the opinions of others where we felt they should receive consideration.

Managers can formulate and officially announce standing plans verbally, or they can distribute them in writing to all concerned. In very small firms (say, those with less than 15 members), verbal pronouncement may be satisfactory; in larger firms, putting standing plans in writing best achieves consistency among all hierarchical levels. For example, neither HCA nor HealthTrust Inc. could exist as an organization in their present form without written standing plans that are clearly presented, widely disseminated, and mutually consistent—from top-level policies to rules formulated at the administrative department level within individual hospitals.

Interestingly, the Joint Commission on Accreditation of Hospitals (JCAH) *requires* that each department of any hospital shall have acceptable written policies and procedures in order to receive accreditation. Our readers should note that JCAH's main objective is to assure that hospital patients throughout the nation will receive the highest quality of care that is consistent with reasonable cost. JCAH regards it as a necessity for the delivery of such care that there be appropriate written standing plans for each and every hospital department. Certainly, the attitude of this prestigious and effective body puts into sharp focus the value of standing plans for any formal organization where quality of services or products is a concern. Of course, standing plans have a number of other purposes, but their use both as a guide and a standard for control in quality assurance is of great importance.

Benefits and drawbacks

Newman and Warren stated, "For any group of people to live or work together, they must be able to anticipate one another's actions. There must be some consistency or pattern of behavior. The more interdependent the activities, the more important the ability to anticipate. . . . This is true for a symphony orchestra, football team, diplomatic corps, ship's crew, bank, coffee plantation, and for any other similar situations."[1] Certainly, this observation is correct. There can be no substitute for standing plans where complex, interdependent activities take place, even if great care has been taken to formulate meaningful and precise goals and objectives extending to every department of an organization. Standing plans certainly prevent many time-consuming "reinventions of the wheel" in the pursuit of goals and objectives.

Standing plans have some negative features, however. Theoretically, managers can formulate standing plans in sufficient detail to control nearly all functions that occur repetitively in organizations engaged in either production or provision of services. One problem is that actions guided too closely become both boresome and burdensome. The stifling of initiative and innovation may reach intolerable limits if standing plans disallow all freedom of thought during an individual's working hours. Some employees will leave an organization from sheer boredom, and others may become disloyal or rebellious. Additionally, the preclusion of innovation and the stifling of initiative constitute in themselves a loss to any business.

The static nature of standing plans also presents a danger. Although most organizations must achieve some level of stability, primarily through organizational structure and standing plans, such plans must be the subject of constant study and change, otherwise operational procedures and methods will cease being state-of-the-art. Many organizations fail to update continuously and thereby lose their position at the cutting edge of technology or become incapable of maintaining an appropriate internal social culture.

Another problem of standing plans is that they cause inflexibility in the handling of unique situations, some of which inevitably occur. Sales have been lost, valuable customers offended, and procurement bargains foregone, all on an appreciable scale, simply because employees felt dutybound to adhere strictly to established policies, procedures, or other standing plans. Completely satisfactory ways to resolve dilemmas that arise in such situations have seldom been discovered.

Many behavioral scientists cite the dangers of "procedural buildup" in inhibiting motivation, and they point out the need for organizations of the future to be adaptive to rapidly changing environments. Our emphasis on the need for continuous strategic and organizational planning reflects these concerns. Certainly, the emphasis on standing plans shows the influence of so-called scientific management on organizational planning, particularly on production methods and procedures. As long ago as

The Decision Maker

"Come with us, and you'll have the widest possible latitude in decision making."

the late 1960s, Gordon Lippitt stated that the organization of the future "will need to remain flexible to cope with ever-changing consumers, services, production techniques, technical skills, changing marketing conditions, social demands, economic forces. . . . A particular theory of management suggesting that an extreme of either scientific management or human relations is the right approach will not be adequate."[2] In this regard, managers who desire to escape all crises and problems through pronouncement of standing plans to cover most areas of management or operational activities must beware. Even greater problems can be created through procedural buildup and choking; stability can easily develop into stagnation.[3]

Many years ago, Chris Argrys, a Yale University behavioral scientist, investigated the effects upon employees of rigid, detailed procedures and methods. His findings indicate that a nearly inevitable trend toward submissiveness, apathy, and frustration develops.[4] One should not ignore the strong evidence assembled by Argrys or the corroborations of numerous others that plans can be too rigid and detailed.

Although the important contributions of "scientific management" must be taken into account, there must be a balance. Managers of an organization must actively seek to achieve the correct balance for that organization by taking into account a wide range of environmental factors, both internal and external to the organization.

As a final word, recognizing the detrimental effects of detailed and rigid standing plans does not relieve managers of the duty to frame some standing plans. With regard to specific repetitive actions that one can predict to occur, there should be some standing plans, even if the primary purpose of these plans is to allow complete freedom in organizational behavior of most types.

Standing plans versus single use plans

To those who read and study both this chapter and Chapter 9, which is on single use planning, the differences between standing plans and single use plans will become rather obvious. Simply, standing plans *stand*, usually on an indefinite basis, to guide and control all organizational behavior that the plans pertain to, unless certain actions or persons have been specifically excluded. In contrast, managers devise single use plans for a specific program or project meant to be accomplished through a coordinated, usually scheduled, set of actions that will not be repeated. One often hears the term *one-time through* in connection with planning required to construct a new corporate headquarters, to enact a 50th anniversary celebration, or to merge with a competitor.

Definitions, applicability, and origins

No clear-cut distinguishing characteristics exist for the numerous kinds of standing plans designated by managers in organizations or identified by authorities in management literature. For each particular organization, then, one can say that a standing plan is what it is called. But even within a particular organization, individuals will have different ideas about the terms used unless specific definitions are given. For example, each of us viewed the word *policy* differently as we wrote this chapter. One believed that any policy was such that exceptions to it could only be made by a higher authority or not at all; the other viewed a policy merely as a general guide to decision making. Having experienced this problem of definition, we advise our readers to designate classifications of standing plans carefully and to be certain to define the classifications explicitly. Regarding our four categories (policies, procedures, methods, and rules), without definition the designation given each would surely receive a number of different interpretations, even among a small number of persons.

Because of the importance of the term *policy* and its wide use, managers should define it very carefully. Also, to indicate whether a policy should be adhered to uniformly, framers ought to signify in the case of each the level of conformance expected.

Cases will arise where an individual believes a specific standing plan has been classified erroneously, for example, where a procedure should have been called a method, or vice versa. However, any misclassification would not negate the binding force of the plan.

Types of standing plans

As noted, a standing plan is a plan that has been formulated and announced and stands indefinitely to provide direction for planning, activities of implementation, or the framing of adaptive responses by and among employees and to set certain limits desired by management. Such limits may be broad or narrow, but preciseness in defining limits allows a more accurate classification of the plan itself.

Standing plans range from giving direction to certain aspects of the behavior and activities of every member of an organization to providing instructions for work techniques or methods used by a single job classification. They can serve as mere guides to thinking or they can even specify whether one should use the left hand or right hand in performing a manual task.

Most authorities perceive that standing plans can function as guidelines for decision making, but some ignore that they also directly control behavior and set the stage for planning of all types. In fact, a standing plan, properly devised, can give guidance to any specific organizational act performed by one or more employees.

Standing plans have a variety of origins, depending on specific situations, on their content and areas of applicability, and on what they are intended to do.

Policies

Newman and Warren state, "A *policy* is a general guide to action."[5] Stoner states, "A *policy* is a general guideline for decision-making."[6] Massie states, "*Policy* is an understanding by members of a group that makes the actions of each member of the group in a given set of circumstances more predictable to other members. A policy is a guide for making decisions."[7] Brown and Moberg, in distinguishing between policies and strategies, state the following:

> *Strategy* refers to an overall plan for the organization to accomplish its goals in the context of environmental forces beyond the control of the organization . . . *Policies* are also guides for behavior and decision making in organizations . . . *strategy focuses primarily on an organization's relationship to the external environment and the competitive situation, while policy focuses primarily on organizational arrangements.*[8]

Despite Brown and Moberg's opinion, we strongly believe a prime function of policies (though not the only function) is to govern or control organizational relationships with the external environment. Although it is difficult to differentiate precisely between policy and strategy (and it is not really important to do so), we believe a strategy should be compatible with formulated policies governing contacts with the external environment. Such policies may exist at the time a strategy is adopted or executives and other managers may formulate them concurrently with the adoption of the strategy.

Our own definition of a policy, which we construe as a kind of standing plan, is as follows:

A policy is a broadly defined guide for organizational members to observe in their behavior or to follow in the performance of their management or operational responsibilities.

Where a policy must serve as an explicit guide, one can add to its written presentation wording such as "no exceptions allowed" or "exceptions allowed only upon the authority of _____" (filling the blank with the title of an officer of the company). In any event, managers had best state whether the policy is intended to effect uniform compliance. Policy makers may, of course, frame separate "rules," but these, in the case of top management pronouncements, usually deal with matters less important than policies.

A statement of policy should indicate to whom it is applicable. If a policy has been formulated and published by a company's board of directors or by top-level managers, one can assume that all departments and the respective members thereof are subject to the policy. If the policy, in being published, is addressed "to all concerned," this should be sufficient to include the entire organization. Top executives may of course formulate policies for application to a particular department (or departments), but in that event the published policy should so state.

Managers of departments and other lesser organizational units can also formulate policies, so long as they are consonant with policies issued at all higher management levels. In essence, in large organizations there invariably exists a hierarchy of policies, and no basic conflicts should exist among them (although exceptions do occur).

In most business firms, managers originate the preponderance of all policies, largely to assure that the preconceived mission and certain general and continuous goals are achieved. A board of directors, in fact, may be involved in formulating policies that are believed to be for the good, or in the best interest, of the firm as a whole. Based on strategic planning, managers at all levels may formulate other and more specific policies that pertain to their restricted areas of responsibility.

Outside agencies (government agencies, etc.) frequently exert pressure on organizations that constitutes a de facto imposition of policy. As already noted, JCAH dictates that certain policies or procedures must be in writing and formally adopted by a hospital in order for it to gain accreditation. To receive funds for Medicare patients, hospitals must follow certain regulations, and as a result they must formulate and implement relevant policies and procedures. In fact, few businesses can exist today without adopting at least some policies or procedures that aim to implement dictates of outside agencies, either governmental or otherwise.

Parenthetically, although formulation of policies in HCA at the corporate level has occurred largely because of the initiatives of managers, a majority of policies at the level of individual hospitals and related health care facilities flow from the need to satisfy either JCAH or governmental agency regulations! In this regard, the health care field may be unique.

Some policies have their genesis directly in operations or at lower hierarchical levels. Unforeseen problems arise that cannot be resolved at these levels, and managers refer the problems upward through established lines of authority for resolution. Although managers may resolve such problems by responding adaptively for a time, continued recurrences constitute grounds for formulating an applicable policy or a standard operating procedure. In some instances, managers may apply resolving responses informally but routinely over such a long period of time that "customs may gradually emerge and achieve the generality, permanence and authority of true policies."[9] This occurs frequently in small firms, but in major corporations, even though such customs may so emerge, they will usually be developed into a formal, written policy or procedure if they are regarded as beneficial. In hospitals, for example, there exists an acute awareness of the ever-present danger of malpractice suits, and experience has shown that protective formal policies set down in writing prove advantageous in tort cases, even though the policy or procedure may have been violated by an individual staff member.

When publishing policies, or any standing plan for that matter, managers should have a date clearly affixed. This informs everyone as to the effective date and allows the easy identification of those policies that need reconsideration in case they have become obsolete.

Procedures

Webber states, "Theoretically, policies are merely guidelines which higher management and staff set down to assist other managers in handling certain anticipated problems. . . . Procedures, in contrast, prescribe specific behavior for managers to follow."[10] Stoner suggests that "policies are carried out by means of more detailed guidelines called 'standard procedures' or 'standard methods.' A *procedure* provides a detailed set of instructions for performing a sequence of actions that occurs often or regularly."[11]

Newman and Warren write, "A procedure details the *sequence of steps* several individuals must take to achieve a specific purpose. When a procedure for dealing with recurring problems becomes formalized, we call it a standard operating procedure."[12]

Some authors have linked procedures to systems, and, indeed, they are an element in all management systems. One must recognize, of course, that of all the loose terms in management, the term *system* is probably near the top of the list. At any rate, over two decades ago Littlefield and Rachel stated, "A procedure is the working level of system; it is an actual guide to employees on how to proceed each time a particular recurring type of work is to be performed."[13] More recently, in contrasting procedures to policies, Massie defined a procedure as "a system that describes, in detail, the steps to be taken in order to accomplish a job. Procedures emphasize details; policies concentrate on basic general approaches."[14]

Over the years, we have come to have a very precise concept of procedures. Together with a group of highly competent department directors at a hospital we managed early in our careers, we formulated a policy and procedure manual for each department, the first time this had been done in Georgia. In each year since, we have dealt with procedures of one type or another in various enterprises related to the health care field. Our concept can be expressed thus:

Whereas policies are guides to thinking and behavioral orientation, procedures deal with sets of definitive acts that are arranged in a sequence and are usually described in terms of who, when, what, where, and how.

Procedures may constitute the working level of systems, the independent means for accomplishing work objectives, or the mechanism for effecting policies (if actions are necessary).

Some procedures form a part of a companywide system. Systems analysts regard these as subsystems or processes. Other procedures may be implemented on a stand-alone basis to effect the independent functions of a single department. Many serve to handle recurring problems related to company policy.

Although there exists considerable diversity of opinion about what a procedure really is, most of the definitions we have reviewed recognize they are composed of steps (acts) arranged in a sequence. Some authorities believe more than one person must participate in a procedure. In most instances, more than one person is involved, but we believe this is not essential. We also believe a procedure may actually be a single use plan, with directions for use in recurring situations if there be such.

Procedures can aid in effecting the work necessary to accomplish organizational goals and objectives. Most apply to localized work at the departmental level, but some cut across two or more departmental lines.

Is there a truly distinguishing feature that sets a procedure apart from a system? Johnson, Kast, and Rosensweig, noted authorities on systems, state, "A system may be defined as an array of components designed to achieve an objective according to plan. . . . A system is an organized or complex whole; an assemblage or combination of things or parts forming a complex or unitary whole."[15] Insofar as organizational systems devised to effect work necessary to accomplish goals and objectives are concerned, procedures are among the array of components to which these authors refer. However, most writers who view organizations strictly from the standpoint of systems refer to procedures as the *activities* of a subsystem (thus avoiding use of the term *procedures* in an apparent attempt to promote systems jargon).

Many procedures in companies having multiple objectives seem to be independent of identifiable companywide systems. In a company having only a single objective or a limited number which are closely similar, one can conceptualize its organization of activities from a systems viewpoint, and procedures (subsystems) fit nicely into the whole as a truly integral component. A textile manufacturing plant with only a few products is a classic example. Where objectives are multiple and diverse, however, and require a broad number of separate specialists for realization (such as in a university teaching hospital), all procedures will not fit into an identifiable system. In such instances, the organization of the entity can only be understood from a departmental standpoint, with some departments utilizing procedures that do not belong to any entitywide system.

Procedures originate basically in four ways: (1) from the mind of managers, (2) from collaborations between managers and operational personnel, (3) from operational personnel directly, and (4) from staff personnel assigned to the task, most frequently those with some knowledge of industrial engineering.

Each of these origins has advantages in certain situations, and all have received considerable elaboration in the literature. Our own experience of collaboration between managers and operational personnel has been extremely favorable. Such collaboration respects the need of those who implement to be involved in planning, the social need to "belong," and the psychological need to develop a sense of worth—all highly important personnel needs. In those instances requiring technical knowledge not available among the involved manager or managers and the operational personnel, a next best option is to add staff personnel who do have that knowledge to the planning group. The social benefits cited will be preserved if the transition is handled correctly. The least desirable approach is to dictatorially impose a procedure. However, in a few instances this may be necessary. Where it has been, we have not hesitated to do it.

In numerous instances during procedure formulation, operational personnel will suggest changes, some of which may be beneficial. Managers should evaluate each suggested change in light of all implications that may be involved. The arbitrary dismissal of ideas emanating from subordinates should occur seldom. However, change merely for the sake of change will accomplish nothing, and some suggestions fall into such a category and have to be rejected.

Problems can arise when operational personnel, without notification to management, arbitrarily change a procedure. This can be especially troublesome where the change affects another department, which then must change some of its procedures. Where the procedure actually forms a subsystem of a firmwide system, such changes can affect an entire organization and create considerable turmoil. Our experience indicates that beneficial changes should be encouraged, but after formalization a procedure should not be changed (except temporarily in unique or urgent circumstances) without full knowledge and assent of management.

Methods

For defining the term *method* we rely primarily on disciplines that take a quantitative approach to management, e.g., industrial engineering, systems analysis, operations research, etc.

We have already noted that a procedure is essentially equivalent to a subsystem or a process as viewed by those who take a quantitative approach. Recall that a process (which those with quantitative backgrounds frequently make reference to) is defined as a series of sequential operations undertaken by one or more persons, generally persons engaged in manufacturing or assembling some type of product. *The term method refers to the operator-task relationships that occur in one or more of the sequenced operations.* As a classic example, a product flows in planned sequence from one work station to another, and at each station operations are performed.

The specific manner in which the operator performs necessary work tasks with prescribed tools or equipment at a particular work station constitutes a method.

Some have used the term *method* to refer to the manner or mode of performing an entire process. It is not surprising that some confusion exists, for method design necessarily first involves the design of the process (procedure) and its separate operations. Only then can the method for performing each composing operation be determined.[16] In any event, we prefer to think of a method as applying to a single operation, and this seems to be the majority opinion among authorities.

Newman and Warren state, "The scientific managers . . . set about to control raw materials, machine maintenance, work flow, tools, training, and other factors that affect output. After such work conditions were controlled, it became reasonable to expect an individual to follow a standard method of work and to achieve a standard output."[17] Although Newman and Warren here seem to construe a method as applying to the work of an individual, elsewhere they refer to methods as if they were entire processes. Numerous industrial engineers also use the term *method* with double connotations.

Some years ago, Haiman expressed precisely our opinion regarding the meaning of the term. He stated, "Whereas a procedure showed us a series of steps to be taken, a method is only concerned with the single operation, with one particular step, and it tells exactly how this particular step is to be performed."[18]

Method, in our opinion, can also be used to refer to the work of an individual at any work station, regardless of whether the tasks being performed compose one step in a series. Thus, one can view the work tasks performed by an individual word processor as a method. Methods analysis, the analysis of procedures, and systems analysis all employ a somewhat standard set of tools for analysis and design. Among these are flow process charts, flow diagrams, operation charts (left-hand–right-hand charts), multiple activity charts, micromotion studies, and principles of motion economy.

Of course, untold millions of methods exist—in an extremely wide range of businesses—that operational personnel and their managers have developed without the involvement of anyone with a background in quantitative approaches. In organizations having detailed and complex manufacturing or service operations, however, the level of technology involved often requires the employment of persons with such a background, either on a full-time or consulting basis.

In many organizations, few positions require the employment of standard methods. In others, most positions do. In all instances where methods have been standardized and formalized, diagrammatic and narrative descriptions prove useful for the guidance of the operators involved and for the orientation and training of new employees.

Working sequentially facilitates the design (in the following order) of systems, of procedures (subsystems or processes), and of methods. In any extensive work improvement program, analysis should also be done in that order. One cannot build from methods to systems anymore than one can build a logical departmentation scheme from the design of individual jobs or anymore than an architect can first design the individual rooms of a hospital and then the hospital as a whole.

Who should be responsible for initiating standard methods? Again, managers may take the initiative, the operators involved may do so, or it may be done as a joint endeavor among managers and operational personnel during the course of designing an entire procedure. In complicated processes, however, those with appropriate quantitative skills should help to devise them, and indeed, they should have the leading role.

Rules

A rule is a positive directive that a specific action must or must not be taken under certain circumstances.

A rule leaves no latitude for an alternative action not specified in the rule itself. The only thing debatable about the application of a rule is whether it is relevant in the given circumstances.

Managers can formulate rules about any aspect of a firm's operation. Rules, if they are extensive, should be categorized. Probably the most familiar category of rules consists of safety rules. Another important category concerns personnel employment and on-the-job conduct. Familiar headings in formal statements of personnel policies, rules, and regulations include:

- hours of work

- behavior and dress codes

- absences from work

- promotional policy

- vacation and sick leave policy

- leaves of absence

- grievance procedures

- employee benefits

Some rules can apply either on a firmwide or a departmental basis. For example, most manufacturing operations have "shop" rules.

Unions demand that there be a set of rules to assure enforcement of contracts with employers. Both management and unions have found that to apply rules to a given category of personnel facilitates the management of the members of any union. In some instances, however, the achievement of management efficiency through the use of rules sacrifices individualism on the job, which is felt as a need by some. Since unions usually deal directly with top management in contract negotiations, rule making originates at the top management echelon. Thus, authority is centralized. These circumstances create a working climate for lower echelon managers and operational personnel nearly the opposite of the environment advocated by a large number of behavioral scientists. Unfortunately, no easy or uniform solution to the problem has been presented, but the mere recognition of the problem may allow both unions and management to plan better in the future.

In the hospital field, JCAH dictates, "The medical staff shall develop and adopt by-laws, rules and regulations to establish a framework of self-government and a means of accountability to the governing body."[19] This standard means exactly what it says, and the hospital not adhering to it will not receive accreditation. It seems probable that medical care at hospitals not adhering to this standard would deteriorate. Some physicians chafe under some of the rules actually formulated, but most recognize the necessity of rules. Someone who decries restraints and other rules imposed arbitrarily upon a specific class may appreciate them when coming into a hospital with his or her own life at stake.

In viewing rules as they are found throughout the business world, it might seem that more exist than are needed. Some rules are picayune; some reflect considerable disregard for those whose behavior is affected. Many persons chafe and fret under rules that obstruct, to some extent, their rational planning and decision-making capabilities. In most such cases, an immediate program of rule revision, or even elimination, should be undertaken. Yet, it is also clear that some rules are necessary for the orderly conduct of business.

Policies and rules have the same relationship to a business firm that laws have to our entire social order. They *must* exist in order to avoid anarchy, especially in large organizations.

Because they are explicit, rules are directly applicable and especially useful in the implementation of the control process. Whereas there can be some debate as to whether a policy was correctly followed in a given situation, there can be little debate as to whether a rule was followed.

In the formulation of standing plans, managers often find themselves in a quandary about whether to guide behavior through a policy or dictate it through a rule. Although no pat principle for deciding holds invariably, there are several questions the originating manager should consider:

1. Is absolute consistency required in the actions or behavior to be affected? If so, a rule is indicated.

2. How damaging will exceptions to or deviations from a policy be to the organization? If the answer is that irreparable damage is possible, a rule should be instituted.

3. Will a contemplated rule be regarded as offensive or picayune? If so, a policy is indicated, especially if the rule would be so viewed by an appreciable number of persons or even by a few if those hold key organizational positions.

4. On balance, will a policy be as effective as a rule? If so, a policy is indicated.

5. Will uniform adherence to the contemplated policy or rule become more important over time? If the importance will probably increase, especially rapidly, a rule may be preferable.

6. Are there possible deviations from the contemplated policy or rule that could result in valuable advantages to the organization? Such a possibility favors creating a policy rather than a rule.

Of course, other considerations may be both relevant and important, but those cited point up the fact that managers should exercise caution in the formulation of rules (which by definition allow no options).

Publication of standing plans

We have already noted the advantages, in all but very small firms, of publishing standing plans in writing and distributing them to those who will be affected. In realizing this, managers then face the question of how best to do it. Here again choices vary, and the most desirable means for a specific firm depends on pertinent considerations such as firm size, type of business, need, and status of plans already published.

Memoranda, letters, policy manuals, procedure manuals, combined policy and procedure manuals, bulletins, and manuals for standard methods are the most common means of publishing standing plans. Top management echelons seldom, if ever, issue manuals for standard methods, and generally, procedure manuals issued from a department pertain only to departmental matters, but not always. Typically, top managers publish policy manuals, policy and procedure manuals, and separate policy statements. The latter most often take the form of memoranda, letters, or bulletins.

Some companies have announced policy through a news release where the policy was of interest to many members of the public, but internal policy statements should always be addressed to those involved.

Managers seldom publish rules solely under that title, although policy manuals or policy and procedure manuals frequently contain "rules and regulations" that are pertinent both companywide and for a given department. Managers issue rules separately at all organizational levels in bulletins and memoranda (they are generally called not rules but regulations). In many instances, a directive will announce a rule that allows no option but that is not designated as a policy, procedure, method, or rule. Supervisors at the lowest hierarchical units publish rules entitled as such more often than do units at higher levels. However, top managers frequently publish policies that result from adaptively responding to recurring problems; these are in effect rules.

In many hospitals, executives publish general policies in a manual, often with the title Policy Manual. Nearly invariably, hospitals publish a personnel policy manual separately. Each department must publish a policy and procedure manual or handbook; this is one of the requirements of the JCAH. Admissions officers distribute patient handbooks, as deemed necessary, to both inpatients and outpatients. The handbooks explain applicable policies and procedures and also contain assuring statements about the hospital and about hospitalization in general.

To effect companywide coordination and the smooth operation of interdepartmental systems, a single department should have on file not only its own policy and procedure manual but those of other interfacing departments. These serve as a reference when changes within the depart-

ment are contemplated and help to assure that such changes will inter-
mesh acceptably with policies and procedures of other departments.
Also, where two departments operate an interdepartmental system, it is
desirable that everyone involved should understand the entire system.

The need seldom arises in any type of business to publish policies,
procedures, methods, or rules in *permanently* bound manuals at any
hierarchical level other than the top. Loose-leaf binders should be used,
for they allow easy additions and revisions to be made as required.

One noted hospital chief executive used the following method for
effecting revisions or additions to departmental policies and procedures:
When a change or addition was formulated, it was forwarded to the
department in three copies—one for immediate inclusion into the department policy and procedure manual, another for display on the department bulletin board for two weeks, and the third for return with the
signature of the department head acknowledging receipt. This executive
used this same procedure to disseminate all types of information, keeping a separate loose-leaf binder to retain file copies for a three-month
period.

Revisions to standing plans

Because published standing plans usually have no expiration date, they
often are regarded as permanent, not only by those most directly
affected, but also by those who formulated them. In addition, pride of
authorship sometimes militates against changes, even when failure or
faults have been demonstrated. Managers at lower management echelons may become aware of the inadequacies of standing plans but refrain
from critically questioning them because of the red tape involved in
making changes or the fear of reprimand. In some cases, when a standing
plan has served a useful purpose for a long time, managers may show a
reluctance to change them, even though changes are plainly indicated.
One or more of these factors sometimes allow unsound or out-of-date
standing plans to remain in force far past their usefulness. This being so,
what is the remedy?

In small and medium firms, an ongoing review of standing plans
may not be possible. Even in these firms, however, an appropriate
manager should explicitly assign to a knowledgeable person the responsibility to see that standing plans are reviewed periodically. In larger
firms (say, those with more than 500 members), standing plans should
receive continual review at both the corporate and departmental levels. In
enterprises with employees numbering in the hundreds of thousands,
few if any reasons exist for there not being a companywide program for
the continuous review and reformulation of standing plans.

Reviewing and revising can be done in many ways, and we will not
attempt to outline the "best" protocol. However, an example from our
own experience may be worthwhile. Several years ago we formed a
hospital committee for the specific purpose of studying policies, procedures, methods, and rules. The best result was the simplification and
formalization of procedures and methods, but both policies and rules
were kept updated and streamlined as needed. The composition of the
committee (about 20 members) included heads of all major hospital

departments. Several subcommittees were formed for specific tasks, such as determining the latest state-of-the-art technology, etc., resolving interdepartmental systems conflict, improving intradepartmental methods, and formalizing procedures. As a result of this work—over approximately a five-year period—the cost per patient day at the institution was reduced to around 15 percent below that of comparable hospitals in Georgia. At the same time, care had improved, morale was higher, and personnel salaries had increased. The experience was extremely gratifying, and we gained insights into management that have not been forgotten. In particular, we learned that studies for improvements in standing plans do result in keeping them up-to-date and completely relevant. A number of other benefits also accrue, not the least of which is that some of the social needs of key personnel are better met.

Summary

Standing plans assist in formulating other plans; guide repetitive actions; define limits of subsequent actions, decision making, and delegations of authority; serve as standards in the control process; and assure acceptable societal behavior among employees. They are necessary in all large organizations to assure both consistency and stability in ongoing operations.

Standing plans fall into many categories. The four discussed in this chapter are (1) policies, (2) procedures, (3) methods, and (4) rules. Standing plans can be issued verbally or in writing, but in most organizations their written publication is necessary.

Although large organizations with interdependent activities could not function without standing plans, such plans can certainly become too restrictive and rigid, leading to undesirable employee behavior. Finding the right "balance" in the use of standing plans is a major task for managers. The solution, however, is not to dispense with standing plans altogether; rather it is to allow some range of freedom of action within the plans as they are developed.

Managers must define the classifications of standing plans used in an organization individually so that no reasonable person could misunderstand the meaning and implications. If this is not done, considerable confusion will occur.

We have defined a policy as "a broadly defined guide for organizational members to observe in their behavior or to follow in the performance of their management or operational responsibilities." Even so, some policies are intended to be strictly observed, and these might be called policy rules or have wording added upon publication, such as "no exceptions allowed" or "exceptions allowed only upon the authority of _____" (filling the blank with the title of a top ranking officer).

Managers at all hierarchical levels can theoretically issue applicable policies, but they usually originate at upper levels. Policies should maintain consistency at all levels and should be dated and state to whom they are applicable.

Whereas a policy is a guide to thinking and behavioral orientation, a procedure deals with definitive acts that relate one to the other within a sequence. Procedures are described in terms of who, when, what, where, and how. They are often equivalent to a subsystem or a process, and managers usually define and describe them in order to accomplish certain actions pertaining to work of one type or another. Once formalized, procedures should change only through a formal process. To abandon procedures on an ad hoc basis usually results in confusion because of their interdependence with other operations.

The term *method* has its origins in so-called scientific management. We have defined a method as consisting of "operator-task relationships that occur in one or more of the sequenced operations of a procedure." Some authorities call a procedure a process and then use the term *method* to refer to one sequence in the process or to the process itself, thus introducing unneeded confusion.

The question arises as to whether the term *method* should be applied to operator-task relationships that occur in operations not in a sequence. It seems appropriate that it should, and in practice we have found it useful to apply the term thus.

Systems, procedures, and methods have been and continue to be studied, designed, and redesigned within several closely related disciplines, all characterized by quantitative approaches to analysis and design. In some complex operations, bringing in experts from these disciplines is optimal, but in less complicated situations, intelligent operators and managers working together can easily achieve efficient solutions to design problems as well as operational problems that arise later.

A rule is a positive directive that a specific action must or must not be taken under certain circumstances. A rule leaves no latitude for alternatives not specified in the rule itself.

Any hierarchical level can formulate rules about various aspects of a firm's operations. Typically, they pertain to safety, personnel employment, and on-the-job conduct. Top management and unions also formulate rules to govern their association and the behavior of union members at work.

Memoranda, letters, policy manuals, procedure manuals, policy and procedure manuals, bulletins, and manuals for standard methods are the most common means for publishing standing plans. Typically, top managers publish policy manuals, policy and procedure manuals, and policy statements. Departmental or divisional levels also publish applicable policy and procedure manuals, with methods and rules most frequently appearing at the supervisory level. Some rules emanate from all management levels, however.

Standing plans should be kept in loose-leaf binders, and each major organizational unit (department, division, etc.) should keep on file for ready reference not only its own standing plans but those of other interfacing units.

One frequently arising problem is the failure to keep standing plans updated. Although small firms may not be able to engage in continuous updating, they can carry out periodic reviews and update as indicated. Larger firms, such as HCA and HealthTrust Inc., should have a continuous review program.

Notes

1. William H. Newman and Kirby E. Warren, *The Process of Management*, 4th ed. (1977), 386. Reprinted by permission of Prentice-Hall, Inc., Englewood Cliffs, N.J.

2. Gordon L. Lippitt, *Organizational Renewal* (New York: Appleton-Century-Crofts, 1969), 23.

3. Ibid., 34.

4. Chris Argrys, *Personality and Organization* (New York: Harper & Bros., 1957).

5. Newman and Warren, *The Process of Management*, 387. Reprinted by permission of Prentice-Hall, Inc., Englewood Cliffs, N.J.

6. James A.F. Stoner, *Management*, 2d ed. (1971), 59. Reprinted by permission of Prentice-Hall, Inc., Englewood Cliffs, N.J.

7. Joseph L. Massie, *Essentials of Management* (1971), 59. Reprinted by permission of Prentice-Hall, Inc., Englewood Cliffs, N.J.

8. Warren B. Brown and Dennis J. Moberg, *Organization Theory and Management* (New York: Wiley, 1980), 274-75.

9. Billy E. Goetz, *Management Planning and Control* (New York: McGraw-Hill, 1949), 65.

10. Ross A. Webber, *Management* (Homewood, Ill.: Richard D. Irwin, Inc., 1975), 324-25.

11. Stoner, *Management*, 135. Reprinted by permission of Prentice-Hall, Inc., Englewood Cliffs, N.J.

12. Newman and Warren, *The Process of Management*, 390. Reprinted by permission of Prentice-Hall, Inc., Englewood Cliffs, N.J.

13. C.L. Littlefield and Frank Rachel, *Office and Administrative Management*, 2d ed. (Englewood Cliffs, N.J.: Prentice-Hall, 1964), 120.

14. Massie, *Essentials of Management*, 59. Reprinted by permission of Prentice-Hall, Inc., Englewood Cliffs, N.J.

15. Richard A. Johnson, F.E. Kast, and J.E. Rosensweig, *The Theory and Management of Systems* (New York: McGraw-Hill, 1973), 4.

16. Ralph M. Barnes, *Motion and Time Study-Design and Measurement of Work*, 7th ed. (New York: Wiley, 1980), 37–38.

17. Newman and Warren, *The Process of Management*, 389. Reprinted by permission of Prentice-Hall, Inc., Englewood Cliffs, N.J.

18. Theo Haiman, *Professional Management* (Boston, Mass.: Houghton Mifflin, 1962), 90.

19. Joint Commission on Accreditation of Hospitals, *Accreditation Manual for Hospitals* (Chicago, Ill.: JCAH, 1978), 83.

Chapter 6

Planning the financial function

Elements of Management
in Corporations

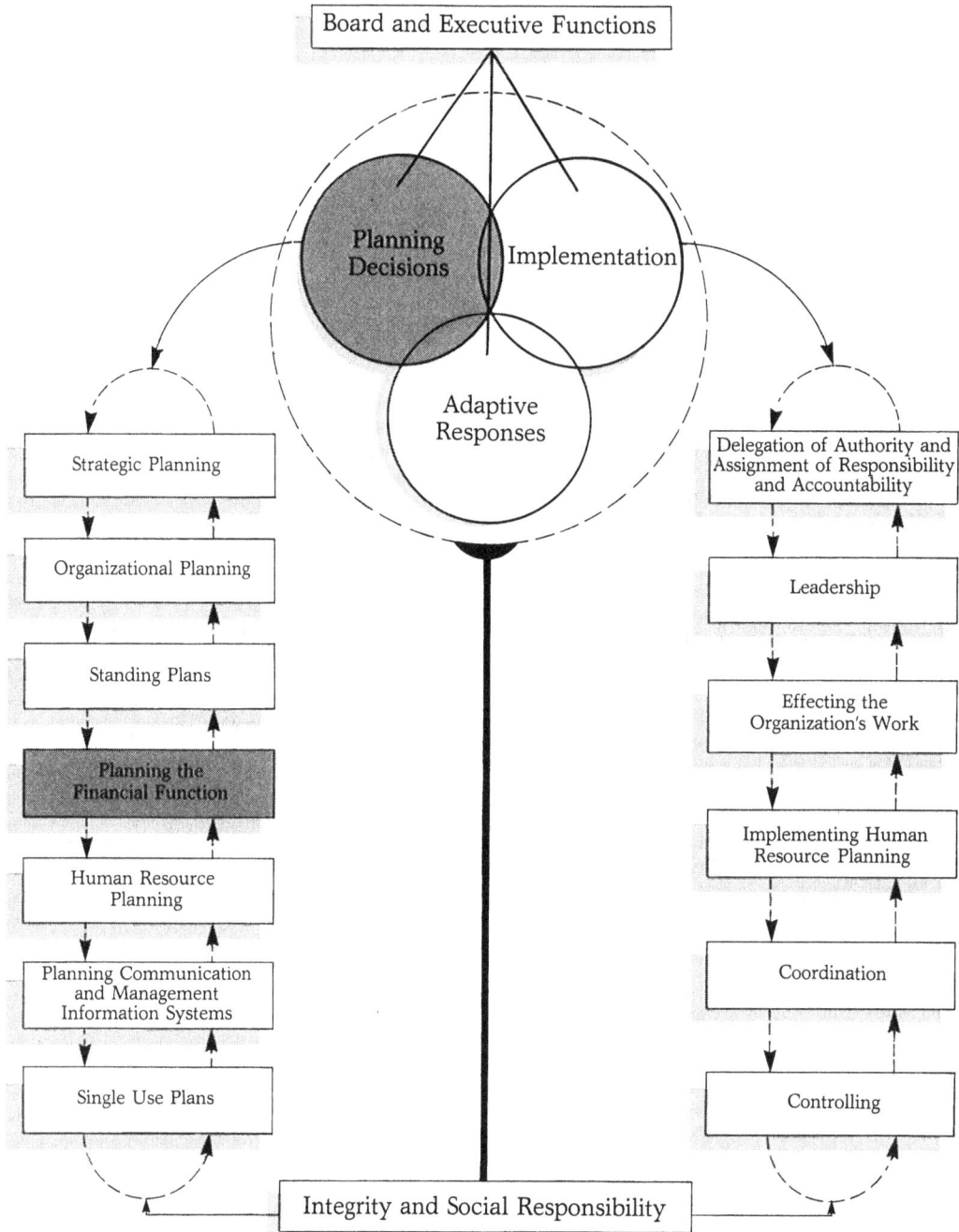

6

Scope and definitions

Because financial gain is one of the top objectives of business firms, the financial function is of primary concern to managers. Usually, the careers of executives hinge on the volume and quality of profits or profitability. Even in not-for-profit organizations, viability and vitality depend on the ability to manage assets effectively and keep revenues acceptably in excess of expenses.

The financial function includes all aspects of financial management and accounting. "The financial function supplies and maintains (manages) the capital or financial resources and provides a system of financial measurement and control (accounting) for the management of the enterprise."[1] Although the range of financial function components is broad and diverse, we will restrict our comments here to five components generally found in major corporations. These are (1) financial planning, in the broadest sense of the term; (2) accounting, both financial and managerial; (3) auditing; (4) tax planning; and (5) risk management. Certainly none of these functions can be said to be more important than the others, but financial planning and accounting consume larger portions of management time in major corporations than do tax planning, auditing, and planning for risk management. (Pension planning has not been discussed due to space limitations in this book.)

Some years ago, Ezra Solomon, the Dean Witter Professor of Finance at Stanford University's Graduate School of Business, stated, "The basic purpose of financial planning is to make sure that capital funds are used wisely."[2] He then noted that the concerns of financial planning are intimately involved in trying to provide systematic answers to three questions. Paraphrased and condensed, the questions are these:

1. What assets should an enterprise acquire and in what form should it hold them?

2. How large should an enterprise become and how much should it commit to expansion annually?

3. How should annually required funds be financed and what should compose the company's liabilities?[3]

Accounting represents the second component of a business organization's financial function. What is accounting? We note that some textbooks on the subject actually fail to define it. Among those definitions we reviewed, that set forth by the Accounting Principles Board (APB) of the American Institute of Certified Public Accountants in 1970 appears to us to be the best. "Accounting is a service activity. Its function is to provide quantitative information, primarily financial in nature, about economic entities that is intended to be useful in making economic decisions—in making reasoned choices among alternative courses of action."[4]

Regarding the APB's definition, Woelfel has observed,

The APB definition of accounting is *goal oriented* rather than process oriented. It emphasizes economic *decision making activities* rather than the recording, classifying, summarizing and interpreting processes of accounting. This interpretation emphasizes the true role of accounting in its modern setting.[5]

We should also emphasize the service aspect of accounting that the APB definition points out. Both of us can be classified as nonfinancial executives, but we are fairly seasoned interpreters of financial information for two reasons: (1) the necessities that have confronted us through the years, and (2) the fact that we have worked with financial executives who made the attempt to provide analyses that were understandable to us. We also know of firms where such attempts seem not to have been made, for one reason or another. Although in both HCA and HealthTrust Inc., many executives have very sound financial backgrounds, many do not, and some of these must make key decisions related to the financial function. Were it not that accountants in each firm clearly regard their activities as a service function, the ability of some executives to make financial decisions would be seriously impaired.

Of course, accounting clearly focuses on control. Granof has stated,

Accountants provide the information required to make decisions as to where to allocate financial resources, and once such decisions are made they provide the data necessary to effectively control such resources. Periodically, as the management process is being carried out, accountants "report the score"—they provide the information by which the results of prior decisions can be evaluated.[6]

Modern accounting is composed of two rather distinct branches: (1) financial accounting and (2) managerial accounting. We will discuss planning for both in this chapter.

William Cleverly has defined financial accounting as "the branch of accounting which provides general purpose financial statements or reports to aid a large number of decision-making groups, internal and external to the organization in a variety of decisions."[7] He further notes, in commenting on accounting in the health care industry, the primary outputs of financial accounting consist of four financial statements:

- Balance Sheet

- Statement of Revenues and Expenses

- Statement of Changes in Financial Position

- Statement of Changes in Fund Balance[8]

Because our comments here directly address the financial function in private business corporations (with stockholders), we only discuss the first three statements named by Cleverly, each of which possesses great significance for profit-making enterprises. The fourth statement we discuss is a statement of shareholders' equity, which has considerable interest for current and prospective investors.

Kaplan, in an excellent text on advanced management accounting, defines the second and newest accounting branch in this way:

> Management accounting is a system that collects, classifies, summarizes, analyzes, and reports information that will assist managers in their decision-making and control activities. Unlike financial accounting, where the primary emphasis is on reporting to people outside the firm, management accounting focuses on internal planning and control activities. Therefore, management accounting requires the collection and analysis not only of financial or cost data, but also data such as prices, sales backlog, product demands on capacity resources, and measures of physical quantities and capacities.[9]

Major corporations approach auditing activities related to their financial statements and their accounting policies, procedures, and controls in two ways. These are (1) having an independent audit prepared, usually on an annual basis, and (2) internal auditing by specifically assigned staff personnel, usually on a continuous basis. The independent auditor, invariably certified in this nation by the American Institute of Certified Public Accountants, follows a process in examining a firm's financial statements that "assures himself (herself) of the fairness of the financial statements, their conformity with generally accepted accounting principles and the consistency with which the accounting principles have been applied from year to year."[10] Internal auditing involves monitoring functions to assure that all ongoing financial and accounting activities follow not only generally accepted accounting principles but also all standing plans that apply to accounting and various other components of the financial function within the individual company.

Tax planning involves interpretation of pertinent tax laws as they apply to both a firm's unusual and routine economic transactions so that tax liabilities will be legally minimized or possibly deferred. Tax planning must closely interface with most other components of the financial function, especially financial planning and accounting. The Tax Reform Act of 1986 will greatly enhance the importance of tax planning in the years immediately ahead.

Risk management involves the protection of an enterprise's assets and profitability against loss caused by "fortuitous, accidental, unexpected circumstances."[11] Risk analysis, which uncovers exposure to losses, is the initial function of risk management. It is followed by the devising of ways to reduce risk, including a sound program of insurance management.

Although in a single chapter we cannot present the numerous facts pertaining to all aspects of planning the financial function in modern organizations, possibly we can point to key facets and stimulate the reader's interest enough that other sources of information will be consulted. See Figure 6-1 for a graphic outline of the components of the financial function discussed in this chapter.

Organizing for the financial function

At the present time, most major corporations place both the financial planning function and the accounting function under a single corporate officer. This promotes coordination and does not compromise control, since financial planning and accounting can remain in separate divisions of the same department. The head of the financial function is most often called vice president for finance or director of finance, and in large firms he or she should be a certified public accountant and should have experience in asset formation, management, and control.

The direct work of the financial function is done primarily by members of the line organization. Although basic work efforts involved in particular financial functions are largely accomplished by staff personnel, line managers either personally accomplish or personally authorize the accomplishment of such functions as asset acquisition, paying bills, buying insurance, compensating employees, etc. Of course, both financial accounting and managerial accounting depend on staff persons for accomplishment and can be called indirect functions owing to the fact the "product of the work is reports and measurements which are the basis for action by general [line] management or other functions."[12]

Organizing considerations

The primary organizing considerations in structuring the financial function are (1) the organizational structure of the business firm, (2) the financial functions to be accomplished, (3) basic accounting safeguards and control, (4) data processing capabilities, and (5) internal lines of communication. Of course, availability of competent personnel will also always affect organizing to some extent; the five considerations noted assume such availability.

Structuring work into components should be done where possible in order to enhance productivity, and each component should have "discrete sets of work objectives for a year or other appropriate period"[13] to allow standards for control of productivity.

We will briefly discuss each of the five considerations noted above.

Organizational structure
Job descriptions of managers should clearly indicate those parts of the financial function for which individual managers will have responsibility and accountability. For every staff position charged with any part of the financial function, the job description should indicate who is the immediate superior and what horizontal lines of communication are to be observed (vertical lines are assumed). Insofar as possible, the physical location of financial and accounting staff should be the same as the line managers to whom they report. For example, a vice president for finance

Figure 6-1

Planning the
Financial Function

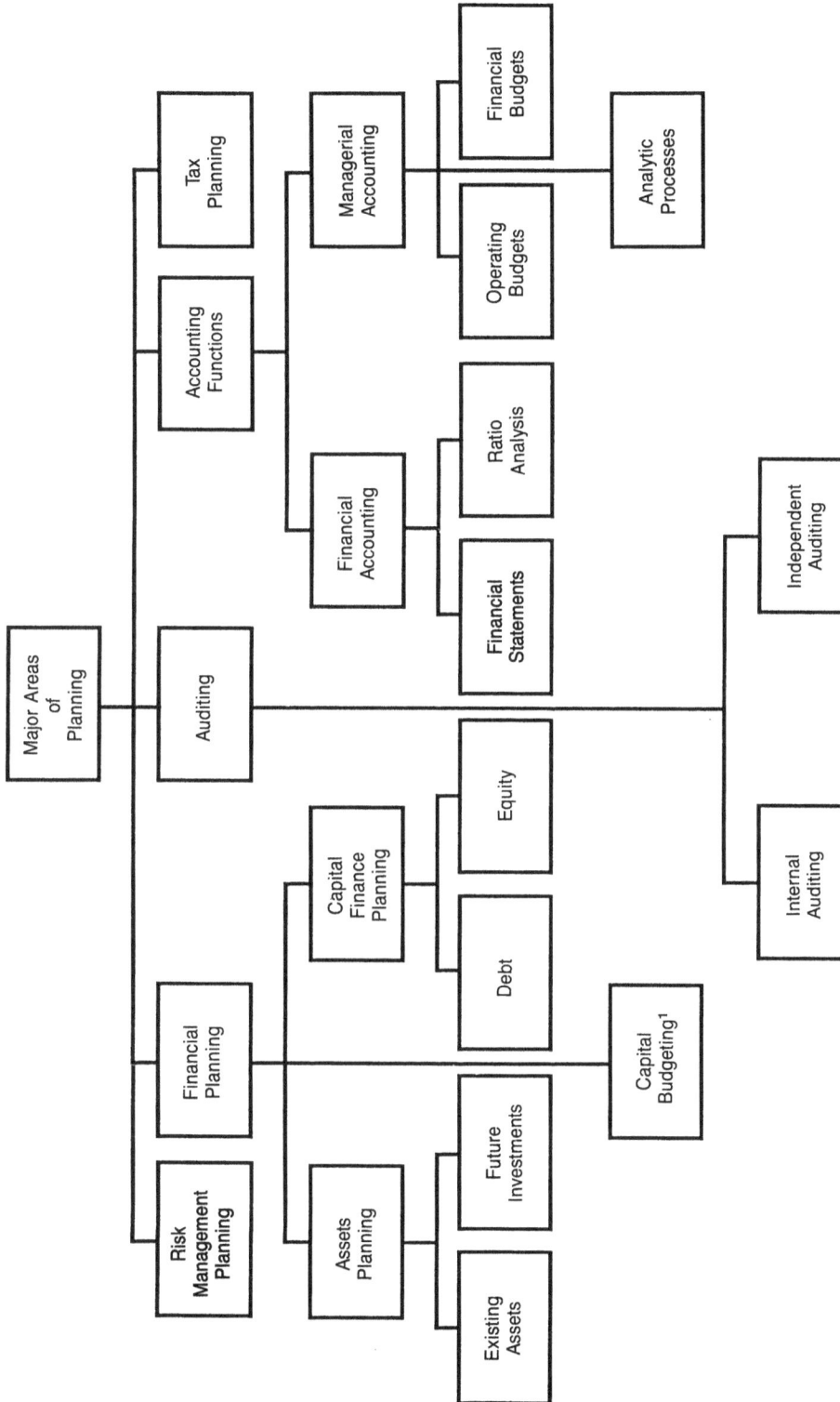

1. Many authorities subsume capital budgeting under Managerial Accounting.

ought to be located at the same site as the president, except under unusual circumstances. This is due to the demands of financial planning as well as accounting.

Decentralized firms may or may not centralize their accounting functions. (General Motors does; General Electric does not.) Most centralize at least part of their financial planning functions, owing to the need to keep a rein on allocations to capital projects. In any event, there should be an organizational chart developed for the department of finance and accounting showing the lines of authority throughout the organization. This chart should be fully understood by all key personnel of the organization. See Figure 6-2 for HCA's organizational chart for its department of finance and accounting.

Financial functions to be planned

The organization of a department of finance and accounting will largely depend on the functions to be performed and the manner of performance. Such considerations are important when a firm is first organized and they continue to be important throughout its life.

At the outset, responsibility for financial planning and the development and installation of an accounting system ought to be assigned to a single person. That person may then delegate authority and assign responsibility and accountability to two separate persons for these two broad functions. Chamberlin has noted, "Failure to establish specific financial positions or components until there is a decision to take action usually results in delay until the financial planning and analysis can catch up with the business decision."[14]

The person assigned financial planning must begin the study of needed assets, together with their financing and acquisition, and develop a system for evaluating asset performance.

The person responsible for accounting must evaluate the nature of the business, identify the types of transactions to occur, and determine an accounting system and its attendant recording devices, along with both recording and reporting forms. This person must develop procedures for record keeping, the preparation of financial statements, and auditing (internal auditing as well as by public accountants). He or she must also develop a system for operating and financial budget preparation (we will discuss capital budgeting under financial planning), tax accounting, and managerial accounting. Controllership must be determined, together with a system for special investigations.

Accounting safeguards and controls

Basic accounting safeguards and controls are very well known and need little discussion. Yet, violations of them continue. The most common in the hospital field probably is the failure to separate purchasing, receiving, and inventory functions. The essence of "checks and balances" is to divide work among "components or positions so that one person does not have complete, exclusive control of a [financial] transaction."[15] Internal and external auditing, to be discussed separately, also are effective protective methods.

Possibly the most basic accounting safeguard in most organizations is to separate custodial functions from recording and reporting functions. A classic example is using separate persons to balance books, reconcile

Figure 6-2

HCA's Department of Finance and Accounting (1986)

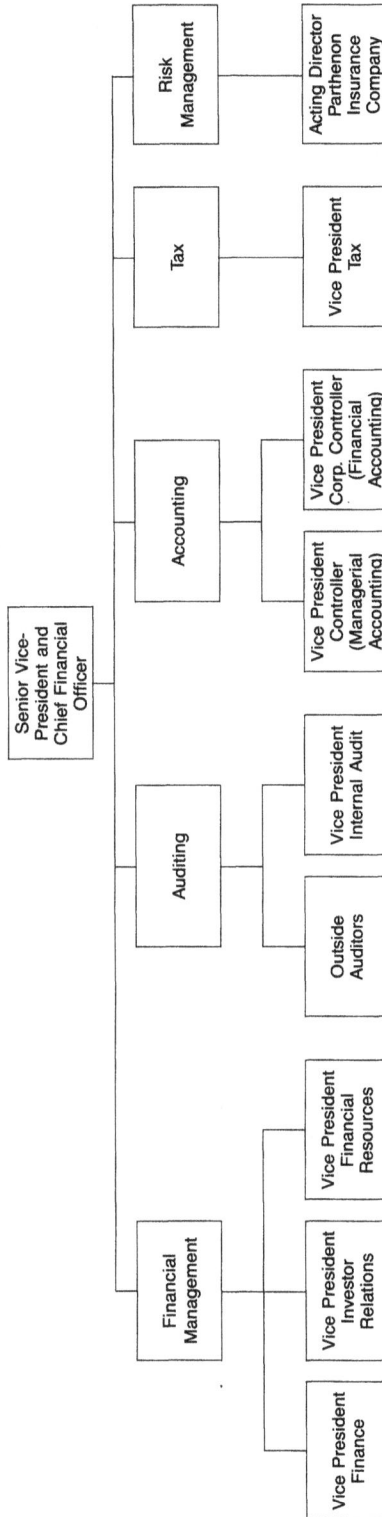

Source: Reprinted with permission of Hospital Corporation of America.

bank accounts, and make payments and deposits. Certainly no single individual should have control of a firm's cash; counting must be independent of recording cash movements. All such considerations, of course, must be respected when devising job descriptions and planning lines of responsibility and accountability.

Data processing capabilities
Over the last two decades nothing has affected the financial function in organizations—especially the accounting function—more than the rapid development of electronic data processing, both hardware and software.

Most organizations desire an integrated management information system. But whether an organization has one or not, it is still necessary that the chief financial officer (CFO) have control over that part of data processing that pertains to things financial. The CFO is directly responsible for capturing records of revenues, costs, payroll, and all disbursements of whatever kind. The CFO also has the responsibility and accountability for maintaining the integrity of all accounting controls and safeguards at the same time. This means that access to certain financial data and information must be restricted to specific individuals on a selective basis.

Not only have evolving data processing capabilities affected the ways in which firms now organize their financial function, but the unique requirements of accounting controls have directly affected planning of management information systems for all firms that possess a financial function. In the give and take that occurs in devising an organizational plan where electronic data processing is involved, this consideration must remain inviolate: *Accounting safeguards and controls must be maintained.*

Internal lines of communication
Managers generally have no difficulties in tracing *vertical* lines of communication (their actual use is sometimes another matter), but failure to communicate *across* lines of authority has usually been blatant. With respect to the financial function, requirements for communication at certain stages of the process should be made a part of established policies and procedures. Job descriptions of financial executives and their subordinates should contain specific references to the nature and frequency of communications that should occur with occupants of other positions, not only in the department of finance and accounting but also in the line organization. See Chapter 8 for a methodology for devising an appropriate communication system throughout any organization having echelons.

One classic example where intradepartmental communication is needed is between budget formulators and the tax planning staff. Communication between financial staff and line staff is needed in the case of all acquisitions of fixed assets requiring financing.

Financial planning

Knowledge required

Appropriate financial planning, like management itself, does not depend on being versed in a single discipline. The essentials of financial planning, as Solomon pointed out several years ago, are directly related to certain strategic components, e.g., setting financial objectives, planning ongoing financial activities in operations, capital budgeting, and planning for an optimal financing structure at various points in the life of the business firm.[16] However, the superior financial executive, we believe, ought to have some in-depth knowledge of economics, data processing, demography, statistics, strategic planning, financial and managerial accounting, societal megatrends, marketing, and actual operations management, if possible. All of these disciplines, in one way or another, bear upon financial management in major corporations and specifically upon good financial planning. If a financial executive deems himself or herself deficient in any of these areas, access to expert sources of relevant information should be developed and maintained.

Role in promotion

Some promoters consider financial planning to be the third phase of promotion of a corporation, the first being discovery of the opportunity for promotion and the second being investigation and analysis. In reality, financial planning begins in the investigation and analysis phase, owing to the fact that financial information must be generated concerning capital funding, operational costs, sales, working capital, cash flow, volumes of accounts receivable, and a host of other considerations. In the financial planning phase proper, promoters take the financial information they have and work with investment bankers or other sources of money, together with financial consultants, such as those found in the Big Eight accounting firms, in order to develop the company's financial structure. Most financial managers construe the term *financial structure* to include the sums of long-term equity and debt securities. A capital plan outlines all types of long-term capital as well as plans for procuring each type. The term *financial plan* is usually construed to mean all short-term and funded liabilities, together with capital stock, surplus, and reserves.

The totality of financial planning carried out in the promotional stage of a corporation having stock sales and a registered debt above certain limits will be reviewed by the Securities and Exchange Commission (SEC) and by all those who have any responsibility for the prospectus, such as underwriters, proposed future directors, and others. Promotion ends when incorporation is complete and directors select officers, who then take over control of the business and start operations.

Initiation by management

The newly elected CEO and the other officers should immediately review the financial plan of the promoters and consider its applicability to both the short-term and long-term future—in other words, start the financial planning of the new company. Certainly, the promoter's work should be given due regard (in many instances, the promoter may be elected either chairman of the board or CEO, or both, of the new company), but financial planning is an *ongoing* activity that requires constant attention from the first day of operations.

If management considers that no changes are desirable in the promotional plan, usually the results of operations will dictate the next moves.

Tasks of financial planning

From the broadest perspective, financial planning involves the following two major categories of activities:

1. *Assets planning.* This planning involves the use of assets or economic resources. Assets planning has two distinct but intimately related categories: (a) planning existing assets usage, and (b) planning future investments, including capital budgeting. Simply, assets planning is done to determine into what funds or assets a company had best allocate its resources, however currently held or currently obtained.

2. *Capital finance planning.* In essence, this planning seeks to determine from what sources a firm should obtain capital to invest in assets or funds for the purpose of promoting profits, profitability, or other financial objectives.

Assets planning

The basic question to be answered in assets planning in a private enterprise is this: Assuming continued liquidity, what asset or combination of assets, either existing or proposed, will provide the greatest net present worth to the enterprise? Answering this question requires the consideration of alternative investments or uses of funds (which always are available for business firms, especially large corporations).

Net present worth can be defined as the "difference between gross present worth and the amount of capital investment required to achieve the benefits being discussed."[17] *Gross present worth* can be defined as "the capitalized value of the flow of future expected benefits discounted at a rate which reflects their certainty or uncertainty."[18]

Financial managers and their staff can, of course, forecast net present worth for a specific investment or a combination of investments or for other assets of all types. The prime object of such forecasting is to assure the business firm that its economic resources individually and collectively are allocated in such a manner that optimum profitability will be best assured. Management should start this forecasting at a firm's beginning and continue it throughout its life.

Planning for existing assets usage
As operations transpire and assets (or funds) are used, a business unit's financial accounting system should record, analyze, and summarize the results obtained. Summarizations finally appear in various financial statements, including each accounting entity's balance sheet. At that time, the recorded profitability can be measured for comparison with previous forecasts and with other specific assets or combinations of assets for which net present worth can be forecasted and considered relative to future acquisitions or reallocations. Thus, two factors predominate in planning existing assets usage: (1) the ongoing evaluation of existing assets to determine if their profitability is optimally desirable, and (2) the assessment of possible reallocations among existing assets or the acquisition of new assets that might occur as a result of the reallocation of funds or the infusion of new capital from a variety of possible sources. Planning

that reflects considerations involving acquisition of new fixed assets is called *capital budgeting*.

Evaluation of existing assets. Considering size and other factors, a business organization may evaluate the profitability of its total assets or the individual components thereof by a number of measuring techniques. Likewise, each investment center within a business firm may evaluate either its total assets or the individual components. An investment center can be considered as any of the following: a department or division (regardless of the basis on which it was created), a given project, or a particular product line that can be sorted out for accounting and investment purposes.

The continuing evaluation of existing assets assures their best use and the optimization of profitability. Three major accounting tools serve to report asset performance and are usually employed periodically, e.g., at the close of a stipulated accounting period. These are (1) the balance sheet, (2) the profit and loss statement, and (3) the return on investment ratio. A balance sheet compares the status of assets and liabilities and allows recognition of trends and comparisons with other accounting entities. A profit and loss statement measures performance of a firm's total existing assets and their productivity.

The return on investment calculation (ROI) undoubtedly is the most common measure of the profitability of existing assets. Also called the *rate of return on assets, all-capital earnings rate,*[19] *book return on investment, return on invested capital,* and *financial statement method of computing return on investment,*[20] the ROI ratio is based on accounting data and is calculated thus:[21]

$$\frac{Sales}{Total\ Assets} \times \frac{Profit}{Sales} = \frac{Profit}{Total\ Assets} = ROI$$

> Some firms measure total assets on a net basis as presented on the balance sheet. Other firms add back the reserve for depreciation to attain a gross asset figure. . . . [Adding back the depreciation reserve] may make for an inherent bias in the figures for reporting a higher return on investment. . . . Whether the net or gross total asset figure is used, the emphasis of the return on investment analysis is to focus on the factors which influence turnover and the factors which influence the profit margin on sales.[22]

We discuss other means of evaluating the profitability of existing assets under our discussions of ratio analyses later in this chapter.

Assessment of reallocations. Plans to reallocate funds among existing assets are based on the evaluations previously discussed. In practice, such planning cannot be separated from planning future investments, which is explained next.

Planning future investments and capital budgeting
Deming and Murdick have noted, "Companies which do not continually and systematically evaluate prospective investments in equipment and buildings against their current capital investments jeopardize their future

existence. Unless they plow back some of their earnings into selective investments, they are merely liquidating their company's capital assets."[23] Several highly visible motel chains have made this mistake, for whatever reasons, and have experienced an obvious decline, both in their reputations and in their earnings.

Our observations and conclusive studies by others show that many companies have no systematic procedures for evaluating prospective investments and fail to assign the responsibility for either suggesting them or for evaluating such suggestions by others.[24]

Fortunately, several years ago, HCA established a formal system for evaluating capital projects suggested by its various hospitals. HCA's finance department, together with members of the executive staff, in addition to their functions in evaluation, has also continually suggested programs of investment, which have then received thorough evaluation for profitability.

Reul has identified three aspects of investment opportunities that should be considered in the evaluation and selection process.[25]

1. *Functional feasibility.* This involves an evaluation of the technical soundness of a product or process, its commercial possibilities, its capability of being produced or implemented, and whether or not a specific firm has suitable production or implementing capabilities for a successful outcome.

2. *Financial acceptability.* This evaluation probes whether it is rational for a specific firm to undertake an investment by weighing the expected profits flowing therefrom against the possibilities of failure and the difficulty for the firm in obtaining the necessary acquisition funds at reasonable cost.

3. *Economic productivity.* This evaluation involves a quantified appraisal of profits from a given potential investment in comparison with alternative investments, along with a comparison of the cost of obtaining required acquisition funds. Production uncertainties should also be weighed against the magnitude of expected rewards.

Reul correctly states, "Although economic productivity is the only one of these three aspects susceptible to quantitative mathematical evaluation, this is not justification for ignoring the others."[26]

Subjectivity necessarily enters into all evaluations of future occurrences. We do not deprecate intuitive judgments if they are appropriately employed. In considering alternative investment opportunities, certainly the thoughts of a highly intelligent, knowledgeable person prove invaluable in identifying clear alternatives and in eliminating some alternatives on the basis of functional feasibility and financial acceptability. Even in the evaluation of economic productivity, some alternatives may be summarily discarded when patent financial deficiencies are observed or when one alternative is so similar to another that no test to show one is better could be devised.

Capital budgeting involves an evaluation and selection process for new investments. Cleverley has pointed out four interrelated steps in this process:

1. generation of project information

2. evaluation of projects

3. decision about which projects to be funded

4. project implementation and reporting[27]

Capital budgeting is a planning process, but step four as noted is implementation and not planning. According to the view propounded in this book, this is an example of the confusion often made between planning and implementation. Project implementation comes after the decision or planning process has been completed. Be this as it may, Cleverley is correct in that decision makers must perform the four steps simultaneously and continually, for information received from the feedback loop of reporting often results in a re-evaluation and alters or reverses previous decisions regarding projects that should be funded. This is a very clear example where planning and implementation are closely intertwined and even inseparable, but at the same time remain clearly distinguishable. (See Chapter 1.)

In any firm, when capital funds are allocated to a proposed investment exceeding a specified minimum amount, the capital budgeting process should dictate that financial feasibility and/or profitability must have been proven using selected standard assumptions for all capital analyses. In HCA, for example, the *Procedure Manual for Processing Requests for Capital* outlines certain standard inputs for capital analyses, such as the cost of capital, long-term interest rate, inflation rate, long-term debt life, payments per period, federal income tax rate, a specified debt-to-equity ratio, etc. HCA has updated these inputs at least annually, and more frequently if indicated.

Solomon suggests four basic criteria for measuring investment worth. Their selective use can provide the basis for determining investments or projects to be included in capital budgets. These criteria are (1) the payback period, (2) the book return on book investment, (3) the internal rate of return, and (4) the contribution to net present worth.[28] Brief discussions of each of these follow, together with a related additional criterion suggested by Cleverley.

Payback period. This ratio is little more than a rule-of-thumb, but as Solomon has observed, it serves as a screening device to weed out undesirable proposals and to identify projects that are clearly high-profit.[29] The ratio can be computed as payback before or after taxes. The before-tax payback equals

$$\frac{\text{Proposed Investment}}{\text{Anticipated Annual Savings}}$$

The result of the computation is the number of years required to achieve the payback.

Book rated return. We discussed this ratio in "Evaluation of Existing Assets" (earlier in this chapter) as the return on investment. Simply, the same ratio is applied to future financial projections of profits from a proposed investment. Solomon points out its shortcomings for comparing alternative future investments. "Apart from the ambiguities involved, the method fails to take into account the timing of expected earnings or of expected outlays."[30] Both timing of expected earnings and expected outlays are highly important in evaluating most proposals for capital expenditures.

Internal rate of return. This is a discounted cash flow technique and has also been called *investor's method* and *true rate of return.*

Solomon defines it as "that rate at which the incremental cash benefits expected from a project (after taxes, but before an allowance for depreciation) have a discounted present value which is exactly equal to the discounted present value of all incremental outlays required for the project's implementation."[31] Reul notes, "The answer obtained by this method may be defined as *the interest rate at which the proposed disbursements would have to be invested in an annuity fund for that fund to be able to make payments equal to and at the same time as the receipts anticipated from the project.*"[32] Davidson et al. state, "*The internal rate of return* of a series of cash flows is the discount rate that equates the net present value of a series of cash flows to zero."[33]

Previously a rather laborious process, the calculations involved in this algorithm have been computerized and can now be done very quickly.

Net present value. Cleverley points to this discounted cash flow analysis as being highly useful in analyzing alternative methods of capital financing. He states, "Net present value simply equals the discounted cash inflows less the discounted cash outflows. In a comparison of two alternative financing packages, the one with the highest net present value should be selected."[34]

Solomon states, "In the present value method, all cash inflows and outflows are discounted, using 'K' [the cost of capital] as the discount rate."[35]

Profitability index. Cleverley stresses the importance of this discounted cash flow method in capital project evaluation "where the benefits of the projects are mostly financial, for example a capital project that saves costs or expands revenue with a primary purpose of increased profits. . . . Thus, those projects with the highest rate of return per dollar of capital investment are the best candidates for selection."[36] However, it is important to evaluate the total portfolio on investment opportunities rather than arbitrarily select one smaller project with a high profitability index. If one makes arbitrary selections, one may then be forced to forego a more significant project, though with a less profitable *percentage* rate of return due to a lack of funds. The profitability index equals

$$\frac{\text{Net Present Value}}{\text{Investment Cost}}$$

Cleverley states that capital review must follow reallocations of investments or new investments after they are made. We agree such definitive review must be implemented by persons specifically assigned to the task.[37] Although this is implementation—in contrast to planning—we should observe that these persons ought to render formal reports about whether project profitability or other project benefits are realized as forecasted.

Capital finance planning

Capital finance planning has a distinct tie-in with all assets planning and, more specifically and directly, with capital budgeting. Planning decisions that take into account evaluations of all investments must necessarily also take into account the cost of capital that can be obtained to make investments. These costs can vary depending on (1) the type and nature of the asset in which investment will be made, (2) the available sources of money, and (3) the various features of the capital financing instrument that can be realized from an available source. Readers should remember that a key criterion in selecting assets is net present worth, and this is defined as the *difference* between the gross present worth and the capital investment required to obtain certain operating results. Certainly, this difference will be greater when the investment required is smaller—which it invariably will be (other factors being equal) when the cost of money or other needed economic resources is low. However, there are other factors involved in obtaining financing, which we will discuss here briefly.

There are two basic sources of capital finance: (1) the sale of equity securities and (2) borrowing through the sale of debt securities. What are the differences between the two? When should a corporation sell equity securities and when should it sell debt securities? What ratios between the two are desirable and at what times and under what conditions? Before we attempt to answer these questions (at least in part), we shall first define these two basic sources of finance.

Definitions of equity and debt

To obtain funding for all types of assets, corporations sell equity securities (to those who buy shares of stock) and borrow by selling debt securities (to lenders who will receive interest on a principal to be repaid at a specified time or times).

Thus, equity capital is that which is paid in by owners—the corporation's shareholders. Debt capital, obtained by a wide variety of loan instruments, creates obligations that must eventually be satisfied. However, satisfaction can be continuously deferred among all creditors through planned refunding, so long as the corporation is able to repay interest on schedule.

Capital structures

Management can devise an optimal capital structure (defined as total equity and debt funding in a planned relationship) through consideration of several factors. Chief among them are (1) the current and projected profitability, (2) the size and nature of the enterprise, (3) the degree of maturity of the business in which the firm is engaged, and (4) the current stage of the individual firm's life cycle.

When a corporation forms, it usually raises capital through the sale of equity securities to those who are willing to provide "venture" capital. As assets are acquired and profitability and reliability increase, the corporate directors may begin to sell debt securities although this also depends on the prospects for rapid growth. After considering the costs involved (as contrasted to equity securities), the degree to which it may appear best to reinvest its own earnings (depending primarily on interest rates), and the willingness to risk creditor control, directors might decide to sell debt securities in the form of a variety of mortgage bonds or debenture bonds. Mortgage bonds, of course, are secured by assets and debenture bonds are of a general credit nature. Corporations also can obtain funds on a short-term basis from banks through "a line of credit" for a variety of reasons, including to consummate "quick deals" and to meet shortfalls in cash flow. In truth, there are nearly as many ways to raise debt capital as the imagination of corporate borrowers and creditors will allow, provided all parties have their objectives and needs met and are satisfied and willing.

Current and projected profitability always affects what a firm may do in terms of equity and debt securities. When profitability is less certain but promising, the sale of equity securities often appears best. When profitability seems more certain and likely to be at a high rate, a combination of equity and debt may appear best. When it becomes fairly certain that the sale of debt securities is a considerably cheaper way to obtain needed funds, then debt securities should be issued, always depending, of course, on the corporation's ability to do so, which in turn depends on projected profitability. When directors can obtain debt at a rate of 7 percent with a fairly certain return of, say, 12 percent on its subsequent investment, no particular brilliance is required to see this would be a good thing to do. Such profits can often be made by allowing lenders of capital funds (at low interest rates) claims against the corporation's net worth. Resulting profits from such borrowing go to the shareholders; the general principle involved is known as "trading on the equity."

Obviously, *the size of an enterprise* influences the volume of sales of both equity and debt securities. Volatility of markets and profitability affect small firms more than larger ones. Thus small firms cannot withstand the "shocks" of recessions as well as larger firms, especially those in mature industries. Equity securities are generally safer, but even a large firm that has an appreciable amount of debt financing should maintain flexibility in its debt-to-equity ratio and be able to change its types of issued securities rapidly.

As to the *nature* of an enterprise, certainly the relationship between debt and equity will be drastically different for a bank (with a high level of cash) than for a retail firm (with a high level of inventory). Industrial firms and hospitals have high levels of fixed assets that further influence this relationship, which is based on the expectations of both investors and lenders.

The *degree of maturity of the business in which a firm is engaged* usually affects the relative amounts of equity and debt financing an enterprise should strive to achieve. In mature industries, where competition is keen, corporate directors by and large should keep debt low. Examples of corporations in such industries are frozen and canned food processors, manufacturers of farm equipment, automobile manufacturers, and manufacturers of refrigerators and many other standard home appliances. Their markets are still growing, of course, but roughly at the same rate as population growth. In young industries, such as a number of segments of the electronics market, where rapidly expanding markets are still possible, debt may be the answer to the demands of growth. Even here, however, when debt securities are issued, consideration should be given to the *time when the market will be matured*, with overextension being avoided. Both Atari and Texas Instruments have had experience with inaccurate predictions of market maturity in the electronics field.

Over the past several years, apparent maturity has come to the inpatient hospital market. Fortunately for hospitals, HCA and HealthTrust Inc. in particular, alternative methods of health care delivery have been rapidly growing. Since the ability to grow in the outpatient area depended to a considerable degree on prior penetration of the inpatient market, HCA has been in an enviable position, even though its original market, inpatient care, appears to be maturing. HCA's debt-to-equity ratio reached 51:49 in 1984, but with the apparent ability to expand rapidly into alternative fields, all of an outpatient nature (with the exception of psychiatric inpatient care, which is still not mature), debt-to-equity had been raised to 62:38 by December 31, 1986. Traditionally, HCA has tried to keep a debt-to-equity ratio of approximately 60:40, but subsequent to debt reductions planned after the restructuring in mid-1987, the debt-to-equity ratio was projected at 57:43.

Many chroniclers have observed that business firms go through cycles during the entire period of their existence. While authorities are not in full agreement about what the stages are, they typically identify the following: (1) emergency or infancy, (2) growth, (3) maturity, and (4) decline or senility. Plainly, these stages are similar to the phases of a particular product market, and firms often diversify into new markets so as to maintain themselves at the stage of maturity and avoid decline.

Obviously, young corporations should avoid issuing long-term, fixed-interest-bearing securities, except possibly to obtain funds for acquiring a valuable fixed asset with a promise of profit, such as was the situation of hospitals in the 1970s.

In growth phases, debt financing may be very attractive, and directors should give judicious consideration to using such financing in some measurable and balanced relationship to equity financing.

In maturity, directors should provide for debt reduction on those of its assets that support the mature portions of its operations. For those that support growth activities, of course, debt financing may still be the preferred choice.

Some firms have a "forever young" policy, that is, they are determined to put new products or new services to market, either through concerted programs of R & D, programs of acquisition, or shrewd market anticipations. Du Pont is the classic example. In such firms, directors must make wise judgments about debt-to-equity ratios and total capital financing for specific segments of the firm's business.

In periods beyond maturity, when declining net earnings can be positively predicted, directors theoretically should make provisions for eventual debt reduction to zero on respective assets and, finally, should make provisions through retained earnings for stockholders to receive, on the last day of the corporation's life, an equitable settlement for the shares of stock they hold. As a matter of fact, however, in the case of larger corporations, the last day of life may never be considered, for it is assumed the ambitiousness of young executives will find a means of healthy perpetuation, chiefly through diversification into new markets.

Our readers should note that the above presents only a smattering of all financing factors that may be important for various types of corporations—quasi-public and private. We have directed our brief comments, of course, primarily to private corporations.

Planning for financial accounting

Background

Although it has been said that financial accounting provides needed information about an economic entity to outsiders—investors, potential investors, creditors, the Internal Revenue Service, the SEC and other governmental agencies, and the general public—it also provides information vital to managers. As a record of past activities, accounting reports can provide invaluable guidance for future activities if carefully studied and analyzed. Financial ratios, discussed later in this section, are especially revealing to managers, as well as to investors and potential investors.

We will discuss here three distinct financial statements. Each has a different purpose and each may be prepared slightly differently from firm to firm, but they all must be prepared using generally accepted accounting concepts and principles.

Independent auditors play a role in demonstrating to the world that the statements they audit adhere to these principles and hence allow consistent analyses, from firm to firm, of financial position and condition. For example, Ernst & Whinney, the elected independent auditors of HCA, in early 1987 issued the statement below to the shareholders and board of directors of HCA. Similar statements appear in the annual reports of major corporations throughout the nation and much of the free world.

> We have examined the consolidated balance sheet of Hospital Corporation of America and subsidiaries as of December 31, 1986 and 1985, and the related consolidated statements of income, shareholders' equity and changes in financial position for each of the three years in the period ended December 31, 1986. Our examinations were made in accordance with generally accepted auditing standards and, accordingly, included such tests of the accounting records and such other auditing procedures as we considered necessary in the circumstances.

> In our opinion, the financial statements referred to above present fairly the consolidated financial position of Hospital Corporation of America and subsidiaries at December 31, 1986 and 1985, and the consolidated results of their operations and changes in their financial position for each of the three years in the period ended December 31, 1986, in conformity with generally accepted accounting principles applied on a consistent basis.[38]

Although space will not permit discussion of the "generally accepted accounting principles" referred to, management must take care to plan their accounting systems in accord with them. Planning an accounting system involves the collection of financial data and the summarization and reporting of financial information. Because accounting is a dynamic profession and new principles and procedures are constantly evolving, the accountants of a firm must also be ongoing students of the profession so that state-of-the-art techniques will be incorporated into routine procedures.

The primary accounting principles, or conventions, involve the following:[39]

1. enforceable property rights

2. an identifiable business entity

3. continuity in operations (going concern)

4. the measurement of money

5. periods of accounting (usually annual)

6. consistency

7. historical costs

8. revenue realization

9. matching of costs and revenues

10. the dual accounting equation

11. reliability of verifiable evidence

12. sufficiency of disclosures

13. conservatism

14. materiality in reporting

15. relevance in application of principles

Besides these conventions, most authorities cite accrual accounting, among others.

Timeliness in reporting

As nonfinancial managers, we have become keenly aware of the importance of timeliness in financial reporting. Although it is seldom discussed in the literature, we point to the fact that many otherwise excellent financial reports become largely worthless to management after the passage of unduly long periods of time. Note that Ernst & Whinney had completed their examination of HCA's records and statements for 1986 by

February 16, 1987. This meant that HCA's accountants had completed their work and that analyses of it were available to HCA officers by mid to late January. Certainly this is an example of the timeliness that managers should expect.

During our tenures as executives of hospitals, we were accustomed to having monthly income and expense statements, plus pertinent analyses, available to us by the 15th of the succeeding month. This degree of timeliness allowed corrections in operations that had to be made promptly if the hospital was not to suffer damage.

Needless to say, we regard timeliness of financial accounting records as extremely important. Sadly, many managers fail to recognize the importance or decide to tolerate the laxness of the accounting system. The result in either case is undesirable. To us, it is axiomatic that all accounting reports should have planned due dates and that implementation should meet the deadline. This means all efforts prior to the reporting—both data collection and summarization—must also be scheduled.

In view of today's dynamic environment, some business enterprises may actually require reporting of selected information on a weekly or even a daily basis. In fact, in implementing some of the new modes of health care delivery, numerous hospital executives have claimed considerable benefits from reports of daily business volumes and expenses.

Financial statements

The preparation of financial statements is one of the main purposes of financial accounting. These statements show the financial condition or position of a firm and the results of operations in such a way as to provide needed information to managers, owners, lenders, governmental agencies, and other interested parties. We will begin with one of the four key statements used by for-profit enterprises: the balance sheet.

Balance sheet

The purpose of the balance sheet (also called the statement of assets and liabilities, the statement of financial condition, and the financial statement) is to present the financial condition of a business entity at a given moment in time. The balance sheet is built around a basic equation:

$$\text{Assets} = \text{Liabilities} + \text{Owner Equity}$$

This can be presented another way:

$$\text{Assets} - \text{Liabilities} = \text{Owner Equity}$$

The totals of the two sides of a balance sheet always balance (are equal), owing to the fact that no matter what business transactions occur, assets are always equaled by the rights of creditors or owners.

The balance sheet, though it is a routine financial statement, requires considerable accounting knowledge and planning for its preparation. One must remember that each item appearing on both sides of a balance sheet occurs as the result of many tasks related to recording it in conformance with accepted accounting principles, which themselves are part of a science or a division of a science (applied mathematics and statistics).

Understanding balance sheet concepts is aided by addressing a series of planning questions posed by Davidson et al. These are as follows:

1. Which resources of a firm are recognized as assets?

2. What valuations are placed on these assets?

3. How are assets classified, or grouped, within the balance sheet?

4. Which claims against a firm's assets are recognized as liabilities?

5. What valuations are placed on these liabilities?

6. How are liabilities classified within the balance sheet?

7. What valuation is placed on owner's equity, and how is owner's equity disclosed?[40]

Table 6-1 displays a balance sheet for the consolidated operations of HCA for the year 1986.

Statement of revenues and expenses
This statement (also called the profit and loss statement, the statement of income, and the operating statement) presents a record of operations over a specific time period. As a statement of performance, rather than condition (which is reflected in the balance sheet), it sets forth a summary of income and expense items in order to show whether operations during the period resulted in a profit or loss—and by how much.

A statement of income and expenses, if submitted periodically and in a timely fashion, allows operational problems to be identified and corrected before they get out of hand. Clearly, planning calls for appropriate timeliness.

The revenue and expense statement supplements the balance sheet in that it accounts for any increase or decrease in owners' equity depending on whether a profit or loss, respectively, has been experienced.

Table 6-2 shows HCA's Consolidated Statement of Income for the period ending December 31, 1986.

Statement of changes in financial position
This statement presents information on the sources (increases) and uses (decreases) of cash during a given period. The major sources of funds (increases) are (1) income-related sources, such as sales; (2) sale of capital stock and borrowed funds; and (3) sale of assets. The major uses of funds are (1) purchase of assets (nonoperating); (2) redemption of stock, either debt or capital; (3) owner distributions; and (4) increases in working capital.

Like the statement of revenues and expenses, the statement of changes in financial position reports *flows*, but whereas the former deals with net assets, the latter deals with cash funds. See Table 6-3 for HCA's Consolidated Statement of Changes in Financial Position for 1986.

Table 6-1

Consolidated Balance Sheet
Hospital Corporation of America

December 31 (dollars in thousands)	**1986**	*1985*
Assets		
Current Assets		
Cash and cash equivalents	$ 150,263	$ 103,092
Accounts receivable, less allowances for doubtful accounts of $248,166 in 1986 and $224,316 in 1985	964,679	885,383
Supplies at cost	116,138	107,278
Other current assets	62,526	76,461
Total current assets	1,293,606	1,172,214
Investments and Other Assets		
Investments of insurance subsidiary at cost	294,901	203,864
Other investments and other assets	608,169	408,280
	903,070	612,144
Property, Plant and Equipment at Cost		
Land	247,660	223,674
Buildings and improvements	2,470,432	2,340,779
Equipment	2,322,531	2,038,334
	5,040,623	4,602,787
Less accumulated depreciation	1,142,549	920,975
	3,898,074	3,681,812
Construction in progress (estimated cost to complete $197,000 in 1986)	274,178	272,933
Cash restricted for construction	4,249	3,350
	4,176,501	3,958,095
Intangible Assets		
Cost in excess of net tangible asset value of purchased subsidiaries	395,538	495,099
Unamortized loan costs	24,657	21,508
	420,195	516,607
Total Assets	$6,793,372	$6,259,060

See notes to consolidated financial statements.

	1986	*1985*
Liabilities and Shareholders' Equity		
Current Liabilities		
Accounts payable	$ 203,545	$ 234,235
Accrued liabilities:		
Salaries and wages	102,270	99,850
Interest	51,707	42,944
Other	186,541	190,487
Income taxes, including deferred taxes of $2,135 in 1986 and $185,300 in 1985	2,135	199,484
Current maturities of long-term debt and bank financing	169,496	40,263
Total current liabilities	715,694	807,263
Long-Term Debt	3,066,893	2,763,241

Table 6-1 continued

Deferred Credits and Other Liabilities

Deferred income taxes	633,735	378,463
Deferred income	1,254	1,877
Reserve for general and professional liability risks	360,413	216,083
	995,402	596,423

Shareholders' Equity

Common Stock, $1 par value		
Authorized—500,000,000 shares		
Issued—81,842,893 shares in 1986 and 86,442,953 shares in 1985	81,843	86,443
Additional paid-in capital	584,819	758,951
Retained earnings	1,388,052	1,268,031
Translation adjustment	(21,766)	(21,292)
Net unrealized loss on marketable equity securities	(17,565)	—
	2,015,383	2,092,133
Total Liabilities and Shareholders' Equity	$6,793,372	$6,259,060

Source: Reprinted with permission from the Hospital Corporation of America 1986 Annual Report.

Table 6-2

Consolidated Statement of Income
Hospital Corporation of America

Years Ended December 31 (in thousands except per share data)	1986	1985	1984
Net operating revenues	$4,930,652	$4,352,306	$3,663,615
Costs and expenses:			
Operating expenses	4,109,528	3,493,325	2,828,026
Depreciation and amortization	294,677	240,730	192,165
Interest	265,060	232,046	187,821
	4,669,265	3,966,101	3,208,012
Income from operations	261,387	386,205	455,603
Investment earnings and other income—net	50,257	81,319	50,356
Income before Income Taxes and Extraordinary Items	311,644	467,524	505,959
Provision for income taxes	137,000	183,800	209,200
Income before Extraordinary Items	174,644	283,724	296,759
Extraordinary items net of income taxes:			
Gain on termination of proposed merger	—	65,400	—
Loss on extinguishment of debt	—	(10,511)	—
Net Income	$ 174,644	$ 338,613	$ 296,759
Average number of common and common equivalent shares	84,116	90,392	88,648
Earnings per Common and Common Equivalent Share:			
Income before extraordinary items	$2.08	$3.14	$3.35
Extraordinary items	—	.61	—
Net income	$2.08	$3.75	$3.35

See notes to consolidated financial statements.

Source: Reprinted with permission from the Hospital Corporation of America 1986 Annual Report.

Table 6-3

Consolidated Statement of
Changes in Financial Position
Hospital Corporation of America

Years Ended December 31 (dollars in thousands)	1986	1985	1984
Funds from Operations			
Income before extraordinary items	$ 174,644	$ 283,724	$ 296,759
Costs charged to income not requiring funds:			
Depreciation and amortization	294,677	240,730	192,165
Deferred credits and other	172,869	148,533	116,156
Funds from operations before extraordinary items	642,190	672,987	605,080
Extraordinary items	—	54,889	—
Funds provided from operations	642,190	727,876	605,080
Funds from Other Sources, Excluding Financing Activities			
Disposals of property, plant and equipment	128,861	116,094	25,657
Proceeds from issuances of common stock	26,065	51,805	61,381
Increase (decrease) in working capital, excluding cash and debt:			
Accounts receivable	(79,296)	(269,337)	(177,221)
Accounts payable	(30,690)	77,856	10,452
Accrued liabilities	7,237	79,256	51,763
Income taxes	32,766	42,809	61,332
Other	5,075	(75,974)	(2,771)
Funds from other sources, excluding financing activities	90,018	22,509	30,593
Funds from (used in) Financing Activities			
Additional borrowings under long-term financing arrangements	528,078	629,007	144,044
Reduction of long-term debt	(156,789)	(232,708)	(225,742)
Increase (decrease) in long-term portion of bank financing	(53,404)	550,391	206,327
Increase (decrease) in short-term bank financing	115,000	(85,000)	85,000
Funds from financing activities	432,885	861,690	209,629
Total funds provided, excluding cash items	1,165,093	1,612,075	845,302
Utilization of Funds			
Additions to property, plant and equipment ($34,000 in 1986, $438,000 in 1985 and $25,000 in 1984 from acquisitions)	635,987	1,110,054	574,940
Repurchase of common stock	204,797	127,455	—
Cash dividends	54,623	53,225	43,635
Investment in Equicor (net of goodwill of $104,000, property of $9,000 and other assets of $12,000 transferred to Equicor)	89,388	—	—
Increase in other investments	40,280	45,219	161,350
Additions to cost in excess of net tangible asset value of purchased subsidiaries	17,145	266,475	18,656
Other applications—net	75,702	(12,305)	26,452
Funds utilized	1,117,922	1,590,123	825,033
Increase in Cash and Cash Equivalents	$ 47,171	$ 21,952	$ 20,269

See notes to consolidated financial statements.

   Source: Reprinted with permission from the Hospital Corporation of America 1986 Annual Report.

Statement of shareholders' equity

This consolidated statement usually presents a multiyear trend in its various items. HCA has typically presented a four-year trend (see Table 6-4). State laws require companies to reveal the sources of shareholders' equity which typically are two: (1) the investment by stockholders in the company and (2) earnings from profitable operations of the company, after taxes. These sources are reflected in both the Balance Sheet Statement and the Statement of Shareholders' Equity in the case of HCA, with its Balance Sheet Statement merely summarizing the contents of the Statement of Shareholders' Equity.

The role of electronic data processing (EDP)

Computers not only affect the ways in which departments of finance and accounting organize, but they affect most work methods for producing various financial statements and reports. However, one must remember that "the development of data processing accounting systems is initially an accounting problem rather than a data processing problem because basic accounting concepts are most important."[41] This being so, all business firms ought to be especially careful to see that accounting personnel work closely with systems analysts and programmers in developing a computerized accounting system which possesses capabilities necessary to render all required financial statements, as well as information analyses desirable in making both short- and long-term financial planning decisions.

The planning decisions related to procuring appropriate computer hardware and designing software to automate an accounting system by means of that hardware are many and often very difficult. Vast sums of money have been wasted by business firms because of ignorance and because of a sophomoric longing for the status that some executives believe results from the ownership and operation of a computer. However, sufficient technical knowledge is now available to avoid the many pitfalls of the past—provided managers formulate an appropriate selection and programming process.

Over the last decade, increased competition among vendors has driven down costs of both hardware and software. At the same time, capabilities have vastly increased, and instantaneous information analyses and statement summarizations of a broad variety can now be programmed in the following areas:

1. order processing/purchasing

2. inventory control

3. accounts payable

4. payroll

5. billings

6. accounts receivable

Table 6-4

Consolidated Statement of Shareholders' Equity
Hospital Corporation of America

(dollars in thousands except per share data)	Common Stock	Additional Paid-In Capital	Retained Earnings	Translation Adjustment	Net Unrealized Loss on Marketable Equity Securities
Balance, December 31, 1983	$86,134	$765,711	$729,519	$(10,456)	$ —
Exercise of stock options and warrants	605	13,572			
Stock issued in acquisition	75	2,743			
Cash dividends ($.50 per share)			(43,635)		
Stock issued under employee stock purchase plan	369	12,052			
Sales of common stock	893	33,890			
Translation adjustment				(7,000)	
Net unrealized loss on marketable equity securities					(11,600)
Net income			296,759		
Balance, December 31, 1984	88,076	827,968	982,643	(17,456)	(11,600)
Exercise of stock options and warrants	1,058	20,291			
Stock issued in acquisition	110	4,890			
Repurchase of 3,615,922 shares of common stock	(3,616)	(123,839)			
Cash dividends ($.60 per share)			(53,225)		
Stock issued under employee stock purchase plan	358	11,668			
Sales of common stock	457	17,973			
Translation adjustment				(3,836)	
Decrease in net unrealized loss on marketable equity securities					11,600
Net income			338,613		
Balance, December 31, 1985	86,443	758,951	1,268,031	(21,292)	—
Exercise of stock options and warrants	376	8,600			
Repurchase of 5,476,200 shares of common stock	(5,476)	(199,321)			
Cash dividends ($.66 per share)			(54,623)		
Stock issued under employee stock purchase plan	348	11,372			
Sales of common stock	152	5,217			
Translation adjustment				(474)	
Net unrealized loss on marketable equity securities					(17,565)
Net income			174,644		
Balance, December 31, 1986	$81,843	$584,819	$1,388,052	$(21,766)	$(17,565)

See notes to consolidated financial statements.

Source: Reprinted with permission from the Hospital Corporation of America 1986 Annual Report.

7. general accounting

8. management information

For further discussion of the role of EDP as it pertains to management information systems, see Chapter 8.

Ratio analysis

Through ratio analysis, accountants can reduce masses of data within individual firms and among the firms of specific industries to comparable bases. This permits trends to be identified, understood, and projected more easily than is possible when dealing with gross numbers. Financial ratio and comparison of trends analyzable because of norms established among a commonly grouped set of enterprises are extremely helpful to executives in managing any business.

Financial ratios also let parties who are not in management ascertain the financial health of a firm, and over the years literally dozens of ratios have been developed as diagnostic tools to pinpoint problem areas while correction is still possible. Although authorities categorize financial ratios in various ways, four currently recognized categories are as follows:

1. *Liquidity ratios* indicate the ability of a firm to meet its obligations as they mature.

2. *Financing ratios* compare the claims of creditors of the firm to owner's equity in order to indicate feasible debt levels and future solvency.

3. *Activity ratios* measure the efficiency of a firm in using its investments.

4. *Profit ratios* measure the profitability of a firm's operations in terms of its sales, total assets, fixed assets, etc.

In all major corporations, executives and accountants should select various ratios and develop parameters and objectives that appear desirable to them. (This should be done both routinely and on special or exceptional occasions.) A schedule for reporting should then be constructed and the reporting made part of routine procedures.

A brief discussion of some pertinent ratios follows.

Liquidity ratios: measuring liquidity
When any firm reaches a point where it has problems in meeting its short-term obligations, a serious liquidity crisis may be at hand. We have known of a number of such crises in the hospital field, and financial officers usually face the problem of obtaining a loan to cover such items as the next payroll. In most instances, lending institutions will apply certain tests, in the form of liquidity ratios, to the troubled firm's balance sheet to try to determine its ability to repay the requested loan plus interest by a certain date.

We have presented four liquidity ratios below. Several others can be used to pinpoint specific causes of a liquidity crisis and indicate what must be done to resolve it.

Current ratio. For many years, this has been probably the most frequently used ratio to determine ability to meet current obligations. Simply, the ratio equals

$$\frac{\text{Current Assets}}{\text{Current Liabilities}}$$

The definition of current assets, in accounting terms, means those that presumably will be converted to cash or used during an operating cycle period (usually one year). Current liabilities mean those that are to be satisfied within an operating cycle period (usually one year).

Since both figures in this ratio are taken directly from the balance sheet, the ratio does not indicate the future. Also, the current assets figure alone does not indicate precisely the liquidity of the assets, which is vital to know in some instances. A long-standing practice in the credit field is to use a value of 2.0 to 2.5 for this ratio.

Because of the obvious shortcomings of the current ratio, credit institutions usually employ another test in conjunction with it, such as the quick ratio or the acid test ratio.

Quick ratio. Since inventory is generally less liquid than the other usual components of current assets (accounts receivable, cash, marketable securities, and prepaid expenses), the quick ratio is often helpful. It equals

$$\frac{\text{Current Assets less Inventory}}{\text{Current Liabilities}}$$

Industrial credit institutions regard a value of 1.0 as an indication of creditworthiness—and hope for a higher value.

Acid test ratio. This ratio indicates the capability of a borrower to repay a loan promptly. It disallows accounts receivable (included in the quick ratio), which can fluctuate rather widely, both in their actual value and their ability to be readily converted into cash. The acid test ratio equals

$$\frac{\text{Cash and Marketable Securities}}{\text{Current Liabilities}}$$

Days in accounts receivable. This ratio is one of the most widely used in the health care field to determine the efficacy of collection efforts (both cash and insurance claims) and the general effectiveness of the credit department. It is easily determined and is an excellent indicator of liquidity. It equals

$$\frac{\text{Accounts Receivable}}{\text{Average Daily Revenue}}$$

Average daily revenue, of course, is computed by dividing the total revenue for a given period (usually six months or a year) by the days in that period.

Not only does this ratio indicate on a gross or net accounts receivable basis the appropriateness of credit policy and the vigor of collection efforts, but an above-average number of days in gross accounts receivable may indicate a high proportion of bad debts, or uncollectibles. Further analyses might then be required to determine the nature and age of the account categories.

Days in inventory. This is another ratio widely used by hospitals, as well as by retail pharmacies. It equals

$$\frac{\text{Total Cost of Goods in Inventory}}{\text{Average Cost of Daily Sales from Inventory}}$$

Some may construe this as an activity ratio, but we have used it as an indicator of liquidity.

Other liquidity ratios. Among others, two ratios are often used in investigations of the causes of liquidity crises. One is the payables index and the other current assets discounted.

Financing ratios: measuring capital structure

Financing ratios, sometimes called leverage ratios and capital structure ratios, indicate the long-term solvency of a firm. Investment bankers and bond rating agencies often use them to determine amounts of debt financing a firm might undertake without unreasonable risks being incurred by lenders. Discussion of three financing ratios follows.

Debt-to-equity ratio. This ratio, probably the most commonly used financing ratio today, measures the percentage of total funds owed to creditors in relationship to assets supplied by owners. It equals

$$\frac{\text{Total Debt}}{\text{Total Equity}}$$

The industry average for commercial enterprises is about 1:3.

Times-interest-earned ratio. This often used ratio indicates the ability of a firm to meet interest payments over time and also reveals how far earnings can fall before a potential deficit occurs. It equals

$$\frac{\text{Profit before Taxes Plus Interest Charges}}{\text{Interest Charges}}$$

Obviously, the higher the value of this ratio, the more likely the firm will be able to repay the interest as it comes due. A standard in the industry is 8:1.[42]

Debt service coverage. Bond rating firms, investment bankers, and financial feasibility analysts all pay close attention to this ratio. In the health care field, for example, most of the Big Eight accounting firms regard a value for this ratio below 2.00 as indicative of risk for hospitals. The ratio equals

$$\frac{\text{Excess of Revenues over Expenses Plus Depreciation Plus Interest}}{\text{Principal Payment Plus Interest Expense}}$$

Other financing ratios. Used frequently in industry, the fixed-charge coverage ratio recognizes both long-term lease assets and long-term lease obligations, in addition to the factors given account in the times interest earned ratio.

Activity ratios: measuring efficiency
Activity ratios involve comparisons between revenues and investments and give indications as to how efficiently a firm turns input (investments in asset accounts) into output (of which revenues are one quantified measure). We will only discuss two of these ratios.

Total asset turnover. This ratio is probably the most common for indicating the efficiency with which a firm's total assets are being used. It equals

$$\frac{\text{Sales}}{\text{Total Assets}}$$

The higher the value of the ratio, the more likely the assets are being used efficiently. However, one must also look at a firm's net-worth-to-debt ratio. In the case of a low ratio, the firm may be trading excessively on the equity. Cleverley[43] reports that several studies of financial statements have shown a standard value of 1.2 for hospitals and McLaughlin[44] reports an industry average of 2.00.

Fixed asset turnover. This ratio takes one category of assets—fixed assets—and measures their turnover in relation to sales. Obviously, this ratio is most meaningful in capital intensive industries. The ratio equals

$$\frac{\text{Total Sales}}{\text{Fixed Assets}}$$

Cleverley[45] reports a hospital standard of 1.75 and McLaughlin[46] reports an industry average of 5.00.

Other activity ratios. Various types of businesses have used a number of other activity ratios that compare total sales to various categories of assets, such as receivables, average inventories, and current assets.

Profit ratios: measuring profitability
Profit ratios relate either certain income statement items one to the other or selected income statement items to certain balance sheet items. These ratios indicate the basic degree of success management has been able to achieve in terms of economics.

Profit margin. This ratio is probably the most commonly used of all the profit ratios and may be the most widely recognized of any type of ratio. It equals

$$\frac{\text{Net Profit after Taxes}}{\text{Sales}}$$

McLaughlin reports the 1977 industry average as 5 percent.[47]

Return on total assets. This ratio has been used by HCA as a primary guide in divestitures, together with the profit-to-fixed-assets ratio. Simply, the return on total assets (ROI, as cited previously) equals

$$\frac{\text{Net Profit after Taxes}}{\text{Total Assets}}$$

When the value of this ratio consistently remains below certain standards, depending on certain factors at a given point in time, HCA gives serious consideration to an individual hospital's divestiture, unless there is some synergistic effect that benefits a sister hospital by its presence and HCA's ownership. McLaughlin reports an industry average for this ratio as about 10 percent.[48]

Profits to fixed assets. This ratio is used in conjunction with the two preceding ones. It equals

$$\frac{\text{Net Profit after Taxes}}{\text{Fixed Assets}}$$

Other profit ratios. Cleverley has reported use in hospitals of the ratio of nonoperating revenue to excess of revenue over expenses,[49] and although we have not used it, it is clearly valuable for analyzing sources of income other than ordinary operations.

Planning for managerial accounting

An evolving function

Management accounting, or managerial accounting as it is sometimes called, originally "evolved from the need to assign costs to products for external financial reports . . . but during the past twenty years . . . texts have expanded their coverage to include the use of cost data for decisions and control within the firm. These texts now treat topics such as cost-volume-profit analysis, budgeting and planning, capital budgeting, and variance analysis of standard cost systems."[50] Of course, we have already treated capital budgeting under the topic of financial planning, where we believe it more properly belongs. However, we point to the fact that some authorities subsume this function, sometimes called capital project analysis,[51] under management accounting.

At the present time, management accounting has become highly technical, and some facets of it still have not been conclusively proved to have practical worth. Considering the limitations of space, we have restricted our discussion to those aspects of management accounting that in most business organizations require routine planning if they are to be implemented. These aspects relate to decision making and control, together with purposes peripheral to these functions. Specifically, we shall discuss the subjects of (1) budgeting, (2) cost accounting, and (3) variance analysis.

Operating and financial budgets

Managers prepare several types of budgets. None of these is a complete plan in itself, but all are essential parts of a complete plan. Budgets are invariably quantified and can be used as a measuring device in the control process. More accurately, a budget develops as a plan, but its quantified elements later serve as a yardstick by which to judge results achieved in the course of plan implementation. (See Chapter 15 on controlling.) Further, budgeting is a planning process used by managers both to foresee probable developments with some degree of accuracy and to assure the outcomes of organizational operations with regard to the deployment and utilization of all types of available resources, including financial.

Capital budgeting is very closely related to both operating and financial budgeting, and in fact many, if not most, authorities classify it as one kind of financial budgeting. As already noted, we discuss it as a part of financial planning rather than of managerial accounting. In any event, capital budgets must be taken into account in the cash flow budget, which is definitely a financial budget.

In recent years, the computer has increased the potential value of budgeting manyfold. Some standard programs now provide the capability to generate complete budgets for very large business firms or for their individual departments. Previously, management's testing of various strategies was a laborious hand-done process and consequently was seldom very extensive. Now, the effects of changes in key parameters or strategies can be determined literally in a matter of seconds, as can the answers to "what if" questions.

All budgets flow from action plans of one type or another, but they will have strategic planning as their original base if strategic planning plays the role it should.

Operating budgets
On the basis of a firm's strategy plan (which provides the starting point for other plans, e.g., a "marketing" plan), certain goals or objectives can be established for every cost center, revenue center, and profit center or for any other defined operational or planning level or entity. From these goals or objectives flow units of service, respective workloads, quantified items of production, or work units, all of which can be budgeted in what some call a statistics budget and others merely "output of the business or management plan."

In HCA, annual management planning has called for the corporate office, field officers, and every service entity (primarily various types of hospitals and outpatient centers) to estimate their units of service and workloads. In a typical hospital, this is reflected in a "service demand budget," and it is from this that both revenue and expense budgets flow for each month of the ensuing year. In other businesses, the basis for revenue and expense budgets may be the number of items manufactured, processed or sold; the number of items bought and sold; or the number of transactions handled (depending on the product line or lines).

In HCA, an "operations budget" flows from the service demand budgets, combines the individual revenue and expense budgets, and finally predicts net income after taxes, by month, by quarter, and for the year—for the entire corporation.

Thus three budgets—the service demand budget, the revenue budget, and the expense budget—compose the operating budget in HCA service entities. These three budgets are formulated in most business firms, although the service demand budget may be designated in various ways, depending on the product or service involved.

Because of space limitations, we have limited our discussion of operational budgeting. We note that many variations of the budgeting process HCA follows do exist. For example, some firms formulate a flexible budget and use a "rolling" or continuous budgeting process rather than an annual preparation process.

We should also note that there can be specific budgets for the individual projects that most firms undertake, as well as a type of specific budgeting called appropriation budgeting. Lastly, many firms follow a "program budgeting" process that is oriented to specific company activities, with breakdowns based on product lines or products.[52]

Financial budgets

Steers, Ungson, and Mowday note, "Operating budgets feed into financial budgets which spell out in considerable detail how the organization will spend money for the same period as well as where the funds will come from."[53] They identify financing budgets, capital expenditure budgets, cash flow budgets, and balance sheet budgets as parts of the "financial budget."[54]

Among the several types of financial budgets prepared, accountants must seek a realistic and workable balance. In the preparation of each, consideration must be given to the other budgets so that the firm can be confident the totality comprises an achievable set of guidelines.

Financing budget. A financing budget merely calls attention to the need for cash to meet the repayment of all borrowed funds, with interest, on required dates throughout some period of time. This can, of course, be done in the cash flow budget.

Capital expenditures budget. See our explanation earlier in this chapter on "Planning Future Investments and Capital Budgeting." The requirements of the capital expenditures budget must be included in the cash flow budget, which is explained next.

Cash flow budget. A cash flow budget records all anticipated movements of funds—necessitated by the outcomes of all other budgets—as a statement of inflows or outflows of cash. Managers must assure that cash will be available when it is needed in the amount needed, or a solvency crisis will ensue.

Managers prepare cash flow budgets for various periods of time. Most firms have an annual cash flow budget, with greater detail focused on the initial two or three months. Many larger firms predict the flow of cash for five-year periods, focusing on the sale or acquisition of major assets and on major borrowings, major sales of stock, and major settlements of long-term obligations.

Cash flow, if insufficient to meet obligations as they occur, may necessitate that revisions be made to discretionary budgets, such as revenue, expense, and capital budgets. If the shortfall is relatively minor at a particular time, managers may make it up with a short-term loan (we have done this in our field) provided that future cash flow will be sufficient for repayment. In any event, the important point is to predict accurately the flow of cash and to act to avoid potential shortfalls well before they might occur.

Balance sheet budget. With the above financial budgets in hand, managers naturally want to know how they will affect the balance sheet. Easily assembled if all its inputs have been previously prepared, the pro forma balance sheet permits executives to see the probable outcome, for an indicated period, of all strategic planning moves, management planning, and financial budgeting already done. After analysis of the pro forma balance sheet outcomes, executives may wish to make changes in previous planning, even back to basic strategic planning.

A budgeting process
Figure 6-3 shows the planning and budgeting process followed in HCA on an annual basis.

The dangers of budgeting
The advantages of budgeting are so obvious that no one would deny its necessity in a responsible business endeavor. However, some drawbacks do appear from time to time. Managers should be aware of the following:

1. Budgets that "challenge" those they affect to make greater efforts may cause resentment over time. Budgets should always be based on *reasonable and realistic expectations.*

2. Budgets sometimes cause tunnel vision. Managers may forgo consideration of suddenly emerging opportunities because "I've got my plans made and I don't want to go through all that budget hassle to pursue anything else." In fact, some managers adhere to their budgets with a certain degree of obliviousness to all environmental occurrences.

3. Budgeting may be overdone and become too costly. There are a certain number of people, among both staff and line personnel, who will put too much time into the budget process in order to purportedly achieve complete accuracy. In one respect this is commendable, but operations and strategic vision may suffer as a result of excessive time expended, not to mention added costs.

4. Unless managers anchor budgeting in soundly conceived and proactive strategic planning, it will deteriorate into a process of making little increases or little decreases to "what happened last year." Budgets developed in this way show no vision and budgeting becomes a rote exercise.

One must remember that technical knowledge of accounting is all that is needed to develop budgets, but that good strategic planning necessitates a variety of investigations and information based on a broad number of disciplines. How well a firm plans strategically does indeed reflect the quality of management and possibly is an indicator of leadership itself.

Figure 6-3

Hospital Corporation of America Annual Planning and Budgeting Process (1986)

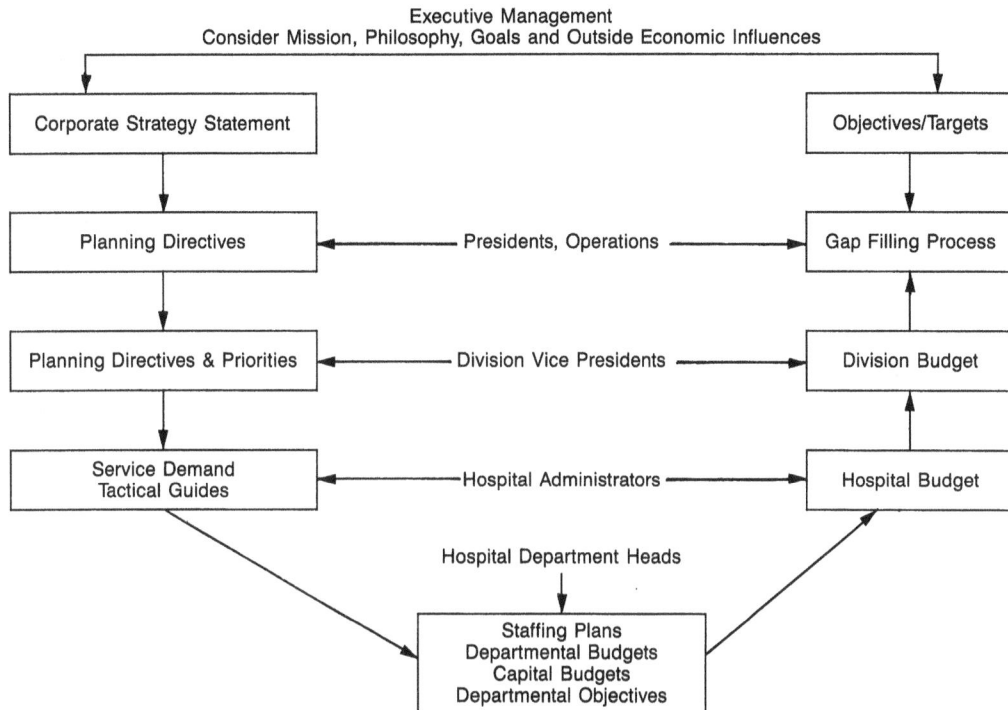

Executive Management
Consider Mission, Philosophy, Goals and Outside Economic Influences

```
┌──────────────────────────┐                                    ┌──────────────────────────┐
│ Corporate Strategy       │                                    │ Objectives/Targets       │
│ Statement                │                                    │                          │
└──────────────────────────┘                                    └──────────────────────────┘
            │                                                               │
            ▼                                                               ▼
┌──────────────────────────┐        Presidents, Operations      ┌──────────────────────────┐
│ Planning Directives      │ ◄───────────────────────────────►  │ Gap Filling Process      │
└──────────────────────────┘                                    └──────────────────────────┘
            │                                                               ▲
            ▼                                                               │
┌──────────────────────────┐        Division Vice Presidents    ┌──────────────────────────┐
│ Planning Directives &    │ ◄───────────────────────────────►  │ Division Budget          │
│ Priorities               │                                    │                          │
└──────────────────────────┘                                    └──────────────────────────┘
            │                                                               ▲
            ▼                                                               │
┌──────────────────────────┐        Hospital Administrators     ┌──────────────────────────┐
│ Service Demand           │ ◄───────────────────────────────►  │ Hospital Budget          │
│ Tactical Guides          │                                    │                          │
└──────────────────────────┘                                    └──────────────────────────┘
            │                        Hospital Department Heads              ▲
            │                                  │                            │
            │                                  ▼                            │
            │                   ┌──────────────────────────┐               │
            └─────────────────► │ Staffing Plans           │ ──────────────┘
                                │ Departmental Budgets     │
                                │ Capital Budgets          │
                                │ Departmental Objectives  │
                                └──────────────────────────┘
```

Source: Reprinted with permission of Hospital Corporation of America.

Zero-base budgeting

In an effort to overcome the negative effects of budgeting by rote (see directly above) and to force managers to prove that continuing specific programs or services would be worthwhile, zero-base budgeting gained some popularity in the 1970s and is still used in some businesses. In zero-base budgeting, each line item in a budget must be justified.

HCA uses a summary level of the zero-base budgeting concept, which *"analyzes operations* and *determines priorities at the program level* (rather than analyzing each activity included in the program)."[55]

See our comments in Chapter 3 regarding zero-base strategic planning.

Cost accounting

Cost accounting has been defined as "an area of accounting whereby costs and related data concerning some object of managerial interest are ascertained, such as the cost of a unit of product, the operating cost of a department, plant, or salesman, or costs associated with a particular investment."[56]

Kaplan recently noted that "cost accounting was developed to fill a need generated by the financial reporting process. Costs had to be allocated so that product-related expenditures could be separated between cost of goods sold and inventory. The emphasis was on fully allocating all costs in an objective and unambiguous way."[57] Despite a simple beginning, cost accounting now employs many sophisticated analytic techniques to solve complex management problems related to both controlling costs and determining prices.

History
In the 1950s and 1960s, accounting systems took into consideration that two types of costs are found in the rendering of services or the manufacture and sale of products. These are (1) fixed costs and (2) variable costs. Conversion to "a direct cost system" was championed by the American Management Association and such authorities as Curtis W. Symonds. In 1966, Symonds stated, "For the vast majority of companies, however, the choice of direct costing is overwhelmingly advantageous (due to its primary characteristic of distinguishing between fixed and variable costs in order to arrive at the 'true' cost of a product at various levels of production)."[58] During the 1970s, many authorities published valuable discussions of topics such as cost definitions, order costing, budgeting, variance analysis, cost allocation, standard costs, direct and absorption costing, and incremental cost.[59] These topics, of course, continue to be discussed, for they relate to managerial accounting procedures in most large and sophisticated business enterprises.

New developments, costs, and validity
The 1980s have seen a fast increasing use of analytic techniques within cost accounting. Regardless of how old the basic knowledge may be, its practical application has been permitted by the computer.

The analytic techniques now employed in managerial accounting necessitate a working knowledge of statistics, probability theory, differential and integral calculus, linear and nonlinear programming, and microeconomic analysis.[60] Students now graduating from our top universities have this knowledge, and they constitute a new breed of experts coming into the business world.

Certainly the cost of using many of the new cost accounting techniques in the real world has to be considered, together with the accuracy and validity of the information after it is in hand. Many managers have raised questions in this regard, and rightly so. However, managerial accounting is a burgeoning science, and many of the analytic techniques have not been completely developed, nor have some found their best areas for application. Our opinion is that, as with other management issues, one has to pay attention to the costs and benefits of applying analytic techniques to various management problems. However, one must also recognize that science will have its say, and no categorical deprecations will obstruct it in the long run. What was it that Jefferson said? "I have sworn eternal hostility toward every form of tyranny over the mind of man." This statement has a message when businessmen, sometimes too practical for their own good and the good of their firms, launch into tirades against "eggheads," "bean counters," and "statistics freaks."

Analytic techniques
Besides the procedures used in direct costing, which provide for the basic differences and individual independence of fixed and variable costs as

they relate to volume changes by product or service, many analytic procedures have been developed that are useful in advanced cost accounting. A sampling of them follows:

- Multiple regression analysis, both linear and nonlinear, is useful in cost estimations and understanding cost behavior variations.

- Cost-volume-profit (CVP) analysis is useful both as a deterministic model and as a model of uncertainty. The deterministic model has proven its usefulness in "profit planning, preparation of flexible budgets, and ex post analysis of operating results."[61] The model of uncertainty has applications pertaining to probabilities relating to product demand levels, profit levels, and achievement of desired profit levels.

- Price-quantity variance analysis is used as a cost control tool in manufacturing operations and to analyze sales and profit performance in many settings.

- Nonlinear programming (NLP) is useful in allocating joint costs to multiple products.

There are many others, and most are either statistical or algebraic algorithms. Also, many, if not most, are inherently involved with quality and productivity.

Planning for cost accounting
How extensively a firm makes use of some of the more esoteric cost accounting techniques for the purpose of problem solving depends on the product or service volumes involved and their monetary value. It also depends on the complexities inherent in production processes, sales efforts, inventory storage, processing of incoming orders and outgoing shipments, staffing, and establishing the best balance among production quality, staffing, and materials cost. Pricing problems may also enter the picture for different product lines jointly produced. The difficulty is to assure an appropriate profit margin on each while at the same time taking into account the effect of competition on product demand. These and many other areas of complexity may necessitate the full-time employment of an accountant skilled in management accounting and more specifically cost accounting. Some firms may wish to employ consultants, and all of the Big Eight accounting firms have qualified people in cost accounting, although some offices in small cities may lack any with the desired level of skills.

Our experience indicates that in firms with low levels of basic management competency, problems requiring expertise in cost accounting may not always be recognized. This being so, consultation overview by qualified consultants is often needed for problem identification. Unquestionably, many businesses are losing untold profits at this moment because of their lack of sophistication in management accounting—as compared with some of their competitors.

Variance analysis

"The motivation behind all variance analysis is to provide insight as to why actual performance differed from that budgeted or expected."[62] The aim, then, of variance analysis is to facilitate "the judging of actual performance against a standard of management expectations. These expectations are established by a budget, profit plan, and standard cost system."[63]

Many examples where performance differed from budgeted expectations arise in all business enterprises, not least in the case of hospitals over the last few years. It is said that to ignore past mistakes dooms one to repeat them. This adage applies to significant operational variations from formally conceived management expectations in business organizations and adequately states the case for variance analysis.

One of the simplest and most frequently encountered problems is where the actual volume of business differs appreciably from the planned volume. Not only should this variation be investigated, but one should also see whether the actual profits have moved as would be expected based on the actual volume and the same costing techniques employed in the original budget. Kaplan has pointed to a number of problem areas where variance analysis should be focused that are separate from the manufacturing process problems to which these analytic techniques were originally applied. One area is constituted by the variations often noted between product sales and profit performances; another is constituted by the computations of mix and yield variances among input materials in a production process (where substitutability exists among the input materials).[64]

For decades, many have debated standards for identifying variances that are sufficiently significant to justify the time and cost of an investigation. No universally accepted model exists. Kaplan concludes, "the value of the proposed models for determining which variances warrant investigations are still to be determined by actual experiment and practice."[65] Nonetheless, all major corporations should develop a procedure and some system of standards for identifying variances deemed worthwhile to investigate in designated areas of budgeted or other quantitatively planned activities or processes.

Kaplan and others have suggested general approaches to decision making in regard to the investigation of variances. Some seem to be better than relying on casual judgment by individual managers. Readers are referred to these sources for information.

Planning the audit function

The independent audit

The Securities and Exchange Commission requires all publicly held companies, with few exceptions, to have an annual independent audit performed. Other firms have such an audit performed for various reasons, not the least of which is to meet requirements by banks, creditors, and insurance companies. In any event, we believe an annual independent audit makes patent good sense. While chief executives of individual hospitals, each of us yearly garnered some consulting advice from auditors that later proved its worth. Although this would not qualify as a reason for an audit, we mention it as a benefit of which others may not be fully aware. Indeed, in selecting an auditor, we would base our selection to some extent on the ability of the auditors to consult with us about the business in which we happened to be engaged. We believe that "putting an audit out to bid" without closely examining the qualifications of the auditors to be assigned is a poor way to select an outside auditing firm, unless of course there are some cogent reasons for doing so.

An independent audit includes an examination of a company's fiscal year-end balance sheet, the statements of income and retained earnings, and the statement of changes in financial position.

A typical auditor's statement appears earlier in this chapter in the "Background" section on "Planning for Financial Accounting." One will note in it the phrase "and accordingly included such tests of the accounting records and such other procedures as we considered necessary in the circumstances." What are these procedures to which reference is made? Alvin Pederson, a partner in Arthur Andersen & Company, noted several years ago the following broad procedures used by auditors:

1. Observation

2. Inspection

3. Confirmation [verification]

4. Comparison

5. Analysis

6. Computation

7. Inquiry[66]

The work of the audit is the responsibility of the auditor alone. The work of preparing for the audit in general and the preparation of all statements the auditor will require for examination is the responsibility of the firm being audited. The firm and the auditor, by working together, can make the audit a meaningful and constructive experience.

Very definitely, the independent audit serves as a monitoring function in the financial management control process. However, the purpose of the independent audit is not to detect fraud, unless of course fraud detection is specifically requested by management. The ultimate responsibility for the financial statements and disclosures presented rests with management, not the auditors.

Internal auditing

Like the auditing performed by independent public accountants, internal auditing also serves as a monitoring function in the financial management control process. Additionally, internal auditing can include appraisals of operational efficiency, depending on the inclinations of managers and the skills possessed by internal auditors. Although the basic purpose of internal auditing is not the disclosure of fraud, it is more likely to detect it than independent auditing, simply because internal auditing involves more detailed examinations.

An internal auditing team performs staff functions, and both its routine and special activities should be clearly understood not only by members of the auditing team itself but by line and other staff managers affected. If this is not so, managers in numerous positions may view the team, particularly when engaged in operational auditing, as something on the order of a "loose cannon."

Specifically, internal auditors should report to an executive *outside* the department of finance and accounting. Preferably, they should report to either the CEO or COO (chief operating officer). Also, they must keep clearly in mind that theirs is a reporting function only. Taking corrective actions is a responsibility of the line organization.

Reports of internal audits should be in writing and given to (1) the managers affected, (2) the auditor's immediate supervisor or manager, and (3) the executive who was assigned responsibility for the internal auditing function.

The main factors that can make internal auditing a success are three:

1. clear communications about all aspects of the auditing function

2. the technical competence of the auditing team, together with the dedication and sincerity with which the work is carried out

3. the follow-up, including needed corrective actions

Planning to establish an internal auditing function involves the same actions and the same type of skills needed for setting up any other company service, with added attention being given to the three factors listed above.

Tax planning

The Tax Reform Act of 1986 will not decrease the importance of tax planning in business enterprises. Indeed, it will increase the complexity of such planning, at least for the next several years.

> Although the top corporate rate has been reduced from 46 percent to 34 percent, Federal revenue from business taxes will increase by a total of more than $120 billion over a six-year period. The sheer magnitude of the new business tax burdens will inevitably increase tax considerations in economic decision making, contrary to the stated goal of tax reform.
>
> Due to the broad scope of this legislation, involving new provisions subject to extensive interpretation, tax payers will be faced with many major planning challenges.[67]

The new federal tax code incorporates changes concerning general business items and the special actions and transactions of corporations. Most major accounting and tax consulting firms have published detailed information regarding these changes, and in any case the subject is too broad for further comment here.

Besides their obligations regarding federal income, excise, and payroll taxes, business organizations must also plan activities necessary for paying all state levies, including income and franchise taxes, property taxes, and sales and use taxes. Local jurisdictions usually impose taxes in some manner, and these too must receive consideration. Multinational companies, of course, must take account of the requirements of countries in which they operate.

Factors that may affect a business firm's tax planning function include the type or types of product or service lines; the firm's size; the type of legal entity it is; the bases used in departmentation as well as the degree of decentralization (see Chapter 4); the number of local, state, and national tax jurisdictions in which the entity operates; and the availability and cost of independent professional tax consultants.

Areas which a firm's tax department should address for purposes of planning include the following:

- Special or extraordinary business actions and transactions, such as the acquisition of major assets and their subsequent use, sales of major assets, corporate acquisitions, liquidations, mergers, reorganizations, etc.

- Scheduling and discharging various tax compliance functions, including required filings and payments. (Although some functions, e.g., the payment of property taxes, may best be decentralized in large corporations, policy making should be retained centrally.)

- Data and information gathering referenced both to special actions and transactions and to compliance functions.

- Audits and examinations, primarily by the IRS.

- Necessary adjustments and settlements.

- Companywide coordination of tax management functions.

The first planning done by any firm regarding taxes should be concerned with organizing a tax department. After appointment of a single person to whom responsibility for tax management is assigned, that person must decide to whom to delegate authority and assign responsibility relating to planning and implementing functions companywide. He or she must also plan for needed communication with other elements of the finance and accounting department and with key executives throughout the organization. The question of how much reliance, if any, will be placed on an independent tax authority and what functions that authority will perform must also be answered.

A key factor involved in tax planning is the ongoing education of all those assigned to accomplish the function. There has been continual change in tax laws, and the new tax reform act will not remain unchanged. Therefore, tax personnel should have a planned program of inservice education. The head of the tax unit should also have an ongoing plan to keep all executives abreast of tax laws and should proactively implement the plan.

Some years ago John P. Kelsey of Price Waterhouse & Company noted, "Probably the most important service to a corporation is the tax planning function which involves the tax department in the dynamic role of changing or modifying events before their completion to achieve a desirable end result. It is imperative that top management of the corporation recognize this fact and create the proper environment to stimulate creative tax planning."[68] This statement still holds true today.

Owing to the extreme involvement of tax managers with the unique problems of their own individual company, a tendency toward tunnel vision may develop. To negate this, all major organizations should have consultations with competent tax advisors who deal with a wide range of enterprises. Adaptations of solutions used in other companies can be suggested by such advisors. If this occurs, their fee (usually rather costly) will be paid many times over. Thus, while independent tax advisors might not be required to perform activities directly involved in tax planning, periodic consultations with them, in our opinion, are highly desirable.

Planning risk management

Frederick C. Church, Jr., defines risk management in this manner: "Risk management therefore is the process of conserving your assets and resources (human, financial, physical and natural) and your revenues against the effects of accidental loss and waste."[69] Church states further, "Risk management's objective is to limit loss, provide catastrophe protection and reduce TCR (total cost of risk)."[70]

HCA has maintained a comprehensive risk management program, and its purpose has been "to minimize exposures to loss through effective quality assurance, loss control, and claims management programs. Also involved are decisions when to retain risk to loss within the corporate family (primarily through HCA's wholly owned subsidiary, the Parthenon Insurance Company) and when to purchase insurance from non-related companies."[71]

The first step in planning for risk management revolves around organizational decisions. The first decision concerns what individual will be responsible for the program of risk management. After organizational planning is under way or even completed, the manager placed in charge of the program and the CEO should draft statements of policy regarding various facets of the program, including steps to prevent loss as well as types and levels of insurance protection against loss when it does occur.

Parthenon Insurance Company, which has had responsibility for risk management in HCA, possesses six basic departments: administration, accounting/finance, quality assurance, loss control, underwriting, and claims. After its organization, Parthenon drafted statements of policy regarding the functions and responsibilities of each of these departments for the guidance of all concerned. Later procedures provided for the implementation of the program throughout the company.

Following organizational planning and formulation of policies, all companies must analyze their exposure to risk. Betterly notes, "Checklists for surveying company risks are available from insurers, trade associations, and other insurance managers."[72] In his recent book *Avoiding Surprises*, Church includes a worksheet for a "Cost of Risk Survey" and checklists for assets (owned, rented, or used), property exposure, and liability exposure.[73]

Church, Betterly, and many other authorities believe that after an analysis of risk has been made, a company must measure or evaluate risk in terms of loss in dollars. The purpose is to determine the possible extent of loss in such areas as property (buildings, inventory, and equipment) and liability (e.g., with regard to products, crime, fidelity, worker's compensation, motor vehicles, etc.). Knowing the areas of loss and the possible extent of loss, management can then plan for controlling it as much as possible and for insuring against it where control fails.

Control programs vary from company to company. HCA's primary control program has been overseen by a quality assurance department (a unit of Parthenon Insurance Company), whose function is

> to give support to HCA affiliates [primarily hospitals] to design and implement hospital based assurance programs, to monitor existing components of quality assurance, to evaluate effectiveness in enhancing patient care and to assist the loss control and claims administration functions of Parthenon Insurance Company in the design and implementation of hospital based risk management programs.[74]

Within each operating entity of HCA, there exists an ongoing, locally managed program of quality assurance, and these have proved very effective in controlling losses from risks. The central department of quality assurance provides assistance, support, and control to each of these decentralized programs. All programs also conform to the standards for such programs published by the Joint Commission on Accreditation for Hospitals (JCAH).

Despite best attempts at controlling losses, they will inevitably occur. Church states that "the effects on your organization can be severe unless a plan exists for dealing with these unfortunate events."[75] HCA has developed detailed procedures and forms for reporting incidents where losses can occur and for managing claims which may flow therefrom, and all major companies should do likewise.

Determining how to finance risk constitutes a major planning task in all risk management programs. Church correctly notes that financing risk can be done either by (1) direct retention within the organization (through a variety of methods) or by (2) transfer of the risk to others (also accomplished in several ways). Decisions about use—considering the types of risks involved and the possible extent of loss attached to each type—are an important part of risk management in any major corporation. In the case of HCA, executives of Parthenon Insurance Company have carried on continuous study and planning concerning this matter and the matter of selecting (1) the best financing plan where risks and costs have been retained by HCA through one means or another (in some instances through insurance policies issued by Parthenon) and (2) the best financing plan where risks and costs have been transferred to others (in some instances by purchase of insurance from unrelated companies). There are many, many aspects of risk financing, and we refer our readers to other sources for full discussions.

Administering the risk management function, depending on the degree of risk, can be a complex undertaking that itself involves major planning activities, such as the development of policies, procedures, methods, and rules, together with budgets, schedules, and a variety of single use plans for nonrecurring events. The risk management department must be involved in planning in order to assure that its needs concerning data processing, records retention, and management information are met. A program of inservice education that will extend throughout the organization must often be planned, with timely updates on methods of loss control being published and distributed to specific organizational units. Reporting must be planned so as to assure the efficacy of the subsequent control process. Typically, reports to top management that include a cost trend analysis should be planned. These reports should be made at least once a year.

Selection of a broker can be a major planning decision, depending on the role a brokerage firm will play in a company's risk management program and on the extent of in-house risk management knowledge. In the case of HCA, Parthenon Insurance Company employs a highly skilled team possessing knowledge about all aspects of risk management, and the selection of a broker, though important, may not possess the significance that it does in smaller firms, where such knowledge may not be available.

Finally, a periodic audit should be planned for any significant risk management program. Accomplished by outside experts, such audits often reveal possible changes that will save appreciable sums, both by controlling loss and by reducing the cost of loss when it does occur.

Summary

Five basic subfunctions compose the overall financial function in major corporations, and some authorities discuss several other more specific activities as financial subfunctions (such as pension planning). The five we have discussed in this chapter are (1) financial planning, (2) accounting, (3) auditing, (4) tax planning, and (5) risk management. HCA's Department of Finance and Accounting has main units for just these same subfunctions.

Financial planning is intended to assure wise use of capital funds. Accounting provides quantitative information about organizational units that is useful in decision making. Auditing is a control function which must be planned; its objective is to see that accepted accounting principles and standing plans are observed in accounting activities and in preparations of financial statements. Tax planning involves interpretation of tax laws to assure that a firm's ordinary and extraordinary economic actions and transactions incur no more tax liabilities than absolutely required. Risk management involves protecting a firm's assets and profitability against fortuitous, accidental, and unexpected circumstances.

The first step in planning the financial function is to devise an organizational plan. No single organizational structure can be cited as ideal, and wide variations exist. All of the usual steps of organizational planning (see Chapter 4) apply in devising a structure for a finance and accounting department.

In establishing the financial accounting subfunction, care must be taken to observe accounting safeguards and controls. Data processing has drastically affected both the organization and the conduct of the accounting subfunction over the last two decades, but one principle still has to be maintained: Accounting safeguards and controls must be respected and accounting information must be limited to those with a right to access.

There are two major activities in financial planning: (1) assets planning and (2) capital financing. Assets planning concerns decisions about the type of investments a firm should make or maintain. Capital budgeting, part of assets planning, involves an evaluation and selection process for new investments. Some authorities believe capital budgets should more properly be subsumed as a budgeting function under accounting, but we disagree.

Capital finance planning involves the cost of capital and the sources of capital finance. The cost of capital depends on the type of asset in which investment will be made, the available sources of money, and the various features of the capital financing instrument used.

The two basic sources of capital funds are (1) the sale of equity securities and (2) the sale of debt securities. Consideration of many factors must be made in order to determine which source a company should use at a given point in its life cycle.

In business corporations, planning for financial accounting requires the preparation of four basic financial statements: the balance sheet, the statement of revenues and expenses, the statement of changes in financial position, and the statement of stockholders' equity. All of these statements must be prepared according to generally accepted accounting principles. They should also be prepared according to a time schedule, with timeliness a top priority, especially for the statement of revenues and expenses.

Electronic data processing continues to have a significant impact on many areas of the financial function, and sound planning is necessary in relation to it. Some of the more common EDP applications pertain to order processing/purchasing, inventory control, accounts payable, payroll, billings, accounts receivable, general accounting, and management information.

EDP can also be used to perform ratio analysis. We discussed a number of ratios in this chapter, including liquidity ratios, financing ratios, activity ratios, and profit ratios.

We limited discussion of the broad field of managerial accounting to three basic components: (1) budgeting, (2) cost accounting, and (3) variance analysis.

In most companies, a service demand budget, a revenue budget, and an expense budget compose the operating budget. (The service demand budget is called by several other names.) Operating budgets feed into financial budgets, which include financing budgets, capital expenditure budgets, cash flow budgets, and balance sheet budgets. Reconciliation of all these budgets is in the best interest of any firm. The cash flow budget, of course, must be positive, and, if not, reconsideration of the others must be accomplished to make it so.

Although no responsible business executive would propose operating without appropriate budgets, there are some dangers in budgeting, primarily psychological, that should be recognized.

Cost accounting is an area where costs and related data concerning some object of managerial interest are ascertained, such as the cost of a product (by unit), the operating cost of a department, a plant, or a salesman, or the costs involved in an investment.

Besides procedures used in direct costing, other analytic cost accounting procedures have been developed. These include (1) multiple regression analysis, both linear and nonlinear; (2) cost-volume-profit analyses (CVP), both as a deterministic model and as a model of uncertainty; (3) price-quantity variance analysis; and (4) nonlinear programming (NLP). Many others exist, representing statistical or algebraic algorithms. Most have involvement with the concepts of quality and productivity.

Variance analysis seeks to determine why actual performance differed from that budgeted or expected. No universal model has been developed, and criteria for when to consider variances differ greatly. Despite this, every company should develop its own criteria for deciding when variance analysis should be performed.

Two types of audits exist in most firms, especially those that are investor owned, such as HCA. The two types are (1) the independent audit performed by outside accounting experts, and (2) the internal audit performed by internal specialists.

The Tax Reform Act of 1986 will not diminish the need for tax planning. Indeed, it will increase this need regarding the federal tax. Of course, the complexities of state and local taxes also demand planning.

Areas that a company's tax unit should address in planning include special actions and transactions, for example, acquisition of assets and their subsequent use, sales of major assets, and corporate mergers, acquisitions, liquidations, and reorganizations. Other areas are scheduling and discharge of tax compliance functions, data and information flow, audits and examinations by the IRS, adjustments and settlements, and coordination of tax management functions.

After organizational planning for the tax function, proactive policies and procedures must be formulated. A plan for educating tax personnel and key executives about dynamic tax laws ought to be developed. The time to anticipate the tax consequences of an action or transaction is *before* it is consummated. Influencing such actions and transactions probably constitutes the greatest contribution of a tax department.

We view periodic outside audits of the tax department's work by independent experts as highly valuable in preventing tunnel vision.

Risk management tries to protect assets and resources of all types, together with revenues, against accidental loss and waste. It also tries to limit loss, provide protection from catastrophes, and reduce the total cost of risk (TCR).

As with the tax function, organizing is the first planning step for risk management. The next step involves the drafting of policy statements about the program as a whole and about each risk management function.

Parthenon Insurance Company possesses overall responsibility for HCA's risk management program. It comprises six departments, most of which are similar to those found in many other major corporations. These are administration, accounting/finance, quality assurance, loss control, underwriting, and claims management.

Exposure to risk must be analyzed, the extent of possible loss due to exposure must be determined, and measures for controlling loss must be devised. Where failure to control can be anticipated, insurance against loss ought to be obtained. Many firms sponsor an insurance company to write policies, or obtain policies through a broker, to cover losses of various types, primarily catastrophic losses.

Planning for risk management also involves data processing programs, records retention, research, and management information distribution. In addition, it includes planning for the control process, primarily through monitoring claims and losses and reporting to top management.

In many firms, selection of an insurance brokerage firm and subsequent dealings with this firm constitute a major area of planning.

Notes

1. George L. Chamberlin, "Organizing the Financial Function," in *Handbook of Business Administration*, ed. H.B. Maynard (New York: McGraw-Hill, 1967), 9–3.

2. Ezra Solomon, "Financial Planning," in *Handbook of Business Administration*, ed. H.B. Maynard (New York: McGraw-Hill, 1967), 9–9.

3. Ibid., 9–10.

4. Accounting Principles Board, Statement No. 4, *Basic Concepts and Accounting Principles Underlying Financial Statements of Business Enterprises* (New York: American Institute of Certified Public Accountants, 1970), par. 40. Copyright 1970 by the American Institute of Public Accountants, Inc. Quoted in Charles J. Woelfel, *An Introduction to Financial Accounting* (New York: McGraw-Hill, 1984), 8.

5. Woelfel, *Introduction to Financial Accounting*, 8.

6. Michael H. Granof, *Financial Accounting*, 2d ed. (Englewood Cliffs, N.J.: Prentice-Hall, 1980), 5.

7. William O. Cleverley, *Essentials of Hospital Finance* (Rockville, Md.: Aspen Publishers, 1978), 9.

8. Ibid.

9. Robert S. Kaplan, *Advanced Management Accounting* (1982), 1. Reprinted by permission of Prentice-Hall, Inc., Englewood, N.J.

10. Alvin Pederson, "The Audit," in *Handbook of Business Administration*, ed. H.B. Maynard (New York: McGraw-Hill, 1967), 10–87.

11. George M. Betterley, "Risk Management," in *Handbook of Business Administration*, ed. H.B. Maynard (New York: McGraw-Hill, 1967), 9–78.

12. Chamberlin, "Organizing the Financial Function," 9–4.

13. Ibid., 9–4, 9–5.

14. Ibid., 9–7.

15. Ibid., 9–5.

16. Solomon, "Financial Planning," 9–10.

17. Ibid., 9–11.

18. Ibid.

19. Sidney Davidson et al., *Intermediate Accounting*, 4th ed. (Chicago: Dryden Press, 1985), 1232.

20. Solomon, "Financial Planning," 9–12.

21. J. Fred Weston, "Evaluating Company Performance," in *Handbook of Business Administration*, ed. H.B. Maynard (New York: McGraw-Hill, 1967), 9–12.

22. Ibid., 3–72, 3–73.

23. Donald D. Deming and Robert G. Murdick, "Equipment Replacement Analysis," in *Handbook of Business Administration*, ed. H.B. Maynard (New York: McGraw-Hill, 1967), 7–65.

24. Ibid., 7–67, 7–68.

25. Raymond I. Reul, "Techniques for Evaluating Prospective Investments," in *Handbook of Business Administration*, ed. H.B. Maynard (New York: McGraw-Hill, 1967), 3–81, 3–82.

26. Ibid., 3–81.

27. Cleverley, *Essentials of Hospital Finance*, 153.

28. Solomon, "Financial Planning," 9–14, 9–15.

29. Ibid., 9–14.

30. Ibid.

31. Ibid., 9–14, 9–15.

32. Reul, "Techniques for Evaluating Prospective Investments," 3–86.

33. Davidson et al., *Intermediate Accounting*, 213.

34. Cleverley, *Essentials of Hospital Finance*, 160.

35. Solomon, "Financial Planning," 9–15.

36. Cleverley, *Essentials of Hospital Finance*, 162.

37. Ibid., 157–158.

38. HCA, *1987 Annual Report* (Nashville: HCA, 1987), 35.

39. David F. Hawkins, *Financial Reporting: Practices of Corporations* (Homewood, Ill.: Dow Jones-Irwin, 1972), 59–69.

40. Davidson et al., *Intermediate Accounting*, 30–31.

41. Richard L. Nolan, "Controlling the Cost of Data Services," in *Catching Up with the Computer Revolution*, ed. Kenneth R. Andrews (New York: Wiley, 1983), 315.

42. Harold J. McLaughlin, *Building Your Business Plan* (New York: Wiley, 1985), 204.

43. Cleverley, *Essentials of Hospital Finance*, 68.

44. McLaughlin, *Building Your Business Plan*, 204.

45. Cleverley, *Essentials of Hospital Finance*, 69.

46. McLaughlin, *Building Your Business Plan*, 204.

47. Ibid., 205.

48. Ibid., 206.

49. Cleverley, *Essentials of Hospital Finance*, 74.

50. Kaplan, *Advanced Management Accounting*, xi. Reprinted by permission of Prentice-Hall, Inc., Englewood Cliffs, N.J.

51. Cleverley, *Essentials of Hospital Finance*, 145.

52. Stephan Landekich, "Budgeting," in *Handbook of Business Administration*, ed. H.B. Maynard (New York: McGraw-Hill, 1967), 10–41.

53. Richard M. Steers, Gerardo R. Ungson, and Richard T. Mowday, *Managing Effective Organizations* (Boston: Kent Publishing Company, 1985), 220.

54. Ibid., 222.

55. HCA, *Corporate Office 1987 Planning Procedures Manual* (Internal document, HCA, Nashville, August 1986), 6–7.

56. L.J. Benninger, "Cost Accounting," in *Handbook of Business Administration*, ed. H.B. Maynard (New York: McGraw-Hill, 1967), 10–13.

57. Kaplan, *Advanced Management Accounting*, 1. Reprinted by permission of Prentice-Hall, Inc., Englewood Cliffs, N.J.

58. Curtis W. Symonds, "Effective Conversion to Direct Cost System," *Financial Executive*, September 1966, 3.

59. Kaplan, *Advanced Management Accounting*, 6.

60. Ibid.

61. Ibid., 181. Reprinted by permission of Prentice-Hall, Inc., Englewood Cliffs, N.J.

62. Ibid., 300. Reprinted by permission of Prentice-Hall, Inc., Englewood Cliffs, N.J.

63. Ibid. Reprinted by permission of Prentice-Hall, Inc., Englewood Cliffs, N.J.

64. Ibid., 308.

65. Ibid., 320. Reprinted by permission of Prentice-Hall, Inc., Englewood Cliffs, N.J.

66. Pederson, "The Audit," 10–89.

67. Ernst & Whinney, *Tax Reform—1986* (1986), introductory page.

68. John P. Kelsey, "Tax Management," in *Handbook of Business Administration*, ed. H.B. Maynard (New York: McGraw-Hill, 1967), 9–68.

69. Frederick C. Church, Jr., *Avoiding Surprises* (Boston: Boston Risk Management Corporation, 1982), 8.

70. Ibid.

71. Parthenon Insurance Company, *Risk Management Manual* (Nashville: HCA, 1986), introductory page.

72. George M. Betterly, "Risk Management," in *Handbook of Business Administration*, ed. H.B. Maynard (New York: McGraw-Hill, 1967), 9–81.

73. Church, *Avoiding Surprises*, 15–49.

74. Parthenon Insurance Company, *Risk Management Manual*, A–7.

75. Church, *Avoiding Surprises*, 131.

Chapter 7

Human resource planning

Elements of Management
in Corporations

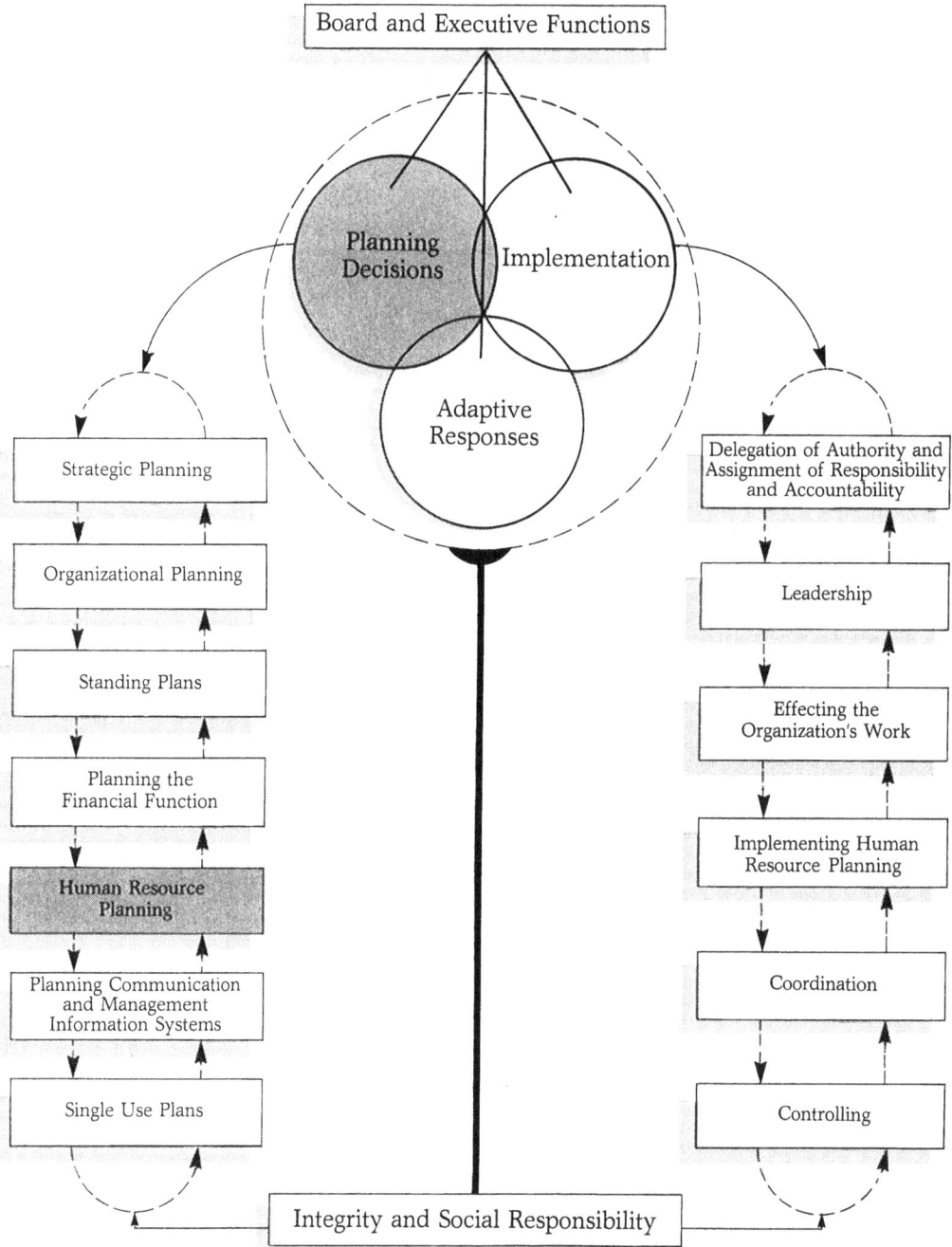

Board and Executive Functions

Planning Decisions

Implementation

Adaptive Responses

Strategic Planning

Organizational Planning

Standing Plans

Planning the Financial Function

Human Resource Planning

Planning Communication and Management Information Systems

Single Use Plans

Delegation of Authority and Assignment of Responsibility and Accountability

Leadership

Effecting the Organization's Work

Implementing Human Resource Planning

Coordination

Controlling

Integrity and Social Responsibility

7

Authoritative perspectives

In an interview with *Fortune* reporter Ann Reilly Dowd, President Reagan stated his personal approach to human resource management (HRM). "Surround yourself with the best people you can find, delegate authority and don't interfere as long as the policy you've decided upon is being carried out."[1] This statement reveals the principle that stood at the heart of the staffing plan for his cabinet and for other high administrative posts: Surround yourself with the best people you can find. Although one may not agree with many or any of the goals sought after and attained by the Reagan administration (nor with the controls instituted), an objective assessment of its first six years (up to the date of Dowd's article) would have to admit that its accomplishments were many. And without detracting from Reagan's personal charisma and other leadership traits, there is little doubt that his simple staffing philosophy contributed greatly to his administration's initial successes. (His lack of understanding of the control process may have contributed to many of its failures.)

In his recent book *Managing*, Harold Geneen revealed the basis for some of ITT's phenomenal success during his tenure as president.

> We set out to hire the very best people in the industry that we could find. I did not want glamorous, glib-talking men who got by on their coiffeured good looks or family connections . . . what we sought were capable, experienced men who were motivated, who wanted to achieve and to make something of their lives, and who were not afraid to work for what they wanted. . . .
>
> In order to attract and to keep these kinds of executives at ITT, we paid our people a base salary 10 percent higher than the industry averages and supplemented these salaries with generous year-end bonuses and salary increases as merited.[2]

Geneen's words enunciate clearly a general policy for both executive selection and compensation.

One of the eight characteristics found by Peters and Waterman to be possessed by America's best run companies is the achievement of productivity through people. Peters and Waterman's findings in this area center on the importance of the contributions of operating personnel (as opposed to those of managers) and reveal that America's best run companies use the proven research findings of the behavioral sciences in the area of motivation to achieve high levels of productivity.[3] Many of these findings pertain directly to specific areas of human resources planning: "Treat people as adults. Treat them as partners; treat them with dignity; treat them with respect. Treat *them*—not capital spending and automation—as the primary source of productivity gains."[4]

Peters and Waterman quote Bill Hewlett about the basis of Hewlett-Packard's phenomenal success: "It is the tradition of treating every individual with consideration and respect and recognizing personal achievement."[5] They also quote from the published philosophy of the highly successful Dana Corporation:

- It is critical to provide and discuss all organization performance figures with all of our people.

- We have an obligation to provide training and the opportunity for development to our production people.

- It is essential to provide job security.

- Create incentive programs.[6]

Peters and Waterman also note some research published in the *Wall Street Journal* about objectives in the employee selection process at Delta Airlines. "Stewardesses, for example, are culled from thousands of applicants, interviewed twice and then sent to Delta psychologist, Dr. Sidney Janus. 'I try to determine their sense of cooperativeness or sense of team work. At Delta, you don't just join a company, you join an objective [team].'"[7] Regarding Delta's promotion, compensation, and employee retention policies, Peters and Waterman found that "the company promotes from within, pays better than most airlines, and goes to any length to avoid laying off workers in a traditionally cyclic industry."[8]

These authors sum up their findings regarding employee training thus: "IBM invests heavily in training. Caterpillar, similarly, takes its people through extensive training. . . . Heavy doses of early on-the-job training also mark HP, P & G, and Schlumbergen."[9]

Finally, Peters and Waterman found highly successful companies generally rely on the free sharing of evaluative information (appearing to some extent as nonevaluative) and peer pressure for application of the control process.[10] Setting objectives (planning), effecting work processes to gain the objectives (implementation), securing and sharing evaluative information (monitoring and reporting), comparing evaluative information with results (measuring), and using peer pressure to correct shortfalls (taking corrective measures) are all general policies of the best run companies.

Beer et al., in *Managing Human Assets*, note that many *Fortune* 500 companies probably do not have consistent policies regarding human resources. They may, in fact, appear to their employees to be inconsistent.[11] "This lack of consistency probably makes it harder for employees to attach a meaning to their relationship with the firm other than one dominated by their own self interest."[12] It seems reasonable that if a sizeable percentage of *Fortune* 500 companies do not have consistent policies regarding their employees, an even higher percentage of other companies also are inconsistent.

Beer et al. further note, "New hires will be motivated to come to work for a company and current employees will stay if they perceive the company's wages, location, organizational climate, advancement opportunities, job security and working conditions as more attractive than those of other companies."[13] No company should offer what it can't deliver. However, every company must be competitive and must realize its human resources are the most valuable of all assets. Further, every company ought to have a philosophy and policies that are consistent and worthy of pride. Each company should then use its philosophy and policy statements as a centerpiece for recruiting and retention efforts.

The outlook at HCA

From the outset, the founders of HCA recognized the importance of high-quality, well-paid people both at the hospital administration level and at the level where patient care is delivered. HCA's administrators, unlike those of most other investor-owned health care systems, have had nearly complete latitude in managing their hospitals, and this has enabled the corporation to recruit the best professionals in the field.

When Don MacNaughton came aboard as chairman and CEO in 1978, it was soon clear he concurred with the philosophy and policies of the founders regarding individual work autonomy (to be tempered with realistic controls). MacNaughton probably stated his philosophy about management of human resources best in a notable guest lecture at a symposium in honor of John T. Conner, who was retiring as chairman of the board and CEO of the Allied Chemical Corporation. MacNaughton said, "Individuals work best and produce most when they (1) know what their job is, (2) know how it fits into the total picture and overall goals, and (3) are permitted to carry it out with a minimum of interference from any one else."[14]

In the same lecture, he presented a brief but excellent statement of philosophy concerning human resource management.

> If you will allow me an oversimplification, I am tempted to say that the sum total of a good manager is one who recruits well, trains well, delegates authority, establishes a simple but sound system of rewards and penalties, a simple but sound system of evaluation and communication, challenges the people to do things and then gets out of the way.[15]

When MacNaughton stepped down from the post of chairman of the board and CEO of HCA, the morale of the company's employees had never been higher and enthusiasm for work probably was at its peak.

Dr. Frist, Jr., who succeeded MacNaughton, obviously possesses the same philosophy of human resources management. In fact, Dr. Frist was one of HCA's founders and thus was among those originally responsible for its personnel-centered philosophy. He seems to be still committed to this philosophy that has undergirded policies toward personnel since the firm's first days of operation.

Our view

In Chapter 17, "Integrity and Social Responsibility," we make the point that employees stake their future on the success of a business organization just as surely as do shareholders. In many instances, their stakes are even greater than those of shareholders. We also argue that attempts to squeeze employees in order to provide short-term benefits to shareholders are self-defeating. Our personal philosophy coincides with the ideas and opinions we have cited above. Both of us, having risen through the ranks, know firsthand the views of operating personnel (we have both worked as operating personnel), first-line supervisors and middle managers (we have served in these capacities), and top management (we have held top positions for appreciable periods, and one of us, after serving as President and COO of HCA, now holds the post of chairman and CEO of HealthTrust Inc.). Our experience, together with constant study of the literature on the art of management, has convinced us that the personnel of any organization is its greatest asset and must be so regarded and managed.

Philosophy and policy

Within the context of this discussion, we will take any given philosophy to be a "theory underlying a sphere of activity" and manifested as a set of expressed "general beliefs, concepts and attitudes of an individual or group."[16] With regard to organizational policies pertaining to human resource planning, the philosophy of top management should constitute the underlying theory. This philosophy, in order to be delineated and eventually implemented, must be expressed. Top management (i.e., the board of directors, where existing, and the executives) expresses the philosophy both directly in explicit statements of philosophy and indirectly through policies and often through goals and objectives that relate specifically to human resources.

Thus, a philosophy should be the basis for policies and goals pertaining to human resource management. Broadly speaking, policies in turn provide the basis for procedures, rules, and methods, and the mission and goals provide the basis for objectives, which may concern various quantitative and qualitative aspects of human resource management, such as numbers and types of employee requirements; employee recruitment, selection, training, development; and so on.

The importance of having a philosophy

Since a firm's philosophy provides the foundation for policies (plans) that pertain to human resource management, the board and the executives should take extreme care in formulating it. Although many, if not most, business organizations have no formally enunciated philosophy in this regard, their omission should not be regarded as appropriate. In fact, we view it as a serious dereliction. Of course, the policies that top management does enunciate will for the most part reflect the philosophy that is held, whether it has been articulated or not. In many instances, however, top management depends on staff personnel and the upper levels of middle managers to formulate policies of all types. With no articulated philosophy to guide such personnel, it is likely that the particular philosophies of a variety of individuals will be manifested in the policies. Consistency will obviously be at risk. One might claim that so long as top management carefully reviews all policies, such policies can be made consistent with the firm's philosophy. Although this may sometimes be true, it certainly won't be true in every case. Further, it is unlikely top management will fully review all policies formulated by lower-level managers.

Formally published statements of philosophy also set the tone for all management actions concerning human resources—the day-to-day interfaces between managers and operating personnel and between managers themselves. These are countless in number, and policies can be piled upon policies without ever creating a general approach to all such interfaces.

Undoubtedly, statements of philosophy serve three important practical purposes: (1) to guide policy regarding human resource management, (2) to set the tone for the conduct of the work of personnel departments, and (3) to establish a frame of reference for all interfaces that occur among personnel (especially managers and operating personnel) that are not covered by policies.

A fourth general benefit of having carefully prepared and formally enunciated statements of philosophy is that they make for good public relations—with regard to the general public, prospective employees, and existing staff. Although some firms with formal statements of philosophy about human resource management may sometimes fail to adhere to them, there is considerable truth in the adage that "you are what you say you are."

Current HRM philosophies

The research findings of the behavioral sciences provide the backdrop for modern philosophies concerning human resource management in organizations.

> The behavioral sciences cover six basic fields: anthropology, political science, economics, sociology, psychiatry, and psychology. In their most elemental sense the behavioral sciences are concerned with the study of (1) human values, or what people want and need; (2) human behavior, or how they act and why; (3) their institutions or what people get; and (4) their power structure, or the nature of power and how it is used.[17]

(We note, as an aside, that the above statement by Robert Sampson supports our opinion that management will never be a separate science, which we expressed in Chapter 1. Management is an art, involving the distillation not merely of the above named sciences but of several others as well.)

The findings of behavioral scientists about human values and needs, motivations, leadership, morale, attitudes, human engineering, training, communications, group dynamics, authority and power, organizational conflict, and resistance to change provide evidence suitable for individuals to develop a philosophy that relates to all specific areas of human resource management. Some of these findings we briefly discuss in various chapters of this text. Others can be found in the wide range of behavioral science literature oriented to organizational management.

No single statement of philosophy will suffice for all firms. Steers, Ungson, and Mowday have convincingly stated, "Perhaps the most important influence on human resource management is the nature of the organization."[18] Certainly, the nature and size of a firm will determine what types of employees are needed (and in what numbers), and various types and numbers of employees will respond somewhat differently to many aspects of a philosophy of human resource management. Generally, however, today's elevated educational levels and high standards of living, together with the keen competition in most job markets and the strong demands for individual freedom and respect, require that there be opportunities for advancement and job satisfaction within the organizations where our nation's labor force seeks employment. We still have blue collar jobs and will continue to have them. But even these exhibit considerably higher levels of sophistication than only a few years ago. Continual advances in education and technology will certainly force work in all employment positions to become increasingly sophisticated.

Nonetheless, the importance of the behavioral sciences in human resource planning must not overshadow the property rights of shareholders and the necessity for retaining solvency and indeed for making a profit. This being so, although we strongly believe that putting the tenets of the behavioral sciences into practice unlocks the initiative and perseverance of employees and helps to achieve both personal and organizational goals, we also strongly believe in the need for effective controls. These are necessary not only to assure the accomplishment of a firm's goals and objectives but also to protect the interests of the vast majority of the employees themselves, together with the interests of the various others who have a stake in the success of the firm.

We noted above that no statement of philosophy about human resource management will be fully applicable to even a large segment of business organizations. However, we provide in Exhibit 7-1 a brief statement of philosophy that may be applicable to a limited number and that may provide guidance to many others.

Policies related to HRM

Policies relating to human resource management should be based on and flow from a consciously formulated philosophy, whether or not it has been articulated in published statements. Of course, we strongly recommend publishing statements of philosophy for the benefit of all, especially rank-and-file employees, who may never find time or feel the inclination to read policies, which are sometimes quite lengthy and detailed.

In Chapter 5, we stated that a policy is a "broadly defined guide for organizational members to observe in their behavior or to follow in the performance of their management or operational responsibilities." Pol-

Exhibit 7-1

The XYZ Corporation Statement of Philosophy on Human Resource Management

The human resource of XYZ Corporation constitutes our single most important asset. Efforts toward societal contributions and profits would be futile without a clear recognition of this fact. Imperatively, we must employ the skilled and talented, and we must provide for their subsequent continuous development and personal advancement. These facts being so, we have formulated and set forth certain statements that reflect strongly held views about human resource management. These statements will be applicable in all interfaces that occur between the corporation and its personnel, either individually or collectively.

I.   To the greatest extent possible, management and personnel should be viewed as partners. Neither can successfully exist without the other. Mutual respect represents an ideal to be actively sought.

II.   Within the context of an equitably determined schedule of salaries and benefits, management will pursue policies derived from these philosophical expressions that result in the employment of the most qualified persons available for respective new positions. However, the concept of "promotions from within" shall be respected.

III.   Management views every personnel position as being important and every person occupying a position as an important team member. Every person employed shall have an opportunity for personal advancement and growth consistent with the success of the corporation.

IV.   The commonly recognized innate needs of all humans shall be respected by the corporation. These are as follows:

1. The need for a physically and emotionally safe and secure working environment.
2. The need for remuneration sufficient to satisfy physiological necessities, with opportunities to advance toward financial security.
3. The need to exercise some degree of control over one's working environment.
4. The need to accomplish, achieve, and succeed.
5. The need for acceptance and esteem by both peers and management.
6. The need for self-expression and eventually, self-actualization.

Although the corporation shall accept significant responsibility for satisfaction of the first three of these listed needs, satisfaction of the final three will depend, in great part, upon individual employee initiative. Finances permitting, management believes that an environment where all these needs can be satisfied should be created.

V.   Management believes that clearly delineated job descriptions should be consummated for every employee, regarding work to be performed, delegations of authority, and assignments of responsibility and accountability, to the greatest extent possible; changes in job descriptions should also be made when tasks and responsibilities change.

VI.   Management views training and development programs as necessary means for improving the effectiveness of personnel and for assisting in the progressive achievements of individual employees.

VII.   Reasonable standards of performance provide a fair means for measuring the degrees of achieved individual success at work.

VIII.   Fairness to all demands that high performers should be rewarded and that those who fail to perform acceptably shall be denied rewards, and, in extreme cases, shall be penalized or weeded out. Management believes that impersonal, objective measurements of performance in all situations constitute the best means for fair determinations of results achieved.

IX.   Management believes that every employee should have an opportunity to provide input to decision-making processes of the corporation, and that a system for assuring this opportunity should be developed.

Exhibit 7-1 continued

X.   Fairness and justice should be the standard used in all cases of controversy arising between employees and the corporation. Accordingly, the right to be heard shall not be abrogated, and appropriate means for assuring this right should be developed.

XI.   Although management may not agree to the letter with all pertinent governmental regulations and reserves the right to work for changes in any that may appear unjust and discriminatory, management believes in basic conformance to the spirit and intent of such regulations until such time that sought-for changes are effected, and will not intentionally stand in violation, either openly or secretly.

Amendments and additions may be made to these statements from time to time, as considered appropriate by the corporation.

Signed: *John Rufus Doe*
President and CEO

icies for human resource management pertain to a number of relationships, including (1) the relationships of managers with other managers, staff personnel, and operating personnel; (2) the relationships of operating personnel (as individuals) with all other personnel; (3) the relationships of corporate personnel staff (usually grouped in a personnel department) with executive staff, line managers and all other employees; and (4) the relationships of all employees, sometimes by category, to the corporation or other business entity.

Job descriptions, organizational structure, policies, and procedures, and specific task assignments spell out for the most part the work relationships managers should have with all other members of a business organization. Other sections of this text cover these relationships in detail.

Job descriptions and procedure manuals generally outline the work relationships operating personnel have with others. We will not specifically discuss these relationships further in this chapter.

Top executives frequently fail (especially in small firms) to establish clear policies regarding the relationships personnel departments have with executives, with other managers, and with rank-and-file employees. They often fail to clearly define the role of the department, the functions the department should perform at various stages of growth, and the nature of the interface between personnel departments and line departments or divisions. Top management also fails, but somewhat less frequently, to outline in formal policy statements the basic purposes and expected benefits of personnel department functions, whether or not these functions have been formally identified.

Formally published "personnel policies" usually outline the relationships that the organization posits for all employees, and these should rest squarely on the philosophical orientation, hopefully explicitly expressed, of the board of directors and the top executive officers.

Role of the personnel department

Top management should establish policies governing the basic role and functions of a personnel department. Subsequently, the personnel department should formulate policies that will guide and control an organization's relationships with employees and submit them for review and approval by top management. Following approval, managers and other supervisory staff can pursue implementation, primarily through the line organization. This is consistent with what Pigors and Myers state about the basic role of personnel administration itself: "Personnel administration is a line management responsibility but a staff function."[19] They add only one qualification: "We believe that the personnel administrator should remain in a staff role, as we have defined it. But in many organizations, especially larger ones facing unions, there has been a tendency to give necessary responsibility for certain personnel functions to the chief personnel or industrial relations executive."[20]

Role expansion

The role of the personnel department has grown considerably in both scope and importance over the last several years. At present, the top executive in the department most frequently is a vice president and reports directly to either the CEO or COO.[21] This claim is supported by research done by The Conference Board, a respected business research organization, which also reported the following:

> The corporate personnel staff unit is emerging in many companies as a primary agency of overall corporate planning and control. These staffs are developing and operating systems to plan and control such key areas of personnel management as:
>
> • The overall staffing of the company, long and short term;
>
> • The overall effectiveness of the organization in terms of worker productivity, employee satisfaction, and the competitiveness of its incentive and reward systems;
>
> • The overall effectiveness of the company's efforts to comply with government agencies, unions and public interest groups in personnel related matters.[22]

At least part of the new focus of personnel departments stems from its emergence "as a primary agency of overall planning and control . . . [and] the major internal enforcement arm of government social intervention in company operation " [e.g., civil rights legislation and related executive orders; the Equal Employment Opportunity Act (EEO) of 1972 (a series of amendments to the Civil Rights Act of 1964); various employment and training programs; the Occupational Safety and Health Act (OSHA) of 1973; the Employee Retirement Income Security Act (ERISA) of 1974; etc.].[23] In all sizeable business firms, authority to keep abreast of the requirements of such programs and to plan responses to them had to be placed somewhere, and the personnel department proved to be the logical department. Janger, author of The Conference Board findings cited above, did report, however, that in some instances staff units separated from personnel may frame or assist in framing policy statements concerning government programs (such as the public affairs or legal staff).[24]

Relationship between role and functions

While acquiring greater scope and added responsibilities, personnel departments have not relinquished any functions inherent in the more traditional role they assumed during the late 1950s and 1960s. In one sense, a role should dictate the functions any given organizational department performs; in another, the functions performed provide evidence of the role that a given department fulfills at any given point in time. Figure 7-1 shows a typical grouping of the various functions for which personnel departments usually have responsibility in some of the nation's largest corporations today. Of course, the grouping may differ from firm to firm, but the range and diversity of functions are typical and indicate the importance of the personnel department's role.

Over the years we have observed that personnel departments may perform a variety of other work (largely investigative) that line managers may not have time or do not wish to perform. Our observations indicate that personnel departments can become a "dumping ground" for activities of this nature and must be protected from this by top management.

Scope of human resource planning

We use the term *human resource planning* with a much broader meaning than most authorities. For example, Glueck has defined human resource planning as "the process by which management determines how the organization should move from its current (human resource) position to its desired (human resource) position."[25] Steers, Ungson, and Mowday state, "More specifically, it involves translating organizational goals and objectives into specific human resource objectives. The nature of the planning process may differ, but generally it involves three major activities . . . forecasting, programming, and evaluation and control."[26] Clearly, these comments limit planning primarily to the quantitative side of staffing. Our view is that human resource planning includes not only these major activities (as functions performed specifically by a personnel department) but also many "qualitative" activities, such as using information from the behavioral sciences in developing approaches to staffing and to all the other personnel department functions.

Also, as we have said, few authorities differentiate between planning and control. We note that the third major "planning" activity cited by Steers, Ungson, and Mowday is not part of planning. Both evaluation and control are implementation activities, not planning activities.

We believe human resource planning includes the following:

1. The development and expression of a philosophy regarding human resource management.

2. The development and promulgation of policies relating to

   - the role of the department of personnel and personnel staff vis-a-vis other departments or divisions, including individual department members

   - the type and fundamental nature of functions to be carried out by personnel department staff and at what locations (the question of

Figure 7-1

Typical Operative Functions of Major Personnel Departments

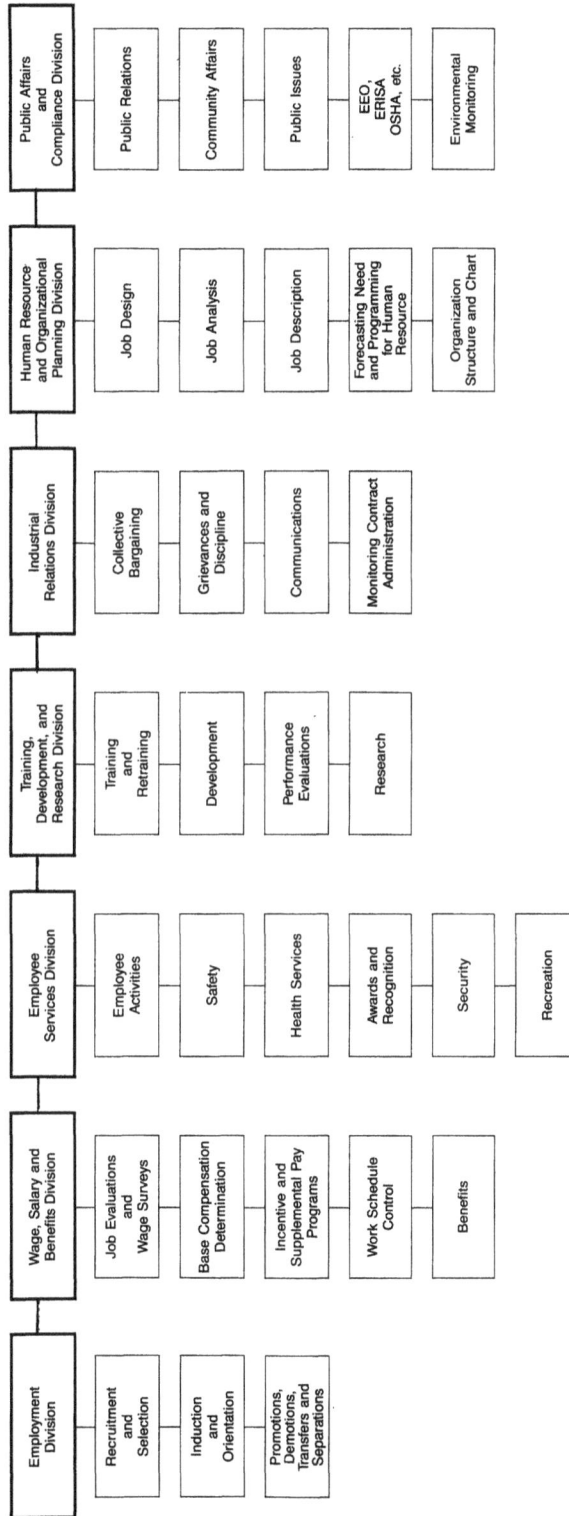

Employment Division	Wage, Salary and Benefits Division	Employee Services Division	Training, Development, and Research Division	Industrial Relations Division	Human Resource and Organizational Planning Division	Public Affairs and Compliance Division
Recruitment and Selection	Job Evaluations and Wage Surveys	Employee Activities	Training and Retraining	Collective Bargaining	Job Design	Public Relations
Induction and Orientation	Base Compensation Determination	Safety	Development	Grievances and Discipline	Job Analysis	Community Affairs
Promotions, Demotions, Transfers and Separations	Incentive and Supplemental Pay Programs	Health Services	Performance Evaluations	Communications	Job Description	Public Issues
	Work Schedule Control	Awards and Recognition	Research	Monitoring Contract Administration	Forecasting Need and Programming for Human Resource	EEO, ERISA OSHA, etc.
	Benefits	Security			Organization Structure and Chart	Environmental Monitoring
		Recreation				

Source: Authors

centralization or decentralization of personnel staff functions must be answered, if applicable; forecasting and programming human resource needs is merely one of the functions performed by most personnel departments)

- the basic purposes and expected benefits to both the company and employees of each distinct set of functions to be carried out by personnel department staff.

3. The development of personnel policies by personnel department staff that will be approved and promulgated by top management and that define relationships between all employees and the company through setting out terms and conditions of employment, organization, compensation, opportunities for advancement, training and development, performance evaluations, employee benefits and services, etc.

4. The development of procedures by personnel department staff for implementing each set of functions to be undertaken, including those pertaining to intradepartmental work activities and to other company activities. Some of these procedures ought to be approved by top management.

Figure 7-2 depicts the elements of human resource planning.

Arguably the development of the procedures noted in (4) above does not constitute human resource planning, but merely involves formula-

Figure 7-2

Elements of Human Resource Planning

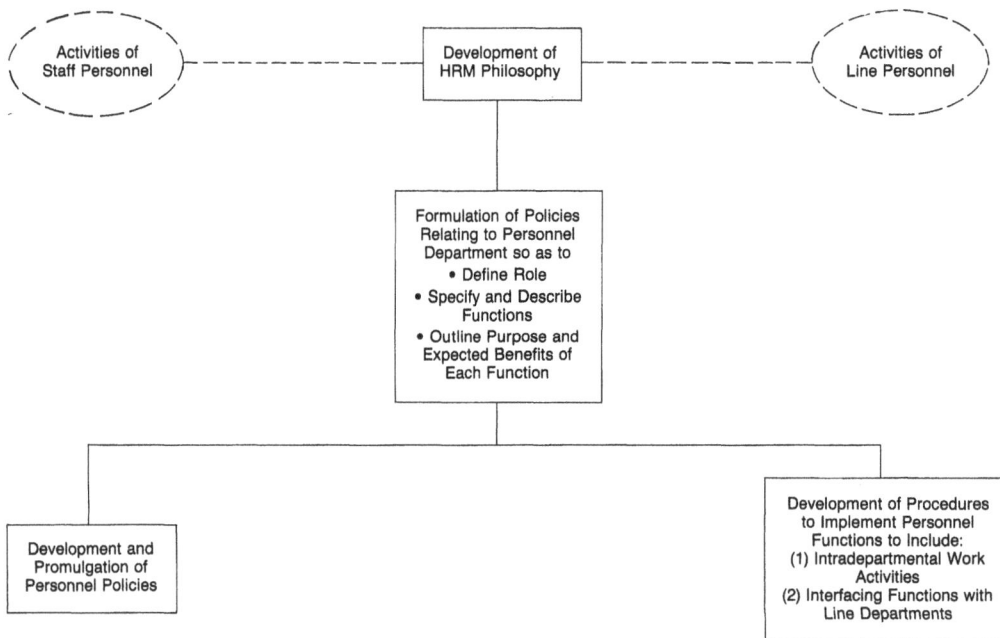

tion of standing plans (discussed in Chapter 5). We admit this, but there are some unique features involved in preparing these standing plans that have made us elect to consider their development as a type of human resource planning. Thus, we set forth a brief discussion of these plans in the final pages of this chapter.

Definitions of human resource planning given by others largely ignore the development of one or more policy or procedure areas we have identified above. Yet all authorities recognize that the formulation (or development) of philosophy, policies, procedures, and even methods is essentially planning. Since the areas of philosophy, policies, and procedures we have identified are essential components of human resource management, their development should logically be classified as human resource planning.

We discuss each of the major areas of human resource planning below.

Areas of human resource planning

Development of a philosophy

In order to demonstrate the logical relationship of human resource management philosophy to human resource planning, we discussed philosophy rather extensively earlier in this chapter. Statements of philosophy set the tone for the development of all policy related to human resource management, and indeed they set the tone for all relationships among employees as well as between the employees and the business organization as a whole.

Development of policies

Policy related to role of personnel departments

Top management should spell out the role of a personnel department vis-a-vis other departments and their individual members. Some executives still insist that since personnel staff render a staff or support function, they should merely provide advice and counsel to personnel in other departments, especially those in line positions. A majority of executives, however, now believe that personnel staff may perform many services directly for line managers, either temporarily or permanently, and should be given the necessary authority for doing so.

One reason that former "directors of personnel" have moved up organizational hierarchies and are now closer to the CEO or COO—and usually have the title of vice president—is that it has become desirable to give them immediate line authority, so they can perform various personnel actions directly in line departments and speak with the authority of the CEO or COO. Haggling between two "down-the-line" departmental entities is thus eliminated, as are subsequent referrals "up-the-line" to get the matter settled (with the attendant complexities).

"How is [personnel] staff expertness made available to and used by the total organization? Is it fed into the top of the organization and channeled to all levels through the chief executive? . . . How do [personnel staff] make their information, advice and services available to those who have most need for them [on a priority basis]?"[27] How do line managers initiate calls for services that need to be rendered by personnel staff? How will costs for such services be handled? Who will have authority, responsibility, and accountability for such services? What freedom or authority (if any) does the top personnel executive have to change personnel procedures that affect other departments, e.g., training and development, performance evaluations, grievance handling, transfers, separations, etc.? How will unresolved disputes between personnel and line staff be settled? What will be the process for changing employee personnel policies? How will official and formal communications between personnel and other departments be recorded?

These are only some of the questions that policy should help to answer.

Policy related to functions of personnel departments

Top line management should explicitly detail through policy pronouncements the functions of human resource management that will be assumed by the personnel department and the interface that should occur between this department and others regarding each function. (This is typically done by the CEO or COO.) This does not necessarily mean that the CEO or COO alone should foresee the need for, and institute actions to initiate, a new personnel department service. Such initiatives are actually most often suggested or undertaken by personnel department executives. However, top line management should officially announce policy for undertaking the service, because of its multidepartmental effects.

Policies specifying the functions a personnel department shall undertake will vary, depending on the size and nature of the organization. In Figure 7-1, we show 32 functions typically carried out by personnel departments in major corporations. These are operative functions and do not indicate the considerable influence personnel department executives have in an organization through the framing of personnel policies, which are separate from policies required to specify operative functions, their purposes, and their expected benefits.

Figure 7-1 depicts one way of grouping functions in a major personnel department. Many readers may have reservations about the grouping shown. Obviously, there exist several considerations to take into account when performing this clustering function. Among them are the following:

- *Kindred nature of the functions.* For example, in Figure 7-1 one can easily note similarities among the subfunctions grouped together.

- *Size of the firm.* In many firms, wage and salary administration and employee benefits are grouped together and assigned to the same person. This assignment makes sense not only because of the reduction in the volume of managerial work, but also because of the kinship between these two major functions.

- *Background and experience of available managers.* This item may evoke some criticism. However, certain situations seem to suggest and even dictate that background and experience be taken into account.

- *Emphasis accorded specific functions and subfunctions.* In emerging firms, executives may fully recognize that some functions and subfunctions should not be activated immediately, and they will group them under a major division and assign them to a manager who is knowledgeable and who will be instructed to advise when activation should begin. The assignment may ignore, for example, kinship with other functions. Of the functions shown in Figure 7-1, recreation, training, and personnel research might compose a set of functions whose activation should be delayed for various reasons.

- *Geographic dispersion of divisions, departments, or other functional entities.* Obviously, a remote unit of a hundred employees will not require a full-fledged onsite personnel staff. There may be a single personnel officer, who indeed may wear a variety of hats and perform a number of largely unrelated duties.

Although for purposes of explanation we have differentiated between policies concerning sets of functions that personnel departments will perform and policies concerning the basic purposes and expected benefits of such sets of functions, we specifically note that policy pronouncements may concern both. (We provide examples of this later.)

Because of space limitations, we will not discuss the entire range of operative functions shown in Figure 7-1. We merely selected those regarded as basic functions found in most corporations.

Governmental compliance activities. Out of a desire for a company to speak with one voice about such programs as OSHA, EEO, ERISA, other civil rights legislation and executive orders, the Equal Pay Act and other acts, together with the need to centralize expert knowledge, sometimes relevant staff is grouped in the personnel department. Janger notes, "Achieving this single voice requires the coordination of many different voices and activities in the company. Such coordination involves the development of policy in each area of regulation and programming."[28]

Labor relations. Most companies that have only professional (or white collar) employees forgo having a labor relations staff. In fact, few companies not threatened by unionization have such staff. However, when threats of collective bargaining appear, usually the need to employ labor relations staff in some capacity arises, even though the company may elect to bargain through specialists in an employer association.

Policy issued by top management should specify the creation of labor relations staff positions, the location of the staff (central headquarters, geographic divisions, plants, hospitals, or other dispersed entities), and at least the general nature of the functions to be carried out. We note that labor relations functions typically evolve over time; issued policy statements should advertise developments in functions as they occur.

In general, management policies should establish what the firm's approach will be regarding at least these three labor relations situations:

1. before any threat of unionization has arisen

2. during the course of union attempts at collective bargaining

3. after unionization

Forecasting and programming staffing needs. These functions alone have been called human resource planning by some authorities. We have outlined a definition of human resource planning that is much broader, as previously noted.

In small companies, line managers usually determine current and future staffing requirements. When the need arises for personnel staff to undertake any activities in this regard, including job analyses, time studies, workload analyses, job descriptions, workload measurements or time budgeting studies, work simplification studies, etc., this fact should be formally announced and policy should be promulgated regarding the role of personnel staff. Particularly in need of clarification is the interface that personnel staff will have with line managers in estimating line staff required for new programs considered in strategic planning (or in downsizing programs).

In concept, forecasting the need for future human resources is very simple. In application, depending on the accuracy of forecasting and the level of staffing efficiency that are desired, it can be complicated. However, all forecasting starts with an inventory of existing employees—by department, by name, by primary and secondary skills, by performance measure or promotion potential, by length of time with the firm and years to retirement. This information can be kept in a computerized "skills inventory." By comparing measured workloads performed by categories of existing departmental staff with anticipated future workloads (derived from the goals and objectives of strategic plans and possibly modified by assumptions about levels of individual employee productivity), the future departmental work force can be calculated. In many instances, these calculations are rather straightforward, but the introduction of new products, new equipment, new procedures, and expense budget requirements can considerably complicate matters.

Typically, personnel department staff work with line managers in forecasting their respective needs for human resources at specific points in the future. Although the tasks required for forecasting can be highly technical, there is no substitute for across-the-table discussions between departmental or divisional managers and qualified personnel staff. On the one hand, line managers impart information about short-range, mid-range, and long-range strategic goals and objectives. (*Short-range* should be interpreted to mean from one month to one year; *mid-range*, from one year to two years; and *long-range*, from two years to five years.) On the other hand, personnel staff can outline the forecasting process required, the possible use of suitable transfers from other parts of the company, and the time required to get additional personnel, either from internal or external sources, on the job.

Personnel staff will need at least one to three meetings with line managers in order to predict the need for future personnel. In some cases, ten or more may be required. The need for such a large number usually develops when detailed analyses of *new* jobs are required. Although such analyses are time consuming and can be quite complicated (readers are referred to other texts for technical details), they are intended to result in an estimation of the specific volume of work one employee can perform in a given unit of time, say, eight hours, a week, or a month. Then, by dividing the total volume of work that must be performed in a given unit of time by the volume that one worker can perform, the total number of employees can be estimated (within certain latitudes). By subtracting available employees (those already on the payroll) from total requirements, the number of new employees can be determined.

After the additions, reductions, or changes in personnel staff (by category or job title) have been determined for a given department, division, or other organizational unit, these should be expressed in terms of a program. Following this, personnel staff and line managers must develop specific procedures for attaining the objectives. Programming generally involves a step-by-step plan to accomplish certain objectives. As in any other plan, who, when, what, where, and how, together with how much (the quantification of expenses), must be determined. Following formulation of a plan, its implementation can begin.

As the personnel staff's role in forecasting and programming evolves, top management should continue to issue policies regarding the stages of the evolution.

Recruitment and selection, induction, and orientation. The functions personnel staff will perform in these regards should be stipulated in announced policy as they are initiated or changed. We define these functions and discuss their implementation in Chapter 13.

Promotions, demotions, transfers, and separations. No more important function exists in any organization than promoting deserving employees, and it is especially important that policy spell out the responsibility of all, including the personnel department, in this matter. By also specifying the nature of the functions personnel staff will perform in potentially controversial actions (such as demotions, transfers, and separations), organizations can avoid many disagreeable and time-consuming situations. Policies may be rather general and leave some latitude for deviations or exceptions in individual cases. However, where authority, responsibility, and accountability rest should be made clear.

Compensation (including incentives) and employee benefits and services. Compensation (formerly more frequently called wage and salary administration) may be determined through a program of job evaluation and employee productivity (or work contribution). Benefits include direct monetary rewards, vacations, sick leave, holidays, paid time off, insurance, retirement plans, etc. Services include the provision of items such as onsite cafeterias, libraries, child care services, etc.

Again, policy should establish the type of functions personnel staff will perform in regard to these matters.

Training and development. "Employee *training* efforts appear to be directed toward increasing skills and abilities relating to the performance of the current job . . . employee *development* efforts are directed toward increasing the level of an employee's knowledge and skills so that advancement is possible."[29] All these programs are marked by diversification.

The nature of the programs to be undertaken, the personnel staff's involvement, the categories of employees to be involved (line managers, line operators, staff managers, and staff operators in the departments to be included), the program responsibilities of line managers (if any), the extent of duration, and the degree of compulsion for participation, if any, should all be specified in policies.

Research. Typically, personnel staff conduct research on absenteeism; turnover; prevalence of alcohol, tobacco, and drug use; utilization of employee benefits and services; and a variety of other simple intracompany conditions or situations. However, personnel staff in very large firms may also perform literature searches and sophisticated social science investigations.

Most research projects undertaken by personnel staff are nonrecurring. This being so, if activities involve other departmental personnel, policy may have to be made on a case-by-case basis. Optimally, direct negotiations between personnel managers and line managers can avoid, in many instances, the involvement of top management.

Employee communications. Top management must establish somewhat specific policies about such things as publication of newsletters, performance of attitude surveys, sampling of opinions through interviews, sponsoring of non-work-related contests, maintaining bulletin boards, publishing employee handbooks, orientation lectures on changing policies, etc. Each program, as it is undertaken by personnel staff, should be announced and its nature described in general terms.

One of the most common and important tasks personnel staff undertake is to publish an employee handbook on personnel policies. Some firms, owing to certain court decisions, do not publish any part of their personnel policies. Top management should issue policies concerning the functions of both line and personnel staff in the preparation, distribution, and updating of such handbooks (if published).

Performance evaluations. Formerly called personnel appraisals or ratings, these evaluations now generally attempt to compare actual results with expected results (quantified, where possible). In some instances, attempts are also made to determine the potential of employees to take on more difficult assignments.

Because of the critical importance and sometimes controversial nature of performance evaluations and also because of their legal implications, top executives must see to it that this matter is handled flawlessly, not only with regard to substantive features but also from an administrative standpoint. Therefore, policy must specify very carefully the functions personnel staff will perform in all related aspects, including determination of methodology, execution, coordination, filing, reporting, etc. Although the processes involved may be determined through the collaboration of executives, line managers, and personnel executives or managers, top management must issue the relevant policy statement after agreements are reached.

Grievance handling. In unionized firms, labor contracts spell out procedure, and in nonunionized organizations, procedures are formulated in a variety of ways.

As with performance evaluations, top management must give specific approval for methodologies developed for grievance handling. In developing and agreeing upon methodology, executives can easily determine the functions of personnel staff, which can then be made a matter of policy.

Miscellaneous. Some personnel staff may do extensive reorganization studies from time to time and work directly with top level executives concerning these studies. They may also perform a variety of other work (largely investigative) relating to specific events and problem employees.

Whatever these duties may be, executives ought to approve them in the form of announced policy.

Policy related to purposes and benefits of personnel functions
As noted previously, a common policy pronouncement may be used to spell out the basic nature of sets of personnel functions and their purposes and expected benefits. This possibility may or may not be present, depending on the continuing evaluation of the functions and on policies already formulated and promulgated.

Owing to space limitations, we will not discuss policy statements pertaining to the purposes and expected benefits of the various sets of functions we have named under previous headings or other functions a firm may implement. We will merely present two examples of such statements in Exhibits 7-2 and 7-3. However, we stress the following: *Personnel managers should develop such policy statements for every set of functions performed by their staff and then have them approved and published by top management.*

Development of personnel policies

With respect to dealing with employees, both individually and collectively, no more important planning function exists than the formulation of personnel policies—those that specify the many relationships and interfaces that employees come to have with a company over time. Even in companies having no more than a hundred employees, managers should develop uniform policies assuring equal, just, and impartial treatment for any individual working in any capacity. After policies have been officially approved at the top executive level, they should be published in a form that can be made available to all managers for ready reference. Many business organizations publish a definitive summary of portions of their policies in a personnel policy handbook.

In reviewing pertinent literature, we seemed to note relatively little emphasis placed on personnel policy handbooks or the basic need to communicate personnel policies to employees in a frank and open manner. Lack of emphasis may be a mistake. Employee good will is invaluable and honesty and openness are essential to its creation.

We realize that legal advisors have warned some companies to refrain from publishing personnel policy handbooks and providing them to employees because the courts, in several instances, have interpreted their contents as a contract, which reduces flexibility for the employer. Individual firms and possibly individual divisions of firms must make the decision to publish or not to publish such handbooks based on their unique situation.

Executives recognize the considerable advantages of standing plans (discussed more fully in Chapter 5), and personnel policies can be classified as such. As with all policies, those pertaining to personnel must undergo periodic change, and routine consideration of changes should occur at approximately two- to four-year intervals. To allay controversy, both policy manuals and employee handbooks ought to be clearly dated and clearly denoted as being subject to change, with the anticipated date of reissue also being stated. In the interim, changes, if required, can be

Exhibit 7-2

Performance Evaluations

POLICY: PERFORMANCE EVALUATIONS FOR STAFF CONSULTANTS

Effective Date: January 1, 1988

Policy Statement

The XYZ Corporation shall objectively appraise the performance of each member of its consulting staff to assure that capable, efficient efforts will be recognized in four distinct areas. These are (1) Technical Performance; (2) Administrative and Supervisory; (3) Client Relations and Development; and (4) Personal and Professional. Performance evaluations shall be executed on a quarterly basis by appropriate managers for each subordinate on January 1, April 1, July 1, and October 1 of each year.

Each evaluation shall be reviewed by the evaluator with the consultant and placed in the consultant's personnel file.

A procedure shall be devised and placed into effect assuring the consultant's right to appeal any evaluation with which he or she is dissatisfied.

Purposes of the Policy

1. Improve the quality of consulting.

2. Provide a basis for promotions.

3. Provide a basis for increased compensation.

4. Assure objectivity and fairness in evaluations.

5. Assure appropriate placements of consultants on projects.

6. Provide a basis for training and further development.

7. Provide an opportunity for face-to-face consultations about strength, weaknesses, and problem areas in the individual's consulting work.

8. Improve the skills of managers in supervising consultants.

9. Create an awareness of the necessity for teamwork between superior, subordinate, and ancillary staff personnel.

10. Improve client relations and assure appropriate ethics in consulting.

Expected Benefits

1. Employee satisfaction and improved morale.

2. Better productivity.

3. Achievement of employee potential.

4. Development of teamwork and coordination.

5. Improvement of communications.

6. Better client relations.

7. Enhancement of company culture.

8. Encouragement of responses to challenges.

Exhibit 7-2 continued

9. Enhancement of "promotions from within" policy.

10. Increase in control.

Procedures

(etc.)

Exhibit 7-3

Policy: Settling Employee Grievances

Filing Number: 111-09-2000   Effective Date: January 1, 1988

Policy Statement

The XYZ Corporation hereby assures each employee the basic right to a hearing related to any company matter, the outcome of which, according to personal perceptions only, appears to place him or her in an aggrieved position. After pursuing a procedure involving three (3) distinct hearings, where the matter can be settled upon agreement with designated company officials in each instance, if the employee still believes that he or she is aggrieved and has not been offered a fair settlement, arbitration can be requested and will be granted by the company. The decision of the arbitrators shall be final.

Purposes of the Policy

1. To assure every employee the basic right to a hearing regarding grievances and thereby effect conformance to the law.

2. To assure every employee fair and impartial treatment in matters of disagreement, where the employee feels aggrieved.

3. To dispose of disputes so that company business can proceed.

4. To assure both the company and employee of fair and equitable settlements of grievances without undergoing legal proceedings.

5. To provide structure to matters certain to arise.

Benefits of the Policy

1. Assures employees that the company respects their rights and thus creates goodwill.

2. Encourages settlements of disagreements without lengthy and expensive lawsuits.

3. Encourages employee retention and helps morale.

4. Brings policy issues into the open and serves to encourage timely revisions.

5. Through the rate of grievances recorded as handled, allows an indication as to the appropriateness of policies and the nature and quality of supervisory acts.

6. Records the company's ability to settle disputes at the level where they occur.

7. Identifies, over time, both managers and employees who are prone to create trouble.

Procedures

(etc.)

made through memoranda. Personnel department managers should devise a process for making changes in policy and for effecting revisions to handbooks. Both the process and proposed changes had best be approved by an appropriate company executive, desirably the CEO or COO.

Exhibit 7-4 sets forth a table of contents for personnel policies which have been in effect at HCA. We believe the contents are typical for large corporations. We know the policy provisions were equitable for all employees of HCA and that employees viewed them as being so. The planning work involved in formulating these policies was considerable, and keeping them updated with approved changes and additions and providing interpretations on an ongoing basis have been major functions of HCA's personnel department.

Many small firms will be able to offer only minimal benefits and services. Regardless, all firms should openly and honestly disclose what they do offer, in an appropriate manner and to the extent possible. At

Exhibit 7-4

HCA's Personnel Policies
Table of Contents
(By Major Headings Only)
(1986)

GENERAL INFORMATION
TABLE OF CONTENTS
  Introduction
  Personnel Policies Approval
EMPLOYMENT INFORMATION
  Equal Employment Opportunity
  Classification of Employees
    Part-Time/Temporary Benefits
  Classification of Exempt and Non-Exempt
    Employees
  Overtime—Non-Exempt
  Employment Date
  Employee Records
    Records for New Employees
    Records During Employment
    Records Returning from Leave of Absence
    Records at Termination
    Retention of Records
    Confidentiality
  Hours of Work
  Time Sheets
  Payment of Wages or Salary
    Payment of Compensation
    Payroll Deductions
    Pay for Partial Period
    Assignment of Wages and Unclaimed
      Compensation
  Garnishments, Levies or Attachments
  Federal, State and Local Withholding Forms
  Applications for Non-Exempt Employment
  Employment of Relatives
  Orientation of New Employees
  Performance Appraisal Process

EMPLOYEE RELATIONS
  Attendance
    Notification of Absence
    Unacceptable Absence
    Excessive Absence
    Evaluation of Excessive Absence
    Weather Related Absence
  Outside Employment
  Dress, Grooming and Appearance
  Telephones
    Business Calls
    Personal Calls
  Presentation of Speeches/Papers
  Leaves of Absence
  Sabbatical Leaves of Absence for Government
    Service
  Reinstatement Following Leave (Other than
    Military Leave)
  Military Duty
  Transfer: Promotional and Lateral
  Employment by HCA International Subsidiaries
  Employee Recourse
    Method of Recourse
  Termination
    Classification of Terminations
    Termination Procedure
    Benefits at Termination
  Reemployment
  Reference Checks
  Benefits Procedure for Employees Changing
    Employment Between HCA and a Subsidiary
    of HCA
  Severance Allowance

least part of the goodwill of employees comes from open communication and forthright disclosures about what they can expect from an employment relationship.

Development of personnel department procedures

All departments in any business enterprise must develop some basic operational procedures for a variety of reasons. (We discuss such procedures in Chapter 5, "Standing Plans.") The personnel department is no exception. Personnel department managers must put the work tasks of individual employees into a sequence in order to carry out the work of the department, which may be defined in terms of goals and objectives or be determined by a previously developed philosophy of human resource management and the policies derived from that philosophy.

As with all other departments, where procedures cut across departmental lines, managers from the involved departments must communicate and assure themselves that the interdepartmental efforts are well

---

EMPLOYEE BENEFITS
  Paid Sick Leave (Non-Exempt Employees)
    Sick Pay Accumulation
    Physician's Statement
    Sick Pay Benefits
    Salary Continuation (Exempt Employees)
  Holidays
  Vacation
    Vacation Accumulation
    Scheduling Vacation
    Unusual Circumstances
    Vacation Pay
    Vacation Accrual Rates
  Jury Duty
  Voting Time
  Bereavement Leave
  Tuition Assistance
  Health Club
  Assignment and Utilization of Company
    Automobiles
RELOCATION INFORMATION
  Employee Relocation Policy A
  Employee Relocation Policy B
    Relocation Benefits Authorization Form
    Reimbursement Procedures
    Indirect Expense Allowance
    House Hunting/Apartment Hunting
    Homesearch Assistance

    Rental Assistance
    Enroute Expenses with Family
    Transportation of Household Goods
    Insurance
    Temporary Living at the New Location (with Family)
    Home Sale Assistance
    Tax Allowance
    Relocation Repayment Agreement
    Time Limitation
    Administration of Policy Interpretation
  Home Purchase Service
    Initiating the Home Purchase Offer
    Qualifications
    Benefits of the Home Purchase Program
COMPENSATION
  Classification of a New Job
  Reclassification of an Existing Job
  Hiring Rates for New Employees
  Processing Payroll Action Forms
  Salary Adjustments
  Geographical Salary Differential
SAFETY AND SECURITY
  Confidential Information
  Possession of Firearms
  Security Program
  Employee Injuries (Work-Related)
  Workers' Compensation

Source: Reprinted with permission of Hospital Corporation of America.

---

meshed. In all such cases, although the next higher echeloned manager may not actively engage in the direct communications and conferences necessary to work out such interdepartmental efforts, he or she should in theory approve the formal procedure so evolved. No reason exists why the higher manager should not engage in these negotiations, but it is not necessary. In the case of the personnel department, many instances occur where personnel staff work actively with line managers to effect certain aspects of personnel policies (which is unique to this department). Since the top personnel department executive usually now reports either to the CEO or COO, there will be little likelihood that he or she, being the next higher echeloned officer, will attend the working sessions between line managers and personnel staff to prepare interdepartmental procedures. Therefore, the initiative to get these procedures worked out rests with the personnel staff. After taking the initiative, however, personnel staff should expect cooperation from the line managers, who have been known to give personnel matters and their own involvement in such matters a rather low priority. Perhaps this is another reason why the chief personnel executive usually now reports directly to the top executive officer. After working out the procedures and agreeing upon them, each line manager should sign off and make appropriate inclusions in the procedure manuals.

Instances where close interdepartmental efforts often prove necessary in effecting personnel-related actions include achieving compliance with governmental social programs; recruitment, selection, and placement; training and development; performance evaluations; compensation and benefits; grievance handling; and promotions, transfers, and separations. In fact, most major sets of personnel department functions require some involvement by other departments.

Of course, another option exists for meshing the activities of personnel staff with those of other departments, and this is by orders from the CEO or COO. However, we believe very strongly in direct interdepartmental communication (see Chapter 8), and we believe, as noted, that personnel staff should initiate negotiations regarding interdepartmental procedures and diligently pursue them. In the rare cases of failure, the matter had best be referred to the immediate superior.

Personnel department staff ought to have greater knowledge about and be more skilled in the several sets of personnel functions previously noted than line managers. This is important in order to avoid some "booing," which can detract from both planning and implementation efforts.

Summary

Academic authorities and practicing managers both agree that appropriate human resource management holds the key to organizational success. Investigations by behavioral scientists have pointed to new philosophies and concepts that have literally revolutionized approaches to human resource management over the last half century. The investigation findings demonstrate the importance of giving individual organizational members recognition and due consideration, the necessity of responding to their needs, and the advantages to be gained from unleashing and stimulating their initiative.

The behavioral science investigations that have been particularly revealing and helpful can be easily found in the literature. They primarily concern human values and needs, motivational theories, leadership, morale, attitudes, human engineering, training, communication, group dynamics, authority and power, organizational conflict, and resistance to change.

The planning involved in human resource management rests on philosophies held and espoused by top management officials. Policies flow from philosophies and implementing procedures flow from policies. Thus, the importance of a firm's philosophy should not be underestimated.

Top managers ought to publish statements of philosophy regarding human resource management. Such statements influence all relationships and interfaces that transpire among organizational members, some of which can never be fully covered by policy statements.

Personnel departments have a key role in human resource management, and top management should clarify it for the benefit of all. Generally, these departments formulate plans either intradepartmentally or in conjunction with other departments or divisions. After approval of these plans by top management, their implementation becomes a line responsibility. Increasingly, personnel staff may perform implementation as a line responsibility under the authority of line managers.

The role of personnel departments has expanded in recent years, and top personnel executives usually now report to either the CEO or COO. This is owing to several reasons, not least of which is that the arrangement provides central coordination for compliance with governmentally sponsored social programs.

In large companies, say, those with 5,000 or more employees, these sets of core functions will typically emerge:

1. government compliance activities

2. labor relations (if unionized or threatened with unionization)

3. forecasting and programming human resource needs

4. recruitment, selection, induction, and orientation

5. promotions, demotions, transfers, and separations

6. compensation (including incentives) and employee benefits and services

7. training and development

8. research

9. employee communications

10. performance evaluations

11. grievance handling

12. miscellaneous

Most authorities use the term *human resource planning* to mean the quantifying of both current and future organizational staffing needs by category. We expand the definition to include the following:

1. development and expressions of philosophy regarding human resource management

2. development and promulgation of policies related to

   • the role of the personnel department

   • the type and nature of functions to be carried out by the personnel department

   • basic purposes and expected benefits of personnel department functions

3. development of personnel policies related to terms and conditions of employment, organization, compensation, opportunities for advancement, training and development, performance evaluations, employee benefits and services, and others

4. development of procedures for implementing each set of activities undertaken by the personnel department

The type and nature of functions to be carried out by a personnel department and the basic purposes and expected benefits of such functions can be set forth in separate or combined policy statements.

Personnel policies governing the many relationships that a company has with its employees should be formulated, published, and distributed to all line managers. A summary of applicable portions usually should be made available to all employees in the form of a personnel policy handbook.

Development of personnel department procedures requires joint efforts by the personnel department and other departments or divisions. This is because implementation of many plans developed by the personnel department will be done jointly with line departments or exclusively by those departments. Where procedures are jointly developed, managers ought to include them in the appropriate departmental policy and procedure manuals.

According to the traditional concept of human resource planning (our concept is much broader), such planning starts when personnel department staff and line managers get together to forecast the staffing requirements of the various organizational units. Subsequently they develop a plan to fulfill the requirements. The first task requires doing an inventory of qualified employees already on the job or otherwise available internally. The next step is to determine total staffing requirements by department and job title or category. Planners make this determination through estimating workloads to be accomplished (using the quantified goals and objectives of the strategic plans) within a given timeframe and dividing these workloads by the amount of work that one employee can typically perform within the same timeframe. Then, by subtracting available internal employees from the total required, the number of employees who must be recruited can be estimated.

Programming involves development of a plan to fulfill the requirements estimated, in terms of who, when, what, where, how, and how much.

Notes

1. Ann Reilly Dowd, "What Managers Can Learn from Manager Reagan," *Fortune*, September 15, 1986, p. 33.

2. Harold Geneen with Alvin Moscow, *Managing* (Garden City, N.Y.: Doubleday, 1984), 132.

3. Thomas J. Peters and Robert H. Waterman, Jr., *In Search of Excellence* (New York: Harper & Row, 1982), 235–78.

4. Ibid., 238.

5. Ibid., 244.

6. Ibid., 248–49.

7. Ibid., 253.

8. Ibid.

9. Ibid., 265.

10. Ibid., 267.

11. Michael Beer et al., *Managing Human Assets* (New York: The Free Press, 1984), 28.

12. Ibid.

13. Ibid., 29–30.

14. Donald S. MacNaughton, "The Art of Management" (Speech delivered at Rutgers University, March 1980).

15. Ibid.

16. *Webster's Ninth New Collegiate Dictionary*, s.v. "philosophy."

17. Robert C. Sampson, "Management and the Behavioral Sciences," in *Handbook of Business Administration*, ed. H.B. Maynard (New York: McGraw-Hill, 1967), 11–16.

18. Richard M. Steers, Gerardo R. Ungson, and Richard T. Mowday, *Managing Effective Organizations* (Boston: Kent Publishing Company, 1985), 452.

19. Paul Pigors and Charles A. Myers, *Personnel Administration*, 9th ed. (New York: McGraw-Hill, 1981), 53.

20. Ibid., 60.

21. Allen R. Janger, *The Personnel Function: Changing Objectives and Organization*, Report #712 (New York: The Conference Board, Inc., 1977), 36–37.

22. Ibid., 11.

23. Ibid., 1–11.

24. Ibid., 23.

25. W.F. Glueck, *Personnel: A Diagnostic Approach*, 3d ed. (Plano, Tex.: Business Publications, 1982), 85. Cited in Steers, Ungson, and Mowday, *Managing Effective Organizations*, 456.

26. Steers, Ungson, and Mowday, *Managing Effective Organizations*, 456.

27. Dale Yoder, *Personnel Management and Industrial Relations*, 5th ed. (1962), 115. Reprinted by permission of Prentice-Hall, Inc., Englewood Cliffs, N.J.

28. Janger, *The Personnel Function*, 41.

29. Steers, Ungson, and Mowday, *Managing Effective Organizations*, 467.

Chapter 8

Planning communication and management information systems

Elements of Management
in Corporations

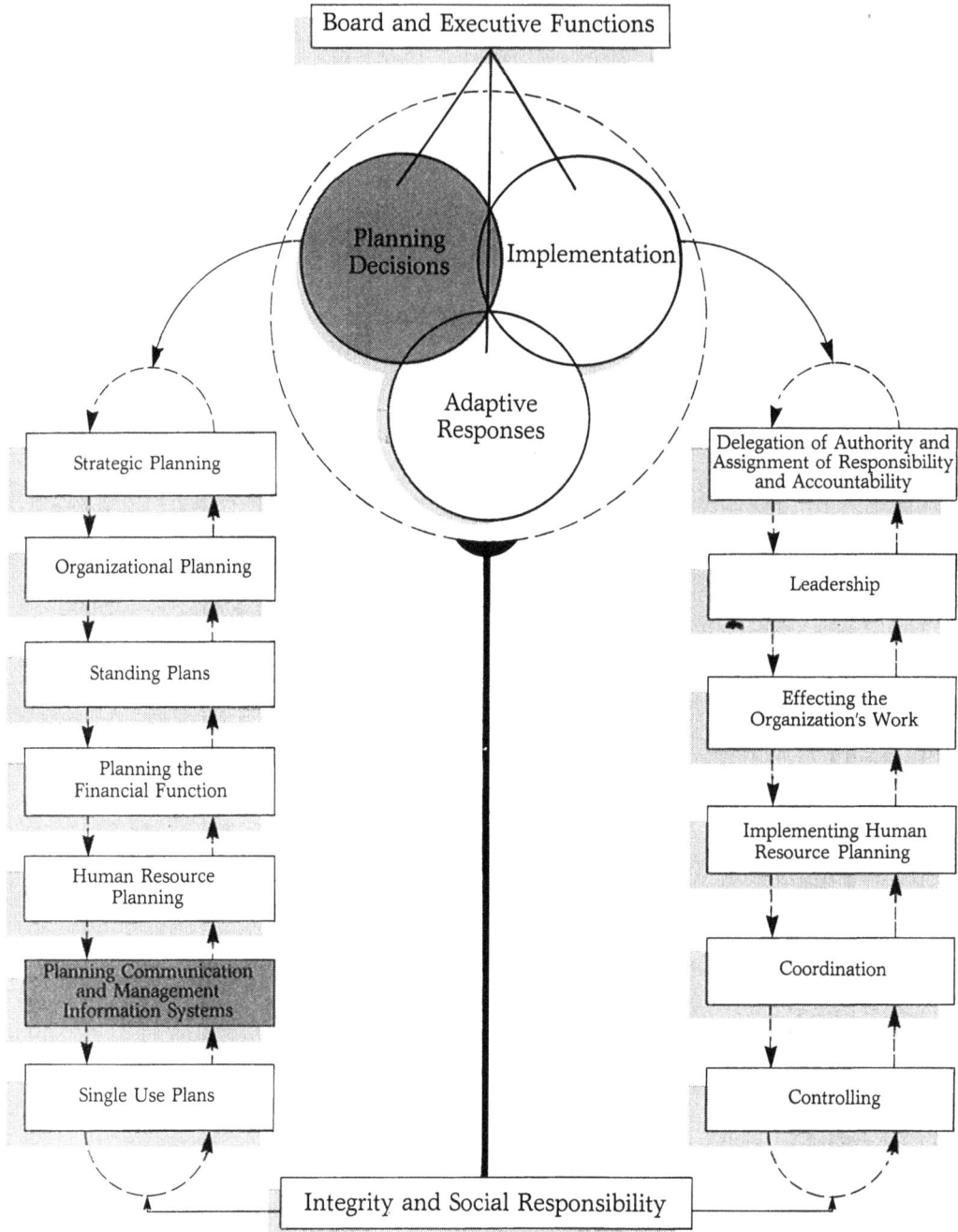

Board and Executive Functions

Planning
Decisions

Implementation

Adaptive
Responses

Strategic Planning

Organizational Planning

Standing Plans

Planning the
Financial Function

Human Resource
Planning

Planning Communication
and Management
Information Systems

Single Use Plans

Delegation of Authority and
Assignment of Responsibility
and Accountability

Leadership

Effecting the
Organization's Work

Implementing Human
Resource Planning

Coordination

Controlling

Integrity and Social Responsibility

8

In recent years, management theorists have devoted considerable study to the field of communication, both inside formal organizations and among individuals and informal groups outside organizations. In this chapter, we discuss communication systems of business organizations and how to plan them so as to assure appropriate exchanges of the operational information necessary to effectively realize the company's mission, goals, and objectives. Further, planned systems of communication should promote unity and morale among organizational members and goodwill between the organization and the public.

A system of organizational communication resembles the nervous system of the human body. Without the nervous system, the human body could not function; indeed, it could not exist. The same can be said of an organization and its communication system. The analogy, however, is limited. None of us had to devote time to planning the nerve connections between our brain and the more than 600 muscles throughout our bodies or the organization of the more than 15 billion nerve units of which the brain is composed. However, if time is not devoted to planning an organizational communication system, parts of the organization will fail to receive the information necessary to the accomplishment of their purposes. Unfortunately, many organizations devote woefully inadequate attention to formal planning of communication systems.

Although the purpose of an organizational communication system is to assure the sending and receiving of vital information, we view such a system as basically a *human* system—a function of organized relationships among organizational members and between the organization and the public. In contrast, management information systems in all major business firms currently are *man-machine* systems, so-called in recognition of the role of computers and other instruments in the recording of data and in the subsequent processing of data for the creation and distribution of management information. Although management information systems roughly qualify as communication systems, we will discuss such systems separately so as to clearly recognize the role of computers or other electronic data processing machines.

Communication

Definition

Some authorities have broadened the term *communication* to include nearly the entire spectrum of human relations in organizations. Such a broad use of the term seems particularly ambitious, especially given that many organizations devote no formal planning to communication as a distinct aspect of management and fail to establish standing plans related to channels, frequency, method, type, format, intent, content, or responsible organizational members. Furthermore, although communication is indeed a distinct element of human relations, conscious formal planning is necessary for effective business communication regardless of what practices are best for human relations in general within a specific firm. Even if the human relations within a firm are exemplary, managers must give specific attention to the timely movement of appropriate messages and information necessary to planning and implementing organizational operations; otherwise, organizational ineffectiveness will likely occur.

Haggblade, in a recent text titled *Business Communication*, gives this definition:

> Communication occurs when a message from one person to another is commonly understood by both parties. Communication occurs when a message actually reaches its destination and is perceived by the receiver as the sender intended.[1]

In our review of definitions of communication by various authorities, none seemed more nearly correct. Note that communication involves at least two parties and that a common understanding of a message is required. Although not explicitly mentioned in the definition, feedback is an important part of communication. Without it, the sender of a message could never be certain that the receiver perceived the message's intent or content correctly. Even so, one may say that *one-way communication* has transpired when a sender knows an intended receiver in fact received a message and the sender is reasonably assured that it was understood—with a complete absence of feedback. In some instances, the sender may not need or desire any feedback. When feedback does occur (and in most instances it is desirable), *two-way communication* will have transpired.

Classifications of communication

Authorities have viewed organizational communication from a number of standpoints. Among them the following have been most common.

According to hierarchical direction
Most corporations have bureaucratic levels, and communication moves both *downward* and *upward* among these levels. *Horizontal* movements can be extremely important from time to time, and they appear to be often neglected. The typical downward movement is from a superior to his or her assigned subordinates; the flow reverses in the case of upward movements. However, diagonally upward or downward movements become desirable from time to time (where a message is given to someone at another hierarchical level who neither is an assigned superior nor assigned subordinate). This usually occurs in emergency situations. Figure 8-1 depicts communication within and between hierarchical levels.

According to method of transmission
Managers frequently debate the relative advantages and disadvantages of *oral* versus *written communication*. Certainly, each has its place, and one

Figure 8-1

Hierarchical Communication

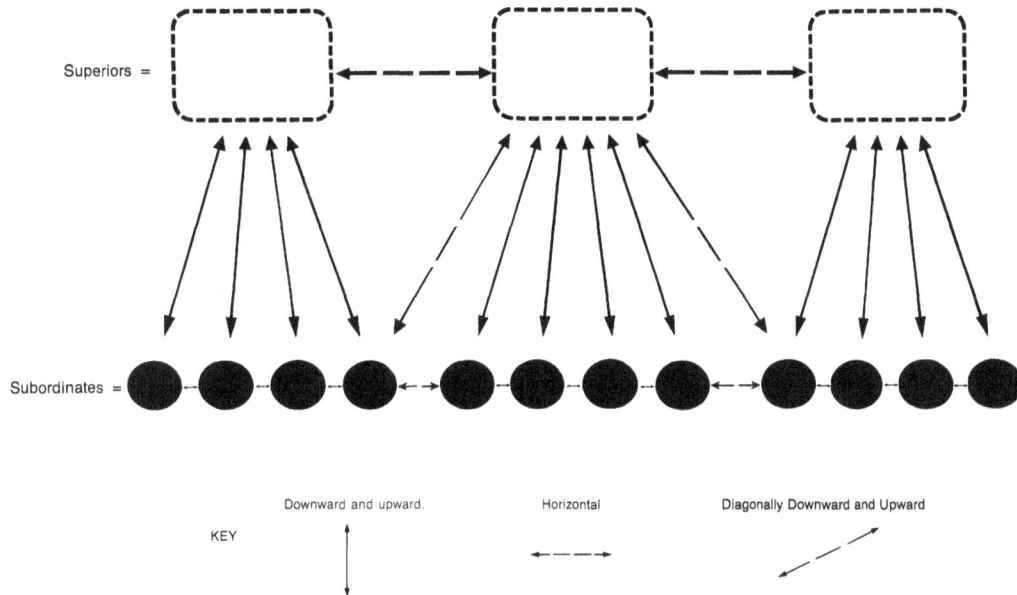

can generalize about which may be more appropriate depending on the senders and receivers involved and on the type of information to be transmitted.

Most authorities now cite a third method of transmission, called *nonverbal communication*. This method transmits "messages that can be inferred from the behavior or actions of others."[2] Little question exists that this third method has considerable importance, but it also frequently allows gross misinterpretations to occur. After being badly deceived or surprised on several occasions by relying on nonverbal impressions, both of us usually await an oral or written confirmation before taking irrevocable actions relating either to a person or a situation.

Our experiences with nonverbal communication include, among numerous others, the following:

- One of the most sloppily dressed individuals we have known was also one of the most outstanding physicians.

- One of the most seemingly naive persons we've met was an imposter.

- One of the richest men we've known drove a pickup truck.

- The trappings of corporate prosperity surrounded the headquarters of a largely bankrupt operation.

Each of us has prided himself on being keenly perceptive about other people. In fact, one of us was formerly prone to brag, "I can tell you most of the life story of a person after a five-minute conversation." At this point, neither of us would make such a statement.

According to content

Steers, Ungson, and Mowday have cited three classifications according to content. These are *technical communication, interpersonal communication,* and *strategic communication.* These authors say that *technical communication* "refers primarily to instructions, policies and procedures related to the performance of jobs in the organization."[3] *Interpersonal communication* "may range from praise from managers for a job well done to inquiries about the health of the employee's family."[4] And lastly, "*strategic communications* involves the future direction and goals of the organization, as well as information related to the external environment."[5]

According to organizational relationships

Communication can be classified as either *internal* or *external* to a specific organization. The terms are self-explanatory. We briefly discuss external communication later in the chapter. Of course, the main thrust of our subsequent comments applies to internal communication, although the headings do not explicitly indicate this.

According to purpose

Citing the classifications of Scott and Mitchell in *Organization Theory: A Structural and Behavioral Approach,* Steers, Ungson, and Mowday note three classifications of communication based on purpose:

1. control the behavior of others, to clarify duties, and to establish or reinforce authority relationships within the organization

2. provide information on which to base important decisions

3. motivate employees and elicit their cooperation and commitment.[6]

We agree these classifications are legitimate, but we have no need to discuss them further, nor will we.

Barriers to communication

Before formally planning and implementing a communication system, managers should assess the organization's specific characteristics and both its internal and external environments. It should be noted that many enterprises have had extreme difficulties with appropriate communication and that analyses of such difficulties have revealed a broad range of problems, which authorities usually group into categories and call *barriers.* Such categories vary widely, depending on the individual authority's viewpoint.

Because we intend to discuss planning for an organizational communication system that involves both internal and external communication, we discuss both internal and external barriers. Further, since organizational messages move in four directions within every organization, we subdivide internal barriers into downward, upward, horizontal, and diagonal (upward and downward) barriers. We do not discuss subdivisions of external barriers.

Internal barriers

Downward communication

Typically, downward communication involves sending messages about policy, procedures, and methods or including instructions, necessary technical information about a host of possible topics, strategic data and information, various kinds of interpersonal information, and items of only incidental management and technical interest. The vast majority of these messages are either oral or written.

The problems we have experienced, together with those reported in the literature, are as follows:

1. *The depth of the hierarchy causes delay in effecting receipt of messages and occasions modifications to their content.* Delay in effecting receipt occurs in both oral and written communication. In oral communication, a message may be so garbled at each level that the content barely resembles the original content by the time it reaches the fourth or fifth level of a hierarchy.

2. *No provisions are made for appropriate feedback.* Many managers issue memoranda, directives, etc., and merely assume receipt by intended receivers and further assume that receivers understood the message as intended. In fact, neither receipt nor understanding may take place. (Misunderstanding is in fact quite common.) "Closing the loop" with appropriate feedback should be duly considered.

3. *The method of transmission is not the best for the message given its content or the degree of understanding or retention required.* In many instances of downward communication, a choice must be made between oral and written communication. Some managers choose oral communication when written communication would be best—often for lack of writing skills. Others issue a formal written directive when a cordial conversation would better suit the occasion. This occurs for a variety of reasons, some of which may relate to a subjective bias stemming from personal inadequacies.

   With regard to written communication, one sometimes must choose between words and graphics (illustrations, graphs, etc.). We have often been impressed with the effectiveness of the latter. Probably the most effective transmission of messages includes both written and oral communication. Writing better assures accuracy and retention and reduces chances for misinterpretation. The spoken word can supplement writing and introduces the personal touch. Also, the spoken word usually engenders feedback. We have often issued written instructions or explanations and followed them up with oral conversations or conferences. On the other hand, we have often held a conference and then had a written report of the discussion (including any agreements) distributed to participants.

4. *Messages lack clarity, completeness, or relevance.* Our own problems in this area have stemmed primarily from impatience. After becoming "fired up" about a matter, we have occasionally "fired off" a memorandum or telephone call which was unclear, incomplete, or irrele-

vant. Although writing must be used in many instances of downward communication, one should compose carefully, for written mistakes have a greater tendency to come back and haunt one than spoken mistakes.

5. *Distrust or lack of knowledge of the sender prevents belief in the contents of messages.* If a receiver does not accept the reliability or veracity of a sender, messages may become suspect either as to content or intent. Communication thus becomes blocked.

   Respect for and trust in a superior by subordinates are intangibles that characterize leadership. They are often difficult to elicit. However, they usually evolve through visual and verbal contact. Managers who isolate themselves in offices and appear pompous, haughty, or even peculiar run a definite risk of never getting either respect or trust. When they do attempt to communicate, their success is minimal. Conversely, a manager who vociferates and handles the truth loosely can expect the same results—not from being unknown, of course, but from being too well known.

6. *Linguistic differences between the sender and receiver prevent the receiver from understanding messages as intended.* Given that this country is the "melting pot" of the world, this problem can be both serious and extensive in a particular company. Ethnic or cultural differences, the country's many sectional differences, the various educational levels, and even the variety of religious backgrounds and moral codes all contribute to considerable differences in the use and understanding of English (or any other language). This being so, a superior must always be cognizant of the person or persons to whom he or she addresses a message and take possible linguistic differences into account. Linguistic differences also extend to the use of technical language or jargon, which a receiver might not understand or might misunderstand.

7. *The receiver lacks the motivation to understand or pay attention to the downward message.* This barrier rarely occurs, and we have seldom encountered it. But obviously the possibility does exist.

8. *Peer pressure at the subordinate levels may prevent accepting a message as intended by the superior.* Again, this rarely occurs, but the literature does record it. Our experience with this problem has been minimal, but we have noted that it can occur among group members performing highly technical work who believe their group interests outweigh the importance of either the message or the sender.

Certainly, the above list does not include all of the barriers to downward communication, but we believe it includes the barriers that occur most frequently.

Upward communication
Although upward communication has markedly improved in organizations over the two preceding decades, it is still probably inadequate. The inadequacy is primarily due to the following barriers:

1. *Subordinates perceive that superiors neither need nor desire communication from them.* This barrier has probably diminished for no other reason than that controlling relies more on formal upward reporting than previously. However, managers still have a long way to go in eliciting the worthwhile ideas and opinions of subordinates. Our opinion that a subordinate manager must learn to exert his or her influence over a superior applies here. When a manager succeeds in managing both upward and downward, everyone benefits, including the organization.

2. *No formal plan exists for communication to flow upward.* Even now some firms lack a formal system of reporting, except for financial data. Then, when disaster or ill times occur, everyone frantically wonders, "How did we arrive at this state?" Counseling also provides a mechanism for upward communication, but once-a-year or even quarterly counseling cannot by itself adequately promote optimal upward flow.

3. *As with downward communication, the depth of the hierarchy may constitute an impediment; the method of transmission may not be optimal; the message may be flawed; the receiver may be distrustful; or there may be serious linguistic differences.* Certainly each of these may pose problems for upward communication.

4. *The subordinate possesses an aversion to the superior.* Each of us has heard this bitter remark: "I'm not going to tell that guy one single thing." Needless to say, to manage one had best have the goodwill and respect of subordinates.

5. *A "brass curtain" may be formed around a superior, especially a superior at a top management level.* Difficulties encountered in getting around a protective secretary or other associate may discourage a subordinate from trying "to get through" to the boss.

6. *The subordinate, for a variety of reasons, may feel like a second class citizen.* We have no quarrel with some of the signs of status, but some managers flaunt the trappings of their position far beyond what is merited by their brainpower. This may have a tendency to "turn off" some subordinates, intimidate others, and create jealousy in still others. In any case, truthful, helpful, and frank communication is stifled.

7. *Peer pressure from an informal group may prove stifling.* Accusations by one's peers about "brownie points," "bucking for a raise or promotion," or "ratting on the group" often prevent upward communication.

8. *The superior receives critical comments with an indifferent, defensive, or hostile attitude.* No one likes to be brushed off or told his or her comments are worthless. Calm, objective discussion is the correct response to critical comments. We have heard many worthless, even some downright foolish, ideas expressed over the course of our careers. However, other ideas have proved to be nearly invaluable. One of the characteristics of a good manager or leader is the ability to

listen objectively and to treat the ideas of others with consideration and respect.

Horizontal communication

Based on our perceptions and the consensus among researchers, we believe horizontal, or lateral, communication in organizations predominates in terms of the total volume of messages transferred. However, the majority are of the informal, interpersonal type that may make relatively little direct contribution to the work of the organization. It seems certain that organizations make less formal provision for horizontal communication than for either downward or upward communication. Also, owing to the structure of chains of command, formal communication does flow vertically rather naturally. If, however, horizontal communication, which can help to achieve optimal coordination on a continuing basis, is to be put to best use, managers must plan for it to occur.

Some barriers to horizontal communication are as follows:

1. *Competition for promotion prevails among those on the same horizontal level more than among those in a vertical chain of command.* This being so, managers on a horizontal level may not wish to extend any assistance to another on the same level, regardless of the fact that the organization itself would be benefited. HCA has experienced this problem among hospital administrators operating hospitals in a common geographic area, and the problem was intensified by competition for growth and earnings. The existence of "watertight" departments in organizations is in part caused by the problem of horizontal competition.

2. *The vertical delegation of authority and assignment of responsibility underscores the importance of vertical, in contrast to horizontal, communication.* The importance of horizontal communication may not be readily apparent to every organizational member. Thus, unless managers from the highest to the lowest echelon each see to it that their subordinates undertake appropriate horizontal communication, it likely will not occur to a sufficient degree.

3. *Except in common work places (shops, restaurants, hospital departments, offices, etc.), physical separation may hamper optimal horizontal communication.* Difficulties may simply arise in getting together those who should communicate.

4. *Many of the problems associated with vertical communication apply to horizontal communication, e.g., inappropriate methods of transmission, flawed messages, distrust, linguistic differences, etc.* Our previous discussion of these problems obviates the need for further comment here.

Diagonal upward and downward communication

In business firms, diagonal communication occurs in relatively small volume and the need for it is much less. Some managers frown on its occurrence, owing to jealousy and suspicion. Although loyalty is very important in any organization, one should not be prejudiced toward a subordinate merely because he or she holds a casual but informative conversation with another manager outside the direct chain of command, either diagonally upward or downward.

We have never formed policies on this kind of communication, nor are we aware of policies having been formed by others. We merely note diagonal communication here to point out the petty jealousy and suspicion it sometimes causes. Where emergency situations arise, such communication becomes very valuable. Perhaps such situations explain why the power inherent in a military officer's rank extends beyond immediate subordinates.

We will not further discuss planning for diagonal communication, believing that managers will perceive when it is desirable or needed and that it will occur as required in emergencies.

External barriers

Most business enterprises communicate at least periodically with several groups outside the organization. Among them are (1) consumers; (2) government agencies; (3) the local public (people living near a plant, factory, or other functional sites); (4) the general public (people living away from functional sites); and (5) competitors.

Each of these parties has different interests, and communication with them differs considerably. In larger companies, specialized staff may handle segmented portions of the entirety of external communications. Executives may directly handle communication with competitors and the local public.

Barriers to effective extraorganizational communication are so numerous that we will not attempt to categorize them. A few of the most obvious barriers are listed below:

- *Poor choice of an advertising or public relations firm is made, with the result that communication is nonsensical, unrealistic, or downright moronic.* We are not sure how many sales are lost because of inept advertising or public relations, but the number must be great. Certainly, millions are spent annually on senseless communication (primarily television advertising).

- *Executives hold themselves aloof from the local public.* The detrimental effect of this barrier has been recognized over the last two decades or so. Rapid improvements have followed, e.g., "good neighbor" policies.

- *Resentment and prejudice toward government cause conflicts with government agencies and result in poor communication.* Every business has a right and a responsibility to protect its best interest so long as the larger interest of the public is not damaged. No business has a right to violate laws, however, except specifically to trigger a "test" case for a questionable law. One has only to read the newspaper to discover companies that have damaged their credibility not only with government agencies but with the general public through either intentional or unintentional violations of government regulations.

- *Bitter antiunion attitudes block optimal communication with unions.* This barrier has diminished dramatically over the last decade, and most executives now deal with unions objectively (and probably much more profitably).

- *The pressing needs of intraorganizational management preclude proper consideration of extraorganizational communication.* Obviously, this occasionally occurs no matter how well managed a firm is.

- *A firm's communication is drowned out by communication emanating from other sources.* Every business "markets" nowadays, often intensely. A resultant barrage of communication reaches the consumer, and unless something unique is sent forth, the communication of a particular firm may be totally disregarded.

Planning an internal communication system

Planning a suitable communication system for a business enterprise involves conscientious preparation of policies and procedures. Policy should be developed by executives and procedures should be developed at each level of the management hierarchy.

We discuss planning employee communications in Chapter 7 and its implementation in Chapter 13. Such communication forms only part of a companywide system. We believe personnel departments do a much better job overall in planning and implementing employee communications than line managers do in communicating among themselves and in planning a companywide downward, upward, and horizontal system for the formal transaction of operations. The reason may be that personnel executives and managers have formal training in a specific area of personnel management called employee communications, while line managers merely depend on the established chains of command to accommodate communication. In fact, chains of command fail to take into account horizontal communication, which possibly promotes coordination more than any other kind of communication. They also do not guarantee that there is any communication (except for the initial act of delegating authority and assigning responsibility and accountability).

Certainly, the inadequacies of communication related to line management do not stem from the fact that policy or procedures for such communication are difficult to understand and formulate. We believe the prime causes of deficiency are (1) the failure to recognize that appropriate communication simply does not occur without planning, (2) sheer neglect, and (3) the failure to implement communication planning even when appropriate policy and procedures have been prepared.

Communication policies and procedures

Every manager in a business enterprise should possess a copy of any company policy statement regarding line communication—downward, upward, and horizontal. Such policy statements should expound the basic roles of both written and oral communication. Every manager should also possess a statement of the communication procedures developed by each assigned subordinate manager in response to this question: *What do you intend to do to assure that adequate communication occurs with your immediate superior, your subordinates, and between you and other managers at the same level?* An additional question is also relevant: *How will you assure that adequate communication occurs among your subordinates?* No manager should settle for or approve anything less than a complete and satisfactory response to these questions. If this strategy is pursued by all managers—from top echelon executives to first-line supervisors—and in conformance with formal company policies on downward, upward, and horizontal communication (including specific requirements for written communication), there will be little chance that a haphazard, hit-or-miss system evolves that allows turmoil and contributes to inefficient, disjointed operations.

Because a policy statement on internal communication can easily be drafted and because communication procedures at each hierarchical level may differ considerably from company to company, we will not set forth examples of each procedure. However, we want to mention two procedures that have served each of us extremely well.

The first is to assemble all immediate subordinates in a group on a periodic schedule (usually weekly or biweekly) so as to promote downward, upward, and horizontal communication (primarily communication about managing operations). The other is to visit personally the offices or workplace of subordinates. This is done in addition to having regular conferences with individual subordinates in one's own office. There is something about going to a subordinate's workplace that calls his or her attention to the need for order and efficiency and at the same time promotes free conversation. This procedure somewhat resembles "management by walking around," which is a characteristic kind of management at Hewlett-Packard. It also resembles a technique reported by Willard V. Merrihue over 25 years ago called "walking the shop and office." Merrihue served as Manager of Community and Business Relations for General Electric Company for a number of years and described this technique in his still remarkable book *Managing by Communication.*[7]

After all, once a manager has planned well and has set in motion implementation (including the implementation of a written reporting system to assure control), he or she should have a primary interest in visual verification and in ferreting out problems that may cause impediments to implementation. Although "management by walking around" or "walking the shop and office" constitutes a very small part of the whole of management, and one we personally would hesitate to call a philosophy (as do some), we have found the technique to be extremely useful in getting at the truth about operations and in identifying problems. Enhancement of the goodwill of subordinates can also occur.

Planning an external communication system

In less hectic and dynamic times, this task may have been relatively simple. However, at present it has assumed great importance and its execution requires mature decision making.

Generally speaking, each external public with which a company must deal should be identified. At least five usually exist (see section on "External Communication" earlier in this chapter). The responsibility for handling each must be assigned and commensurate authority must be delegated. A CEO may wish to retain personal responsibility for one or more publics, especially in small to midsize companies and local branches of larger companies.

No conflicts should exist among the policies developed for these publics, although a separate policy should be developed for each. The diversity of interests that form the relationship between an individual firm and these publics makes the formation of separate policies imperative.

After policy has been developed and responsibility assigned, those who are given responsibility should draft implementing procedures. Such procedures ought to outline an operational protocol based on the existing environment, and rarely are two environments the same. For example, we have dealt with a press in one area that was extremely friendly and with a press in another that was frankly hostile.

With regard to communicating with the local public, one procedure might address relations with the local newspapers; another, relations with radio stations; and still another, relations with television stations. One must be mindful that jealousies exist among the various types of media and that evenhanded policies and procedures avoid animosities.

Some managers still believe if you operate a legitimate business and sell a quality product or service, public relations will automatically be good. In fact, we held that belief years ago. However, with competition currently being what it is, we believe a proactive approach is needed for dealing with a firm's external publics. More than ever, firms must wisely plan and diligently implement.

Mechanical and electronic communicating devices and systems

The hardware systems and devices now on the market to promote many specialized areas of communication are mind boggling and far too extensive to discuss here. Many organizations (e.g., hospitals) use the telephone, radio, television, computer, and even pneumatic tube systems to effect the transmission of messages, either oral or written, or both.

The telephone, however, remains the company workhorse, and its capabilities have grown enormously. As an example, to avoid using traditional answering machines or answering services, at least one company has successfully developed digital voice exchange equipment and operates it under client contracts. Along with receiving messages, the equipment allows users to create, send, store, reply to, and forward voice messages to one or more individuals. Users need only a push-button telephone to use the system at any hour of the day anywhere in the world. This system, in addition to reducing the average telephone bill, puts an end to "telephone tag," and it greatly increases the number of completed two-way communications.

No third person is involved, and if desired, identical messages can be expeditiously sent to literally hundreds of persons on the system. The system is especially helpful to companies with geographically dispersed offices and agents or with employees who must constantly travel, and it assures complete confidentiality by allowing each user his or her individual access code. Obviously, this system has application in many firms and can enhance upward, downward, horizontal, and diagonal upward and downward communication.

Planning a management information system

Definitions and overview

Henry C. Lucas, Jr., in a notable text entitled *Information Systems Concepts for Management*, defines an information system as "a set of organized procedures, which, when executed, provides information to support decision making."[8] Lucas further notes, "We define information as a tangible or intangible entity which serves to reduce uncertainty about some future state or event."[9]

Ralph H. Sprague, Jr., and Eric D. Carlson, in *Building Effective Decision Support Systems*, opine that decision support systems (DSS) are an evolutionary step beyond management information systems (MISs).[10] Although this may or may not be true, we view a sophisticated MIS as including DSS, and therefore we have elected to use the broader term. As for the claim of some that the MIS approach is aimed only at middle managers, we believe this represents a misconception. We used the kind of information purportedly supplied by DSS *before* the term *decision support system* was popularized. This suggests *management information system* is the more inclusive term. Further, this is consistent with the existence of systems (DSS) that supply information specifically needed by top executives. Sprague and Carlson correctly state our view of DSS: "DSS comprise a class of information systems that draws on transaction processing systems and interacts with other parts of the overall information system to support the decision-making activities of managers and other knowledge workers in organizations."[11] We believe, however, that in formulating plans for an effective MIS, one should make provisions for supplying the kind of information that DSS purport to supply.

John Gessford, in *Modern Information Systems*, uses the terms *business information system* and *business data system* interchangeably, and he states that "data is what a well organized system can produce. Information is what the user hopes and tries to get from the system."[12] Gessford, in attempting to establish an appropriate relationship between data and information, further observes, "Data must be both *relevant* [to the concerns of management in decision making] and *newsworthy* to qualify as information."[13]

Austin defines the terms *data* and *information* in a way that conforms to our long-held view of the matter. He states that "*data* refers to raw facts and figures which are collected as part of the normal functioning of the hospital [or other business]. Information . . . is defined as data which have been processed and analyzed in a formal, intelligent way, so that the results are directly useful to those involved in the operation and management of the hospital [or other business]."[14]

In distinguishing between data and information, Austin makes a point that should be noted by all who may become involved in the planning and design of management information systems. It is this: *The basic objective of an MIS is to provide to managers at various levels of an organizational hierarchy information—as opposed to data—that will be useful in planning, implementation, and framing adaptive responses.* Most authorities focus on the use of information for decision making (planning). However, much of the information produced by an exemplary MIS serves in the monitoring step of the control process, which is a distinct element of implementation (according to this text). Regarding adaptive responses, certainly their effective formulation depends many times directly on the immediate availability of relevant information. Thus, we would emphasize that information serves the needs of managers in *all* areas of management, not just in decision making.

Austin observes that "all too often, voluminous computer printouts gather dust in the desk or shelves . . . because insufficient thought went into the preparation of useful reports, both in form and content. Alternatively, computerized data banks, accessible through terminals or microprocessors, may exist but be little used because of the lack of planning in the retrieval and analysis of the information for purposes of management planning and control."[15] (Note that Austin is one authority who recognizes the use of information beyond the realm of decision making.)

The problem Austin has cited arises most often from a lack of involvement in system planning by those who need and use certain information in their management (or operational) functions. So-called computer experts, who usually have limited knowledge of the information required by managers at specific hierarchical levels, plan and design the system; those who use the system then belatedly discover that it does not respond to their needs. That many systems are built on what a programmer can program rather than on actual needs is well known.

Also, in a lesser number of instances, because of management naiveté, lack of clear-cut job descriptions, or lack of organization in decision-making and control functions, some managers actually don't know what information they need. When this occurs, the blind are leading the blind, and there is no sure solution.

Be this as it may, Austin's further point is worthy of note: "An essential element for the successful development of hospital information systems [or those for any business enterprise] is carefully planned teamwork by administrative and technical (systems) personnel in information systems development."[16]

Many authorities and computer experts fail to specify the important differences between a management information system (MIS) and an operational information systems (OIS). Thus managers in some firms, when a satisfactory OIS has been developed, believe they have done their duty regarding the development of an MIS.

Burian and Fink observe that "*operational systems* involve production, marketing, distribution, and other business processes. Data produced by the operational systems serve as input to the operational information systems."[17] These authorities further note, "*Operational information systems* accept data from the operational systems and provide information about the functioning of these systems."[18]

In hospitals, for example, data that are generated by an admitting department, a collections department, a supply function, or a laboratory and then processed as information become part of an operational information system.

Burian and Fink also state that "while operational information systems provide information on day-to-day operations, *management information systems* provide information for all levels of decision making including developing long range plans and procedures."[19] Undoubtedly, long-range plans and procedures should be taken to include the major types of planning discussed in this text, such as strategic planning, human resource planning, financial planning, etc.

Burian and Fink point out that "the heart of many management information systems is *the data base*, a structured file containing historical records, forecasts, plans, programmed decisions, rules and models."[20] They also correctly note that some management information systems develop from teleprocessing systems and that management information is available from the systems on demand, either according to a schedule or by exception.[21]

Obviously, operational information system planning and management information system planning overlap and cannot be logically separated. Therefore, they should be undertaken simultaneously and as a part of one development effort.

Austin observes that "computers are in a sense only incidental to the entire process of information systems development" and "an essential element for the successful development of . . . information systems is carefully planned teamwork by administrative and technical (systems) personnel in information systems development."[22] Although Austin's comment about computers being only incidental to the development of a management information system is perfectly true, certainly no sizeable business organization would attempt to develop any comprehensive information system today without using computers. Therefore, how to employ them becomes a necessary consideration in the development of such systems. Their capabilities, capital and operational costs, unique characteristics, personnel requirements, and effects on organizational planning are factors of great significance in planning both operational and management information systems and cannot be ignored.

Organizational planning

Because planning an MIS and undergirding operational information systems or subsystems is a multidisciplinary effort, relevant decision-making authority should be placed at top-level management echelons. In small to midsize firms (say, those from 10 to 1,000 employees), this responsibility might be retained by the CEO or COO. In larger firms, it should be retained no lower than a second echelon executive who has or is given coordinating responsibility for a broad number of departments. To delegate authority and assign responsibility for planning "data processing" exclusively to the head of a "data processing department" is a mistake of the first order and greatly increases the probability that considerable effort and money will be expended wastefully.

In many instances where this is done, the appointed head of the data processing department has an appropriate amount of technical knowledge regarding computer hardware, programming systems design, data preparation, etc. However, in a majority of organizational settings, the appointed head will not know the pertinent decisions which must be made up and down the management hierarchy concerning, for example, strategic planning and its implementation, planning for implementation of the financial function, human resource planning and its implementation, organizational planning, and controlling (from a variety of standpoints). As noted, the classic remedy is to do the following: *Assign responsibility for planning and developing a management information system to an executive at a hierarchical level above the technical (systems) personnel and above most managers who will need to derive information from the system.* This top echelon manager should then appoint a committee (in some instances, a task force) to develop guidelines and specific recommendations regarding the planning and design of the management information system. All major organizational departments must be represented among the appointees and every department should have input through at least one appointee. Many organizations call such a committee the MIS Planning and Development Committee.

This committee or task force should convene at the call of the involved executive as needed. The meetings should occur at least once a month, even after the MIS is fully developed and implemented, to assure the resolution of problems as they arise and to formulate any planned system additions and alterations that are indicated. Thus, the committee will deal with aspects of both planning and implementation—and of course adaptive responses, as the need for them occurs.

Subcommittees usually have to be formed for investigations and recommendations relevant to specific areas of systems planning and development.

The committee should give careful consideration to employing an independent consultant who specializes in the development of systems for firms in similar lines of business. An expert's outside viewpoint will prevent tunnel vision and allow more objectivity when considering the needs of individual departments. Priorities can also be more logically developed. The consultant should possess a track record of successful system installations and must not be a representative of an equipment sales or manufacturing firm. In the event a firm does not have appropriate technical expertise in-house, employing an outsider becomes imperative.

There are two phases in planning an MIS, and these will be discussed below. The actual work involved in both phases must be assigned to specific individuals within departments, and time must be set aside for these persons to perform their tasks. The nature of these tasks will become evident as we discuss the planning steps below. Technical personnel within an established MIS can serve as resource consultants for these assigned departmental individuals, as can outside consultants if they are employed to assist in the undertaking, which we recommend.

It would be difficult to overemphasize the importance of appropriate time commitments by committee or task force members to the planning and development of an MIS. The assigned executive should authorize the required time and, if necessary, *redefine* each member's job to take account of such planning and development.

The MIS planning process

A fairly distinct process can be followed in planning for a management information system. This process involves two basic phases, each of which can be ordered into steps. Figure 8-2 shows the relationship of these phases, the first of which can be called Analysis and Evaluation of Information Needs and the Existing MIS and the second, Planning Steps in Designing and Implementing an MIS.

Phase I: Analysis and evaluation of information needs and the existing MIS
Many organizations have no mission statement; some have only a basic goal of "making a profit." Although making a profit is commendable,

Figure 8-2

Planning Management Information Systems in Business Firms

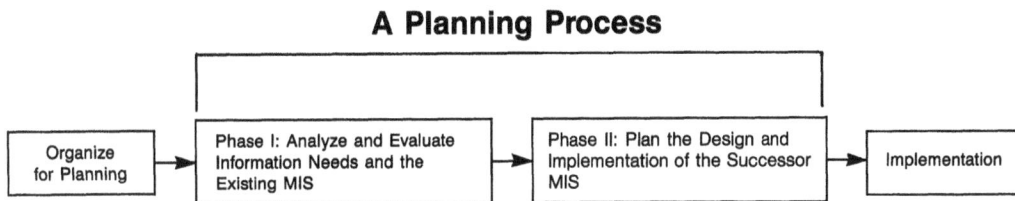

A Planning Process

| Organize for Planning | → | Phase I: Analyze and Evaluate Information Needs and the Existing MIS | → | Phase II: Plan the Design and Implementation of the Successor MIS | → | Implementation |

quantified goals and objectives allow definitive targets toward which work efforts can be directed. Appropriate MIS planning includes considerations related to the basic outlook and nature of the firm.

Steps 1 and 2: Document mission, goals, objectives, and work procedures. Planning an MIS provides management with the opportunity to examine or re-examine the existing nature of the firm and to think about possibly more desirable proactive approaches to doing business. In taking advantage of this opportunity, the company mission and goals should be documented, as well as the objectives of departments (divisions, plants, etc.) and functional units (if any). For our purposes here, we will define a *functional unit* as a component of a department (or other administrative unit) that pursues one or more identifiable work procedures and produces measurable output.

By identifying current goals and objectives and the work processes needed to attain them, one can then better conceptualize the information required for formulating appropriate goals and objectives periodically (usually annually) and for controlling work processes resulting from a variety of planning decisions, most of which can be improved by relevant, timely information. The best MIS will supply pertinent information about what a company and its departments and functional units *plan* to do (in terms of goals and objectives) according to specific work policies and procedures that have resulted from formal planning efforts.

Step 3: Document data and information needs. As previously noted, a management information system builds on an operational information system. Information needed by operational personnel to guide and control their work processes and information needed by managers to plan and implement must be determined jointly. This step conceptualizes the information needed by both operational and management personnel, including information required by top executives.

The types of planning (decisions) done by managers that can be substantially improved by appropriate information supplied by an MIS are as follows:

1. strategic planning (see Chapter 3)

2. planning in various areas of financial management (see Chapter 6)

3. human resource planning (see Chapter 7)

4. organizational planning (see Chapter 4)

5. standing plans, including the procedures and methods of operational systems (see Chapter 5)

6. single use plans (see Chapter 9)

Regarding implementation, the control process cannot properly function in most businesses without in some way quantifying planned output. Many other aspects of implementation also benefit, for example, in the implementation of human resource planning (see Chapter 13) and in effecting various types of work (see Chapter 12).

Step 4: Analyze the existing system. Obviously, any firm should base MIS planning on information that it should be getting rather than on what it is getting from an existing system. Although determining what it should be getting can start with what an existing system is supplying, analyses should extend far beyond this point, as has been explained.

While the last statement above is true, one can also document data and information outputs of a current system *after* conceptualizing what a company actually needs. The inclusion of this documentation in Step 4 reflects this approach, which is essentially based on the notion that analysts may become biased by what is being produced and thereby mentally make compromises. Whether determining output is done before or after conceptualizing need, the objective is to identify gaps and deficiencies between the data and information which the existing system is producing and the data and information that should be optimally supplied for the purpose of operating and managing the business enterprise efficiently and profitably.

Other elements within this step include flow charting the existing system, narratively describing its processes and attributes (good and bad), evaluating processing equipment from both functional and physical standpoints, documenting the various costs of operations, and making notations about the feasibility of further development (from the standpoint of both hardware and software). Needless to say, vast amounts of time are required in most firms to accomplish these tasks.

Step 5: Identify current information gaps, deficiencies, and excesses. Having determined what the existing system is supplying in terms of data and information to operational personnel and managers—from top executives to the supervisory level—and having conceptualized what it should be supplying, one can then document gaps, deficiencies, and excesses, if any. This is the key objective of the analysis and evaluation phase (Phase I), although there are others, which have been noted. The determination of deficiencies has been planned for and naturally follows the preceding four steps.

Step 6: Summarize findings and conclusions of the analysis and evaluation. The purpose of this step is to provide members of the MIS planning and development committee, the CEO, and possibly other key executives with a concise and easily understandable statement of findings and conclusions of the study. This summarization will allow the committee to formulate a recommendation whether or not to proceed with Phase II of the MIS planning and, if the recommendation is to proceed, to give some specific direction to the process. Final authority as to further planning work and its direction rests with the CEO (or another authorized executive), and his or her assent should be obtained. One can expect, however, that if the analysis and evaluation phase has been properly carried out, the CEO will agree with its conclusions and with the recommendations of the MIS planning and development committee.

Figure 8-3 diagrams the steps of Phase I: The analysis and evaluation of a firm's information needs and its existing MIS.

Phase II: Planning steps in designing and implementing an MIS
Seven basic steps characterize this phase. Although many authorities have noted most aspects of designing an MIS, we have attempted to order these steps in logical fashion so as to form a process that will best assure an optimal outcome. Figure 8-4 diagrams the steps of Phase II.

Step 1: Formulate system requirements. This step involves making some initial assumptions about what data and information will actually be supplied to both operational personnel and managers rather than what one might wildly dream of having supplied. The very definition of information implies relevance as opposed to mere factual interest. One of the mistakes made over the years in MIS planning has been, in many areas, to supply more data (to be distinguished from information) than managers use or need for decision making and control. However, a more serious problem, due to a lack of manager involvement in planning, has been the supplying of insufficient or erroneous information. Technical personnel of the "data processing department" often merely supply what an equipment manufacturer has advised. Certainly, some of the best examples of "muddling through" have arisen from "installing the company computer."

The approach to this step should be on a manager-by-manager basis (referenced to positions established or to be established) from the top of the hierarchy to the supervisory level. Operational processes must be considered, including work processes or procedures used or to be used. The consideration should be companywide and department by department, and should even extend to functional units.

Users, both managers and operational personnel, should work with technical personnel to develop the information requirements. The users should be in control. Report formats, timeliness, accessibility, and cost estimations should all be discussed, with some consideration given to input requirements.

At this stage of the process, optimism should prevail: If certain information will truly be needed to make key decisions, for example, it should not be disregarded just because of supposed costs or difficulties in programming.

Step 2: Establish development priorities. Austin has clearly noted the purpose of establishing priorities for information systems development: "The list [of priorities] should include all functional areas . . . and should be rank ordered in the recommended sequence for systems development. For example, the task force might determine that financial control is the

Figure 8-3

Phase I:
Steps in Analysis and Evaluation
of Information Needs and Existing
MIS

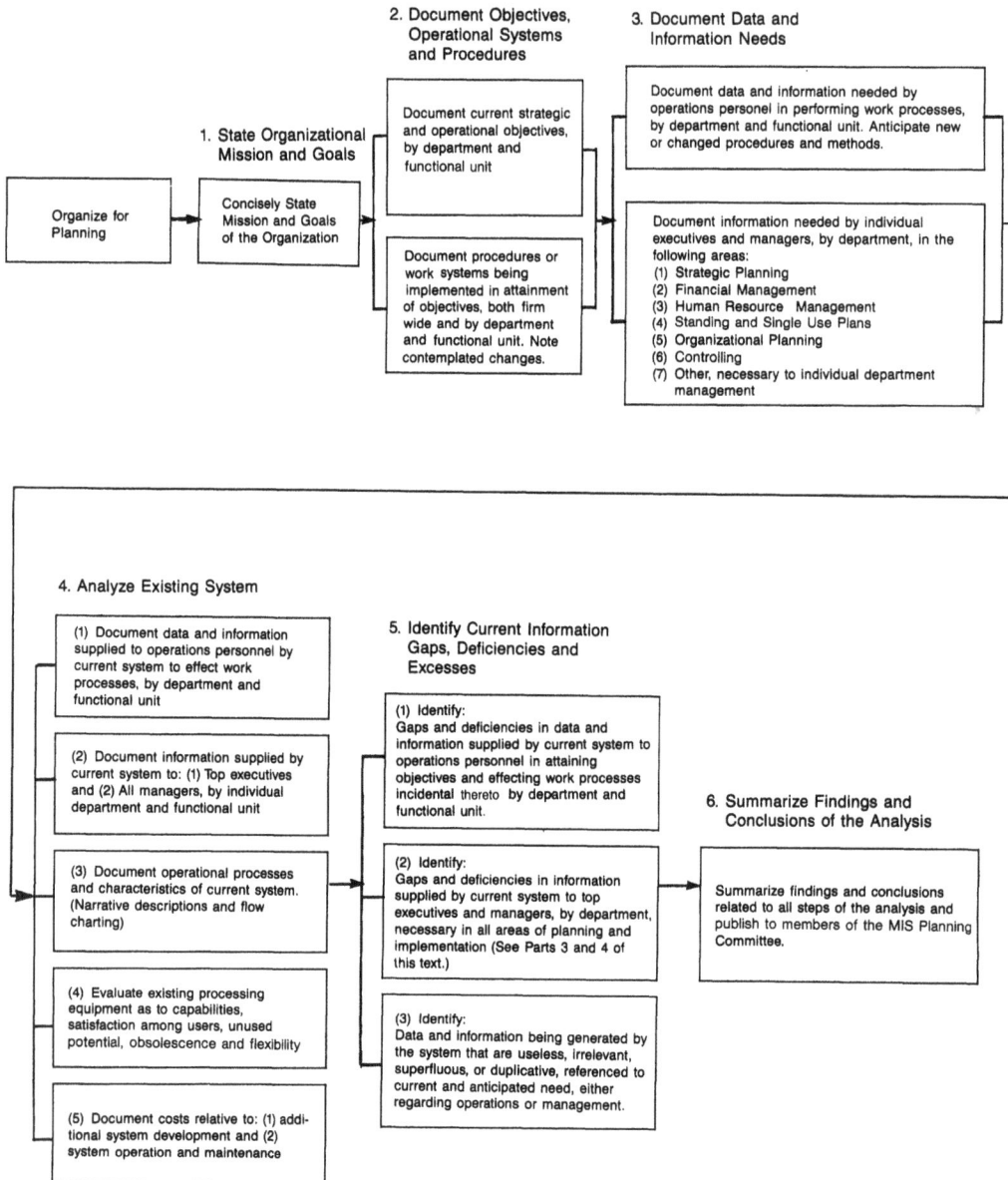

2. Document Objectives, Operational Systems and Procedures

3. Document Data and Information Needs

1. State Organizational Mission and Goals

Document current strategic and operational objectives, by department and functional unit

Document data and information needed by operations personel in performing work processes, by department and functional unit. Anticipate new or changed procedures and methods.

Organize for Planning

Concisely State Mission and Goals of the Organization

Document procedures or work systems being implemented in attainment of objectives, both firm wide and by department and functional unit. Note contemplated changes.

Document information needed by individual executives and managers, by department, in the following areas:
(1) Strategic Planning
(2) Financial Management
(3) Human Resource Management
(4) Standing and Single Use Plans
(5) Organizational Planning
(6) Controlling
(7) Other, necessary to individual department management

4. Analyze Existing System

(1) Document data and information supplied to operations personnel by current system to effect work processes, by department and functional unit

(2) Document information supplied by current system to: (1) Top executives and (2) All managers, by individual department and functional unit

(3) Document operational processes and characteristics of current system. (Narrative descriptions and flow charting)

(4) Evaluate existing processing equipment as to capabilities, satisfaction among users, unused potential, obsolescence and flexibility

(5) Document costs relative to: (1) additional system development and (2) system operation and maintenance

5. Identify Current Information Gaps, Deficiencies and Excesses

(1) Identify:
Gaps and deficiencies in data and information supplied by current system to operations personnel in attaining objectives and effecting work processes incidental thereto by department and functional unit.

(2) Identify:
Gaps and deficiencies in information supplied by current system to top executives and managers, by department, necessary in all areas of planning and implementation (See Parts 3 and 4 of this text.)

(3) Identify:
Data and information being generated by the system that are useless, irrelevant, superfluous, or duplicative, referenced to current and anticipated need, either regarding operations or management.

6. Summarize Findings and Conclusions of the Analysis

Summarize findings and conclusions related to all steps of the analysis and publish to members of the MIS Planning Committee.

Figure 8-4

Phase II:
Planning Steps in Designing and
Implementing a Management
Information System

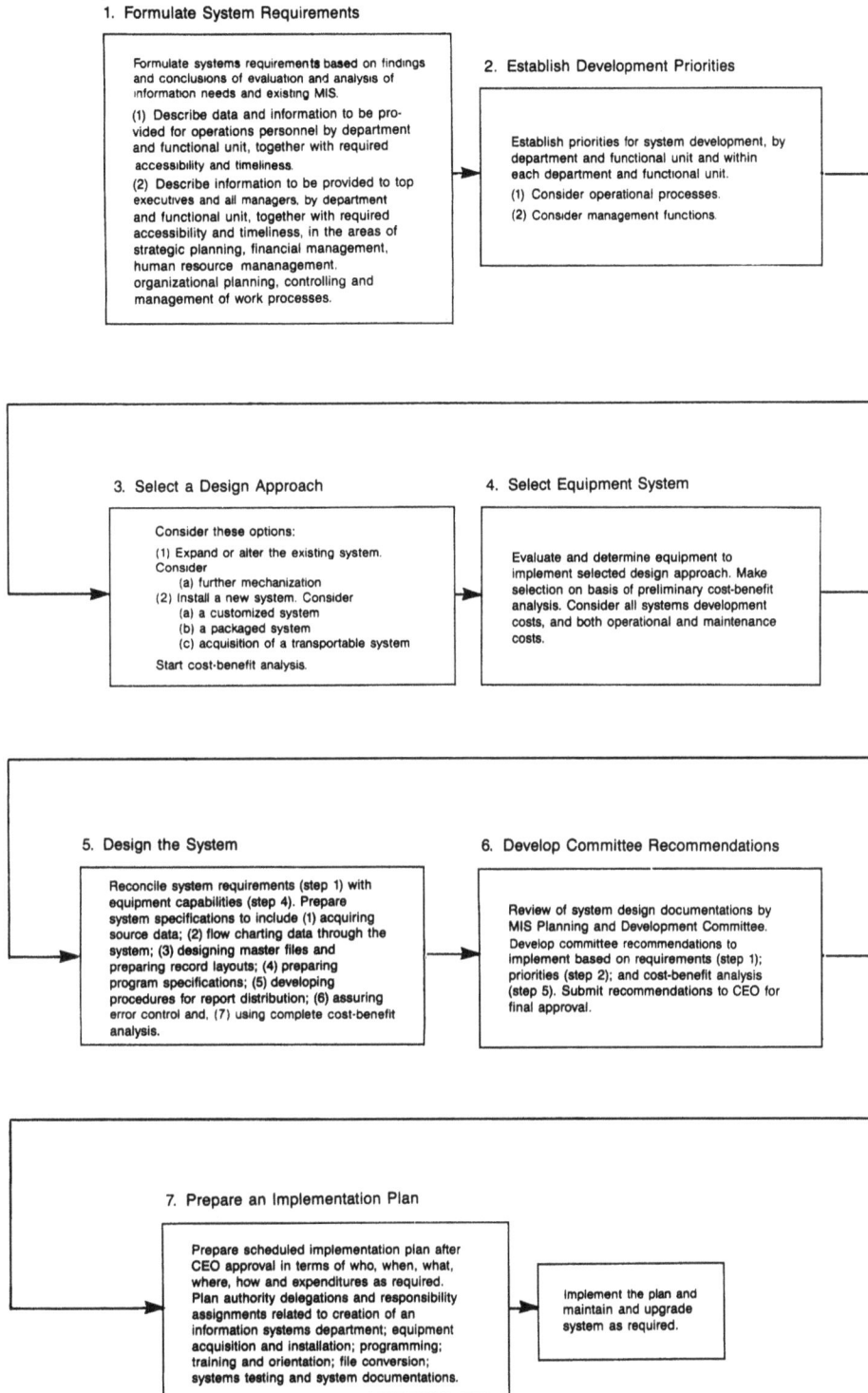

1. Formulate System Requirements

Formulate systems requirements based on findings and conclusions of evaluation and analysis of information needs and existing MIS.

(1) Describe data and information to be provided for operations personnel by department and functional unit, together with required accessibility and timeliness.

(2) Describe information to be provided to top executives and all managers, by department and functional unit, together with required accessibility and timeliness, in the areas of strategic planning, financial management, human resource mananagement, organizational planning, controlling and management of work processes.

2. Establish Development Priorities

Establish priorities for system development, by department and functional unit and within each department and functional unit.

(1) Consider operational processes.

(2) Consider management functions.

3. Select a Design Approach

Consider these options:

(1) Expand or alter the existing system. Consider
    (a) further mechanization
(2) Install a new system. Consider
    (a) a customized system
    (b) a packaged system
    (c) acquisition of a transportable system

Start cost-benefit analysis.

4. Select Equipment System

Evaluate and determine equipment to implement selected design approach. Make selection on basis of preliminary cost-benefit analysis. Consider all systems development costs, and both operational and maintenance costs.

5. Design the System

Reconcile system requirements (step 1) with equipment capabilities (step 4). Prepare system specifications to include (1) acquiring source data; (2) flow charting data through the system; (3) designing master files and preparing record layouts; (4) preparing program specifications; (5) developing procedures for report distribution; (6) assuring error control and, (7) using complete cost-benefit analysis.

6. Develop Committee Recommendations

Review of system design documentations by MIS Planning and Development Committee. Develop committee recommendations to implement based on requirements (step 1); priorities (step 2); and cost-benefit analysis (step 5). Submit recommendations to CEO for final approval.

7. Prepare an Implementation Plan

Prepare scheduled implementation plan after CEO approval in terms of who, when, what, where, how and expenditures as required. Plan authority delegations and responsibility assignments related to creation of an information systems department; equipment acquisition and installation; programming; training and orientation; file conversion; systems testing and system documentations.

Implement the plan and maintain and upgrade system as required.

most pressing problem . . . and direct that development of a financial information system take priority."[23] Installation time, ease of installation, cost, and importance are all factors to consider in determining the priority list, together with relationships between information needed by one department and information needed by another.

After approval of the priority list by the MIS planning and development committee, the list should be given to the CEO (or an executive authorized by the CEO) and various other interested executives. The CEO or authorized designee should give formal approval.

Step 3: Select a design approach. A summary of alternatives that are available as design approaches in planning MIS systems today has been discussed by Austin. He cites the following:[24]

1. development of individual independent systems

2. modular design

3. fully integrated approach

4. distributed processing approach

Each of these approaches has application in various business firms depending on type, nature, and size.

Small businesses may well select the individual independent system approach because limited applications are needed and all personnel may be grouped in contiguous office suites or other functional areas, with easy access to each system as is necessary and allowable. As a business grows, however, inability to transfer data and information from one system to another presents many problems.

Hospitals have most frequently chosen the modular design approach, owing to independent needs for information by departments in some functional areas and shared needs where work processes or systems cut across departmental lines. Numerous other businesses have similar needs.

Many large hospitals are now installing fully integrated systems which feature a central data base. HCA is currently installing such a system, and the current trend in data management is toward establishment of a central data base,[25] especially among large business enterprises.

Distributed data processing systems feature some level of processing at various geographic locations, with communication between the remote processors and a large central computer on either a real-time or batch processing basis.[26] The success of minicomputers has led to the great current interest in distributed systems.

With regard to this step in planning by an individual firm, the MIS planning and development committee has two basic choices: (1) to alter and possibly expand the existing system using one or a combination of the four approaches just cited, and (2) to select a new approach.

As a practical matter, if an organization decides to make a basic change from its current system, there are usually three alternatives regarding the acquisition or development of software to meet system requirements. (Note that the selection of a software system will determine the equipment required.) These three alternatives are as follows:

1. Design a customized system. (This may be very costly.)

2. Purchase a packaged system. (This has the advantage of quick usage, but it usually requires retooling. It may be the predominate approach today.)

3. Acquire transportable software from a firm with a similar organization that pursues similar business objectives. (One advantage is the probable low cost. Such software may or may not satisfy requirements.)

Each of these alternatives can be compared in terms of meeting established requirements and costs. Their comparison forms a basic part of a cost-benefit study, which can be started earlier but should be started *no later* than this step. Regardless of the approach selected by the committee, the CEO or authorized designee should approve it.

Step 4: Select an equipment system. Equipment selection is a logical follow-up to the choice of a design option, which itself necessarily involved some consideration of equipment capabilities. This step may involve considerable costs, so the selection made should also receive tentative top executive approval. The cost-benefit analysis started earlier should be continued in this step.

Step 5: Design the system. This step requires a vast amount of technical work on the part of personnel of the information systems department. However, such personnel must work closely with managers throughout the organization to see that requirements for data and information are met (Step 1) as fully as possible and according to the development priorities established in Step 2.

As Burian and Fink have noted, design is really a reconciliation of systems requirements with the capabilities of the equipment to be used.[27]

The cost-benefit analysis started in the previous steps should be finalized and submitted to the full committee for study and approval, together with a summarization of the system design.

Step 6: Development committee recommendations. The MIS planning and development committee members should be given ample time to review the systems design and the cost-benefit analysis. Even in this step, the opportunity exists to alter previous decisions before proceeding to implementation. At the call of its chairperson, the committee should meet and formulate its final recommendations. These recommendations, together with the cost-benefit analysis and an executive summary of the system design, should then be given to the CEO or authorized designee for approval.

Step 7: Prepare an implementation plan. After CEO approval, the MIS planning and development committee should authorize preparation of an implementation plan. This plan can be prepared by personnel of the information systems department or by an outside consulting firm. In either case, the plan should be complete and in terms of the parameters specified in the creation of any single use program (explained in Chapter 9).

Authority delegations and responsibility assignments regarding positions and individual departments must be specified. The details of equipment acquisition and installation must be specified, including the vendor, schedule, placement, and costs. Programming must be scheduled. Provisions for training and orientation must be made. Additional scheduling must be done for file conversions, system testing, and final system documentations.

The implementation plan should be comprehensive and largely completed *before* implementation so as to prevent getting "the cart before the horse." The plan should possess many provisions, too numerous to name here, but those responsible should remember that any plan can be tested for completeness by examining it to see that it clearly specifies who will do what, where it will be done, in what manner tasks will be carried out, when tasks will be performed (scheduling in a sequence), and what costs will be involved (usually in the form of a budget).

After committee approval, implementation can proceed with the assurance that haphazard, tangential, and other ill-conceived actions have been avoided. Overall, time will have been saved as a result of the orderly procession due to sound planning, and mistakes will have been prevented (mistakes which usually necessitate repetitive planning actions).

Summary

Conscious formal planning is a requisite for effective business communication. Communication, the sending of messages that are understood by the receivers in the same way as by the senders, forms the basis for all acts of management in business firms. Thus, planned systems of communication are extremely important.

Where electronic machines, including computers, are used in communication, a man-machine system is said to exist. Written and oral messages form a human communication system.

One can classify human communication systems according to hierarchical direction, method of transmission, content, organizational relationships, and purpose. Each method of classification is useful from time to time in planning.

Improved planning results from recognition of certain barriers to communication. Regarding downward communication, these are the most common barriers: depth of the hierarchy; a lack of provision for feedback; erroneous selection of best method of message transmission; lack of clarity, completeness, or relevance in the message; distrust or lack of knowledge of the sender by the receiver; linguistic differences between sender and receiver; lack of motivation to understand the message; and peer pressure perceived by the subordinate.

Frequently cited barriers to upward communication include the perception by subordinates that a superior neither needs nor desires communication from them; a lack of formal planning; depth of the hierarchy; erroneous selection of best method of transmission; flawed messages;

distrust by the receiver; linguistic differences; a subordinate's aversion for the superior; a "brass curtain" surrounding the superior; a sense of inadequacy felt by the subordinate; peer pressure; and a defensive or hostile attitude exhibited by the superior.

Barriers to internal horizontal communication include competition among peer managers; a lack of appreciation for the importance of horizontal communication; physical separation; inappropriate methods of transmission; flawed messages; distrust; linguistic differences; etc.

Communication occurs between an organization and extraorganizational publics including (1) consumers, (2) government agencies, (3) the local public, (4) the general public, and (5) competitors. Appropriate communication results from planning based on the individual features of each of the five publics. Again, recognition of barriers to communication will result in better planning. Some of the more common are poor choice of an advertising or public relations firm; aloofness of executives; prejudice toward government agencies; expressed antiunion attitudes; lack of sufficient management time; and intense competition in marketing by other firms.

Planning internal communication systems involves conscious preparation of company policies and procedures pertaining thereto. Each manager should make sure that each subordinate has prepared a written plan to initiate and continue upward, downward, and horizontal internal communication.

Three ways of effecting upward, downward, and horizontal communication are (1) scheduled conferences among departmental managers and their superior, (2) visitations by the superior to the workplaces of subordinates for the purpose of formal or informal fact finding, and (3) written memoranda, including directions, reports, confirmations, agreements, schedules, etc.

In planning an external communication system, the five publics noted must be given individual consideration, with separate but non-conflicting policies being drawn up regarding interfaces with each. Basically, an evenhanded policy that shows goodwill and neighborliness is preferable. However, in contrast to past times, a proactive stance must be assumed to assure that the goodwill of the various publics is manifested in return. This is due to the extreme competitiveness that currently exists in the business environment.

Management information systems (MISs), if properly planned and implemented, will produce the information generally purported to be supplied by decision support systems (DSS). Therefore, our planning steps have been directed toward MISs, which we have construed as including DSS.

In planning and implementing an MIS, a planning and development committee should be formed, at least in most sizeable companies. An upper echelon executive should have charge of the committee's work in order to assure consideration of user needs throughout the organization. Technical analysts and systems designers will work within the information systems department and perform such work as the committee may direct.

Because an MIS and an operational information system (OIS) overlap (an MIS usually builds upon an OIS), we have also included comments about OISs in our planning steps.

To assist in the planning of an MIS, we believe an independent consultant should advise the planning committee about each step of the process involved. This will insure against subjectivity, bias, and possible lack of experience internally.

We began by assuming the existence of a company that already has a data and information system of some type. We then set forth certain steps necessary in evaluating and analyzing not only the existing MIS but also the actual need for data and information.

The first step in the evaluation and analysis process is to examine or re-examine the firm's mission and goals. Sadly, many information systems have been installed in disregard of what the organization was supposed to be doing. System analysts have frequently taken into account only current work processes, whether or not they were indicative of the longer-term mission and goals.

The second step is to document departmental objectives and the procedures or work systems being used to accomplish them. This allows a review of current policies, procedures, and methods, and it provides an opportunity to change them for greater efficiency.

The third step is basically intended to answer the question, "What data and information are needed for planning activities necessary to the ongoing work of goal and objective formulation and for implementing activities required for goal and objective attainment?" Special consideration must be given to strategic planning, financial management, human resource management, organizational planning, control measures of a broad variety, and supervisory activities at all individual department and functional unit levels.

The fourth step is to analyze what the current system produces, how it operates, and how much it costs (in terms of some type of work unit). Also, analysts should evaluate existing processing equipment as to additional capacity, obsolescence, flexibility, and general functionality.

The fifth step is to identify gaps and deficiencies in data and information supplied for all purposes, together with any useless or duplicative reports that may be regularly issued by the existing system.

The sixth step is to summarize findings and conclusions based on the evaluation and analysis. The summarization is then placed in the hands of all members of the MIS planning committee and its chairperson. The CEO or authorized designee should also receive a copy of this summarization and give it due consideration and (hopefully) approval.

We suggest a seven-step process for designing an MIS and planning its implementation.

The first step is to formulate system requirements concerning the data and information that need to be supplied to operational personnel and managers throughout the management hierarchy, including top executives. In this step, information necessary to both planning decisions and implementing activities (e.g., controlling) must be considered.

The second step is to establish development priorities (by department and functional unit) so as to schedule implementing activities based on degrees of need and costs. Both operational and management needs must be considered.

In Step 3, the planning committee selects a design approach. There is a basic choice between (1) expanding or altering the existing system to satisfy the identified data and information requirements and (2) installing a new system. If it is decided to install a new system, the committee is confronted with five basic alternatives: (1) a system composed of independent processing units; (2) a modularly designed system; (3) a fully integrated system; (4) a distributed processing system; and (5) a combination of two or more of the preceding kinds of system. In making a choice among these alternatives, the committee must decide on (a) a customized system, (b) a packaged system, or (c) a transportable system.

In step 4, consideration is given to the selection (based on all attendant costs) of an equipment system that is capable of implementing the selected design option (Step 3).

The fifth step is to design the information system. Seven standard work segments characterize this step. The first six pertain to preparing system specifications. They are (1) acquiring source data; (2) flow charting data through the system; (3) designing master files and preparing record layouts; (4) preparing program specifications; (5) developing procedures for report distribution; and (6) devising methods for error control. The seventh and final segment involves completion of the cost-benefit study started in Step 4.

Step 6 involves a review of the system design by all members of the MIS planning and development committee. The committee also reviews the results of the cost-benefit analysis. Assuming committee approval, the CEO or authorized designee should review the committee's recommendations and hopefully give approval for developing a plan to implement the system as designed.

The seventh and last step is to prepare an implementation plan. The plan should deal with creation of an information systems department (the current successor to the data processing department), equipment acquisition and installation, programming, training and orientation, file conversion, systems testing, systems conversion, and systems documentation. Implementation should follow.

Notes

1. Berle Haggblade, *Business Communication* (St. Paul, Minn.: West Publishing Company, 1982), 6.
2. Richard M. Steers, Gerardo R. Ungson, and Richard T. Mowday, *Managing Effective Organizations* (Boston: Kent Publishing Company, 1985), 385.
3. Ibid., 388.
4. Ibid.
5. Ibid.
6. Ibid., 390–91.
7. Willard V. Merrihue, *Managing by Communication* (New York: McGraw-Hill, 1960), 173.
8. Henry C. Lucas, Jr., *Information Systems Concepts for Management* (New York: McGraw-Hill, 1978), 5.
9. Ibid.
10. Ralph H. Sprague, Jr., and Eric D. Carlson, *Building Effective Decision Support Systems* (Englewood Cliffs, N.J.: Prentice-Hall, 1982), 4–18.
11. Ibid., 9.
12. John Evens Gessford, *Modern Information Systems* (Reading, Mass.: Addison-Wesley, 1980), 4.
13. Ibid.
14. Charles J. Austin, *Information Systems for Hospital Administration*, 2d ed., with contributions by William J. Harvey (Ann Arbor, Mich.: Health Administration Press, 1983), 3.

15. Ibid., 3–4.

16. Ibid., 4.

17. Barbara J. Burian and Stuart S. Fink, *Business Data Processing*, 2d ed. (1982), 48. Reprinted by permission of Prentice-Hall, Inc., Englewood Cliffs, N.J.

18. Ibid. Reprinted by permission of Prentice-Hall, Inc., Englewood Cliffs, N.J.

19. Ibid., 50. Reprinted by permission of Prentice-Hall, Inc., Englewood Cliffs, N.J.

20. Ibid. Reprinted by permission of Prentice-Hall, Inc., Englewood Cliffs, N.J.

21. Ibid. Reprinted by permission of Prentice-Hall, Inc., Englewood Cliffs, N.J.

22. Austin, *Information Systems for Hospital Administration*, 46.

23. Ibid., 50–55.

24. Ibid.

25. Burian and Fink, *Business Data Processing*, 101.

26. Ibid., 462–64.

27. Ibid., 424.

Chapter 9

Single use plans

Elements of Management
in Corporations

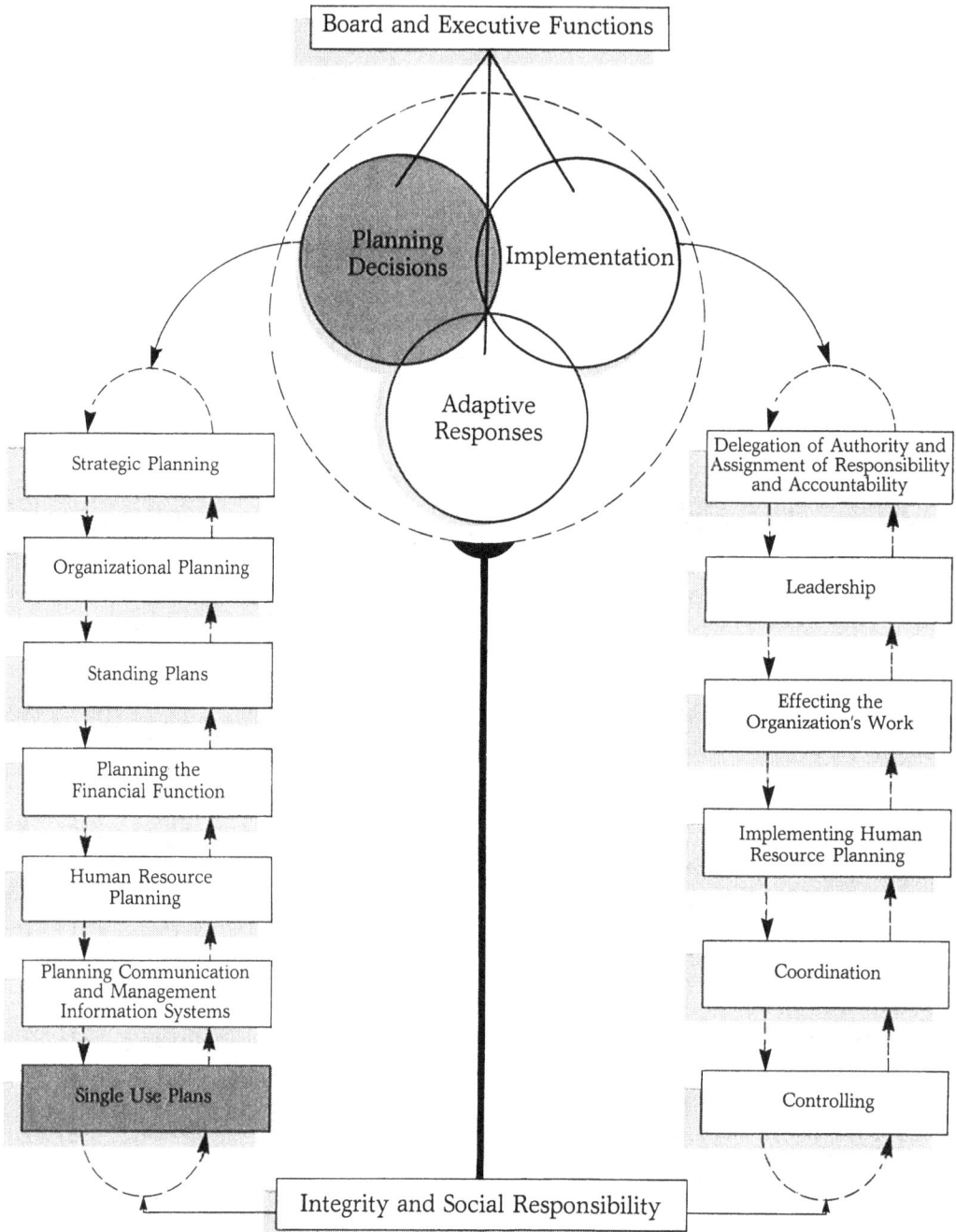

Board and Executive Functions

Planning Decisions

Implementation

Adaptive Responses

Strategic Planning

Organizational Planning

Standing Plans

Planning the Financial Function

Human Resource Planning

Planning Communication and Management Information Systems

Single Use Plans

Delegation of Authority and Assignment of Responsibility and Accountability

Leadership

Effecting the Organization's Work

Implementing Human Resource Planning

Coordination

Controlling

Integrity and Social Responsibility

9

Background and definitions

The term *single use plan* is essentially self-explanatory. Whereas organizations employ standing plans time and time again to guide recurring activities that are routine and ongoing in the conduct of operations and management, they devise and employ single use plans (1) to resolve a particular problem (such plans are often part of an adaptive response), (2) to gain a one-time objective or set of objectives, such as those formulated in strategic planning, and (3) to conduct the activities inherent in a unique event. Like standing plans, single use plans are regarded by most authorities as operational plans. Some authorities refer to operational plans in general as action plans, but apply the term *action plan* more frequently to single use plans than to standing plans. This probably is because standing plans concern not only routine operations but routine management behavior and decisions as well.

Newman and Warren explain single use plans in terms of programming, projects, and schedules. They state, "The basic characteristic of single use plans can be explained best in terms of programs; other forms, such as schedules and projects, can then be viewed as particular kinds of programs."[1]

Stoner states, "The major types of single-use plans are programs, projects and budgets."[2] He further states, "A *program* covers a relatively large set of activities. The program shows (1) the major steps required to reach an objective, (2) the organization unit or member responsible for each step, and (3) the order and timing of each step. The program may be accomplished by a budget or a set of budgets for the activities required."[3] With reference to projects, Stoner writes, "*Projects* are the smaller and separate portions of programs. Each project has limited *scope* and distinct directives concerning assignments and time."[4]

Newman and Warren basically agree with Stoner about the meaning of the term "program," but they seem to broaden Stoner's concept of a project. They state, "Often a single step in a program is set up as a project. Actually, a project is simply a cluster of activities that is relatively separate and clearcut."[5] Thus, according to them, a project can be part of a program, but it needn't be.

Lee, in *Management by Multiple Objectives*, does not specifically define programming, but he states, "Programming action plans basically involves laying out the best possible approach to follow in order to achieve set objectives."[6] Additionally, he states, "An action plan must specify what, how, when and by whom a certain activity or a set of activities should be undertaken in order to achieve objectives."[7]

J.P. Barger, president of Dynatech Corporation, some years ago defined programs as follows: "Detailed characteristics of the paths to be taken, methods and resources to be used or acquired, and functional interrelationships of all factors required for successful accomplishment of the goals."[8] Barger did not employ the terms *single use* or *project* in relation to programming or in any other context.

Brown and Moberg neither define nor discuss single use plans or projects, but they do define a program as "a detailed formulation of a plan to accomplish a particular task. It will probably include a number of job assignments along with a specific allocation of resources. Mechanisms for coordinating the activities may also be specified. In addition, a program typically includes a budget and other control measures."[9]

The preceding references demonstrate, again, the lack of precisely defined terms pertaining to a specific area of management. However, some common threads appear among the comments of the authorities cited, indeed more so than with regard to many other subjects discussed in this text. All seem to agree upon the general nature of a program, and those who mention the term *project* do not seem to be in any basic disagreement. There is general agreement, including among authorities not cited, on the meaning of the term *single use plan*.

Two types of programs

Many programs have a high probability of success. Given our conception of projects, they have an even higher probability of success. However, not all programs and projects can be laid out neatly as a series of time-sequenced events or tasks that will inevitably result in the attainment of a desired goal or objective. Sometimes managers establish a strategic goal or objective with the full knowledge that programming plans may fail in implementation. On other occasions, a complete programming of all actions necessary to attainment may be impossible because of unknowns and unknowables. The best strategy for management may be to program for the short-term future so as to allow *later* longer-term programming that will provide guidance for actions more likely to attain goals and objectives. Programming performed for the short-term future, in such instances, must be flexible and must not preclude later programming involving one of several possible routes to goal or objective attainment.

Some authorities use the term *commitment programming* to refer to that programming or project planning possessing a high probability of success regarding goal or objective attainment.[10] Others refer to such planning as *static programming*.[11] We prefer the former term.

Where programming or project planning is performed "in the face of the quickened pace of change and greater uncertainty of the environment," the term *adaptivising* has been used.[12] Some authorities employ the term *adaptive programming*.[13] One of the older texts called programming in the face of unknowns and unknowables *dynamic programming*, which we regard as an appropriate designation.[14] Since the terms *adaptivising* and *adaptive programming* seem similar in meaning to our term *adaptive responses*, we have chosen to use these terms instead.

The true nature of single use plans

Planning is one of only three basic functions performed by managers, and although many hold that managers fail to devote sufficient time to it in organizations, there may be more time so expended than is commonly recognized. We believe single use plans, particularly, have not been recognized as being the large consumers of management time they actually are. Not only do single use plans serve directly in pursuit of organizational goals and objectives and in preparing to implement a unique event, but managers formulate them as adaptive responses to problems arising from a host of causes (see Chapter 16).

The authorities we have quoted above dwell on complex, multistepped programs and projects composed of clusters of activities. But single use plans also include plans prepared within hours or even minutes and with no more formalization than notes jotted on a writing pad. Each of us has prepared such plans for a variety of purposes, not the least of which has been to "put out fires" (i.e., respond adaptively). For example, as line managers we prepared a plan within less than an hour in response to a unique event which arose early in our careers. The situation developed as follows.

In soliciting donations for a not-for-profit hospital, a letter was sent (over the CEO's signature) to one of the wealthiest men in the United States, who owned a hunting preserve of over 10,000 acres in an adjoining county. This individual, who we will call Mr. O, had still made no reply after a month or so, although his presence on his property for the hunting season was well known.

At approximately 1:00 P.M. on a Friday, the CEO's secretary announced that "Mr. O is calling." Mr. O's voice sounded rather urgent. "My wife has been thrown from her horse, and she's badly bruised, and her right knee is swollen twice normal. There may be some broken bones. I'm leaving with her in the back of my station wagon within a few minutes and should be at your emergency room within 45 minutes. Could you watch out for us? By the way, after she's settled, I'd like to see some of your hospital, and we'll discuss your letter, which I have at the top of my correspondence."

Most CEOs seek advice when an event of this type arises, and the one of us who was the CEO called the other, who was serving as his assistant. We then worked out the following plan.

- Alert the emergency room. Both of us would be at the entrance upon Mr. and Mrs. O's arrival.

- Alert the chief radiologist that x-rays would probably be taken.

- Alert the admissions office that Mrs. O might be admitted if bones were broken and admission indicated.

- Alert a member of our board of trustees, a personal friend of Mr. O's, and see if he could come to the hospital and chat with Mr. O.

- The CEO would take personal charge of Mr. O, and the assistant would remain in the emergency room area to assure Mrs. O of our personal interest and to relay information to the CEO's office, where Mr. O would be retained until the emergency results were known.

- The CEO's secretary would alert each station on a standard 20-minute "tour" route (customarily used for some categories of visitors) that the CEO and Mr. O might be around within the coming two hours.

- After the tour, return Mr. O to the CEO's office to await disposition of the patient.

One will note that every element of a complete plan received attention: who, when, what, where, and how. Implementation of the plan was exact. After emergency examination, the emergency physician referred Mrs. O to radiology with an announcement that broken bones were "unlikely." During the time Mrs. O was in radiology, Mr. O was guided by the CEO through the standard tour and then returned to the CEO's office to chat with his personal friend (one of our board members), who had by that time arrived. Mr. O voluntarily brought up the matter of the request for a donation and assured us that his foundation would act favorably upon our request.

After 30 minutes of examination, Mrs. O was released from x-ray (no fracture seen) and it was announced she did not need to be admitted as an inpatient. A pleased couple then departed for home, with nothing required beyond the filling of a prescription for pain.

(For our readers who might have become intrigued with the human interest element, we can report that the hospital did receive a sizable donation and that Mrs. O retained her interest in horses, which was clearly evidenced when the most notable of them won the Kentucky Derby some years later!)

In contrast to the above, we have also constructed programs that involved the expenditure of millions of dollars (billions in total) and altered the basic nature of some very large hospitals.

We here pose a series of questions and provide answers to them that demonstrate our views about various types of single use plans, including certain aspects of them.

1. *What is the difference between a program and a project?*
There are no clear-cut differentiating criteria. Managers use both *program* and *project* without a clear sense of difference. Either a project or a program should be described in terms of who, when, what, where, how, and how much (if funds are involved). Generally, we view a program as having a much broader scope than a project, but we do not believe that a project has to be an integral part of a program. Many "projects" entirely stand alone.

2. *Is a budget a single use plan?*
Strictly speaking, a budget is a financial plan, and financial plans are invariably geared to other types of plans with a broader scope, whether they be strategic, operational, capital, developmental, etc. We would not consider a budget a complete single use plan, but only part of such a plan. Typically, budgets are components of business plans, management plans, or annual operating plans, all of which can be classified as single

use plans. A budget also serves as a yardstick, during implementation of a plan, in controlling.

3. *How do budgets relate to strategic planning and operational planning, especially to single use operational plans?*

Financial planning and resource allocations are basic integral parts of strategic planning. Detailed budgeting should follow when operational planning (programs and projects) is undertaken to establish guides for implementation. Strategic planning often fails because planners have not truly incorporated financial planning into it. They fail to consider resource allocations until operational planning is undertaken, with the result that grandiose goals and objectives are established that, because of insufficient available funding, can't possibly be attained.

Too much power can also be left in the hands of financial managers, who sometimes make allocations on their own initiative and with some degree of disregard for what other managers have previously agreed upon in strategic planning. In essence, managers should establish strategic goals and objectives that are realistic in terms of resource allocations, and budgets should reflect those allocations when operational plans, particularly single use plans, are formulated.

4. *Is a schedule a single use plan?*

Again, a schedule does not constitute a complete plan but is an integral part of a program or project. It is also used in controlling.

5. *What would be a correct designation for the brief plan described earlier in this chapter?*

Management authorities have ignored brief, informal plans of this type, and they have not been regarded as true planning, even by the individuals preparing them. Many managers view planning as being something abstruse and mysterious, but at the same time might refer to the brief example plan as "my plan to _____." To respond to the question directly, we should say we do not believe a generally accepted designation exists.

6. *Are there any universal characteristics of single use plans?*

All complete single use plans, and there are many so-called plans that are incomplete, should be conceptualized in terms of "who (if humans are involved), when, what, where, and how."[15] If funds are involved, how much should be designated. "Although physical models; mathematical, diagrammatical and/or statistical models; flow diagrams; PERT charts; [financial budgets]; narrative descriptions, etc. may each be used as descriptive techniques, the whole concept of . . . plan is grounded in this simple conceptual context."[16]

Certainly managers should clearly spell out multistep programs or projects involving many activities and persons, with conscious attention to the factors we have cited and with employment of quantitative approaches and appropriate scheduling and descriptive techniques. Simple day-to-day adaptive responses and informal planning need not be detailed, and who, when, what, where, and how may be implied rather than explicitly stated. The level of detail must be left to the judgment of managers involved in specific situations, but one should never forget that the factors we have cited are involved in *every* complete single use plan.

Approaches to programming

The complexity of programming and project planning varies quite widely, depending on the scope of what one is trying to accomplish. For example, if an individual entrepreneur wishes to establish a franchised paint store, he or she might confer with a lending institution, an accountant, the owners of buildings in which the store might be located, and the paint manufacturer. Following this fact finding, a program, most probably a brief business plan, can be formulated, including a budget and a Gantt chart. The program can spell out with due care the necessary information about who, what, when, where, and how. Then, if the prospective lender responds favorably, the program or plan can be implemented, hopefully with success. In building a major hospital or industrial plant, however, the vast amount of work involved will require a hierarchy of programs prepared by a wide range of planners, consultants, and contractors.

Figure 9-1 diagrams the major activities involved in most large hospital building programs. With minor modifications, the same process could be used in the planning, design, and construction of factories and plants of a broad variety. Each of the blocks in the figure represents one or more programs, and several would necessitate some project planning work. It will be noted that the first step in such a process is strategic planning, which is the subject of Chapter 3 of this text. Strategic planning, financial planning, physical and functional evaluations, regulatory planning, and facilities opening actually represent the only groups of activities hospital staff are ordinarily capable of performing acceptably, and even regarding these activities hospital boards and executives usually employ outside consultants to make significant contributions.

Most of the groups of activities require, at the very least, a detailed Gantt chart, and PERT can be well used in the construction and facilities opening phases. Figure 9-2 shows a typical Gantt chart of a tax-exempt bond financing process and Figure 9-3 shows a simplified PERT chart.

Managers in business firms and other organizations may regard many plans as single use that have really been adapted from common or standard approaches for similar situations in a given business or other organizational field. For example, Chrysler might decide to erect and put into operation a new plant at a certain location in a given year. This would be a one-time objective within the company's strategic plan. The company would indeed formulate a single use plan for reaching the objective. However, the consultants employed to assist in the planning (architects, engineers, planners, etc.) would probably introduce standard approaches and merely adapt them to the local situation. We ourselves have done so in the planning and construction of hundreds of hospitals. Most professional consultants apply standard approaches time and time again in solving one-time problems within specific organizations. Although the plans so formulated are truly single use for the organization involved, they may be plans that have been employed elsewhere and minimally revised for the project at hand.

Figure 9-1

The Planning, Design, and Construction Process

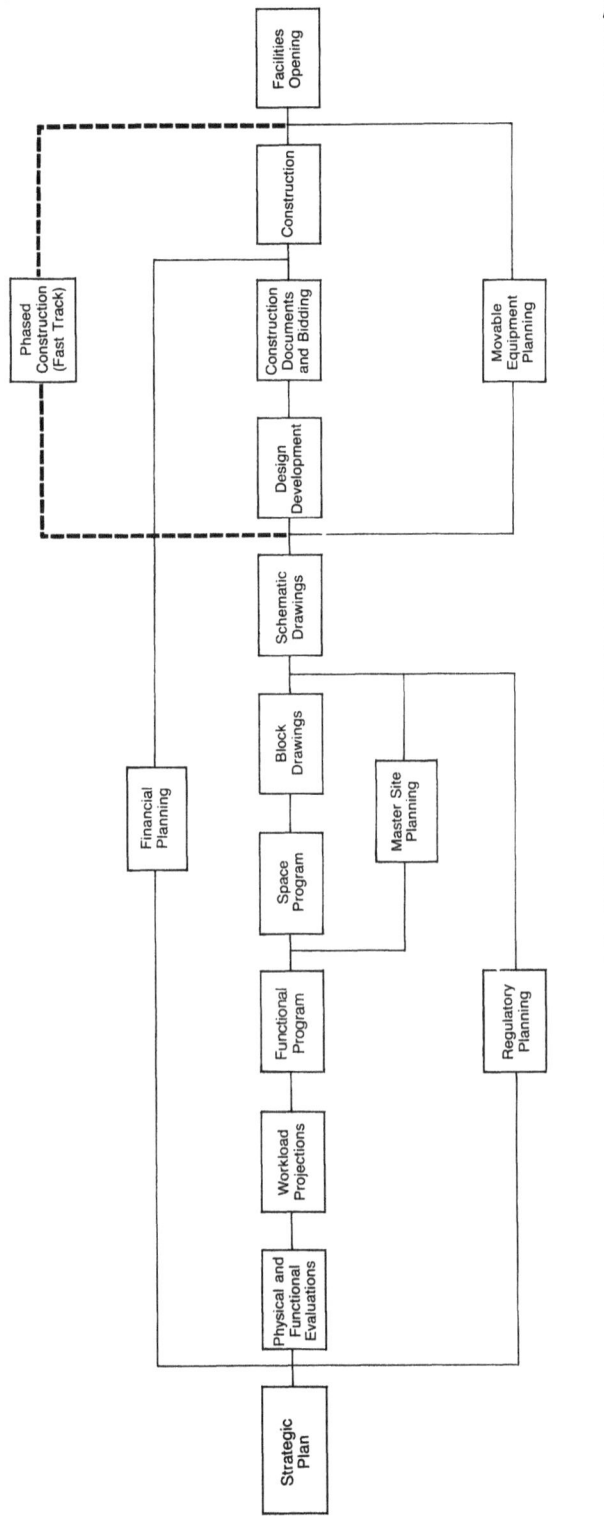

Source: Reprinted from *Hospitals: The Planning and Design Process*, 2d ed., by O.B. Hardy and L.P. Lammers, Aspen Publishers, Inc., © 1986.

Figure 9-2

Example of Financial Planning Model, Typical Tax-Exempt Bond Financing Process

LEGEND

Functional Planner   Architect/Engineer

Investment Banker   Legal Counsel

Hospital Officials   Contractor

Financial Feasibility Consultant

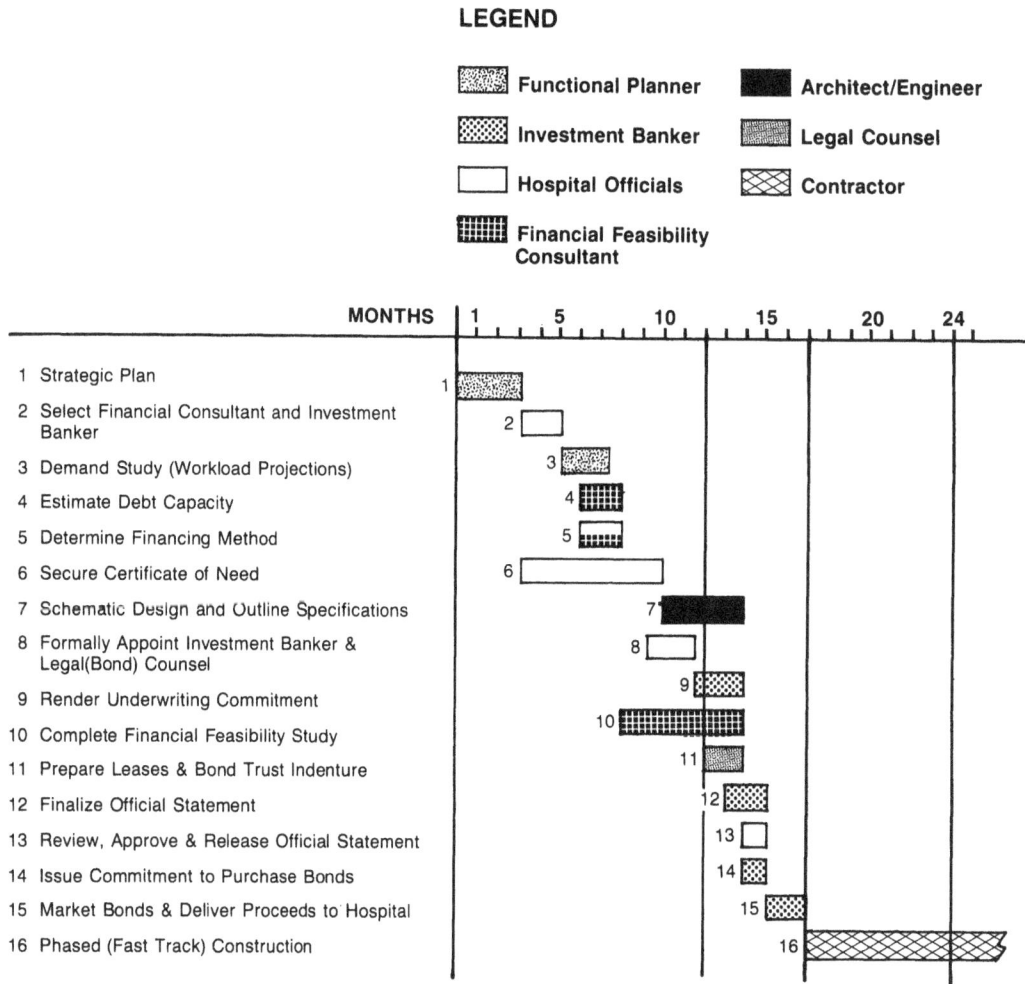

MONTHS | 1 5 10 15 20 24

1 Strategic Plan
2 Select Financial Consultant and Investment Banker
3 Demand Study (Workload Projections)
4 Estimate Debt Capacity
5 Determine Financing Method
6 Secure Certificate of Need
7 Schematic Design and Outline Specifications
8 Formally Appoint Investment Banker & Legal(Bond) Counsel
9 Render Underwriting Commitment
10 Complete Financial Feasibility Study
11 Prepare Leases & Bond Trust Indenture
12 Finalize Official Statement
13 Review, Approve & Release Official Statement
14 Issue Commitment to Purchase Bonds
15 Market Bonds & Deliver Proceeds to Hospital
16 Phased (Fast Track) Construction

Source: Reprinted from *Hospitals: The Planning and Design Process* by O.B. Hardy and L.P. Lammers, p. 108, Aspen Publishers, Inc., © 1986.

Some programs may be simple (as in the paint store example); some may be complex (as in the building of a major industrial plant); some may be original, in that no similar one has ever been prepared before; and some may have been prepared by consultants to solve a class of similar problems through minor adaptations. However, all original program or plan development should involve a process that is logical, methodical, and almost universally applicable to formal (and sometimes informal) single use planning in organizations.

The amount of actual work required in the development of single use plans differs for a variety of reasons, the most obvious being that some

Figure 9-3

Example of Simplified PERT
(Major Events in Production of an
Airplane)

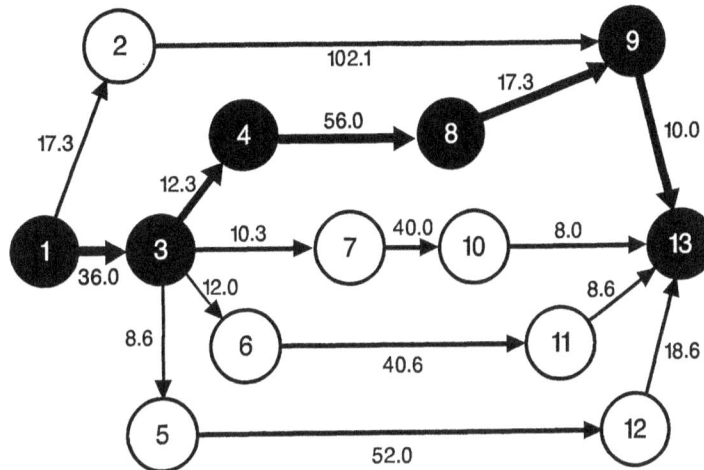

Events (each major milestone of progress) are: 1—program go-ahead; 2—initiate engine procurement; 3—complete plans and specifications; 4—complete fuselage drawings; 5—submit GFAE requirements; 6—award tail assembly subcontract; 7—award wings subcontract; 8—complete manufacture of fuselage; 9—complete assembly of fuselage-engine; 10—receive wings from subcontractor; 11—receive tail assembly from subcontractor; 12—receive GFAE; 13—complete aircraft. **Note:** GFAE is government-furnished airplane equipment.

Source: Reprinted from *Management: A Systems and Contingency Analysis of Managerial Functions,* 6th ed., by H. Koontz and C. O'Donnell, p. 693, with permission of McGraw-Hill Book Company, © 1976.

plans are simple and some are complex. Another reason is that starting points and basic assumptions may differ widely from situation to situation. The classic example involves the development of a program to gain one or more objectives already adopted in a strategic plan. No two strategic plans have the same content and character, and the level of detail about the goals and objectives developed in each is seldom the same. For example, regarding strategic planning, we have tended to view the consideration of basic courses of action for attaining goals and objectives as a part of such planning. Our reasoning is that one should not adopt as part of a formal plan goals or objectives that are not feasible economically or in some other way. Other planners, however, merely assume feasibility and do not consider any alternate approaches to implementation in the strategic planning process. This approach involves considerably more "carry over" work in programming than the approach we usually use. Even so, a vast majority of situations will allow employment of a basic process.

The process we outline is methodical and substantially restrains the human tendency to jump to conclusions based on imagined flashes of brilliance. However, it does not prevent incorporation of genuinely brilliant ideas; in fact, it enhances the probability of such incorporation. It militates against forgetfulness. In major undertakings, it necessitates considerable documentation, which can be later used in controlling during implementation. Also, in major undertakings, those who will be responsible for implementation will typically be involved in the programming.

If there are any negative aspects of the process, they are due to the required thoroughness, which can cause programming to drag and delay implementation unless managers demonstrate a predilection for action (as they should). We offer further comments about this matter later in this chapter.

Figure 9-4 diagrams the process that is explained below.

Steps in the programming process

1. *Organize for the programming or project planning effort and develop a procedure for review and approval of the plans to be formulated.*

It is impossible to devise a set of principles that apply universally, owing to the wide range of variations. However, persons who will have the authority and responsibility to implement the plan should be intimately involved in the development, or at the very least have a vital review function.

2. *Formulate a clear statement of the objective or objectives to be attained through development of the single use plan.*

If such a statement has not been prepared in strategic planning, it must be prepared as part of programming or project planning. This is so elementary it seems superfluous to mention, yet the necessity to give conscious consideration to the matter is sometimes overlooked. It is then realized at the end of programming that "this is not what we wanted to do in the first place."

In preparing programs or project plans not related to strategic planning, one must likewise give careful thought to precisely defining the objective(s) of the efforts about to be made.

Figure 9-4

A Programming Model in 10 Steps

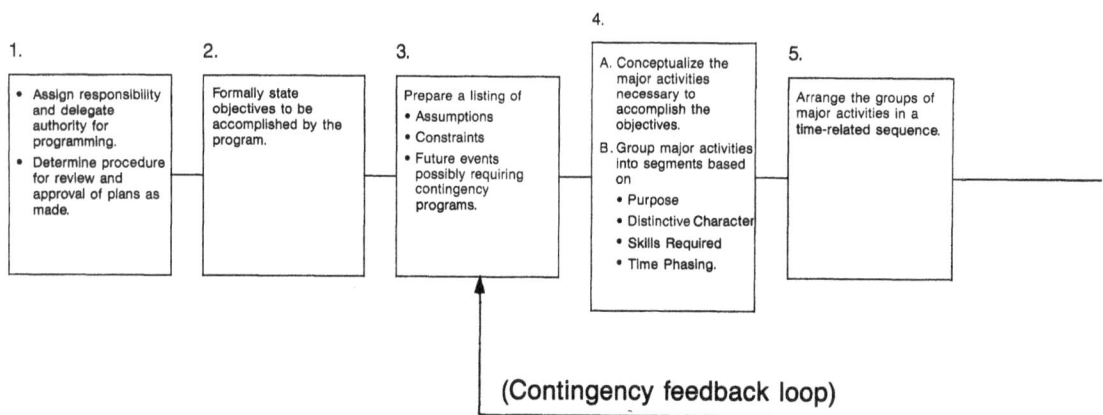

1.	2.	3.	4.	5.
• Assign responsibility and delegate authority for programming. • Determine procedure for review and approval of plans as made.	Formally state objectives to be accomplished by the program.	Prepare a listing of • Assumptions • Constraints • Future events possibly requiring contingency programs.	A. Conceptualize the major activities necessary to accomplish the objectives. B. Group major activities into segments based on • Purpose • Distinctive Character • Skills Required • Time Phasing.	Arrange the groups of major activities in a time-related sequence.

(Contingency feedback loop)

3. Prepare a list of assumptions or constraints regarding the programming or project planning, together with a list of future events whose unknown outcome may necessitate contingency programming, fallback positions regarding objectives, or other adaptivising.

The assumptions or constraints should be set forth under headings that imply who, when, where, what, how, and how much (if finances are involved). If the programming is derived from strategic planning, the assumptions involved can be ascertained from that documentation in most instances. Development of assumptions or constraints usually results from considering how to resolve problems (framing an adaptive response, usually) or from planning special events. Several sources of help for achieving resolutions will usually be evident, not least among them the manager's own knowledge and the opinions of both subordinates and superiors. In situations requiring special technology, programmers should consult an appropriate expert.

In visualizing the future, programmers must take note of events that could cause a drastic change in the requirements for attaining objectives or goals. If such events are likely to occur, it should be determined whether contingency programs ought to be developed. We have developed contingency programs on some occasions where the probability of an event necessitating considerable program changes was as high as 40 to 50 percent. Examples of where we prepared contingency programs include proposals (in effect, proposed programs) to government agencies for approval of construction projects and programs for the development of a number of diagnostic and treatment services for various health care facilities. On some occasions, approval of only part of a proposal could be anticipated, and therefore we caused fallback positions to be taken and contingency programs developed on that basis.

In a majority of instances where a future event could be anticipated that might require program changes, however, we either depended on later program adjustments to lead to the desired outcome or deliberately carried programming to the point when the event might occur. Whether the event did occur or not then dictated subsequent programming efforts.

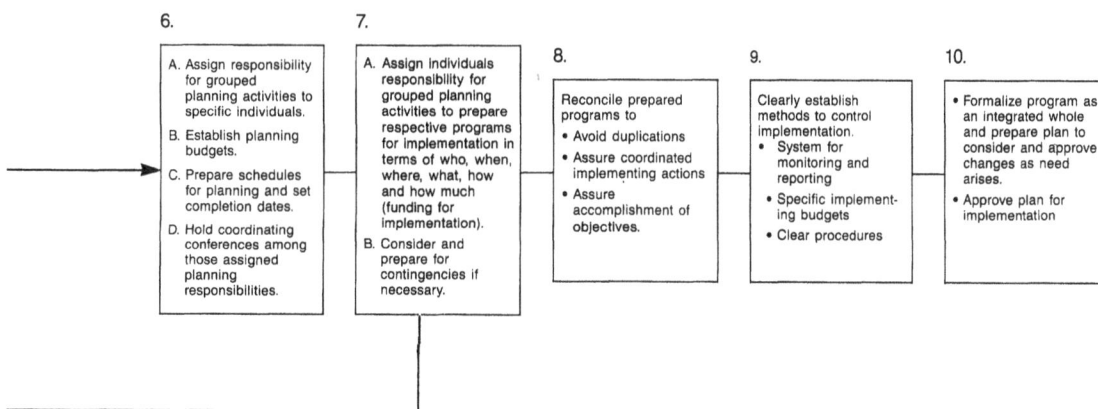

6.

A. Assign responsibility for grouped planning activities to specific individuals.

B. Establish planning budgets.

C. Prepare schedules for planning and set completion dates.

D. Hold coordinating conferences among those assigned planning responsibilities.

7.

A. Assign individuals responsibility for grouped planning activities to prepare respective programs for implementation in terms of who, when, where, what, how and how much (funding for implementation).

B. Consider and prepare for contingencies if necessary.

8.

Reconcile prepared programs to
• Avoid duplications
• Assure coordinated implementing actions
• Assure accomplishment of objectives.

9.

Clearly establish methods to control implementation.
• System for monitoring and reporting
• Specific implementing budgets
• Clear procedures

10.

• Formalize program as an integrated whole and prepare plan to consider and approve changes as need arises.
• Approve plan for implementation

We know for certain that hospitals throughout the nation have literally wasted millions of dollars by developing complete architectural and other plans based on anticipated approval of government agencies or on the assumption that money could be obtained for capital funding of ambitious building projects. When such assumptions or anticipations were found to be incorrect, redesign and repeated consulting work required payment of expensive fees and in a few instances even project abandonment. Thus managers should regard the anticipation of future events capable of altering the course of programming as quite important.

4. *Conceptualize the major activities required to accomplish the objective or objectives and group them into segments based on purpose, distinctive character, or skills required for performance (in some instances, time phasing may also constitute a basis for segmentation).*

Refer to Figure 9-1. This diagram shows the segmentation of major activities required to develop a major hospital. Not one, but several bases determined the groupings.

Strategic planning provides the objectives for program development. Strategic planning activities are distinctive and require special skills for performance. In Chapter 3, we describe a basic process for strategic planning.

A *physical evaluation* requires architectural and engineering skills and a *functional evaluation* comprises tasks to be performed by a functional planner. The two evaluations together indicate the worth of an existing physical resource (existing facilities) for further use in fulfilling the objectives of the strategic plan. Purpose, the distinctive character of the activities, and required skills for performing them form the bases for this group.

Workload projections are the dependent variables flowing from independent variables (inpatient admissions and outpatient visits) determined in the strategic plan. Dependent variables indicate a hospital's annual volume of demand in terms of inpatient days and all types of diagnostic and treatment modalities (x-ray visits, laboratory tests, etc.). The quantitative calculations of these, together with staffing quotas, determine the number and type of workstations and rooms throughout a hospital. The distinctive nature of this work, together with the statistical skills required to perform it, provides the basis for this group.

The next block in Figure 9-1 shows *functional programming.* Based on information developed in the strategic plan, physical and functional evaluations, and workload projections, planners can then methodically list all required spaces, either new or modified. It will be possible to determine physical relationships among these spaces and to indicate the exact use of each. Again, purpose (development of a basic policy document to be handed as instructions to an architect) and the unique required skills are the bases for this group.

The next group of activities constitutes *space programming.* Although separate from functional programming, it should be done concurrently. The distinctive skills required for performance necessitate the separation. A space program involves taking the list of individual rooms or areas developed in the functional program and assigning specific space allocations to each. It also involves calculating the differentiated totals of square footage, including those for new space, altered space, or unaltered space.

At the conclusion of space programming and functional programming, qualified estimators can fairly accurately develop cost figures for the envisioned building program.

Financial planning and *regulatory planning* both develop in stages over periods of time, as shown. Their purposes, distinctive characteristics, and the unique skills required to perform them form the bases for grouping both of these classes of activities. In each instance, planners use information as it is obtained through the other groups of activities shown to refine and further develop the activities composing financial and regulatory planning until their programming is completely implemented.

The work of the architects begins with *block drawings*. Based on departmental totals developed in the space program and on instructions contained in the functional program, an architect prepares single line drawings of each level. This work determines the circulation scheme and massing of the building. The group, as noted, results from similarity of skills required for performance.

Together with block drawings, *master site planning, schematic drawings, design development,* and *construction documents and bidding* all include activities performed by architectural and engineering consultants. Why were they not lumped together as a single group of activities, since they are all to be performed by the same specialists? The answer is in part that each is a discrete set of activities subject to individual approval by an owner. Also, the start or completion of other activities depends upon timing related to these discrete segments of the total A/E work.

Movable equipment and interiors planning also is a logical segment because of the unique characteristics and special skills required to perform the work.

Construction can be phased or it can be performed on a single bid basis. Both options are shown in the diagram. Purpose, distinctive character of the work, and skills required for performance all serve as bases for this group.

Facilities opening is the final group, and all three of the bases cited for construction apply here as well.

5. *Arrange the groups of major activities in a time related sequence.*

Figure 9-1 also shows how this can be done. In some situations, a Gantt chart or critical path chart may be the preferred means for demonstrating the time required to perform each group and to obtain the necessary approvals. From the basic Gantt chart, the programming for each group can proceed.

6. *For each group of activities, decide who will be responsible for further planning and performance, establish tentative planning budgets and completion dates, and hold planning conferences among those assigned responsibilities.*

We realize assigning of responsibilities constitutes an act of implementation. As we have previously stated, planning and implementation can always be differentiated but they cannot (and should not) always be separated in the course of goal and objective attainment. The planning conferences serve to assure coordination among subsequent programs and work performances.

7. *For each group of major activities, conceptualize the work to be performed in terms of who, what, when, where, how, and how much (referenced to funding) and prepare a program.*

Planners typically use both narrative descriptions and graphic depictions to present these programs. Gantt charts, the critical path method (CPM), and PERT all are classic graphic means used singly or in combination. In this step, top executives should confer with those assigned responsibility for each group to assure overall program coordination. Again, the principle that those responsible for performance ought to have a major role in planning for that performance should be adhered to.

Programmers should consider alternate programs in this step to assure selection of the most feasible. Selection criteria usually concern total cost, quality of anticipated results, cost effectiveness, timing, risk, policy, avoidance of undesirable consequences, flexibility, etc.

8. *Reconcile the programs for individual groups of activities.*

Obviously this must be done or else various duplications and conflicts will emerge to later hinder implementation. Programmers must assure overall coordination.

9. *As a part of programming or project planning, establish clear methods of controlling implementation.*

In reality, this should have been accomplished as part of Steps 6, 7, and 8. If appropriate budgeting has been done, definite dates for completion of the grouped activities established, and responsibilities for performance clearly assigned, little will remain to be done in this step. However, we have inserted it because of the importance of controlling and because a definitive system of reporting should be made known to all concerned. The manager responsible for the entire programming effort should pause here and give some careful thought to control and how reports on performance should be made (including what kind of reports and how they should be scheduled).

10. *Formalize the total program and prepare a plan for the approval of changes as the need arises.*

Most comprehensive programs generate literally volumes of documentation and seldom allow presentation under a single cover. Many of lesser size, however, can be formalized and presented through charts and narrative descriptions contained in a single binder.

In planning and constructing a new hospital or making major alterations and additions to an existing one, owners cannot prepare programs for all the segmented groups of activities simultaneously. This is because plans made in one group frequently affect the planning to be done in another. For example, in the process shown in Figure 9-1, all subsequent programming depends on the goals and objectives established in strategic planning, all design work has to await preparation of functional and space programs, etc. Thus, programming for a major undertaking may extend over several years. In fact, programming for a major hospital building project typically lasts one to three years, and can even extend to four years if architectural and engineering work is included as part of the programming.

As a major program proceeds to implementation, the need to make changes almost invariably arises, whether or not those preparing the program are able to foresee events whose outcome will demand directional changes and necessitate the use of contingency programs or adaptivising. Because requirements to make changes do occur so frequently, managers should prepare a plan for reviewing individual instances and enacting approvals as indicated at the outset of any major programming effort (see Step 1).

A plan for planning

Harold Geneen, the legendary former head of ITT, stopped "long-range planning" at ITT on one occasion owing to the time it was taking away from planning and implementing activities related to quarterly earnings.[17] Obviously, one of the most aggressive managers of our time found himself in a common situation regarding strategic planning, management planning, and complex programming. The situation arises when planning tasks consume inordinate amounts of time and overwhelm line managers. Where the importance of planning is recognized, management usually allocates appreciable time for strategic planning and management planning as part of the annual routine. On some occasions, however, available time runs short, and if the need arises simultaneously to allocate larger blocks of time to complex single use planning, managers are placed in an acute dilemma. Some planning activities may be delayed, and planning that is not timely can be as bad as, and sometimes worse than, no planning at all. What is the answer?

No simple answer exists. One can state that all managers must manage their own time efficiently, but of course this is a truism. Our own experience indicates that good managers—those with unswerving professional dedication—give whatever it takes to succeed in difficult situations. When 40 hours a week will not suffice, twice that many hours can be devoted on occasion to keeping abreast of necessary work. Both of us have done this, and neither is the worse for wear. However, this advice is also trite.

One other possibility we have had experience with is "to plan for planning." In anticipation of a time-consuming programming effort for one of the largest medical centers in the nation (Chicago's Rush-Presbyterian-St. Luke's Medical Center), one of us directed the preparation of a plan for planning that served to guide a program for major expansions in the early 1970s. Although this was a consulting effort, the plan for planning did give all those engaged in formulation of this important programming timely information about their responsibilities during fairly well-defined time periods. Those involved regarded the information developed as worthwhile at the time it was provided, and its worth was definitely proved over the following four years.

Admittedly, to prepare a plan for planning seems to be heaping planning upon planning and creating an overabundance, but in some instances it is sensible and helpful. Consider the diagram in Figure 9-1. Some of the participants in major hospital expansions have little or no knowledge about many of the activities necessary to the process. By preparing a plan for planning that explains the basic activities, provides reasons for the sequencing, and announces a total schedule (including probable time requirements of key participants), each manager will be able to more accurately plan his or her time commitments.

Situations where a plan for planning is indicated are certainly rare. However, when those situations do occur, it is better to provide managers who will be responsible for the planning early information about the nature of their involvement and the amount of time they will have to commit than to allow them to be surprised and not have the opportunity for scheduling (with regard not only to their own time but also that of their subordinates). We know that in such cases a plan for planning done at the outset does conserve management time in the long run.

Use of consultants

Business firms employ consultants for single use planning probably more than for any other type of management activity. One of the advantages in using a consultant is that they possess specialized professional knowledge. For example, the vast majority of business firms cannot afford to employ an operations research analyst full-time, but many of these firms do occasionally encounter situations where such a specialist is needed. The same can be said about industrial engineers, financial analysts, strategic planners, functional planners, architects, and a host of others. These specialists usually work on either a contractual or per diem basis, and their assistance with special activities, including single use planning, can be invaluable.

Another advantage in using consultants is that it conserves the time of managers. As previously noted, nearly overwhelming management time requirements sometimes occur in the preparation of major single use plans. A business firm can employ a consultant to contribute planning time during such occurrences as well as to provide relevant expertise.

Great care should be used in seeking out and employing consultants. Although many small firms offer well-qualified individuals, some do not. In larger firms, some of the best qualified consultants may be overburdened with work and their fees can be very high. On balance, however, it is preferable to contract with a large firm possessing a good reputation than to look for bargains.

Since the quality of services one receives from a consulting firm depends almost directly on the project director assigned to assist on a specific job, careful investigation of that person should be made and his or her time commitments ascertained.

Controlling

One of the most serious derelictions that occurs in programming or project planning is to fail to control the process after it is set into motion. Failure most frequently occurs with regard to staying on schedule and on target (i.e., accomplishing the planning work as envisioned originally). Many managers agree at some point with subordinates on the planning work to be accomplished and the schedule and then ignore the matter entirely. We have often observed planning efforts stray so far afield from original objectives that the program produced had scant resemblance to what was intended. Also, it is not uncommon to see planning considerably delayed and the quality of finished plans fall far below what a good manager would expect.

The avoidance of all of these problems and the useless planning that may result can be achieved by instituting a good system for reporting on planning progress. There is a tremendous difference between giving a subordinate no responsibility to report progress or the reasons for delays and informing the subordinate that a definitive completion schedule has been agreed upon and that percentage-of-completion reports must be submitted periodically. The same applies to staying on target and to maintaining planning quality. Control of the planning process is itself clearly very important in the formulation of single use plans.

At the outset of a programming or project planning effort, an initiating manager usually has a definite idea about when implementation should start so that the value of timing can be respected. Plans must be completed by that time, and they obviously should give clear guidance in terms of who, when, what, where, and how. If plans are not completed, the timing of implementation may become so inappropriate that it will be indefinitely postponed or canceled. This is embarrassing for all concerned, but most especially for the responsible manager, whoever that may be.

Management texts are replete with discussions of the negative aspects of control. Considerably less seems to have been written about the negative aspects of failure to control. Although we completely reject dictatorial forms of controls, we continue to believe that abandonment of controlling is equivalent to an abandonment of the responsibility to manage.

One can draw an analogy from the military. In both noncommissioned and commissioned officer training, one learns very early about two basic aspects of getting something done. First, one must give an order for it to be done, and second, one must check back to see that it has been done. In the business world, one must first have an agreement that certain activities are going to be accomplished and that reports of accomplishments will be made at agreed times. Secondly, one must diligently see to it that agreements are fulfilled. This basic philosophy applies both to formulation of plans and implementation of plans.

Summary

Managers prepare single use plans to resolve problems, gain one-time objectives, or conduct activities inherent in a unique event. Typically used once, single use plans contrast to standing plans, which are applied recurringly to various activities.

Authorities have used the terms *programming* and *project planning* to refer to single use plans. We regard the difference between the programming and projected planning as primarily related to scope, with programming being the more comprehensive of the two.

There are two basic types of programming. Commitment programming is certain of being completed and, after completion, of being implemented. Adaptive programming (also called adaptivising) must be accomplished in the face of unknowns and possibly unknowables, and thus it requires either a set of contingency programs that can be used for probable eventualities or partial, flexible programming that can be used to adapt to whatever the future brings (adaptivising).

Single use plans vary from those requiring many volumes of documentation to those that can be jotted on a note pad. Managers and other organizational members refer to many incomplete plans as single use plans, for example, budgets and schedules. These in fact are parts of single use plans. A complete single use plan should invariably include information, either explicit or implicit, on who, when, what, where, how, and how much (if money is involved).

A basic approach we have used for formal single use planning of some appreciable scope consists of a series of steps, summarized as follows:

1. Organize for the programming or project planning effort and develop procedures for review and approval.

2. Clearly define the objectives of the single use plan to be developed.

3. Prepare a list of constraints regarding implementation and a list of possible future events whose occurrence may require contingency programs, fallback positions regarding objectives, or other adaptivising.

4. Conceptualize the major activities required to accomplish objectives and group them based on purpose, distinctive character, or skills required for performance. A grouping based solely on time phasing may also be necessitated.

5. Arrange the groups of major activities in a chronological sequence.

6. Assign responsibility for further programming and subsequent performance related to each group of major activities, establish tentative planning budgets and completion dates, and hold planning conferences among those receiving assignments.

7. Conceptualize work to be performed in each group of major activities in terms of who, when, where, what, how, and how much (referenced to finances). Consider alternatives; select one; prepare a program.

8. Reconcile programs for individual groups of activities to assure future coordination and avoidance of duplication.

9. Clearly identify methods of controlling implementation.

10. Formalize the total program or project plan and prepare a plan to effect changes when they are needed.

Because implementation follows planning and often becomes useless unless accomplished in a timely manner, managers cannot allow planning to fall victim to delays, which can happen for a variety of reasons. To prevent these delays, managers must manage their personal time well and make whatever efforts are necessary to keep up with planning schedules (which should always be carefully worked out and contain specific completion dates). We have also found that plans for planning can be helpful at the start of large, comprehensive programming or project planning efforts. These plans educate those who will be involved and provide information about the probable time commitments of key participants. Seemingly superfluous, such plans in practice have proved their worth both in saved time and improved quality of plans.

In formulating single use plans, consultants can play a vital role. Not only can they bring special skills to the process, but they can conserve large amounts of management time.

Many managers fail to control a planning process after they have set it in motion. We regard controlling as indispensable in the preparation of any major program or project plan, and it can be done in a manner that avoids all the negative effects cited so frequently in management literature.

Notes

1. William H. Newman and Kirby E. Warren, *The Process of Management*, 4th ed. (1977), 403. Reprinted by permission of Prentice-Hall, Inc., Englewood Cliffs, N.J.
2. James A.F. Stoner, *Management*, 2d ed. (1982), 134. Reprinted by permission of Prentice-Hall, Inc., Englewood Cliffs, N.J.
3. Ibid. Reprinted by permission of Prentice-Hall, Inc., Englewood Cliffs, N.J.
4. Ibid. Reprinted by permission of Prentice-Hall, Inc., Englewood Cliffs, N.J.
5. Newman and Warren, *The Process of Management*, 406. Reprinted by permission of Prentice-Hall, Inc., Englewood Cliffs, N.J.
6. Sang M. Lee, *Management by Multiple Objectives* (New York: Petrocelli Books, 1981), 124.
7. Ibid, 121.
8. J.P. Barger, "The Managing Process," in *Handbook of Business Administration*, ed. H.B. Maynard (New York: McGraw-Hill, 1967), 1-8.
9. Warren B. Brown and Dennis J. Moberg, *Organization Theory and Management* (New York: Wiley, 1980), 278.
10. Ibid., 280.
11. Newman and Warren, *The Process of Management*, 407.
12. Brown and Moberg, *Organization Theory and Management*, 280.
13. Newman and Warren, *The Process of Management*, 407.
14. William H. Newman and Charles E. Summer, Jr., *The Process of Management* (Englewood Cliffs, N.J.: Prentice-Hall, 1961), 420.
15. Owen B. Hardy, "Systematic Processes Applied to Health Care Planning," *Hospital Administration* 16 (Winter 1971): 420.
16. Ibid.
17. Harold Geneen with Alvin Moscow, *Managing* (Garden City, N.Y.: Doubleday, 1984), 47.

Part IV

Implementation

The vast importance accorded decision making over the last several decades has seemingly resulted in de-emphasizing implementation, which is of equal importance. Managers may make decisions correctly and efficiently, and decisions that have the capability of elevating a company to one of the foremost in the land, but without implementation, such decisions go for naught. Actions consonant with decisions are equally as important as the decisions themselves.

Implementation is the partner of planning—dissimilar to be sure, but tightly yoked and inseparable. Planning and implementation often occur so nearly simultaneously that the distinction between the two becomes blurred. However, close analysis of what a manager is actually doing at a specific time will reveal identifying characteristics. Primarily, planning involves making decisions about actions to be taken and implementation involves exercising the means by which the actions are carried out.

Part IV contains six chapters, each explaining in some detail various aspects of implementation. Collectively, the subjects they address constitute the very essence of implementing actions.

Despite a current propensity among authors to point to a single aspect of management and through words build that aspect into a monument of impressive proportions, not one subject addressed in Part IV can be ignored. The manager who does so will remain, except through sheer luck, at lower or middle management levels. The manager who strives for a working knowledge of all aspects of implementation—and all aspects of planning and adaptive responses—will almost inevitably rise to the top.

In this part, as throughout the text, we have attempted to provide balanced and reasoned viewpoints on each subject discussed. The ability to conceptualize correctly a whole, its components, and their relationships within the whole is extremely important for those aspiring to become topflight managers. To say "this is the central key" or "that's the answer to all management problems" exhibits immaturity of thought or ignorance about the many aspects of management, or both. Management is a very broad subject, and although none of its components are inscrutably abstruse, conceptualization and knowledge of the whole truly presents a considerable challenge.

Chapter 10

Delegation of authority and assignment of responsibility and accountability

Elements of Management
in Corporations

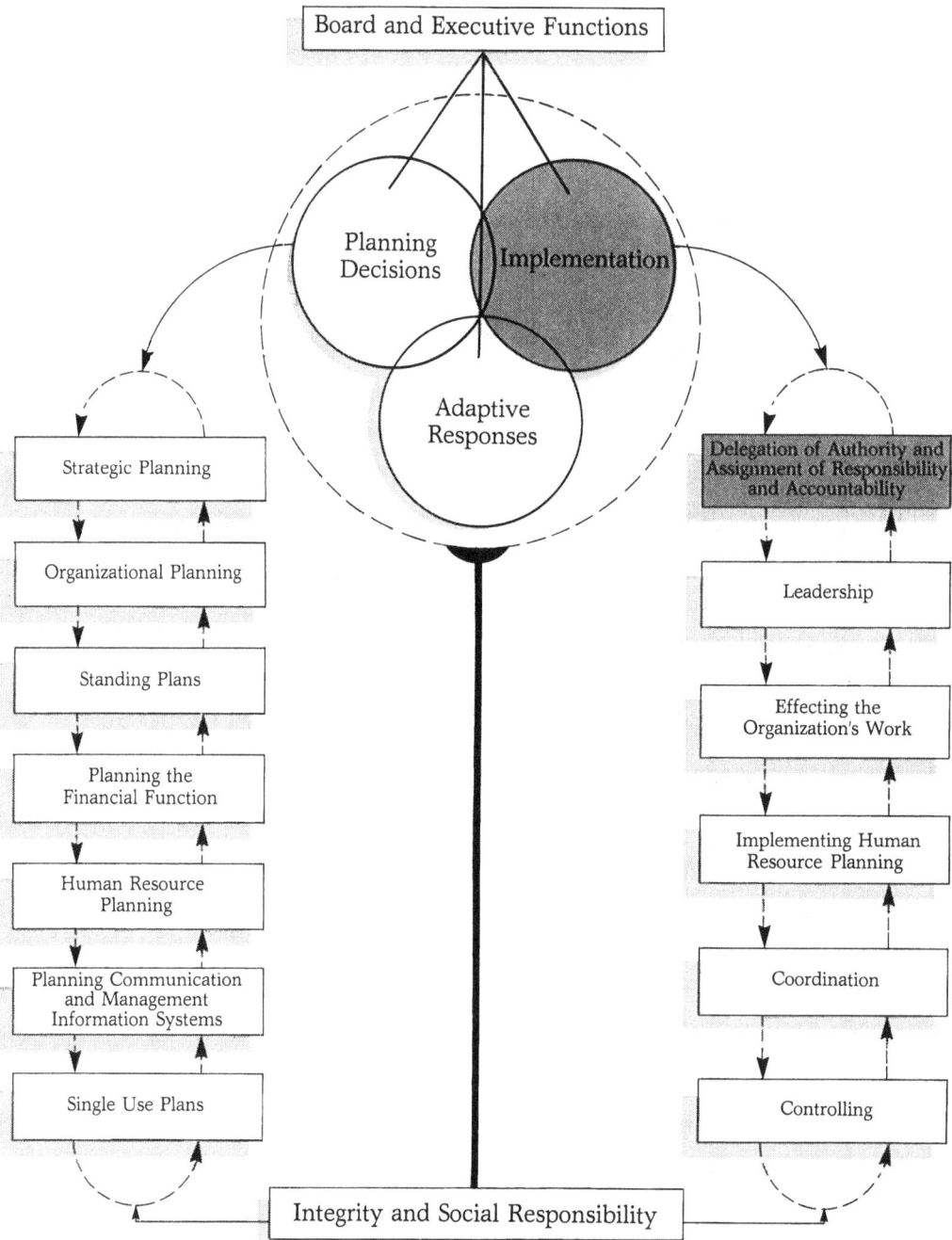

Board and Executive Functions

Planning
Decisions

Implementation

Adaptive
Responses

Strategic Planning

Organizational Planning

Standing Plans

Planning the
Financial Function

Human Resource
Planning

Planning Communication
and Management
Information Systems

Single Use Plans

Delegation of Authority and
Assignment of Responsibility
and Accountability

Leadership

Effecting the
Organization's Work

Implementing Human
Resource Planning

Coordination

Controlling

Integrity and Social Responsibility

10

Background

Although greatly outnumbered by other types of business entities, private corporations conduct far and away the major portion of business activities and commerce in this nation and indeed in most nations of the Western world. Partnerships and individual proprietorships account for a small percentage, and public service corporations for most of the remainder. Each entity (of whatever type) requires an organized set of efforts, and the delegation of authority and the assignment of responsibility and accountability are among the means by which organizing is effected and subsequent operations carried out.

Each corporation receives its authority to do business from one of the fifty states. Clauses contained in the articles of incorporation effect the legality of authority for operations, upon approval by the appropriate secretary of state. The extent of authority is implied by the stated purposes and objectives of the corporation, together with powers expressly conferred under pertinent laws.

The state makes no express grant of authority in the case of partnerships and individual proprietorships. The laws related to property ownership and the rights of individuals to conduct business through trading, contracting, and various other commercial activities provide the authority for the functions of such organizations. In both these instances, however, the authority to operate is vested in the owners and organizers just as surely as it is vested in the "artificial person" known as a corporation.

Through *delegation*, each entity—whether a corporation, partnership, or individual proprietorship—passes the authority vested in it, by whatever means, to those who will actually carry out the business of the organization. Concomitantly, each entity usually divides up the total body of activities anticipated and assigns *responsibility* for carrying out the resulting groups of activities to specified individuals. Hopefully, the authority to perform and the scope of assigned activities will be commensurate. If not, the results may not be completely successful.

Accountability should also accompany the delegation of authority and assignment of responsibility for activities to be performed. This is because the law does not recognize the relinquishment of responsibility by the organization itself as represented by its top officers or board of directors. Thus, responsibility may only be assigned and not actually transferred. Thus, when it is assigned, the assignor has the right to expect that the assignee will be accountable. Like responsibility, accountability cannot be relinquished. Even though there may be a multilevel organizational hierarchy in place, the president and board of directors of a corporation still possess responsibility for all of a company's operations and can be held accountable for infringements on the rights of others by employees.

Problems

Problems have always occurred in delegating authority and assigning responsibility and accountability. One reason is the complexity of human personalities, and another is the difficulty in achieving a perfect meeting of the minds between those who delegate and assign and those who receive. Also, assignors of responsibility and accountability frequently have gaps in their assignments (no one has been given the assignment) or overlaps (two or more persons have been given the same assignment). In some instances, this is intended (for any one of a number of reasons), but we believe it mostly occurs from sheer forgetfulness or sloppiness in performance of a basic management function.

Some years ago McFarland noted some of the pitfalls associated with unrelated, unclear, and imperfect delegations of authority.

> Management writers have been prolific in describing effects of unclear lines of authority in organizations. To leave executives in doubt as to the scope of authority they possess can only lead to confusion and conflict. If executives are not sure of their authority, their capacity to act is impaired. Their failure to act can slow up the work of the organization and cause other problems to arise. Also, it paves the way for usurping illegitimate authority.[1]

> Likert has noted failures to clarify assignments of responsibility. "A number of recent studies are providing disturbing evidence that communication between managers and supervisors fails to make clear to subordinates precisely what the job is and what is expected of them."[2]

In our own field, we have observed many unclear delegations of authority and both gaps and overlaps in assignments of responsibility and accountability. These have proved to be problematic, especially with the recent fast growth of HCA's owned-hospital divisions, management company, and psychiatric company.

With respect to the individual hospital level, Cline, in an unpublished study of three hospitals in the Washington, D.C., area, found that of nine subordinate managers and three assistant administrators, all of them differed in opinion from their superiors as to how much authority they possessed.[3] Although there have been improvements in delegations of authority and assignments of responsibility and accountability in recent years at the individual hospital level, we are aware of cases where these tasks are far from being optimally performed.

Some difficulties for the student of management in understanding how best to delegate authority and assign responsibility and accountability may arise from the wide variation of opinion among supposed experts on management. The behavioral scientists generally favor broad, somewhat loosely circumscribed authority delegations and work assignments;

Delegation's Pitfalls

The Iran-Contra Fund Diversions

"I didn't know anything about it."
President Reagan

"Col. North was a loose cannon."
Republican Congressional Members

"I managed Col. North very loosely and didn't tell the President about the diversions."
Admiral Poindexter

"What was Col. North's job description?"
A Manager

"I didn't do anything on my own. I had the authority to do everything I did."
Col. North

"They're all lying."
Democratic Congressional Members

these purportedly allow the development of initiative and enhance motivation, thus increasing productivity and job satisfaction. Those who pursue mechanistic approaches favor precisely delineated delegations and work assignments; the intent is to achieve better coordination and control and in that way increase productivity and job satisfaction. We do not endorse or condemn either approach. Depending on the individual situation, managers may use both in the same organization at the same time. Several pertinent factors are (1) the specific type of work to be performed, (2) the qualifications of the person or persons involved, (3) the kind of personalities involved, (4) the degree of timeliness required, (5) the requirements for success, and (6) the benefits, if any, resulting from innovation.

Some problems of perception, about delegations of authority especially, may be encountered as a result of the semantic morass frequently found in management literature. Also, many viewpoints exist regarding sources of authority, and experts have presented a variety of definitions of responsibility. (However, seemingly little disagreement has arisen about the nature of accountability.) Interestingly, Dessler states emphatically, "But while authority can be delegated, *responsibility* cannot."[4] Stoner seems to disagree. He states, "We define delegation as the assignment to another person of formal authority and responsibility for carrying out specific activities."[5]

Purpose of this chapter

Although we agree with Dessler that responsibility cannot be delegated, we will not argue semantics or confirm or deny various concepts of delegation or assignment which have been advanced. Rather, we will discuss—from the standpoint of implementation—how managers can best effect delegations of authority and clearly and positively assign responsibility and accountability.

We intend to (1) discuss four basic components of all delegations of authority and parallel assignments of responsibility and accountability, (2) set out one way for implementing the act of delegation or assignment, and (3) note certain means for effecting commitments from those persons to whom authority is delegated and responsibility and accountability assigned.

Role of law and the behavioral sciences

Many managers are seriously deficient in their knowledge of the various laws of the state or states in which their corporation (or other formal organization) carries out its intended operations through the acts of its agents or employees. Although we regard application of the principles of organizational sociology and psychology as being of prime importance in organizational management, when a manager's concepts of these sciences and their influence on his or her managerial practices conflict with basic adherence to established truth and doctrine as they flow either from applicable tenets of English common law or to federal law and state statutes, we believe that the law must come first.

From a sociological and psychological standpoint, it may seem desirable in some instances to delegate authority and assign responsibility as broadly as possible—in effect to say, "Go out and do your own thing in your own way and only report to us the results you achieve." Alas, from a legal standpoint, this course poses many dangers. While such a course sometimes succeeds, it can also bring about nearly ruinous results. The latitude given to E.F. Hutton managers in handling checks is a recent example. While this company may continue to show profits, the stigma now attached to it and the reduction of profits from what they might have been indicate that delegations of authority and subsequent control measures should have taken legal implications into account much more stringently. It behooves all managers to be students not only of sociology, psychology, motivation and leadership theory, etc., but also of legal principles. Indeed, in many instances, managers should have ongoing consultations with appropriate legal counsel in conducting organization operations.

Superior and subordinate

The vast majority of delegations of authority in formal organizations occur between just two parties. The two parties involved are (1) the person or persons transferring the authority and charged by the organization to complete an agreement both as to the scope of it and the scope and types of responsibility that will be assigned and (2) the person receiving the authority and with whom the agreement about the authority and responsibility is made. The first party is usually called the superior and the second is called the subordinate. In most organizations, a hierarchical succession of agreements exists from a legal standpoint, and views about the several concepts of authority and about whether authority in reality flows upward or downward matter very little.[6]

Collective bargaining has narrowed the areas in which agreement may be negotiated between individual superiors and subordinates in those firms that have been unionized. "The terms of collective agreements, . . . the interpretation . . . of those agreements and . . . the spread of arbitration as a means of resolving grievances" has certainly reduced "the [entire] scope of managerial discretion."[7] This especially applies to individual managers and their ability to delegate authority directly to individual employees and to effect agreements about responsibility and accountability. Nonetheless, through their assent to union bargaining, union members accept the delegations of authority and assignments of responsibility and accountability agreed to by their union representatives, usually in sessions with top management. Thus, delegations and assignments actually occur, but somewhat indirectly.

Relationships created by agreements

An agreement reached between a superior and subordinate creates either the relationship of employer and employee or the agency relationship. In some instances, an agreement may create both, based on specific acts to be done by the subordinate. Subsequent amendments are mere extensions of the original agreement, but in each instance the objective should be to achieve a basic meeting of the minds of the involved parties.

What are the elements of a perfectly consummated delegation of authority and assignment of responsibility and accountability for acts of work to be performed? They are as follows:

1. mutual consent and agreement about the establishment of the relationship between both parties

2. mutual agreement as to the type and scope of acts and duties which the subordinate will perform on behalf of the superior

3. delegation of authority by the superior to the subordinate for performance of the acts and duties as mutually agreed upon

4. assent or commitment by the subordinate to assume an obligation and accountability for performance of the agreed-upon acts or duties (this assumed obligation and accountability does not relieve the superior relative to third parties or a higher superior).[8]

The process as outlined definitely establishes that the subordinate is accountable to the superior with regard to the success or failure of the acts or duties to be performed. Credit or blame, whichever is warranted by the results, must be accepted by the subordinate. This is implied, if not expressly stated, by the employing agreement as consummated.

Stoner has well noted, "For managers, the concept of accountability has an added dimension: Not only are managers held accountable for their own performance, but they are also held accountable [from a legal standpoint] for the performance of their subordinates. In fact, accountability for the actions of subordinates is one of the defining characteristics of a managerial position."[9] Stoner's remarks are valid from a legal standpoint and confirm that accountability cannot be delegated but merely assigned. (They also seemingly contradict an earlier quotation from Stoner about responsibility.)

Legal consequences

Although the typical employee does not have authority to contract with third parties on behalf of an employer, an agent can do so, and where the agency relationship is created, a perfect meeting of the minds between the superior and subordinate becomes particularly important. This is because this relationship, subsequent to its creation, depends not entirely on what was privately intended, but partly on what appears to the outside world to have been intended. Court interpretations will be based on implications of and inferences from the actions and words of both parties, together with outward circumstances.[10] Undoubtedly, perfect understanding and agreement by the parties generally reduce intended and inadvertent misinterpretations of the relationship. In creating perfect understanding and agreement, managers should precisely describe the intended relationship in writing.

As noted in Chapter 2, most top corporate executives occupy a position of general agent in a significant legal sense. Thus, if a hospital administrator or executive director is involved, for example, the parties to the agreement should put the agreement in writing so as to define specifically the extent of delegated authority in relation to third parties. This will prevent unintended interpretations of the scope of both authority and responsibility. Also, to carry the example a step further, the top executive should exercise like precautions in consummating agreements with those who report to him or her at the next lower hierarchical level and also where a limited agency relationship must be created for certain functions and purposes.

In all organizations where employees have ongoing contacts with the public and where opportunities for tort cases arise, it is important that clear and complete agreements exist between the employer and the employees. This is because the courts will interpret delegations of authority and assignments of responsibility in light of what seems to have been intended and not what may have been intended by the employer or, for that matter, what may have been in the minds of the employees. A clear written relationship puts each party at least in an intended position and, we believe, allows an employer to reduce the probability that employees will perform acts which may bring about a tort case through unauthorized acts or acts erroneously performed.

Simultaneously formulated procedures and later amendments to them (if any) can reflect agreed delegations and assignments; documentation of both procedures and amendments will protect against tort cases.

A classic example is the installation of side rails around the bed of an irrational hospital patient. If left to individual judgment of a variety of nurse managers throughout a hospital, in some cases the responsible nurse will not see to it that such rails are in place at the appropriate time for preventing an injurious fall by a patient. If, by a clear agreement, the nurse consents to be responsible for putting the rails in place, given a described condition, and that consent is reflected in a clearly worded procedure, it will be more probable that the rails will be appropriately installed. Even if the nurse fails to install the rails and the patient is injured, the courts will usually render a verdict more favorable to the hospital, because due care was at least shown in assigning responsibility for actions that would have prevented the injury had they been carried out. We have not reached these conclusions through conjecture. We have learned them through experience—the hard way!

> Thus, by factual interpretation, organizational delegation [and assignment of responsibility] is not purely a matter of sociological or psychological concern, although these aspects are highly important. Neither is it a subject of academic and theoretical conjecture. *Rather it is a relationship established between superior and subordinate which is firmly grounded in the laws of the place where the delegation is consummated.*[11]

Achieving coordination

Management authorities have long recognized that delegation constitutes a prime means of organizational coordination, not only with vertical hierarchical relationships but with horizontal relationships as well. Most centralized organizations function as a coordinated system, and in many instances, the degree of coordination directly determines the measure of success. Even in the case of geographically decentralized companies or divisions, coordination between many geographically remote operations and a centralized corporate headquarters is necessary. Both General Motors and HCA are classic examples of this.

Thus, whether in the confines of a localized workplace, where jobs must mesh with each other to achieve production objectives, or among vast operations geographically dispersed throughout a nation, delegation is the means by which authority to implement organizational activities is transferred. At the same time, managers must make corresponding assignments of responsibility and accountability, and if they make such delegations and assignments clearly and flawlessly, they will greatly increase the probability of achieving effective coordination.

Of course, other means exist for achieving coordination. Supervision, leadership, directing, etc., are typical examples. However, current research overwhelmingly indicates that close supervision has a stultifying effect. Leadership, viewed as that behavior of a manager which is so perceived that it results in voluntarily personal efforts by organizational members (in this case, efforts to coordinate actions with others)—may not be the most certain means for achieving coordination. Although directing in some cases can be efficacious, by itself, or even in concert with leadership and supervision, it may be inefficient regarding coordination.

To digress a bit, many authorities have noted there is a need for job security, job satisfaction, and control over their environment on the part of employees and managers at lower levels. We completely agree that this need exists, but we also believe that executives' peace of mind, security, job satisfaction, and control over work environment must be considered. Most executives have serious responsibilities not only to employees, but also to investors, lenders, boards of directors, consumers, and the public in general. Not surprisingly, we have found our own executive tasks and duties much less confused and much more satisfying when we have delegated authority and assigned responsibility and accountability appropriately than when we have attempted to operate in a fashion where every person beneath us had considerable leeway to pursue tangential courses of action based on uncertain predilections.

Thus, one can argue that flawless delegations and assignments are the preferred means of coordination and are highly effective in structuring organizational activities. Research at Ohio State University and elsewhere has provided good evidence that structure is correlated with increased productivity and cost control. We thus conclude that failing to delegate authority and assign responsibility in the classic manner (as outlined in this chapter) is a mistake   and, in truth, a serious dereliction of managerial duty. If the failure stems from mere inadvertence or a lack of knowledge, one's qualification for being a manager might well be questioned.

The following presents in a very simple and understandable way the importance of flawless delegation of authority and assignment of responsibility.

> During childhood and the young adult years, most persons come to belong to a competitive team of one kind or another. Few are unaware that the members of a football team, for example, undertake a specific role and that the success of the team depends in no small measure upon how well the actions or functions inherent to one role are performed in relation to those of another role. That the actions or functions to be undertaken by one team member are largely predetermined in consideration of the actions or functions to be undertaken by each of the other members would be largely unquestioned. The same underlying factors apply when delegations [and responsibility and accountability assignments] are made in an organizational context. Simply, the content of a delegation made with regard to one individual should take into consideration and be related to the content of those delegations made with organizational teammates if optimum productivity through coordinated efforts is to be attained.[12]

This analogy clearly applies to the production and marketing of computers, hamburgers, cars, soap, and soup and to the implementation of all organizational activities of whatever kind where degrees of teamwork are required.

Anyone can easily see on reflection that delegations and assignments must be based on good planning, especially planning related to organizational structure and strategy (including the setting of goals and objectives) such as has been outlined in earlier chapters. Certainly, system and subsystem functions must receive consideration, particularly functions one individual will perform that are related to those that others will perform. In some instances, a single individual must have work assignments in more than one system. The delegating and assigning agreement consummated with the individual can reflect this very easily. Some agreements will delegate a minimum of decision making and almost exclusively concern operational activities. Others will almost exclusively concern decision making. In both instances, however, the agreement should be made in order to coordinate work activities and should delegate the appropriate authority to see that the coordination is carried out.

Effecting delegations of authority and assignments of responsibility

Job design (in the case of newly forming or expanding organizations) and job redesign (in the case of existing organizations seeking to streamline operations or to enrich jobs) are planning tasks that can result in job descriptions forming the basis for an agreement whereby responsibility and accountability for performance of specific activities and duties are assigned and the authority for carrying them out is delegated. (We discuss both job design and redesign in Chapter 4.) However, even though great care has been taken in job design or redesign to see that there are few work overlaps or omissions in a system or in subsystems, implementation requires that a superior and a subordinate understand each other thoroughly to assure that coordinated activities are achieved and a minimal number of misunderstandings occur later on.

Many organizations, particularly hospitals, use standard, vaguely worded job descriptions which are nearly meaningless. A job description should accurately reflect that which was agreed upon by the superior and subordinate; if this means rewriting it after mutual understanding of the terms of employment has been achieved, we believe the effort will be worthwhile. (Note: The term *job description* is used in this book in reference to both operational personnel and managers. Many authors reserve the term *position description* to refer to the outline of a manager's duties, authority, responsibility, and accountability.)

A conference provides the best setting for attaining mutual understanding by a superior and a subordinate where a delegation of authority is to be made and responsibility and accountability are to be assigned. Ideally, the superior should have a clear idea of the nature of the work *before* the conference and may have a prepared job description in hand reflecting this idea. If so, the tentative description can provide the basis for discussion. Under no circumstances, however, should the superior hand a job description to a prospective subordinate and give the impression that "here it is; take it or you don't have a job." Such an approach will almost certainly engender rebellion on the part of the subordinate, either overt or covert. The thoughts and aspirations of the subordinate should be carefully considered, for a perfect meeting of the minds about what is to be done and the scope of delegations and assignments is one of the objectives. The conference may not yield a fixed, precise job definition. Nonetheless, the matter must be initially discussed and understanding reached, with both parties in clear concurrence as to the tasks to be undertaken and the general boundaries of the authority delegated and the responsibility and accountability assigned.

After a commitment to perform has been made (based on the understanding reached) and the subordinate has assumed his or her obligations, there should be a subsequent conference for evaluating the original agreement. In most instances, questions will arise about the work and possibly about the scope of authority delegated. Interfaces with other members of a work team usually present problems that require some explanation or further discussion. As with a football team, perfect teamwork sometimes proves difficult to achieve. The follow-up conference should be held within a month or so of the subordinate's assumption of duties so that aggravations, if any, will not be allowed to fester.

At the follow-up conference, changes in the original job description should be made verbally where indicated. If they are substantial, they should be put in writing as soon as is practicable, with both parties retaining copies of the amended document. Ideally, a third conference will be held within six months. This shows that the manager is concerned and creates goodwill for the organization, besides uncovering dissatisfactions that may have developed. Usually, a third conference will involve only minor adjustments, assuming good organizational planning has provided appropriate job design at the outset.

Managers in every echelon of an organization should have at least one annual conference with each immediate subordinate with the specific objective of reevaluating the job description. Such conferences allow for fine tuning coordination and provide an opportunity to learn of problems that may be rankling.

Work team conferences

We have mentioned the difficulty in delegating and assigning in such a way that complete coordination of work team activities will result. Organized efforts throughout the centuries have encountered this problem. It can be overcome in many ways, but we have found that face-to-face meetings of team members are especially effective. We have always been proponents of holding a weekly meeting of department heads in hospitals during our careers as hospital administrators, having read Fayol's clear statement to the effect that there is no substitute in this regard.[13]

Many chief executives of hospitals only hold meetings with department heads on a quarterly, semiannual, or annual basis. Our study of the operations of industrial and other organizations reveals similar situations elsewhere. We believe that in such situations executives are either afraid to face their subordinates in a group or that they are partly managing by intimidating their subordinates individual by individual. In each case, there is a clear indication the manager is aware of personal inadequacies and has a basic lack of the courage needed to be a manager.

We cannot recommend too strongly having these face-to-face group conferences with subordinates—and at least monthly in a vast majority of cases. They serve as an efficacious adjunct to delegating agreements in bringing about optimal coordination. A manager's job is likely to be more secure if the manager takes the heat and dissipates it as it occurs rather than if he or she awaits the big blast of a possible crisis situation later on.

In holding group meetings, we have found that some members of the group may be reluctant to speak out about dissatisfactions regarding his or her own work or about the work of others. We have successfully employed the technique of asking each member present a point-blank question about whether there are any troublesome aspects of operations, especially those related to coordination. This prevents anyone from maintaining silence and harboring animosities. Although members may occasionally elect to maintain silence, even in the face of the point-blank question, most eventually recognize their silence as being a violation of integrity and will usually seek a personal conference with the manager involved to discuss problems.

By holding these group meetings, managers often perceive needed revisions to delegations of authority and assignments of responsibility and accountability, together with desirable changes in policy and procedure manuals.

Role of job descriptions

The basic purpose of a job description is not to put together a set of stereotyped generalities in order to fulfill a dull management policy. At present, many job descriptions are so vague that they border on being absurd and in no way describe the actual scope of authority and work assignments of an individual manager, agent, or specialized organizational operator.

The purpose of job descriptions is to reflect accurately and in some detail the understanding reached between superiors and subordinates about delegated authority, assigned work, and the attendant responsibility and accountability. Such job descriptions, executed for each and every member of an organization and continually reviewed at conferences between superiors and subordinates, can become vital management tools. (See Exhibit 4-1, p. 114, as an example of a job description for a specialized operator.)

Some hospitals defer job descriptions for top-level executives on the grounds that they can stifle initiative or that misplaced authority might be delegated. We have no cause to believe this is unique to hospitals, and in fact our literature searches confirm that other businesses use the same bad reasoning. McFarland dismissed such an approach years ago when he stated, "No job is so nebulous that its characteristics and responsibilities cannot be defined, unless complete organizational anarchy is to prevail."[14]

Thus, to make job descriptions so vague as to be worthless or to omit them entirely constitutes an outright violation of a basic management function. To compensate for the absence of a vital mutual understanding with and commitment from individual employees, a manager must employ much less desirable means to get work done, such as close supervision, personal admonitions, and possibly even disciplinary acts. Often an organization merely hobbles along, operating at a level of efficiency far below its potential. The chief executive and the subordinate managers may hold their jobs, but the cost in terms of job satisfaction, bottom-line profits, and optimal results is untold.

Summary

Delegated authority flows from organizational charters and bylaws throughout business organizations by means of a succession of agreements between superiors and subordinates. Corresponding assignments of responsibility and accountability should form parts of the same agreements. However, responsibility and accountability cannot be delegated (transferred) from one manager to another. Once vested, these are retained, even though from a functional standpoint they can be assigned to individual subordinates in a manner commensurate with delegated authority.

Four essential elements compose an agreement between a superior and a subordinate wherein authority is delegated and responsibility and accountability assigned:

1. mutual consent to establishment of the relationship

2. agreement as to the scope and type of work or duties which the subordinate will perform on behalf of the superior

3. delegation (transfer) of authority by the superior to the subordinate for performance of the acts and duties mutually agreed upon

4. assent or commitment by the subordinate to assume an obligation and the accountability for performance of the agreed upon acts or duties (the assumed obligation and accountability does not relieve the superior relative to third parties or a higher superior).

Managers use such agreements to divide up the total work of an organization. They thereby become important tools for achieving coordination of tasks performed by individuals as a part of work systems and subsystems. Other techniques can be used to supplement the coordination achieved by these agreements, such as supervision, leadership, and group conferences (e.g., meetings between a superior and a team of subordinates formed to accomplish certain goals and objectives). Our own experience leads us to believe the communication between a superior and subordinates and among subordinates that results from regularly scheduled group conferences is highly effective as a supplement to formal superior-subordinate agreements in achieving ongoing coordination of work efforts.

The agreements between superiors and subordinates provide the basis for meaningful job descriptions for all employees of an organization. In contrast to the vague, stereotypical statements common in many organizations, such job descriptions, constantly updated through regularly scheduled superior-subordinate conferences, can become a vital tool in achieving efficiency, job satisfaction, and increased bottom-line profits.

Notes

1. Dalton E. McFarland, *Management: Principles and Practices*, 2d ed. (New York: Macmillan, 1964), 300.
2. Rensis Likert, *New Patterns of Management* (New York: McGraw-Hill, 1961), 52–53.
3. Raleigh Cline, "Decentralization and Managerial Job Satisfaction" (Unpublished report, Department of Health Care Administration, George Washington University, 1965).
4. Gary Dessler, *Organization and Management* (Reston, Va.: Reston Publishing Company, 1982), 67.
5. James A.F. Stoner, *Management*, 2d ed. (1982), 313. Reprinted by permission of Prentice-Hall, Inc., Englewood Cliffs, N.J.
6. Chester I. Barnard, *The Functions of the Executive* (Cambridge, Mass.: Harvard University Press, 1938), 163–69.
7. Marten Estey, *The Unions*, 3d ed. (New York: Harcourt Brace Jovanovich, 1981), 135.
8. Owen B. Hardy, "Delegation: The Administrator's Challenge," *Hospital Administration* (Winter 1970): 11.
9. Stoner, *Management*, 315. Reprinted by permission of Prentice-Hall, Inc., Englewood Cliffs, N.J.
10. Hardy, "Delegation," 12.
11. Ibid., 13.
12. Ibid., 15.
13. Henri Fayol, *General and Industrial Management* (London: Sir Isaac Pitman and Sons, Ltd., 1961), 205.
14. McFarland, *Management*, 205.

Chapter 11

Leadership

Elements of Management
in Corporations

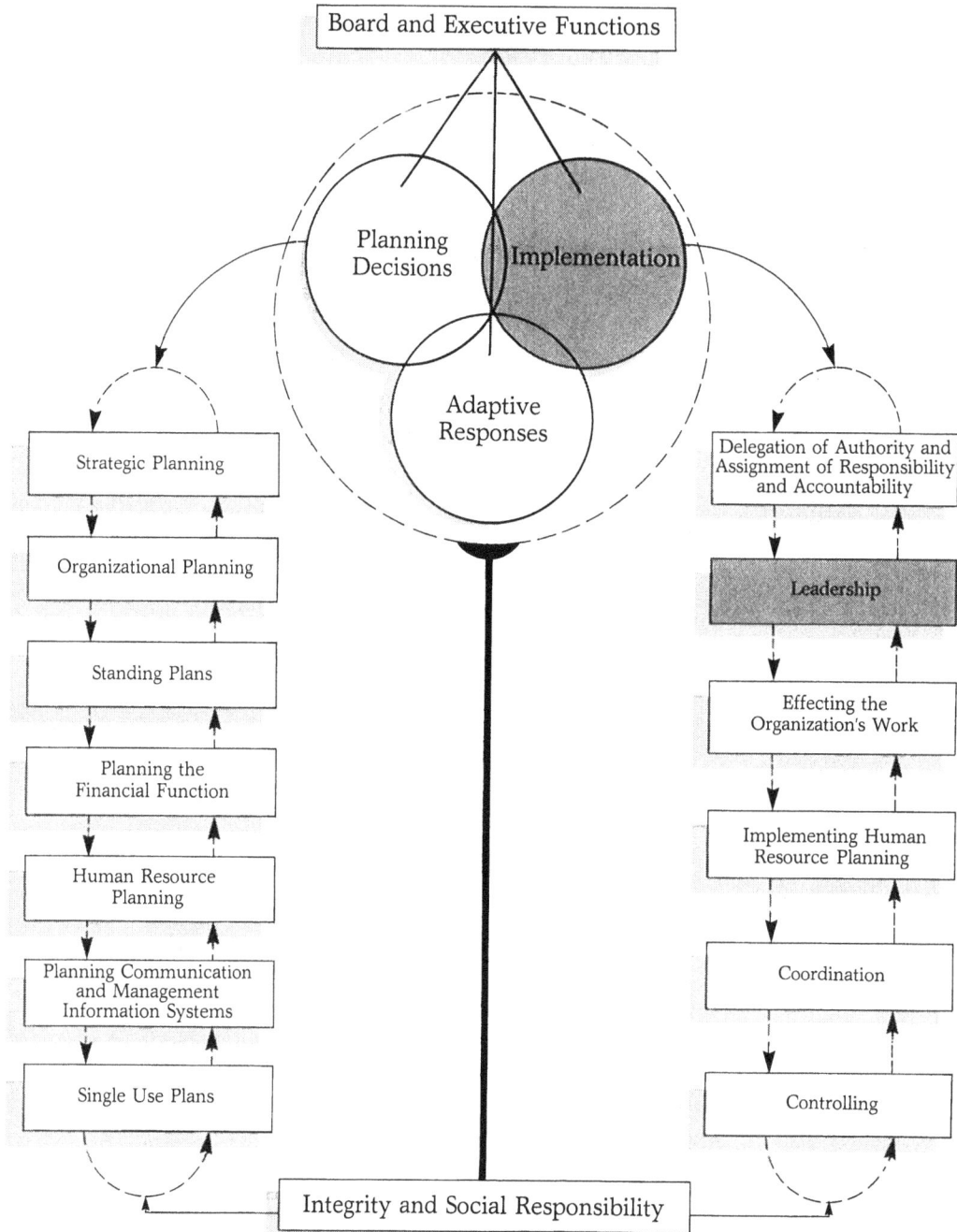

Board and Executive Functions

Planning Decisions

Implementation

Adaptive Responses

Strategic Planning

Organizational Planning

Standing Plans

Planning the Financial Function

Human Resource Planning

Planning Communication and Management Information Systems

Single Use Plans

Delegation of Authority and Assignment of Responsibility and Accountability

Leadership

Effecting the Organization's Work

Implementing Human Resource Planning

Coordination

Controlling

Integrity and Social Responsibility

11

Leadership is a variable in management effectiveness which is extremely difficult to measure. That it constitutes a prime factor, few would deny, but many continue to define it in various ways and debate its characteristics, situational aspects, relationships with power and authority, and means of development. Less seems to be heard about leadership in organizations than was heard a few years ago, but this may be owing to the current consuming interest in the larger subject of management.

Leadership was, is, and always will be a means used by human beings to induce other human beings to act in particular desired ways to achieve particular desired ends. This certainly does not differentiate leadership from a number of other means whereby desired ends are also attained, but it does indicate that leadership in organizations should be subsumed under the general category of management functions we have called implementation. At present, planning for leadership usually occurs informally (largely in the minds of individuals). However, the time may come when such planning will be done formally in many business organizations. We state this despite only a few positive results from leadership training, at least according to current research.

Some of the confusion about the precise nature of leadership arises from the fact that it has been referred to as "a function, a characteristic, a combination of traits, a position, a relationship, a person or groups of persons, a process, an ability, an influence, a method of guidance, and even mere supervision; some also broaden the term to include any action a purported leader might take."[1] Further, many use the term *leadership* in reference to "politicians, military commanders, civil rights workers, playground supervisors, executives, moderators of discussion groups, chairpersons of committees, religious spokesmen, and a host of diverse positions in which varying amounts of authority have been vested."[2]

In short, *leadership* continues to be one of the most loosely used terms in our language. Even a brief survey of available literature on the subject will reveal that some of the most effusive praises that could be framed by the human mind have been heaped upon it. This has occurred despite the fact that there literally is no general agreement among authoritative groups as to what it really is.

In this chapter we attempt to define leadership as it relates to organizational management. In doing so, we examine some of the perceptions and theories concerning the subject that have been expressed over the last several decades. We also review a number of views that seem false to us. Finally, we express an opinion as to how to select organizational

"Which one?"

*" . . . And you characters
had better get the job done."*

"I know we can do it."

leaders and, for an aspiring manager who wants to improve his leadership potential, briefly discuss a sound method for doing so.

The importance of leadership has been underestimated in recent years. This may be owing to the greater reliance of most organizations on money and job satisfaction to provide sufficient motivation among employees for the accomplishment of work objectives. In our own area of management—the health field—leadership remains particularly important because of the necessity to deal with organizational structures that comprise highly diverse elements and over which the chief executive officer and other top managers do not have complete control. Leadership has been observed to be effective in achieving coordination and efficiency in the operation of hospitals in particular.

Leadership theories

The trait theory

This theory centers on the personality traits of individuals who have been regarded as leaders in a variety of environmental settings. It searches for traits common to at least a majority of leaders in a majority of situations. The theory holds that if such traits can be positively identified, then individuals who possess them can be deliberately selected for those positions where leadership is required, thereby assuring a successful outcome.

The trait theory derives from the great man theory of leadership, originally propounded by Thomas Carlyle, a Scottish historian. Carlyle feared democracy and contended that "the history of the world is but the biography of great men." Others, however, soon recognized that great leaders of the past have not uniformly contributed to the well-being of humankind and that their personal characteristics have varied quite widely. These insights subsequently stimulated extensive research aimed at discovering "good" traits among "good" leaders in attempts to save the trait theory.

Although debates about leadership traits continue, most authorities agree that leadership cannot be defined as a trait or a combination of traits. After considerable research, Eugene E. Jennings, associate professor of business administration at Michigan State University, commented, "Fifty years of study have failed to produce one personality trait or set of qualities that can be used to discriminate between leaders and non-leaders. This failure to identify leadership traits in individuals has led us to look elsewhere for keys to leadership."[3] Even so, there is some value in identifying certain personality traits which it might be desirable for a person to have who is to be put in a position of leadership within a given situation. Of course, identifying desirable traits relative to job positions is generally helpful, whether or not leadership is a recognized job requirement.

In discussing intelligence, social maturity and breadth, inner motivation and achievement drives, and human relations attitudes, Keith Davis noted that "studies show that there is a better-than-chance probability that a leader will have more of these traits than the general population and sometimes even more than the average of his followers."[4] Even here, despite citing valid research, Davis recognizes there are no universal traits of leadership. However, he indirectly confirms the value of striving to fill leadership positions with persons perceived as possessing a small number of valued traits. In a sense (and probably without being aware of it), Davis confirms the plausibility of the situational leadership theory, which is discussed next.

The situational leadership theory

This theory focuses on where leadership occurs and characteristics of the environment. To a large extent, it assesses situational aspects apart from an assessment of so-called leadership traits as researched by those adhering to the trait theory. However, many students of the situational school have believed the nature of a situation may indicate characteristics or traits which the leader of a given group should possess at a given time. Obviously, as time passes and the situation changes, traits originally indicated may no longer be desirable. Thus ongoing leadership (i.e., having a specific individual occupying a specific leadership position over a period of time) will rarely continue to meet the needs of a situation.

From another standpoint, one can argue that those thrust into leadership positions based largely on situational factors are

> often mere group tools, voicing already formed opinions, fulfilling expressed desires and taking demanded actions. However, skillful as the person may be in the use of these tactics and in meeting situational needs, he is not necessarily exercising leadership and is, in a sense, the follower of the group. This reasoning, of course, cannot exclude from the ranks of leaders those who so gain top echelons and who later exercise true leadership. In some cases, the latter event obtains, and these instances may

have been mistakenly interpreted to strengthen further the situational theory of leadership.[5]

Most authorities have now recognized the fallacies of the situational leadership theory. Even so, many continue to use this theory in the development of others more useful to overall management theory.

Interaction or relationship theories

Douglas McGregor, one of the most notable pioneers in the application of behavioral science research to the field of management, stated the following in the early 1960s:

> There are at least four variables now known to be involved in leadership: (1) the characteristics of the leader; (2) the attitudes, needs, and other professional characteristics of the followers; (3) the characteristics of the organization, such as its purpose, its structure, the nature of the tasks to be performed; and (4) the social, economic and political milieu. The personal characteristics required for effective performance as a leader vary, depending on other factors. This is an important research finding. *It means that leadership is not the property of an individual but a complex relationship among these variables.*[6]

Although McGregor's statements show great insight, we disagree with his conclusion. Leadership only emerges if there is a leader present. However the behavior of the leader may be perceived and however it may be affected by the situational elements that are present, leadership is still vested in that leader. In short, without a leader there can be no leadership. We hasten to add that we believe McGregor is essentially correct in noting the variables that he does.

Fred E. Fiedler's contingency theory of leadership is actually an interaction theory that holds that leadership effectiveness is contingent on the interaction or relationship between the style of the leader and the favorableness of the situation. The effectiveness is measured in terms of (1) leader-member relations, (2) task structure, and (3) the degree of formal authority vested in the leader's position.[7] Fiedler's work, which has continued for more than 20 years, involves systematic methodologies for measuring how the interaction of leadership styles (e.g., autocratic, permissive, etc.) and situational variables affects the performance of work groups.

The path-goal theory of leadership, developed by Robert J. House, is essentially an interaction or relationship theory based on the relationship between leader behavior and responding employee behavior. This theory also draws on the expectancy theory of motivation. Essentially, the theory postulates that being a leader involves devising rewards for goal attainment by subordinates and making the path to these rewards and to the work goal itself satisfactory or desirable in the minds of the individuals involved.[8]

Many others have investigated numerous interactions and relationships that occur in various types of organizational settings and how they affect the success of leaders. One problem common to all of these investigations is the difficulty in establishing suitable means for measuring both causes and effects. Thus, while it seems plausible that each of the interaction and relationship theories mentioned here has elements of truth, incontrovertible proof is lacking for all of them, and it is safe to predict that such proof will never be found. However, this does not detract from the basic worth of the theories as objects of study for students of management.

Behavioral theory

In contrast to the trait theory, behavioral theory focuses on what the leader does rather than on inherent characteristics. However, behavioral theorists depend on the observations of those around the leader to determine perceptions of the leader's acts, thereby taking account of the fact that it is not so much what the leader does that affects the performance of others as how it is perceived.

Ohio State University researchers have probably done some of the most comprehensive studies of leader behavior ever attempted. Beginning over 25 years ago, these studies produced the Leader Behavior Description Questionnaire (LBDQ), which in various versions is used as an instrument for measuring and describing leader behaviors in a wide range of research settings.[9]

The Ohio State version of the LBDQ is based on the view that there are two prime areas of leader behavior: (1) initiating structure and (2) consideration.[10] Initiating structure includes constructing performance standards, scheduling, supervising, coordinating, etc. The performance of the leader in initiating structure is measured by items on the LBDQ, and high scores have indeed shown a correlation with certain performance measures, e.g., cost and productivity.[11]

Leader consideration is simply the degree of considerate behavior toward employees that is in evidence. Genuine concern and care for employees usually result in friendship, trust, and, in most instances, respect. The LBDQ measures consideration through a number of items, and a correlation has been demonstrated between high scores and various desirable characteristics of employee groups, such as high job satisfaction, low employee turnover, and reduced grievance rates.[12] There has not been a consistent correlation between high scores on consideration and high productivity, as regards both individuals and groups.[13] This fact, however, does not detract from the considerable worth of low employee turnover and reduced grievance rates.

The Ohio State research indicates that the two basic characteristics of leader behavior (initiating structure and consideration) function independently of each other, and the extent that "a manager uses one of them does not help predict the amount of the other that he is using."[14] Consequently, Reddin noted that these two factors can be charted at right angles.[15]

In the 1950s and 1960s, behavioral science researchers also carried out extensive work at the University of Michigan that corroborated the Ohio State work, in that the two basic factors of task orientation (initiating and employee-centered relationships consideration) are indeed present in leader behavior. However, the Michigan findings differed from the Ohio State findings in that as a manager's behavior became more task oriented, it became less concerned with employee-centered relationships, and vice versa.[16]

We regard the studies accomplished at Ohio State University and the University of Michigan, together with other later work based on those studies, as of considerable value to managers and students of management. Although the LBDQ has not been shown to have significant value as a predictive tool regarding leadership, certainly the central message of the research is loud and clear: Managers are well advised to structure the workplace of employees to some (optimal) degree and to be considerate to them. Behavioral theory has certainly influenced our own management styles over the years and has contributed to our definition of leadership, as will be seen later in this chapter. We regard behavioral theory, as it now exists, to be acceptable as a practical approach to getting organizational work accomplished.

As research has generally shown, a consistent correlation between high job performance and high employee satisfaction has not been demonstrated. Yet managers (leaders) have a responsibility in all situations to strive for the achievement of both.

Leadership styles

Numerous researchers have studied styles of leadership over the years. McGregor's Theory X and Theory Y implied two styles, each stemming from a different way in which a leader might regard his or her employees. A Theory X leader is presumed to view employees as generally indolent and irresponsible and in need of very close supervision. A Theory Y leader views employees as motivated, concerned, creative, and desirous of an optimal degree of control over the individual workplace.[17] Chris Argyris continued and broadened McGregor's work, but Argyris's general approach to style remained consistent with it.

During the 1930s, Donald Lippitt and Ralph White performed a number of now famous experiments under the direction of the late Gestalt psychologist Kurt Lewin. They tested three "styles of leadership" (authoritarian, democratic, and laissez-faire) so as to determine effects on individual and group behavior. Each of the test groups comprised five 11-year-old children as well as an adult who purported to exercise leadership based on the three styles of leadership.[18] In general, the democratic style proved to be most effective. It is merely a surmise, of course, but we believe an authoritarian style of leadership would prove much less desirable in business organizations (and most others) today than appeared to be the case in the 1930s. As to the laissez-faire style, we recognize there are some situations where it has applicability, but we could not argue too strongly against using the laissez-faire style continuously *without* controls characterized by definitive parameters, even in the R & D departments of many large corporations, where nearly total freedom is often allowed to researchers.

With reference to these tests, leadership styles have varied widely in terms of degrees of supervision, and the results obtained from the tests have without doubt been instrumental in guiding leaders toward the "democratic" style (with variations in the degree of democracy). On the whole, leadership styles have tended to vary from being more employee centered to being more task or goal oriented. Achieving the appropriate balance between the two extremes remains a constant leadership responsibility.

Robert Blake and Jane Mouton's popular managerial grid takes into account both a people orientation and a task orientation, and in doing so it identifies five basic styles within its continuum.[19] Rensis Likert, a researcher at the University of Michigan, set forth four styles in a continuum: (1) exploitive autocratic, (2) benevolent autocratic, (3) participative, and (4) democratic.[20]

More recently, Lin Bothwell outlined a continuum of ten leadership styles. These, too, vary essentially from the autocratic to the laissez-faire. Bothwell does, however, provide a methodology for determining which of the ten styles managers should employ at a given time. The determination depends on (1) the task and its deadline for completion, (2) the existing environment, (3) the characteristics of the employees (or followers), and (4) the tendencies of the leader in making decisions (e.g., whether the leader tends to act alone or let a team decide).[21] Although we have not formally used Bothwell's methodology, it is based on one principle that we *have* used: It is not necessary and indeed not desirable to use the same leadership style in all situations. Some situations require an authoritarian approach and others require a laissez-faire approach. However, in a majority of instances, some variation of the democratic approach is to be preferred.

Erroneous views about leadership

Many have expressed false or questionable views about leadership. This will undoubtedly continue to be the case. Nonetheless, it will be useful to briefly consider a few of these erroneous views as a way of approaching the question of how to define leadership in the field of management.

To begin with, we do not believe that leadership in its true sense results from the mere possession of organizational authority or from the use of power derived from such authority.

Some years ago, Dubin stated, "Leadership in organizations involves the exercise of authority."[22] Argyris also implied that leadership involves use of power.[23] During that same period, however, Newman and Summer, adherents of the process school of management thought, viewed leadership as completely separate from authority, power, and force, and they discussed it as an individual process.[24] Likert, viewing the issue from a sociological standpoint, also espoused the belief that leadership is not to be confused with threats and force, and he emphasized that leadership should be understood in terms of relationships (see the section above on interaction or relationship theories of leadership).[25]

More recently, Lin Bothwell stated specifically in regard to organizations that "leadership, perhaps more than anything else, involves the use of power."[26] In contradiction to that statement, Robert Albanese has opined that "people follow leaders *voluntarily* and for reasons of their own choosing," and he defined leadership as behavior that elicits voluntary follower behavior beyond that associated with required performance on the job.[27] We agree with this and believe that this same opinion is held by a majority of management authorities today.

Because leadership in formal organizations cannot be studied apart from a leader's position in the organizational hierarchy, and also because managers are loosely referred to as leaders whether or not they are, a superficial analysis of leadership might lead one to believe it is synonymous with the total range of duties, obligations, and activities inherent in an organizational position. But this is far from true. Again, leadership is something beyond the basic use of management skills.

Another view about leadership that we believe to be false concerns decision making. Some earlier writers seemed to imply that some decisions constitute leadership because they are policy making in nature and affect greatly not only the organizations in which they are made but the lives of employees as well. Selznick espoused this view,[28] and Jennings held that the leader is an initiator of plans which are carried out by an executive.[29] In contrast, another author has said,

> Because many noted leaders have also been men of acute vision and imagination, and because their decisions in some instances mark milestones in the affairs of the human race, decision making has tended to become confused with leadership; creativeness in decision, particularly, has been frequently identified as leadership. It is possibly in these areas that the greatest controversy now exists with respect to the true meaning of organizational leadership.[30]

At present, the view that decision making constitutes leadership persists, but it is possibly less widespread than previously. The term *manager* has come to replace the term *leader* in most writings about management (which incidentally was almost universally called *administration* 40 years ago). To some extent, the change is merely one of semantics. In any case, most authorities now believe decision making to be the responsibility of a manager, and they regard it largely as a planning function, not an implementation function.

Victor Vroom and Philip Yetton have made a distinct contribution to decision making in organizations in recent years through development of a model concerning "leader" styles in the process of decision making. These authors outline three main styles for reaching solutions to group problems: autocratic, consultative, and group. Each style involves a different degree of potential participation by employees.[31] On cursory review, the model may seem to presuppose that decision making per se is leadership, but in reality it is the *style* by which decisions are reached that the authors regard as leadership. If these authors had used the terms *manager* and *management* in describing these styles rather than *leader* and *leadership*, greater consistency with current terminology might have resulted.

Organizationl decision making is certainly a managerial responsibility that derives from organizational charters and bylaws. But while leadership behavior does not exclude decision making, most decision making occurs as a planning activity. Thus, decision making and leadership are not equivalent, despite what some have seemed to believe. However, it shouldn't be concluded that an incompetent decision maker could become a great leader in the business world. Perceptions of a given person as someone who exhibits competence in decision making may contribute toward his or her image as a leader.

A number of authors in recent years have bandied about the erroneous notion that being a leader and having the capabilities of a manager are somehow mutually exclusive. Quite to the contrary, in the business world today, if someone does not have good problem-solving capabilities, can't make good decisions, doesn't focus on organizational goals, and doesn't have quite a few management skills of a fairly technical nature, there would be a high probability that that person would be laughed right out of any reputable business organization. In the case of a person with such managerial deficiencies, the opportunity to exercise leadership would never present itself. In our opinion, the very first requisite for becoming a leader is to have good management skills, which can be thought of as the stepping stones to leadership in the business world. Nonetheless, having the very best management skills will not necessarily make someone a great leader.

Our definition of leadership

What then is leadership? Is it so inextricably intertwined with the mechanistic and legalistic functions of management that it cannot be isolated? Is leadership in organizations something that had best be disregarded, with new emphasis placed instead on "directing"? Is it now so confusing that we should cease worrying about it? We think not. While it may be a bit fuzzy and ill defined, there is no substitute for that extra "something" in the perceived behavior of a manager which causes employees to give a little more, to exhibit organizational loyalty, and to voluntarily coordinate their actions with those of others to produce products of superior quality or to achieve organizational objectives on time and within budgets.

This is our definition of leadership within formal organizations:

> *Leadership is the perceived behavior of a manager that causes a motivation within subordinates, other organizational members, and possibly peripherally related individuals to strive voluntarily toward achievement of organizational goals and objectives. The motivation that results from the manager's behavior is detectable in a work situation, even if it is not completely separable from motivations caused by other sources.*

As has been noted by many others, leadership is not a precisely defined characteristic of managers. Leading (or exercising leadership) is essentially a matter of causing motivations in persons to act in certain ways (for the good of the organization); and, their becoming motivated often depends on their perceptions of a manager's behavior. Not all persons will perceive the actual behavior of a manager in the same way. As well, the degree to which a person becomes motivated and the importance of the motivation for performance levels in achieving organizational goals and objectives will vary from person to person in the organization.

Practicing leadership

Considering the several variables involved, a manager, in dealing with a broad range of organizational members, cannot expect to uniformly cause appropriately motivating perceptions in the minds of all parties with whom interfaces occur. The manager can, however, in face-to-face contacts with individuals, consciously behave in such ways that there will be a high probability of perceptions occurring that will cause desirable motivations. This assumes sensitivity and a basic knowledge of the social sciences on the manager's part. But in the end, the manager must exhibit some consistency in behavior and hope that the behavior will be fitted to and largely accepted by a *majority* of those with whom interfaces occur. This involves gaining knowledge of the social backgrounds, propensities, likes, dislikes, and needs of those with whom relationships are established. It also involves keeping sight of the fact that one should strive for more than mere personal acceptance or popularity. A manager must never forget that a manager's basic function is to achieve the organization's goals and objectives, either directly through personal efforts or through the efforts of others. And a manager must also never forget that these efforts should be ethical, within the bounds of decency and propriety, and in conformance with the law.

Two basic situations

Two basic situations occur where managers, especially those in top echelons, should be acutely aware of the implications of our definition of leadership and of the other facts and opinions expressed in this chapter. These are (1) where it is necessary to select persons for positions where perceived leadership behavior will be greatly desirable (this is the case with most upper level management positions), and (2) where managers wish to enhance their effectiveness through the exercise of leadership. The second situation occurs with regard to nearly all managers at some time or other.

Selecting persons for leadership positions

When a person must be selected for a position where perceived leadership behavior would be desirable, a list should be drawn up of the types of behavior which would tend to cause favorable perceptions among some or all of the following: subordinates, persons in lateral hierarchical positions and the person or persons who will be superior to the person who fills the position. This list, of course, is entirely separate from the list of position skills that can be somewhat objectively evaluated. One should certainly require that the standards set for position skills should be met by any candidate for the job. As for the first mentioned list, those preparing it should consider the environmental situation in all its aspects, e.g., persons, time, exigencies, constraints, goals and objectives, etc. After completing the list of desirable behavioral characteristics, the selection process can continue with a candidate search and subsequent interviews of eligible persons.

The list of desirable behavioral characteristics should include those from the two dimensions of leader behavior identified by Ohio State researchers: (1) initiating structure and (2) consideration. We point out, however, that any list so prepared ought to be modified to take into account the peculiarities of the individual situation.

In regard to initiating structure, the Ohio State researchers found there were five basic leader behaviors. A leader

1. maintains definite standards of performance

2. expresses clear attitudes

3. asks that standard operating procedures be followed

4. assigns particular tasks

5. emphasizes the meeting of deadlines.

Similarly, the findings about consideration can be summarized as follows. A leader

1. displays warmth and concern in personal relationships and is friendly and approachable

2. elicits trust

3. exhibits readiness to explain actions taken

4. demonstrates a willingness to listen to subordinates and to allow them to participate in decision making

5. treats employees as equals.

With regard to individual situations, the listed behavioral characteristics can be weighted in terms of their considered importance in view of the various environmental aspects. In essence, a basic factor analysis would be desirable (see the section on application of criteria to yield objective selections in Chapter 3).

Obviously, it will be difficult to measure candidates in this regard who are being considered from outside the employing organization. Such measurement is relatively easy for candidates with a record of several years within the organization.

Although traits have generally been impossible to evaluate in terms of their ability to predict employee behavior, the following general traits identified by Keith Davis should be considered as indicators of leadership potential:

1. intelligence

2. social maturity and breadth

3. inner motivation and achievement drives

4. human relations attitudes.

We wish to add a fifth trait. This trait, which we consider to be of the utmost importance in the long run, is *integrity*. Integrity is especially important at this time. One has only to scan the daily newspapers to become aware of the considerable volume of reported white collar crime, which undoubtedly is in small proportion to the volume of *undetected* stealing, cheating, and general dishonesty. We believe integrity will merit increasing attention, in contrast to previous years, when candidates were often merely assumed to possess the trait.

Enhancing perceptions of leadership

What can a manager do to create or enhance perceptions of his or her behavior so that leadership will be effected? Is there a simple formula? Is self-analysis and adoption of a specific style worthwhile?

A manager cannot adopt any simple, easy formula regarding leadership. Although various simplistic recipes being currently published may be helpful in some situations, we think they have been put forward primarily for pecuniary gain and for increasing personal status. As stated in our opening chapter, management (of which leadership is an intangible part) is not the abstruse riddle hidden in an enigma that some hold it to be. On the other hand, neither management nor leadership is so easy that it can be learned by an overnight perusal of a number of magical Dos and Don'ts.

The student of management aspiring to be a leader must pursue a concentrated study of the published literature on leadership, sociology, and psychology in management. Simultaneously, periodic self-analysis regarding style will be helpful. No single style of leadership will suffice in all situations, but in a majority of them (at least in the Western world), consideration for subordinates is a requisite.

Several authorities have devised various concepts of leadership and leadership styles, and we recommend study of the following:

- *Leadership and Decision Making*, by Victor H. Vroom and Philip W. Yetton, published in 1976.

- *The Art of Leadership*, by Lin Bothwell, published in 1983.

- *Leadership*, by Leonard R. Sayles, published in 1979.

Lastly, in effecting perceptions of behavior that will bring about desirable results, the manager must

1. be ever cognizant that increasing effectiveness and efficiency in attaining goals and objectives is the major purpose of business leadership (although it may be the most important purpose, others follow closely behind, such as the achievement of job satisfaction by employees of the organization)

2. recognize that consistent behavior designed for the long term will be more effective overall than behavior suited for the exigencies of the short term

3. adopt a sensitive social consciousness directed both inside and outside the organization

4. realize that the conjunction of "goodwill" and respect among organizational personnel is generally a reflection of appropriate leadership

5. understand that leadership behavior affects three groups: superiors, subordinates, and those in lateral positions (a fourth group may be important in some situations, i.e., where peripherally related individuals not actually part of the organization contribute to the attainment of goals, objectives, and goodwill)

6. communicate clearly, frequently, and incisively about matters pertinent to planning, implementation, and adaptive responses, and also exhibit a businesslike attitude, but avoid arrogance

7. know that personal behavior serves as the primary basis for organizational members' perceptions of leadership (since both actions and words make up behavior, a manager must constantly evaluate his or her personal on-the-job conduct and exercise prudence in all communications)

8. realize that the unlocking of initiative and voluntary cooperation and coordination among organizational members is directly linked to increasing their personal need satisfaction.

Summary

Leadership is a loosely used, imprecisely defined term, and one of the major objectives of this chapter is to construct a suitable definition for use in business organizations.

Authorities have advanced many theories about leadership. Most of the theories fall into one of four major classifications, depending on whether the given theory focuses on (1) traits, (2) situations, (3) interactions and relationships, or (4) behaviors. Researchers have also identified and studied a rather broad range of leadership "styles." These generally vary from being more task or goal centered to being more employee centered. The majority of authorities concur that no single leadership style applies in all situations.

We defined leadership within formal organizations as the *perceived* behavior of a manager that causes a motivation within subordinates, other organizational members, and possibly peripherally related individuals to strive voluntarily toward achievement of organizational objectives with a greater intensity of effort than would have otherwise occurred.

Two situations, with variations, exist in organizations where managers should be especially knowledgeable about leadership theories and styles. These are (1) where leaders must be selected to fill manager positions throughout the hierarchy, especially at top levels; and (2) where a manager already occupies a position and wishes to enhance his or her leadership style. Regarding the first situation, we believe it is useful to do a basic factor analysis for each candidate for a position, using factors relating to initiating organizational structure and consideration for employees. This has special merit in the case of candidates within the selecting organization, where a valid record of managerial behavior has already been established. For candidates outside the organization, evaluation of five traits may be useful (in addition, of course, to evaluating whether the candidate is technically qualified for the position). The five traits are (1) intelligence, (2) social maturity and breadth, (3) inner motivation and achievement drives, (4) human relations attitudes, and (5) integrity.

Regarding the second situation, all managers who aspire to leadership should be students of organizational leadership. These managers must

1. be aware that the achievement of organizational goals and objectives is the major purpose of leadership

2. realize that behavior suited for the long term is usually more effective overall than behavior especially tailored for the short term

3. develop a sensitive social consciousness

4. know that good will and respect are common indicators of leadership

5. understand that leadership behavior has effects upward, downward, and laterally within the organization and also many times outside the organization

6. communicate frequently and meaningfully about planning, implementation, and adaptive responses

7. know that personal actions (including communications) are the basis for others' perceptions of leadership and that each manager must constantly evaluate his or her on-the-job behavior

8. realize that personal need satisfaction unlocks initiative and voluntary cooperation and coordination among organizational members.

Notes

1. Owen B. Hardy, "Leadership and the Hospital Administrator," *Hospital Administration* 13 (Winter 1968): 35.
2. Ibid.
3. Eugene E. Jennings, "The Anatomy of Leadership," *Management of Personnel Quarterly*, Autumn 1961. Quoted in *Essentials of Management*, 3d ed., ed. Harold Koontz, Cyril O'Donnel, and Heinz Weihrich (New York: McGraw-Hill, 1982), 425.
4. Keith Davis, *Human Behavior at Work* (New York: McGraw-Hill, 1972), 103–4.
5. Hardy, "Leadership and the Hospital Administrator," 37.
6. Douglas McGregor, *Leadership and Motivation*, ed. Warren G. Bennis and Edgar H. Schein, with the collaboration of Caroline McGregor (Cambridge, Mass.: MIT Press, 1966), 73.
7. Fred E. Fiedler, "The Leadership Game: Matching the Man to the Situation," *Organizational Dynamics*, Winter 1976, pp. 5–12. Copyright by AMACOM, a division of the American Management Association.

8. Robert J. House, "A Path-Goal Theory of Leader Effectiveness," *Administrative Science Quarterly* 16 (September 1971): 321–338.

9. Robert Albanese, *Management: Toward Accountability for Performance* (Homewood, Ill.: Richard D. Irwin, Inc., 1975), 484.

10. Ralph M. Stogdill and Alvin E. Coons, eds., *Leader Behavior: Its Description and Measurement*, Research Mimeograph no. 88 (Columbus, Ohio: Ohio State University, Bureau of Business Research, 1951). Also see an updated literature review of the Ohio State research by Steven Kerr, Chester A. Schriesheim, Charles J. Murphy, and Ralph M. Stogdill, "Toward a Contingency Theory of Leadership Based upon the Consideration and Initiating Structure Literature," *Organization Behavior and Human Performance*, August 1974, pp. 62–82.

11. Albanese, *Management*, 485.

12. Ibid.

13. Ibid., 485–86.

14. W.J. Reddin, *Managerial Effectiveness* (New York: McGraw-Hill, 1970), 21.

15. Ibid.

16. Ibid., 21–22.

17. Douglas McGregor, *The Human Side of Enterprise* (New York: McGraw-Hill, 1960), 33–176.

18. Donald Lippitt and Ralph K. White, "An Experimental Study of Leadership and Group Life," in *Readings in Social Psychology*, rev. ed., ed. Guy Swanson, Theodore Newcomb, and Eugene Hartley (New York: Henry Holt & Co., 1952).

19. Robert R. Blake and Jane S. Mouton, *The New Managerial Grid* (Houston, Tex.: Gulf Publishing Company, 1976), 9–15.

20. Cited in Lin Bothwell, *The Art of Leadership* (Englewood Cliffs, N.J.: Prentice-Hall, 1983), 217.

21. Ibid., 237.

22. Robert Dubin, *Human Relations in Administration* (Englewood Cliffs, N.J.: Prentice-Hall, 1961), 348.

23. Chris Argyris, "Personal vs. Organizational Goals," *Yale Scientific Monthly*, February 1960, pp. 40–50. Reprinted in Dubin, *Human Relations in Administration*, 72–73.

24. William H. Newman and Charles E. Summer, Jr., *The Process of Management* (Englewood Cliffs, N.J.: Prentice-Hall, 1961), 475–93.

25. Rensis Likert, *New Patterns of Management* (New York: McGraw-Hill, 1961), 170, 172.

26. Bothwell, *The Art of Leadership*, 153.

27. Albanese, *Management*, 478.

28. Philip Selznick, *Leadership in Administration* (Evanston, Ill.: Ron Peterson and Co., 1957), 30–37, 62–64.

29. Eugene E. Jennings, "The Anatomy of Leadership," *Management of Personnel Quarterly*, Autumn 1961. Reprinted by permission in Harold Koontz and Cyril O'Donnell, eds., *Management: A Book of Readings* (New York: McGraw-Hill, 1964).

30. Hardy, "Leadership and the Hospital Administrator," 35–50.

31. Victor H. Vroom and Philip W. Yetton, *Leadership and Decision Making* (Pittsburgh, Pa.: University of Pittsburgh Press, 1976), 93–122.

Chapter 12

Effecting the organization's work

Elements of Management
in Corporations

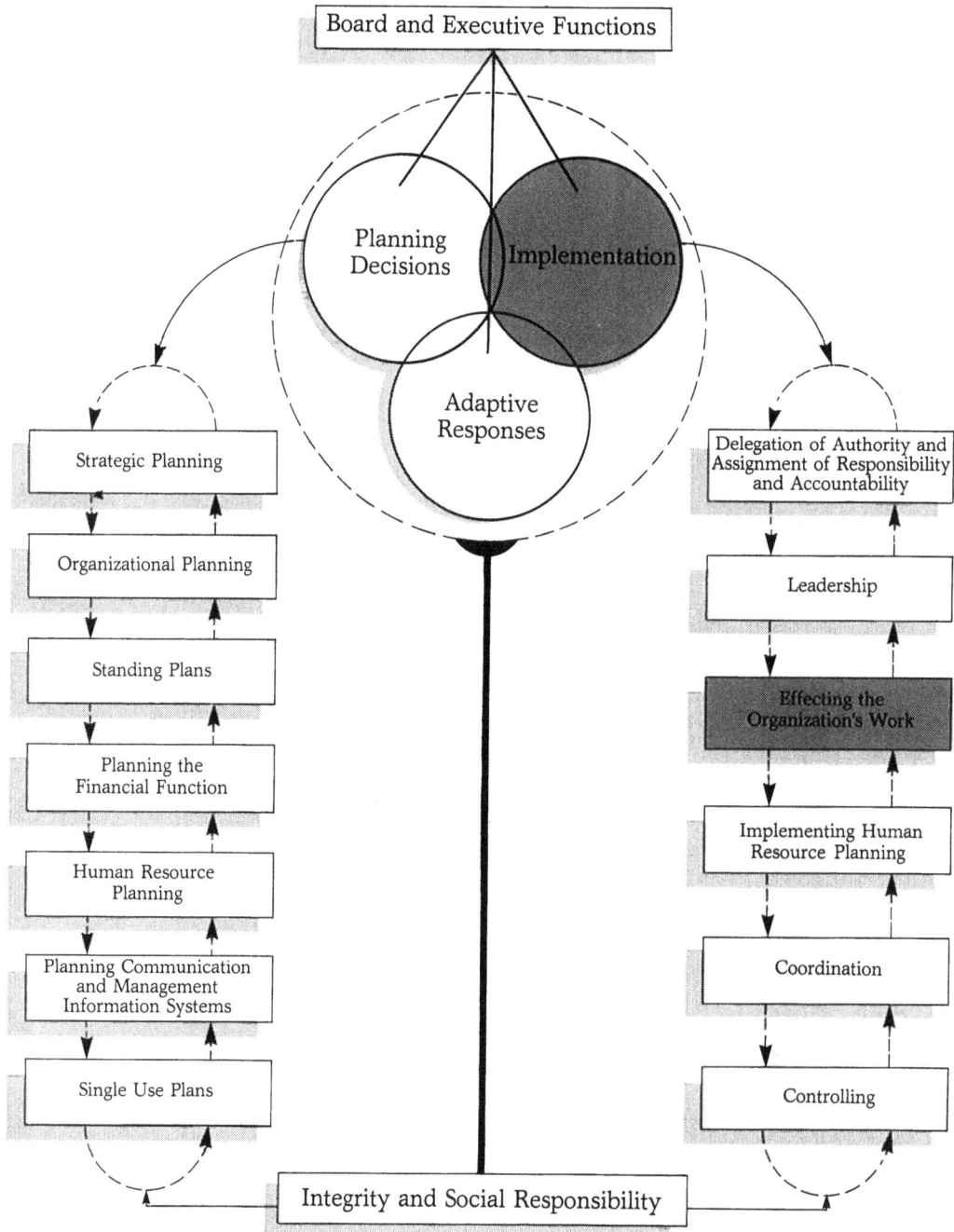

Board and Executive Functions

Planning
Decisions

Implementation

Adaptive
Responses

Strategic Planning

Organizational Planning

Standing Plans

Planning the
Financial Function

Human Resource
Planning

Planning Communication
and Management
Information Systems

Single Use Plans

Delegation of Authority and
Assignment of Responsibility
and Accountability

Leadership

Effecting the
Organization's Work

Implementing Human
Resource Planning

Coordination

Controlling

Integrity and Social Responsibility

12

The purpose of management in a business organization is to assure the accomplishment of work, either operational or managerial, and thus help to realize the organization's mission, goals, and objectives. Nothing can be achieved without work, mental or physical, or both. There may be some who feel disdain when the word *work* is used. However, accomplishment of work occurs either when a chief executive officer sits in an office overlooking Madison Avenue drafting an order directing the investment of millions or when a cleaning person comes in that evening to empty wastebaskets. When the miner carefully places explosives, when the backhoe operator manipulates hydraulic controls, when a computer programmer analyzes steps in a process, when an accountant balances debits and credits, and when a special staff assistant labors over a monthly report, work is being done. Even planning encompasses work efforts aimed at determining what implementing work will best realize the mission, goals, and objectives. Literally all business organizations depend on successful work of one type or another for their existence and perpetuation.

This chapter has little to do with work systems to achieve productivity. Determining how to organize for work and provide appropriate equipment, facilities, and layout occurs in planning of several types already discussed. Our intent here is to examine actions for getting work accomplished by individual organizational members (some of whom function in groups). The examination is from the standpoint of a manager who relates to other managers and to subordinates. We discuss broad strategies for getting work done as well as some methods and techniques for the actual accomplishment. Our remarks concern management implementation as opposed to planning, but it is evident that managers must see to it that the work involved in planning also gets done.

We do not differentiate to any significant degree between line and staff work, nor between management work and operations work. Line, staff, management, and operational personnel are all human beings and all must make organizational work contributions. The concepts discussed will apply in some, and possibly most, situations and environmental settings. In short, all management efforts in effecting accomplishment of work throughout any organization in the Western world at this point in time have some characteristics in common.

All managers who pursue the profession of management eventually face such questions as these: How can I get the most from my subordinates? How can I use my position and my abilities in such a way as to achieve the mission, goals, and objectives of the organization? What are the factors that will motivate organizational members, working as individuals or as members of groups, to make optimal work contributions? Why do some individuals achieve high performance levels consistently while others are consistently low achievers? Are there certain techniques I can use to become a better hands-on manager?

Although we do not answer each of these questions directly, our purpose is to provide a framework that will allow all managers to respond to these questions (and possibly other similar questions) in ways best suited to each.

Review of the literature

In reviewing the vast body of management literature now existing, one will find that authorities have cited a considerable number of ways managers effect organizational work and strive to achieve high performance levels from organizational members. In this section, we define and briefly discuss the most commonly cited means of effecting work. We occasionally express our own ideas, which have been distilled from both study and experience.

Directing

This term, like the term *leadership*, remains ill defined in management literature. After conversing with numerous managers about its meaning, we have concluded managers are much closer to a consensus on a definition than are academic authorities.

Ernest Dale listed directing as one of seven management functions and defined it thus:

> Since no one can predict just what problems and opportunities will arise in the day-to-day work, lists of duties must naturally be couched in rather general terms. The manager must, therefore, provide day-to-day direction for his subordinates. He must make sure that they know the results he expects in each situation, help them to improve their skills, and in some cases tell them exactly how and when to perform certain tasks. If he is a good manager, he makes his subordinates feel that they want to do the best possible job, not merely work well enough to get by.[1]

In the same book, Dale further explained the meaning and intent of directing: "The directing phase of the management job is what many people think of as management itself: telling people what to do and seeing that they do it. Not only must the manager have plans he wants carried out, not only must he divide the work and hire people who are capable of doing it, he must also compel or induce people to use their capabilities."[2]

After defining directing, Dale then entered into discussions of industrial psychology, leadership, supervision, motivation, group dynamics, and improved matches of types of jobs and employees.[3] Obviously, considerable overlaps exist among these subjects as well as between them and the six remaining management functions Dale discussed—planning, organizing, staffing, control, innovation, and representation.[4]

In the early 1970s, Massie also listed directing as one of seven functions of management (the list otherwise differs from Dale's list) and defined it as "the process by which actual performance of subordinates is guided toward common goals."[5] He then commented as follows on four perceived elements of directing:

> Directing concerns the total manner in which a manager influences actions of subordinates. First, it includes the issuing of orders that are clear, complete, and within the capabilities of subordinates to accomplish. Second, it implies a continual training activity in which subordinates are instructed to carry out the particular assignment in the existing situation. Third, it necessarily involves the motivation of workers to try to meet the expectations of the manager. Fourth, it consists of maintaining discipline and rewarding those who perform properly. In short, directing is the final action of a manager in getting others to act after all preparations have been completed.[6]

Blake and Mouton, in *The New Managerial Grid*, cited directing as one of five "responsibilities" of managers, but fail to further define it.[7] They apparently presume everyone knows what it is. In fact, agreement as to a precise definition does not exist among management authorities, as has been noted.

More recently, Brown and Moberg defined directing as "defining and implementing an internal organizational environment conducive to utilizing human resources for goal attainment."[8] This definition seems to us somewhat inconsistent with common usage, and it differs considerably from the definitions of the other authorities whose writings we have surveyed. These authors also observe that "generally, the management process of directing involves providing a social environment suitable for job performance."[9]

In his comprehensive text *Management*, Stoner does not discuss directing as a management function.[10] Apparently, he prefers to use the term *leading* rather than *directing*. Newman and Warren, in *The Process of Management*, use the word *activating* as a substitute for both *leading* and *directing*.[11]

Managers perform a function in business organizations that should be called directing, and for such settings we have prepared a definition based not only on our experiences but on the opinions of approximately two dozen top managers we have quizzed on the matter. The definition is this:

> *Directing consists of issuing directives, orders, and authoritative pronouncements regarding decisions made and plans adopted; it is the appropriate exercise of legitimate authority by top echelon managers in the initiation, regulation, and maintenance of courses of action for defined divisions or units of an organization.*

Chief executives and other officers of major business firms spend a large part of their time initiating and pursuing top-level planning.

Another major concern should be monitoring and controlling at the top level, which are elements of implementation. Still another concern—hopefully, a much lesser one than the two previously mentioned—is responding to unforeseen issues and occurrences (i.e., making adaptive responses). Among several other concerns is the function of directing, which is entirely an implementing action—getting work accomplished.

Directing implies the ability to bring about involuntary actions of subordinates; leading implies behavior that brings about voluntary actions (besides those obtained through directing). However, even though authority may clothe a directive and the manager may have the ability to apply force through penalties, a situation rarely develops in the business realm where a subordinate has no alternative but to comply. The law allows no type of forced labor, and any person can leave the employment of a business enterprise at any time. This may not be the most desirable option, but the point is that a person in a business organization (or any other where membership is voluntary) cannot be *made* to do anything involuntarily, at least from a legal standpoint.

Chester Barnard conceptualized the acceptance theory of authority on similar grounds, i.e., that all management authority is useless unless it is accepted by subordinates.[12]

We regard directing as a top echelon function of implementation. Although many authorities seem to avoid completely the term *supervising*, it seems more appropriate for lower level management, where the exercise of management authority is generally implicit.

Leadership

Leadership is one of the most loosely used terms in our language. However, if one were to ask a cross section of managers the question, "Is leadership one of the means by which employees become motivated to accomplish work in business enterprises?" we believe that the answers would be nearly unanimously in the affirmative. Certainly, leadership is a key factor in determining employee motivations. Although its effects are not highly predictable and conscious attempts at its exercise often result in failure, especially among managers in middle and lower hierarchical echelons who stand face to face with subordinates on a daily basis, no one can reasonably hold that providing leadership should not be a goal. Our own philosophy is that it is best to concentrate first and foremost on being a good manager. One of the implications of a body of research done at Ohio State University affirms that by being a good manager, a person's total behavior may be construed as leadership.

We discuss leadership at some length in Chapter 11. The definition we set forth there seems correct and, therefore, we will recite it again:

Leadership is the perceived behavior of a manager that causes a motivation within subordinates, other organizational members, and possibly peripherally related individuals to strive voluntarily toward achievement of organizational goals and objectives. The motivation that results from a manager's behavior is detectable in a work situation, even if it is not completely separable from motivations resulting from other sources.

Many authorities who adhere to the process school of management have discussed leadership as one of five or six elements in the process. It is truly an important aspect of management—a distinct means by which employees become motivated to better work performance.

Exercise of authority

Authority in organizations has long served as a means of getting all types of work accomplished. There is probably as much consensus about the definition of the term as exists for any other term in management. Even so, four theories about the actual source of authority stand out in the literature.

Albanese presents a traditional definition (or "traditional theory") of authority, which follows:

> Authority may be considered as the right of a person to issue orders and to direct the behavior of those over whom the authority is exercised. Although authority resides in a person (only a person can issue orders), it arises out of the demands of positions in organizations. Thus, a person in an organization has authority by virtue of the requirements of the job position in the formal structure of the organization. . . . When authority is exercised by a person through the act of issuing orders the authority is intended to guide the behavior of those to whom the order was issued; authority implies the capacity to exact compliance.[13]

One clearly recognized source of authority is the charter of a corporation, which can be issued by any one of the 50 states. The charter grants a corporation the right to pursue its stated purposes by all legal and lawful means available to it. This grant of authority then is delegated by an incorporating board of directors to company officers, who in turn delegate authority to other managers and agents as required for running the business. In our view, whether or not any operational or other person ever accepts the fact that authority is vested in the board of directors and subsequently in company officers or other managers of the corporation does not change the fact that it has been vested in them from a legal standpoint.

We believe that the "acceptance theory," although it is reasonable, unfortunately ignores this fact. From a practical standpoint, managers must recognize and respect the acceptance theory. It holds that regardless of the amount of authority that may flow from a state to a corporation, if subordinates do not accept the authority as duly delegated to managers, it remains useless. In fact, this is true.

The "competence theory" holds that authority derives from the competence, knowledge, and expertise of those placed in positions of traditional authority. First, competence is presumed to be the factor that causes a person to qualify for and receive a specific position. Subsequently, competence is the factor that induces subordinates or others to accept the authority of the person granted it. This theory more or less ignores the existence of owner-officer roles in closely held companies. Sometimes the only thing such persons possess that makes them stand out is money. But money may in fact prove to be the basic ingredient needed for success. Such cases are problematic for the competence theory.

The "contractual theory" holds that the source of a manager's authority flows from the employment agreement between an organization and a specific manager. This agreement may be written or implied. As noted in Chapter 10, we affirm the truth of the contractual theory from a legal standpoint. We see no real conflict between this theory and the traditional theory.

Regardless of whether it has a single source or multiple sources, authority has rightfully been recognized as an important means for effecting work accomplishments.

Power and force

Many have noted that traditional authority is equivalent to "legitimate" power, and as such it is recognized nearly universally as a means for getting work done. Albanese, among others, has well noted that the power actually possessed by a manager may far exceed his or her authority (or legitimate power). Conversely, in the case of weak managers who engender little respect from subordinates, their power to get work done may be less than their authority (this is consistent with the acceptance theory). Albanese states the following:

> In work organizations many people exert power over others even though the power goes beyond the requirements of job position. Subordinates often infer power to their manager that cannot be explained in terms of the legitimate demands of the job. Managers can and have coerced their employees by subtle threats of withholding salary increases, promotions, or desired fringe benefits. Power can be viewed as the potential capacity to exert influence over others.[14]

From the remarks of Albanese, one may get the sense that illegitimate power is rather sinister. Indeed, opportunities for abusing power do exist. However, power per se is neither sinister nor evil.

Brown and Moberg recognize that power may extend beyond legitimate authority. They state,

> Some individuals are personally very powerful regardless of the amount of authority formally given to their position. The basis of this personal power lies with an individual's competence, charisma, and personal leadership skills. Unlike authority, the use of personal power is not legitimized by the organization. Yet it is a typical occurrence in organizational life. It can be employed on behalf of organizational effectiveness as well as personal gain.[15]

French and Raven have identified five sources of power in organizations that may exist at any hierarchical level:[16]

1. *Reward Power*. This kind of power is based on the ability of one person to reward another in a variety of ways.

2. *Legitimate Power*. As already noted, this kind of power derives from legitimate or traditional authority.

3. *Coercive Power*. As the negative side of power, this type reflects an ability to inflict penalties or withhold rewards.

4. *Expert Power*. Due to possession of specialized knowledge or expertise, a person may hold power beyond that considered inherent to the position occupied from the traditional viewpoint.

5. *Referent Power*. Based on a manager's prestige or charisma, derived from one source or another, subordinates and others may sense an expanded base of power and thereby respond beyond normal expectations.

Many years ago, Robert Bierstedt attempted to put power, force, and authority in their proper relationship. Nothing expressed since that time has refuted his view. Bierstedt stated,

> We want therefore to propose three definitions and then to examine their implications: (1) power is latent force; (2) force is manifest power; and (3) authority is institutionalized power. The first two of these propositions may be considered together. Of course, they appear to be circular definitions and, as a matter of fact, they are. If an independent meaning can be found for one of these concepts, however, the other may be defined in terms of it and the circularity will disappear. . . . Unlike force, incidentally, power is always successful; when it is not successful it is not, or ceases to be, power. Power symbolizes the force which may be applied in any social situation and supports the authority which is applied. Power is thus neither force nor authority but, in a sense, their synthesis.[17]

Certainly, power manifests itself as force in business organizations less than ever before. Yet, if it were not present at all, management's task would be far greater than it is. Few people want to be fired and to have this fact on their personnel record. Thus, power may play a greater role than we sometimes believe.

Influence

Stoner defines influence as "actions or examples that, either directly or indirectly, cause a change in behavior or attitude of another person or group."[18] Massie states that "influence implies a voluntary, and even unconscious, manner of affecting the actions of others through persuasion, suggestion and other methods."[19] Albanese states that "influence is a term that covers both authority and power. . . . A manager can have influence through authority, power, or both. The sources of influence can include job position, personality, seniority, persuasive abilities, job competence, and expertise, among others."[20]

All three of these authors differ widely in their perceptions of what actually constitutes influence in organizations, but all three discuss it in conjunction with authority and power and under the general heading of organizing.

We regard influence essentially as a means of work implementation but recognize that delegating authority occurs within the context of implementing organizational planning.

Dessler subsumes authority, power, and influence under leadership and thus further compounds the confusion in the literature. He states this about influence: "Influence is usually defined as the art of producing an effect of somehow getting someone or something to take to action."[21]

Despite the considerable disagreement in the literature about what influence really is, each author who discusses it (and many do not) believes it is a factor in the performance of work. We also believe this.

Supervision

Supervision, in the broadest sense, is the overseeing of work processes or of the performance of subordinates and their equipment, if any. In this sense, supervision exists in every part of an organization and at all management levels where either staff or operational work is performed. In management jargon, however, the term *supervision* often refers to the work of a supervisor, i.e., a management person directly in charge of an operational workplace. In manufacturing and many types of industrial enterprises, a supervisor is the first-level management person directly responsible for operations and employee performance in a shop, a specific part of a shop, an assembly line, a specific part of an assembly line, or any other operational workplace. In hospitals, the nurse directly in charge of other nurses rendering patient care often receives the title of *nurse supervisor*.

Lester R. Bittel, one of the nation's foremost authorities on supervisory management, has defined a supervisor as "anyone at the first level of management who has the responsibility for getting the 'hands-on-the-work' employees to carry out the plans and policies of the higher-level management."[22]

The Taft-Hartley Act of 1947 says that a supervisor is

> any individual having authority, in the interest of the employer to hire, transfer, suspend, lay off, recall, promote, discharge, assign, reward, or discipline other employees, or responsibility to direct them, or to adjust their grievances, or effectively to recommend such action, if in connection with the foregoing the exercise of such authority is not of a merely routine or clerical nature, but requires the use of independent judgment.[23]

These definitions of a supervisor, of course, reflect some implications of the meaning of *supervision*. They also reveal the great importance of supervisors and of their management responsibilities. Indeed, Massie has stated that the supervisor's position is the major link between management and actual operations. "The supervisor's task is made more difficult by the fact that to the individual worker he *is* the management. The supervisor's daily contact with the workers and his interpretation of company policies places him in a strategic position. He represents an important medium through which the workers can communicate with top management."[24]

Several authorities have written extensive volumes on management without mentioning supervisors and supervision, except to say that close and dictatorial supervision is not a desirable management technique (we fully agree). However, ignoring supervision will not eradicate it as a major means for getting work done in business organizations.

Peter Drucker, as early as 1954, wanted to rid management of the term *supervisor*. He stated, "I do not like to quarrel with terms as such. But the term 'supervisor' describes the opposite of what the job should be. I believe the term itself to be such an impediment that it would be better to change it to 'manager' altogether."[25] Despite Drucker's wishes, the term *supervisor* is as prevalent today as most other management terms which were in vogue in 1954.

In discussing the deficiencies in the tasks and responsibilities of the supervisor in 1954, Drucker penned words which, it can now be seen, were among the most cogent and prophetic ever enunciated by any management authority:

> What the supervisor needs to discharge his job is first of all clear cut objectives for his own activity. These objectives must be focused directly on the objectives of the business. Like all true objectives they must contain goals both in terms of business results and in respect to the realization of basic beliefs and principles. They must balance the requirements of the immediate and the long-range future.
>
> The supervisor needs the authority that goes with the responsibility for reaching these objectives. He needs knowledge about the company's operations, its structure, its goals and its performance without which his own objectives cannot be meaningful. He needs the means to reach these objectives and the measurements that focus on their attainment. In fact, everything that is necessary to achieve the objectives of his department should be under his control—otherwise he cannot be held responsible.[26]

Although we have no research findings that would confirm supervisors do now supervise more in terms of goals and objectives and with better knowledge of company operations than in 1954, it is almost obvious that they do. Drucker's contribution in this regard has been considerable.

Despite the negative implications of supervision, despite the fact that management by objectives may be more prevalent than ever, and despite the fact that many organizations no longer even use the term *supervisor*, the truth remains that supervision, defined either broadly or narrowly, still is one of the chief means for getting work accomplished in business enterprises today.

Effecting group synergy

The actions of groups accomplish many and various types of work in organizations. In industry and a multitude of service organizations, managers often form work teams when individuals acting alone cannot perform the combined tasks necessary for achieving basic objectives. Also, valid research has conclusively shown that groups properly formed and motivated will perform at higher levels than individuals acting alone, both qualitatively and quantitatively. This phenomenon we will call *group synergy*. However, groups improperly formed and motivated can be detrimental to work accomplishment and the achievement of goals and objectives. In some instances, groups have become downright harmful, with destructive or disruptive tendencies that originated either directly or indirectly from associations formed within the group.

Since some work processes require the actions of groups, managers cannot avoid their formation. Thus, the managerial objective relating to groups should be to effect group synergy to an optimal degree during the course of their existence. The complement of that objective is to avoid group motivations that produce untoward consequences.

Many types of aggregations of persons can loosely be called groups. As we use the term here, however, it has a restricted meaning, and even from its definition some implications for managers seem apparent.

> A group, then, may be defined as a plurality of individuals who are in contact with one another, who take one another into account and who are aware of some significant commonality.
>
> An essential feature of a group is that its members have something in common and that they believe that what they have in common makes a difference.[27]

Managers, from executive to supervisory levels, must at times form groups, which they then must manage to some degree. Some groups may have a purely advisory role on an ad hoc basis; some, through a majority vote, may make important decisions and wield great power; some are primary work groups that produce something or render a service on a day-to-day basis. Whatever the roles may be of groups established through the acts of managers, they can all be called *formal* groups. Further, these are the groups that managers must seek to energize for the basic accomplishment of goals and objectives. These are the groups in which managers must strive to effect synergetic efforts among composing individual members.

Many authorities have also cited the need for synergetic efforts among formal working levels and groups. Rensis Likert's famous linking pin theory addresses this possibility. Based on research by Pelz and confirmed by numerous others, a supervisor of a primary work group forms a "linking pin" between that work group and his or her supervisor.[28] Likert stated in *New Patterns of Management*,

> These results [of research by Pelz and others] demonstrate that *the capacity to exert influence upward is essential if a supervisor (or manager) is to perform his supervisory functions successfully.* To be effective in leading his own work group, a superior must be able to influence his own boss; that is, he needs to be skilled both as a supervisor and as a subordinate. In terms of group functioning, he must be skilled in both leadership and membership functions and roles.[29]

We consider being able to manage an immediate superior to be one of the basic skills that middle managers need to possess. In order to achieve results at any middle management level, a manager has to communicate and manage in upward, lateral, and downward directions.

Figure 12-1 contains Likert's original graphic depiction of the linking pin function. Regarding this function, Likert stated the following:

> An organization will not derive the full benefits from its highly effective groups unless they are linked to the total organization by means of equally effective overlapping groups. . . . The use of highly effective groups in only one part or in scattered portions of an organization will fail, therefore, to achieve the full potential of such groups. . . .
>
> The higher an ineffective group is in the hierarchy, the greater is the adverse effect of its failure on the performance of the organization. . . .
>
> To help maintain an effective organization, it is desirable for superiors not only to hold group meetings of their own subordinates, but also to have occasional meetings over two hierarchical levels. This enables the superior to observe any breakdown in the linking pin process as performed by the subordinates reporting to him.[30]

Note the agreement of Likert's statement about holding group meetings with Fayol's statement about department head meetings, which we discussed in Chapter 10.

Group dynamics
Most authorities construe *group dynamics* to mean changes that occur within groups during their existence, together with the influence exerted

Figure 12-1

The Linking Pin

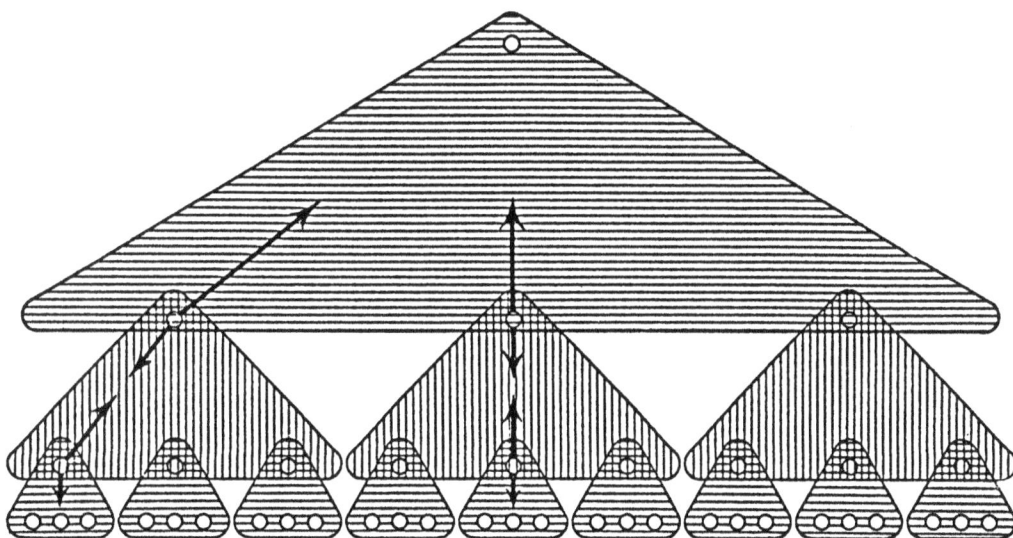

(The arrows indicate the linking pin function)

Source: Reprinted from *New Patterns of Management* by R. Likert, p. 113, with permission of McGraw-Hill Book Company, © 1961.

by the groups on their individual members. However, *group dynamics* was a term coined originally to refer to an approach to the study of group behavior.[31] Its originator was Kurt Lewin, the famed Gestalt psychologist who emphasized wholes and totalities as opposed to individual stimuli and responses. Group dynamics is essentially equivalent to field theory, the theory developed by Lewin that is about groups. Deutsch, in commenting on field theory, stated, "All psychological events (thinking, acting, dreaming, hoping, etc.) are conceived to be a function of the life space which consists of the person and the environment as *one* constellation of interdependent factors."[32] Group dynamics basically involves the study of a group as a group, together with all of the influencing factors impinging upon the group and its members, both internally and externally.

Informal groups

Researchers have directed their studies not only to formal groups but also to those informal groups with which managers also must deal. Most informal groups form very naturally (and function innocuously) in organizations as a result of the basic social needs of human beings. Individuals who are in close proximity to each other and who have some commonality of interests, either on or off the job, will naturally form a group. Immediately, the psychological forces that affect groups will come into play and they may continue to act indefinitely, depending on a host of fairly obvious factors.

As indicated, informal groups usually prove helpful in satisfying social needs on the job that are not satisfied within formal groups. However, some informal groups can be harmful to management. For example, the common factor that originally pulled an informal group together may have been a dislike for a management policy or even a manager. Owing to psychological reinforcements that accrue in such situations, an informal group can be potentially dangerous. (Viewed from another standpoint, a group's causing a *change* in erroneous or bad policy could be beneficial.)

Our basic view of informal groups makes us believe they should be encouraged, but the astute manager will be sensitive to the potentially adverse behavior that can come from them.

Research findings

Following are some findings derived from research relative to groups (largely from a group dynamics standpoint) that have relevance to management situations today.

1. Group influence on members springs in considerable measure from group cohesiveness—the bonding among group members. Cohesiveness results from several pertinent factors, one of which is group size. Findings indicate cohesiveness starts to decrease beyond a total membership of about 20.[33] Loss of cohesiveness is reflected in increased disagreements and hostilities among members. Other factors influencing cohesiveness are age, education, performance levels, common interests, and in some instances, status.[34]

2. Highly cohesive groups have an increased capability for high performance. Groups with low cohesiveness, on balance, have a decreased capability. Highly cohesive groups whose members agree on high performance goals tend to achieve them.[35] However, highly cohesive groups may establish lower performance goals, for one reason or another, than management desires, and they are capable of controlling output at the lower levels.[36] The apparent corollary is that managers should strive to achieve cohesiveness within groups and then to stimulate the adoption of high, but achievable, performance goals.

3. Cohesiveness positively affects uniformity of output among group members, either at high levels or at low levels, depending on the group's attitudes toward management, established work objectives, and other factors.[37]

4. Intergroup competition enhances the cohesiveness of groups; intragroup competition tends to be detrimental to cohesiveness. However, there are hazards in intergroup competition, especially possible bad effects of defeat on groups that lose in the competition.[38]

5. Stable groups tend to be cohesive; unstable groups—those continually rearranged or whose membership changes frequently—tend to be less cohesive.[39]

6. Cohesive groups tend to have greater control over the various norms (behavioral standards) of the group, such as the setting of goals and performance levels, the degree of adherence to policies, and various social aspects of membership conduct. Nondeviating members exercise control over deviating members through rewards given and punishment administered. Rewards and punishment are manifested variously, e.g., by extending or withholding assistance during the course of interdependent work procedures. Actual physical punishment has occurred on numerous occasions.[40]

7. Groups with a low level of cohesiveness, where pressures to conform are not strong, tend to have outputs that are often inconsistent with the norms.[41]

8. Solutions to problems by groups usually prove better than those found by individuals. (Of course, this assumes the individuals in the group and those functioning alone are equally intelligent and knowledgeable.)

9. As already indicated, groups are likely to establish norms (standards) regarding the behavior of individual members. The more important a norm is to a group, the more likely the members are to use the norm as a guide to behavior and the more likely the group is to enforce it as such a guide.[42]

10. Many of the norms established by a formal work group have nothing to do with management's policies or objectives, but are of a social

nature, e.g., dress, lunch habits, types of salutations, etc. Such norms invariably emanate from an *informal* organization that forms within a formally organized group. However, this informal organization often becomes sufficiently strong to affect performance levels. The famous Bank Wiring Room Study, conducted in Chicago at the Hawthorne works of the Western Electric Company during 1927, revealed that an informal organization among a group of 14 employees in a special test room did just that. The employees involved clearly controlled output of work through a very cohesive informal social organization.[43] The basic conclusion reached by the investigators was that one must always take into account informal social organizations that form in work groups, including their relationship to the total organization (formal and informal) of the enterprise or business.[44]

11. Groups, on balance, reach riskier decisions than do individuals deciding alone.[45]

12. In on-the-job problem solving regarding work processes or procedures, participating in the decision making increases the acceptability to group members of the decisions reached.[46]

13. The skills of a group's leader, primarily in promoting communication and assuring that all members have a part in discussions and decision making, tend to affect the group's performance.[47]

14. More than one leader may emerge in the same group. For example, Benne and Sheats identified two types of group function which sometimes correlate to the roles of two types of group leader. The two types of function are (1) task functions and (2) maintenance-oriented functions.[48] Task functions are concerned with getting group work done. Most often the leader associated with task functions is that person designated by management, but not always. An informal leader, backed by the general approval of the informal organization within the formal group, may supplant the officially appointed leader.[49] Often an intragroup member who commands the respect of the group but who has not been given any official role by management in effect takes over maintenance functions (i.e., those concerned with group well-being, development, and informal communication).

Nearly three decades ago, Dorwin Cartwright, director of the Research Center for Group Dynamics at the University of Michigan, enunciated the following principles of group behavior. These principles, among others, were derived from valid research. Some of them duplicate to a degree the comments listed above.

a. The more attractive the group is to its members, the greater is the influence the group can exert on its members.

b. In attempts to change attitudes, values, or behaviors, the more relevant they are to the basis of attraction to the group, the greater will be the influence the group can exert upon them. . . .

c. The greater the prestige of a group member in the eyes of other members, the greater the influence he can exert.

d. Efforts to change individuals or subparts of a group which, if successful, would have the result of making them deviate from the norms of the group will encounter strong resistance.

e. Creating a shared perception by members of the need for change, thus making the source of pressure for change lie within the group, brings strong pressure for group change.

f. All relevant people in the group must share information relating to the need for change, plans for change and consequences of change.

g. Changes in one part of a group produce strain in other related parts which can be reduced only by eliminating the change or by bringing about readjustments in related parts.[50]

There have been many additional findings reported from research conducted within and among groups. Some are irrelevant to managers, but the astute manager will carefully review research findings as they are reported in current literature.

Main types of formal groups
Managers create groups of certain basic types at a variety of organizational levels for a variety of work purposes. The types are as follows:

1. *Operational Work Groups.* These groups appear throughout all industrial and service enterprises. They may be the most common type of work group in the Western world today.

2. *Staff Work Groups.* These groups engage in administrative activities not directly involving line work. Some of them may serve line managers, but they do not engage directly in producing products for or rendering services to customers. However, some may directly interface with customers.

3. *Committees.* According to our personal observations, committees abound in most businesses where more than 200–300 persons are employed. In many instances, outside agencies dictate that there be certain committees (hospitals are notorious in this regard).

4. *Ad Hoc Committees.* Ad hoc committees mostly serve for a specific one-time purpose and can be very useful. However, some managers appoint them to dodge the responsibility of framing a plan or making an appropriate adaptive response to an unforeseen situation. Some ad hoc committees result from a desire to delay a decision. We know these

statements are true, because both of us have admittedly acted thus. Even so, we may be less guilty than most managers.

5. *Task Forces.* Task forces often perform extensive investigations related to broad-scale operations. HCA has employed them on several occasions to good advantage.

Management attitudes and actions in effecting synergy

We cannot emphasize too strongly the need for continuing research on both formal and informal groups in business enterprises of all types. At the same time, managers must keep currently abreast of research findings and conclusions as they are published. Also, all managers who create formal groups and have responsibility for their performance should continuously monitor that performance in light of the dynamics occurring as a result of the totality of internal and external influencing factors impinging on the group and its members. The factors can be psychological or of some other nature.

We have specified five basic types of formal groups found in business organizations. Since each type has distinctive characteristics, each organization exhibits differences, and each individual group functions separately in a distinct environmental setting, one would be foolish to state there are hard and fast principles which apply to every group and its situation. (One might opine that the truest and most reliable management principle is that there are no universally applicable management principles where relationships among humans are concerned.)

However, on the basis of our literature searches, our experience, and the experience of other managers we have had the opportunity to talk to, we can provide some worthwhile generalities about forming, managing, and controlling groups for the purpose of effecting synergy to achieve optimal work performance. We have gathered these generalities in the three sections that follow. Although we have framed our statements in a rather positive fashion, we emphasize that these are generalities and that exceptions to each will occur. Some may have no applicability in many situations.

Forming groups

1. In forming a group, one should clearly define its purpose, most frequently in writing, together with its goals and work objectives.

2. The formal head of the group—chairperson, leader, supervisor, manager, or director, whatever title is most appropriate—should receive a specific appointment, unless circumstances indicate that the group should elect its own head.

3. The authority of the group as a group, if any, ought to be clearly specified. If authority is vested only in the head of the group, that too should be specified. Clearly written documents are the preferred means of delegation.

4. There should be agreement between the superior forming the group and the named head of the group (or between the superior and each

individual group member, if indicated) as to delegated authority, assigned responsibility and accountability, and the work to be accomplished, including at least general agreement on the method of accomplishment. Most frequently, such agreements had best be put in writing, with affected persons retaining copies.

5. The superior should designate at the outset the methods and timing of reports by the group. The superior should clearly set forth the responsibility of the head of the group in this regard and also make certain stipulations concerning the records that are to be maintained.

6. The workplace or meeting place of the group and a schedule of activities of the group ought to be specified at the outset, if applicable.

7. One objective of any person forming a group should be to achieve group cohesiveness. Factors affecting cohesiveness are as follows:

   - Size is an important factor. Our experience indicates greatest cohesiveness occurs in groups having 5 to 12 members. Research findings clearly show that cohesiveness begins to deteriorate in groups having more than 20 members.

   - Common interests, common skills, interdependent skills, and status are factors that affect cohesiveness and group harmony. Our own opinion that this is true is confirmed by the literature and by other managers.

   - Age may or may not be a factor, depending on the type of work the group is to accomplish.

   - Whether the head of a group has the ability to achieve cohesiveness among group members (taking into account the work to be accomplished) should be carefully considered *before* formal appointment.

   - The stability of the personalities of group members also merits evaluation *before* the members are appointed to the group.

8. The person forming a group should try to ascertain that the members named, appointed, or hired do not have potential tendencies to be disloyal to the individual business or firm. Those chosen to be members should be considered the most likely to achieve the goals and objectives of the group as agreed upon. If necessary deviations from established goals and objectives seem likely, each member's outlook ought to be such that pursued deviations will be in the best interest of the formal organization (as opposed to pursuits by an informal group bent primarily on self-gain).

9. The creator of a group should be certain that sufficient potential exists in the group for maintenance needs to be satisfied and for task-oriented direction, leadership, or supervision to occur.

10. Political realities of formal organizations usually dictate that appropriate managers or department heads or their handpicked designees receive appointments to advisory or problem-solving committees and task forces, especially when the group membership spans more than one hierarchical level. In choosing members for a group, such political realities may outweigh the desirability of achieving certain group attributes. Giving in to such realities may not result in the best functioning of the group, but it may keep the creator of the group free from political "traps." (We make this point as a consequence of some of our own "battle scars.")

Managing groups

Managers may designate or install the heads of groups in numerous ways, but all formal groups require an officially recognized and approved director, leader, chairperson, manager, supervisor, or other titled head. Whoever receives appointment as the head of the group must then manage or supervise its actions in the most appropriate manner for achieving its goals and objectives effectively and efficiently. The following points may be useful to group leaders.

1. The goals and objectives of the group as they relate to work accomplishment are the group's top priority. At the same time, the maintenance needs of the group members must be met, and a reward system should be in place that provides gratifications for individual group members (including the head) as sustained work efforts proceed.

2. Research has clearly shown performance levels will be higher in structured situations rather than in unstructured situations.[51] At the same time, a democratic style of group leadership or supervision has also been demonstrated to be more effective than authoritarian or laissez-faire styles. Truly, structure and democracy need not be at variance. Sharing with group members relevant knowledge, information, and experience, together with giving explanations pertaining directly to work methodologies and other aspects of the group's actions, will cause them to become motivated to strive for high performance levels. Allowing participation in decision making provides an added impetus.[52] One caution: Close and dictatorial supervision should be avoided. An impersonal application of requirements is optimal, e.g., democratically adopted rules and regulations as opposed to those personally imposed and enforced by a manager.

3. The general attitude and outlook of a group manager often is reflected in the attitudes and outlooks of group members. One can draw a classic example from the nursing profession. After working with hundreds of hospitals, both of us feel confident we could fairly accurately describe the personality of the director of nurses in any hospital of 200 beds or less—if we were allowed to visit several nursing stations. We also feel confident we could describe the general attitudes of the nurses as a body if we were allowed a 30-minute conversation with the director of nurses. Of course, some hospitals are so large that the director's influence becomes dissipated before it reaches floor duty nurses, and the personality of some lesser but

more closely associated figure will "rub off." Our experience is consistent with research findings on the influence of group leaders in other situations. Thus, those who manage groups had best set good examples of personal behavior, for that behavior has some probability of being emulated by group members.

4. A manager or other titled head of a group should identify, where possible, with group members, but at the same time always maintain the respect of the group. Again, structure, democracy, impartial and fair controls, concern for maintenance needs, supportiveness, and a reward system come into play.

5. Regarding the chairing of committees and task forces specifically, the following suggestions merit consideration:

   • Distribution of a predetermined agenda to group members at least 24 hours before a meeting is scheduled to convene, together with certain pertinent information about each agenda item, is of great value in expediting conduct of the meeting and in reaching better decisions.

   • The duration of a meeting should be announced at least 24 hours prior to its scheduled start time, and even earlier if members must travel from a distance.

   • Meetings should begin on time and close according to schedule. The attention span of those present will deteriorate considerably after 90 minutes of discussion.

   • The chairperson should state at the beginning of the meeting what the meeting should accomplish.[53]

   • Anthony Jay formulated seven rules for chairing committee meetings, and we generally agree with them:

     —Control the garrulous.

     —Draw out the silent.

     —Protect the weak.

     —Encourage the clash of ideas.

     —Watch out for the suggestion-squashing reflex.

     —Come to the most senior people last.

     —Close on a note of achievement.[54]

     To Jay's list we might add this: Adhere to the agenda until it is completed, then talk about extraneous items.

- Regarding the attainment of a consensus within a deliberative body, Jay Hall offered five guidelines, which are summarized as follows:

  —Do not argue for your position after having clearly stated it. Wait for reactions from other members.

  —Do not resolve arguments from a win-or-lose posture. Seek the best alternatives.

  —Do not seek a resolution based on the desire for harmony. Demand logic.

  —Do not bypass logic and resolve conflicts through votes, bargaining, flipping a coin, etc. Also, because the ideas of some members will not be adopted, do not bargain for their advantage on some unrelated point for purposes of mollification.

  —Get everyone into the discussion so as to work from a broad information base and thereby provide an opportunity for the best solution.[55]

  We would add this to the list: Don't lose your temper.

6. "The work group is an organization for which you [the supervisor] are expected to provide direction and inspiration, and not moral judgments."[56] This statement, by Lester R. Bittel, could not be more true in most situations. However, a supervisor or manager should not tolerate either illegal or immoral activity on the job.

7. Objectivity, based on factual data and information, has many advantages over possibly biased subjectivity in dealing with all group problems. At the same time, one must remember in dealing with both individuals and groups that perceptions and not facts often are of greatest importance. One initial problem may be to get members to perceive things as they are. Failing this, a manager may have to deal with members' perceptions as if they were facts.

8. Presenting opinions and arguing about possible solutions to problems already solved in a less-than-desirable manner (second-guessing) seldom accomplishes anything except ill will. Accept a situation as it is, and proceed on a positive note from there. However, if after objective counseling, tempered with compassion and supportiveness, a group member continues repeatedly to err, either willfully or from incompetence, he or she should withdraw or be removed from the group. The psychological effects of keeping a "bad apple" in a group prove just as detrimental to the productiveness of other members as do intemperate actions by the manager.

9. Insofar as possible, manage groups so that members thereof are treated as ends rather than means. However, the principle that all members of the *organization* should be treated as ends rather than means should usually take precedence when there is a conflict.

Likewise, the principle that all humans should be treated as ends rather than means ought to take precedence in setting the goals and objectives of an enterprise.

10. A manager or supervisor of a group should know and be concerned about the status of each member with respect to the physiological, safety, social, self-esteem, and self-actualization needs enunciated by A. H. Maslow.[57] This knowledge and concern should stem, not from a desire to manipulate, but from a desire to be as supportive as possible. Genuine concern usually creates rapport, and rapport stimulates performance. The point can be made by asking yourself, "Do I want to work face to face with someone who has no concern for my well-being?" Common sense says the answer will be no and findings from a variety of research support common sense in this instance.

11. The head of a group should also be knowledgeable about reference groups to which group members belong. Often such groups greatly influence on-the-job behavior, not only of persons working in groups but of those working largely independently.

12. Although specialization stands at the very heart of current civilization's material wealth, it produces undesirable results if carried to an extreme. For example, in many small and medium enterprises, especially service organizations, group cohesiveness and customer satisfaction can both suffer. A finished, observable achievement is satisfying in itself to the members of the group that accomplished it.[58] Team action performed during consulting engagements, construction projects, the assembly of a customer's order, the delivery of health care to patients, and a host of other endeavors can be a source of pride when the end product can be observed by the team members.

    As to customer satisfaction, one can draw a good example from the nursing profession. "Functional nursing" is based on job specialization; each service rendered to patients is performed by special individuals, e.g., giving intravenous fluids, administering medications, making beds, delivering food, etc. Although this approach may be economical, a patient becomes confused by the variety and volume of traffic in the hospital room and confused as to who has responsibility for care and treatment. At the same time, the specialty work becomes very impersonal and boring to those individuals performing it. As a remedy, "team nursing," which limits all patient care to a small group headed by a "team leader," came into vogue.

13. The person who heads a group, especially where group members are in constant association on the job, should be continuously aware that the goals of informal associations certain to arise may conflict with the work objectives. Thus, group leaders should strive to assure that the goals of these informal associations do not adversely affect work performance. Many strategies for solving this problem exist. Some of these concern the formation of the group while others concern day-to-day operations. Some involve ongoing associations of the group head with group members and others involve demonstrating in a variety of ways that the enterprise is responsive to the social needs of the group.

Controlling group work

We have separated these comments from those above to show our regard for the special importance of implementing control. Chapter 15 contains many suggestions applicable to controlling group work. Points having special application are cited below.

1. In many work groups, organizational goals and objectives apply to the actions of the group as a whole, with control of the output of individual group members often being left to the discretion of the person heading the group. A variety of techniques exist for effecting control of individual group members. Some relate to operating procedures devised for the group and others are based on personalized job descriptions and agreements (see Chapter 10). However, many situations occur where direct supervision is the most obvious method of control. In such instances, a supportive approach will allow peer pressure from other group members to become effective. Peer pressure, then, flowing from group cohesiveness, can become the prime method of increasing individual performance that does not measure up to reasonable expectations.

2. Despite the effectiveness of peer pressure, one cannot overlook the fact that direct supervision represents a legitimate and appropriate method of control, and it remains possibly the prevalent method in business enterprises today. Supervision, in our opinion, is not only a means of getting work done but also a means of governing quality, quantity, cost, timeliness, etc.

3. An important point about small group control is that it is desirable to get immediate feedback about actual results and compare them to expected or planned performance. In many instances, such feedback should be provided daily. Nothing can be more demoralizing to a group than out-of-date feedback, which leave members feeling that "if we had just known in time, we wouldn't have looked so bad."

4. Where the achievement of performance levels of all types depends to some degree on group teamwork, the system of rewards should take that into account. This promotes self-control among individual group members.

5. The best way to avoid the unpleasant and undesirable aspects of controlling—including the eventual firing of some group members for poor performance—is to take due care in the formation of a group and then to manage it properly. Thus, the points set out in the previous two sections indirectly contribute to optimal control of group performance.

Work contracts

At present, many business enterprises "farm out" substantial portions of their work. This applies especially to manufacturing firms, whose officers often find cheaper labor can be supplied in other nations or in other areas of the United States. Although numerous "network" (or "vertically dis-aggregated") companies have sprung up, many currently vertically inte-grated companies also contract for work related to the manufacture of parts and, in some cases, finished products. Most of the automobile manufacturers farm out work to one degree or another, or at least con-sider it.

In contracting for work, the nature of the agreement and its eventual enforcement must be conceptualized and put into a definitive legal con-tract. This will involve the assistance of competent legal counsel. One caution: If the contract is for labor to manufacture a specific product that is separate from the vendor's ordinary course of business for a general market, failure to deliver what was ordered will probably not place the agreement under the Statute of Frauds.[59] Therefore, managers must exercise extreme care in drafting such contracts, which should contain meaningful and enforceable penalties for failure to perform according to specifications. The problem is compounded, of course, when labor is contracted in foreign nations.

Motivation

A manager should never substitute expedient manipulation for appropri-ate effectuation of motivation. As we have already noted, a strategy of consistently treating any group of people only as means will ultimately bring undesirable results. "In short, emotional excitation and involve-ment, when substituted for just and fair rewards (both extrinsic and intrinsic) may accomplish limited objectives, but, in effect, a short-chang-ing of the subordinate [and others] occurs which will sooner or later be rejected."[60]

However, we agree with Gellerman that

> It would be wrong for a supervisor [or any other manager] *not* to take whatever deliberate steps he could to help make the indi-vidual employee (and, by extension, the organization as a whole) more productive. It would be wrong for a supervisor not to help make that sizable fraction of an employee's life that is spent on the job more meaningful to him . . . [a manager] also has responsibilities to society as a whole . . . because his deci-sions affect the ways in which resources of talent and energy are allocated.[61]

In other words, managers, through means that do not bring harm to others and that supply just rewards to subordinates, have a responsibility to provide both a physical and psychological environment that causes a motivation within employees, either as individuals or as members of a group, to strive for optimal productivity.

Certainly, meeting this management responsibility is easier said than done. Every situation requiring hands-on management is unique. Further, no scientifically proven protocols exist that can be universally applied. The research findings of the behavioral sciences are extremely helpful, however, and the thoughtful manager will be a constant student of them.

Employees on the job are primarily motivated by perceptions of individual needs. Outside influences, or motivational forces, can affect, either positively or negatively, an employee's perceptions of individual needs as they relate to work. Thus, it may seem that the manager's task is to provide influences that positively affect the employee's perceptions of his or her needs in such a way that the employee becomes optimally productive. One can readily see that it is impossible to be specific when one realizes that a manager may not be dealing with realities but with perceptions possibly in conflict with other perceptions. Also, an employee's genetically inherited capabilities and past experiences are significant parts of the equation, as are the employee's current cognitive orientations. When Winston Churchill described Russia as "a riddle wrapped in a mystery inside an enigma," he gave us a phrase that could aptly be applied to the topic of motivation, especially motivation in situations where optimal work performance is sought after.

However, managers can follow some general strategies in trying to bring about motivations of employees at work. In doing so, four basic factors should be kept in mind:

1. an individual's perceptions of his or her personal needs

2. an individual's cognitive orientations—information held, the understanding of role, position and relationship to other personnel, the concept of organizational mission, goals, objectives, and culture, and the sense of "fit" to the general work environment

3. an individual's capabilities—genetic characteristics as enhanced by education and experience

4. an individual's perceptions of those motivational forces that management has control over and that affect him or her at the workplace.

Although no one can formulate precise algorithms to provide worthwhile quantifications regarding the above, certainly one can conceive of the kind of desirable work environment that would be regarded by a *majority* of employees as a positive motivational force. Of the four factors listed, it is easy to see the final one *directly* involves management. Management can only do what management can with the resources that it possesses and has control over.

After taking into consideration an employee's current cognitive orientations and individual capabilities, clearly what management deals with and should be striving to affect favorably is the *totality* of perceptions about optimal work performance. Since perceptions cannot be discussed as a totality, we have broken them down into the seven kinds listed below. The list is not in order of importance (if indeed there is such). We will not cite factual findings and their sources owing to limitations of space and time. However, all of these kinds of perception have been shown by valid research to result in employee motivation toward optimal work performance. See Figure 12-2 for a diagrammatic portrayal of these seven kinds.

Figure 12-2

Seven Employee Motivational Perceptions

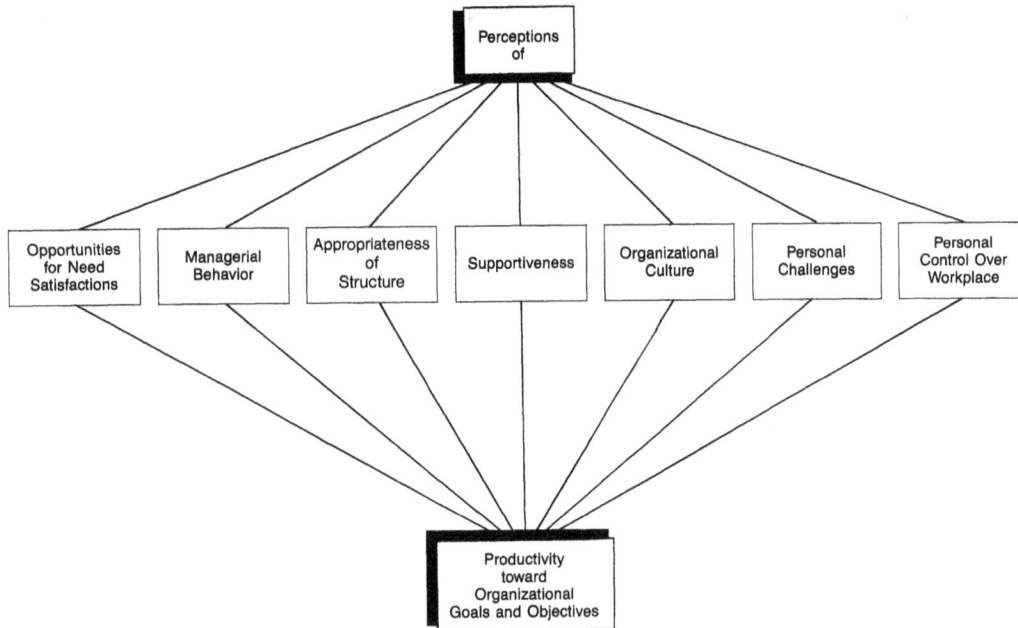

1. *Perceptions that opportunities exist for satisfaction of personal needs (as these needs are personally perceived).* We are speaking here, of course, of A. H. Maslow's hierarchy of needs as set forth in his famous *Motivation and Personality.*

2. *Perceptions that managerial behavior, especially that of immediate superiors, is worthy of respect and emulation.* As pointed out elsewhere, the example set by a superior's behavior will be mirrored to some extent in the attitudes and behavior of subordinates. All managers must be extremely careful in their relationships and interactions with all subordinates, taking care that no actions derogate work performance and that all actions ultimately enhance it. Maintaining respect is a key element in effecting employee motivation.

3. *Perceptions that the structure and system inherent in work situations are appropriate.* Although individuals generally differ about what is appropriate, the overwhelming body of research shows productivity is greatest in fairly highly structured situations. We have cited elsewhere the advantages of impersonal structuring as opposed to personal or dictatorial structuring.

4. *Perceptions that supportiveness will result from positive work efforts and that fair penalties will be imposed for less-than-positive efforts.* Managers should use penalties only in an impersonal manner and as a last resort. However, to deny that penalties should ever be used is analogous to suggesting we abolish law enforcement systems in society as a whole.

5. *Perceptions that the organizational culture is in harmony with personal values and attitudes.* For example, few citizens would feel comfortable in a Mafia-controlled organization if they were aware of the fact.

6. *Perceptions that work situations will challenge one's capabilities and allow for growth, but that goals and objectives are attainable.* This possibly has greater importance than ever owing to the current Yuppie culture with its emphasis on self-fulfillment.

7. *Perceptions that personal control over personal work will be equal to the amount of personal control desired.* Each employee must be considered as an individual and be given as much desired control over his or her work as is feasible. Managers have developed many programs in various types of enterprises as a response, e.g., job enrichments, realignments, etc.

The real problem for managers is to determine how each of the above kinds of perception applies to immediate subordinates and to those in lateral and higher level positions. This is certainly a challenge of immense proportions. Seldom, if ever, does management optimally achieve all of these perceptions among its employees.

All seven kinds of perception can serve as general goals for human resource planning and are achievable through appropriate planning and implementing actions. With regard to implementing actions, most can be traced as a direct follow-up to specific plans. However, in some instances (e.g., category 5, which concerns the fit of organizational culture with personal values and attitudes), implementing actions may only relate to an organizational climate created by the total body of plans and other implementing actions.

When contemplating the many ways of accomplishing work in business organizations, it can be seen that in each case the behavior used in implementation will affect the perceptions of individual employees. A specific behavioral pattern cannot be devised that affects the perceptions of all employees in the same way. Therefore, managers must use behavior that has the highest probability of engendering favorable perceptions in a majority of employees. Of course, individual employees may sometimes become motivated in response to the use of more selective means, at least to some extent.

Summary

This chapter discusses the various direct means managers use in effecting the accomplishment of work (by individuals and by groups). Of course, the whole culture of an organization affects the perceptions of employees and their degree of motivation. For brevity's sake we have limited our comments (except in one instance) to what might be called "hands-on" approaches. The major approaches are

1. directing

2. leadership

3. exercise of authority

4. using power and force

5. influence

6. supervision

7. effecting group synergy

8. work contracts

9. motivation.

We view *directing* as an approach largely used by top echelon managers and chief executive officers. It includes the exercise of legitimate authority and involves the issuing of directives, orders, and authoritative pronouncements regarding courses to be followed and actions to be taken.

Leadership is an approach that tries to elicit voluntary actions of organizational members (and possibly others). Leadership can be a powerful adjunct to other approaches that are pursued throughout the organizational hierarchy. We define leadership as the perceived behavior of a manager that results in a motivation of another person to strive voluntarily toward organizational goals and objectives to a greater degree than otherwise would have occurred.

Exercise of authority can occur and does occur at every management level. The traditional theory of authority holds that the authority vested in any manager is derived from the organizational charter. The acceptance theory holds that authority flows from the bottom up, owing to the fact that in free nations consent is necessary for the exercise of authority. Actually, both theories have elements of truth. Authority is legally vested in organizational managers whether or not it is ever used. However, authority so vested remains useless unless organizational members accede to it.

Managers use *power and force* as means for effecting work accomplishments; both are components of vested authority. As one writer has stated, "(1) power is latent force; (2) force is manifest power, and (3) authority is institutionalized power."[62]

Influence refers to the ability of one person to change the behavior of another by any means, either direct or indirect. Direct influence is usually associated with authority, power, and leadership.

Supervision remains the predominant means of effecting work in organizations, although its nature has changed dramatically over the past 25 years. The term *supervision* typically applies to getting work done at lower management levels, although upper level managers "supervise" their immediate assistants, such as clerical and secretarial help.

Effecting group synergy involves a broad range of strategies for increasing performance in formal and informal groups. Of course, management is chiefly concerned with formal groups—those created by management to accomplish work.

Cohesiveness is a desirable group characteristic, because cohesive groups have been shown to be capable of high performance, provided that the attitudes of members toward organizational goals and objectives are favorable. Conversely, cohesive groups, because they tend to establish and control adopted norms, may restrict performance if members regard objectives excessive or unreasonable.

Long-term membership within a group creates stability, and stability promotes cohesiveness, as does strong and effective group leadership.

Groups solve problems better than do individuals, owing to the greater total knowledge possessed by the members. Further, being involved in the problem solving process tends to make members more accepting of the solutions or decisions. Groups also often reach riskier decisions than do individuals.

Groups have both task- and maintenance-orientated functions. Often, each of these two kinds of function are performed by two separate leaders within the group. Usually, an appointed group leader performs task functions; maintenance functions may be done either by the appointed leader or by an informal leader recognized and accepted by the group.

There are five basic types of formal groups: (1) operational work groups, (2) staff work groups, (3) standing committees, (4) ad hoc committees, and (5) task forces.

A number of general guidelines may be useful in effecting group synergy. We discussed these under three headings: (1) forming groups, (2) managing groups, and (3) controlling group work.

Generally, managers should use great care in forming groups, with the details of formation being put in writing. Objectives, authority, methods and timing of reporting, and a designated workplace should all be described and a general understanding clearly reached between group members and the appointed group leader. To achieve cohesiveness, the following factors, among others, should be considered: the size of the group (under 20 members), common interests, the age of members, the stability of personalities, the management potential of the appointed leader, and company loyalty. Our experience indicates that political realities had best be respected, especially in the appointment of committees, even though performance may suffer slightly.

As to actual management or supervision of a group, predetermined company work goals and objectives constitute the top priority. However, maintenance needs and other personal needs of group members should be met to the extent feasible. Both structure and democracy in leadership are desirable objectives, and they need not be at variance. The example set by the head of a group can have a powerful influence on member behavior. Thus, group leaders must be careful that all their actions and attitudes are conducive to the accomplishment of work goals and objectives and engender adherence to company policies.

Special techniques and protocols are helpful in managing committees or task forces, such as providing an agenda and related information well before scheduled meetings, keeping meetings to a prescribed length, controlling discussions, seeing that all have a chance to express opinions, encouraging the clash of ideas, and closing meetings on a positive note.

Certain guidelines also apply to the conduct of committees or task forces members during meetings. Do not frame issues as win or lose propositions, but remain open to compromises. After having clearly stated an opinion, give others an opportunity to react. Do not seek resolutions for harmony's sake alone, but demand logic. Do not offer promises about unrelated matters so as to gain harmony on the matter at hand. Get all members involved in the discussions so as to provide the broadest information base for solutions. Finally, hold tempers in check.

To be effective as a group manager, one must be objective and seek facts in resolving problems. Nonetheless, the perceptions of group members may be the most important realities that need to be dealt with. One might begin by trying to align facts and perceptions. Second-guessing members is unwise in most situations, but repeated errors by a work group member should not be tolerated indefinitely. After counseling and sincerely attempting to be supportive, if errors continue, the member should be removed from the group to avoid negative reactions from other members.

A manager or supervisor should seek to understand each group member's needs and motivations. Group members almost invariably regard concern shown by a leader with favor.

Group member satisfaction often comes from observing end products of group work and from knowing that goals have been attained. Also, a true leader constantly strives to see that no basic conflicts exist between organizational goals and objectives and those arising from informal personal associations within the group.

As to controlling group work, the basic principles of control given in Chapter 15 apply. In small work groups supervision is necessary, and it should be done supportively. If the majority of a cohesive group perceives supervision as supportive, pressure from peers will often make a deviating member conform.

Self-control is an ideal that can now often be attained, and impersonal measurements of work, together with rapid feedback referenced to such measurements, make it easier to achieve.

Contracting for work is not a new idea, but it has become more prevalent owing to the availability of cheaper labor in other countries and some areas of this country. Extreme care must be taken in drafting contracts to assure that they contain enforceable penalties for nonperformance or for performance not conforming to specifications.

Motivation is a highly complex subject. Measurable facts or realities rarely can be isolated, thus precluding use of precise protocols or algorithms.

Four basic factors are involved in employee motivations:

1. an employee's perceptions of personal needs

2. an employee's cognitive orientations

3. an employee's capabilities, both genetic and acquired

4. an employee's perceptions of motivational forces that management controls and that may impinge on him or her in the workplace

Managers have the task of favorably affecting the *totality* of perceptions about work performance. We have separated the perceptions into seven kinds, each of which has been shown by research to be capable of causing motivations of employees toward optimal work performance:

1. Perceptions that opportunities exist for satisfaction of personal needs. Reference is to the personal needs outlined by A.H. Maslow in *Motivation and Personality*.

2. Perceptions that managerial behavior and especially that of immediate superiors, is worthy of respect.

3. Perceptions that structure and system are appropriate. Structure has been shown to have favorable effects on productivity.

4. Perceptions that good work efforts result in supportiveness and that fair penalties will be imposed when necessitated.

5. Perceptions that there is a fit between organizational culture and personal values and attitudes.

6. Perceptions that challenges and potential for growth exist in work situations and that goals and objectives are attainable.

7. Perceptions that employees will have as much personal control over work as is feasible.

Motivational theory applies to each of the ways work is done in specific organizations, with the exception of contract work, and then it applies to the contracted organization.

Notes

1. Ernest Dale, *Management: Theory and Practice*, 2d ed. (New York: McGraw-Hill, 1969), 6.
2. Ibid., 424.
3. Ibid., 425–52.
4. Ibid., 6–7.
5. Joseph L. Massie, *Essentials of Management*, 2d ed. (1971), 7. Reprinted by permission of Prentice-Hall, Inc., Englewood Cliffs, N.J.
6. Ibid., 99. Reprinted by permission of Prentice-Hall, Inc., Englewood Cliffs, N.J.
7. Robert R. Blake and James Mouton, *The New Managerial Grid* (Houston, Tex: Gulf Publishing Company, 1978), 17–18.
8. Warren B. Brown and Dennis J. Moberg, *Organization Theory and Management* (New York: Wiley, 1980), 663.
9. Ibid., 412.
10. James A.F. Stoner, *Management* (Englewood Cliffs, N.J.: Prentice-Hall, 1982).
11. William H. Newman and Kirby E. Warren, *The Process of Management*, 4th ed. (Englewood Cliffs, N.J.: Prentice-Hall, Inc., 1977), 540–619.
12. Chester I. Barnard, *The Functions of the Executive* (Cambridge, Mass.: Harvard University Press, 1938), 163–66.
13. Robert Albanese, *Management: Toward Accountability for Performance* (Homewood, Ill: Richard D. Irwin, Inc., 1979), 256.
14. Ibid., 247.
15. Brown and Moberg, *Organizational Theory and Management*, 94–95.

16. John R.P. French and B.H. Raven, "The Bases of Social Power," in *Group Dynamics: Research and Theory*, 2d ed., ed. D. Cartwright and A. Zander (Evanston, Ill.: Row Peterson, 1960), 607–23.

17. Robert Bierstedt, "Power and Social Organization," in *Human Relations in Administration*, 2d ed., ed. Robert Dubin (Englewood Cliffs, N.J.: Prentice-Hall, 1961), 242–43.

18. Stoner, *Management*, 304. Reprinted by permission of Prentice-Hall, Inc., Englewood Cliffs, N.J.

19. Massie, *Essentials of Management*, 76. Reprinted by permission of Prentice-Hall, Inc., Englewood Cliffs, N.J.

20. Albanese, *Management*, 247.

21. Gary Dessler, *Organization and Management* (Reston, Va.: Reston Publishing Company, 1982), 349.

22. Lester R. Bittel, *What Every Supervisor Should Know*, 4th ed. (New York: McGraw-Hill, 1980), 3.

23. Taft-Hartley Act of 1947, quoted in Bittel, *What Every Supervisor Should Know*, 4.

24. Massie, *Essentials of Management*, 102. Reprinted by permission of Prentice-Hall, Inc., Englewood Cliffs, N.J.

25. Peter Drucker, *The Practice of Management* (New York: Harper & Row, 1954), 328.

26. Ibid., 322–23.

27. Michael S. Olmsted, *The Small Group* (New York: Random House, 1959), 21–22.

28. Rensis Likert, *New Patterns of Management* (New York: McGraw-Hill, 1961), 113–14.

29. Ibid., 114.

30. Ibid., 114–15.

31. Olmsted, *The Small Group*, 109.

32. Morton Deutsch, "Field Theory in Social Psychology," in *Handbook of Social Psychology*, vol. 1, ed. Gardner Lindsey (Cambridge, Mass.: Addison-Wesley, 1954), 182–85. Quoted in Olmsted, *The Small Group*, 109–10.

33. Stanley F. Seashore, *Group Cohesiveness in the Industrial Work Group* (Ann Arbor, Mich.: Survey Research Center, University of Michigan, 1954), 90–95. Quoted in Dessler, *Organization and Management*, 403.

34. Dessler, *Organization and Management*, 403–8.

35. Albanese, *Management*, 540–43.

36. Ibid.

37. Dessler, *Organization and Management*, 410–11.

38. Ibid., 403–4.

39. Ibid., 404.

40. Ibid., 404–11.

41. Stoner, *Management*, 333.

42. Albanese, *Management*, 542.

43. Based on F.L. Roethlisberger and William Dickson, *Management and the Worker* (New York: Wiley, 1939); and Henry Landsberger, *Hawthorne Revisited* (Ithaca, N.Y.: Cornell University Press, 1958). Reported in Dessler, *Organization and Management*, 408–10.

44. Dessler, *Organization and Management*, 408–10.

45. Ibid., 416.

46. Ibid., 416–17.

47. Ibid., 414.

48. Kenneth J. Benne and Paul Sheats, "Functional Roles of Group Members," *Journal of Social Issues* (Spring 1948): 42–47. Reported in Albanese, *Management*, 487.

49. Dessler, *Organization and Management*, 412.

50. Dorwin Cartwright, "Achieving Change in People: Some Application of Group Dynamics," in *Readings in Human Relations*, ed. Keith Davis and William G. Scott (New York: McGraw-Hill, 1959), 219–30. Originally published in *Human Relations*, no. 4 (1951): 381–92. Reported in Ernest Dale, *Management*, 441–42.

51. Albanese, *Management*, 484–86.

52. Bittel, *What Every Supervisor Should Know*, 53.

53. Anthony Jay, "How to Run a Meeting," *Harvard Business Review* 54 (March-April 1976):43–57. Reported in Stoner, *Management*, 346.

54. Ibid.

55. Jay Hall, "Decisions, Decisions, Decisions," *Psychology Today*, November 1971, p. 86. Reported in Stoner, *Management*, p. 347.

56. Bittel, *What Every Supervisor Should Know*, 57.

57. Abraham H. Maslow, *Motivation and Personality*, 2d ed. (New York: Harper & Row, 1970), 35–58.

58. William H. Newman and Charles E. Summer, Jr., *The Process of Management* (Englewood Cliffs, N.J.: Prentice-Hall, 1961), 148–49.

59. William R. Anson, *Principles of the Law of Contracts*, ed. Thomas H. Patterson (Chicago: Callaghan and Company, 1939), 132.

60. Owen B. Hardy, "Leadership and the Hospital Administrator," *Hospital Administration* 13 (Winter 1968): 46.

61. Saul W. Gellerman, *Management by Motivation* (American Management Association, 1968), 36.

62. Maslow, *Motivation and Personality*, 35–58.

Chapter 13

Implementing human resource planning

Elements of Management
in Corporations

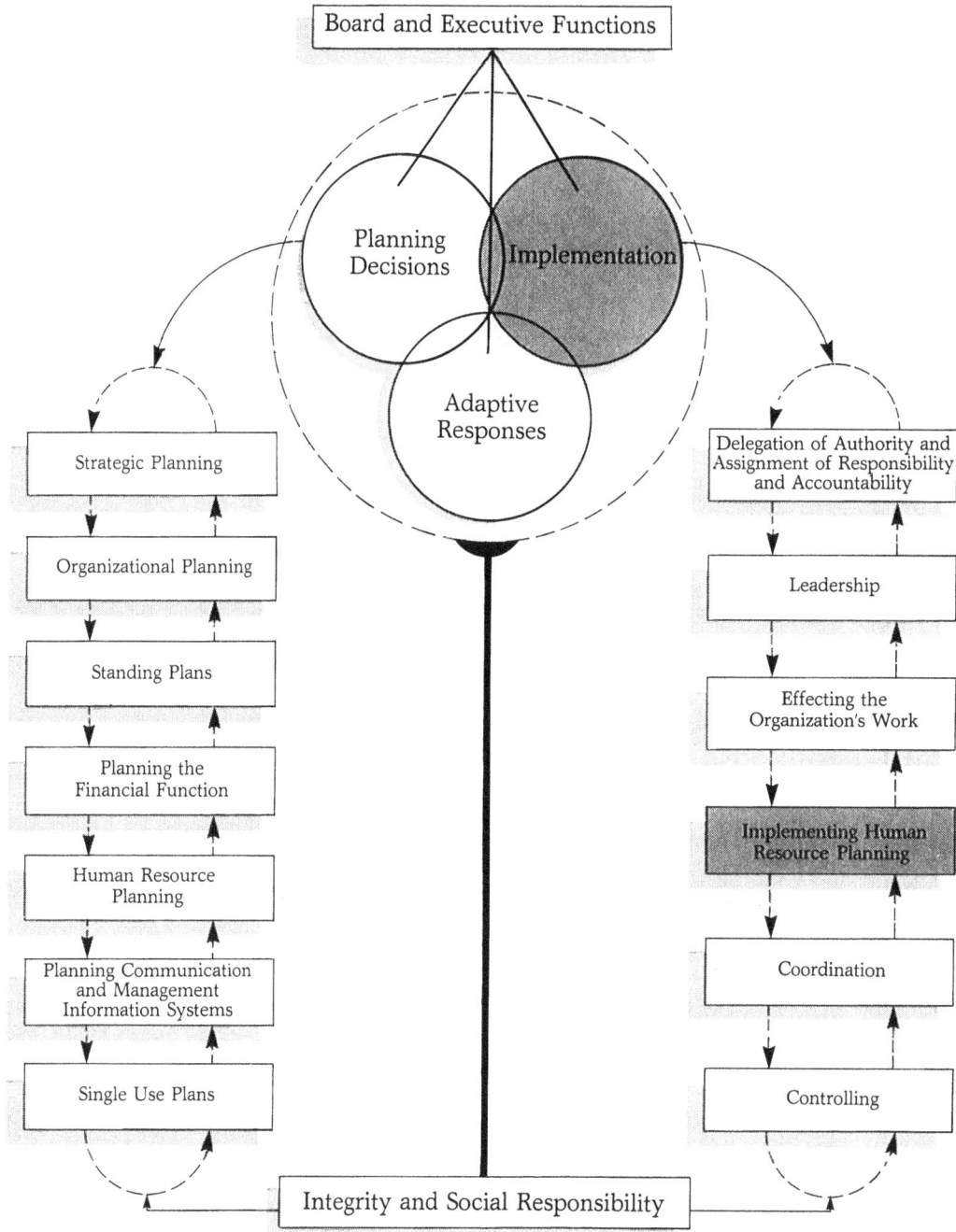

Board and Executive Functions

Planning Decisions

Implementation

Adaptive Responses

Strategic Planning

Organizational Planning

Standing Plans

Planning the Financial Function

Human Resource Planning

Planning Communication and Management Information Systems

Single Use Plans

Delegation of Authority and Assignment of Responsibility and Accountability

Leadership

Effecting the Organization's Work

Implementing Human Resource Planning

Coordination

Controlling

Integrity and Social Responsibility

13

Definitions

In its broadest sense, human resource management involves all formal interfaces that managers have with operating personnel and with other managers in the course of conducting a company's business. Its action or implementing phases extend into every aspect of management.

Planning for human resource management creates managerial attitudes and orientations which are eventually reflected, through *implementing actions*, in an organization's cultural environment—an environment that hopefully will be conducive to productivity and the satisfaction of employee needs. *Statements of philosophy* enunciate management's beliefs and attitudes. *Policy pronouncements* reveal management's intentions regarding implementation of philosophical beliefs and attitudes. *Procedures* set forth the specific steps for carrying out intentions related to the formal interfaces that management personnel have with individual members of the organization.

Are all policies, procedures, and methods of an organization—and the activities necessary to implement them—the direct concern of human resource management? The answer is no. Human resource management is concerned only with those policies and procedures (and occasionally methods) that directly involve the human aspects of management's interfaces with personnel, both individually and collectively. Indirectly, however, the implementation of every type of plan involves humans, even those plans that are entirely work oriented, and therefore aspects of human resource management inevitably enter into the implementation of all policies, procedures, and methods of all organizations. A plan may not specifically refer to the human relations factors occurring in phases of implementation, but such factors may play an even greater role in achieving successful results than the basic technical correctness of the plan itself.

Because it would be impractical, indeed impossible, to spell out in all of a company's work-oriented policies, procedures, and methods just how a manager should interface with subordinates and others who engage in implementation, we stressed in Chapter 7 the importance of published statements of philosophy. Such statements can at least encourage certain attitudes among managers regarding supervising, directing, influencing, leading, and controlling, all of which will at one time or another be employed in implementation.

Scheer eloquently expresses the view that we hold in the following words: "A company program built around procedures, even though each separate instrument is a technical masterpiece, is lifeless. Programs made up of techniques but not understanding have a shell for a body and an ache for a soul."[1]

Again, human resource management, in its broadest sense, involves all of management. Plan implementation, as one of the basic elements of management, necessarily relies on human resources and must always take into account the fundamentals of human behavior and relationships. Thus, successful organizations respect both the behavioral sciences and their financial responsibilities as they undertake to carry out those activities required to accomplish their missions, goals, and objectives (or carry out their plans).

Chapter 7 concerned human resource planning. In this chapter, we discuss implementation of the several categories of plans described there. The four main kinds of human resource planning are as follows:

1. Development and publication of a philosophy regarding human resource management.

2. Development and promulgation of policies related to the role, functions, basic purposes, and expected benefits of a personnel department. (The forecasting and programming of human resource needs constitutes one of these functions.)

3. Development of a full range of personnel policies.

4. Development of procedures for implementing each set of activities (or function) undertaken by a personnel department.

We discuss below implementing activities for each of these categories.

Implementation of a human resource philosophy

The implementation of an organization's philosophy of human resource management occurs primarily through implementation of other plans. Thus, policies, procedures, and methods, not philosophical pronouncements, are mainly what require specific acts of implementation. Statements of philosophy, however, serve as a guide for acts of implementation occurring throughout an organization.

In Chapter 12, we outlined a number of ways used by managers to effect organizational work and achieve optimal performance levels from organizational members. Among them were directing, leadership, exercise of authority, use of power and force, influence, supervision, techniques for effecting group synergy, and methods for effecting employee motivation. In each instance, management style may be considerably affected by statements of philosophy that a manager has internalized. For example, few policies or procedures exist in organizations that address style per se. Yet, suppose a manager reads the following in a relevant statement of philosophy on human resource management: "To the extent possible, management and the personnel body should be viewed as a partnership. . . . Mutual respect represents an ideal to be actively sought. . . . Management views . . . every person occupying a position as an important team member. . . . The right to be heard shall not be abrogated." When those statements are supported by other statements reinforcing the idea that every employee is important, it seems doubtful a manager would use a domineering style in dealing with either subordinates or equals. Nor would one expect a manager to act arbitrarily or peremptorily toward employees.

No reputable management authority would deny that style is a very important element in leadership. At Ohio State University, in fact, researchers found that "employee turnover rates were lowest and employee satisfaction highest under leaders who were rated high in consideration." Conversely, leaders who were "rated low in consideration and high in initiating structure had high grievance and turnover rates among their employees."[2] Researchers at the University of Michigan found that "the most productive work groups tended to have leaders that were employee-centered [showed consideration] rather than production-centered."[3]

The evidence seems clear that although statements of philosophy depend directly on relevant formulations of policies, procedures, and methods for their implementation, they certainly influence nearly every formal action taken by managers in an organizational context.

Top managers who enunciate the organization's philosophy can assure its implementation both in direct or indirect ways by continually stressing its importance. If the philosophy is published and then filed away in a company's archives, there will be little likelihood of its continuing influence. Prominent posting and frequent references to it will instill a sense of its importance in managers that is bound to be reflected in their actions and ultimately in the actions of others.

Implementation of policies related to personnel departments

Implementing the department's role

For our purposes here, we will assume appropriate policies have been developed outlining the role that a personnel department will fulfill and the functions it will perform, together with the purposes and expected benefits of each function. This, of course, is an optimistic assumption, for as Scheer, among others, has well noted, "Too often, personnel programs grow without any real plan of organization."[4] However, most business enterprises start small, and before they are able to support the full range of functions found in the personnel departments of large corporations, they must reach a certain level of financial capability. Even so, in starting small, executives would do well to envision adding functions (by steps) until there is a full range. In any set of circumstances, there should be a plan of organization which can be implemented immediately or over time.

Appointing the head of a personnel department

From the standpoint of a chief executive officer, the first step in implementing role definition and policies for a department of personnel is to delegate authority and assign responsibility and accountability to a person who will serve as head. This seems elementary, but many executives encounter great difficulty in entrusting a vice president for personnel administration (or whatever the title) with the decisions and acts of implementation this person had best undertake. Additionally, the degree of functional authority the personnel head will possess should be determined at this time and should be clearly included in the job description. Too often, executives give a personnel administrator some functional authority orally but fail to communicate the fact to line managers. Conflict inevitably occurs. To avoid this, delegating executives should accurately communicate to line managers the nature and degree of functional authority which has been delegated to the department of personnel.

Chapter 10 discusses practical means for delegating authority and assigning responsibility and accountability. Of course, how much authority is delegated by an executive and how much responsibility or accountability is assigned can vary widely and may be open to individual interpretation. However, delegating and assigning should be done clearly enough that it does not become a subjective matter. Unless deceit is to be served, it seems reasonable that a personnel administrator should know fairly accurately what his or her duties and responsibilities are.

Conferences

After delegating and assigning, especially in the early stages of implementation, the CEO should confer frequently with the personnel department head, for adaptavising may be necessary. During stages of growth, many issues arise, especially concerning the employment of key personnel and even groups of operating personnel, that the personnel head cannot and should not decide alone (full recognition of this fact should be made at the outset). Additionally, conferring promotes coordination and allows the CEO to provide suitable guidance in nonroutine matters.

The decisions that have to be made about employment are usually related to this simple question: "Should we staff in anticipation of increased work volumes or should we wait until work volumes force the employment of necessary staff?" Depending on a number of considerations, one alternative or the other will usually be best. In any case, such decisions should not be made exclusively by the director of personnel without input from the CEO and possibly a COO or division or department executive.

Grouping personnel functions

After the CEO has delegated and assigned (hopefully flawlessly and with clarity), the personnel head must do likewise with respect to his or her subordinates. Before doing so, the type and fundamental nature of functions to be carried out by the personnel staff must be considered, based on the assignments made by the CEO. Relying on education and experience, the personnel head will group activities into logical department sections, envision growth in phases, and make delegations and assignments on such bases. We regard the grouping of functions as an act of planning, but delegations and assignments as definite acts of implementation. Considerations related to the grouping of functions are outlined in Chapter 7.

Assigning grouped functions

Regardless of the bases for groupings or of the groupings actually made, the next implementing step involves the head of the personnel department assigning the functions to specific persons. This act of implementation necessitates the delegation of authority and the assignment of responsibility and accountability to specific individuals, just like any other such act. Again, delegating and assigning should be done flawlessly, with clarity, and, in most instances, in writing.

Further delegations and assignments
In large firms, implementing policies pertaining to the personnel department necessitates employing personnel specialists to work as assistants to those managers who serve as heads of functional groupings or divisions. Appropriate delegations and assignments must of course be made.

Before employing these specialists, heads of functional groupings and the chief personnel executive must at least envision procedures by which implementing activities will be carried out. If this is not done, meaningful job descriptions cannot be worked out. We discussed such procedures in Chapter 7 and we comment on their implementation later in this chapter.

If delegations and assignments for these specialists are made properly, a structured department will have been created that will stand ready to perform as a team and with a considerable degree of coordination. Conversely, if managers have not performed these implementing tasks properly, one can expect a considerable amount of infighting, power grabbing, futile activity, and a number of other undesirable results.

Achieving the purposes and benefits of policies

With policies in hand, with personnel functions appropriately grouped, and with an organized staff whose every member has been given appropriate authority, and assigned responsibility, and accountability, the personnel department will be ready to achieve the purposes set forth in the policies concerning the department's functions. Exhibits 7-3 and 7-4 provide examples of statements of purposes and benefits related to performance evaluations and the handling of grievances, respectively. Evaluating performance and handling grievances are only two of a broad range of functions for which policies may have to be implemented.

Implementation of policies is accomplished through pursuit of established procedures, with further guidance being afforded by supervision, direction, and leadership. All of the means commonly used for implementing work may come into play (see Chapter 12). Also, management by objectives can be utilized without difficulty owing to the ease of translating expected benefits into statements of objectives. Managers should exercise control with either approach. Formulations of objectives should be stated so as to allow easy measurement of accomplishments where quality or quantity is involved. (See Chapter 15 for related discussions.)

Some personnel departments implement some of their functions through management by objectives and others merely through ongoing guided procedural work. Some work, of course, depends entirely on demonstrated demands, with demands being governed by forces unrelated to personnel staff. In such instances, objectives may be difficult to formulate. In others, managers may quite easily formulate objectives, such as an annual enrollment in a pension plan, the start-up of a new personnel program by a definite date, or the complete staffing of a new organizational unit within a projected timeframe.

Exhibit 13-1

Policy: Sick Leave Pay

Filing Number 111-07-1000

Effective Date: January 1, 1984
Revised Date: January 1, 1988

Policy Statement

The XYZ Corporation shall provide economic protection in the form of Sick Leave Pay to employees who are necessarily absent from work due to personal illnesses or nonoccupational accidents. Sick leave pay shall extend to both regular full-time and regular less-than-full-time employees. Eligible days for sick leave pay shall correlate with length of employment time. In some instances, outlined herein following, proof of illness will be required. Provisions for accrual of sick leave, within prescribed limits, shall be made.

Purpose

To provide the benefit of economic protection to employees during periods when they cannot earn pay due to bona fide illnesses or nonoccupational accidents; to demonstrate the concern of the Corporation for the welfare of its most valuable asset—its employees; and to assure the loyalty and good will of the entire employee body.

Procedures

1. Any employee who reports for work and who later on the same day becomes ill shall report to the Company Clinic. With concurrence of the Duty Nurse, the employee may leave work for the remainder of that day and will be paid in full and with no charge being made against entitled sick leave time.

2. The following schedule shall govern entitlement to days of regular pay for employees who are absent by reason of personal illness or nonoccupational injuries.

Wage-Hour Employees

Employment Period	Sick Leave Pay Entitlement (Workdays)	Maximum Accrual of Unused Sick Leave Days (all previous years)	Waiting Time to Entitlement (Workdays)*
0-3 Months	0		
4-9 Months	7		2
2nd Year	10		1
3rd Year	10	4	0
4th Year	10	8	0
5th Year	10	12	0
6th Year	15	16	0
7th Year	15	22	0
8th Year	15	28	0
9th Year	15	34	0
10th Year	15	40	0
After 10 Years	15	46	0

*No waiting time shall be required for any sick leave absence of 7 or more days upon presentation of a written doctor's certificate of illness to the Duty Nurse in the Company Clinic.

Implementing personnel policies

Each major heading listed in HCA's personnel policies represents a policy, and each policy must be supported by an implementing procedure. To show the relationship of an implementing procedure to a relevant policy, we provide in Exhibit 13-1 an example of a policy on sick leave pay and the corresponding procedure. Note that the procedure

	Salaried (Exempt) Employees		
Employment Period (Years)	Sick Leave Pay Entitlement (Workdays)**	Maximum Accrual of Unused Sick Leave Days (all previous years)	Waiting Time to Entitlement (Workdays)
1	10		0
2	10		0
3	10	4	0
4	15	8	0
5	15	12	0
6	15	18	0
7	15	24	0
8	15	30	0
9	15	36	0
10	15	42	0
After 10 Years	18	46	0

**A sick and absent employee shall be paid for the entire week during which entitled days expire, provided he or she possesses eligibility for pay under any aspect of company policy.

3. Each employee has the responsibility to establish the fact of his or her illness or disability when absent in order to receive entitled sick leave pay. This responsibility can be met by calling in to respective, appropriate administrative supervisors by 10:00 a.m. on the first day of absence or having a spouse, other family member, or physician call in.

4. Any employee failing to give proper notification of his or her illness or disability shall not receive entitlement to sick leave pay, except in extreme cases of hardship or catastrophic conditions where notification could not have been reasonably expected to have been given as noted. Where notification is not properly given, the matter will be considered on its merits by the appropriate administrative supervisor at the time notification is received.

5. Any employee absent for more than three (3) work days due to personal illness or injury, when returning to work, shall report to the Duty Nurse in the Company Clinic to be cleared for duty. At the discretion of the Duty Nurse, an employee may be required to furnish a physician's statement pertaining to his or her fitness. The Duty Nurse shall hand a "Clearance for Work" to the returning employee, if fitness for duty is established, and the employee shall remit same to the appropriate administrative supervisor prior to the assumption of work tasks.

6. On or shortly after respective employment anniversaries, the Company will submit to each employee a statement of sick leave used during the previous year and the number of potentially entitled days, including accrued days, for the coming year.

7. The Company has purchased a group disability insurance policy to provide weekly payments to employees during long-term illnesses, after sick leave pay as outlined under this policy has been exhausted. See Policy entitled "Group Disability Insurance."

8. The Company reserves the right to deny sick leave pay in instances of obvious abuse, and where such is strongly suspected, involved employees may be required to establish proof of illness, either through the Company Clinic or by the statement of an attending physician.

possesses the characteristics of a complete plan (i.e., designations of who, when, what, where, and how). Thus, implementation of personnel policies actually occurs through implementation of relevant procedures in a majority of instances.

Responsibility

Who has responsibility for implementing personnel policies? Actually, every member of an organization possesses this responsibility—both managers and operating personnel. After their formulation and publication, all managers have the responsibility of seeing that implementing procedures are followed. Operating personnel have the responsibility of adhering to policies by not committing violations, either through omission or commission. Personnel policy handbooks facilitate this by increasing employees' knowledge of personnel policies. Personnel department managers have a special responsibility to monitor faithful execution of policies throughout a firm by all organizational members. Because managers in a personnel department are often solely concerned with implementation of some policies, they must carry primary authority and responsibility—and accountability. In instances where personnel managers and managers in line departments coordinate their actions in the execution of an implementing procedure, the procedure should spell out the responsibilities of each clearly and accurately.

Although personnel department managers have a responsibility to monitor appropriate adherence to policies and implementing procedures throughout the organization, they do not have the responsibility to take corrective action in most situations affecting line departments or divisions; that responsibility lies with line managers. Of course, job descriptions and procedures provide the opportunity for these responsibilities to be properly coordinated.

Effecting implementation

Assuming that all planning has been accomplished and that the personnel department stands fully ready to effect implementation of one or more personnel policies, how do managers initiate action? The answer is to exercise one of the classic means of getting any type of organizational work done, namely, directing. At least one noted author defined direction (or directing) as "the management function of stimulating action to take place."[5] Who gives the directive to initiate a specific policy (or policies) on a certain date? Depending on its importance, the CEO or COO may do so through an official pronouncement—or the chief personnel officer may do so.

Although directing should be used to actually start implementation and may be used as a means of continuing it, all other means for effecting work may later be employed, including supervising, influencing, leading, providing motivational stimuli, exercising power, authority, and force, and controlling. (With respect to controlling, few situations exist where control procedures should not be at least readied for use.)

Implementing personnel department activities

We stated in Chapter 7 that personnel department staff should develop procedures for implementing each set of functions to be undertaken, including those that pertain to intradepartmental work activities and to other company activities as well. We also stated that some of these procedures should be approved by top management.

While the absence of procedures for carrying out the work of the personnel department does not preclude assigning the head of the department or other managers responsibility for groups of functions, it does militate against clarity in delegating authority and assigning responsibility and accountability to working specialists. However, this is not to say that specialists are never hired without work procedures being in place. In fact, specialists are perhaps more often brought in prior to the formulation of procedures. Many managers are content to "muddle through" and depend on the specialists themselves to establish procedures. We have even observed some departments (probably many exist) where working procedures have never been formulated. Managers have simply hired specialists, told them what they wanted accomplished, and put them to work. Internal interfacing among specialists and external interfacing with line and other personnel occurs under the direction of the personnel department managers.

Regardless of how procedures for carrying out the work of a personnel department may be formulated, we will assume for our purpose that they have been formed and in fact govern implementation of work carried out by the personnel department in certain functional areas. So no reader will be confused as to the procedures being referred to here, we stress we are *not* referring to procedures used in administering a personnel policy. Instead, we are referring to the procedures necessary to carry out the functions discussed below, which are the same "core" functions we cited in commenting on their implementing policies and procedures in Chapter 7.

Government compliance activities

Responsibility to comply with governmental regulations extends throughout an organization, but responsibility to interpret regulations, educate organizational personnel, post notices, monitor reported conformance, and prepare for the submission of required reports most often rests with the personnel department. Additionally, in matters of hiring (the selection process and the respecting of privacy), compensation, employee benefits, monitoring hours worked, filing compliance reports with proper agencies, and interpreting the legal implications of labor laws, the personnel department usually has many direct implementing responsibilities.

Just where the working staff involved in monitoring, performing implementing acts, or filing reports will be located varies widely from firm to firm. In some, these functions may be carried out almost exclusively by a corporate headquarters unit; in others, many of them may be performed in decentralized operating units. In all instances, however, duties must be assigned and delegations of authority and assignments of responsibility and accountability must be made.

Conformance to a major new regulatory requirement usually necessitates an initial period for the orientation of top executives and top personnel officers. The orientation may involve study of the law and expert interpretations of it, briefings by governmental officials, attendance at seminars, etc. Following the orientation, the CEO orders policy to be developed by designated personnel staff and determines who will be assigned responsibility for its implementation. In most instances, both line managers and the personnel department staff are involved. In the case of the personnel department, the top personnel executive holds overall responsibility for its functions. This executive then assigns specific tasks to others. In Figure 7-2, we arbitrarily placed monitoring, reporting, and educational functions pertaining to EEO, ERISA, and OSHA in the Public Affairs and Compliance Division of the (theoretical) personnel department. However, there are other functions, including some in the other personnel divisions, that must be assigned by the division heads to specific persons.

Generally, compliance activities include not only *new* implementing efforts related to orientation, notification, monitoring, and reporting, but also efforts related to modifying already established functions, such as employment and compensation.

After the degree of compliance is monitored and the results are reported to the relevant government agency and to the persons in the organization who are responsible for compliance, the question arises as to who should be responsible for any corrections that are indicated. Invariably, responsibility should be given to those managers who initially received delegations and assignments regarding the implementation of the compliance activities. If this is not done, the will to implement can be materially weakened. Monitoring and reporting can easily be assigned as a staff function; taking corrective actions should continue as a line function.

The implementing work to be performed by the personnel department will eventually involve the various methods for effecting work that were discussed in Chapter 12. Managers will do well to become intimately familiar with them and also to organize their thinking and activities in terms of planning, implementing, and framing adaptive responses. Conceptualizing all organizational work becomes simplified when this is done, and it greatly reduces the incidence of that horrible question that occasionally presents itself to all managers: "What am I going to do now?"

Labor relations

Implementing activities by a personnel department regarding labor relations should reflect policies and procedures currently in effect. In Chapter 7, we cited three situations requiring different policies: before threats of unionization, during attempts at unionization, and after a union contract has been consummated. However, one factor is common to all situations with regard to policy formulation or policy implementation. Miner and Miner have stated it simply: "A personnel manager should be thoroughly familiar with the field of labor relations whether the firm's employees are unionized or not."[6] In other words, personnel managers should be ready to serve as experts in labor relations under any circumstances—for the benefit of their employers.

Overall, unions have had a salutary effect on the evolution of personnel policies and their implementation throughout the nation, even in nonunion firms. "It is generally conceded that employees most susceptible to union organizing appeals are those who are dissatisfied."[7] Probably in most cases, the dissatisfaction has stemmed from inequities or omissions in personnel policies and a general disdain for employees in the workplace. When employee dissatisfaction becomes evident to managers, they often effect improvements and thus remove the impetus that might have pushed employees toward unionization. In those companies that have responded properly, the threat of unionization is reduced and management can devote time and energies more effectively toward increasing productivity, raising living standards for employees further, and giving shareholders a good return on their investments.

Responsibility for labor relations varies, but very often, even in small firms, the chief personnel officer may receive the assignment. "A large multiplant corporation . . . may have an entire department staffed with experts in wage and salary administration, insurance and pension planning, contract negotiation, labor law, and the like."[8]

In contract negotiations, a personnel manager nearly always serves on the negotiating committee so as to provide experience and to become prepared for participation in the administration of a contract, if one is signed. Also, the personnel department usually has responsibility for wage and benefit surveys, determination of area personnel practices, and whatever other such research may be desirable. The personnel manager may also serve as an expert advisor to other members of management's negotiating team (provided the manager has fulfilled the professional obligation to become knowledgeable about labor relations).

In contract administration, personnel departments carry out those parts of the contract that implicate their usual functions. Usually, continued negotiations are required, and personnel staff may enter into these if top management so decides.

Although variations occur in contract administration, one can infer which functions are normally implemented by a personnel department from the contents of a typical labor contract. Some items most often included are listed below:

1. Union recognition: the exclusive right to represent employees.

2. Extent of bargaining unit: who is, and is not, included.

3. Management rights: guarantee of noninterference in operations.

4. Union security and status: good faith partnership.

5. Strikes and lockout: the rules of conduct.

6. Union activities and responsibilities: ability to function.

7. Wage determination: pay scales (single rate for grades or ranges), job evaluation, shift differentials.

8. Wage administration: raises (calendar or merit), premium pay, incentives, bonus.

9. Overtime: at what rate and when applicable.

10. Benefits: insurance, pension, unemployment.

11. Security and protection: job bidding, transfers, promotions, layoffs, recalls.

12. Seniority: regulations to be followed.

13. Health and safety: concern for employee welfare.

14. Working conditions: hours, schedules, services, conveniences.

15. Time not worked but paid: vacations, holidays, rest periods.

16. Discipline and discharge: warnings, penalties, suspension.

17. Grievances: procedure for handling [and arbitration of unresolved grievances].[9]

In administering a union contract (implementation), management should stick as close as possible to its terms and not make further concessions. Miner and Miner have cited the dangers of being intimidated by militant union leaders, especially when a new contract is first administered.[10] Concessions usually occur in attempts to reduce or prevent internal conflicts, but conflict reduction should not exceed the limits beyond which the solvency and viability of the enterprise become adversely affected.

Again, during implementation, duties and responsibility and accountability must be assigned and appropriate authority delegated if the job is to get done. Throughout, monitoring and reporting provide the means for effecting control.

Forecasting and programming human resource needs

Forecasting human resource needs is a planning function and has no direct implementing activities attached to it. Its implementation takes place through other functions that are primarily activity oriented, such as recruiting and selection.

Programming translates forecasted human resource needs "into specific *personnel objectives* and goals."[11] From these, specific action plans must be developed, which are then reflected in such functions as recruitment and selection, training and development, performance evaluation, etc. All of these functions require specific implementing activities, some of which are discussed elsewhere in this chapter.

Recruitment, selection, induction, and orientation

Recruitment
Recruiting "matches the preferences and goals of individuals with the needs and preferences of organizations."[12] Prior to recruitment, a careful job analysis should be done to determine the skills required for the particular position that needs to be filled. Assuming policy favors inside recruiting (we believe it should), the personnel specialist must first survey current employees. If a qualified person is not found within the organization, attention then turns to the outside.

Regardless of whether recruiting is focused inside or outside, personnel specialists must be mindful of laws pertaining to unfair discrimination. Screening should be strictly confined to tests and standards that apply to skills necessary for satisfactory discharge of the duties of the position. Otherwise, minorities or other classes of people can level charges of unfair discrimination. Some very large court awards have been made in recent years based on such charges.

In seeking outside applicants, business firms go to a variety of sources depending on the type of organization. For example, Ernst & Whinney specialists annually visit those college campuses known to have strong accounting and MBA programs; construction companies advertise through various publications and, if they are not unionized, regularly call employment agencies; hospitals contact professional associations and a wide variety of other sources (owing to the wide variety of skills necessary in modern hospital care). A list of possible sources of outside recruiting follows:

- state employment offices

- private search firms, especially those oriented toward professionals and executives

- professional organizations

- schools, including trade schools, high schools, business schools, colleges, universities, and hospital-sponsored schools (e.g., nursing schools)

- work forces of competitors

- advertising (in a broad variety of publications)

- state agencies (e.g., for the handicapped)

- employee referrals from a variety of outside contacts

- voluntary walk-ins and call-ins

- unions

Selection
Selection should employ a well-defined process in every firm, and unless some overriding reason arises, neither personnel specialists nor executives should circumvent the process. Some of the most unfortunate incidents of our careers have resulted from a failure to check references carefully. In one instance, for example, we hired a person who proved to be a complete imposter, posing as a Ph.D. but possessing only a high school diploma. We reasoned that to contact this man's current employer would only start a bidding war regarding salary, and thus we failed to check with that key reference. In fact, the current employer was in the process of uncovering the deception and voluntarily informed us of the imposture about a month after our "steal."

Scheer notes that selection actually involves a process, and there are a number of points at which candidates may be rejected. They are as follows:

1. Preliminary interview

2. Submission of executed application

3. Interview

4. Check on references

5. Physical examinations

6. Testing (mental, skills)

7. Multiple interviews

8. Final selection[13]

Obviously, an employer learns more about a candidate at each step. Except perhaps during earlier steps, when charges of discrimination might be made, the manager always has the opportunity to reject a candidate. We believe this process or some variation is what most major firms currently use.

The basic objective of the selection process is to hire a person who will fill a given position in an exemplary manner. No magic formulas exist, and the executive who believes that he or she possesses a God-given talent for quickly picking the "right" person will experience some rude awakenings. Our best judgment is that a thorough process of selection should be followed, and as closely as possible.

Induction and orientation
The key to a high retention rate for new employees is to have an appropriate process of indoctrination and orientation. The steps in such a process will vary according to the nature of the position the new employee will occupy and also according to his or her past experience. Often, new employees must be given on-the-job training or other types of instruction before being placed on their own. Some companies utilize "sponsors" for acclimatizing new employees. Most have a set induction program that lasts a day or two, followed by orientation, which often takes some form of "show-and-tell." Most organizations satisfactorily provide such introductory induction and orientation programs, but many fail to place sufficient emphasis on agreements about the content of individually tailored job descriptions. Where this occurs, the new employee's first reaction at the job site may be, "This is not what I thought I would be doing." Already surprised, the next reaction is, "I don't like what I'm being forced to do." Not long afterward, the employee leaves.

One can avoid losing many an employee by first carefully reaching an understanding about specific tasks to be performed, authority to be delegated, and responsibility and accountability to be assigned. Then, with proper orientation at the job site (possibly with a sponsor), the new employee can settle in and find the satisfaction originally anticipated. As stated in Chapter 10, after a new employee has assumed a position, the manager should hold conferences with the employee at appropriate intervals to determine whether any adjustments should be made in the job description. These conferences can produce goodwill and they sometimes result in worthwhile suggestions for changes in policies, procedures, or methods being made.

Promotions, demotions, transfers, and separations

Promotions

Once policies and procedures for promotions have been developed, they are ready for implementation. Assuming that policy favors promotions from within, the manager possessing responsibility for making a choice should carefully consider all eligible candidates by reviewing their personnel files. If the personnel department has faithfully filed records about original recruitment, psychological and physical testing, prior promotions, performance evaluations, etc., each file should present overall a fairly objective profile of the candidate's qualifications.

From the records (without considering outward personal characteristics), the candidates should be ranked in terms of their qualifications to perform in the position for which they are being considered. Too often, a top professional person without management qualifications receives a promotion to a key executive position—with disastrous results.

In making the ranking, intelligence, experience, seniority, education, and past performance can be evaluated using the files. After the initial ranking, outward demeanor, attitude, health, and stamina should receive careful attention. Of these, stamina is very important. J.L. Pilcher, a former U.S. congressman and an astute business executive, often opined that stamina is the single greatest ingredient for success in any position. Although we are not prepared to fully endorse that statement, a candidate's ability and will to stay on the job for long hours and under arduous circumstances certainly should be taken into consideration.

Interpersonal skills can be ascertained from the record. However, general appearance and a pleasing demeanor have some value inasmuch as making a good initial impression is important for many jobs.

If a promotion to a sensitive executive position is being considered, those with whom the candidate will be associated may have worthwhile opinions which can be discreetly ascertained. Note, however, that those who do not have responsibility for making the choice may express their biases, and this must be taken into account.

Loyalty to the firm and loyalty to superiors have received little attention in the literature. Yet, R.W. Woodruff, former chairman of the board of the Coca Cola Company, and General R.K. Mellon both considered loyalty very important when selecting those who would surround them.[14] Neither of us would tolerate having a direct subordinate who did not possess managerial honesty and had not demonstrated loyalty to the firm.

Managers can easily construct a ranking of candidates based on demeanor, health, stamina, loyalty to the firm, and the anticipated "fit" with associates. This ranking, together with that made from the personnel record, should allow a sound selection.

Making a selection and notifying the person selected is the easy part of the entire process. Notifying those who knew they were being considered that they failed to get the promotion is the most difficult part. The sensitive manager may mitigate an employee's disappointment by expressing appreciation for current performance. Promises about the future, however, should usually be avoided.

Obviously, managers must observe all regulations concerning equal rights when considering promotions of any type.

Demotions

A demotion will create a corporate saboteur faster than any other management act of which we are aware. Demotions should be avoided, if possible, except in rare instances when the recipient has actually requested a move to a lesser position or where health factors are involved.

When HCA merged with Hospital Affiliates International, there were certain adjustments necessary regarding titles and positions. Several persons became disgruntled and operated at half speed until they found other jobs outside HCA.

Because of the demoralization that almost inevitably occurs when demotions are made, one should consider terminating without prejudice the person who might be demoted and extending whatever assistance can be given in the search for a new job elsewhere.

Transfers

"A transfer involves shifting an individual to another job, at the same grade level, as determined by job evaluation."[15] Transfer procedures can be very specific, and one should carry them out fully but with some sensitivity. A transfer, like a demotion, can be demoralizing when not desired by the transferee.

To effect the transfer, all steps in establishing any person in a new position must be observed, including delegations, assignments, agreements about job description content, etc.

Separations

Separations include layoffs, resignations, firings, retirements, and deaths. Because uncomfortable situations occur almost invariably with layoffs and firings and even occasionally with resignations and retirements, procedures should be well defined and carried out in the prescribed manner (tempered with good judgment). Being sensitive to the feelings of the affected person is of considerable importance.

We will not dwell at length upon any of the kinds of separation, but we will offer some brief comments on firings. Line managers, rather than staff personnel, should consummate a firing. We have had, as line managers, considerable success in consummating firings, and we have generally adopted the procedure described below:

1. Confront the employee directly and in an unemotional, businesslike manner about the purported dereliction, with a nonaffected subordinate present. Listen carefully to the employee's rebuttal, if one is made. Clearly make the point that corrections must be made or termination will result. Close the conference with an agreement about the corrections and set a date for reviewing whether or not they have occurred.

2. At the next conference, in a similar setting, review whether or not the corrections have been made as agreed upon. Assuming they haven't, one must face whether to give additional time for them. In most instances, we have given additional time, but less than after the first conference. We add the proviso that at the next conference, if corrections have not been made, the person should bring a resignation along, for termination will be certain.

3. At the next conference, assuming corrections have not been made and that the person does not bring along a resignation, make the termination then and there. Strangely, several people have come very near to apologizing to us at this time. This is because we stated that their actions were reflecting on our own reputation and credibility and to tolerate the continued derelictions would jeopardize our own positions—all of which was true.

In matters involving confessed or proven moral turpitude, we have several times made peremptory firings; these were easy to do and were usually completely accepted by the parties involved.

In firings, emotions must be put aside. We have, as noted, sometimes assumed the posture of the aggrieved party. But even in these cases we "kept our cool."

Exit interviews

Exit interviews prevent many ill-advised company-initiated separations, for managers know the separated employee will "spill the beans" (if there are any to be spilled). This, however, is not the main purpose, which instead is to allow the exiting employee to divulge to someone in the personnel department any information that might be useful in preventing other employees from quitting in the future. Exit interviews also promote goodwill, for they allow those leaving an opportunity to ventilate their grievances without fear of reprisal.

An exit interview should follow a structured format and the comments of the person interviewed should be recorded. Results of the interview ought to be copied and provided to the employee's immediate superior and to the immediate superior of the person conducting the interview; a copy should also be put in the file of the exiting employee. Further pursuit of the matter is left largely to the interviewer's superior.

Compensation (including incentives); employee benefits and services

Compensation (including incentives)

Modern compensation policy appears to be roughly the same in many organizations. Our literature review showed that the opinions of Steers, Ungson, and Mowday essentially represent the current consensus. These authors call attention to two separate dimensions of equity. "*External equity* is maintained when compensation is comparable to that employees might earn in other organizations by performing the same work."[16] To determine what that compensation is, personnel departments conduct surveys and investigations concerning salary levels in other organizations. *Internal equity* involves decisions "about the value of specific jobs to an organization and the relative compensation to be offered employees in different positions."[17]

In most cases, a modern organization, in order to determine the value of specific jobs relative to others inside and outside of the organization, will institute a job evaluation program, which according to Metzger has the following eight basic steps:

1. Agree on the objectives to be maintained and the job to be covered.

2. Select a job evaluation committee and the type of evaluation to be used.

3. Conduct a job analysis.

4. Convert the job analysis into a usable form.

5. Perform the evaluation.

6. Make a wage survey in the industry and in the community.

7. Assign rates to each job.

8. Maintain the job evaluation program.[18]

Steers, Ungson, and Mowday have called attention to the concept of *comparable worth*. This concept "suggests that comparisons between *different* jobs are important. Comparable worth reflects the contributions of different jobs to the organization and suggests that equal wages be paid to men and women [and minority members] performing tasks of equal value."[19] We might comment that most business firms find avoiding the implementation of this concept to be very difficult, owing to the presence of unions and pervasive government regulations.

Incentive pay involves tying raises to higher levels of productivity, evidenced either in the form of bottom-line profits, items produced, sales made, tasks performed, etc. Incentive pay most often is geared to some type of quantification, but quality may also be taken into account by the plan that is adopted.

Bonuses are sums of money given in addition to wages, usually as a gift from the employer. Such gifts may be based on performance. Strictly speaking, a bonus, as opposed to incentive pay, is awarded without the recipient knowing ahead of time.

Compensation includes myriad factors, possibilities, and aspects about which volumes have been written. We have only mentioned a few key points so as to set the stage for our brief comments on implementation.

Assuming a compensation program has been properly planned and procedures devised, how can it be successfully implemented?

1. All managers, and especially executives, must be knowledgeable about and support the program. The personnel department has the responsibility for orientation. To help accomplish this, a copy of the

wage program, together with the Job Evaluation Manual and pertinent job description, should be placed in the hands of all managers.[20]

2. The program should be administered uniformly throughout the organization, and deviations from the program should be a matter for separate policy provisions. For example, long-time seniority at the same position (often a "dead-end" position) might require such provisions.[21]

3. There should be a designated contact in the personnel department whom managers (and those referred by managers) can direct inquiries to and who will provide explanations.

4. The program, including job descriptions, job analyses, the Job Evaluation Manual, wage surveys, etc., must be kept up to date.[22] Implementation problems invariably arise when personnel departments fail to keep the information current.

5. The personnel division having responsibility for creating and maintaining a compensation program and must follow a schedule for accomplishing all facets of its work. Otherwise, the program will become outdated, thus allowing employees to be lost to competing firms.

6. The personnel department ought to query line managers from time to time about problems they encounter. Awareness of problems allows the development of solutions.

7. The department or division maintaining the compensation program must be well organized internally and work as a team. Authority, responsibility, and accountability should be properly placed and explicitly set out in the job description for each staff member.

8. Prepare appraisals of performance independently of any action to be taken (e.g., merit raises, promotions, etc.). Otherwise, performance appraisals will merely become justifications for actions already decided on subjectively.[23]

9. In large companies where authority for administration of a compensation program has been delegated and responsibility assigned to a number of division or department heads, audit and control measures must be carried out to assure that those managers properly implement the program.[24] Otherwise, unjustified deviations will occur.

10. Compensation in the form of monetary pay (and other benefits) will not by itself be an adequate response to the needs of employees. The absence of other satisfiers may cause employees to readily express dissatisfaction with compensation. Thus, even though a compensation program may be fair and in many other ways admirable, managers should administer it in combination with other need satisfiers, such as opportunities for socialization, recognition of accomplishments, personal control of the work environment, etc. This is impor-

tant under all wage options, but especially those not based on pay incentives.

11. In wage incentive systems, the manager's role changes. Rather than concentrating attention solely on employee motivation, a manager must also be concerned with providing optimal conditions for maximum productivity and not "stand in the way" of an employee's attaining maximum earnings.[25]

12. When changes are made in a compensation program, resistance to them will usually occur. Realizing this, sensitive managers assure that those affected will receive a complete orientation and be given personal explanations.

Employee benefits and services

Benefits. Scheer cites this definition of employee benefits: "Anything which benefits the employee directly or indirectly in the form of extra income or services in excess of established straight-line earnings, whether required by law or not."[26] If one excludes certain things an employer may provide employees for their enjoyment, convenience, or general edification, we agree with that definition.

Many authorities do not distinguish benefits and services and most do not differentiate them clearly. Some call a specific provision for employees a benefit and others call the same provision a service. We believe, however, a benefit involves the provision of something material, whereas a service does not (although of course morale may be improved, enjoyment and convenience increased, or education enhanced). Benefits are provided to employees individually, usually according to a well-defined plan. Services are provided uniformly and may, without prejudice, be accepted or rejected. Benefits constitute a part of a total compensation package; services usually do not.

Miner and Miner note that benefits "are not intended to encourage task motivation. Little effort has been made to use fringe benefits as inducements or rewards, with a view to maximizing the effectiveness of role behavior . . . benefits may be used as an inducement to continued organizational membership. A further objective . . . is that such benefits are a valuable asset in recruiting potentially effective employees."[27]

The benefits usually valued most by employees fall into four categories: (1) direct payments of money or paid time off; (2) various types of insurance, paid for by the employer; (3) retirement and disability pension provisions, sponsored and paid for by the employer; and (4) certain personal services required by the employee which have material value and are provided by the employer.

The concept of a *compensation package* for employees includes benefits, and many employees make decisions about employment based on the value of benefits (assuming monetary remuneration among area employers is roughly equal). Thus, implementation of a compensation program covers the award of benefits. (See previous section for 12 points concerning implementation of a compensation program.)

Where the compensation package includes a number of benefits, as often is the case, employees and prospective employees will be more satisfied with the program if quality of benefits is high. Thus, implementation is enhanced where the personnel department has a person dedicated to evaluating, costing, and overseeing the administration of benefits. For example, many types of medical and hospitalization insurance coverages exist, and costs range widely. A selection process is required, and the decisions that must be reached do not come easily. Careful evaluations of costs and efforts to assure efficiency in administration of the program will almost certainly have to be done by the personnel department. After benefits have been selected and implemented, the department will also have the responsibility of monitoring satisfaction.

Services. Services include such things as an onsite library, a cafeteria, recreational facilities, a medical clinic, child care facilities, etc. Many such services reflect decisions made by top management (including the top personnel executive). However, their administration (implementation) may be the responsibility, not of the personnel department, but of a line department manager or of another staff department, such as supply or logistical support. In any case, such implementation involves an operation such as that found in independent businesses of a similar character. Proper organization, including delegations of authority and assignments of responsibility and accountability, assumes great importance, together with other factors discussed in Chapter 12.

Training and development

As noted in Chapter 7, *training* refers to the teaching of skills and abilities. It may, as Stoner believes, apply primarily to nonmanagerial personnel.[28] *Development* refers to instruction that is intended as preparation for employee promotion (see Chapter 7). Stoner notes that management development should be regarded as consisting of "programs that attempt to improve the technical, human relations, and conceptual skills of managers."[29]

Regardless of exact meanings of the terms, we regard training and development programs very highly. Not only do companies receive benefits from the rising level of skills and abilities, but those enrolled in such programs are more dedicated to task accomplishment and exhibit better morale. (We have found no valid research proving increased levels of morale, but based on close observations of our own employees over the years, we believe morale is improved.)

Training and development programs should accurately focus on specific areas where increased skills and abilities would prove useful to the sponsoring firm. Although line managers can arrange on-the-job training to be given to both junior managers and technically skilled operational personnel, classroom instruction by staff personnel is usually a required supplement. With respect to hospitals, for example, we regard an institution as having no program of in-service education unless there exists formal classroom instruction. We have also observed that programs organized and carried forward by line personnel, in addition to their other duties, tend to fail. Simply, training and development tend not to receive the attention necessary for success. An ideal program has staff teachers periodically giving pertinent classroom instruction that is coordinated with the work being done by employees at their worksites.

Many companies sponsor programs of job rotation. For example, in small hospitals, laboratory and radiological technicians may be cross trained so that night call duties can be rotated. Small business companies sponsor job rotations of similar kinds.

Apprenticeship training has an ancient history. In apprenticeship, a skilled worker takes a student worker and imparts certain skills during the course of work. Many universities have used the residency or internship approach to complete formal requirements for degree programs. Business firms cooperate in these programs and sometimes independently sponsor similar programs.

When a business rapidly expands, there usually arises a need to change some skilled operational personnel who "know the business" into managers. In many instances, such personnel have no inkling of the basics of management and often perform poorly. At the very least, some organized instruction in the elements of supervision and the necessary management procedures must be provided. Just recently, on a consulting engagement, one of us encountered such a situation. The new managers stated, "We managed to survive, but for three months we just floundered around and learned by the mistakes we made." Thus, lack of a properly focused management development program can sometimes cause serious problems.

Advancing technology has caused many companies to undertake retraining programs. Government has assumed some responsibility in resolving problems related to laid off workers with obsolete skills. One of the sad things is the number of middle-aged people who must be completely retrained to find employment. But one should also remember the problems of top managers who struggle to retrofit an entire enterprise so as to keep pace with new companies, both here and abroad. Problems abound at every level of many aging companies, and retraining—by a variety of means—must be carefully planned and vigorously implemented.

Both staff and line personnel have to be intimately involved with training and development. Most of the time, staff personnel engaged in such programs will have had courses in education (how to teach) and they will understand how individuals learn and how instruction can best be carried out in most situations to facilitate learning. But many line managers will have had no formal courses in education. Perhaps the most fruitful strategy to use at the initiation of any training or development program is to give some instruction on recognized techniques of effective teaching to all who will be involved.

Very large firms send promising young managers through management development programs that are offered at some of our major universities. For example, in the early years of his brilliant career, Harold Geneen attended such a program at Harvard. We have a high regard for these programs, and recommend them especially for managers who have already demonstrated the toughness and intelligence needed to rise from the bottom ranks to middle management.

After assessing the many training and development programs we have either sponsored or observed over the years, we concluded that the most effective exhibited the following characteristics:

1. There was a correlation between, on the one hand, student needs and aptitudes and, on the other, training or development course materials.

2. The qualifications of the instructors, both their skills and abilities as teachers and their technical knowledge, was high.

3. There was meaningful involvement and helpful supervision at the workplace.

4. Classroom instruction, using relevant textual materials, was provided in addition to on-the-job training.

5. Recognition or some other reward for successful completion of the program was given.

Research

Yoder defined research as being "purposive, systematic investigation, designed to test carefully considered hypotheses or answer thoughtfully framed questions."[30] Many personnel departments investigate personnel-related problems, but often in a loosely structured manner that may or may not produce valid answers. Except in the very largest firms, little highly structured personnel research occurs.

Assuming for the moment that a company's policy is that personnel-related research will be undertaken by the personnel department, the problem of implementation must receive consideration when a question arises requiring systematic investigation. Following are several guidelines personnel executives may wish to observe in undertaking research:

1. Authority to conduct research should be delegated and responsibility and accountability assigned to one specialist who will perform within guidelines concerning staff, budget, and time (even though the guidelines may not be rigid).

2. The person assigned the research ought to have a background as a researcher, unless the question posed can be definitively answered by techniques of simple descriptive statistics. Persons unskilled in research tend to frame questions or hypotheses for investigation so broadly as to defy data accumulation of sufficient scope and validity to produce answers that are reliable or valid.

3. The researcher should submit to the assigning executive a synopsis of the intended research process and a model of the report he or she intends to render upon completion of the investigation. This not only informs the executive but forces the researcher to think carefully about the research methodology. Executives should be mindful that research in social relations can sometimes be offensive, both in the investigative processes and in the reporting.

4. The nature and frequency of progress reports and the time required for completion should be agreed upon at the outset.

5. Findings of most research had best remain confidential until the assigning executive chooses to release appropriate information. On a few occasions we have observed that the assigning executive was literally among the last to be informed of the research results.

The above provides only a smattering of information about research. Although executives cannot be expected to be skilled in every technical function undertaken by an enterprise, many are especially uninformed about bona fide research. They should at least briefly explore the field prior to spending perhaps as much as hundreds of thousands of dollars on what may be a very nebulous project.

Employee communications

Employee communications include company-sponsored publications of a wide variety, e.g., printed manuals and broadcasts by electronic and other media. Smaller firms generally publish a simple employee newsletter and little else. Very large firms may use a variety of means to channel desired information to personnel. In most instances, responsibility for employee communications devolves on the personnel department.

In Exhibit 7-2, we placed employee communications in an industrial relations division of the department, but in nonunionized firms where no such division exists, this function could be placed in an employee services division.

Preferably, a person with a major in journalism should have responsibility for this function. Implementation aspects include those we discussed in Chapter 12.

The following guideline ought to be given the person in charge of this function: Potentially controversial matters require approval from the assigning executive prior to reporting. A guideline for the assigning executive is this: Company-related information that will inevitably circulate via the grapevine should seldom be banned from publication.

Performance evaluations

As organizations grow, need for fair, objective evaluations becomes apparent. To assure justness and fairness and to convince employees that the evaluations are just and fair, management must seek a valid and reliable system of appraising the performance of individual employees. That a perfect system for performance evaluation of individuals within specific employment categories has not as yet been devised does not relieve management from the duty to strive to plan and implement a system that has both objectivity and validity. Scheer has well noted,

> Performance rating is useful in any personnel action, but should be done independent of the action taken. To be effective, it should be done when nothing is at stake, then referred to when some action is called for. To be fair and impartial, and thereby meaningful, it should not be done in connection with a salary increase, promotion, discharge and the like. Done at a time when the employee is under consideration for some action, the rating becomes window dressing to support the recommendation.[31]

Exhibited personal characteristics formed the bases for the oldest methods of appraising effectiveness on the job. Because of the considerable risk of bias by raters, however, methods increasingly focus on evaluating performance in terms of results achieved. Especially since the advent of MBO has the achievement of objectives been used as a basis for formal appraisal. Managers thereby become able to focus on possibly more accurate measurements of results rather than on personality traits, and they thus avoid embarrassing, subjective discussion points during performance appraisal interviews. Even so, imperfections remain, because an individual's effort often cannot be accurately determined in situations involving team effort.

Stoner has noted four ways organizations perform appraisals:[32]

1. using a superior to rate subordinates

2. using a group of superiors to rate subordinates

3. using a group of peers to rate a colleague

4. using subordinates to rate superiors (used rarely in business organizations).

For operational personnel, managers still primarily rely on the first way. Many organizations rely on the second for rating junior managers, and some rely on the third for appraising managers at upper levels.

We know of one consulting firm that uses a combination of self-evaluation and evaluation by respective superiors on each consulting assignment.[33] The superior discusses his or her evaluation of the subordinate's work with the subordinate, and the two forms are then conjoined and placed in the subordinate's personnel file, possibly to be reviewed if and when a promotion or raise is placed under consideration. The self-evaluation forces the subordinate to appraise objectively his or her own performance and to try on the next assignment to improve it. This approach also allows the subordinate to compare the self-evaluation with the evaluation of others. Although subjectivity still is a problem, this approach seems to be effective as a motivator of performance improvement. (See Exhibit 13-2.)

Using material presented by Porter, Lawler, and Hackman in *Behavior in Organizations*, Steers, Ungson, and Mowday consider performance evaluation approaches involving (1) comparisons of employees with others in some scheme of ranking and (2) ratings according to various types of scales.[34] The first approach corresponds roughly to "grading on the curve," a technique used in some schools. The second approach uses absolute standards and offers considerable opportunity for objectivity but no guarantee of it.

Regardless of the type of evaluation approach employed and the type of form used to record ratings (and there are a plethora of both), the entire system should culminate in scheduled periodic interviews (held at least once a year) between a superior and a subordinate. These interviews provide an opportunity to extend congratulations on progress and suggest areas for improvement in performance. Each interview should be cordial and should focus on performance rather than on personality traits. Thirty minutes is usually ample, though less or more may be used in individual instances. The superior ought to place a brief factual account of the interview in the subordinate's personnel file.

Exhibit 13-2

Example Form for Performance Review

ERNST & WHINNEY
PERFORMANCE REVIEW FORM

Mcs Staff

Staff member_____ Self-Review □   Yes □   No □

Intern □   Staff □   Advanced Staff □   Senior □   Supervisor □   Manager □

Date of promotion to current staff classification _____

On this
Engagement from _____ to _____
Client _____ Approximate Hours _____

Reviewed by _____ Date Prepared _____

Give a general description of the assignment, including the degree of difficulty, and the type of work performed by this person:

_____
_____
_____

Provide supplemental comments on performance in each of the four major areas:

Technical
_____
_____
_____

Administrative and Supervisory
_____
_____
_____

Client Relations and Development
_____
_____
_____

Personal and Professional
_____
_____

P53 (11/79) Printed in U.S.A.

If this person were assigned to a similar engagement for you, would you assign him or her more advanced work?

Yes___ No___ Explain _____
_____

Other comments (include comments on special circumstances which might have affected performance and other matters which might help in this person's development):

_____
_____
_____
_____
_____
_____

Does this person understand and follow the ethics of the profession and the policies of the firm? Yes___ No___

If no, explain the circumstances and what corrective actions have been taken. _____

This review was discussed with the individual on _____   Date _____

Instructions

1. The performance review is to serve as a summary of the performance of a professional staff member and is the basis of the Staff Development System.

2. A performance review should be completed for each person who works for 80 or more hours on an assignment. In addition, reviews may be prepared on other assignments considered significant, groups of assignments, or time periods.

3. Review forms are to be prepared independently by both the individual and his or her superior on the assignment.

4. The summary evaluation line at the end of each major area should represent your overall evaluation in that area. This overall evaluation should be expressed by a single checkmark in the appropriate column.

5. Written comments should be included for each of the requested items.

6. Review forms should be completed and discussed with the individual at the completion of the individual's work on the assignment and then turned in to the SDS coordinator.

7. Separate performance review forms are available for audit, tax, mcs and administrative.

PERFORMANCE REVIEW — MANAGEMENT CONSULTING SERVICES

Following is the level of performance of this person observed on this assignment, relative to the performance expected of most persons with experience in this staff classification similar to that of the reviewer, and considering the difficulty of this assignment and any other factors you consider pertinent:

		Performance	
Not Applicable	Less Than Expected	Expected	Better Than Expected

Technical Performance

1. Performed assigned functions without an unusual degree of supervision and assistance.
2. Communicated ideas and information both orally and in writing.
3. Produced appropriate working papers, reports, proposals, or letters.
4. Understood how his or her assigned tasks were related to the overall assignment objectives.
5. Knew current developments in his or her field and applied them to the assignment.
6. Used imagination and creativity when seeking solutions to problems.
7. Diagnosed client's problems and proposed appropriate solutions.
8. Demonstrated an objective point of view.

Summary of Technical Performance

Administrative and Supervisory

9. Planned his or her own work, and the work of assigned staff where applicable, in appropriate priorities and sequences.
10. Controlled his or her own work, and the work of assigned staff where applicable, so that it was completed in an appropriate time.
11. Kept superiors, and client service executive where appropriate, informed on the status of work for which he or she was responsible.
12. Completed assigned work and wrapped up loose ends.
13. Assessed the capabilities of assigned staff and provided needed guidance and information. (Not applicable for staff)
14. Provided climate for high level of motivation for assigned staff. (Not applicable for staff)
15. Reviewed staff performance and communicated needed improvements. (Not applicable for staff)

Summary of Administrative and Supervisory

P33 (11/79B) Printed in U.S.A.

PERFORMANCE REVIEW — MANAGEMENT CONSULTING SERVICES

		Performance	
Not Applicable	Less Than Expected	Expected	Better Than Expected

Client Relations and Development

16. Obtained the cooperation of client personnel, assured client understanding of the nature of the work to be performed by client personnel, and worked closely with client personnel assigned to the engagement.
17. Established and maintained effective contacts with appropriate client personnel and others.
18. Was knowledgeable of the professional capabilities of E&W and related these to the client's needs.
19. Kept abreast of client service opportunities through meetings and discussions with client personnel and E&W executives.
20. Demonstrated ability to present and sell ideas.

Summary of Client Relations and Development

Personal and Professional

21. Inspired confidence and respect from associates and the client.
22. Assumed responsibility for his or her work.
23. Demonstrated maturity and sound business judgment.
24. Used tact in relationships with associates and client.
25. Demonstrated a positive attitude toward our firm and our profession.

Summary of Personal and Professional

Source: Reprinted by permission of Ernst & Whinney's Chicago office.

Grievance handling

A grievance occurs when an employee formally expresses dissatisfaction caused by a perception of having been wronged in connection with some company matter. Where a union contract exists, fairly specific guidelines define what constitutes a grievance and set out a resolving process. In nonunion firms, grievance procedures are less likely to be definitively outlined, but most major firms do now have such procedures in force.

Where a union contract exists, a manager has no choice but to follow the agreed upon procedure, and usually avoidance of any deviations is the wisest course of action. Managers should also avoid displays of anger or ridicule and other emotional excesses. When the grievance procedure has been fully implemented and a settlement made (possibly by an arbitrator), managers should again "play it cool" and be truly statesman-like. If management "loses," a show of retaliation would be undesirable, but managers should not hesitate to continue exercising perceived rights under the contract.

If no union contract exists but the company possesses grievance procedures, the attitudes of involved managers play a key role in the implementation of procedures. Here again, emotional displays must be avoided and a calm problem-solving attitude exhibited. Usually the following steps should be implemented:

1. *Receive and record the expressed grievance.* During this first step, the manager should attempt resolution and treat the complainant fairly and with respect. Careful listening usually allows true understanding of the problem. The manager must remember it is not his or her responsibility to define the problem; putting words into an employee's mouth should be avoided. However, the manager should be certain the aggrieved employee agrees with the recorded definition.

2. *Ascertain the relevant facts.* Decisions made on the basis of provable facts are to be preferred. In some instances, this may not be possible, and managers then may rely on the hearsay of responsible persons. In any event, truthfulness is of paramount importance. A thorough, honest recording of relevant facts in the form of "completed staff work" is the objective.

3. *Render a decision.* The manager, on the basis of his or her investigation, should confer and negotiate with the employee. The decision reached by the manager and its rationale ought to be carefully explained. Fairness requires giving the employee ample opportunity to rebut, and the manager should accurately record rebutting remarks. Maintaining a relaxed, cordial atmosphere best facilitates settlement. If a settlement cannot be reached, the employee should be told whom the matter will be referred to as well as the time and place of the next conference. However, Van D. Kennedy has well noted that "the overwhelming majority of grievances can and shall be informally adjusted and disposed of at the foreman-steward [lowest management] level."[35]

4. *Finalize the resolution.* Formal procedures usually move decisions on grievance settlements (in steps known to employees) up to top executive levels, depending on the size of the organization. But until it

reaches the level at which the organization says, "This is our response, and it is final," the whole matter should be handled in a businesslike manner, tempered with cordiality. Even if the aggrieved employee receives absolutely nothing else in response to the grievance, respectful treatment gives some satisfaction and proves the decency of management.

Throughout the entire handling of a grievance, managers ought to act both fairly and in the interests of the company. Usually, protecting company interests will best be done by striving to settle grievances in a just and equitable manner.

If the grievance cannot be settled by management, unionized and some nonunionized firms incorporate arbitration into the settlement process. When a grievance ends in arbitration, management presents its case by a previously prescribed method. Whatever the decision of the arbitrators, emotional displays should be avoided by management. Of course, the exercise of its rights always remains management's prerogative and has no necessary relationship to displaying emotions or not.

Miscellaneous

Personnel staff frequently develop plans of organization or reorganization under policies or directives laid down by top management. In fact, consideration of reorganizations and realignments of organizational elements of HCA has been ongoing within the personnel department.

The prime point to remember here (other than the usual requisites for getting work accomplished) is that the plans submitted for implementation should be as complete and detailed as possible. Many seemingly wonderful organizational plans fall apart when consideration of details is undertaken. Few executives wish to approve a half-baked plan of reorganization and in implementation find it contains several concealed flaws that render it unworkable or even a serious embarrassment. Periodic reporting of progress is desirable, and when approval is requested for a specific plan, it should be complete in all its aspects.

The personnel department often receives assignments of other miscellaneous work, but these usually have a one-time-through plan that can be implemented by the methods described in Chapter 12.

Summary

Implementing human resource planning involves implementing the range of plans outlined in Chapter 7. In this chapter, we discussed the following implementing activities:

1. implementation of a human resource philosophy

2. implementing policies related to the personnel department

   • role of the department

   • grouping personnel functions

   • achieving the purposes and benefits of policies

3. implementing personnel policies

   - responsibility

   - effecting implementation

4. accomplishing major personnel department activities

   - government compliance activities

   - labor relations

   - forecasting and programming human resource needs

   - recruitment, selection, induction, and orientation

   - promotions, demotions, transfers, and separations

   - compensation (including incentives) and employee benefits and services

   - training and development

   - research

   - employee communications

   - performance evaluations

   - grievance handling

   - miscellaneous

Generally, implementation of all functions performed by the personnel department involves the various aspects of effecting organizational work discussed in Chapter 12. Readers should carefully review the suggestions set forth there. Of course, study of Chapter 7 ("Human Resource Planning") is a prerequisite for full appreciation of this chapter ("Implementing Human Resource Planning").

In this chapter, we merely attempted to point out certain unique aspects of implementing each type of human resource planning and thus supplement our discussion of effecting organizational work in Chapter 12. Of course, the range of duties assigned to personnel departments throughout the nation are extremely broad, and several options usually exist for accomplishing facets of various tasks. Considering this, we know our readers must refer to other works for full understanding of both the planning and implementing work inherent in human resource management. We only hope we have ordered our presentation in a way that will facilitate further study.

Notes

1. Wilbert E. Scheer, *Personnel Administration Handbook*, 2d ed. (Chicago: Dartnell Press, 1979), 30.

2. James A.F. Stoner, *Management*, 2d ed. (1982), 473. Reprinted by permission of Prentice-Hall, Inc., Englewood Cliffs, N.J.

3. Ibid., 474. Reprinted by permission of Prentice-Hall, Inc., Englewood Cliffs, N.J.

4. Scheer, *Personnel Administration Handbook*, 1.

5. Edwin B. Flipp, *Principles of Personnel Management*, 2d ed. (New York: McGraw-Hill, 1966), 67.

6. John B. Miner and Mary Green Miner, *Personnel and Industrial Relations* (New York: Macmillan, 1977), 477.

7. Ibid., 484.

8. Ibid., 490.

9. Scheer, *Personnel Administration Handbook*, 840.

10. Miner and Miner, *Personal and Industrial Relations*, 502.

11. Richard M. Steers, Gerardo R. Ungson, and Richard T. Mowday, *Managing Effective Organizations* (Boston: Kent Publishing Company, 1985), 457.

12. Ibid., 459.

13. Scheer, *Personnel Administration Handbook*, 159–60.

14. Comments made to Owen B. Hardy, circa 1959.

15. Miner and Miner, *Personnel and Industrial Relations*, 461.

16. Steers, Ungson, and Mowday, *Managing Effective Organizations*, 473.

17. Ibid., 474.

18. Norman Metzger, *Personnel Administration in the Health Care Industry*, 2d ed. (New York: SP Medical and Scientific Books, 1979), 63–64.

19. Steers, Ungson, and Mowday, *Managing Effective Organizations*, 474.

20. Scheer, *Personnel Administration Handbook*, 664.

21. Ibid.

22. Ibid.

23. Ibid., 618.

24. Randolph S. Driver, "Wage and Salary Administration," in *Handbook of Business Administration*, ed. H.B. Maynard (New York: McGraw-Hill, 1967), 11-105.

25. H.B. Lawson, "Wage Systems," in *Handbook of Business Administration*, ed. H.B. Maynard (New York: McGraw-Hill, 1967), 11-159.

26. Scheer, *Personnel Administration Handbook*, 714.

27. Miner and Miner, *Personnel and Industrial Relations*, 516.

28. Stoner, *Management*, 542.

29. Ibid. Reprinted by permission of Prentice-Hall, Inc., Englewood Cliffs, N.J.

30. Dale Yoder, *Personnel Management and Industrial Relations*, 5th ed. (Englewood Cliffs, N.J.: Prentice-Hall, 1962), 585.

31. Scheer, *Personnel Administration Handbook*, 688.

32. Stoner, *Management*, 547–48.

33. The firm is Ernst & Whinney.

34. Steers, Ungson, and Mowday, *Managing Effective Organizations*, 472; citing L.W. Porter, F.E. Lawler, and J.R. Hackman, *Behavior in Organizations* (New York: McGraw-Hill, 1975).

35. Metzger, *Personnel Administration*, 263; citing Van D. Kennedy, *Principles of Grievance Adjustment*.

Chapter 14

Coordination

Elements of Management
in Corporations

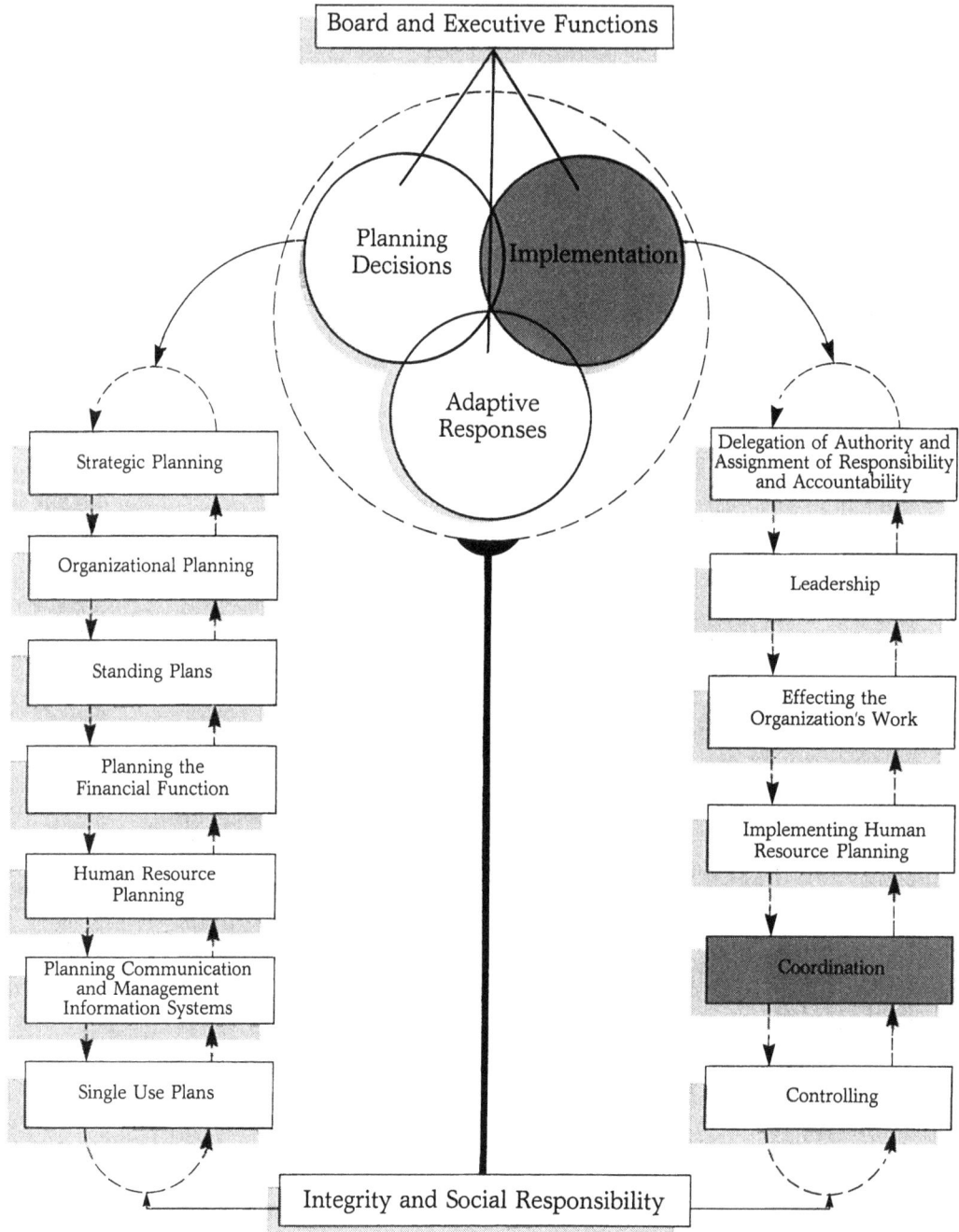

Board and Executive Functions

Planning
Decisions

Implementation

Adaptive
Responses

Strategic Planning

Organizational Planning

Standing Plans

Planning the
Financial Function

Human Resource
Planning

Planning Communication
and Management
Information Systems

Single Use Plans

Delegation of Authority and
Assignment of Responsibility
and Accountability

Leadership

Effecting the
Organization's Work

Implementing Human
Resource Planning

Coordination

Controlling

Integrity and Social Responsibility

14

Background

Mary Parker Follett's famous words about coordination are just as applicable today as they were when she wrote them many years ago.

> For a business to be a going concern, it must be unified. The fair test of business administration, of industrial organization is whether you have a business with all of its parts so coordinated, so moving together in their closely knit and adjusting activities, so linking, interlocking, interrelating that they make a working unit, not a congeries of separate pieces. . . . The efficiency of many plants is lowered by an imperfectly worked out system of coordination. In some cases all the coordination there is depends on the degree of friendliness existing between the heads of departments, or whether they are willing to consult; sometimes it depends on the mere chance of two men coming up to town on the same train every morning.[1]

Although managers, on the whole, know more about coordination and how to attain it than they did in Follett's day, there has also been an increasing need for it. This need is largely the result of the increasing specialization required by the greater complexity of skills, the growth in complexity and size of enterprises, and the demand for greater efficiency and productivity. These factors and others now operative worldwide will undoubtedly lead to failure or at least second-rate status for many poorly coordinated business firms.

Inexplicably, many management authorities largely ignore coordination. Others seem to confuse it with cooperation (which is similar but distinct). Still others mention it only as a function of organizing. However, those who have produced the body of "classic" management literature and have devoted their attention to the whole of management clearly have believed that coordination is a basic element of management. Without it, no large organization could exist, and most small ones (even those with only three or four employees) discover it is a requisite for total success.

Church and Alford, writing in 1912, stated, "The coordination of effort is an inseparable counterpart of the division of effort. By coordination is meant the pre-arrangement of a number of separate efforts in such a manner as to produce a definite end."[2]

Fayol, in his famous pioneering text *General and Industrial Management*, lists coordination as one of five elements of management, the others being planning, organizing, command (directing), and control. About coordination, Fayol wrote the following:

> To coordinate is to harmonize all the activities of a concern so as to facilitate its working, and its success. It is giving to the material and social, functional, organic whole such proportions as are suitable to enable it to play its part assuredly and economically. It is to bear in mind in any activity whatsoever, technical, commercial, financial or other, the obligations and consequences such action involves for all the functions of the business. It is to keep expenditure proportionate to financial resources, equipment and tools to production needs, stocks to rate of consumption, sales to production. It is to build the house neither too small nor too big, adapt the tool to its use, the road to the vehicle, the safety precautions to the risks. It is to relegate the secondary to second place after the principal. It is, in a word, to accord things and actions their rightful proportions, and to adapt means to end.
>
> In a well co-ordinated enterprise the following facts are to be observed—
>
> 1. Each department works in harmony with the rest. . . .
>
> 2. In each department, divisions and sub-divisions are precisely informed as to the share they must take in the communal task and the reciprocal aid they are to afford one another.
>
> 3. The working schedule of the various departments and sub-divisions thereof is constantly attuned to circumstances.[3]

Turning to the reasons why coordination fails in some organizations, Fayol penned words which seem to describe conditions existing in many enterprises today.

> 1. Each department knows and wants to know nothing of the others. It operates as if it were its own aim and end, without bothering either about neighbouring departments or the business as a whole.
>
> 2. Water-tight compartments exist between the divisions and offices of the same department as they do also between different departments. Each one's prime concern is to take cover from personal responsibility behind a piece of paper, an order or a circular letter.
>
> 3. No one thinks of the general interest; initiatve and loyalty are nonexistent.
>
> This attitude on the part of the personnel, so disastrous for the concern, is not the result of preconcerted intention but the culmination of nonexistent or inadequate co-ordination.[4]

In the 1940s, James Mooney defined coordination as "the orderly arrangement of group effort, to provide unity of action in the pursuit of a common purpose," and he listed it as one of the principles of organization.[5] In the 1960s, Ernest Dale stated that coordination is actually part of organizing rather than a separate function. With reference to organizing, he wrote,

> The objectives and the work that will be necessary to attain them dictate the skills that will be needed. In organizing, the manager decides on the positions to be filled and on the duties and responsibilities attaching to each one. But the work done by the members of the organization will necessarily be interrelated; hence some means of coordinating their efforts must be provided. Coordination is, in fact, an essential part of organization rather than, as Gulick (and many others) suggested, a function in itself.[6]

We partly agree with Dale, but coordinating reaches far beyond organizing. Although planning for coordination starts with organizational planning, its implementation involves leadership, basic cooperation, good communications (which Dale subsumes under directing), and day-to-day managerial directing, supervision, influencing, use of authority and power, and controlling.

In the 1980s, Stoner, seemingly influenced by Dale, stated that coordination was part of organizing, but then discussed it as if it were an independent function. However, Stoner did not note the vital role of voluntary cooperation and coordination in unifying organizational actions, and he presented only the mechanistic or structural aspects of coordination.[7]

Definition

The several comments quoted above in definition of coordination seem satisfactory in whole or in part, but here we give our own definition:

> *Coordination is the orchestrating of the activities of a person or a group of persons with the activities of others so as to achieve common organizational objectives through team play. Coordination within an organizational hierarchy must occur both vertically and horizontally, and usually it must be done according to some sequencing of the tasks to be carried out.*

Indirectly, coordination also implies a balance and rhythm among the functioning parts of a whole.

Role of specialization

The advent of specialization drew the need for coordination of work efforts into focus. In *The Wealth of Nations*, Adam Smith set forth an often-quoted account of the advantages of specialization by describing the manufacture of pins. Smith wrote, "One man draws the wire, another straights it, a third cuts it, a fourth points it, a fifth grinds it at the top for receiving the head. . . ." By specializing in this manner, ten men could produce 48,000 pins a day, whereas each man working by himself might have been able to produce 20 pins a day.[8] The principle cited by Smith, i.e., breaking down production jobs into separate, easily performed tasks so as to increase total productivity geometrically, has been proven and is now accepted worldwide.

The principle of specialization is at the very heart of modern civilization and it effects, in some measure, every human endeavor. The modern hospital is a perfect example of task specialization. Most hospitals have between 25 and 40 specialized departments, each performing a specialized service, and many departments have a number of branching specialized subfunctions. When one reflects on the matter, one realizes that nearly every corporate activity in the land builds on specialized activities in order to provide a better service or make a better product (and with greater efficiency).

We stress the importance of specialization in order to make the point that it is here to stay. No amount of decrying its disadvantages and its untoward psychological effects on workers will decrease it overall. Accepting this, one then has to consider (1) how best to coordinate the specialized activities inherent in a total service or production endeavor so as to achieve optimal results and (2) how to satisfy the sociological and psychological needs of those engaged in specialized tasks. The first consideration directly relates to the purpose of this chapter, and we report certain research findings and authoritative opinions regarding the second in several sections throughout this text.

Small and large groups

Where very small work groups are involved, say six to eight persons, the best approach to coordinating work efforts may be to depend largely on self-coordination. This is especially true where the activities of the group are not required to mesh precisely according to a stringent timetable. Through observations of the actions of other group members and through discussions, one member can easily "fit in" appropriately with little or no supervision, without detailed job descriptions, and with only minimal procedural directions.

In the case of larger organizations, however, management must take care to effect coordination through careful management.

Relationship to other management processes

Managers develop approaches to coordination in planning phases and carry them out in implementation. Strategic planning, organizational planning, planning for communication networks and information systems, and the construction of standing and single use plans all should take coordination into account through structured, mechanistic processes. In implementation, opportunities to coordinate occur during the process of assigning work, delegating authority, supervising, communicating, monitoring and controlling, etc. When implementing, managers should strive to achieve an extra measure of voluntary coordination among subordinates, superiors, and individuals or groups in lateral positions. Leadership techniques that elicit voluntary cooperation can be used, as can other techniques, such as applying appropriate motivational stimuli, holding group meetings to discuss how best to accomplish specific work activities, and encouraging group decision making.

We shall set forth our suggestions regarding coordination under three basic headings: (1) mechanistic means, (2) hands-on management, and (3) voluntary cooperation. We also discuss each of these at some length in other sections of this book.

Figure 14-1 presents the three groups of means of coordination ordered in a sequence that often occurs in organizations where conscientious attempts are made to achieve coordination.

Mechanistic means

Mechanistic means of coordination include those deliberately planned, structured, and made a part of organizational patterns, policies, procedures, systems, and methods.

Organizational structure

Organizational structure refers to the formal arrangement of an organization's departments and the job positions within each. As stated in Chapter 4, managers usually effect departmentation in one of four ways or in some combination thereof: by function, geographic area, product, or type of customer. Each of these ways of organizing may best facilitate coordination of work efforts in specific situations, depending on an enterprise's line or lines of business, the products made or sold, the services rendered, the availability of specialized personnel, and appropriate physical facilities. The volume of products made or services rendered, the number of personnel, and the technical complexity of operations also influence how best to organize in order to effect coordination.

Obviously, one would expect to encounter less difficulty in coordinating the work of a few employees in unskilled or semiskilled tasks than in coordinating many employees in complex tasks. Extremely large manufacturing and assembly plants, for example, have been shown to be so cumbersome that decentralization and departmentation along product lines is now an accepted way of simplifying both coordination and control.

The span of supervision in some enterprises may be a factor in determining the type of organizational structure adopted, and in some instances limits to this span may work in favor of coordination, for work units can be kept small and the number of persons whose work requires coordination can be limited.

Hospitals have been traditionally organized by function, and considering the diversification of functions and the large number of departments, coordination has been and remains a distinct problem in the care and treatment of patients. In recent years, coordination of supply functions has improved markedly through the use of a supply processing and distribution system which cuts across all functional departments and operates largely as an independent, coordinated system. Also, the

Figure 14-1

Achieving Organizational Coordination

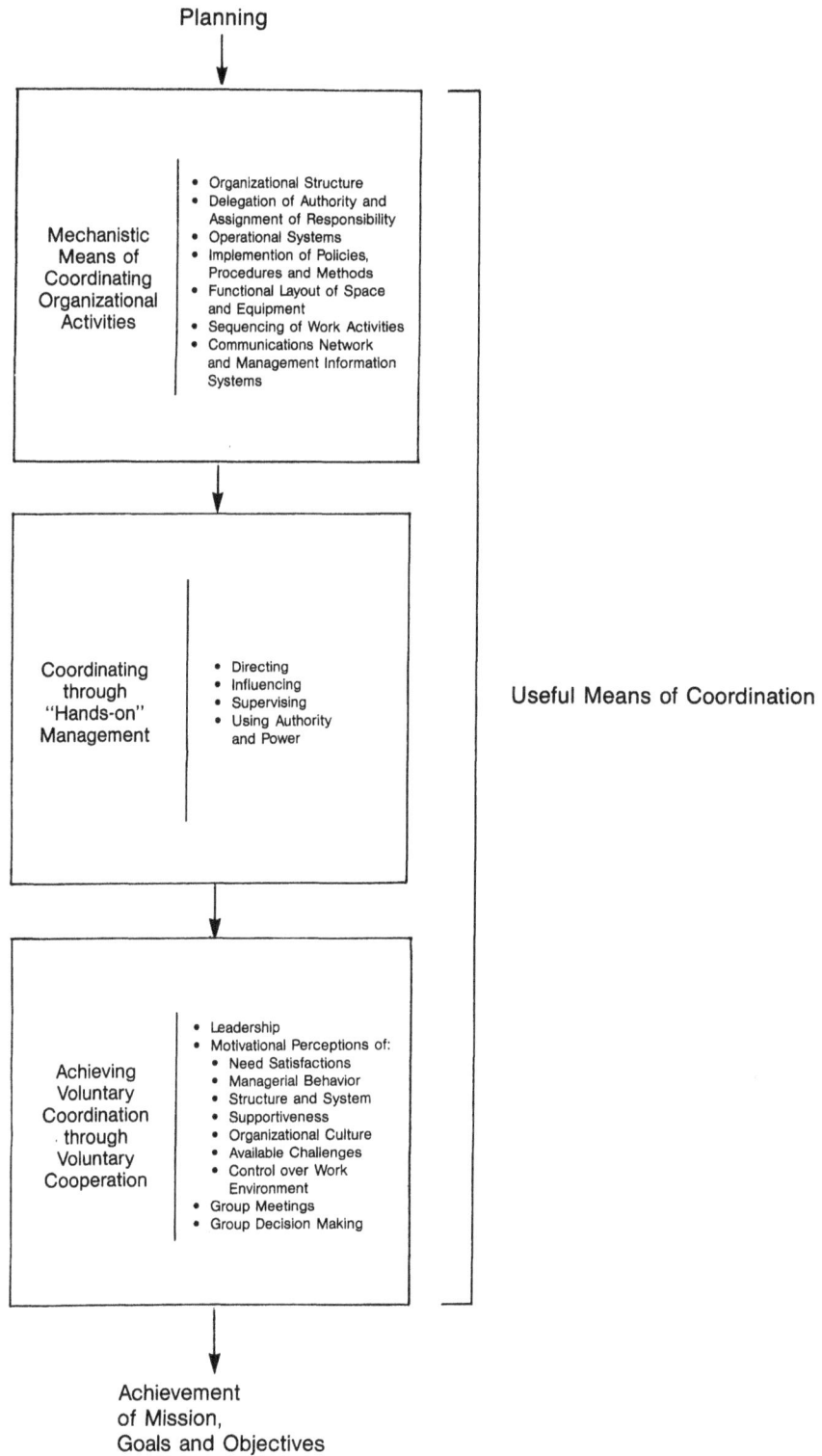

Planning

| Mechanistic Means of Coordinating Organizational Activities | • Organizational Structure
• Delegation of Authority and Assignment of Responsibility
• Operational Systems
• Implemention of Policies, Procedures and Methods
• Functional Layout of Space and Equipment
• Sequencing of Work Activities
• Communications Network and Management Information Systems |

| Coordinating through "Hands-on" Management | • Directing
• Influencing
• Supervising
• Using Authority and Power |

Useful Means of Coordination

| Achieving Voluntary Coordination through Voluntary Cooperation | • Leadership
• Motivational Perceptions of:
  • Need Satisfactions
  • Managerial Behavior
  • Structure and System
  • Supportiveness
  • Organizational Culture
  • Available Challenges
  • Control over Work Environment
• Group Meetings
• Group Decision Making |

Achievement
of Mission,
Goals and Objectives

removal of many outpatient functions from inpatient facilities has occurred, which is in part a result of the difficulties encountered in coordinating inpatient and outpatient functions within the traditional departmental structure. This applies especially to large hospitals.

These problems of coordination in hospitals parallel similar problems in all types of businesses, depending on individual situations. Obviously, no solution applies universally.

Delegations of authority and assignments of responsibility

Delegations of authority and assignments of responsibility are decided on during organizational planning and executed during implementation. To emphasize that such delegations and assignments are an important means of achieving coordination in operations, we discuss them separately from organizational structure.

Managers can conceptualize coordination as a harmonizing of operational relationships—among management personnel, among operating personnel, and among managers and operating personnel together. Another conception of coordination directs attention to vertical and lateral relationships within the structured hierarchy. Certainly, by delegating authority and assigning responsibility clearly and in perfect accord with a plan of coordination for specialized activities, the probability increases that coordination will be attained.

We have already outlined (in Chapter 10) the use of formal job descriptions to effect the teamwork necessary for attaining objectives. The preparation of job descriptions obviously depends very much on the procedures that will be used to accomplish the necessary work. If each job description reflects in detail the work that an employee will actually perform within a coordinated total effort, the employee, in giving consent to the job description, in effect agrees to coordination (and in a particular manner) even before the work is undertaken. We realize it is difficult to devise such detailed, well-meshed job descriptions, but they are desirable to achieve coordination through their use.

Operational systems

The formal planning, delineation, and operation of production or other work systems, where input and output are clearly defined and sequential steps in a process identified and established, is a mechanistic form of coordination. The system may be either continuous or intermittent, depending on the breakdown of work sequencing, which in turn depends on the type of product made or service rendered. In either case, however, well-defined methods—independent of voluntary cooperation and coordination—serve to coordinate the work efforts of organizational members within the system. The systems approach to operations has been shown to be a highly effective coordinating mechanism, since systems, procedures, and methods are explicitly detailed in terms of *"who, when, where, what and how.* This is a point seldom clearly outlined in the now considerable body of literature pertaining to systems analysis and engineering."[9]

Implementing policies, procedures, and methods

Standing plans promulgated to appropriate departments of an organization have long provided guidance for the coordination of activities. Usually, policies give directions for coordination among departments, procedures outline approaches to coordinating work intradepartmentally, and methods describe individual work tasks that will mesh both laterally and vertically within departmental procedures.

As noted in Chapter 5, in our early careers we guided the preparation of a procedures manual for each department of a hospital we were then managing. Thereafter, our orientation for each new employee included a study of the procedures manual of the relevant departments. The employee then received a certificate attesting to satisfactory completion of the study of the relevant procedures manual or manuals and also to satisfactory understanding of the specific work about to be undertaken as outlined in a written job description. We found this approach greatly enhanced coordination of work efforts, and the cost per patient day at this institution was significantly reduced as a result. For several years, HCA's hospitals have frequently used this approach to effect coordination and efficient team activities on an intradepartmental basis. HealthTrust Inc. also plans to use this approach.

Management engineers have made great contributions in the area of coordination, especially at the work level, where standard operating procedures and standard methods are important. However, the dangers of work dissatisfaction are inherent in any situation where procedures and methods are "forced" upon individuals. Perhaps our success with standard procedures and methods resulted from the fact we always instituted new ones with appropriate periods of education and that new employees always received adequate orientation. The most basic point, however, is whether one would rather forgo the opportunity to attain coordination through standard procedures and methods in accomplishing repetitive tasks or try to gain high morale through self-coordination, even in large group endeavors. The reply nearly cries out: Go with the standard procedures and deal with possible work dissatisfaction in a rational manner.

Although we have not seen any research results on the level of worker satisfaction in situations without planned guides to the coordination of repetitious specialized tasks, we can only imagine it would be low. In fact, such situations may not even exist, for production would probably reduce to naught. Thus, the main problem is not whether procedures and methods should be used, but rather which procedures and which methods are best and who should devise them. With regard to the latter point, it seems obvious management should take the initiative in devising procedures, but hopefully with appreciable input from specialized operators.

Functional layout of space and equipment

Well-designed layouts of space and equipment can enhance coordination of work efforts. One has only to monitor a sample of workplaces to conclude that the layout of facilities in probably thousands of businesses hinders rather than helps the coordination of work efforts. Millions of people go to work every day at facilities that literally obstruct work, and yet surprisingly few question the situation. Each building is an overpowering reality, and that it could have been designed to be flexible but also to accommodate optimally the work conducted inside never occurs to many people, including some top managers.

Hospitals have vastly improved in terms of functionality over the past two decades, owing to the advent of a new discipline called functional planning, which is concerned with establishing appropriate proximities among departments and achieving short and direct traffic flows, both inter- and intradepartmentally. The layout of space and equipment at the work level increasingly conforms to the principle that form follows function.

Functional planning for the design of any building utilized for work as well as the location and layout of equipment therein can pay rich dividends in terms of coordination and increased productivity. At the same time, it can remove many aggravations which operating personnel usually experience in performing tasks where "one has to go around one's elbow to get to one's nose."

Sequencing of work activities

From a mechanistic standpoint, scheduling and its implementing aspect, the sequencing of work activities, offer excellent (and constantly used) means of coordination. Although schedules in their strictest sense merely establish "the specific time when a job or some task is to be accomplished,"[10] they can be supplemented with details concerning who, what, and how. They also usually imply, either implicitly or explicitly, where the activities will be accomplished.

Schedules that reflect the sequencing of work tasks vary quite widely in their levels of detail, their methods of preparation, and the types of activities involved. Executives often schedule activities that apply to special programs and projects, and lower level managers and operational programmers usually schedule production or service activities. Executive level scheduling is oriented more toward broad conceptual overviews related to strategic plans and total operations; that at lower management levels may concern closely sequenced departmental activities where queuing theory, computer simulation models, shortest processing time, and other statistical approaches may be important. In all instances, however, one of the prime objectives of implementing such sequencing is coordination.

Systems of communication

Planned communication networks and management information systems are definitely mechanistic means of enhancing coordination. The need for answers regarding when, where, and how to commit resources of one type or another can be met only if that information is available in the form needed on a timely basis. In Chapter 8 we elaborate on this matter at some length.

The same reports used in the control process and the same system used to generate such reports also prove useful in coordinating the various activities related to who, when, what, where, and how, both in repetitive work and in special one-time-through programs and projects.

We have not discussed controlling as a mechanistic means of coordination, but certainly the structure involved in that process and the feedback derived therefrom have considerable usefulness in seeing that work is efficiently coordinated (see Chapter 15). One might reason that in a sense controlling implies coordination, but it is a negative sense. Therefore, we have not pursued this line of thought.

Hands-on management

Directing

Certainly directing can serve as a means of coordinating, one of several that qualifies as a form of hands-on management. Typically, directing initiates action (generally viewed as starting in the top echelons) and, in many organizations, continues it. Its use as a means of coordination probably varies inversely with the effectiveness of mechanistic means. However, directing will never be completely dispensed with, owing to failures, even if only occasionally, among mechanistic approaches.

Influencing

At some levels of an organizational hierarchy and also in the case of nonmembers whose efforts are needed by the organization, influencing is one choice for coordinating work efforts. Managerial sensitivity will reveal when it should be employed.

Supervision

In Chapter 12, we discussed supervision at some length, including its current role in effecting work during the course of plan implementation. Like policies, procedures, and standard methods, supervision is an enduring element of management, despite the fact that its practice will become decidedly different than in previous years.

It is safe to say that occasionally all of the mechanistic means of coordination discussed will fail, either singly or collectively, in their ability to appropriately coordinate work efforts. Direct, hands-on supervision is another means, and a very effective one, that can supplement these mechanistic means.

Many current academicians who author management texts seem to have become "gun shy" of expressing opinions about supervision owing to adverse criticism from social scientists; they therefore might barely mention the subject in the entire contents of a typical 400-page text. Although we fully understand and appreciate the independent and innovative spirit of the Yuppie generation, we also know that the efforts of all individuals in modern day corporations must be coordinated. We understand and appreciate the considerable contributions of social scientists to management and know the dictatorial (authoritarian) brand of supervision evidenced in industrial and other types of enterprises in years past is not now ordinarily acceptable for getting work. We understand and acknowledge that provision of positive support is preferred in nearly all facets of hands-on management of people, including the coordination of their efforts. However, we also see no need to "throw the baby out with the bathwater." Supervision still has a highly important role as a distinct management function. Without it, no large business enterprise could long exist.

Therefore, we can forthrightly state that supervision is an important adjunct to coordinating the teamwork of most organizations. How it should best be implemented depends on many factors, including the time, the place, the individuals involved, and the work to be accomplished.

Use of authority and power

We discussed this means of hands-on management in Chapter 12 and will not elaborate on it here. However, in urgent situations or where recalcitrant attitudes cannot otherwise be overcome, the appropriate employment of authority and force (the manifestation of power) may be justified in assuring coordination of work efforts. As we previously noted, the use of authority, power, and force has its place and should not be eschewed when appropriate.

Voluntary cooperation

A bridge building example

One of us served as a combat platoon commander in the Corps of Engineers during early manhood. In the course of this service, activities included the building of a number of "fixed span" and "floating" Bailey Bridges—each kind basically an erector-set type of bridge designed for fast construction under combat conditions. The British designed and initially used both kinds. Both were adaptable to transfer on trucks in a disassembled state to locations previously designated for erection. Comprehensive manuals set forth specifications and building directions that small working units of combat engineers could use to accomplish specialized construction tasks. The erector-set instructions included exact sequences of assembly, and it was necessary to follow them precisely. Both during practice and during construction in combat zones, battalion officers clocked the time required for comparison with standard times.

In the course of building a number of these bridges, a few at night under complete blackout conditions, it became apparent that despite every precaution to obtain perfectly coordinated work efforts, such was impossible. The answer lay in engendering a willingness among work units to help each other and, within work units, a willingness among individuals to do more than their precise share for the common cause. With frequent shouts of "Latch on and catch up" (the precise wording), every man was galvanized into concerted action and fixed his attention on achieving the work required.

Neither the commissioned officer nor the noncommissioned officers rested on their authority or dignity. All had dirty hands and a sweaty brow when the work was done. No job was beneath any person. A singleness of purpose pervaded the construction squads—*get the bridge built!* Consequently, the units usually considerably bettered the recommended construction times.

There is a lesson to be learned here: Certain motivational forces, if brought into play at the right time, can be of material assistance in the accomplishment of work objectives in most organizations. In the case of the bridge building, through perceived leadership and a basic inner drive for survival, voluntary cooperation sharply increased and resulted in a coordination of effort well beyond that anticipated.

Back to the business world

A considerable number of business enterprises must coordinate their work with other businesses, independent specialists, and sometimes government agencies. On some occasions, an organization's management may not have de facto control over persons within its own hierarchy. We will again use hospitals as an example, but schools and many service organizations, such as consulting firms, could also be used. In a hospital, the medical staff functions to a considerable extent outside the range of the chief executive's power; auxiliary groups wish to contribute their services, but desire very loose control. In governmental and quasi-governmental units, various outside officials may cast at will their lengthy shadows in management's path. In all these situations, mechanistic means of coordination, plus techniques of hands-on management, may not be sufficient to coordinate all necessary activities.

Also, those whose efforts should respond to mechanistic means may not give their fullest measure of cooperation, and the best coordination possible will still fail. Therefore, other ways of achieving a greater level of coordination must be sought.

Two management subprocesses

The answer to achieving coordination that might otherwise not be realized (i.e., by merely using mechanistic means and hands-on management) lies in two subprocesses of management previously recognized by only a few management authorities. One of them, *voluntary cooperation*, arises primarily as a function of leadership, together with certain other motivational perceptions. The other, *voluntary coordination*, arises in part from two-way communications but mostly from voluntary cooperation. Managers and others often confuse these two subprocesses (or subfunctions), but they are quite distinct.

Newman and Summer regard voluntary cooperation as primarily an emotional response that leads to willing and enthusiastic participation in carrying out plans and striving toward organizational objectives.[11] These authors seem to believe that most voluntary cooperation develops as a consequence of motivations caused by initiating leadership behavior within a management's hierarchy. Certainly, voluntary coordination would depend to some extent on effective two-way vertical communication (as has been surmised by certain authorities).

It follows, then, that voluntary coordination, as opposed to that obtained through ways already described, would include coordination generated largely by voluntary cooperation, which in turn is largely the result of the perceived leadership behavior of a manager or managers. Although voluntary coordination does involve vertical relationships, we agree with Mary Parker Follette's opinion that it develops, for the most part, through interpersonal horizontal relationships voluntarily undertaken in response to motivational influences that are not directly part of the mechanistic techniques or hands-on management previously cited (see Figure 14-1).[12]

Although most voluntary coordination may result from voluntary cooperation initiated by perceived leadership incentives, many employees have other motivational drives not associated with management's efforts at all, such as the desire to achieve promotion or otherwise satisfy personal ambition.

Certainly, the extra measure of coordination that comes from voluntary cooperation and that a manager may be able to consciously evoke originates partly as a result of perceived leadership behavior. Even if the voluntary cooperation is based directly on the personal ambitions of subordinates or others, a manager's supportive attitude will probably have a beneficial effect.

As indicated, voluntary coordination depends to some extent on both vertical and horizontal relationships fostered by two-way communications. This being so, managers should remember the art of listening nearly always enhances leadership. A manager must generate confidence and trust in subordinates and other associates, and this will not be possible without providing ample opportunity for feedback, whether positive or negative.[13] Since all coordination in some sense occurs as a result of communications, it follows that having an optimal communication system and the necessary accommodating devices is very desirable. We discussed communication networks in Chapter 8.

Recommended actions

Any executive or manager who seeks to procure voluntary coordination among employees should consider doing the following:

1. Imbue those under his or her leadership and also those at its fringe with a profound psychological commitment to the objectives of the organization.[14] "Objectives should be unified to the extent possible and a dominant objective established."[15] Some recent authorities decry leadership that uses strong emotional appeals. However, when such appeals are not made to stir motivations which substitute for rightful individual needs but rather are for the more successful achievement of legitimate societal benefits, no harm is done and much good can be gained.[16]

2. "Arrange and encourage face-to-face contacts among the key people of groups whose action must be coordinated."[17] No less an authority than Fayol recommended weekly department head meetings, a technique we have employed to tremendous advantage. We have also used both standing and ad hoc committees for the purpose of achieving voluntary coordination.

3. "Encourage group decision making . . . not only will voluntary cooperation be enhanced thereby, as previously cited, but voluntary coordination can also be developed through the ego-involvement of those making the decision."[18]

4. "Nurture and use the informal organization." Most organizations have informal channels of communication and at least the rudiments of one or more informal organizations, which typically cut across departmental lines and extend outside the organizational hierarchy. The presence of informal organizations "may be recognized, encouraged and utilized for several purposes, not the least of which is voluntary coordination. Barnard recognized their value in producing this response when he described the organization as being formal when the activities of two or more persons are consciously coordinated toward a given objective, and as being informal when interpersonal relationships are without conscious joint purpose, even though pro-

ducing common or joint results.[19] Further, informal organization is born and sustained among friends, and certainly those who maintain friendly relations will coordinate their efforts without compulsion much more readily than those who are near strangers."[20]

Although informal organizations exhibit considerable irrationality at times, the perceptive manager can often use them constructively, in particular, to help achieve voluntary coordination.

To sum up, voluntary cooperation and voluntary coordination appear sometimes elusive and may not be achievable through mechanistic means or hands-on management. We have suggested some approaches which we have found beneficial in operating organizations that are among the most complex in today's world.

Balance

We have already cited Fayol's remarks about the need for separate departments of an enterprise to achieve an appropriate degree of proportion (or balance) based on operational requirements and contributions. Many managers (including ourselves) have encountered difficulties in this regard. Such difficulties usually develop as a consequence of the following two situations: (1) an optimal balance has not truly been determined and (2) turf builders, empire builders, or others with ambitions inconsistent with the interests of the enterprise deliberately expand their staff, their space, and their operations beyond what is truly needed.

Achieving balance starts with a priority ranking of goals and objectives in strategic planning and continues in implementation when means and funds are aligned with required actions. Typically, imbalances form during planning when some managers "pad" their budgets for one reason or another. Of course, the converse also happens, i.e., some managers reduce their budgets below what they need. Top managers have a responsibility to see that these imbalances do not occur.

Especially in construction programs are empire builders liable to make their play, powerfully and persuasively demanding space allocations well beyond true needs. Outside consultants can often assist in preventing this.

In essence, coordination implies a balanced operation, with departmental activities contributing to the whole whatever is required for realizing the goals and objectives in an efficient manner and in accordance with a timetable.

Summary

Authorities on management have viewed coordination variously, with some believing that it is merely an outgrowth of organizational planning and its implementation and others believing it is a distinct process. Our own view is that coordination must be given careful attention during all types of planning and that it must be conscientiously implemented by a number of management methods and approaches. Coordination must be an objective of all management actions, for coordination of the actions of specialized personnel or groups of personnel is at the very heart of management in organizations.

We defined coordination as "the orchestrating of the activities of a person or group of persons with the activities of others so as to achieve common organizational objectives through team play." Coordination within an organizational hierarchy must occur both vertically and horizontally, and usually according to some sequencing of the activities to be carried out.

Coordination occurs during the implementation of previously made plans, usually by means of a number of identifiable management actions. We categorized the ways to coordinate under three headings: (1) mechanistic means, (2) hands-on management, and (3) voluntary cooperation.

The mechanistic means we listed included (1) organizational structure; (2) delegation of authority and assignment of responsibility; (3) operational systems; (4) implementing policies, procedures, and methods; (5) functional layout of space and equipment; (6) sequencing of work activities; and (7) systems of communication. All of these must be well planned and carefully established or carried out during implementation.

Techniques of hands-on management, including directing, influencing, supervision, and use of authority and power, are probably the oldest known means of coordination. Close dictatorial supervision often achieves less than optimal results, and social scientists have justifiably been very critical of it. As a result, management authorities devote relatively little attention to supervision in general, even though it necessarily occurs in nearly every facet of management and operational activities in organizations everywhere. Supervision, reasonably carried out, must continue to serve as a distinct means of coordinating the work of organizations.

Managers can achieve voluntary coordination of work efforts by begetting a spirit of voluntary cooperation among subordinates, superiors, and peers, as well as among persons on the periphery who may influence work outcomes. Voluntary cooperation occurs as a result of leadership behavior by managers or as a result of inner drives associated with personal needs (drives which may perhaps be influenced by management actions).

There are at least four ways in which a manager may elicit voluntary cooperation so as to achieve voluntary coordination:

1. Imbue subordinates and other organizational associates with a profound psychological commitment to the objectives of the organization.

2. Arrange and encourage face-to-face contacts among the key persons of groups whose actions must be coordinated.

3. Encourage group decision making.

4. Nurture and use any informal organizations that exist.

Balance among departmental and certain specific operational activities partly results from the priority ranking of goals and objectives set in strategic planning. By then allocating budgeted funds in true accordance with needs, turf building can be eliminated or reduced to a minimum.

Notes

1. Mary Parker Follett, *Freedom and Coordination*, ed. L. Urwick (London: Management Publications Trust, 1949), 61–76. Reprinted in *Classics in Management*, ed. Harwood F. Merrill (New York: American Management Association, 1960), 337.

2. Alexander H. Church and L.P. Alford, "The Principles of Management," *American Machinist* 36 (May 30, 1912): 857–61. Reprinted in *Classics in Management*, ed. Harwood F. Merrill (New York: American Management Association, 1960), 204.

3. Henri Fayol, *General and Industrial Management*, trans. Constance Storrs (London: Sir Isaac Pitman and Sons, 1949), 103–4.

4. Ibid., 104.

5. James Mooney, *Principles of Organization* (New York: Harper & Brothers, 1947), 5.

6. Ernest Dale, *Management: Theory and Practice*, 2d ed. (New York: McGraw-Hill, 1969), 5–6.

7. James A.F. Stoner, *Management*, 2d ed. (Englewood Cliffs, N.J.: Prentice-Hall, 1982), 281–89.

8. Adam Smith, *The Wealth of Nations* (New York: Modern Library, 1937), 3–4.

9. Owen B. Hardy, "Systematic Processes Applied to Health Care Planning," *Hospital Administration* 16 (Winter 1971): 17.

10. Richard M. Steers, Gerardo R. Ungson, and Richard T. Mowday, *Managing Effective Organizations* (Boston: Kent Publishing Company, 1985), 245.

11. William H. Newman and Charles E. Summer, Jr., *The Process of Management* (Englewood Cliffs, N.J.: Prentice-Hall, 1964), 497.

12. *Dynamic Administration: The Collected Papers of Mary Parker Follett*, ed. H.C. Metcalf and Lyndall F. Urwick (New York: Harper & Bros., 1941), 297 ff.

13. Owen B. Hardy, "Voluntary Cooperation and Coordination," *Hospital Administration* 2 (Fall 1966): 39.

14. Ibid., 41.

15. Ibid.

16. Ibid.

17. Ibid., 42.

18. Ibid.

19. Chester I. Barnard, *Functions of the Executive* (Cambridge, Mass.: Harvard University Press, 1949), 122.

20. Hardy, "Voluntary Cooperation and Coordination," 42–43.

Chapter 15

Controlling

Elements of Management
in Corporations

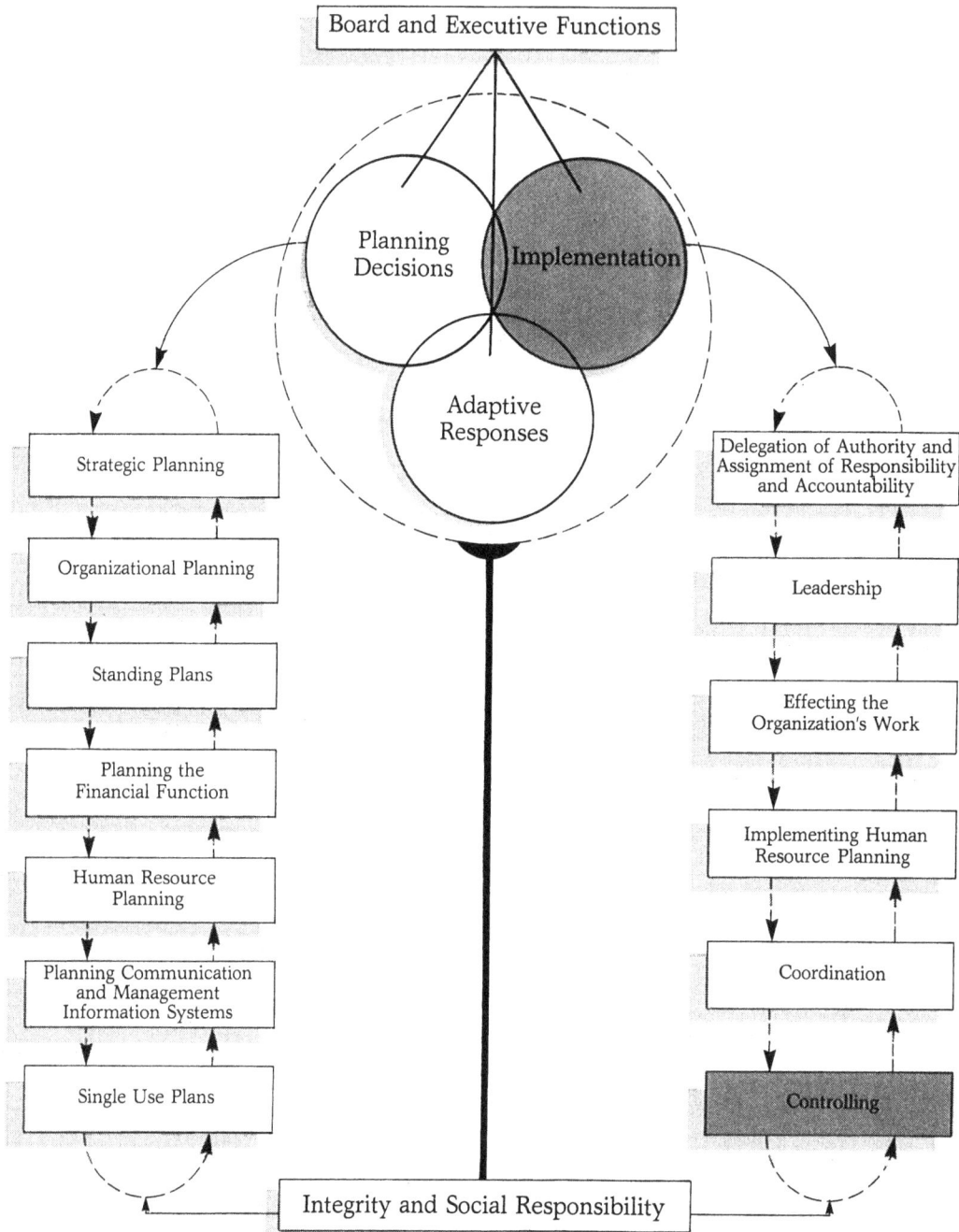

Board and Executive Functions

Planning Decisions

Implementation

Adaptive Responses

Strategic Planning

Organizational Planning

Standing Plans

Planning the Financial Function

Human Resource Planning

Planning Communication and Management Information Systems

Single Use Plans

Delegation of Authority and Assignment of Responsibility and Accountability

Leadership

Effecting the Organization's Work

Implementing Human Resource Planning

Coordination

Controlling

Integrity and Social Responsibility

15

Background

We enter into a world of controls at birth. At an early age, we learn that standards for human behavior exist and that conformity to them is expected. Parental controls, as they interlock with social controls, are the first with which we become acquainted. We confront controls at school soon afterward. For example, grading of scholastic performance is at the heart of our school system. In the course of maturing, we learn that legal statutes exist stipulating standards for human conduct and that violations of them result in undesirable consequences. Thus, by the time a young person accepts employment in a formal organization with a definitive mission and goals, he or she understands the general nature of controls, whether or not any reflective thought has been devoted to their characteristic aspects or elements.

Again, each of us learns very early in life that failure to conform to expected standards of performance or behavior usually results in denial of desirable rewards and occasionally in outright punishment. Punishment, especially, can be very unpleasant to children or adolescents when administered as a way of enforcing obedience. Thus, many people probably initially bring to places of employment a dislike of controls, or at least of the dictatorial manner in which they are sometimes enforced. Either consciously or subconsciously, many adults distrust subjective work appraisals by a superior, probably as a result of earlier experiences.

Research has clearly shown that close supervision of work, subjective evaluation of performance, and the arbitrary administration of a system of rewards often cause employees to rebel against both authority and responsibility.[1] Considering that anarchy is the natural result of an absence of controls—in society as a whole or in any large organization—management must develop a philosophy of control that will result in the most advantageous climate for organizational achievement. Following adoption of such a philosophy, care must then be taken to see that implementation is carried out in a manner which does not derogate it.

Our purpose here is to describe a philosophy of control appropriate for the management of most business organizations and to delineate an accommodating process that can result in high organizational productivity and employee satisfaction. The reader will soon see that we advocate using impersonal, objective measurements of results, measurements that can then be compared to objectives or standards previously established in planning. In many instances, those whose work is affected can actually

"We've come
a long way,
but it's still
control."

THEN ...

"O.K. 10 LASHES UNLESS YOU
START BREAKING THE PIECES
SMALLER."

NOW...

"THE COMPUTER REPORTS I HAVEN'T
REACHED MY TARGET, BUT I'LL RESPOND
IMMEDIATELY BY IMPLEMENTING A
CONTINGENCY PLAN."

establish these standards. At least, those whose performance is measured should have full knowledge of the planned targets or objectives. Ideally, the targets or objectives should be jointly set or agreed to by affected superiors and subordinates, as explained in Chapters 3 and 10. Except in the most urgent circumstances, managers should avoid subjective, arbitrary, or dictatorial applications of the control process.

The role of planning

Continuing to follow tenets enunciated by Fayol in the early part of this century, most management authorities believe that the management control function "involves setting a target, measuring performance and taking corrective action."[2] This is correct, except that the formulation of goals, objectives, and targets constitutes a distinct planning function. Monitoring, measuring performance, and taking corrective actions are all functions involved in implementation. Although controlling will not be optimal without the formulation of a goal, objective, target, or other yardstick, this does not mean that controlling is planning or that planning is controlling. Two separate functions are involved: planning and controlling. Further, controlling very definitely forms a part of a broad group of activities best called implementation.

Most organizations, in addition to goals and objectives, have established standing plans—policies, procedures, and regulations—within whose scope work will be performed. Managers then expect conformance to such plans by all personnel. These plans serve as standards or yardsticks by which the actions of everyone affected can be measured and the degree of conformance determined. Thus, managers can, by using standing plans as standards, exercise control over behavior in the same manner as they exercise control in the accomplishment of goals and objectives.

Additionally, a number of organizational efforts, mandated by government or outside agencies, must be undertaken which may not constitute organizational goals or objectives as such (i.e., as far as the mission or purpose of the organization is concerned). These efforts concern conformance to regulations or standards for quality. In the case of hospitals, a plethora of such regulations and standards exists. In the case of industry and other businesses, there are OSHA and EPA regulations, among others. Although pressure for performance may come from outside the organization, planning must take these regulations into account. In fact, the standards and targets can still be said to flow from planning performed by the organization.

Goals and objectives used as standards to measure accomplishments can be either short or long range and may pertain to financial, programmatic, or other operational aspects. They may also relate to single use (one-time-through) plans or to the ongoing pursuit of specific business lines.

When managers fail to establish goals and objectives at each level of its hierarchy, they lose the opportunity to achieve ideal control. We know of many hospitals that do no strategy planning other than that related to budgeting, and often the budget receives little or no attention after its formulation. Happily, this has not been the case at HCA, which may account for a considerable part of HCA's success.

In order to control well, a business must plan well. Even those businesses having purely adaptive roles can almost invariably establish managerial objectives which are meaningful and can serve as yardsticks in measuring performances. When we hear any manager state, "Not much planning can be done in our business," our almost involuntary reaction is that it probably hasn't yet been tried.

Our primary focus here is on controlling as it applies to accomplishing business objectives, but, as already indicated, every sizeable organization finds controlling necessary regarding adherence to policies, procedures, and regulations. These operate to create what has become popularly known as the culture of an organization, or its "ways of doing things." The control process operates in such instances only when nonconformance is evidenced.

Controlling and controversy

A great deal of controversy about controlling has arisen during the past several decades. Many social scientists believe humans function best in an environmental setting where initiative and good intentions remain largely uninhibited. Those who use a structured, mechanistic approach to management have traditionally believed assured attainment of goals and objectives requires a system of rewards and penalties (perhaps restricted to the denial of rewards).

Although we are not attempting to straddle the fence, we believe in any fairly broad range of formal organizations, there will be situations calling for the application of each of these theories. For example, in many service organizations, such as accounting and consulting firms, public relations firms, law firms, etc., the exercise of initiative by highly educated professionals has proven to be an absolute requisite for success. These situations call for only minimal control. Even here, however, managers set targets for sales, revenue, and earnings during the course of planning and measure performance during implementation, with both planning objectives and control activities being attached, in the final analysis, to the work of the individual.

In organizations requiring a great deal of specialization and simultaneous team play, although initiative usually should not be stifled, fairly rigid structuring may be desirable to attain goals and objectives efficiently. Consider again the analogous case of a football team. One can hardly imagine a coach in the NFL saying, for example, "I want you men to go out and use your initiative this afternoon; do your own thing. I may send in a few plays, but regard these merely as suggestions. And, to make you even happier, we won't review any films tomorrow to see how well you performed." Certainly, many business organizations require nearly as much specialization and teamwork as do sports teams, including most production-oriented businesses from fast-food restaurants to car assembly operations.

Social scientists have often attacked various aspects of scientific management and traditional management, in many cases justifiably. Some of the particular reasons why controlling has been criticized are as follows:

- Control measures, in the absence of appropriate objectives or standards established during planning, can be carried out in an authoritarian or dictatorial manner by superiors exercising authoritarian or dictatorial supervision.

- Superiors might arbitrarily set objectives and standards with no agreement from subordinates. Some employees then feel pressures which they cannot cope with.

- Methods of monitoring and measuring results can be accomplished by means regarded as offensive and unfair.

- Those affected sometimes do not understand the methods being used for monitoring and for measuring results because of ad hoc extemporaneous improvisations by managers.

- Superiors sometimes change the standards which a subordinate may have agreed to without getting further agreement. This can occur during implementation of control and for reasons not understood by the subordinate.

- The standards imposed may not be mutually consistent. For example, standards regarding cost and quality frequently exhibit inconsistencies.

However, from the standpoint of many managers, there may be other reasons why employees resent controls. Intellectual stubbornness or physical lethargy (or both) may cause some subordinates—managers and operators—to resent even control measures that were agreed to. Some degree of unreasonableness is likely to occur just as frequently among subordinates as among superiors throughout an organization.

Our own thesis is that each manager's basic purpose should be to gain business objectives. Popularity should not constitute a goal in itself, although it will hopefully be a result of managing properly. Also, stimulating personal initiative among personnel should not be a primary goal, although such stimulation may prove beneficial in attaining business objectives. Most individuals will hopefully achieve wealth and self-actualization, but in business organizations not everyone can be president or vice president or even a middle manager. No utopia has ever existed, and while we may desire perfection and may try to achieve it within an organization, it is doubtful that it will ever be attained and that every employee will be totally satisfied.

Thus, in managing, one should apply controls to the degree that best serves one's purpose in gaining objectives and with a keen sensitivity at all times regarding the social, physical, mental, and materialistic needs of all members of the organization. We believe that over the total range of business organizations within capitalistic economies, the degree to which managers should apply controls will vary quite widely, but, as a function of implementation, the characteristics of controlling remain essentially the same. Controlling is a basic process and can be explained in basic terms. The degree to which controls are applied and the specific methods of application can be left to the discretion of managers and will depend on the nature of the organization, the work to be accomplished, and the special qualifications and needs of affected individuals.

Authority and responsibility for control

As an ideal, self-control has currently captured the imagination of many practical managers. We also favor self-control, as will be seen later in this chapter. However, the question arises as to who in a given business enterprise possesses the authority and responsibility for exercising control over implementing activities.

All authority and responsibility of whatever kind is originally vested in a corporation's board of directors. As previously noted, board members and executives then delegate authority and assign responsibility throughout the organization among managers, generally following a hierarchical chain and with the scope of both adjusted to the work anticipated to be performed. Authority and responsibility (and accountability) for controlling, as a part of the total, are distributed along the same hierarchical chain, and every subordinate manager comes into possession of a sufficient amount of authority and responsibility to exercise appropriate control over the work agreed upon, unless a specific omission is stipulated by a higher superior. Thus, controlling becomes a responsibility (accompanied by accountability) that cannot legally be avoided by managers. This is as it should be, considering both the economic and the social roles which business organizations should fulfill.

Although a subordinate manager's organizational responsibility for controlling may seem obvious and, we believe, attaches to the management position legally, nonetheless it should be fixed by arriving at a clear understanding with an immediate superior. This can be done orally, but organizational structure will evidence greater stability and there will be a higher probability of positive control if managers routinely put assignments in writing. A carefully prepared job description serving as an agreement between a superior and a subordinate is an appropriate means for avoiding needless misunderstandings.

Besides those managers who possess responsibility for control, many people in operational and staff positions participate in its execution. Employees who have no authority to take corrective action often perform data collections and comparisons with standards. For example, the nurse who records the temperature of patients for the use of other nurses and physicians and the internal auditor who reports his or her findings to the director of finance have no authority regarding the complete control process, yet each plays a vital role in it.

Assigning responsibility and accountability and delegating authority to a subordinate manager for a given control function do not relieve the CEO or the board of directors of responsibility in relationship to third parties. In fact, there can be no divestiture of ultimate responsibility for control regarding any aspect of any work that is performed throughout the organization, as was explained in Chapter 10.

Control defined

Although most practitioners of management now understand the control process, in order to establish a frame of reference we shall review authoritative definitions.

The following statement, made by Henri Fayol and first published in 1916, has continued to serve as a basis for other definitions up to this very day.

> In an undertaking, control consists in verifying whether everything occurs in conformity with the plan adopted, the instructions issued and principles established. It has for object to point out weaknesses and errors in order to rectify them and prevent occurrence. It operates on everything, things, people, actions. From the management standpoint it must be ensured that a plan does exist, that it is put into operation and kept up to date.[3]

In reviewing Fayol's definition, one readily sees he recognized that the respective yardsticks or standards used to measure results are developed during planning (or as a part of the "plan adopted").

Newman and Summer, in the mid-1960s, stated,

The aim of control is to assure that the results of operation conform as closely as possible to established goals. Three elements, or phases, are always present in the control process. These are:

1. Standards that represent desired performance. These standards may be tangible or intangible, vague or specific, but until everyone concerned understands what results are desired, controls will create confusion.

2. A comparison of actual results against the standards. This evaluation must be reported.

3. Corrective action. Control measurements and reports serve little purpose until corrective action is taken when it is discovered that current activities are not leading to desired results.[4]

The similarities between the two definitions are appreciable. Fayol's definition, when analyzed, reveals the same elements as Newman and Summer's definition.

More recently, Rakich and Darr stated,

The controlling process monitors organizational performance by measuring it and comparing it against standards which are a derivative of organizational objectives [established in planning]. The controlling process consists of collecting information, determining whether organizational activity is consistent with the standards, and taking corrective action should there be deviations.[5]

Like the previous definitions, this one includes (1) measuring performance against standards and (2) taking corrective action should there be deviation from the standards. However, Rakich and Darr note in particular that standards "are a derivative of organizational objectives."

Brown and Moberg state that "controlling is maintaining organizational activities in conformity with plans and goals."[6] Here again, these authors relate controlling to actions taken during implementation so as to assure conformance of results with goals and objectives. In recent years most authorities have agreed that standards by which results are measured in controlling should be established during planning and, further, that they should be formulated at every level of a management hierarchy.

A strategy for controlling

As Fayol noted, control "operates on everything, things, people, actions." Our purpose here, however, will not be to examine the myriad mechanical, electrical, and other physical mechanisms used throughout industry to control various types of devices and machines as well as various aspects of specific environments. Our purpose is to consider the control of people—who in making use of available technology, eventually control both things and actions.

As discussed in Chapter 3, organizational goals and objectives should be established in planning in such a form that results achieved in pursuing them can be compared with them. Four basic aspects of objectives are usually important in this regard: quantity, quality, time, and cost.[7] A fifth aspect, the method of achieving the objectives, is also sometimes important, as is a sixth aspect, namely, location (e.g., "Our objective this year is to establish a production center at such-and-such address").

Managers can best accomplish controlling within the limits of the established policies and procedures of an organization. If policies and procedures for controlling have not been included among an organization's plans, then such policies and procedures should be formulated and made a part of standing plans. (See Chapter 5 for further comments in this regard.)

Our basic strategy for controlling embraces ten points, which are stated below. Adherence to them will reduce resentments to a minimum and render outright hostility ineffectual.

1. Superiors and subordinates should jointly agree on the objectives or standards (established in planning) against which results achieved will be measured.

2. Ideally, objectives and standards should be expressed in such a manner that results can be easily measured against them and the outcome of the comparison quantitatively described (see Chapter 5).

3. The actual comparison of results with objectives or standards should be performed in an impersonal manner and according to procedures fully understood and agreed to by the persons whose performance is being measured. In many instances, self-measurements of perform-ance may be advisable, provided the appropriate superior under-stands and agrees to the methodology used.

4. Those whose achievements are to be measured should have a clear understanding of any compliments or criticisms that might result from their success or failure, respectively. Such an understanding hopefully should occur at the time objectives are formulated, but certainly no later than the time implementation is undertaken.

5. The monitoring of progress toward objectives as well as reports generated therefrom should be valid and should not in themselves cause any embarrassment to those whose performance is being measured.

6. Monitoring and reporting of progress ought to be timely and suffi-ciently frequent so that the probability of failure before corrective actions can be taken is reduced to an acceptable minimum—from the standpoint of both the superior and the subordinate.

7. When reports that monitor progress (reports of measurements of results achieved) indicate corrective actions must be taken, both the superior and the subordinate should agree on such actions and the subordinate should be delegated the authority and assigned the responsibility for executing the actions (unless, of course, the subor-dinate's ability to perform has come into serious doubt).

8. The monitoring and reporting system should record the causes of failure if such causes are not obvious.

9. Self-acknowledgement of failure or partial failure to achieve agreed objectives is the desired outcome of controlling (assuming, of course, that failure or partial failure has occurred).

10. If a situation indicates that a system of incentives might be desirable in meeting or exceeding objectives, the incentives should be clearly understood and agreed upon by both the superior and the subordinate. The administration of the system should be fair and impartial.

As early as 1954, Peter Drucker realized the importance of management by self-control. In his now famous book, *The Practice of Management*, he stated, "Indeed, one of the major contributions of management by objectives is that it enables us to substitute management by self-control for management by domination."[8]

As regards self-control, no less an authority than Lee Iacocca holds that it is currently practical. In discussing a quarterly review system, Iacocca states, "In my experience, after ninety days are up, the guy who hasn't succeeded [in achieving objectives] will come in and explain apologetically that he didn't make his goal before the boss says anything. . . . He comes to realize that this is *his* problem—and not the boss's fault."[9] According to Iacocca, "Even then, there's usually time to take some constructive action."[10]

In their statements, both Drucker and Iacocca are assuming that objectives or standards have been properly established and agreed upon by superior and subordinate, appropriate reporting of progress is being carried out, and self-measurement of performance can be readily accomplished. But what happens when these conditions do not occur and may not be possible to effect? How should a manager react when that rare subordinate defies all control? We have already given an answer: One of a manager's basic responsibilities, one it is rarely possible to escape legally, is to assure that control, as a function, applies directly to implementing activities. Although a manager should make every effort to follow our ten points for effecting control in a manner that builds goodwill, stimulates motivation, and engenders the least amount of resentment among subordinates, the fact remains that no one should abandon controlling or shirk the responsibility for its implementation—in all of its aspects.

The strategy we describe above for controlling is one that most managers in most business organizations can use effectively. However, controlling, in its application, is an extremely tedious element of management, and managers usually confront a number of implementing problems as it is carried out in specific organizations. Among the most difficult objects to achieve are the following:

- assuring that results are monitored and then measured against objectives or standards in a valid and efficient manner

- assuring that during the monitoring and measuring of results, support rather than harassment is shown toward those whose results are being measured

- communicating appropriately with those whose results are monitored and measured (in particular, the timeliness, method, and attitudinal orientation should be appropriate)

- making sure that corrective measures are undertaken and completed, hopefully through the initiative of the subordinate or subordinates involved (this assumes, of course, that the results achieved were unsatisfactory).

The process of control

The control process comprises three basic functions, which closely interface with two others (one is a planning function and the other is a human resource management function). Figure 15-1 graphically depicts the process discussed below.

The three controlling functions are as follows:

1. *Monitoring*. This consists of tracking progress toward objectives, checking conformance to policies and procedures, and rendering reports about progress and conformance to affected managers and possibly others.

2. *Measuring Performance*. Performance results or activities are compared with predetermined standards. The standards are devised in planning and usually take the form of stated goals and objectives (with reference to results) or the form of policies and procedures (with reference to activities).

3. *Taking Corrective Actions*. This involves making changes in either implementing activities or plans so as to bring performance in line with original or revised expectations.

Invariably, before control becomes possible, managers must devise a standard by which performance results as well as other activities can be measured. Goals and objectives formulated in planning are what an organization wishes to accomplish, and they serve as standards. Policies and procedures provide the standards for other activities.

A system of rewards, devised in human resource planning, will also be closely connected with the control process. If a manager, or for that matter a staff or operating person, consistently meets or exceeds expectations (i.e., meets or exceeds objectives or other performance standards), then he or she should receive whatever rewards are merited. Our comments on this matter are contained in a later section ("Rewards as Merited").

Monitoring

In Chapter 8, the importance of planning communication networks and management information systems (MIS) was noted. This work, like the formulation of goals and objectives, makes up a part of planning. Such planning should take into account the information needed in the process of control and should make certain it is provided on a timely basis to those who require it in monitoring results.

Once efforts to achieve goals and objectives begin to be made, monitoring results should also begin (the first step in the control process). The basic means to effect monitoring are four: (1) written or printed reports, (2) oral reports, (3) a combination of written and oral reports, and (4) personal observations. Each proves satisfactory in certain circum-

Figure 15-1

The Process of Control

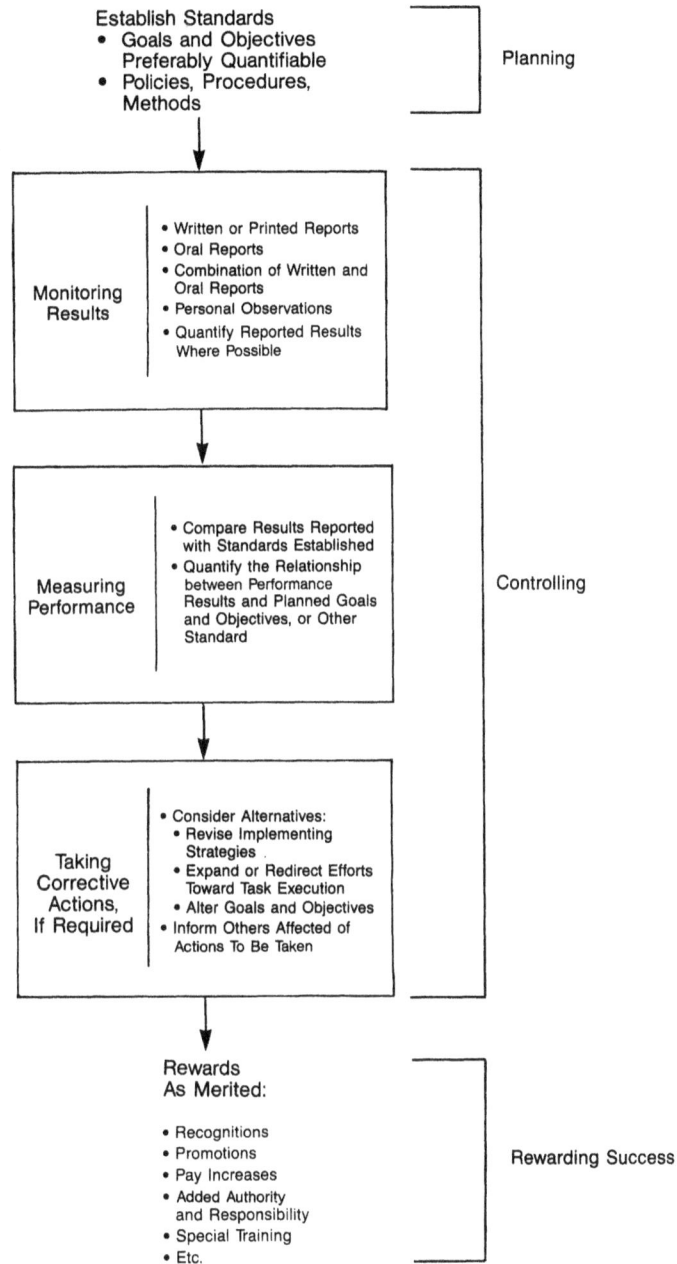

stances, and some situations need a combination or even all four together.

There is definitely no substitute for formal written reports in any organization which has several hundred employees or more. Managers ought to schedule reports on ongoing activities to be provided at least monthly. Special programs and projects require written reports tailored to their individual needs. In some instances, oral discussions about the written report between superior and subordinate managers prove beneficial. Particularly where problems are identified, oral discussions should immediately follow submission of the written report. Oral reports by themselves can be used for special activities arising on a daily basis or used in the interim as a supplement to scheduled written reports. In manufacturing, quality control reports may be necessary on a daily or even an hourly basis, but there the prime concern is product rather than personnel control.

Direct observations also play a key role in most performance monitoring. Managers can use visits to divisions, departments, or other work sites to audit reports which have been made in writing. Such visits, if conducted properly, will also exhibit management's concern for and interest in operational activities.

Where possible, routine written reports should have a brief, standardized format, somewhat like a check list, and aim at strategic control points. Reports on special projects should also usually be brief, but their requirements vary according to the situation.

Reporting by exception has received a great deal of attention in the literature over the years. The basic idea is that as long as the results of routine operations remain within previously defined limits, no report is deemed necessary. Reporting is required only by any exceptions to the standards. This approach may be satisfactory in manufacturing operations, where thousands of items of like nature are produced, but service organizations such as hospitals, airlines, vendors of consumer goods, and banks deal almost entirely with human beings. Our own experience in health care delivery indicates reporting will fall by the wayside if it is not done routinely. Thus the "exceptions," even if they could be properly identified, might not be reported. One can easily see that both a superior and a subordinate are in far different positions when the subordinate can say, "I just forgot to report that embarrassing exception" and when he or she must choose between routinely reporting the truth or a falsehood—and elects to report a falsehood which may be detected later. We conclude that reporting by exception should be considered only very cautiously by most businesses, except where manufacturing or processing of things is what is being monitored.

In most businesses, financial reporting has become quite sophisticated. This is probably because a large number of schools now turn out many graduates in finance and accounting. Other types of reporting may still be deficient, however, because businesses vary so extensively in their types of activity. No possible standards could be devised for activity reporting as precise and widely adapted as financial ratios, for example. Despite this fact, in every business, if one can establish a performance objective, one can devise a reporting system that will check on progress toward it and finally reveal whether it has been attained within a given time period.

Measuring performance

When a manager receives progress reports on performance, he or she should then compare the results reported with those expected upon conclusion of the work. Difficulty often arises in relating interim reports and interim results to those results that will finally be achieved as they pertain to a goal or objective to be attained within a specified timeframe.

One solution that should not be overlooked is a prior division of the work into segments or time-related phases with reports being due upon completion of each.

Again, controlling intermeshes with planning. If a manager has planned well and devised a good work schedule, interim reports can often be used to predict accurately a final outcome (basing the prediction on a reasonable set of assumptions).

One can express the measuring of performance thus:

$$\frac{\text{Performance Results}}{\text{Plans}}$$

This ratio assumes the planning objective, as well as the results achieved, can be expressed quantitatively. For example, if a hospital has the goal of attaining a market share of 60 percent of the inpatient admissions in its service area by the end of a given reporting year and finds it is receiving, at that time, 55 percent, one can state that goal attainment was 92 percent successful.

Few calculations will be as simplistic as this example. Some performance results will not be quantifiable. Perhaps most measurements, other than those prepared in financial and statistical accounting, will not be completely valid. However, where possible, the measurement should be accurate, and one can always achieve greater accuracy through quantified expressions than through any others. Objectivity is imperative. The accurate measurement of performance—done in a timely manner and by means of a valid standard expressed previously within an accepted plan—is probably the most vital element in the control process. It is also one of the key functions in all of management.

Taking corrective actions

The phrase *taking corrective actions* has unpleasant connotations to many people who give superficial study and consideration to the control process. Possibly the phrase *adjusting to standards* might better be substituted. However, *taking corrective actions* has become widely used and we have decided to retain it.

When results show deviations from plans, in terms of time, quality, quantity, or some other standard, it is usually desirable to effect changes in the approach to achievement. One may change the plan itself (alter goals and objectives), revise implementing strategies and tasks, or expand or redirect efforts being expended in task execution. The control process, through the monitoring system, should reveal the causes of the deviation(s), and the measurement of performance should reveal the extent.

If interim reports indicate undesirable results are being obtained, the manager directly involved should begin to take corrective measures, but at the same time report these measures to the superior next above. If the superior has objections, he or she should immediately voice them. Alternatively, the subordinate may discuss contemplated corrective actions with the superior before initiating them. In some instances, there may be more than one superior and one subordinate involved, depending on the extent operations have been segmented in order to obtain some overall goal.

Suppose a subordinate manager at the work level is failing to achieve objectives that have been freely agreed to. The corrective actions taken, regardless of who devises them, should be reported up the line of authority and responsibility to all levels where higher goals and objectives may be substantially affected. At each of these levels, the manager involved not only possesses the right of approval or disapproval, but also the right (and responsibility) to receive assurances that such corrective actions are in the best interest of the organization.

Suppose a subordinate manager is failing to achieve agreed objectives and has full knowledge of the fact through timely reports. Further, suppose he or she inexplicably takes no corrective actions. What then? One should act directly and unhesitantly. Discussions with that manager should be initiated by the superior next above and the situation rectified.

Rewards as merited

Rewarding those who have achieved their objectives within the limits of time and other constraints is not part of the basic control process, and we have provided a discussion of reward and incentive systems elsewhere in this text. However, we will repeat here that providing satisfying rewards for high performance demonstrates the fairness of management. Indeed, it also is effective in sustaining top performance over an extended time period and helps to assure the attainment of business objectives. Bennett sums up the matter by stating, "The purpose of linking rewards and performance is to reward employees for extra effort, to motivate them to higher levels of productivity and performance, and to have them gain satisfaction in work well done."[11]

The notion of linking rewards and performance is not new. However, in our own field, insufficient progress has occurred in this area. Typically, job descriptions are formally tied to a salary scale, and management makes few attempts to provide incentives. The investor-owned systems have certainly been the leader in rewarding outstanding performance; the institutions operating under civil service regulations have probably done the least.

Social scientists have presented conclusive evidence that money and other materialistic rewards are often limited in their effectiveness as motivators. Desirable results may also be short-lived. Maslow has presented a powerful argument that every individual possesses certain needs, ranging from basic physical needs to higher needs, such as the need for self-actualization.[12] We agree with Maslow's theory in nearly all its aspects and discuss it in other chapters.

Regarding Maslow's theory, a manager must seriously study the social background of each subordinate and assess the status of his or her needs. This, of course, can be time consuming and provide much opportunity for error, but we strongly believe the effort is worth it. Afterwards, the manager can individually tailor rewards as merited, at least to some extent. However, there are some dangers even here, e.g., the lack of uniformity tends to alienate employees who perceive others as having received rewards that are unmerited.

Under Maslow's theory, money may be the best motivator to those who need it. The degree of need for money varies according to individual perceptions. A middle manager, for example, who has a comfortable home and several thousands of dollars in the bank may not feel an acute need for money. On the other hand, a top executive living in a mansion with an expensive life-style may feel a dire need for money, even though his or her net worth may be ten times that of the middle manager.

Although Maslow's continuum of needs embraces only five hierarchical levels and it is stipulated that the satisfaction of needs at one level introduces a different set at the next level above (until the highest level of self-actualization is reached), the possibilities for particular need satisfiers in an incentive or reward system are staggering, considering the wide range of perceptions of the various individuals in a large organization. Management faces this question: What can be offered as an effective incentive to X (an employee) at Y (a hierarchical level) for attaining Z (an objective) that, if awarded, will fully or partially satisfy a specific need perceived by X? (Keep in mind that perceptions may be myriad.)

At the same time, the manager may know there are a limited number of different types of incentives or rewards that can be offered—usually very few as compared to the many types of possible need. These are complex problems, and although every solution may be less than ideal, a manager should still try to provide one. Also note that in most instances being a Monday morning quarterback is infinitely easier than actually calling signals on Sunday afternoon.

Among those incentives or rewards commonly used are pay increases, bonuses, profit sharing, recognition (an extremely broad category), promotions, special training, assurances of security (e.g., tenured positions), special privileges, improvements in the working environment, and added authority and responsibility.

Management must give careful consideration to the provision of rewards and incentives and administer programs involving them according to a clearly established policy, especially in larger firms. Even in those firms with fewer than 100 employees, caution, objectivity, and fairness must be constant features of any program of incentives, or else animosities will quickly materialize.

Many well-managed firms make little use of a separate reward system and instead rely on a basic sense of belonging and participation to motivate employees. Although we support the idea of trying to engender a sense of belonging as well as the idea of participatory management, we also support the use of merited rewards.

Summary

Controls operate throughout society and are not unique to business organizations. Although controls are a necessity, their use has received a great deal of criticism over the last several decades, primarily owing to the authoritarian and arbitrary manner in which managers have enforced them in many organizations.

Planning meshes closely with controlling, although they are two distinct functions. Planning formulates goals and objectives at each level of an organizational hierarchy, and from them standards and yardsticks are fashioned to use during the control process in measuring the results of implementing efforts. Managers also use an organization's policies, procedures, and regulations (plans) in measuring the on-the-job behavior of all personnel. In many instances, schedule planning and resource allocation planning are performed parallel to the control process, and one can truthfully say that if a manager fails to plan well, he or she will also fail to control well. Nonetheless, planning is not controlling.

The control process operates through the use of policies, procedures, and regulations as standards in effecting behavioral control and, in the same manner, through the use of objectives and goals as standards in effecting performance control. We elected to confine our discussions in this chapter largely to controlling through the use of goals and objectives, since controlling of the other type is so similar.

From a legal standpoint, line managers of a business or organization possess responsibility for controlling, unless a higher manager has expressly withheld it. At the same time that work assignments are made, authority is delegated, and responsibility is fixed, the requirement to control is also vested, whether stated or not. However, the requirement should be explicitly noted and made part of an agreement between superiors and subordinates at the outset of employment.

We recommend ten guidelines for implementing control.

1. Superiors and subordinates should reach an agreement during planning about objectives or standards to be used in measuring results.

2. Objectives should be quantified, where feasible, so that the results to be measured against them can also be quantified.

3. Measuring results against objectives (or standards developed therefrom) should be done objectively, validly, impersonally, and according to fully understood methods. Self-measurement is desirable where feasible.

4. All the possible consequences of a failure or partial failure to achieve planned objectives should be fully understood by those whose performance is measured.

5. Progress monitoring and reporting should not embarrass those whose performance is measured (i.e., apart from the results that may be revealed).

6. Monitoring and reporting should be timely and sufficiently frequent for corrective actions to be implemented before failure occurs.

7. Both the superior and the subordinate should agree on corrective actions when they prove necessary; the subordinate should then undertake to perform them.

8. Reporting should also record the causes of failure or partial failure.

9. If failure or partial failure occurs, controlling should encourage and accommodate acknowledgement of the fact by those responsible for the failure.

10. Any system of incentives or rewards used in conjunction with the control process should be fair and impartial.

The process of controlling has three basic functions which interface closely with certain functions of planning, e.g., strategic planning and human resource planning. The three controlling functions are

1. monitoring and rendering reports on progress being made in achieving objectives

2. measuring performance results as they occur against standards or yardsticks developed from goals and objectives formulated during planning

3. Taking corrective actions to bring results in line with objectives (when measuring indicates such actions are required).

Monitoring involves gaining information about progress toward goals and objectives in four ways, which can be used in combination: (1) written (printed) reports, (2) oral reports, (3) a combination of written and oral reports, and (4) personal observations. We believe any sizeable business organization had best require written reports.

We do not think reporting by exception is practicable in most service organizations, but we recognize its applicability in manufacturing and other kinds of industrial organizations.

Measuring performance can be quite tedious, but it can be expressed quite simply as a ratio:

$$\frac{\text{Performance Results}}{\text{Plans}}$$

The phrase *taking corrective actions* has some negative connotations, and some organizations use *adjusting to standards*. When results do not conform to plans in terms of quality, quantity, time, cost, or method, changes in implementation may have to be made—or even the goals or objectives may require altering if they prove to be unrealistic.

Ideally, the subordinate whose achievements are not meeting objectives should begin taking corrective actions and simultaneously report such actions to his or her superior and to others affected. Affected superiors have the right to disapprove such actions and to hold discussions regarding them so as to achieve an understanding with the subordinate. Alternatively, a subordinate may hold such discussions with the superior *before* initiating corrective actions.

Managers devise incentive and reward systems for motivational purposes and to give fair rewards to those who accomplish their objectives. Some options should be possible in granting rewards, and these options ought to take into account the fact that motivational stimuli differ quite widely among individuals at different hierarchical levels and even at the same level. At the same time, such a system must be administered fairly and objectively, or else animosities will develop among affected personnel.

Incentive or reward systems commonly include pay increases, bonuses, profit sharing, several types of recognition, promotions, special training, assurances of security, special privileges, improvements in the working environment, and added authority and responsibility.

Notes

1. Rensis Likert, *New Patterns of Management* (New York: McGraw-Hill, 1961).
2. Gary Dessler, *Organization and Management* (Reston, Va.: Reston Publishing Company, 1982), 586.
3. Henri Fayol, *General and Industrial Management*, trans. Constance Storrs (London: Sir Isaac Pitman and Sons, 1948), 107.
4. William H. Newman and Charles E. Summer, Jr., *The Process of Management* (1964), 561–62. Reprinted by permission of Prentice-Hall, Inc., Englewood Cliffs, N.J.
5. Jonathan S. Rakich and Kurt Darr, eds., *Hospital Organization and Management: Text and Readings*, 2d ed. (New York: SP Medical and Scientific Books, 1978), 277.
6. Warren B. Brown and Dennis J. Moberg, *Organization Theory and Management* (New York: Wiley, 1980), 295.
7. Peter Drucker, *The Practice of Management* (New York: Harper & Row, 1954), 131.
8. Ibid.
9. Lee Iacocca with William Novak, *Iacocca: An Autobiography* (New York: Bantam Books, 1984), 49.
10. Ibid.
11. Addison C. Bennett, *Improving Management Performance in Health Care Institutions* (Chicago: The American Hospital Association, 1978), 216.
12. Abraham Maslow, *Motivation and Personality*, 2d ed. (New York: Harper & Row, 1970), 35–58.

Part *V*

Adaptive Responses

No manager can always plan or implement with perfection. Therefore, planning and its implementing activities will occasionally fail to accomplish desired goals or objectives (for any one of a host of reasons), and managers must be able to respond adaptively.

Because planning capabilities are much greater now than they were even five years ago, those who take advantage of them will forge quickly ahead of those who do not. However, the environment in which business enterprises operate is also rapidly changing, and enhanced planning capabilities are required to keep abreast. Thus, the need to respond adaptively will not disappear, and indeed some authorities believe it will increase, despite expanding sources of data and growing computer capabilities. Although we do not share this opinion (even while conceding the environment is more rapidly changing), we know that at any given moment a multitude of managers will be frantically attempting to rectify some situation gone awry owing to imperfect planning.

To our knowledge, no authority has previously recognized responding adaptively as constituting a major element of management. Even so, based on our own experience and on observations of managers in a multitude of environments, we know an appreciable part of management time is spent in framing and implementing adaptive responses. In the case of some managers, in fact, the major portion of their time is spent thus.

Some managers apparently remain content to "muddle through," and some seemingly enjoy making rapid-fire responses, even if these may not be efficient or achieve results equal to those attainable through rational planning. However, we do not maintain that adaptive responses necessarily indicate failure or dereliction on the part of managers. There are, in truth, many instances where planning decisions must be made in the face of unknowns or unknowables. Inevitably mistakes occur, and when they do, it is best to recognize them and respond adaptively and adequately.

Managers need to strive for increased skill in all their activities. Whether or not a manager realizes what a great amount of time is spent in "putting out fires," changing directional courses owing to unforeseen environmental influences, or adjusting to new internal circumstances, the fact is that increased skills in making adaptive responses will add to his or her ability to manage. Our following comments hopefully will assist in this regard.

Chapter 16

Framing and implementing adaptive responses

Elements of Management
in Corporations

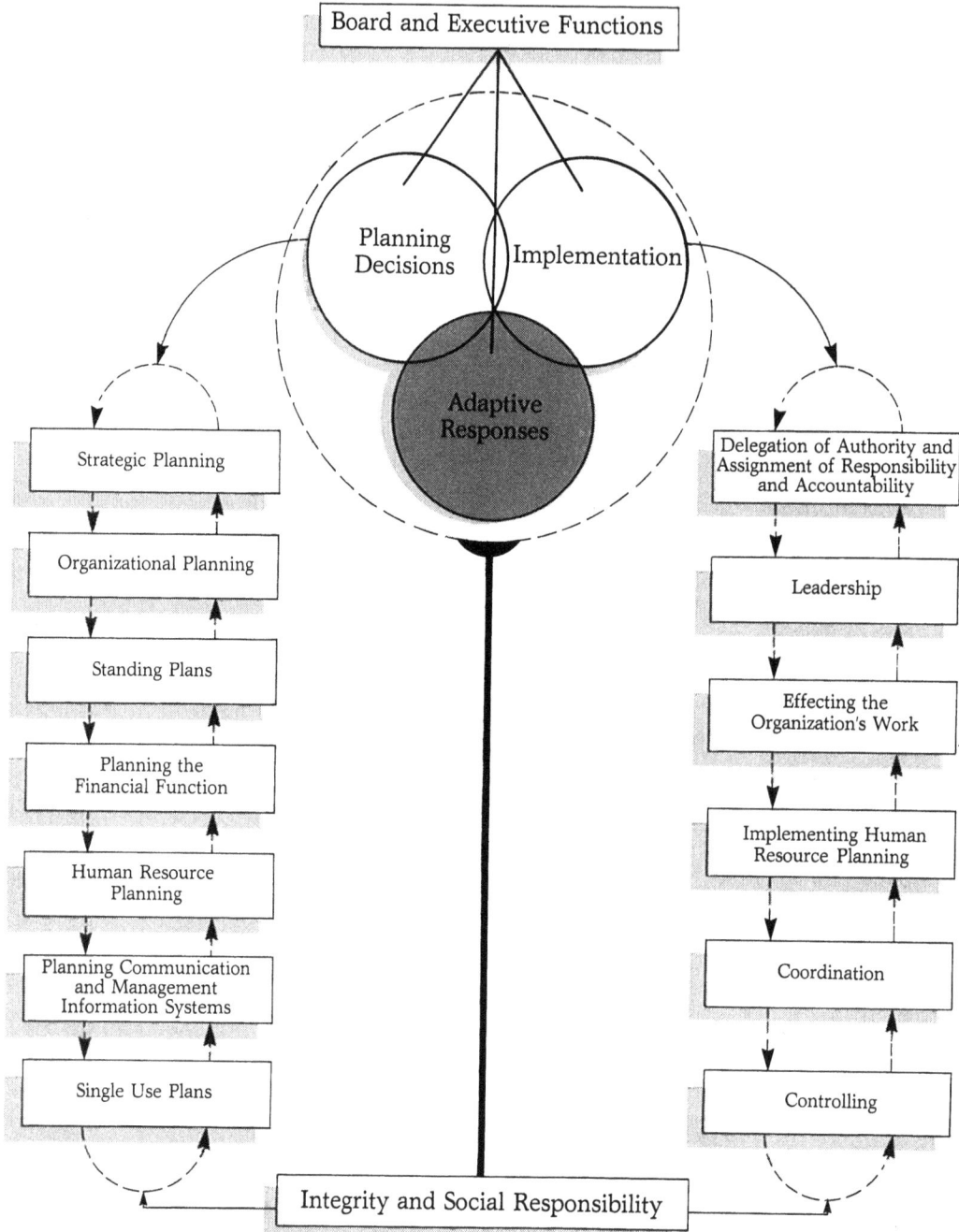

16

Relevance of adaptive responses

Although we are sure the organizational time devoted to the framing of adaptive responses is inversely proportional to the quality of appropriate planning, we also know managers will never be able to envision the future so clearly and precisely that they can entirely avoid major or minor crises. Indeed, the certainty that managers will need to respond adaptively (and often) to future circumstances they cannot foresee completely justifies, we believe, our view that adaptive responses constitute a major category of management functions. Also, these functions have characteristics that distinguish them from routine planning and implementation functions and therefore should be considered separately.

Adaptive responses are not unique to business firms. They are needed in all human organizations, and their occurrence does not relate to any particular organizational missions or purposes. Beyond this, humans cannot so order their organizations that they will be free from the necessity to respond adaptively to at least some circumstances which cannot be foreseen. Therefore, this chapter possesses implications for all those who are engaged in managing organized efforts.

Previous recognition of adaptive responses

Although no authority has previously regarded adaptive responses as a major category of management functions, several have recognized the imperfections of planning and the unavoidable conflicts that occur as the result of an often uncontrolled or uncontrollable environment.

Sayles, in his text on managerial leadership, uses the term *contingency responses*, which is obviously similar to our term. He states,

> In the perfect organization, confronting neither internal problems nor external change, the managers would act like those scientific management paragons; plans would be converted into procedures and assignments, and the forthcoming work processes would be maintained by automatic inter-worker coordination. . . .
>
> But, of course, nature (and a lot of other things) often conspires to destroy that clockwork perfection. Subordinates get testy: they fail to complement one another; other departments are unable to fulfill their commitments; breakdowns and short-

ages (or surpluses) occur. The managers' job is to get the system going and to keep it going by their own actions.[1]

Sayles then offers some cogent suggestions, based primarily on the behavioral sciences, about appropriate contingency responses. He discusses these suggestions, as a group, in a chapter entitled "Working the Hierarchy," with a focus on the vertical exchanges required by an echeloned organization.[2] Sayles also recognizes the importance of lateral communications in framing contingency responses.[3]

In his book, *Theory Z*, which is concerned with the characteristics of Japanese management, Ouchi recognizes that in industrial organizations, adaptive changes must sometimes be made, including both conventional operating changes and strategic changes to account for major environmental shifts.[4] However, Ouchi does not discuss such adaptations comprehensively, nor does he recognize they frequently occur in all organizations.

We have already mentioned the term *adaptive planning* in previous chapters. Brown and Moberg briefly discuss adaptive planning, and some of their comments accord with our view of adaptive responses, although they have an orientation to planning only. They state, "An adaptivising approach [to planning] should take into account the fact that our knowledge of the future falls into three different categories: certainty, uncertainty, and ignorance. Each category requires its own special planning technique: *commitment, contingency,* and *responsiveness.*"[5] Basically, these authors say there should be comprehensive planning—with a particular orientation toward future organizational activities—based on what is known at the time about future environments or events. We agree, but we also fully recognize that planning may become so comprehensive as to be impractical, and our experience indicates that those engaged in planning will never be able to foresee all situations necessitating adaptive responses. Clearly, managers must deal with such situations, and advice about how generally to respond to them could well be beneficial.

In recognizing the critical importance of strategic planning, Stoner briefly discusses an approach to strategy making which he calls adaptive. He states,

> The *adaptive* mode has been called "the science of muddling through."[6] Where the entrepreneur confronts the environment as a force to be controlled, the adaptive manager reacts to each situation as it arises. Where strategy in the entrepreneurial organization consists typically of dramatic leaps forward in the face of uncertainty, the adaptive organization moves ahead timidly in a series of small, disjointed steps. And where the entrepreneur constantly seeks to beat competition to the punch, the adaptive manager tends to react defensively to the actions of competitors.[7]

Stoner's remarks are generally correct, but we have known some managers who were extremely aggressive in framing adaptive responses. In the absence of planning, however, one is forced to react continuously and, strive as one may, an overwhelming set of circumstances eventually arises. In many instances, such circumstances are in part due to the existence of a competitor who is committed to planning and to acting on the basis of plans.

Newman and Warren discuss adapting (or adaptation) as it occurs within the context of an outmoded management style. They state, "Actually, a modern manager goes well beyond adapting; he exercises a positive influence to make things happen . . . he is a dynamic innovating force."[8] Although we completely agree, we would add that a manager cannot exercise a positive influence or be a dynamic innovating force unless he or she has developed a vision of the future through forecasting and has formulated appropriate plans. If this is not done, adapting will be the manager's way of life, just as it was for many managers several decades ago and as it continues to be for more managers than one would like to believe.

Whereas Newman and Warren decry adaptation as a passive adjustment to circumstances and Stoner deplores the actions of an adaptive manager, we see the framing of adaptive responses as an activity that, although drastically reducible by careful planning, can never be eliminated.

Both Alvin Toffler and William R. Boulton have stressed the need for organizations to be able to adapt in periods of rapid changes, including, as they see it, the current period. Toffler, in *The Adaptive Corporation*, states that "instead of being routine and predictable, the corporate environment has grown increasingly unstable, accelerative, and revolutionary."[9] Boulton, in *Business Policy: The Art of Strategic Management*, states, "Our concern today is that unstable and turbulent environments are causing greater uncertainty, complexity, and conflict within organizations."[10] We agree with both Toffler and Boulton that we probably live in a period containing more rapid change than ever before. However, we stress, much more than they, that managers cannot create an adaptive organization by merely having a willing mind and a flexible nature. In the face of great change, the need to plan becomes paramount. Further, organizations can plan with the assurance that appropriate data of all types—demographic, social, and economic—are more readily available than in the past, that computers can process such data more rapidly, and that statisticians abound who are capable of examining various courses of action in terms of a variety of parameters.

Our experience indicates that new planning capabilities very definitely compensate for the new uncertainties of local, regional, or national environments. The capability to pursue extended, fixed courses of action over periods of many years may never be possible again (though this itself is not entirely certain). But for now one can plan more validly, at least for the short term, than at any time in history. Our zero-base concept of strategic planning (see Chapter 3) represents an approach that unquestionably will allow any firm to respond to the vicissitudes of change in a most timely manner, provided the other types of planning we have discussed are also conscientiously and properly done.

Adaptive responses defined

One of the great problems in discussing various facets of management is the lack of a common set of terms. As early as 1961, Harold Koontz pointed to this problem and to the confusion that existed (and still exists) owing to the number of diverse approaches to management theory taken by various "schools" of management thought.[11] To help the reader understand what we mean by the term *adaptive responses*, we now set forth a definition of it that takes into account organizational management as currently practiced.

> *Adaptive responses are managerial reactions to unforeseen environmental occurrences internal or external to the organization.*

As noted in our opening chapter, adaptive responses have as their object the avoidance of undesirable results or the reaping of attractive rewards. On many occasions, they necessitate at least some changes in formal plans. The majority are short-term corrections to ongoing operations, though they are needed in a variety of situations.

Adaptive responses, though usually devised urgently and implemented within a short timeframe, sometimes even lead to a paradigmatic change in the mission of many similar organizations or in their approach to doing business itself. For example, over the last decade or so, adaptive responses have changed both the manner in which forecasts and strategic plans are accomplished and the basic nature of the plans themselves for organizations engaged in the delivery of health care, especially hospitals.

Once a response has been formally incorporated into the routine planning and implementation processes of an organization, however, it ceases to be an adaptive response (in our sense of the term). Certainly, the response (or responses) so incorporated would continue to represent an adaptation to environmental impingements, but it would then be handled on an ongoing basis within routine planning and implementation processes. It is clear, then, that adaptive responses are one-time-through activities. Note, however, that often in operations the same mistake or conflict occurs twice, thus necessitating the same response twice. In such instances, we would still classify the response as adaptive. Only when it is made routine and incorporated into formal planning and implementation processes does a response cease to be an adaptive response.

Elements of adaptive responses

Adaptive responses are composed of planning, nonfunctional decision making (as contrasted to planning), and implementing activities (see Figure 16-1).

In considering the framing and implementing of adaptive responses, one might again ask why we have singled them out as a separate kind of management function, since they are composed primarily of the other two major kinds of management activity we have identified, namely, planning and implementing. And although it is true that nonfunctional decision making (i.e., making immediate choices among available options) is sometimes necessary, the vast majority of management time consumed in making adaptive responses is spent in short-term planning and in performing the activities of implementation. The answer lies in the

Figure 16-1

**Components of Adaptive
Responses**

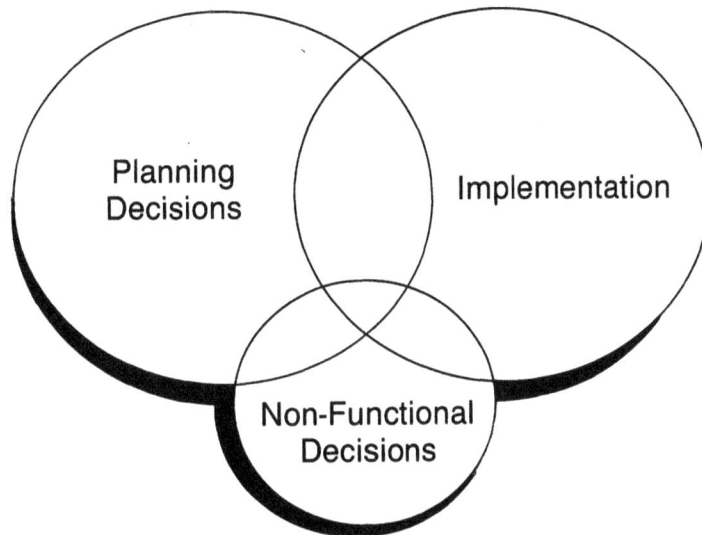

fact that each situation requiring an adaptive response is basically unstructured. As in the case of football, soccer, or baseball, circumstances arise that the playbook does not cover. When this occurs, players must assess at a glance the existing situation and react appropriately. Unique improvisations, either to avoid undesirable consequences or to exploit an opportunity, are common.

The contrast between deliberate acts of planning and implementation (discussed in previous chapters) and adaptive responses should be apparent. We maintain that the general randomness and structurelessness of the situations in which adaptive responses are needed, the several approaches available for formulating and implementing them, and the frequency of their occurrence are all factors that justify conceiving them as constituting a major class of management functions. This conception can then lead to the serious study of adaptive responses as a long-neglected element of management.

Willingness to respond adaptively

Some managers exhibit great reluctance in admitting planning errors and acknowledging poorly executed acts of implementation. Pride and fear of lost prestige or ridicule often cause managers to "stay the course" to the bitter end, or at least a mediocre end. Sometimes they drag others, including shareholders and employees, into the mire along with themselves. We regard this as inexcusable. When monitoring of results (hopefully an effective monitoring process exists) indicates formal planning and implementation are not achieving objectives, economic and other, it shows infinitely more character and wisdom to recognize, evaluate, and admit errors than to cover them over with verbal smokescreens and continue perpetuating the same mistakes. In such instances, adaptive responses become imperative.

We have observed some managers to fail to respond to unforeseen circumstances from an unwillingness to admit the realities of a situation. For example, few hospitals have shown exemplary leadership in responding to the national rebellion against high costs and charges for inpatient care. Rather, many hospital executives have been carried kicking and screaming into the new era, with a profuse number of justifications for past failures.

Role of planning

Adaptive responses differ from formalized planning in their urgency, short duration, and uniqueness. They are generally one-time-through activities and their plans are single use plans. Managers frame most adaptive responses in reaction to problems that demand urgent or immediate attention. In such cases, managers function "under the gun" and perform necessary planning within relatively brief time periods. If, however, the planning inherent in responding adaptively carries forward as an activity separate from routine, formal planning and no need exists to incorporate it into the routine process, its duration would not be characteristic and might be unlimited.

As already noted, planning required for adaptive responses should be incorporated into the routine planning activities of an organization (if feasible), because sometimes many separate problems demand to be resolved simultaneously and these together can overwhelm the individual managers confronting them. If it becomes obvious that the same problem (or very similar problems) will arise frequently, standing plans should be amended so that the resolution can be carried out routinely. This will relieve managers of "reinventing the wheel" each time the problem occurs, thus saving time that can be used for anticipating other problems. It must always be remembered that the framing and implementing of adaptive responses is usually an inefficient (though necessary) expenditure of management time.

Categories of adaptive responses

Adaptive responses can be classified in several different ways, but one way that can be useful in their framing and implementation is very simple, involving only two categories. By consciously placing each new case into one of the two categories, managers will be able to easily devise a basic procedure for handling cases within each category. Undoubtedly, the two procedures will not accommodate all cases placed in the categories, but at least a start will have been made. Readers should keep in mind we are writing about *unforeseen* problems or opportunities that cannot be handled under existing plans or established customs. The two categories are as follows:

1. adaptive responses to problems or opportunities that can and should be handled by the affected manager alone, without assistance from

other managers positioned either laterally or vertically in the management hierarchy

2. adaptive responses to problems or opportunities that transcend the authority and responsibility of a single manager or that cannot be handled without assistance from other managers.

Formulating category 1 responses

After a manager recognizes the existence of the unanticipated problem (or opportunity) and determines that he or she, together with assigned operating personnel, can and should handle it without the assistance of other managers, the following steps are appropriate. On occasion, a situation may be extremely urgent and no more than a fast mental review will be possible. Yet, if one trains oneself to be a reflective thinker (see John Dewey's definition on pp. 59–60), these steps can be done with the necessary speed.

1. Define the problem in objective terms. In numerous instances, we have observed managers whose greatest failure occurs at this early point. Some indulge in wishful thinking and get lost musing about how things "ought" to be, wondering about what others believe or hope, or brooding about preventive actions already impossible to execute. All such assessments are useless and can lead to early failure. No, it is essential to define the problem exactly as it is. Keep in mind, however, that although the perceptions of others involved may not correspond to reality, they indeed have these perceptions—which may need to be taken into account despite their inaccuracy.

Where quantification is possible, it should be accomplished as a part of an objective assessment.

2. Conceptualize alternative solutions to the problem. Sometimes the solution will be so obvious that only brief consideration is required. However, acting on a prematurely conceived solution occurs all too frequently. Each alternative should be conceptualized in terms of who, when, what, where, how, and how much (if funds are involved).

In this step, a manager will be wise to consult with those who will implement the plan, time permitting. We believe it is usually preferable to get those who will be assigned the responsibility for implementation to be involved in the planning.

If time allows, a manager should state in writing the alternatives believed worthy of consideration. Even if this is for individual use only, it still assists in ordering one's thinking. Usually, a manager will wish to consult with some key operating personnel, and written statements facilitate discussions.

3. Formulate and apply selection criteria to each alternative. Usually selection criteria will vary from case to case, but in business organizations there are several criteria that apply to many different situations. These include effectiveness, risk, timing, total cost, unit cost, avoidance of undesirable consequences, flexibility, anticipated revenues, etc.

We stress again the importance of valid, objective quantification. Only when one reduces generalities to numbers can they be validly compared. Of course, some criteria cannot be quantified. With respect to these, one had best obtain expert opinion, even though past experience often (but not always) can prove helpful.

4. Adopt the alternative that appears to be best in terms of the selection criteria. This step essentially involves the formulation of a plan.

5. Prepare a communication describing the plan in terms of who, when, what, where, how, and how much (if funds are involved). Managers must judge, on each occasion, whether the plan should be communicated orally or in writing. We lean toward written communications, because they tend to be clearer and more difficult to misinterpret. Also, managers usually wish to give some justification for the plan, and this is often the best time for doing so.

6. Devise a plan for control. This may involve no more than an intent to check back at completion of the work. However, it may involve a rather detailed system of measurement and reporting, and planning is certainly the best time for devising such a system.

7. Discuss the plan with those who will implement it. Rarely should a plan be delivered in the form of orders to subordinates, whether they be managers or operating personnel. However, if time does not permit discussion, this may serve as the most practical method.

After timely communication of the plan, implementation follows, which we discuss under a subsequent heading.

Formulating category 2 responses

If a situation occurs that cannot or should not be handled through application of standing plans or accepted customs and if the affected manager has determined that resolution of the problem (or exploitation of the opportunity) cannot be achieved within the scope of his or her authority and responsibility, the following steps can usually be followed to good advantage. Because other managers will be involved, however, the process may be somewhat difficult to control.

1. Define the problem (or opportunity) objectively and determine which managers will be involved in or significantly affected by its resolution. The precautions we have noted above in discussing the first category apply here also, but objectivity may be more difficult to achieve, because the significance and scope of the problems tend to be greater than for the first category.

Obviously, other managers with a pertinent interest in the unforeseen problem or opportunity should be notified and consulted. Yet, many managers attempt to keep unexpected problems and opportunities "close to the vest," usually for bad reasons. They then often find themselves in trouble and with little sympathy from their colleagues.

2. Communicate with other affected managers, positioned both horizontally and vertically in the organization's hierarchy, and with key operating personnel (if indicated). Confirm the authority and responsibility for resolution. This step involves developing the teamwork that may be required for both planning and implementation. Some ignore this step from overly aggressive tendencies or a desire to demonstrate leadership qualities. Of course, sometimes urgency may require a manager to forge ahead and circumvent colleagues. The manager may even usurp authority to effect resolution, if indicated. (In fact, we have done this.) Ordinarily, however, it is best to be a team player.

We know of nothing more unpleasant in organizational management than to be confronted with a big surprise, especially when it unnecessarily occurs through the actions of a fellow manager. When another manager may be appreciably affected by one's planning or implementation of an adaptive response, one should almost always communicate with that manager. Timely communication is the foundation of coordination, and not only does it increase the probability of success, but it is a requirement of managerial honesty.

3. Establish time limits for resolution of the unforeseen occurrence. After getting feedback from fellow managers, reviewing information about the situation and its degree of urgency, and making a tentative assessment of required resources and existing constraints, one should establish time limits for (1) framing a plan for action and (2) implementing the plan. This step also involves determining the priority ranking of the resolution (i.e., its degree of importance vis-à-vis the importance of other managerial responsibilities).

If other managers are involved in any facet of the occurrence's resolution, they will be able to budget their time much more wisely by knowing the probable timeframe.

4. Formulate alternative solutions. Seldom is a major problem or opportunity simple. Generally, managers should formulate two or more possible resolutions in terms of necessary funds (a quantified estimate), who will act, what they will do, when and where the actions will be done, and in what manner. This step is equivalent to Step 2 for Category 1 adaptive responses, but the formulations should involve consultations with at least those managers most vitally affected by the outcome, including those positioned laterally and vertically in the hierarchy.

5. Formulate and apply selection criteria. Managers should use appropriate selection criteria, such as total cost, life cycle cost, effectiveness, timing, risk, avoidance of undesirable consequences, flexibility, bottom line, etc., to test each hypothetical resolution being considered (if time permits). Relevant criteria should be adopted, and factual information and informed opinion should be assembled regarding how each resolution stands with respect to each criterion.

Of all steps, this one requires the greatest technical knowledge. In small firms, such knowledge may not be available among organizational members, and consultants may be used if the importance of the matter so indicates. The technical knowledge required is basically for gathering valid, objective, quantified data and for performing statistical comparisons. Not only does quantification, if valid for comparisons, force objectivity into testing, but much time can be saved and hurt feelings avoided by elimination of a considerable amount of "jawboning."

6. Adopt the solution which appears most feasible in terms of the selection criteria. This represents, in essence, selection of one alternative as a plan to be followed. Although advice may have been obtained in each of the steps up to this point, the manager possessing authority and responsibility for resolving the occurrence should make the selection. In this way, plan resolution can be kept at the hierarchical level where it should be, and the integrity of authority and responsibility will be maintained. This pinpointing also helps to develop the abilities of managers in regard to basic planning and decision making.

7. Devise a control system. Where several managers are involved, this becomes doubly necessary.

8. Communicate the plan to appropriate organizational personnel, especially affected managers. Such communication anticipates the need for approval and coordination during execution. Direct discussions prove most effective.

Again, this communication should describe the plan in the usual terms—who, when, what, where, and how. It may also disclose financial parameters, if applicable.

With this communication, implementation can begin.

Nonfunctional decision making

The literature is replete with information about decision making, especially the writings of one or two decades ago. Of course, decision making does pervade all of management and is in no way unique to the making of adaptive responses. Perhaps we have been remiss in not discussing it directly and at more length in preceding portions of this text, but note that all planning is actually decision making, though restricted to determining future courses of action. We have devoted seven chapters to planning and have delineated two similar but separate planning methodologies immediately above.

However, managers sometimes face the need to make choices that will not basically affect future courses of action. For example, one might have to select from among equipment items that do the same job or from among insurance firms that provide equal coverage and charge equal premiums. One might have to choose one manager from among many to receive a routine award, choose one vendor from among several having essentially equal prices, quality, and capabilities, choose staff from among a number of applicants, most of whom possess acceptable qualifications, or choose an architect, consultant, or other expert from among several qualified outsiders. One classic example is when a temporary staff member has to be selected to cover the unexpected absence of a key operating person. No change in plans is required; one merely has to choose who the substitute will be.

Each of these cases involves a response in the form of a simple choice that has little or no bearing on the direction of an already determined course of action. Although such choices may be made while a plan is being created, they do not constitute a plan themselves and occur most often when re-evaluation of a part of a plan becomes necessary. Admittedly, only a fine line exists between these nonfunctional decisions and the true planning decisions that occur either as part of routine planning or of planning required in making adaptive responses. However, thoughtful consideration will reveal the differences.

A good way to distinguish a nonfunctional decision from a planning decision is to try to answer this question: Does the decision involve a simple choice among largely equal alternatives, and is it such that no matter what choice is made, the future outcomes of either related or unrelated plans will almost certainly not be affected? If the answer to this question is yes, the decision can definitely be classified as nonfunctional.

Nonfunctional decisions are most frequently made in the process of responding adaptively, and thus we recognize them as an integral, though small, subelement of adaptive responses. Although in the case of most adaptive responses managers must formulate action plans prior to implementation, sometimes they need only make nonfunctional choices.

For this reason, we have elected to discuss decision making as a function separate from planning. We repeat: All planning (making decisions about future courses of action) is decision making, but not all decision making is planning (which excludes simple nonfunctional decision making).

Types of decision making

Authorities have described two predominant types of decision-making processes: the *rational process* and the *creative process*. Dewey's *reflective thought process*, the *scientific method*, and the *systems approach to planning* stand prominent among other decision processes. We briefly discuss the rational and creative processes below. The reader is referred to other publications and to the preface to Part III for explanations of the other three methods cited, as well as use of the rational process for planning.[12]

The rational process
Where only simple choosing is involved, the following steps compose the rational process.

1. Determine the available choices that appear to be feasible.

2. Establish selection criteria and apply them to each choice. Selection criteria usually have to be determined from scratch owing to the wide variations among alternatives. However, "best qualified for the purpose intended" is often used. We should stress here, as we did for planning, that quantification brings objectivity to the comparison of alternatives. Factor analysis, at least, can be quickly done.

3. Select the alternative which appears best in terms of the criteria. In effect, the decision occurs at this point.

4. Communicate the decision to those who will act on it (or implement it).

    At this point, the decision awaits implementation. Some authorities mistakenly list implementation as a step in the decision-making process ("the carrying out of the decision," as it is usually put). Carrying out a decision is unequivocally separate from making it. The only connection is that decision making should take into account the feasibility, cost, and timing of carrying out the various alternatives under consideration.

The creative process
Newman and Warren have noted the following stages of the so-called creative decision-making process, based on the testimony of inventors and scientists.[13]

1. *Saturation.* This involves becoming mentally steeped in the problem, so that all its aspects are internalized.

2. *Deliberation.* In this stage, the mind analyzes, notes relationships, and searches for solutions based on what is known about the problem and what the desired attributes are of any solution.

3. *Incubation.* Here the mind turns from conscious solution seeking and analysis and instead relaxes, allowing the subconscious to work.

4. *Illumination.* The mind suddenly perceives a promising solution.

5. *Accommodation.* This involves testing the solution for feasibility while further refining it at the same time.

Our own experience in reaching innovative solutions to problems with which we were deeply involved indicates these stages do in fact occur. We want to stress that few innovations occur without deep mental immersion in a given problem. This means that those who consider matters casually seldom achieve "bright ideas." We also believe, based on our observations and experience, that decision makers should test all so-called bright ideas in terms of appropriate criteria in a cold and sober manner, based on objective quantifications. It is surprising how many times we have seen an apparently brilliant idea reveal serious flaws when it is objectively tested.

Validity in decision making

Decision making is importantly involved in general planning and also in making the simple choices sometimes required for responding adaptively. Indeed, some authorities, notably Herbert Simon, the 1978 Nobel Prize winner in economics, come very close to equating decision making (including what we call planning) with management.[14] Considering that the best plans and most expertly made choices have little or no value unless they are implemented, we hesitate to go that far. But we do believe that, in the affairs of any organization, planning and nonfunctional decision making are together the equal of implementation as far as importance.

Steers, Ungson, and Mowday note the inability of humans to be completely rational in decision making, both in its broadest sense (including planning) and in the sense of making simple choices. Based on previous work by Simon, they note that humans, for the most part, are only "intendedly rational, or seeking to be rational in the face of incomplete information and computational abilities."[15] This may be true, but we maintain it is better to intend to be rational than to ignore rationality, as we have sometimes observed managers to do. Also, the ability to achieve rationality depends directly on three factors: (1) the mental capabilities and objectivity of the decision maker, (2) the valid data pertaining to the problem at hand, and (3) the computational capabilities that are available.

Some very prominent executives have castigated "bean counters," "MBA upstarts," "whiz kids" and all who rely heavily on quantification, perhaps with some justification. Certainly a problem exists when one can't see the forest for the trees. However, early in our careers we had a famous CPA give us this advice: "When you are trying to solve a problem or win an argument, there is a possibility you will fail, even with the very best facts available, but when you have pertinent facts, the probability of being successful increases manyfold."[16] We have always held this opinion in high regard, and although we are skeptical of "principles" of management, this comes about as close to truly being one as any we've come across.

We should note that a number of authorities, in their despair over the inability of humans to achieve complete rationality, largely dismiss the rational decision-making process and then turn to examining how managers "really make decisions." When one considers that the rational decision-making process and the scientific method are very similar, this question leaps forward: How can scientists, who are also human, achieve the rationality that has allowed us to progress from living in caves to placing a man on the moon? If we had continuously despaired about the process of scientific investigation and its shortcomings, we might still believe the world is square.

Objectivity, based on valid information and precise measurements, has been the hallmark of scientific investigation, which usually involves use of the scientific method. The characteristics of the scientific method closely resemble those of the rational decision-making process. In making important decisions, the same objectivity that characterizes scientific investigation can now be brought to bear, provided decision makers obtain valid information and apply appropriate computer-aided statistical computations. Progress will continue in this area, and the future will belong to those who bring it about.

Situations necessitating adaptive responses

As we have already stated, adaptive responses are usually spawned in a variety of problem situations, although some arise when unanticipated opportunities appear. Typical problem situations are as follows.

1. *Inadequate or inappropriate planning.* Many managers have few plans to follow and they literally come to their offices and wait for things to happen. They may not be aware of it, but they are pursuing a basic strategy of reacting rather than acting. "Putting out fires" becomes a way of managerial life. A basic theme of this text, of course, is that planned actions avoid the constant need for reactions and that planning increases the probability of success in operations.

2. *Breakdowns in communication and coordination.* The causes of such breakdowns are almost innumerable, but basic inattention to the necessity to communicate is a major one. Of course, having ill-defined and nebulous communication policies and channels is another.

3. *Failures to implement properly.* Some firms plan well and then lack leadership or other management abilities needed to get operations going and to keep them functioning smoothly.

4. *Resistance to change.* Ordinarily, resistance should and can be avoided by appropriate planning and implementation, but not all things can be read from the minds of humans. Therefore, no one will ever overcome resistance to change completely (nor would this be desirable). It will continue to occasionally necessitate the framing and implementation of adaptive responses.

5. *Conflicts among personnel.* Many authorities have written about person- nel conflicts, including their stimulating and enervating effects. Dynamic tension does produce some beneficial results, as does planned or at least envisioned competition. However, we regard playing "the old administrator's game," whereby subordinates are deliberately pitted against each other, as reprehensible and basically unethical, regardless of any results it might achieve. Some have employed this technique to place subordinates in a somewhat depend- ent and subservient position, and we deplore this as well. (We have come across situations in organizations where conflicts created in this manner were so bad that we were certain some of those involved were carrying pistols!) In any case, conflicts among personnel will continue to require adaptive responses on some occasions.

6. *General personnel problems.* Deaths, sudden illnesses, unannounced absences, sudden necessities to fire (discharge), sudden resignations, and other unexpected occurrences not covered by standing plans are typical examples.

7. *Unanticipated external events or conditions.* It would be impossible to list all of these owing to their number and variety. However, unexpected governmental interventions, sudden economic changes, and so-called acts of God constitute a sizeable number. Each of these may bring advantages or disadvantages to the affected firm.

Some readers, given their own managerial experiences, may be able to think of other situations necessitating adaptive responses, but the above constitute the major portion. See Figure 16-2 for a graphic depic- tion of some sources of adaptive responses.

Implementing adaptive responses

Perspective

The same factors that affect planning that occurs as part of an adaptive response also affect implementation. As noted, adaptive responses tend to be urgently needed, of short duration, and unique.

Managers find that implementing adaptive responses usually dis- rupts organizational work routines. Unless implementation is carried out properly regarding each occurrence, operational personnel can become testy, managers affected may engage in "scapegoating," and some of those involved may wallow in self-pity. If the necessity occurs to imple- ment too many adaptive responses too fast, some may make remarks to the effect that "someone has got to do something about this disorganized mess around here."

Although we deplore management where planning is nearly nonex- istent and managers constantly flail about trying to resolve one crisis after another (many of which could have been avoided through appropriate planning), the manner in which one plans and implements adaptive responses often reveals one's managerial mettle. Because implementing activities are most visible to operational personnel and affect them most, these activities may constitute the basis of their judgments of managers.

Figure 16-2

Adaptive Responses: Originating Sources

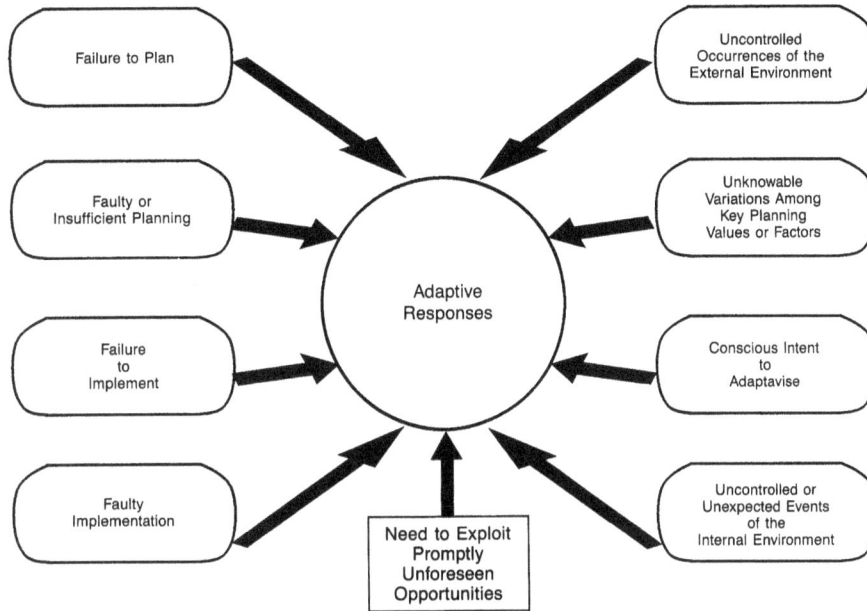

Successful and satisfactory planning and implementation of an adaptive response that personnel (both managers and operating personnel) can agree was necessitated by an occurrence whose prevention could not reasonably have been expected can engender enhanced cooperation and voluntary coordination, both in routine work and in future adaptive responses. Conversely, if a manager fails in implementation or successfully implements, but in a manner that reduces the respect of his or her subordinates and fellow managers, they may withhold wholehearted support in the future.

Sadly, many people erroneously judge the leadership qualities of managers more by their implementation of adaptive responses than by the planning and implementing work done to accomplish the mission, goals, and objectives of the organization. Be this as it may, one cannot deny the importance of framing and implementing adaptive responses. Certainly, adaptive responses, if not handled properly, can seriously impair organizational activities and can decrease the respect of others for a manager's capabilities. This can occur even where the adaptive response is an attempt to exploit an opportunity.

General nature of implementation

Implementations of whatever kind, including implementations of adaptive responses, will occasionally involve all of the factors and activities we have cited in Part IV. Certain of those factors and activities pertain to *all* implementations. For example, the persons who will actually perform the implementating activities must be informed of that fact in one way or another and must accept the authority, responsibility and accountability for doing so—this is basic to getting any work done. Control measures, determined in planning, must be carried out in implementation. Group dynamics will occur in work done both in routine operations and in adaptive responses, and in each case can be similarly influenced by managers.

However, probably because of the urgency and the necessarily short timeframe for executing many adaptive responses, their implementation seems to cause a greater number of problems of two kinds than does the implementation of planning for routine operations. We have often observed that when adaptive responses are being implemented, there is increased resistance to change and more conflicts among personnel. We discuss these two problems briefly below and refer readers to Chapters 4 and 12 for further discussion.

Resistance to change
Years ago, Sartain et al. noted, "Perception is a joint function of the stimulus situation and of the perceiver and his emotions, attitudes and frames of reference."[17] We believe that owing to the urgency of responding adaptively to some situations, there may be insufficient time for many affected persons to gain an accurate perception of the need for the response or the manner in which it must be accomplished.

Likert has noted that changes "which are superimposed by authority meet with strong resistance."[18] Since managers necessarily implement many adaptive responses through direct orders, they therefore meet some resistance.

Conflict
If not handled properly, adaptive responses will occasion organizational conflict. For example, in urgent situations an executive may decide on a plan and then instruct a staff person to relay the plan to a line manager for implementation. (We have done this.) The line manager immediately resents this, viewing the staff person as a usurper of authority. Conflict results.

Many conflicts occur as a result of communication obstacles, one of the causes of conflict noted by Miles.[19] The urgency of making some adaptive response simply does not permit adequate communication to be effected.

Conflicts may also come about merely because the exigencies of some situations do not allow managers to coordinate adequately.

Categories of adaptive responses and their implementation

Implementation is the execution or fulfillment of planning—good, bad, or indifferent. The implementing activities of adaptive responses serve to fulfill planning done to resolve unexpected problems or exploit unexpected opportunities. One can therefore consider these activities in light of the two categories of adaptive responses noted previously:

1. adaptive responses to problems or opportunities that can and should be handled by the affected manager alone, without assistance from other managers positioned either vertically or horizontally in the management hierarchy (of course, the implementation of these responses will usually involve operational personnel)

2. adaptive responses to problems or opportunities that transcend the authority and responsibility of a single manager or that cannot be handled without assistance from other managers (again, one would expect involvement of operational personnel in implementation).

Owing to the uniqueness of the problems and opportunities that arise, the uniqueness of the plans for resolving them, and the variety of organizational environments where implementation takes place, we consider it impossible to formulate any reliable stepped or staged process for implementation regarding any classification of adaptive responses. However, we note below certain differences between the implementation of adaptive responses and the implementation of routinely planned work activities. Also, we briefly discuss differences related to the two categories of adaptive responses previously cited.

Implementing category 1 responses
The urgency, short duration, and uniqueness of adaptive responses affect their implementation. These factors also tend to force special actions to be done quickly, which often proves to be inefficient and disruptive to ongoing operations. Peremptory or arbitrary orders meet resistance and cause conflicts among personnel. Problems with coordination also occur in greater numbers than in the case of routine operations.

Regarding Category 1 responses, the probability of events getting out of hand may be less than for Category 2 responses, owing to the fact that the sphere of action does not extend beyond the purview of a single manager.

Depending on the kind of operations being performed routinely by operational personnel, the amount of cohesiveness of the operational group, and the degree of rapport enjoyed with an informal group leader, the manager may find the most effective method of implementation is to outline his or her plan in terms of when, where, what, and applicable financial parameters, and leave specific work assignments and performance methodologies to the group. Where a cohesive group does not exist or where a manager decides making specific assignments will be more effective, he or she should do just that. However, we have always regarded group conferences with subordinates—to clarify work assignments and suggested work methodologies—as beneficial, for they allow the airing and discussion of perceived problems. Managers must always remember that the successful implementation of the adaptive response is the true objective—not ego satisfaction. Furthermore, many operational employees, although not versed in management, have an excellent sense of coordination, and most people will exhibit a higher level of cooperation if they feel involved.

In adaptive responses (more so than in routine operations), subordinates will have greater respect for an assigning manager and will evidence greater cooperation when the manager also remains involved. To make arbitrary assignments with firm, tight deadlines and then leave with a promise to return late in the day after eighteen holes of golf seldom wins many avid supporters. Subordinates, superiors, and other organizational associates judge one's leadership just as much by what one does as by what one says (probably even more than by what one says).

In making the arbitrary assignments that are sometimes necessary in implementation, the *manner* in which an assignment is made is often as important as the nature of the assignment. Treating subordinates respectfully rates very high; a willingness to compromise, without being spineless, nearly always wins support. Being aware of what a subordinate has to do routinely is frequently helpful in making appropriate assignments and prevents burdening the subordinate unduly.

We have often traded favors with subordinates in situations where organizational policy would not be violated (e.g., "You do this for me, and I'll do that for you at some later time"). Many adaptive responses may necessitate overtime for operational personnel; company policy should be followed in this regard.

We have observed that managers who are most successful in implementing adaptive responses where subordinates are involved are those who, for whatever reason, enjoy a good rapport with their subordinates. Demonstrated firmness and genuine concern for persons, coupled with a positive work attitude, seem to generate such rapport more than any other factors.

As noted previously, we have found no pat formulas for handling adaptive responses. One must rely on one's best judgment and on one's management and leadership abilities.

Implementing category 2 responses
The chief difference between implementations of Category 1 and Category 2 adaptive responses concerns the difficulty in coordination. In Category 2 responses, not only may managers in a vertical hierarchical relationship be involved, but frequently so may those in a horizontal relationship. One might assume that a manager in the highest echelon can always take charge, but often the problem is more pertinent and of more concern to a manager in a lower echelon. Also, the manager in the highest echelon might in effect say, "You work it out."

In such situations, the implementing manager must rely solely on the cooperativeness of all managers involved, except those, hopefully, over whom he or she exercises authority. Thus, an opportunity arises to test one's skills as a negotiator, an exchanger of favors, a politician, a compromiser, and, in a sense, a leader.

Direct discussions with other managers will be most effective. Here, again, feelings of being involved elicit cooperation. After the responsible and initiating manager has explained his or her plan for implementation and the decision-making process used in devising the plan, the other managers can offer suggestions and advice. Compromises often prove necessary, but in the end there hopefully will be acceptance of the assignments in the plan and of a starting point for work. The responsible manager should also discuss his or her control plan and implement control activities while the general implementation of the adaptive response progresses.

As in the case of Category 1 adaptive responses, we can recommend no step-by-step implementing process, except to say that the plan made must be communicated, work assignments effected, and a control system established. Just how this will be done will depend on the unique features of each situation and the abilities of the various managers involved.

Summary

Through appropriate planning, managers can significantly reduce time devoted to framing and implementing adaptive responses. However, organizations can never be free of them, owing to human inability to foresee the future with complete accuracy. Because of this and the frequency with which adaptive responses occur, we have conceived them as constituting a third major category of management functions—the other two, of course, are planning and activities of implementation.

Although our review of management literature has not been exhaustive, it has been comprehensive. We concluded that no authority has heretofore classified adaptive responses as a major category of management functions.

We have defined adaptive responses as managerial reactions to unforeseen environmental occurrences internal or external to the organization. They have three primary components: planning, nonfunctional decision making (simple choices among alternatives as opposed to planning), and implementing activities. Since the two main components of adaptive responses are planning and implementation, one might logically ask why we believe it necessary to put them in a separate category. The answer is that they are basically unstructured compared to routine operations.

The distinguishing characteristics of adaptive responses are urgency, short duration, and uniqueness. These dictate that planning, decision making, and implementation will often be very different than for routine operations.

In general, responding adaptively is not an efficient use of management time. Where managers can foresee the continued occurrence of problems or opportunities that have occasioned adaptive responses, they should incorporate required planning and decision making into policies, procedures, and methods, with implementing activities being incorporated into routine operations.

To facilitate the study of adaptive responses, we divided them into two categories:

1. adaptive responses to problems or opportunities that should be handled by a single manager and with no assistance from other managers

2. adaptive responses to problems or opportunities that transcend the authority and responsibility of a single manager or that cannot be handled without assistance from other managers.

Planning for Category 1 responses comprises these steps:

1. Define the problem or opportunity.

2. Conceptualize alternative solutions.

3. Formulate and apply selection criteria to each alternative.

4. Adopt the alternative deemed best in terms of the criteria.

5. Prepare a communication that reflects the plan in terms of who, when, what, where, how, and how much (if funds are involved).

6. Devise a plan for control.

7. Communicate the plan to those who will implement it.

   Planning for Category 2 responses comprises the following steps:

1. Define the problem or opportunity and determine other affected managers.

2. Communicate the defined problem or opportunity to all affected managers.

3. Establish and communicate time limits for resolution to other affected managers.

4. Formulate alternative solutions.

5. Formulate and apply selection criteria.

6. Adopt the solution deemed best in terms of the criteria.

7. Devise a plan for control.

8. Communicate the plan in terms of who, when, what, where, how, and how much (if funds are involved) to affected managers and key operational personnel.

   Both rational and creative decision making prove useful in making the nonfunctional choices that are sometimes necessary in framing adaptive responses.
   The following situations, among others, typically generate the need for adaptive responses:

- inadequate or inappropriate planning

- breakdowns in communication and coordination

- failure to implement properly

- resistance to change

- conflicts among personnel

- opportunities requiring quick exploitation

- unanticipated external events or conditions

- conscious intent to adaptivise

- unknowable variations among key planning values or factors.

The implementation of the plan and of any nonfunctional decisions is the final component of an adaptive response. Implementation can involve, from time to time, all of the factors and activities cited in Part IV of this text. Some of these factors and activities occur in all adaptive responses, e.g., assignment of authority, responsibility, and accountability and employment of the control process. Others may occur infrequently. There seem to be two kinds of problems with a high incidence of occurrence: resistance to change and conflicts among personnel. Their high incidence may result from the characteristics of adaptive responses—urgency, short duration, and uniqueness.

In Category 1, implementations where only a single manager and operational personnel are involved, the manager's rapport with the operational personnel is very important. Depending on group cohesiveness (see Chapter 12), the manager may merely turn the matter over to the group after describing the desired objective and setting a deadline for achieving it.

An involved manager who is respected by subordinates for his or her concern, supportiveness, and businesslike approach to work situations will be able to implement adaptive responses quite handily.

Coordination usually proves to be a much greater problem in the case of Category 2 implementations where several managers, both vertically and horizontally related, may be involved. The initiating and responsible manager must achieve rapport with these colleagues, and he or she must be able to gain their support and cooperation or else defer to a responsible manager in a higher echelon. Discussions, explanations, and clear elucidations of adopted plans are desirable in dealing with Category 2 problems and opportunities. Compromises, exchanges of favors, and the willing involvement of others are frequently found necessary for success. Regardless of the approaches, techniques, and methodologies that may be used in implementation, managers should not relinquish their responsibility to control.

Notes

1. Leonard R. Sayles, *Leadership: What Effective Managers Really Do and How They Do It* (New York: McGraw-Hill, 1979), 27.
2. Ibid., 113–24.
3. Ibid., 71–92.
4. William G. Ouchi, *Theory Z* (Reading, Mass.: Addison-Wesley, 1981), 89.
5. Warren B. Brown and Dennis J. Moberg, *Organization Theory and Management* (New York: Wiley, 1980), 280.
6. Charles E. Lindblom, "The Science of Muddling Through," *Public Administration Review* 19, no. 2 (1959).
7. James A.F. Stoner, *Management* (1982), 106. Reprinted by permission of Prentice-Hall, Inc., Englewood Cliffs, N.J.
8. William H. Newman and Kirby E. Warren, *The Process of Management*, 4th ed. (1977), 4. Reprinted by permission of Prentice-Hall, Inc., Englewood Cliffs, N.J.
9. Alvin Toffler, *The Adaptive Corporation* (New York: McGraw-Hill, 1985), 1.

10. William R. Boulton, *Business Policy: The Art of Strategic Management* (New York: Macmillan, 1984), 204.

11. Harold Koontz, "The Management Theory Jungle," *Journal of American Management*, December 1961, pp. 174–88.

12. Owen B. Hardy, "Systematic Processes Applied to Health Care Planning," *Hospital Administration* 16 (Winter 1971): 7–24.

13. Newman and Warren, *The Process of Management*, 249.

14. Richard M. Steers, Gerardo R. Ungson, and Richard T. Mowday, *Managing Effective Organizations* (Boston, Mass.: Kent Publishing Company, 1985), 169.

15. Ibid., 177.

16. From a statement by Charles H. Anderson, CPA, circa 1956.

17. Aaron Sartain et al., *Psychology: Understanding Human Beings* (New York: McGraw-Hill, 1962), 250.

18. Rensis Likert, *New Patterns of Management* (New York: McGraw-Hill, 1961), 191.

19. R.H. Miles, *Macro Organizational Behavior* (Santa Monica, Calif.: Good Year, 1980). Cited in Steers, Ungson, and Mowday, *Managing Effective Organizations*, 422, 425.

Part VI

Keeping Society's Trust

Newspaper reports appear daily about scandals involving dishonesty in business. The Federal Bureau of Investigation reports that white collar crimes are rising. However, one must remember that human nature has probably changed very little over the course of recorded history and probably infinitesimally during the last century or so. The recorded rise in crime is most likely the result of two factors: (1) more thorough recording and reporting of crime and (2) rapid changes in the social environment.

The first factor is of little moment, and indeed it may be of benefit in the fight against crime. However, the second factor is a cause for worry, not only for the business community but for all lawmaking and law enforcement bodies. In fact, we should all be concerned, for social order and lawabidingness are the pillars on which our entire civilization rests. Thus, each manager has a responsibility not only to practice honesty, but to ferret out and expose the dishonesty of others. Lawmakers and law enforcement agencies have a special responsibility to devise new ways to identify and detect criminality in business, both in current conditions and in the conditions that are expected to evolve. We should not attempt to deter progressive business operations so as to assure the long-term efficacy of *current* laws and their enforcement. The challenge lies in keeping laws and their enforcement abreast of changing conditions.

We also believe educators and management authorities have a responsibility to stress integrity and social responsibility at this particular time, which is why we include Part VI in this book. Paying no attention to a problem wrongly suggests that no problem exists, or that if it does exist, its discussion has no value. Certainly the current lack of ethical behavior and integrity in the business world does constitute a problem, one that should be confronted directly and discussed openly.

In this part, we stress several factors which have served Western civilization very well. None of us can afford to sacrifice them and risk losing the gains our capitalistic society has given us.

Chapter 17

Integrity and social responsibility

Elements of Management
in Corporations

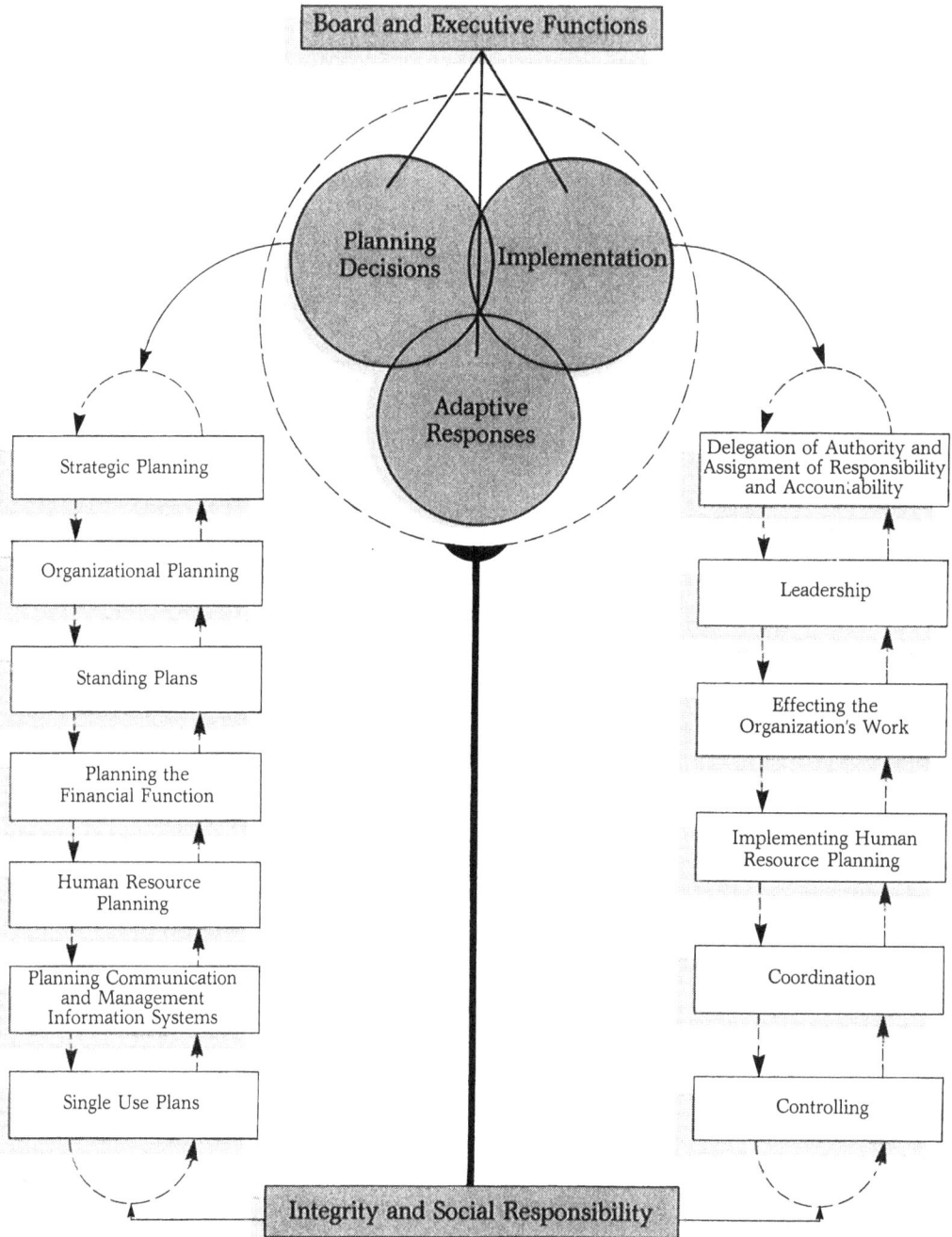

Board and Executive Functions

Planning Decisions

Implementation

Adaptive Responses

Strategic Planning

Organizational Planning

Standing Plans

Planning the Financial Function

Human Resource Planning

Planning Communication and Management Information Systems

Single Use Plans

Delegation of Authority and Assignment of Responsibility and Accountability

Leadership

Effecting the Organization's Work

Implementing Human Resource Planning

Coordination

Controlling

Integrity and Social Responsibility

17

Management responsibility and the current situation

Managers have a primary professional responsibility to strive toward the attainment of the goals and objectives of the organizations they serve. Although we feel very strongly about this, we feel just as strongly that they should not in the process sacrifice integrity and social responsibility. In fact, we espouse the theses that (1) the ability to gain organizational objectives will be thwarted in the long run by forsaking basic honesty and (2) the ultimate goal of all organized business should be to provide societal benefits. At the very least, no business organization should adopt an objective or goal that it knows will be detrimental to humans, either directly or indirectly.

Our opinion about the social responsibilities of business enterprises may not be in complete conformity with the classic view—supported by court decisions—that the basic purpose of a corporation is to maximize profits for shareholders, at least in the long run. However, in most large and highly visible corporations, providing societal benefits and maximizing long-term profits may actually be in harmony, for a corporation or other business which does not produce or assist in producing societal benefits will probably not survive to maximize long-term profits.

We know many arguments have developed as to what is socially beneficial. There are numerous instances where business activities occasion debate as to their harmful or beneficial effects. Also, it is sometimes extremely difficult to draw a line between honesty and dishonesty, and in some instances even between legality and illegality. Nonetheless, in a day when arrests for fraud and embezzlement are increasing[1] and when, according to a poll conducted in 1983 by the Gallup organization, only 18 percent of our national population believe standards of honesty held by business executives are "high" or "very high,"[2] the subject of integrity urgently needs discussing. In fact, another Gallup poll conducted during 1983 revealed the public believes that business values are declining.[3] Ongoing Wall Street scandals and other scandals recently publicized have certainly done nothing to reverse public opinion.

In this chapter, we intend to address the conduct of managers in their organizational lives only. Although we believe most managers cannot easily apply two sets of principles—one in their personal lives and another in their organizational lives—we specifically deny any direct or

"Much Ado about Deaver"
May 26, 1986 — pp. 20, 21

"The Fall of Wall Street Superstar:
Ivan Boesky Pays 100 Million to Settle
The Biggest Insider Trading Case Ever"
November 24, 1986 — pp. 71-74

"Peddling Influences"
March 3, 1986 — pp 26-36

"Ghost Story: The Teamster's
Boss Is Indicted"
May 26, 1986 — p. 22

"All Eyes on Accountants: A Once
Comfortable Profession Undergoes
Unprecedented Scrutiny"
April 21, 1986 — p. 61

**"Dark clouds over
Wall Street: History's
Largest Insider — Trading Case
Stuns the Investment World"
May 26, 1986 — pp 48, 49**

"Washday Blues: Scandal
Strikes Shearson"
July 7, 1986 — p. 46

Source: Random sample of 24 issues of *Time* Magazine, 1986.

indirect concern with conduct in personal affairs. In fact, both of us have strongly argued on many occasions that what an employee does away from the job should be considered little or not at all in evaluating performance on the job. Thus, our remarks are aimed exclusively at managers' conduct in the process of doing organizational work and at their contacts with associates and clients within the context of their organizational roles.

Our purpose here is also not to present an essay on religion or religious beliefs. Nonetheless, Western moral ideals are derived primarily from the Hellenic and Judeo-Christian traditions, whose tenets have shaped our thinking, and through the medium of English common law, also shaped legal statutes throughout every state of our nation. Regardless of what one may think about our ideals or their background, laws truly exist and their violation is punishable—and rightfully so. The sad but harsh truth is that in management today there are enough persons sufficiently lacking in integrity to put the business world into a state of anarchy were it not for the penalties imposed in the process of enforcing the laws. As for social consciousness, undoubtedly OSHA and EPA regulations would not be in effect today if they were not needed.

Lack of integrity

Black's Law Dictionary defines integrity as "soundness of moral principle and character, as shown by one person dealing with others in the making and performance of contracts, and fidelity and honesty in the discharge of trusts; it is synonymous with 'probity,' 'honesty,' and 'uprightness'."[4] Webster defines it as "an uncompromising adherence to a code of moral, artistic, or other values: utter sincerity, honesty and candor: avoidance of deception, expediency, artificiality or shallowness of any kind."[5]

We have always thought that to have integrity was simply to be honest (honesty being defined as "adherence to the facts; freedom from subterfuge or duplicity; truthfulness, sincerity"). However, demonstrating a lack of integrity involves committing crimes as well as straying from the truth, resorting to duplicity, or infringing principles of business ethics.

In thinking about failures of integrity, it will be useful to categorize them, as we do below. Other categorizations are of course possible.

1. *Crimes.* Crimes are broadly divided into felonies and misdemeanors. Fraud, bribery, embezzlement, price fixing, and stealing compose the majority of crimes perpetrated within business operations today.

2. *Misrepresentations and Subterfuges.* This category includes lying about matters of substance and intentionally portraying facts in such a manner that those to whom the portrayal is made will reach invalid conclusions. These infractions are not sufficiently serious to be called crimes.

3. *Breaches of Moral Obligation.* Most managers have a professional status of one type or another. Even many without such a status have responsibilities toward others in their organizational roles. Breaches of professional and role responsibilities make up the majority of this category.

We shall now discuss each of these categories in turn.

Crimes

The specific causes of criminal activity among managers and others in organizations arise from many sources. Greed, including individual greed and greed for increased company profits, is probably the most common cause. Ivan Boesky and Dennis Levine were likely motivated by greed, for example. Many commit crimes on behalf of organizations in financial difficulty. Some of John DeLorean's alleged illegal acts are probably attributable to the fact his car company was in deep financial trouble. Several years ago, we were acquainted with a famous man whose private firm was also on the verge of bankruptcy. His actions resembled those of a wounded animal at bay, and there was little question but that he would have committed crimes, subterfuges, and breaches of responsibility in order to save his company. Indeed, he did demonstrate a lack of integrity, and the fact that he eluded prison is little short of a miracle.

We could recount many other anecdotes concerning the criminal activity of managers, but it would serve no useful purpose. Criminality in business is a fact of daily life and no amount of wishful thinking or sophomoric denials can change that.

Probably most crime is initiated by a single individual (possibly aided by an accomplice) and done purely for self-gain. Of course, there are also crimes committed by a group of three or more, but again the motive is usually self-gain. Finally, some organizations, through actions of their officers, make decisions that result in the commitment of one or more crimes. The motives are various, but most are economic in nature. For example, in 1977, Revco Drug Stores, Inc., a major Medicaid provider, was found guilty of a computer-generated double-billing scheme that illegally took more than half a million dollars in Medicaid funds from the Ohio Department of Public Welfare.[6]

Computer-related crime may become a matter of grave concern in the near future. Donn B. Parker has warned, "But the reason for great concern is not the past incidence of computer crime, but rather its potential harm to society, both in incidence and loss. I am optimistic about limiting loss. We will be in a close race with criminals over the next few years."[7] Some of these criminals will unfortunately occupy management positions in organizations.

Needless to state, a manager who engages in criminal activity, either for self-gain or for the company, courts personal disaster. If the manager is apprehended, his or her professional career will be so tarnished that it may never recover. Any anticipated personal gain will be negated many times over. If the purpose was to benefit the organization, the likely result will be serious losses (either direct or indirect, through reduced prestige and goodwill).

Middle managers sometimes receive pressure from higher managers to perform illegal acts. In such cases, a serious dilemma may develop for the subordinate manager, who might confront loss of a job, withholding of a promotion, outright demotion, or denial of a justified pay raise. In the face of such threats, what should the subordinate's response be?

To begin with, no one should perform criminal acts. Criminal activity always proves to be detrimental in the long run to the individuals involved, the organization or organizations involved, and the business community in general. Apart from that point, there is no clear-cut answer as to what the specific reaction to such pressure should be. Sometimes the best solution is to resign the position and seek other employment, at least if it seems the proposed criminal act will be unique. However, if the criminal activity is proposed to be carried out over a period of time, the subordinate should provide information to appropriate law enforcement authorities and seek assistance from them. We have stated elsewhere our belief that management is a profession and that one of its responsibilities is the policing of its own ranks. For the individual manager, this entails acting to rid the profession of crooks, regardless of whether they happen to be superiors or subordinates.

Misrepresentations and subterfuges

Literally, thousands of ways exist in which any manager can sacrifice integrity through misrepresenting information and resorting to subterfuge. However, most incidents involve verbal or written communications.

The most common form of misrepresentation is simple lying. Perhaps in some cases it is wise to "bend the truth," but the mature person will know when these occur. They rarely occur in regard to business-related matters of any substance.

For example, a subordinate manager might tell a superior, "I like the new suit you are wearing today," when in fact he or she really abhors it.

No harm has been done and the superior probably feels better. The matter is nonsubstantive, and in any case the suit might be beautiful to some, since beauty is in the eyes of the beholder, at least to some extent. Suppose, however, a young manager informs his or her superior that an absence from work is necessitated and provides some reason. The superior ascertains the reason given is not true. This small matter, which the superior may never mention, creates distrust. From that point on, the superior will question the words of the young manager, and doubly so after a second such incident. Not only has the young manager acquired a handicap, but troublesome doubt exists in the mind of the superior.

Dealing with a liar is always burdensome, and not merely because of the consequences resulting from false information, although they can be extremely costly on occasion. After a person shows a tendency to prevaricate, it is necessary to expend a considerable amount of time and thought in differentiating truth from falsification on each occasion that information is exchanged. This can be very aggravating to a superior and often results in lost opportunities for advancement for the subordinate and sometimes in outright dismissal. We can unequivocally state that adherence to the truth should always be observed with regard to matters concerning the conduct of business.

Unquestionably, lying about substantive matters will eventually impair a manager's capability to manage and will damage management as a function in any organization. We believe a manager seriously impairs his or her influence, leadership, and promotion potential, as well as creates uncertainty and perplexity for others when prevarications are made habitually about many nonsubstantive matters. Sissela Bok's book *Lying: Moral Choice in Public and Private Life* cogently argues that society itself can only exist where truth in communications among humans predominates.[8]

Risks associated with lying increase in written communications, because detection will not allow denial. It is reported that Howard Hughes deliberately used written communications infrequently so as to avoid being "tied down." We have often said that if a person can't put something in writing, he or she either doesn't understand it, doesn't want to accept responsibility, or is afraid of being caught in a lie. Confusion in any organization is greatly diminished when managerial intents are put in writing—truthfully, that is. Again, we have generally followed this principle: It is not enough to be honest and truthful; a manager should leave a record that he or she has been honest and truthful. Following this principle will keep one out of trouble on most occasions—if the record is accurate.

Using subterfuges (artifices or expedients for evading unfavorable consequences) leads to many sorts of devious ploys, most of which, if exposed, place a manager in a much worse light than would otherwise have resulted. Subterfuges often accompany lying or half-truths.

Subterfuges typically surface in accounting and statistical reports, especially where the person responsible for results is also responsible for reporting. We have been acquainted with several chief executives who were barely competent and would routinely "hide" or "bury" certain unfavorable figures in reports to governing boards. While both of us understand a manager's concern about possible consequences of unfavorable results, we have held to the principle that if there are unfavorable results to be reported, the manager responsible should report them first. If a manager is objective in reporting, he or she will usually receive assistance in correcting the situation; if not, distrust soon mounts and dismissal may result.

Some large corporations actually use subterfuges in the preparation of reports for stockholders, a few to such an extent that the reports become primarily a form of public relations. Needless to say, such reports often eventually work to the disadvantage of those who prepare them and to the corporation itself.

Breaches of morality in obligations

The managers of business enterprises have many moral obligations, some of which substantially conflict with others. These obligations have been the subject of considerable study by philosophers and social scientists for over a century, but especially during the last three decades. We will briefly discuss some of the opinions resulting from this study and then consider the main ways in which managers breach their moral obligations.

Aristotle and Plato are probably the founders of the philosophy that in any work situation each individual has a basic obligation to perform his or her job, trade, or profession well. This philosophy applies to business enterprises in the Western world today, and it is generally held that operating personnel should seek proficiency in their special tasks and that management personnel should provide adequate remuneration, humane treatment, and a healthful working environment for operating personnel (as well as members of their own ranks).

According to philosopher Norman Bowie, justification for the moral position that one should perform one's functions in an organization to the best of one's ability can be given within the framework of both deontological and utilitarian ethics.[9] Regarding deontological ethical theory (*deontological* derives from the Greek term *deon*, meaning duty or obligation), Bowie states, "According to deontological ethical theory, the relationship one has to those affected by one's actions is a relevant consideration in determining what one ought to do."[10] He also states, "Deontological theory incorporates society's view of the importance of role or station as an element in deciding the actual obligations one has."[11]

Regarding utilitarian ethics, Bowie states, "For a utilitarian, what one ought to do is determined solely by the consequences that result. One ought to act so as to bring about the best consequences one can. A utilitarian would argue that the assumption of role obligations by individuals holding the role leads to good consequences."[12]

Resolving questions of moral conduct

In every organizational role, there will inevitably arise occasions when "what one ought to do" is difficult to ascertain and possible courses of action are in conflict regardless of what set of moral values is held. Problems also arise when, within the same organization or among peer organizations, what one ought to do on the basis of one's role conflicts with what others ought to do on the basis of their roles. Can all such dilemmas be resolved through the application of deontological or utilitarian theories? Obviously, the answer is no. Bowie then poses the question, "Is there a higher morality that supersedes role morality?" He holds, and we agree with him, that moral precepts exist which undergird the practice of all business and the conduct of all organizational management. One should, then, rely on them in those instances where role morality falls short of providing answers to dilemmas.

Moral precepts. Moral precepts can be defined as those whose systematic violation would undermine all business practice and reduce commercial transactions to anarchy. Of course, this presupposes business as practiced in the Western world, where Hellenic and Judeo-Christian moral and intellectual traditions predominate. One needn't be prejudiced to suggest that it is among Western and Western-influenced nations that business practice has become most productive and that as a result of the productivity, living standards have attained a level never before equaled at any time or in any place on earth. Although scientific research has not proved that Western commerce, conducted under precepts flowing from the background influences as cited, correlates directly with the high levels of material wealth, one has only to compare our prosperity with that of countries operating under other precepts to reach a tentative conclusion.

Kant's categorical imperative. The German philosopher Immanuel Kant constructed a formal deontological theory which has been widely used to try to determine whether or not proposed business actions are moral. This theory requires that proposed actions meet certain formal standards and "conform whatever the consequences, to a universally recognizable and universally valid, logical structure."[13] Of all moral theories, Kant's famous doctrine of the categorical imperative probably elicits the greatest respect from ethicists.

Kant enunciated three interrelated standards by which an action might be morally judged. Summarized, they are as follows:

1. The performer of the act sincerely believes the principle on which one acts could beneficially become a universal law.

2. All individual human beings would be treated as ends in themselves and not merely as means.

3. Both the initiator of the act and those whom it affects can rationally affirm its justness.

Through these standards Kant tried to provide for consistency among actions, i.e., by having people act according to universal precepts, show respect for all members of humankind, and mete out basic justice as required. Bowie uses the Kantian expressions to argue for the relevance of morality among business enterprises and plausibly submits that business could not survive without certain moral standards. (Without attempting to detract from Kant's widely recognized genius, we note that the categorical imperative has obvious similarities to the golden rule, of which Kant was undoubtedly aware.)

There have been opponents to the moral views of both Kant and Bowie. Bowie admits this, even citing Albert Z. Carr's article "Is Business Bluffing Ethical?"[14] Carr challenges Kantian morality in the following ways. First, he states that an understanding of business can be gained from playing poker. Second, he claims that competition and negotiation inherently involve deceptions, including conscious misstatements and concealments of pertinent facts. Third, he claims that success in business requires that a business person must "do unto others as he hopes others will not do unto him."[15]

Of course, anyone who has ever played poker knows that although it does involve the deceptions Carr cites, it also has its own explicit rules of conduct so as to give each player fair and equal chances. These rules allow for consistency and in this respect poker is exactly equivalent to Kantian ethics.

Competitive puffery versus breaches of morality
Bowie concedes that businesses do engage in a great deal of puffery—especially in the areas of advertising and vying for sales—and with the full knowledge and condonement of society. But he also cites concrete instances of deceptive and fraudulent practices that violate the Kantian philosophy and undermine the conduct of business itself. As regards competitive puffery, the courts in this nation have recognized but disregarded it, except in those cases where deceptions or untruths occasion harm to other persons. Some difficulties have arisen, of course, in ascertaining when the deceptions or untruths actually resulted in, or could result in, harm.

On the basis of our own experience and the recorded experiences of other people in business, we believe the following are the primary ways in which managers breach their moral obligations. There may be some overlapping of this category of infraction with the categories discussed previously, i.e., (1) crimes and (2) misrepresentations and subterfuges. Undoubtedly some of these actions would provide the basis for civil litigation.

1. intentionally neglecting to perform the duties inherent in one's organizational position to the best of one's ability

2. consciously being disloyal to the organization for which one works at any level of its hierarchy, unless the expected loyalty is clearly superseded by a higher professional moral principle or by a higher universal moral principle

3. deliberately abrogating formal promises and contracts, except where a higher universal moral principle so dictates, e.g., in order to avoid a harm greater than the abrogation

4. willfully withholding payment of just debts when payment is possible

5. knowingly offering false or partially false guarantees

6. knowingly perpetuating unfair trade practices as defined by statutes or regulations or unlawfully or unethically restricting fair competition

7. intentionally discriminating against certain classes of persons, usually on the basis of race, creed, color, or sex

8. consciously concealing pertinent facts from anyone who has a right to know such facts

9. consciously or neglectfully endangering personnel, clients, or other parties through the existence of physical hazards at a workplace or on other property for which a manager is responsible

10. committing minor theft, fraud, bribery, embezzlement, or any other act that, except for its insignificance, would be punishable as a crime

11. consciously or neglectfully violating lawful regulations protecting the rights of others

12. concealing criminal or immoral acts of those whose actions fall within the purview of one's managerial responsibility

13. failing to protect and enhance the interests of a business's owners, balanced against the interests of other stakeholders in the business (stakeholder interests are defined and further discussed in a later section of this chapter)

14. deliberately using persons as means rather than ends, especially when the result is detrimental to them.

Many managers commit breaches of one or more of their moral obligations, either because of ignorance or because of careless neglect. Of course, neither of these reasons is acceptable as far as the courts are concerned. Only careful and responsible consideration will assure that one's moral obligations are always met.

To sum up our views about integrity, we believe that a manager's professional career could not long survive without it, and neither could a given business organization. In fact, business as we know it might completely cease. Every game must have its rules and those rules must be kept somewhat inviolate for the game to even exist. The competitive business world is not an exception. (In the case of business, of course, civilization itself has a prime stake.) The players must understand what the rules are and sufficiently respect them so as to assure the survival of the business game. It will be primarily through the integrity of business managers, both individually and collectively, that this can be achieved.

Social responsibility

Since 1962, when the Kennedy administration popularized the phrase *the public interest*, there has been an ongoing debate about the social responsibility of business corporations and other business firms. Milton Friedman and Theodore Levitt have probably done more to promulgate the conservative view than any other spokesmen. Friedman, in talking about free economies, states, "In such an economy, there is one and only one social responsibility of business—to use its resources and engage in activities designed to increase its profits, so long as it stays within the rules of the game, which is to say, engages in open and free competition, without deception or fraud."[16] Levitt has stated, "The function of business is to produce sustained high-level profits. The essence of free enterprise is to go after profit in any way that is consistent with its own survival as an economic system. . . . Welfare and society are not the corporation's business. Its business is making money, not sweet music."[17]

An opposing view is stated by Robert A. Dahl. "Today it is absurd to regard the corporation simply as an enterprise established for the sole purpose of allowing profit making. We the citizens give them special rights, powers and privileges, protection, and benefits on the understanding that their activities will fulfill purposes. Corporations exist only as they continue to benefit us. . . . Every corporation should be thought of as a social enterprise whose existence and decisions can be justified only insofar as they serve public or social purposes."[18]

We believe each of these opinions is flawed. For example, when Friedman states that "there is one and only one social responsibility of business—to use its resources and engage in activities designed to increase its profits," we believe he is wrongly imposing his view about a matter which it is the business of each business to decide. If a corporation or other business desires to make a limited profit or to carry on purely altruistic activities in addition to its commercial activities (and regards itself, in either case, as performing one of its responsibilities), it exercises, in essence, a rightful prerogative. Additionally, every business operates at the pleasure of the country in which its activities are carried on, and in the final analysis society will say what the responsibilities of businesses are—not an economist.

We regard Mr. Levitt's statement as something of a posture, especially when he claims that a corporation's "business is making money, not sweet music." If Levitt and other ultraconservatives who opine that the single function of a corporation is to make money are right, then shouldn't the quickest way to make money be the best way? So why not engage, without any compunction, several expert engravers, retire to a secluded island, and go at it? In our opinion, the conservative cause suffers damage by such posturing.

We also disagree with Dahl when he states that "every corporation should be thought of as a social enterprise whose existence and decisions can be justified only insofar as they serve public or social purposes." Indeed, most corporations in this nation receive charters quite simply to provide "pecuniary gain" to shareholders. To think that their "decision" must be justified (to whom?) on the basis of "public or social purposes" (based on what definition?) is quite unreasonable.

Of the three opinions, we tend to favor Mr. Friedman's. However, unlike Friedman, we believe a business has responsibilities to categories of people other than shareholders. Although any business must have a primary loyalty to investors and must see to it that all reasonable actions are taken to assure profits, at least in the long run, we also know time is money and that the time which employees invest in the business gives them a stake in it. Other groups also have a stake in the affairs of most businesses.

Stakeholders

In his book *Beyond the Bottom Line*, published in 1985, Tuleja notes the broadening of the constituencies to whom business enterprises are believed to have obligations.[19] In 1977, J. Scott Armstrong wrote about essentially the same groups.[20] Each referred to several groups as *stakeholders*, i.e., people who have a vital material interest in the conduct of a given business corporation or other kind of organization. We discuss below the same groups as Tuleja, with some variations (see Figure 17-1). We also address the question whether or not there are societal benefits that result from an enterprise's meeting its supposed responsibilities regarding each of these stakeholder groups.

Stockholders as stakeholders

Investors unquestionably organize and finance a business enterprise simply for pecuniary gain in most cases. Few businessmen would undertake the risks involved if financial gain was clearly not possible. If financial gain does not eventually appear, an investor will usually withdraw his or her investment and put it where there exists a brighter hope of gain (provided the investment has not been lost through the incompetence of managers or unfavorable circumstances).

Can societal benefits be realized because investors, acting merely for self-gain, put up their money for the organization and development of a

Figure 17-1

Stakeholders in the Management of Corporations

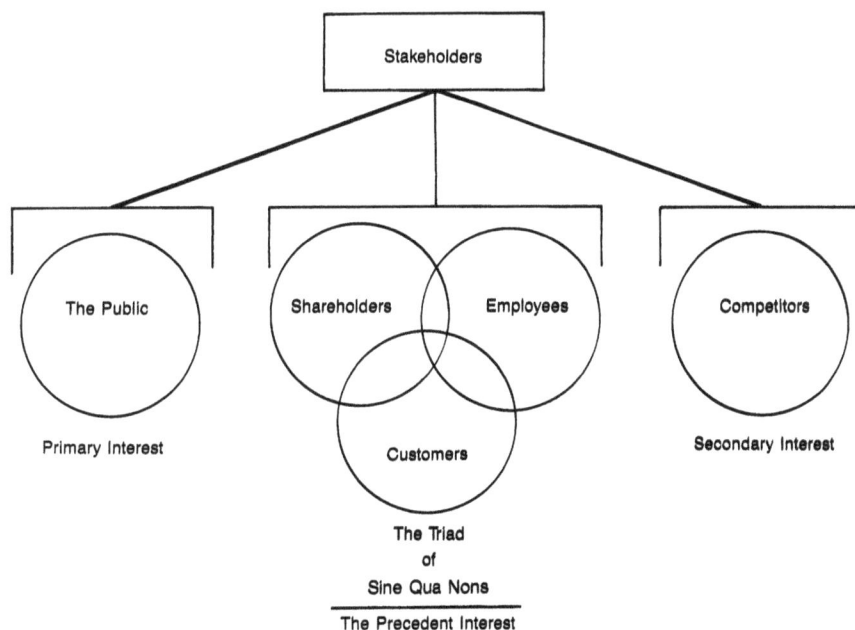

business enterprise? The answer is yes. Businesses create jobs, perform services for the public, and produce products that are both useful and enjoyable. But businesses would not exist were it not for investors, and all businesses owe a responsibility to their owners, whether their investments have been made through the purchase of stock shares or otherwise. Society very definitely benefits because businesses return profits to investors, for receiving profits is the usual motive for investing in a business in the first place.

Although we acknowledge that businesses have responsibilities to groups other than stockholders, clearly stockholders are the initial stakeholders, and they continue to be essential stakeholders throughout the life of major businesses. While we don't say they are the most important stakeholders, clearly none are more important.

Employees as stakeholders

When employees undertake to manage and operate an investor-owned business, each individual employed gambles to some extent his or her future welfare on the success of the venture. Although an employee always has the option of resigning and looking elsewhere for work, we believe any respectable corporation owes its employees the opportunity to satisfy their needs, both economic and personal. Boards of directors should not sacrifice this obligation merely to pay shareholders a maximum profit, despite the claims of ultraconservative economists. Indeed, attempts to squeeze employees so as to provide short-term benefits to shareholders will be self-defeating, for competent employees will get the message and look elsewhere for jobs. Thus, in order to assure long-term profits for shareholders, those who run the business, invest their time, and risk their very future must receive ample remuneration.

The question arises whether there are any societal benefits that result from responding to such needs of employees as have been identified and enunciated by social scientists over the past half century? Again, the answer is yes. We will have a healthier, better educated, and more competent work force throughout society if businesses properly respect and meet employee needs. Indeed, placing the interests of employees on a par with those of shareholders will most likely result in stronger and more profitable business enterprises and lead to a better and more stable society.

Customers as stakeholders

What about customers? Does a business enterprise have a social responsibility to them as well as to shareholders and employees? Each business had better acknowledge that it does—that is, if it wants to continue as a business.

The hospital industry is a classic example. Suppose an investor-owned hospital system, in order to maximize short-term profits, decides to sacrifice adequate patient care. Any shareholder, economist, or other sane person who becomes a patient within that system will quickly decide that it does have at least one responsibility other than to maximize profits. That system, or any other, clearly has a responsibility to provide the care it says it is providing, and this responsibility, in our view, equals or even exceeds its responsibility to shareholders. Again, failure to meet this responsibility will be completely self-defeating. Very shortly, the public will get the message and seek care elsewhere. Long-term profits will be sacrificed to short-term profits, because of lost market shares and possibly adverse judgments in malpractice liability suits.

Although the implications of not satisfying obligations to customers usually will not be as clear as in the case of hospitals, we believe any serious study of a given business corporation or other type of firm will reveal that such obligations (or responsibilities) do exist.

Do any societal benefits result from a company's meeting its responsibility to customers? This can hardly be denied. In fact, in a capitalistic form of economy, where most services and products are provided to society through business enterprises, chiefly corporations with shareholders, such important social goals as order, security, and individual physical well-being would be impossible if companies did not meet their responsibilities to customers. Any corporation which denies it has such a responsibility and does not act to meet it cannot and should not long exist. William Henry Vanderbilt's statement "The public be damned" was unfortunate in his day and would be deplorable if spoken now. Unfortunately, similar remarks are still being made, although they tend to be less straightforward and are uttered with a certain wariness.

Members of the public as stakeholders

In previous years, many corporations (primarily industrial corporations) damaged the environment horrendously and denied any responsibility to protect it. While some still surreptitiously abuse it, their numbers have been dwindling, thanks to federal, state, and local regulations. After the properties of innocent citizens were ruined, rivers and streams were polluted, and the atmosphere was filled with noxious fumes, it was finally recognized that business enterprises have a responsibility to the general public not to render it harm through operational activities.

Responsibility to the public has two faces. There is a generally recognized responsibility not to do harm to the environment, property, or person of any individual living adjacent or in near proximity to the place where an enterprise's operations transpire. Like any individual (and corporations are regarded under the law as persons, although artificial), a business enterprise should be a good, law-abiding neighbor.

The issue whether corporations should be helpful neighbors to those in close proximity to operations or worksites continues to be debated. Conservative economists say a manufacturing plant, for example, has no responsibility to try to benefit the community where it is located and that so long as laws and regulations are obeyed (usually while keeping up vigorous efforts to have them annulled), a business need not do anything to make the community a better place in which to live; after all, such actions might cost shareholders some of the profits to which they are rightfully entitled. The opposing view is that community involvement of corporate officials—on company time—is indeed an obligation owed to the local public, not to mention the duty of corporations to financially support their communities' "worthy causes."

Although most businesses now do participate as good neighbors in the communities where they are located, and at the expense of profits to shareholders, we believe that such neighborliness should have limits, i.e., actions benefiting a local community should not jeopardize an enterprise's survival. Just as the public does not expect a poor person to support "worthy" causes, it should not expect struggling corporations or other businesses to do so either. Furthermore, like an individual, a business enterprise should retain complete autonomy in deciding which worthy causes to support and what the nature and degree of support should be.

The other face of the responsibility to the general public involves the avoidance of harm to the environment, property, or person of individuals or groups of individuals, no matter how remote they may be to the base of operations of a given enterprise. Obviously this makes good sense, if for no other reason than to avoid the tort actions which will surely occur if such responsibility is disregarded.

Do national or multinational corporations have affirmative responsibilities throughout the entire geographic area in which their products are sold or their services provided? We believe this question is best decided by individual businesses through their boards of directors. If a company believes there is an issue, it may wish to assume such a responsibility.

As to whether societal benefits result from an enterprise's meeting its responsibility to the general public, the answer seems clear: Avoidance of wrongful harm to members of the public, whether located near or far from an enterprise's operations, accrues to the benefit of all, including shareholders and all other stakeholders. Affirmative good neighbor actions in appropriate localities also provide societal benefits. However, if survival of an enterprise becomes jeopardized by such actions, it is reasonable to forgo them in the interests of the long-term benefits that will result from the continuation of the enterprise.

Competitors as stakeholders

When one has spent the greater part of one's life fighting competition, sometimes seemingly internicine competition, one has some difficulty in accepting that a responsibility to competitors does exist. However, every business has a responsibility to its competitors to play according to "the rules of the game." The reason we said Friedman's view of social responsibility may be the best among the three cited earlier is that even though he claims the single social responsibility of business is to increase its profits, he adds "so long as it stays within the rules of the game which is to say, engages in open and free competition without deception and fraud." In other words, each business owes a responsibility to competitors to play fair, which limits the first part of Friedman's statement, i.e., that the single social responsibility of business is to increase profits.

Certainly, any business owes a duty to all segments of society, including competitors, to stay within established laws and regulations governing the conduct of commerce and business. That is to say, business has a duty not merely to know the law but to refrain from attempting to break it. The only exception is when a test case in regard to a controversial regulation may be undertaken so as to assure that the controversial regulation itself is within established law.

We realize there are many aggravating regulations governing the conduct of business in this country. Both questionable business ethics and enthusiastic government officials have played their roles in bringing about this state of affairs. Even so, a business enterprise should stay within current regulations and owes its competitors that duty.

Tuleja holds "that competing firms do have moral claims on a business. Two, that these claims are widely, if not consciously, recognized. And three, that if they are not honored, free enterprise itself becomes threatened."[21] We agree with these statements.

Some of the more common infringements of morality among business competitors include the following: ignoring conflicts of interest, being unfair to rivals; making false or deceptive statements about one's own practices, products, or services; placing unfair pressure on clients not to patronize a competitor; dispensing bribes, including gifts deliberately designed to sway the decisions of clients; dispensing kickbacks; spying on the works or activities of competitors when such spying constitutes an invasion of privacy or filching; price fixing and other collusions among a limited number of enterprises to the detriment of others; and deliberately "raiding" the personnel body of another firm so as to reduce its effectiveness.

To the question whether any societal benefits result from an enterprise's meeting its responsibility to competitors, the answer is again yes. In order to preserve our capitalistic economy, business must play according to the rules of the game (i.e., without deception and fraud) if the game itself is to be preserved. Capitalism has demonstrated its ability to make truly the "Great Society," and the unscrupulous and untrammeled greed of a few must not destroy that which provides for the needs of all our citizens. All business enterprises unequivocally owe to their competitors the duty to stay within the laws and regulations governing commerce and business and also to practice business in an ethical manner, with specific avoidance of the derelictions we cited above.

A statement concerning the social responsibility of business enterprises

We recognize and accept that the first responsibility of private business enterprises is to earn profits. Without profits, there could be no business as we know it today. Profits divided among investors—who make a given enterprise possible in the first place—is a necessary condition. Without hope of return on investments, investors would put their money elsewhere, and businesses could not operate in a capitalistic economy.

We do not believe, however, that the only responsibility of a business enterprise is to *maximize* profits for owners. It also has responsibilities to employees, customers, members of the public, and competitors. The dictum that "business would not exist without profits to shareholders" is true; it also would not exist without employees and customers. These *three* groups form an inseparable triad on which all businesses rest. Thus, every business must recognize all its responsibilities and try equally hard to meet each one.

Here, then, is our view of the responsibilities of current day business enterprises. *The basic responsibility of private business enterprises is to return a competitive profit to investors while at the same time fulfilling certain equally stringent responsibilities to employees, customers, the public, and competitors.*

Rather than *maximum profit*, we have used the term *competitive profit*. The point is that profits must be at least sufficient to attract ongoing investment and thus assure the continuance and economic health of the enterprise.

Summary

The integrity of individual managers and of managers acting as groups on behalf of business enterprises is the "glue" that holds together individual organizations and, in truth, our capitalistic society and our nation. Business without integrity would pose such a problem to government in our pluralistic society that it could not exist in its present form. Because of increasing failures of integrity among managers in business enterprises, governments have already enacted many laws and regulations in order to police commerce and business. Without question, such laws and regulations will increase unless businesses develop more respect for certain ethical precepts which underlie all human relationships.

The moral infractions committed within business can be divided into three basic categories: (1) punishable crimes, (2) misrepresentations and subterfuges, and (3) breaches of moral obligation. All of these detract from the quality of business life in this nation and among the community of nations.

Crimes, lies, and subterfuges are very serious violations and possibly cause more harm than breaches of moral obligation. However, it is generally clear what constitutes a crime, a lie, or a subterfuge, and our discussion of them is brief. What are the moral obligations of businesses and people in business are relatively more difficult to determine. Moral obligations result from role and professional obligations to do the best one can in one's position within the company. Thus, if all employees did the best they could at their jobs, only good consequences would result for all. However, to resolve questions about what one ought to do in a particular role, especially when there seems to be a conflict with what others ostensibly ought to do in interfacing roles, it is necessary to consider higher or overriding principles of morality.

Many regard Immanuel Kant's categorical imperative as a worthy principle of higher morality. According to Kant, one should apply three rules when trying to decide if an act is morally correct:

1. The principle acted on could beneficially be made into a universal law.

2. In doing the act, one treats the affected human beings as ends rather than solely as means.

3. Both the initiator of the act and those affected can confirm its justness.

A reasonable application of these standards to a given act (i.e., an act whose moral correctness is not clearly determined by one's role) can provide practical answers regarding business morality. Practical applications may not yield utopian answers, but one need not search for utopian answers—merely practical ones for issues of practical moral obligation.

We listed 14 common derelictions of moral obligation. Most would not constitute a criminal act (some would if sufficiently serious), but each one might provide the basis for civil litigation, depending on the circumstances and the extent of damage to a plaintiff.

Our view of the social responsibility of businesses is at variance with both extremely conservative and extremely liberal opinions. A simple statement of it follows: The basic responsibility of private business enterprises is to return a competitive profit to investors while at the same time fulfilling certain equally stringent responsibilities to employees, customers, the public, and competitors.

We reject the view that business has a single responsibility to make maximum profits for shareholders. Recognizing the importance of initial investments for organizing and starting a business enterprise and for subsequently developing and expanding it, we hold that competitive profits must be made, or else investors will refuse or withdraw their support. At the same time, business organizations could not operate without both employees and customers, who must therefore also be treated fairly. Such treatment may tend, in fact, to increase profits.

In addition, business organizations have a responsibility to the public not to harm or injure any individuals. We believe they should also act as good neighbors and extend assistance to the communities in which they have their operations, provided such actions are not a threat to survival (as a result of denying competitive profits to shareholders).

Finally, business enterprises have certain responsibilities to their competitors. The basic responsibility is to "play according to the rules of the game," that is, to respect the laws and regulations applicable to the conduct of business and commerce and also to respect certain moral precepts. Material societal benefits result from fulfillment of these responsibilities, because on them rests the survival of private enterprise as we know it today.

Notes

1. Department of Justice, Federal Bureau of Investigation, *Crime in the United States* (Washington, D.C.: Federal Bureau of Investigation, Department of Justice, 1984).
2. Tad Tuleja, *Beyond the Bottom Line* (New York: Facts on File Publications, 1985), 3–4.
3. Ibid., 4.
4. *Black's Law Dictionary*, 4th ed., s.v. "integrity."
5. *Webster's Third International Dictionary*, s.v. "integrity."
6. Diane Vaughan, *Controlling Unlawful Organizational Behavior* (Chicago: University of Chicago Press, 1983), 1–9.
7. Donn B. Parker, *Fighting Computer Crime* (New York: Scribner, 1983), x–xi.
8. Sissela Bok, *Lying: Moral Choice in Public and Private Life* (New York: Pantheon Books, 1978).
9. Norman Bowie, *Business Ethics* (Englewood Cliffs, N.J.: Prentice-Hall, 1982), 5–12.
10. Ibid., 10–11.
11. Ibid., 11.
12. Ibid.
13. Tuleja, *Beyond the Bottom Line*, 22.
14. Albert Z. Carr, "Is Business Bluffing Ethical?" *Harvard Business Review*, January-February 1968, p. 45.
15. Bowie, *Business Ethics*, 55.

16. Milton Friedman, *Capitalism and Freedom* (Chicago: University of Chicago Press, 1962), 133–36. Quoted in *Ethical Theory and Business*, ed. Tom L. Beauchamp and Norman E. Bowie (Englewood Cliffs, N.J.: Prentice-Hall, 1979), 136.

17. Theodore Levitt, "The Dangers of Social Responsibility," *Harvard Business Review*, September-October 1958. Quoted in *Ethical Theory and Business*, ed. Tom L. Beauchamp and Norman E. Bowie (Englewood Cliffs, N.J.: Prentice-Hall, 1979), 138–39.

18. Robert A. Dahl, "A Prelude to Corporate Reform," in *Corporate Social Policy*, ed. Robert L. Heilbroner and Paul London (Reading, Mass.: Addison-Wesley, 1975), 18–19. Quoted in *Ethical Theory and Business*, ed. Tom L. Beauchamp and Norman E. Bowie (Englewood Cliffs, N.J.: Prentice-Hall, 1979), 148.

19. Tuleja, *Beyond the Bottom Line*, 247–48.

20. J. Scott Armstrong, "Social Responsibility in Management," *Journal of Business Research* 5 (September 1977).

21. Tuleja, *Beyond the Bottom Line*, p. 136.

Appendix A

Glossary

Accountability. Answerability for certain obligations assumed on behalf of an employer or under the terms of a contract.

Accounting, Cost. Accounting that ascertains costs and related data concerning some object of managerial interest.

Accounting, Financial. The branch of accounting that provides financial statements and reports for assisting both internal and external organizational groups in decision making.

Accounting, Managerial. A process of collecting, classifying, summarizing, analyzing, and reporting information for managers to assist in both planning and control functions.

Accounting Safeguards. Measures taken to establish checks and balances in financial functions so as to prevent mistakes and fraud.

Adaptive Response. A managerial reaction to unforeseen environmental occurrences internal or external to an organization.

Adaptive Responses, Category 1. Adaptive responses that require no approval by or consultation with other managers.

Adaptive Responses, Category 2. Adaptive responses that require either approval by or consultation with one or more other managers.

Adaptivising. Altering plans as dictated by environmental changes.

Affirmative Good Neighbor Actions. Actions done by a business in recognition of its social responsibility to its community, including active support of worthy causes.

Agent, General. One to whom a principal delegates authority and assigns responsibility and accountability for operating an entire business or performing all transactions or functions of a specific kind. Usually a general manager in business organizations.

Agent, Special. One to whom a principal delegates the authority and assigns the responsibility and accountability for performing a specific act.

Art. An occupation requiring specialized knowledge or skills.

Audit, Independent. A monitoring function performed by independent auditors as a part of the financial management control process.

Audit, Internal. A monitoring function performed by designated organizational personnel as a part of the financial management control process.

Authority, Acceptance Theory of. The theory that regardless of the amount of authority flowing from a state to a legally organized entity, if subordinates do not accept the authority of managers it remains useless.

Authority, Competence Theory of. The theory that authority is derived from the competence, knowledge, and expertise of those placed in positions of traditional authority rather than from delegation by a superior.

Authority, Express. Authority given explicitly, either orally or in writing.

Authority, Implied. Authority which is not express, but which devolves on someone as a result of circumstances.

Authority, Traditional Theory of. The theory that a person's authority to issue orders and direct the behavior of others is derived from a legally binding contract or charter.

Balance Sheet. A financial statement that presents the financial condition of a business entity at a given moment in time; it is built around the basic equation: Assets = Liabilities + Owners' Equity.

Big Eight Accounting Firms. The eight largest public accounting firms in the nation.

Board of Directors. Persons elected by common stockholders to run a corporation.

Bond. A certificate or evidence of a debt.

Bonus. A reward given to an employee for outstanding work; it has monetary value and is awarded without the employee's prior knowledge.

Book Rated Return. The return on investment (ROI) ratio applied to future financial projections of profits from a proposed investment.

Bottom-Up Approach to Organizational Planning. Starting planning with individual jobs of workers and managers.

Budget, Balance Sheet. A pro forma balance sheet statement to indicate the probable outcome of financial budgeting previously done.

Budget, Operating. A statement of anticipated revenues and expenses to predict and control the outcomes of organizational operations for a specified time period.

Budget, Program. A budget relating to a specific company activity, with breakdowns based on product lines.

Budgeting, Capital. Planning that reflects considerations involving acquisition of new fixed assets.

Budgeting, Zero-Base. Budgeting that requires justification of each line item, regardless of justifications in prior years.

Bureaucratic Model of Organization. Arrangement of managers in hierarchical levels, starting with the chief executive officer and going through middle management levels to a lowest supervisory level.

Capital Financing. The planning and implementation involved in obtaining capital for investment in assets or funds that will best promote profits, profitability, or other financial objectives.

Capital Structure. Total equity and debt funding in a planned relationship.

Categorical Imperative. A set of three interrelated standards by which an action may be judged in regard to its morality. Developed by Immanuel Kant.

Chain of Command. In corporations, the person-to-person route of authority and control flowing from a board of directors through hierarchical ranks to the lowest management level.

Classic Management Theory. The theory that management can be viewed as a set of universal principles and functions.

Common Law. Those principles and rules of action deriving from usages and customs of immemorial antiquity or from judgments and decrees of courts; the ancient, unwritten laws of England, which formed the basis for much of the law in the U.S.

Communication. A message sent by a person which is perceived by a receiver as the sender intended.

Communication Barriers. Impediments to optimal human-to-human communication.

Communication, Diagonally Downward or Upward. Communication which reaches outside a specific line of authority to another line and traverses either upward or downward to another hierarchical level.

Communication, Downward. Communication initiated at a higher management level and directed to a lower level (or levels).

Communication, External. Communication which purposefully occurs (as a company function) between organizational personnel and a member or members of an external public.

Communication, Horizontal. Communication between or among managers at the same hierarchical level.

Communication, Internal. Communication between or among persons in the same organization.

Communication, Lateral. Communication which flows from one manager to another, both of whom are at the same hierarchical level in an organization.

Communication, Nonverbal. Messages that can be inferred from the actions or behavior of others.

Communication, Strategic. Communication that involves the future direction and goals of the organization, together with information pertaining to the external environment.

Communication, Technical. Communication primarily about instructions, policies, procedures, and methods related to performance of jobs in an organization.

Communication, Upward. Communication initiated at a lower management level and directed to a higher level (or levels).

Comparable Worth, Doctrine of. The view that persons holding jobs of equal value should be given equal compensation, regardless of individual personal differences.

Compensation, Employee. Remuneration (money and benefits) received by an employee for work performed.

Compensation Package. Direct remuneration plus benefits.

Competitive Puffery. Harmless touting of one's own products or services in the hope of besting the competition.

Conflict. Discord which occurs between or among employees due to real or imagined infringements.

Consideration. Genuine care and concern for subordinates evidenced by behavior on the part of a superior.

Contingency Approach to Organizing. Planning an organizational structure based on specific situations and conditions.

Controlling. Monitoring activities, measuring results, and taking corrective actions to assure conformance to previously established goals, objectives, or other standards.

Cooperation, Voluntary. Willing participation in performance of duties or assignments.

Co-optation. Joining with likely dissidents in planning to preclude future opposition.

Coordination. The interrelating of organizational activities in order to achieve objectives through teamwork.

Coordination, Involuntary. Coordination which results from a distinct obligation or from authoritative orders or other instructions given by a superior.

Coordination, Voluntary. Coordination which results from voluntary actions, without any threat of force from an external source.

Corporation. An artificial person or legal entity created by or under the authority of a state or nation.

Corporation, Business. A private corporation formed to transact business of one or more kinds.

Corporation, Closely Held. A corporation owned by a small number of stockholders and whose stock is not traded on public stock exchanges.

Corporation, Private. A corporation founded by and composed of private individuals for private purposes (as opposed to governmental purposes) and having no guaranteed responsibilities.

Corporation, Public. A corporation formed by the state to act as an agency of government administration, generally within a defined location in the state, e.g., a city, town, or village.

Corporation, Quasi-Public. A corporation not strictly organized for governmental purposes but which will perform functions for the good of the public, e.g., gas, water, and light companies and certain not-for-profit hospitals organized by governmental bodies.

Crime. A positive or negative act in violation of a penal law.

Critical Path Method (CPM). An arrow diagram showing all activities of a single use plan in a defined sequence, calculated as to the longest or critical path through it. Originally based on a single time estimate.

Culture. The totality of management approaches in a specific organization; the environment within an organization in all its aspects.

Data. Raw facts and figures which, when processed and analyzed, yield information pertinent to a business entity.

Debt Security. An instrument given by a debtor to a creditor that assures the payment of debt in case of failure to meet an obligation as specified.

Decentralizing. Dividing management duties (as opposed to operational functions) among persons and locations by means of delegations of authority and assignments of responsibility and accountability.

Decision Making, Rational. A process for selecting the best available alternative based on factual information, expert opinion, research, or experience.

Decision, Nonfunctional. A choice made between two or more alternatives, none of which has a material or direct effect on future courses of action.

Decision, Planning. A decision that directly determines certain aspects of future courses of action.

Decision Support System (DSS). A system that draws on transaction processing systems and interacts with an overall information system to support decision-making activities.

Decisional Law. Law which is based on decisions of judges presiding over a court.

De Facto. Actual although not based on law.

De Jure. Legitimate or lawful.

Delegation of Authority. The transfer of authority from one person to another, usually from a superior to a subordinate.

Deontological. A deontological ethical theory is one that holds actions are right or wrong, not on the basis of their consequences, but on the basis of whether they conform to moral principles or are duties in themselves.

Departmentation. The segmenting of operational work processes into workable or manageable units.

Departmentation, Functional. Creation of departments based on groupings of similar functions.

Departmentation, Geographic. Creation of departments based on geographic territories.

Departmentation, Product. Creation of departments based on products made or types of services rendered.

Departmentation by Types of Customers. Creation of departments based on the needs or demands of particular types of customers.

Directing. The art of issuing directives, orders, and authoritative pronouncements that initiate, regulate, and maintain courses of actions for defined divisions or units of an organization; directing is usually a function of top echelon managers.

Discipline. A subject capable of being codified in a form suitable for instruction; a field of study or professional work.

Due Care. The kind of care that would be exercised by a reasonably prudent person in a similar situation.

Echelon. One of the levels of management personnel in an organization.

Economic Productivity. A quantified appraisal of profits from a proposed investment.

EDP. Electronic data processing.

Employee Benefits. Benefits accruing to an employee that add to his or her income or reduce his or her personal expenses; benefits having monetary value.

Employee Communications. Usually, communications emanating from a personnel department and distributed to all employees, such as newsletters, explanations of policies, etc.

Employee Development. Educational efforts directed toward increasing knowledge and skills in order to enhance the possibility of promotion.

Employee Incentive. Extra remuneration for performance that exceeds the normal expectations for a job or position.

Employee Services. Services available to employees that add to his or her convenience or quality of life.

Employee Training. Educational efforts directed to increasing skills and abilities relating to the performance of a job.

Equity, Stockholders. The sum of common stock and all retained earnings.

Equity Securities. Shares of stock.

Ethic. A set of moral principles or values.

Executive. For the purpose of this book, the chief executive officer of a corporation and his or her immediate subordinates; other officers appointed directly by a board of directors; and heads of largely autonomous corporate divisions, plants, or other business units and their immediate subordinates.

Exit Interview. A formal interview of an employee immediately prior to organizational separation; usually performed by a member of the personnel department.

Extrapolate. To project.

Feedback. Informational output from operations that is used in controlling.

Fiduciary Relationship. A relationship where there is a special confidence reposed in a person such that he or she is then bound to act in good faith and with due regard to the interests of the party reposing the confidence.

Financial Acceptability. The magnitude of probable reward compared to the probability of attainment while also taking into account the cost of financing required outlays and the probability and consequences of failure.

Fixed Assets. Assets that are relatively permanent in nature and used in a business operation.

Force. Power that is manifested.

Forecasting. Projecting or predicting a future event or condition, usually based on rational study and analysis.

Function. A particular kind of work performed or intended to be performed.

Functional. (1) Able to perform a function with ease or efficiency (e.g., a functional organization) or (2) able to accommodate the performance of a function in an easy or efficient manner (e.g., a functional physical facility).

Functional Feasibility. An aspect of an investment opportunity featuring technical soundness, commercial possibilities, and the capability of being successfully implemented by means of a firm's available resources.

Functional Unit. A department, component of a department, or other administrative unit that pursues one or more identifiable work procedures and produces output that can be measured.

Gantt Chart. A bar and event chart. Shows time-related accomplishment of each task in a program (each related to the others) so that progress can be easily monitored. Named for its originator, Henry Gantt.

Generally Accepted Accounting Principles. Accounting concepts, measurement techniques, and standards used in presenting financial statements.

Goals. Broad ends toward which the efforts of the organization as a whole or specific divisions of it are directed.

Golden Rule. The moral principle that one should do to others only what one desires that others do to oneself.

Government Compliance Activities. Activities that identify, interpret, communicate, and seek compliance with all government regulations that apply to an organization (especially personnel department activities).

Grievance. An employee's expressed feeling of dissatisfaction caused by a perception of having been wronged in connection with a company-related matter.

Grievance Handling. The process used by a firm to evaluate and rectify (if need be) an employee grievance.

Gross Present Worth. The capitalized value of the flow of future expected benefits discounted at a rate which reflects their certainty or uncertainty.

Group. Several individuals (or more) who are in contact with one another, take one another into account, and are aware of some significant commonality.

Group Cohesiveness. The degree of influence that a group has over its members.

Group Dynamics. (1) An approach to the study of group behavior originated by Kurt Lewin; (2) changes that occur within a group and the influences exerted by the group upon individual members.

Group Synergy. The harmonizing of work in a group that results in a better total performance than would have occurred by each individual acting alone.

Group, Formal. A group formed by management for a certain purpose (or purposes).

Group, Informal. A group that voluntarily forms based on one or more positive or negative social interests.

Hierarchical Level. An echelon in a hierarchical or bureaucratic organization.

Hierarchy. The order or ranking that exists in an organized body, e.g., the ranking of managers.

Implementation. Performance of acts to carry out the various organizational plans.

Induction. Bringing a new employee into a firm.

Influence. The power of producing an effect without apparent exertion of force or direct orders or instructions.

Information. Data that have been processed in a formal, intelligent way so that the results are useful to those in the operation and management of a business.

Initiating Structure. Actions taken by a superior to maintain definite standards of performance, give clear directions, assure conformance to standard operating procedures, assign definitive tasks, and place emphasis on meeting deadlines.

Insider Trading. The trading in shares of publicly held stock by someone (an insider) who is privy to information that may affect the value and price of the shares.

Integrity. Soundness of moral principle and character shown by one person in dealing with others.

Intra Vires. When an act of a person or corporation is within the scope of the legal powers or authority of the person or corporation.

JCAH. Joint Commission on Accreditation of Hospitals.

Job. The total set of tasks and responsibilities assigned to an individual.

Job Analysis. Analysis of a job in terms of tasks and necessary skills.

Job Depth. The degree of control an employee has over his or her environment so as to effect completion of a work process without supervision.

Job Description. A narrative or diagrammatic delineation of the assigned tasks, responsibilities, authority, accountability, and reporting relationships that attach to a person who assumes a position in an organization.

Job Design. The assignment of specific task activities, duties, and responsibilities to an individual job.

Job Enrichment. Adding variety to a job and providing greater autonomy.

Job Rotation. Moving an employee from one job to another, usually to relieve boredom or to cross train.

Job Scope. The number and types of tasks included in a job.

Labor Relations. Usually, relations with unions or other organized labor groups.

Leadership. Perceived behavior that causes a motivation within subordinates, other organizational members, or peripherally related individuals to strive voluntarily toward achievement of organizational goals and objectives.

Leadership Behavior Description Questionnaire (LBDQ). A research tool devised at Ohio State University for measuring and describing leader behaviors.

Leadership, Behavioral Theory of. The theory that leadership depends on perceptions of the behavior of an individual rather than on his or her traits.

Leadership, Contingency Theory of. The theory that leadership effectiveness depends on an interaction between leadership style and a given situation; effectiveness is measured in three ways: (1) leader-member relations, (2) task structure, and (3) authority vested in the leader's position.

Leadership, Great Man Theory of. The theory that historical change or development is basically caused by the actions of great men or born leaders.

Leadership, Path-Goal Theory of. The theory that leadership depends on rewards for goal attainment, with the path to these rewards being both ascertainable and desired by subordinates. Developed by Robert House.

Leadership, Situational Theory of. The theory that the fundamental needs of a situation dictate the traits that an individual must have to exercise leadership.

Leadership, Trait Theory of. The theory that leadership results from certain personality traits possessed by an individual.

Leadership Style, Authoritarian. A style featuring autocratic leader behavior.

Leadership Style, Democratic. A style based on participatory decision making.

Leadership Style, Laissez-Faire. A style in which the leader allows free exercise of initiative by followers.

Level of Cognizance. An organizational position possessing a distinctive planning outlook.

Line Managers. Managers who occupy positions in a direct line of authority established to accomplish organizational goals and objectives.

Linking Pin Function. The linking which the supervisor of a primary work group effects between that work group and the supervisor's superior. Originally recognized by Rensis Likert.

Liquidity. The state of having the money to pay debts as they fall due.

Management. (1) a body of organizational managers; (2) functions performed by organizational managers regarding human and material resources.

Management by Objectives (MBO). The setting of performance goals for each manager (usually through agreement between a superior and a subordinate), with subsequent results used as a measure of successful accomplishment.

Management Information System (MIS). A system (usually computerized) designed to provide information to managers that will be useful in planning, implementation, and framing adaptive responses.

Management Principle. A universally applicable management precept.

Marketing. Creation of organizational programs to establish exchange relationships with various categories of persons.

Maslow's Hierarchy of Needs. A. H. Maslow's view that humans will be motivated by the prepotent need at a given time. Generally, he held that needs range upward from physiological needs to security, social, esteem, and self-actualization needs, with the satisfaction of one initiating the motivation to satisfy the next highest.

Matrix Organization. Where product or task force employees under an assigned line manager are combined with dually reporting specialists at corporate or divisional levels, for the purpose of accomplishing some specific project or purpose.

Method. The specific manner in which an operator performs certain necessary work tasks with prescribed tools or equipment in a particularly arranged work station.

MIS. Management information system.

MIS Planning and Development Committee. A committee established to analyze and evaluate the organization's information needs and the capabilities of an existing MIS to supply them; the committee then plans, designs, and implements a successor MIS.

Mission. The basic purpose of an organization (its raison d'être).

Motivation. An inner stimulus causing one to perform a certain act (or actions); the inner stimulus may arise from one perception or a broad range of perceptions.

Net Present Value. In regard to a proposed financing package, that value which equals the discounted cash inflows less the discounted cash outflows.

Net Present Worth. The difference between gross present worth and the amount of capital investment required to achieve certain benefits.

Net Profit Margin. Sales divided by net profits.

Objectives. Specific ends for accomplishment within a distinct time-frame, the degree of achievement of which can be measured by some quantified means.

Operational Information System (OIS). A system that accepts data from operational systems and provides information about the functioning of these systems. Usually computerized.

Operations Personnel. (Also called *operational personnel*.) Those engaged in line work or in work directly devoted to producing products or rendering services.

Organization. A body of persons related one to the other by means of a systematic structure.

Orientation. Instructions that familiarize a new employee with the company and the job he or she is to hold; also, instructions for those who move from one job to another.

Owner's Equity. Excess of assets over liabilities.

Paradigmatic Event. An event that clearly represents a change from a previous order of things to a new order.

Partnership. A voluntary contract between two or more persons to place all or a specified sum of their material resources, labor, and skill into a business, with the understanding that there will be a proportional sharing of profits or losses among them.

Payback Period. The time required for earnings or savings to pay back the cost of an investment.

Perception. The result of a combination of factors, including the perceiver's stimulus situation and his or her frame of reference, attitudes, and emotions.

Performance Evaluation. Evaluating on-the-job performance of employees. Also called *performance rating* or *performance review*.

Personnel Benefits. Direct monetary rewards, vacations, sick leave, paid time off, insurance, retirement awards, etc.

Personnel Policies. Policies that specify the nature of relationships and interfaces that employees come to have with a company over time.

Personnel Services. Services which provide a convenience or enhance the quality of on-the-job life, such as cafeterias, libraries, playgrounds, child-care programs, etc.

PERT. Program evaluation review technique. An ordered, time-related diagram showing the relationships among a network of discrete events and thereby describing an entire program.

Philosophy. A very broad theory underlying a sphere of activity and manifested as a set of expressed general beliefs, concepts, and attitudes.

Plan, One-Time-Through. A plan for accomplishing a specific one-time goal or objective. Same as a single use plan.

Plan, Single Use. A plan devised to define and accomplish a one-time goal or objective or to resolve a unique problem. Same as a one-time-through plan.

Plan, Standing. A plan that is permanent or that has no time limit. Standing plans have been categorized in this book as policies, procedures, methods, and rules.

Planning, Assets. On the assumption of continued liquidity, making decisions related to an asset or combination of assets that will provide the greatest benefits to a specific business entity.

Planning, Contingency. Formulating alternative plans based on possible future events.

Planning, Financial. (1) Planning for the use of assets or economic resources, both existing and future; (2) capital finance planning.

Planning, Human Resource. Planning related to (1) human resource management philosophy and policies, (2) functions to be undertaken by a personnel department, and (3) personnel policies and procedures. Most authorities limit human resource planning to staffing quantifications.

Planning, Long-Range. Formulating organizational mission and goals for a three- to ten-year period.

Planning, Operational. Includes formulation of both standing and single use plans, especially those that directly relate to implementing acts.

Planning, Strategic. Planning which establishes mission, goals, and objectives for time periods of one to five years (or more); the planning is in regard to finance, productivity, sales, procurements, personnel needs and responsibilities, performance dates, locations, and programs for implementation.

Planning, Tax. Making or influencing decisions pertaining to economic transactions that will hopefully legally minimize or defer tax liabilities.

Planning Decision. A decision regarding a future course of action.

Policy. A guideline for organizational members to observe in their behavior or to follow in the performance of their management or operational responsibilities.

Position Description. Usually, the job description of a manager. May be more oriented to describing results to be achieved than to a detailed listing of duties to be performed.

Power. The ability to apply force in getting others to perform certain acts; latent force.

Power, Coercive. Power derived from the ability to inflict penalties or withhold rewards.

Power, Expert. Power derived from the possession of specialized knowledge.

Power, Legitimate. Power derived from legal authority.

Power, Referent. Power derived from one's prestige or charisma.

Power, Reward. Power derived from the ability of one person to reward another.

Practice. The continuous exercise of a profession.

Predicting. Forecasting on the basis of observation, experience, or scientific reason. When a projection is altered on the basis of any of these, it becomes a prediction.

Procedure. Acts related to each other in a sequence for the purpose of accomplishing defined work and usually described in terms of who, when, what, where, and how.

Process. A series of actions or operations to accomplish certain goals, objectives, or other ends.

Productivity. The rate of production of goods or services by some unit of manpower.

Profession. A vocation, calling, occupation, or employment involving labor, skill, education, special knowledge, and compensation or profit. The labor or skill involved is predominantly mental or intellectual rather than physical or manual.

Profitability Index. The ratio of net present value to the investment cost of an investment. Often used to indicate a method of calculating the true ratio of return on a proposed investment.

Program. A comprehensive single use plan for accomplishing a major goal or objective by means of a stepped approach, each step of which is described in terms of who, when, what, where, how, and how much (if funds are involved).

Programming, Adaptive. Programming that is tentative and devised so as to allow events to determine the next steps (see *Adaptivising*).

Programming, Commitment. A program whose goals and objectives have a high probability of being attained.

Programming, Functional. In facility planning, the programming of functions to be carried forward in new or altered construction (in terms of type, quantity, and procedures).

Project. Usually, but not necessarily, one part or phase of a program and characterized by a limited scope.

Project. To extrapolate, extend, or expand past trends of known indices into the future and results in a projection.

Promotion. The tasks involved in organizing and developing a corporation up to the day operation begins.

Ratio, Debt-to-Equity. Ratio of total debt to total equity employed in a business.

Ratios, Activity. Ratios that compare revenues and investments and indicate how efficiently a firm turns investments in asset accounts into revenue output.

Ratios, Financing. Ratios that indicate long-term solvency.

Ratios, Liquidity. Ratios that focus on a firm's ability to meet short-term financial obligations, especially ratios that focus on the relationship between current assets and current liabilities.

Ratios, Profit. Ratios that measure profitability in terms of income statement items one to the other or of income statement items to balance sheet items.

Recruiting. Matching the preferences and goals of prospective employees with the needs and preferences of employers.

Reflective Thought Process. A rational method of thinking, making decisions, or reaching conclusions. First enunciated by John Dewey.

Reporting. The second step in the management control process, the first being monitoring and the third being corrective action. (Many authorities cite setting a standard as step one, but in the strictest sense that is planning, not controlling.)

Reporting by Exception. Reporting to higher management levels only significant deviations from established standards or goals.

Resistance to Change. The tendency of humans to maintain situational stability and offer some resistance when it is disturbed.

Responsibility. An obligation to perform or to refrain from performing certain acts and to answer for injuries or other ill consequences that result from not meeting the obligation.

Retained Earnings. The part of stockholders' equity that results from profits and is retained.

Retraining. Training given to those with obsolete skills; retrofitting.

Return on Investment (ROI). Earnings divided by total assets.

Revenue and Expense Statement. A performance statement setting forth a summary of income and expense items so as to show whether operations resulted in a profit or loss—and how much of one—for a stated period.

Risk Management. Functions related to protecting a firm's assets and profitability against loss caused by accidental or unexpected circumstances.

Role. A behavioral pattern that a person in a particular business or social position is expected to conform to.

Rules. A directive that a specific action must or must not be taken under certain circumstances.

Scientific Management. The theory of Frederick Taylor and others that efficiency in operations can be obtained primarily through time-and-motion studies, work analyses, improved methods, specialization of tasks, intensive training of workers, and incentive pay.

Selection. The process of hiring a person capable of filling a position.

Selection Criteria. Criteria for evaluating an alternative in a planning or decision-making process.

Self-Actualization. Self-fulfillment; realization of one's full potential.

Self-Coordination. Coordination resulting from one's own initiative.

Separations. Organizational layoffs, resignations, firings, retirements, and deaths.

Shareholder. Someone who owns a share in property or stock in a corporation.

Sine Qua Non. Something that is indispensable; an event, condition, or object that is necessary for the existence of some other event, condition, or object.

Social Responsibility. The responsibility that every business has to society not to perform harmful acts.

Span of Control. The span of subordinates that a superior must direct, supervise, or control.

Staff Positions. Management positions established for the performance of duties that are supplementary to those of line managers. Such positions are often advisory, and they sometimes are delegated functional authority to veto certain line decisions.

Stakeholder. Someone who has a vital material interest in the conduct of a business firm.

State of the Art. The best currently existing method of performing a particular act or set of tasks.

Statement of Changes in Financial Position. A statement containing information on the sources (increases) and uses (decreases) of cash during a specific period for an accounting entity.

Statute. A law expressed in writing that has been enacted by a legislature.

Structure. The manner in which one part of an organization is related to others and the organizational form by which managers are related to each other.

Subordinate. Someone who reports directly to a person at a higher hierarchical level in an organizational setting.

Subsume. To put subordinate or component elements within a larger class or whole.

Subsystem. An identifiable set of related tasks in a larger system.

Subterfuge. An artifice or expedient employed to evade unfavorable consequences.

Sui Generis. One of a kind.

Superior. A manager who has subordinate managers or operational personnel reporting directly to him or her in an organizational relationship.

Supervision. Overseeing work processes and the performance of subordinates and their equipment. Used primarily when referring to lower level managers.

System. An organized whole; a combination of things, parts, or persons that somewhat harmoniously work together as a unified whole.

Systems Approach to Planning. A methodology for identifying and evaluating alternative courses of action and preparing a development program. Developed by the General Electric Company.

Task Identity. An individual work assignment that upon completion results in an identifiable object, product, or process.

Theory X. A theory that presumes employees require close supervision. Identified by Douglas McGregor.

Theory Y. A theory that presumes employees are responsible and motivated and desire a certain degree of control over their workplace. Identified by Douglas McGregor.

Top-Down Approach to Organizational Planning. Starting planning with a structure based on production processes, equipment, and human capabilities viewed from an overall standpoint.

Transactions. Business events that are measured in terms of money.

Transfer. Shifting an employee to another job at the same grade level.

True Rate of Return. (Also called *internal rate of return* and *investors' method.*) A measurement of the economic productivity of a proposed investment in terms of an interest rate.

Trustee. A person in whom an estate, interest, or power is vested for administrative purposes or for the benefit or use of another.

Ultra Vires. Beyond the scope of the legal powers of a corporation.

Underwriter. An investment banking firm that sells a corporation's stock to the public.

Utilitarian Ethics. The theory that actions are morally correct inasmuch as they bring about good consequences.

Variance Analysis. An analysis that compares actual performance against a standard of management expectations.

Vertical Integration, Backward. Undertaking a business that supplies the resources to run the main business.

Vertical Integration, Forward. Undertaking a business that brings the main business into closer contact with customers so that they will be more likely to use company products or services.

Vest. To give someone (or some group or organization) possession of authority, power, property, etc. If authority is vested in a person (or, in other words, if that person is invested with authority), he or she has a right to exercise that authority.

Workload Projections. Quantified projections of the output of a department or other administrative unit.

Zero-Base Strategic Planning. Hypothesizing the elimination of each and every existing goal and objective so as to consider whether there are more feasible ones (given the framework of conducting business).

Appendix B

Bibliography

Albanese, Robert. *Management: Toward Accountability for Performance.* Homewood, Ill.: Irwin, 1979.

Albers, Henry. *Principles of Management: A Modern Approach.* 4th ed. New York: Wiley, 1974.

Albrecht, William P., Jr. *Economics.* 2d ed. Englewood Cliffs, N.J.: Prentice-Hall, 1979.

Anson, William R. *Principles of the Law of Contracts.* Edited by Thomas H. Patterson. Chicago: Callaghan and Company, 1939.

Argyris, Chris. *Management and Organizational Development.* New York: McGraw-Hill, 1971.

_____. *Personality and Organization.* New York: Harper & Bros., 1957.

Armstrong, J. Scott. "Social Responsibility in Management." *Journal of Business Research* 5 (September 1977).

Asman, David, and Meyerson, Adam, eds. *The Wall Street Journal on Management.* Homewood, Ill.: Dow Jones-Irwin, 1985.

Austin, Charles J. *Information Systems for Hospital Administrators.* 2d ed. Ann Arbor, Mich.: Health Administration Press, 1983.

Barnard, Chester I. *Organization and Management.* Cambridge, Mass.: Harvard University Press, 1948.

_____. *The Functions of the Executive.* Cambridge, Mass.: Harvard University Press, 1966.

Barnes, Ralph M. *Motion and Time Study: Design and Measurement of Work.* 7th ed. New York: Wiley, 1980.

Bassett, Glenn A. *Management Styles in Transition.* New York: American Management Association, 1966.

Beauchamp, Tom L., and Bowie, Norman E., eds. *Ethical Theory and Business.* Englewood Cliffs, N.J.: Prentice-Hall, 1979.

Beer, Michael, et al. *Managing Human Assets.* New York: The Free Press, 1984.

Bennett, Addision C. *Improving Management Performance in Health Care Institutions.* Chicago: American Hospital Association, 1978.

Benton, Lewis, ed. *Management for the Future.* New York: McGraw-Hill, 1978.

481

Bierman, Harold, Jr., and Smidt, Seymour. *The Capital Budgeting Decision.* 6th ed. New York: Macmillan, 1984.

Bittel, Lester R. *What Every Supervisor Should Know.* 4th ed. New York: McGraw-Hill, 1980.

Blake, Robert R., and Mouton, Jane S. *The New Managerial Grid.* Houston, Tex.: Gulf, 1978.

Blau, Peter M., and Scott, W. Richard. *Formal Organizations.* San Francisco: Chandler, 1962.

Block, Lee F., ed. *Marketing for Hospitals in Hard Times.* Chicago: Teach 'em, 1981.

Bok, Sissela. *Lying: Moral Choice in Public and Private Life.* New York: Pantheon Books, 1978.

Bothwell, Lin. *The Art of Leadership.* Englewood Cliffs, N.J.: Prentice-Hall, 1983.

Boulton, William R. *Business Policy.* New York: Macmillan, 1984.

Bowie, Norman. *Business Ethics.* Englewood Cliffs, N.J.: Prentice-Hall, 1982.

Brandt, Steven C. *Strategic Planning in Emerging Companies.* Reading, Mass.: Addison-Wesley, 1981.

Brown, Warren B., and Moberg, Dennis J. *Organization Theory and Management.* New York: Wiley, 1980.

Brown, Wilfred. *Exploration in Management.* New York: Wiley, 1960.

Burian, Barbara J., and Fink, Stuart S. *Business Data Processing.* 2d ed. Englewood Cliffs, N.J.: Prentice-Hall, 1982.

Carr, Albert L. "Is Business Bluffing Ethical?" *Harvard Business Review,* January-February 1968, pp. 36–47.

Cheek, Logan M. *Zero-Base Budgeting Comes of Age.* New York: AMACOM, a division of American Management Association, 1977.

Church, Frederick C., Jr. *Avoiding Surprises.* Boston: Boston Risk Management Corporation, 1982.

Clark, George L. *Summary of American Law.* Rochester, N.Y.: The Lawyers' Cooperative Publishing Company, 1949.

Cleverley, William O. *Essentials of Hospital Finance.* Rockville, Md.: Aspen, 1978.

Costello, Timothy W., and Zalkind, Sheldon S. *Psychology in Administration.* Englewood Cliffs, N.J.: Prentice-Hall, 1963.

Couvey, H. Dominic, and McAlister, Neil Harding. *Computer Choices: Beware of Conspicuous Computing.* Reading, Mass.: Addison-Wesley, 1982.

Coxe, Weld. *Marketing Architectural and Engineering Services.* New York: Van Nostrand Rheinhold, 1971.

Cumming, Paul W. *Open Management.* New York: AMACOM, a division of American Management Association, 1980.

Dale, Ernest. *Management: Theory and Practice.* 2d ed. New York: McGraw-Hill, 1969.

Dauten, Paul M., Jr., ed. *Current Issues and Emerging Concepts in Management.* Boston: Houghton Mifflin, 1962.

Davidson, Sidney; Hanowille, Leon; Stickney, Clyde P.; and Weil, Ronald L. *Intermediate Accounting.* 4th ed. Chicago, Ill.: Dryden, 1985.

Davis, Keith. *Human Behavior at Work.* New York: McGraw-Hill, 1981.

Dessler, Gary. *Organization and Management.* Reston, Va.: Reston Publishing Company, 1982.

Dewey, John. *How We Think*. Boston: Heath, 1933.

Domanico, Lee. "Strategy Planning: Vital for Long Range Development." *Hospital and Health Services Administration*, Summer 1981, pp. 25–50.

Dowd, Ann Reilly. "What Managers Can Learn from Manager Reagan." *Fortune*, September 1986, pp. 33–41.

Drucker, Peter F. *Management: Tasks, Responsibilities, Practices*. New York: Harper & Row, 1974.

———. *The Practice of Management*. New York: Harper & Row, 1954.

Dubin, Robert. *Human Relations in Administration*. 2d ed. Englewood Cliffs, N.J.: Prentice-Hall, 1961.

Ernst & Whinney, *Tax Reform—1986*. 1986.

Estey, Marten. *The Unions*. 3d ed. New York: Harcourt Brace Jovanovich, 1981.

Fayol, Henri. *General and Industrial Management*. Translated by Constance Storrs. London: Sir Isaac Pitman and Sons, 1967.

Federal Bureau of Investigation. *Crime in the United States*. Washington, D.C.: Department of Justice, 1983.

———. *Crime in the United States*. Washington, D.C.: Department of Justice, 1985.

Ferguson, William A. "Agency." In *Modern American Law*, vol. 2, Chicago: edited by Eugene A. Gilmore. Rev. ed. Blackstone School of Law, 1963.

Fiedler, Fred E. "The Leadership Game: Matching the Man to the Situation." *Organizational Dynamics*, Winter 1976, pp. 5–12.

Flippo, Edwin B. *Principles of Personnel Management*. New York: McGraw-Hill, 1966.

Follett, Mary Parker. *Dynamic Administration: The Collected Papers of Mary Parker Follett*. Edited by H.C. Metcalf and L. Urwick. New York: Harper & Bros., 1941.

Follett, Mary Parker. *Freedom and Coordination*. London: Management Publications Trust, 1949.

Foulkes, Fred K., and Livernash, E. Robert. *Human Resources Management*. Englewood Cliffs, N.J.: Prentice-Hall, 1982.

Friedman, Milton. *Capitalism and Freedom*. Chicago: University of Chicago Press, 1962.

Gailbraith, John Kenneth. *Economics and the Public Purpose*. Boston: Houghton Mifflin, 1973.

———. *The New Industrial State*. Boston: Houghton Mifflin, 1967.

Gellerman, Sam W. *Management by Motivation*. New York: American Management Association, 1968.

Geneen, Harold, with Moscow, Alvin. *Managing*. Garden City, N.Y.: Doubleday, 1984.

George, Claude S., Jr. *The History of Management Thought*. Englewood Cliffs, N.J.: Prentice-Hall, 1968.

Gessford, John Evans. *Modern Information Systems*. Reading, Mass.: Addison-Wesley, 1980.

Gilbert, Thomas F. *Human Competence*. New York: McGraw-Hill, 1978.

Goetz, Billy E. *Management Planning and Control*. New York: McGraw-Hill, 1949.

Granof, Michael H. *Financial Accounting*. 2d ed. Englewood Cliffs, N.J.: Prentice-Hall, 1980.

Green, Laura. *Computers in Business and Industry.* New York: Franklin Watts, 1984.

Grossman, Lee. *The Change Agent.* New York: AMACOM, a division of American Management Association, 1974.

Haas, Kurt. *Understanding Ourselves and Others.* Englewood Cliffs, N.J.: Prentice-Hall, 1965.

Haggblade, Merle. *Business Communication.* St. Paul, Minn.: West, 1982.

Haimann, Theo. *Professional Management.* Boston: Houghton Mifflin, 1962.

Haire, Mason. *Psychology in Management.* New York: McGraw-Hill, 1964.

Hardy, Owen B. "Systematic Processes Applied to Health Care Planning." *Hospital Administration* 16 (Winter 1971): pp. 7–24.

————. "Voluntary Cooperation and Coordination: Requisites for Effective Hospital Administration." *Hospital Administration* 11 (Fall 1966): pp. 34–43.

————. "Delegation: The Administrator's Challenge." *Hospital Administration* 15 (Winter 1970): pp. 8–19.

————. "Leadership and the Hospital Administrator." *Hospital Administration* 13 (Winter 1968): pp. 35–50.

Hardy, Owen B., and Lammers, Lawrence P. *Hospitals: The Planning and Design Process.* 2d ed. Rockville, Md.: Aspen, 1986.

Harvard Business Review. *On Human Relations.* New York: Harper & Row, 1979.

————. *On Management.* New York: Harper & Row, 1975.

Hawkins, David F. *Financial Reporting Practices of Corporations.* Homewood, Ill.: Dow Jones-Irwin, 1972.

Heller, Robert. *The Supermanagers.* New York: Dutton, 1984.

Henn, Harry C., and Alexander, John R. *Laws of Corporations.* St. Paul, Minn.: West, 1983.

Herzberg, Frederick; Mausner, Bernard; and Snyderman, Barbara Block. *The Motivation to Work.* 2d ed. New York: Wiley, 1967.

Hospital Corporation of America. *Corporate Office 1987 Planning Procedures Manual.* Nashville, Tenn.: HCA, 1986.

House, Robert J. "A Path-Goal Theory of Leader Effectiveness." *Administrative Science Quarterly* 16 (September 1971): 321–38.

Hunt, Pearson; Williams, Charles; and Donaldson, Gordon. *Basic Business Finance.* 3d ed. Homewood, Ill.: Irwin, 1966.

Hymes, Dell, ed. *Reinventing Anthropology.* New York: Random House, 1972.

Iacocca, Lee, with Novak, William. *Iacocca.* New York: Bantam, 1984.

Janger, Allen R. *The Personnel Function: Changing Objectives and Organization.* New York: The Conference Board, 1977.

Johnson, Richard A.; Kast, Fremont E.; and Rosenzweig, James E. *The Theory and Management of Systems.* 2d ed. New York: McGraw-Hill, 1967.

Joint Commission on Accreditation of Hospitals. *Accreditation Manual for Hospitals.* Chicago: JCAH, 1978.

Kaplan, Robert S. *Advanced Management Accounting.* Englewood Cliffs, N.J.: Prentice-Hall, 1982.

Kerr, Steven, et al. "Toward a Contingency Theory of Leadership Based upon the Consideration and Initiating Structure Literature." *Organization Behavior and Human Performance,* August 1974, pp. 62–82.

Koontz, Harold. "The Management Theory Jungle." *Journal of the Academy of Management*, December 1961, pp. 174–88.

Koontz, Harold, and O'Donnel, Cyril. *Management: A Book of Readings.* New York: McGraw-Hill, 1964.

Koontz, Harold; O'Donnel, Cyril; and Weihrich, Heinz. *Essentials of Management.* New York: McGraw-Hill, 1982.

Kotler, Philip. *Marketing for Non-Profit Organizations.* Englewood Cliffs, N.J.: Prentice-Hall, 1975.

_____. *Marketing Management, Analysis Planning and Control.* 4th ed. London: Prentice-Hall International, 1980.

LeBoeuf, Michael. *The Greatest Management Principle in the World.* New York: Putnam, 1985.

Lee, Sang M. *Management by Multiple Objectives.* New York: Petrocelli, 1981.

Levinson, Robert E. *The Decentralized Company.* New York: American Management Association, 1983.

Lifton, James, and Hardy, Owen B. *Site Selection for Health Care Facilities.* Chicago: American Hospital Association, 1982.

Likert, Rensis. *New Patterns of Management.* New York: McGraw-Hill, 1961.

Lindberg, Donald A.B. *The Computer and Medical Care.* Springfield, Ill.: Thomas, 1968.

Linneman, Robert E. *Shirt Sleeved Approach to Long Range Planning.* Englewood Cliffs, N.J.: Prentice-Hall, 1980.

Lippitt, Gordon L. *Organization Renewal.* New York: Appleton-Century-Crofts, 1969.

Lippitt, Ronald, and White, Ralph K. "An Experimental Study of Leadership and Group Life." In *Readings in Social Psychology,* edited by Guy Swanson, Theodore Newcomb, and Eugene Hartley. Rev. ed. New York: Henry Holt and Co., 1952.

Littlefield, C.L., and Rachel, Frank. *Office and Administrative Management.* 2d ed. Englewood Cliffs, N.J.: Prentice-Hall, 1964.

Lucas, Henry C., Jr. *Information Systems Concepts for Management.* New York: McGraw-Hill, 1978.

Lundberg, Louis B. *The Art of Being an Executive.* New York: The Free Press, 1984.

McCabe, Douglas M. "The Morale Indicators." *Presidential Airways Magazine* 1 (June-July 1986), p. 20.

McConkney, Dale D. *How to Manage by Results.* 4th ed. New York: American Management Association, 1983.

McFarland, Dalton E. *Management: Principles and Practices.* 2d ed. New York: Macmillan, 1964.

McGregor, Douglas. *The Human Side of Enterprise.* New York: McGraw-Hill, 1960.

_____. *The Professional Manager.* New York: McGraw-Hill, 1967.

McLaughlin, Harold J. *Building Your Business Plan.* New York: Wiley, 1985.

Manning, Frank V. *Managerial Dilemmas and Executive Growth.* Reston, Va.: Reston Publishing Company, 1981.

March, James G., and Simon, Herbert A. *Organizations.* New York: Wiley, 1967.

Maslow, Abraham. *Motivation and Personality*, 2d ed. New York: Harper & Row, 1970.

Massie, Joseph L. *Essentials of Management*. 2d ed. Englewood Cliffs, N.J.: Prentice-Hall, 1971.

Maynard, H.B., ed. *Handbook of Business Administration*. New York: McGraw-Hill, 1967.

Meigs, Walter B., and Meigs, Robert F. *Accounting: The Basis for Business Decisions*. 6th ed. New York: McGraw-Hill, 1984.

Merrihue, Willard V. *Managing by Communication*. New York: McGraw-Hill, 1960.

Merrill, Harward F., ed. *Classics in Management*. New York: American Management Association, 1960.

Metzger, Norman. *Personnel Administration in the Health Services Industry*. 2d ed. New York: SP Medical & Scientific Books, 1979.

Miller, Robert W. *Schedule, Cost, and Profit Control with PERT*. New York: McGraw-Hill, 1963.

Milling, Bryan E. *Financial Tools for the Non-Financial Executive*. Radnor, Pa.: Chilton, 1983.

Miner, John B., and Miner, Mary Green. *Personnel and Industrial Relations*. New York: Macmillan, 1977.

Mooney, James B. *The Principles of Organization*. Rev. ed. New York: Harper & Row, 1947.

Moyer, R. Charles; McGuigan, James R.; and Kretlow, William J. *Contemporary Financial Management*. 2d ed. St. Paul, Minn.: West, 1984.

Naisbitt, John. *Megatrends*. New York: Warner, 1982.

Newman, William H., and Summer, Charles E., Jr. *The Process of Management*. Englewood Cliffs, N.J.: Prentice-Hall, 1961.

Newman, William H., and Warren, E. Kirby. *The Process of Management*. 4th ed. Englewood Cliffs, N.J.: Prentice-Hall, 1977.

Nolan, Richard L. "Controlling the Cost of Data Services." In *Catching Up with the Computer Revolution*, edited by Kenneth R. Andrews. New York: Wiley, 1983.

Olmstead, Michael S. *The Small Group*. New York: Random House, 1959.

Optner, Stanford L. *Systems Analysis for Business and Industrial Problem Solving*. Englewood Cliffs, N.J.: Prentice-Hall, 1965.

Ouchi, William G. *Theory Z*. Reading, Mass.: Addison-Wesley, 1981.

Parker, Donn E. *Fighting Computer Crime*. New York: Scribner, 1983.

Parsons, Talcott. *Sociological Theory and Modern Society*. New York: The Free Press, 1967.

Parthenon Insurance Company. *Risk Management Manual*. Nashville, Tenn.: HCA, 1986.

Peiffner, John M., and Sherwood, Frank P. *Administrative Organization*. Englewood Cliffs, N.J.: Prentice-Hall, 1960.

Peters, Thomas J., and Waterman, Robert H., Jr. *In Search of Excellence*. New York: Harper & Row, 1982.

Pigors, Paul, and Myers, Charles A. *Personnel Administration*. 9th ed. New York: McGraw-Hill, 1981.

Rakich, Jonathan S., and Darr, Kurt, eds. *Hospital Organization and Management*. 2d ed. New York: SP Medical and Scientific Books, 1978.

Reddin, W.J. *Managerial Effectiveness*. New York: McGraw-Hill, 1970.

Reuschlein, Harold Gill, and Gregory, William A. *Agency and Partnership*. St. Paul, Minn.: West, 1980.

Samuelson, Paul A. *Economics*. 11th ed. New York: McGraw-Hill, 1980.

Sartain, Aaron Roy; North, Alvin J.; Strange, Jack Roy; and Chapman, Harold Martin. *Psychology: Understanding Human Beings*. McGraw-Hill, 1962.

Sayles, Leonard R. *Leadership*. New York: McGraw-Hill, 1979.

Scheer, Wilbert E. *Personnel Administration Handbook*. 2d ed. Chicago: Dartnell, 1979.

Scheim, Edgar H., and Bennis, Warren G. *Personnel and Organizational Change through Group Methods*. New York: Wiley, 1965.

Schoderbek, Peter P. *Management Systems*. New York: Wiley, 1967.

Scott, William G., and Mitchell, Terrence R. *Organization Theory*. 3d ed. Homewood, Ill.: Irwin, 1976.

Selznick, Philip. *Leadership in Administration*. Evanston, Ill.: Ron Peterson and Company, 1957.

Shapiro, Irving S., with Kantman, Carl B. *America's Third Revolution*. New York: Harper & Row, 1984.

Shaw, Marjorie. "A Comparison of Individuals and Small Groups in the Rational Solution of Complex Problems." *American Journal of Psychology* 44 (July 1932), pp. 491–504.

Simon, Herbert A. *Administrative Behavior*. 2d ed. New York: The Free Press, 1957.

Smith, Adam. The *Wealth of Nations*. New York: Modern Library, 1937.

Sprague, Ralph H., Jr., and Carlson, Eric D. *Building Effective Decision Support Systems*. Englewood Cliffs, N.J.: Prentice-Hall, 1982.

Steers, Richard M.; Ungson, Gerardo R.; and Mowday, Richard T. *Managing Effective Organizations*. Belmont, Calif.: Kent, 1985.

Steiner, George A. *The New CEO*. New York: Macmillan, 1983.

Steiner, George A., and Miner, John B. *Management Policy and Strategy*. New York: Macmillan, 1977.

Stogdill, Ralph M., and Coons, Alvin E., eds. *Leader Behavior: Its Description and Measurement*. Research Mimeograph no. 88. Columbus, Ohio: Ohio State University, Bureau of Business Research, 1951.

Stokes, Paul M. *A Total Systems Approach to Management Control*. New York: American Management Association, 1968.

Stoner, James A.F. *Management*. 2d ed. Englewood Cliffs, N.J.: Prentice-Hall, 1982.

Summer, Charles E., and O'Connel, Jeremiah J. *The Management Mind*. 3d ed. Homewood, Ill.: Irwin, 1973.

Sweeny, H.W. Allen, and Rachlin, Robert. *Handbook of Budgeting*. New York: Wiley, 1981.

Symonds, Curtis W. "Effective Conversion to Direct Cost System." *Financial Executive*, September 1966, p. 3.

Taylor, Frederick W. *Principles of Scientific Management*. New York: Harper & Bros., 1911.

Taylor, W. Bayard. *Financial Policies of Business Enterprises*. 2d ed. New York: Appleton-Century-Crofts, 1956.

Tead, Ordway. *The Art of Leadership*. New York: McGraw-Hill, 1951.

Toffler, Alvin. *The Adaptive Corporation*. New York: McGraw-Hill, 1985.

Tuleja, Tad. *Beyond the Bottom Line*. New York: Facts on File Publications, 1985.

Urwick, L. *The Elements of Administration*. New York: Harper & Row, 1943.

Van Gundy, Arthur B. *Managing Group Creativity.* New York: American Management Association, 1984.

Vaughan, Diane. *Controlling Unlawful Organizational Behavior.* Chicago: University of Chicago Press, 1983.

Vroom, Victor H., and Yetton, Phillip W. *Leadership and Decision Making.* Pittsburgh, Pa.: University of Pittsburgh Press, 1976.

Warner, D. Michael; Holloway, Don C.; and Grazier, Kyle L. *Decision Making and Control for Health Administration.* 2d ed. Ann Arbor, Mich.: Health Administration Press, 1984.

Webber, Ross A. *Management.* Homewood, Ill.: Irwin, 1975.

Woelfel, Charles J. *An Introduction to Financial Accounting.* Santa Monica, Calif.: Goodyear, 1980.

Wormser, Maurice. "Private Corporations." In *Modern American Law,* vol. 4, edited by Eugene A. Gilmore. Rev. ed. Chicago: Blackstone School of Law, 1965.

Wren, Daniel A. *The Evolution of Management Thought.* New York: The Ronald Press Company, 1972.

Yoder, Dale. *Personnel Management and Industrial Relations.* 5th ed. Englewood Cliffs, N.J.: Prentice-Hall, 1962.

Index

Balance sheet budget, 178, 468
Behavioral science, 14, 284
  human resources, 201-202
Board, 31-32, 468
  adaptive response, 20, 21
  audit committee, 45
  chief executive officer, 41-43
    advice, 44
  committee structure, 45-46
  compensation and human resource
    committee, 46
  corporate assets, 43
  corporate relations and ethics
    committee, 46
  election of officers, 36
  executive, 41-43
  executive committee, 46
  fiduciary relationship to, 43
  finance committee, 46
  formal legal functions, 43
  functions, 34, 38-46, 40, 42-46, 64, 92,
    124, 144, 196, 226, 256
    overview, 38-39
  implementation, 20, 21
  legal functions, 31
  management outcomes, 45
  meetings, 45
  organization committee, 45
  outside members, 44-45
  planning, 20, 21
  powers, 36
  selection process, 44-45
  shareholder, 41
  strategy review committee, 46
  talent development, 45
Bond, 468
Bonus, 366, 468
Book rated return, 155, 468
Budget
  operational planning, 261
  single use plan, 260-261
  strategic planning, 261
Budgeting
  advantages, 178
  drawbacks, 178
Budgeting process, 178, 179
  Hospital Corporation of America, 179
Building program, 262, 263

C

Capital, availability, 83
Capital budgeting, 154-155, 155-159, 176,
  177, 468
  steps, 156-157
Capital finance planning, 154-162
Capital financing, 468
Capital structure, 159-162, 468
Cash flow budget, 177-178
Categorical imperative, 469
Certified public accountant, 147
Chain of command, 469

Chief executive officer
  board, 41-43
    advice, 44
  legal function, 52-53
Chief financial officer, data processing, 152
Classic management theory, 469
Coercive power, 321
Commitment programming, 258
Committee, 329
  chairing, 333-334
Common law, 469
Communication, 13, 227-239, 469
  adaptive response, 435
  barriers, 230-236, 469
  classifications, 228-230
  content, 230
  coordination, 391
  defined, 227-228
  downward, 228
  electronic communicating devices and
    systems, 238
  employee, 372, 471
  external, 230
  external barriers, 235-236
  hierarchical direction, 228, 229
  horizontal, 25, 228
  internal, 230
  internal barriers, 231-235
    diagonal upward and downward
      communication, 234-235
    downward communication, 231-232
    horizontal communication, 234
    upward communication, 231-234
  internal lines, 152
  interpersonal, 230
  mechanical devices and systems, 238
  network, 23
  nonverbal, 229
  one-way, 228
  oral, 228-229
  organizational relationships, 230
  personnel policy, 215
  planning, 21-22, 23
  policies, 236-237
  procedures, 236-237
  purpose, 230
  standing plans, 126, 138-139
  strategic, 230
  strategic planning, 73
  technical, 230
  transmission method, 228-229
  two-way, 228
  union, 235-236
  upward, 228
  vertical, 25
  written, 228-229
Communication system
  planning, 236-238
    external, 237-238
    internal, 236-237
    policies, 236-237
    procedures, 236-237

importance, 72
Group synergy, 323-326, 473
    linking pin theory, 324-325
    management attitudes, 330
Guidelines, 125

H

Halsey, Frederick, 8
Hands-on management, 392-393
    authority, 393
    directing, 392
    influencing, 392
    power, 393
    supervision, 392
HealthTrust Inc.
    market maturity, 161
    strategic planning, 73
Hierarchy, 473
    Maslow's, 475
    number of levels, 111
    span of control, 111
Hospital
    departmentation by function, 102, 103
    design, 118
Hospital Corporation of America
    balance sheet, 166-167
    board, 44-45
        committee structure, 46
        outside members, 44-45
    budgeting process, 179
    departmentation by geographic location,
        105-108, 109
    departmentation by service, 106, 108
    factor analysis worksheet, 86
    goals, 77
    human resources, 199
    independent auditors, 162
    market maturity, 161
    mission, 76
    personnel policy, 218-219
    risk management, 186-188
    statement of changes in financial
        position, 168
    statement of income, 167
    statement of shareholders' equity, 170
    strategic planning, 66
Human relations attitudes, 299
Human resource management. *See also*
        Personnel deparment
    behavioral science, 201-202
    characteristics of successful, 197-199
    defined, 349-350
    Hospital Corporation of America, 199
    philosophy, 200
        importance, 200-201
    philosophy, implementation, 350-351
    policy, 200, 202-204
Human resource planning, 23, 195-220.
        See also Personnel department
    defined, 206
    elements, 206-208

implementation, 347-378
    need forecasting, 360
    personnel department procedure
        development, 219-220
    personnel policy development, 215-219
    philosophy development, 209
    policy development, 209-215
    scope, 206-209
Hypothesis, 59
    testing, 59

I

Iacocca, Lee, 51
Identification of constraints, 80
Implementation, 19-20, 277, 473
    accountability, 25
    adaptive response, 435-436, 437-438
    approaches, 24-25
    authority, 25
    background, 23-24
    contract, 24
    definition, 23-24
    executive, 50-51
    general nature, 437-438
    group synergy, 25
    human resource planning, 347-378
    job description, 24
    leadership technique, 24
    management by objectives, 24, 25
    personnel policy, 355-356
        responsibility, 356
    responsibility, 25
    supervision, 24, 25
    task assignment, 24
Incentive pay, 366
Induction, 362-363, 473
Influence, 321-322, 473
    defined, 321
Information, 473
    defined, 239
Information base, strategic planning,
        80-83
Initiating structure, 473
Insider trading, 473
Integrity, 447-465, 473
    defined, 450-451
    lack of, 450-457
    leadership, 308
Intelligence, 299
Internal rate of return, 480
Inventory, days in, 173
Investment
    book rated return, 157-158
    economic productivity, 156
    financial acceptability, 156
    functional feasibility, 156
    internal rate of return, 158
    net present value, 158
    payback period, 157
    planning future, 155-159
    profitability index, 158

Vertical integration
  backward, 480
  forward, 480
Vertically disaggregated company, 337
Vice president for finance, 148
Voluntary cooperation, 393-394, 394-396, 470
Voluntary coordination, 394-396

W

Work contract, 336-337
Work team conference, 290-291

Workload projection, 268, 480
Workplace functionality, 94, 118-119
  aesthetics, 118

Z

Zero base, 76-77
Zero-base
  budgeting, 179, 468
  strategic planning, 49, 480

About the Authors

Owen B. Hardy, FACHE, FAAHC, has provided consulting services to some of the world's most prestigious medical centers, including Rush-Presbyterian-St. Luke's Medical Center and Northwestern Memorial Hospital in Chicago, Illinois; Tulane University Medical Center and Ochsner Foundation Hospital in New Orleans, Louisiana; Erie County Medical Center in Buffalo, New York; University of Cologne Hospital in Cologne, West Germany; Ottawa General Hospital in Ottawa, Ontario; Washington Hospital Center in Washington, D.C.; and Park View Medical Center, Nashville, Tennessee.

Over a twenty-year span of consulting, Mr. Hardy has supervised the preparation of hundreds of reports in every aspect of hospital planning. The value of hospital construction for which he has provided planning services runs into billions of dollars.

For ten years, Mr. Hardy has held the position of National Health Care Planning Advisor with the firm of Ernst & Whinney, Chicago, Illinois. He formerly was president of Medicus Planning, Inc., vice-president of Friesen International, Inc., and for 14 years a hospital chief executive officer. He is a co-author of the award winning book, *Hospitals: The Planning and Design Process*, and stands eminently qualified to co-author a comprehensive text on management such as this. Mr. Hardy is a frequent contributor to the nation's top hospital professional publications and is widely known throughout the United States and abroad.

R. Clayton McWhorter, FACHE, as Chairman and Chief Executive Officer, is responsible for the overall leadership and management of HealthTrust Inc., with regard to strategic planning, external affairs, and corporate management.

Prior to his participation in the formation of HealthTrust Inc. in September 1987, McWhorter served as President and Chief Operating Officer of Hospital Corporation of America from 1985.

McWhorter joined HCA in 1970 as administrator of Palmyra Park Hospital in Albany, Georgia. In 1973 he was promoted to division vice president and in 1976 joined HCA's executive management staff as senior vice president of Domestic Operations. McWhorter became executive vice president in 1980, adding international operations to his responsibilities in 1983, and continuing in that position until becoming President and Chief Operating Officer in 1985.

Prior to joining HCA, McWhorter was assistant administrator of Phoebe Putney Memorial Hospital in Albany, Georgia. He also served as administrator of Sumter Regional Hospital in Americus, Georgia and West Georgia Medical Center in LaGrange, Georgia.

McWhorter attended The University of Tennessee, Knoxville, pre-pharmacy, 1951-52, and earned his B.S. degree in pharmacy in 1955 from Samford University in Birmingham, Alabama. His professional and business activities include serving as a Fellow of the American College of Healthcare Executives and a member of the Board of Directors of the Federation of American Health Systems. He is also director of Third National Bank in Nashville, and a member of the Board of Directors of the Foundation of State Legislatures, the National Association of Manufacturers, and the Wessex Corporation.

www.ingramcontent.com/pod-product-compliance
Lightning Source LLC
Chambersburg PA
CBHW082120210326
41599CB00031B/5818